LONELY PLANET PUBLICATIONS

KARLA ZIMMERMAN
LISA DUNFORD
NATE CAVALIERI

CHICAGO

CITY GUIDE

INTRODUCING CHICAGO

The city of Chicago rises high across the blue waters of Lake Michigan

The line spills out the door and curls clear around the corner. You do the right thing and wait with the mod crowd, stomach growling with each warm, spicy waft of air. Finally, you're in! But ordering presents a challenge – will it be the blue cheese pork with cherry-cream sauce and dried apricots, or the sesame-ginger duck?

The former, you decide, and when it arrives you almost faint after the first flavor-packed morsel hits your mouth. The national press has been hinting that Chicago is the country's new culinary star, and you couldn't agree more.

Funny thing is, you're eating at a hot dog stand.

Granted, it's a gourmet hot dog stand (called Hot Doug's and beloved by foodies everywhere), but it sums up Chicago's essence in a bite – this is a city that loves and seamlessly merges high culture and earthly pleasures.

Take the Art Institute, revered house of impressionism and home to more than a quarter million works. What happens come Super Bowl time? The museum straps giant fiberglass Bears helmets onto its front entrance lion sculptures. Or look at Crown Fountain, another creation that design critics laud. Venerated as high art by locals? Nope, it's just a water park to splash around in.

That's not to say Chicago doesn't take its greatness seriously. It gets irritated by the whole 'Second City' thing, the name implying inferiority to the cities on the coasts. Please. Didn't *Saveur* magazine just rank Chicago over New York as having the nation's best restaurant scene? And didn't Chicago just beat LA to win the US 2016 Olympic bid? Thought so.

CHICAGO LIFE

Chicago bullheadedly proclaims its own cultural trends and lifestyle niches: to hell with coastal fads. That maverick spirit is most visible in the city's creative realms, from Pilsen artists making canvases from stuffed-animal innards to Lincoln Park chefs toasting peanut-butter sandwiches by heat gun.

On the business side, the area is home to industry titans such as Boeing, McDonald's, Motorola and, of course, Oprah. Chicago actually determines the future of all American retailing and thus, popular culture – this is where companies come to test new products, be they Broadway shows or Costco caskets. Whether they make it to your local shelf depends on what the pragmatic but open-minded people of the Windy City have to say.

During the past five years, the pace of change here has been fast and grand. An architectural boom swept through downtown and spilled over its edges. Mod Millennium Park led the way, then the Calatrava-designed Spire joined in, set to become the USA's tallest building in 2011. Meanwhile, developers condo-ify every decrepit meat warehouse and abandoned church they can get their hands on.

The surge does come with urban planning conundrums. To tell the truth, the issues have been around for a while: traffic gridlock (Chicago ranks second only to LA); historic building demolition; and the long legacy of public-housing mismanagement and racial segregation. If Chicago truly wants to succeed in its 2016 Olympics bid, it'll have to address these challenges sooner rather than later. And rest assured that when it does, it'll do things in its own, fiercely independent way.

Hit Chicago's eating streets for an encounter with a local legend: the humble deep-dish pizza (p166)

HIGHLIGHTS

CITY OF FESTIVALS

The Windy City whoops it up like there's no tomorrow. Between March and September alone it throws 200 free festivals. Whether they honor Mexican independence or giant floating turkeys is irrelevant – Chicago just wants an excuse to crank tunes, blast fireworks and party in the streets.

❶ Chicago Blues Festival
Rock to fret-bending licks at the world's largest blues fest (p14).

❷ Taste of Chicago
Unloosen the belt before gorging on a park-full of food (p14).

❸ Lollapalooza
Bodysurf through three days of rock bands (p15).

1

1 Gallery Districts
Admire art showrooms bunched in the West Loop (p97), Pilsen (p102) and River North (p66).

2 Pilsen Murals
See eye-popping scenes splashed across Little Mexico's buildings (p102).

3 Art Institute of Chicago
View a quarter million Monets, Renoirs and other colorful masters (p52).

4 Green Mill
Relive Chicago's dark past: tipple martinis and get jazzed at Al Capone's old speakeasy (p183).

CULTURE APPRECIATION

Chicago treats its world-class operas and circus-punk marching bands with equal reverence. Same goes for its glitzy Broadway-style theaters and roll-the-dice-for-admission-price storefront stages. While you can find anything in a museum or on a stage here, specialties include blues, jazz, improv comedy and theater.

2

3

4

FOODIE FAVORITES

For years epicures wrote off Chicago as a meaty backwater. Then a funny thing happened: chef by chef, restaurant by restaurant, the city built a scene of plenty. Suddenly, foodies are bypassing reservations on the coasts, coming instead to the heartland. And critics agree: the eateries here might just be the USA's best.

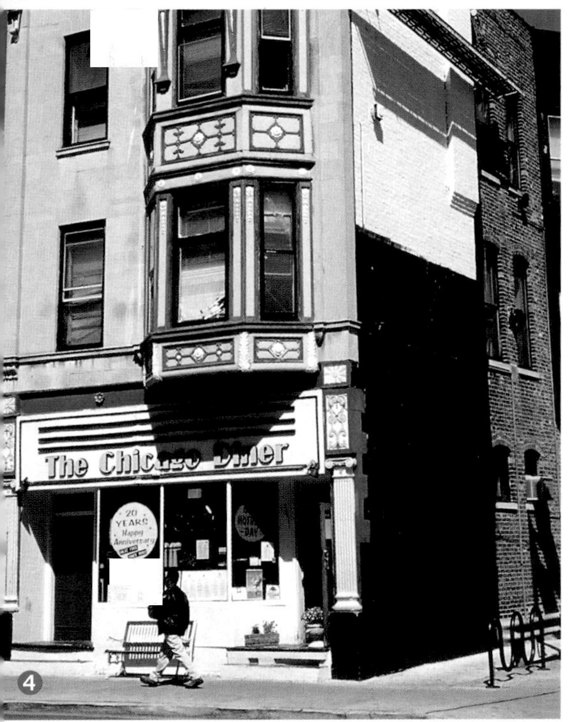

❶ Farmers' Markets

Reduce your food miles by eating locally sourced items (p140).

❷ Ethnic Eats

Fire up your tastebuds at Vietnamese, Indian and Greek joints, or Mexican restaurants like Nuevo Leon (p164).

❸ Chicago Hot Dog

Bite into a famed Vienna dog laden with peppers, pickles and more (p158).

❹ Neighborhood Joints

Seek out eateries buried deep in local 'hoods, such as vegetarian fave Chicago Diner (p152).

1 Sears Tower
Skyrocket to the top of the USA's tallest building (p56).

2 Rookery
See Frank Lloyd Wright's atrium overhaul (p57).

3 Millennium Park
See the sun glint and the city reflect off the swooping silver Bean (p53).

4 Tribune Tower
Identify shards from global monuments in the gothic building's base (p62).

STEELY SKYLINE

Hard to believe all this height came compliments of a cow. When Mrs O'Leary's bovine kicked over the lantern that burned down the city in 1871, it created the blank canvas that allowed Chicago's mighty architecture to flourish. Chicago put up the world's first skyscraper in 1885, and hasn't looked down since.

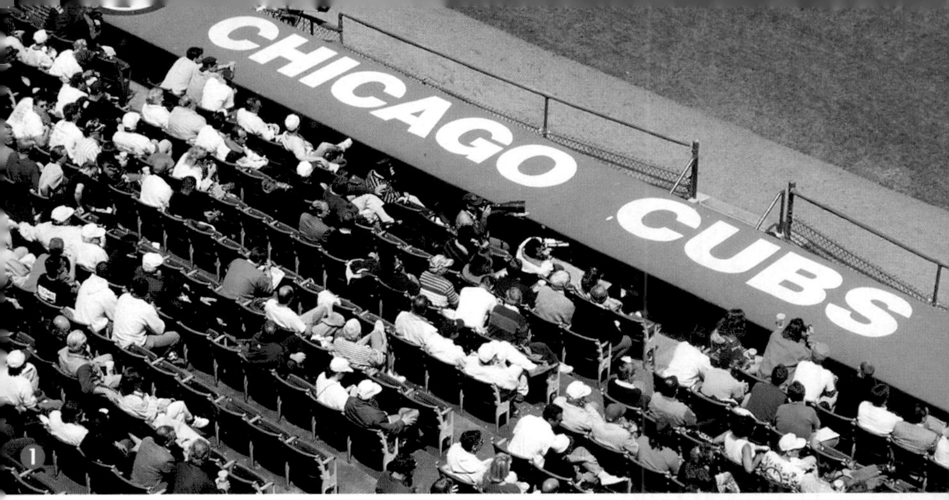

SPORTS FANATICS

When the weather warms, Chicagoans dash like sun-starved maniacs for the parks and beaches to cycle, swim and skate. When the weather sucks, they hibernate inside (often in bars) and watch sports on TV. And during all seasons, they head to the stadiums to cheer on their baseball, football and basketball teams in action.

1 Chicago Cubs
Watch baseball's favorite losing team play at historic Wrigley Field (p210).

2 Lake Michigan Beaches
Build sandcastles, spike volleyballs or swim in the waves (p209).

3 Watch a Game in a Bar
Join locals anytime, anywhere in the city's favorite pastime (p170).

4 Lasalle Bank Chicago Marathon
Join one million spectators feeling the pain of 45,000 runners (p17).

CONTENTS

Continued from previous page.

THE AUTHORS

Karla Zimmerman

Karla lives in Chicago, where she has been eating deep-dish pizza (Giordano's preferred) and cheering on the hopeless Cubs for the past 19 years. She's a bit silly in love with her town and will talk your ear off about its sky-high architecture, green-glinting lakefront, global neighborhoods and character-filled dive bars. Come wintertime, the words she uses get a bit more colorful, especially if she's just shoveled her car out of a snowbank.

Karla writes travel features for newspapers, books, magazines and radio. She has authored or co-authored several of Lonely Planet's US and Canadian titles. For this book, she wrote the Background, Neighborhoods, Shopping, Sports and Day Trips & Excursions chapters.

KARLA'S TOP CHICAGO DAY

I take the El downtown and the skyline zooms into focus. Soon the train is rumbling through the Loop. I disembark near Millennium Park (p53), stopping to admire 'the Bean' (p56) and smile at Crown Fountain's gargoyle-people (p53) as they spit water. I then visit the Chicago Cultural Center (p58) to see the gorgeous interior and a free lunchtime concert.

Next, I hop on the Red Line and head to Wrigley Field (p81) to catch a Cubs game. If the sun is shining and the breeze is blowing, nothing beats an afternoon here; if the sun is obscured and the breeze blizzardlike, at least tickets are easier to come by. I order a hot dog and Old Style beer, sighing as the Cubs get clobbered.

Nothing heals the soul like retail therapy, so it's off to Division St (p120) in Wicker Park/Ukrainian Village. The boutiques offer stylish clothes and oddball accessories, but I confess: my favorite places here are dive bars like the Gold Star (p176). After a drink I'm hungry. The neighborhood can easily solve my problem. Organic pizza? Swank vegetarian? Mexican? I decide on comfort food at Feed (p161).

It's getting late, but I make one more stop at the Hideout (p185), a tucked-away bar hosting indie rock, folk and country musicians. I head in for a set, then cab it home, convinced once again that Chicago is my kind of town.

Nate Cavalieri

When Nate first took in the twilit skyscrapers and hazy shoreline from atop the Sears Tower after a day of hot dogs and impressionists, his 10-year-old mind held one thought: *this* is a city. Two decades later, that awe hasn't diminished. A native of Michigan, Nate studied music and writing at Oberlin College and spent a brief stint in Chicago clubs as a musician – he now lives in Sacramento, California. Nate wrote the Eating, Drinking, Nightlife and Arts chapters.

Lisa Dunford

Born in East Chicago, one of Lisa's fondest childhood memories is of her grandmother taking her to Lincoln Park Zoo. Her father's hotel-industry career moved them around the country and back again. No wonder she writes about travel and reviews hotels – she was signing room service bills as soon as she could print. Lisa returns to Chicago often to visit her sister, cousin, aunt and uncles – Lou Malnati's pizza is a requirement each time. Lisa wrote the Walking Tours, Sleeping and Transportation chapters.

LONELY PLANET AUTHORS

Why is our travel information the best in the world? It's simple: our authors are independent, dedicated travellers. They don't research using just the internet or phone, and they don't take freebies in exchange for positive coverage. They travel widely, to all the popular spots and off the beaten track. They personally visit thousands of hotels, restaurants, cafés, bars, galleries, palaces, museums and more – and they take pride in getting all the details right, and telling it how it is. Think you can do it? Find out how at **lonelyplanet.com**.

GETTING STARTED

So you've decided to visit the Windy City. Excellent choice. You'll be well entertained, given all the festivals and attractions. The top sights are conveniently plunked near downtown – and what's not in the center is easily accessible by public transportation (ie the El trains) – so you don't have to worry about having a car. And Chicago's prices won't break the bank, especially with a bit of advance planning. What are you waiting for? Let's go…

WHEN TO GO

Wicked weather slaps the city between November and March. It gets nastiest in January, with temperatures hovering around 24°F (-4°C) and blasting snow and wind added for emphasis. This is when everyone stays inside and drinks.

When the sun begins to shine again and warmth creeps through the skyscrapers, from April through October, everyone flings open their doors and makes a greedy dash for the outdoor festivals, ballparks, beaches and beer gardens. This is the best time to visit Chicago. It's no surprise that this is also the city's peak season, specifically June through August, when summer temperatures average 85°F (29°C).

FESTIVALS

Chicago stages an insane number of festivals, concerts and events. The moment the thermometer registers a single degree above freezing, you can count on some group lugging a stage and speakers to Grant Park to celebrate the good news. Between March and September alone, the city throws 200 free day- or weekend-long shindigs.

Grant Park hosts most of the outdoor biggies, like Blues Fest, Jazz Fest and Taste of Chicago. Many of the major parades take place nearby along S Columbus Dr. We've highlighted some of our favorite events here, but this is by no means a comprehensive list. For the whole enchilada, check with the Mayor's Office of Special Events (☎ live 312-744-3315, recorded 312-744-3370; www.cityofchicago.org/specialevents). Another good resource is www.chicagofests.com. The Arts (p192) and Nightlife (p182) chapters contain further information on music, theater, dance, film and literary festivals.

January & February

BLACK HISTORY MONTH

☎ 877-244-2246

The city hosts events and exhibits from north to south and everywhere in between to celebrate African American history throughout February.

CHICAGO AUTO SHOW

☎ 630-495-2282; www.chicagoautoshow.com

Detroit, Tokyo and Bavaria introduce their latest and finest vehicles to hordes of excited gear-heads in a huge, mid-February show at McCormick Place.

CHINESE NEW YEAR PARADE

☎ 312-225-0303

Loads of spectators line Wentworth Ave in Chinatown to watch dragons dance, firecrackers burst and marching bands bang their gongs. The exact date varies according to the ancient Chinese calendar.

March

HELLENIC HERITAGE GREEK PARADE

☎ 773-775-4949; www.chicagogreekparade.org

Hellenic pride overtakes Greektown in this celebration and parade, held the last Sunday of the month. The action centers on Halsted St, from Randolph to Van Buren Sts.

POLAR PLUNGE

☎ 312-527-3743; www.chicagopolarplunge.org

Watch over 650 people experience extreme shrinkage as they jump into Lake Michigan from North Ave Beach. Held the first Sunday in March, the event is a fundraiser for the local Special Olympics.

ST PATRICK'S DAY PARADE

☎ 312-942-9188; www.chicagostpatsparade.com

It's a city institution: after the parade along S Columbus Dr, the local plumbers union dyes the Chicago River shamrock green (pouring in the secret, biodegradable coloring near the N Columbus Dr bridge). Then everyone drinks beer.

April

ANARCHIST FILM FESTIVAL

home.comcast.net/~more_about_it

Fight the power by checking out this two-day festival's works by and about anachists. Topics might cover everything from revolution in Oaxaca, Mexico to national identity card usage in the UK. Screenings usually occur during a late-month weekend; check the website for locations.

ART CHICAGO

☎ 312-587-3300; www.artchicago.com

The Merchandise Mart gets all chi-chi for this late-month event showcasing contemporary and modern art. Featuring more than 3000 artists, it is a Very Big Deal in Chicago's art world. Several museums and galleries hold simultaneous events.

CHICAGO IMPROV FESTIVAL

☎ 773-935-9810; www.chicagoimprovfestival.org

You'll get some good yucks from the Improv Fest, which runs for a week in mid-to-late April at stages around the city.

GREEN APPLE FESTIVAL

www.greenapplefestival.com

This carbon-neutral event coincides with Earth Day and features musical performances at venues throughout town, including kid-friendly freebies at the Peggy Notebaert Nature Museum and Lincoln Park Zoo.

SMELT SEASON

☎ 312-742-7529; www.chicagoparkdistrict.com

From April 1 to April 30, the wee fish known as smelt swarm into Chicago harbors to spawn. They're met by flocks of amateur anglers armed with nets and deep-fat fryers, who stake out piers up and down the lakefront.

May

BIKE THE DRIVE

☎ 312-427-3325, ext 251; www.bikethedrive.org

There's one day a year when you don't need to worry about cars knocking you off your bicycle. It's the Sunday before Memorial Day, when, starting at 5:30am, automobiles are banned from Lake Shore Dr and the road becomes a sea of two-wheelers. Riding along the car-free lakefront as the sun busts out from the horizon is a thrill. It costs $40 to participate; proceeds benefit the Chicagoland Bicycle Federation.

CINCO DE MAYO FESTIVAL & PARADE

☎ 773-843-9738

This annual bash celebrating the Mexican army routing the French in 1862 draws more than 350,000 people to Pilsen with food, music and rides on the first Saturday in May. The colorful parade begins at the intersection of Cermak Rd and Damen Ave, and proceeds to Douglas Park where the festival lets loose.

GREAT CHICAGO PLACES & SPACES FESTIVAL

☎ 312-744-3370; www.greatchicagoplaces.us

This festival includes boat, bike and walking tours of Chicago's major architectural treasures – including peeks into many spaces that aren't regularly open to the public. It's held on the third weekend in May.

LOOPTOPIA

☎ 312-782-9160; www.looptopia.com

Looptopia is a newcomer to the fest scene (it started in 2007), offering an all-night bash on a Friday in early May. More than 100 Loop stores, theaters, restaurants and bars stay open through the wee hours and provide special food, music and arts programming both indoors and out.

POLISH CONSTITUTION DAY PARADE

☎ 773-745-7799; www.may3parade.org

Accordion-fueled polka'ing and lots of kielbasa bring out Chicago's mighty Polish community (the world's second-largest after Warsaw). The event celebrates Europe's first democratic constitution, signed in 1791. It's held on the first Saturday in May on S Columbus Dr.

June

ANDERSONVILLE MIDSOMMARFEST

☎ 773-664-4682; www.andersonville.org

The Swedes in Andersonville gather round the maypole mid-month to sing, dance and eat lingonberries.

CHICAGO BLUES FESTIVAL

☎ 312-744-3370; www.chicagobluesfestival.us

It's the biggest free blues fest in the world, with four days of the music that made Chicago famous. More than 750,000 people unfurl blankets by the multiple stages that take over Grant Park in early June.

CHICAGO COUNTRY MUSIC FESTIVAL

☎ 312-744-3370; www.chicagocountrymusicfestival.us

Grant Park fills up once again, this time with cowboy-boot-wearin' folks on the last weekend of the month. The music spans the gamut from slick new artists to old-school favorites like Loretta Lynn and Kenny Rogers.

CHICAGO GOSPEL FESTIVAL

☎ 312-744-3370; www.chicagogospelmusicfestival.us

Praise the lord and say hallelujah for the choirs singing their souls out on three stages in Grant Park; the fest usually takes place in early June.

GAY & LESBIAN PRIDE PARADE

☎ 773-348-8243; www.chicagopridecalendar.org

Colorful floats and risqué revelers pack Halsted St in Boys' Town on the last Sunday in June.

GRANT PARK MUSIC FESTIVAL

☎ 312-742-7638; www.grantparkmusicfestival.com

The top-notch Grant Park Orchestra plays free pop and classical concerts in Millennium Park's Pritzker Pavilion most Wednesdays, Fridays, Saturdays and Sundays from mid-June through mid-August.

PRINTERS ROW BOOK FAIR

☎ 312-222-3986; www.printersrowbookfair.org

This popular event, sponsored by the *Chicago Tribune*, features thousands of rare and not-so-rare books for sale, plus author readings. The browsable booths line the 500 to 700 blocks of S Dearborn St in early June.

PUERTO RICAN PARADE & FIESTAS PUERTORRIQUEÑAS

☎ 773-292-1414; www.prparadechicago.com

Chicago's substantial Puerto Rican community takes to the streets downtown in the middle of June for the parade along S Columbus Dr, followed by pork-filled eats at the festival in Humboldt Park.

SUMMERDANCE

☎ 312-742-4007; www.chicagosummerdance.org

Enjoy the music as free bands play rumba, samba and other world music preceded by fun dance lessons at the Spirit of Music Garden (601 S Michgan Ave) in Grant Park. Lessons start at 6pm Thursday to Saturday, and 4pm Sunday, from mid-June through August.

TASTE OF CHICAGO

☎ 312-744-3370; www.tasteofchicago.us

This 10-day food festival in Grant Park coincides with the Fourth of July fireworks bash. More than 70 local eateries serve some of the greasiest food you've ever tried to rub off your fingers. Bring your wallet, bring extra napkins and bring your patience for long lines and crowd-jostling. Live music also features on several stages.

July

CHICAGO FOLK & ROOTS FESTIVAL

☎ 773-728-6000; www.oldtownschool.org/festival

Mid-month, one of Chicago's coolest organizations – the Old Town School of Folk Music – throws this two-day party in northside Welles Park, featuring everything from alt-country to Zimbabwean vocalists.

CHICAGO OUTDOOR FILM FESTIVAL

☎ 312-744-3370; www.chicagooutdoorfilmfestival.us

Running from mid-July to the end of August, this Grant Park festival is like a drive-in but without all the obnoxious cars. Screened on Tuesdays at sundown, the films are all classics, and are preceded by Chicago shorts. Bring your blankets and lawn chairs to where Monroe St meets Lake Shore Dr.

FOURTH OF JULY FIREWORKS

☎ 312-744-3370

The city pulls out all the stops for this spectacular concert, in which fireworks burst over Lake Michigan in a lengthy display while the Grant Park Orchestra plays a stirring rendition of Tchaikovsky's

1812 Overture. The festivities happen on July 3, the day before Independence Day. For the best view of the light show, try the embankment east of Randolph St and Lake Shore Dr.

PITCHFORK MUSIC FESTIVAL

☎ 312-744-3315; www.pitchforkmusicfestival.com
It's sort of Lollapalooza Jr, only for bespectacled indie-rock fans. Sonic Youth, the New Pornographers and other indie heroes shake up Union Park (1501 W Randolph St) on a typically sweltering weekend, Friday through Sunday, in mid-July.

VENETIAN NIGHT

☎ 312-744-3370
Yacht owners pimp their rides with lights and parade the glowing boats through Monroe Harbor to an 'ahh'ing' crowd. Fireworks follow. The event takes place late in the month.

August

AFRICAN FESTIVAL OF THE ARTS

☎ 773-955-2787; www.africainternationalhouse.org
Hip-hop music and ethnic eats bring crowds to Washington Park (5700 S Cottage Grove Dr) for this annual event, usually held over the Labor Day weekend.

BUD BILLIKEN PARADE

☎ 877-244-2246; www.budbillikenparade.com
Held on the second Saturday of the month, this huge parade (the USA's largest African-American one) features drill teams, dancers and floats; it runs along Martin Luther King Jr Dr, from 39th St to 51st St, and wraps up with a picnic in Washington Park afterwards.

CHICAGO AIR & WATER SHOW

☎ 312-744-3370; www.chicagoairandwatershow.us
On Saturday and Sunday afternoon, the third weekend in August, the latest military hardware buzzes the lakefront from Diversey Pkwy south to Oak St Beach, rattling all the buildings' windows in between. North Ave Beach is the best place for viewing.

CHICAGO JAZZ FEST

☎ 312-744-3370; www.chicagojazzfestival.us
Chicago's longest-running music fest attracts top names on the national jazz scene. Miles Davis, Dave Brubeck and Charlie Haden are among those who have topped the bill. It's always held over Labor Day weekend in Grant Park.

CHICAGO UNDERGROUND FILM FEST (CUFF)

www.cuff.org
Independent, experimental and documentary films from around the world screen at CUFF, the edgier, younger sibling of the Chicago International Film Festival (see p16). Venues include various small theaters and galleries held over five days in later August.

ELVIS IS ALIVE 5K

☎ 773-305-3338; www.fleetfeetchicago.com/htm/events_races_elvis.asp
Shimmy into your white jumpsuit, glue on the sideburns and energize with a peanut-butter-and-banana sandwich for this annual race through Lincoln Park, held the Saturday before Elvis' August 16th birthday. There's also a post run concert in the park.

LOLLAPALOOZA

☎ 888-512-7469; www.lollapalooza.com
Once upon a time, this mondo rock fest traveled city to city. Now its permanent home (at least through 2011) is here in Chicago. It's a raucous event, with 130 bands – including many big names – spilling off seven stages in Grant Park. It's usually held the first weekend in August.

Ticket prices vary, depending on how early you buy. In 2007 a limited batch went on sale in early March. These are the cheapest to obtain, since the band line-ups haven't been finalized and you're buying on spec. The next ticket round was in early April; you get a bit more information on who's playing at this point, so tickets cost a bit more. By show-time, a three-day pass costs about $195; day passes are about $75. While tickets did not sell out in '07, advance purchases can help you save significant bucks. Keep a close eye on the website for updates.

NORTH HALSTED STREET MARKET DAYS

☎ 773-883-0500; www.northalsted.com/maket_days.php
More than 250,000 people, gay and straight alike, descend onto this neighborhood

street festival to check out crafty vendors and listen to live music; prepare to see some wild costumes and booths. It's held in early- to mid-August.

VIVA! CHICAGO LATIN MUSIC FESTIVAL

☎ 312-744-3370; www.vivachicago.us
The Latin Music fest, held during a late-month weekend in Grant Park, features *cumbias* (Columbian folk music), merengue, salsa and ranchero music delivered by some of the biggest names in the industry.

September

CELTIC FEST CHICAGO

☎ 312-744-3370; www.celticfestchicago.us
Bagpipers, storytellers and Celtic culture abound at this mid-month weekend festival. The 'Men in Kilts Leg Contest' on Saturday evening is a hairy good time.

DAY OF THE DEAD CELEBRATIONS

☎ 312-738-1503; www.nationalmuseumofmexicanart.org
The National Museum of Mexican Art in Pilsen puts on exciting Day of the Dead events running from late September to mid-December.

GERMAN-AMERICAN FESTIVAL

☎ 630-653-3018; www.germanday.com
This good-time Oktoberfest happens mid-month in the heart of the old German neighborhood at Lincoln Sq (4700 N Lincoln Ave). On Saturday of the weekend event, the Von Steuben Parade marches through (*Ferris Bueller's Day Off* fans will remember this as the parade Ferris joins for his float singing).

MEXICAN INDEPENDENCE DAY PARADE

☎ 773-328-8538
You'll see lots of cute kids dressed to the nines at this colorful and loud event, held in early September along Columbus Dr.

WINDY CITY WINE FESTIVAL

☎ 847-382-1480; www.windycitywinefestival.com
Vendors pour more than 250 global vinos in Daley Bicentennial Plaza – a cool $25 gets you 10 tastings plus some free music acts. It's held the second weekend in September.

WORLD MUSIC FESTIVAL

☎ 312-742-1938; www.cityofchicago.org/worldmusic
Musicians and bands from around the world tote their bouzoukis, ouds and other exotic instruments to Chicago for a week's worth of performances late-month. Shows take place at venues throughout town, with the Chicago Cultural Center anchoring it all.

October

AROUND THE COYOTE ARTS FESTIVAL

☎ 773-342-6777; www.aroundthecoyote.org
A great introduction to the alternative world of the Wicker Park and Bucktown arts community, this series of gallery open houses and performances features hundreds of local artists in and around the Flat Iron Building at 1579 N Milwaukee Ave. It's typically held on the second weekend in October.

CHICAGO BOOK FESTIVAL

☎ 312-747-4999; www.chicagopubliclibraryfoundation.org
The Chicago Public Library organizes special readings, lectures and book events throughout the month at its citywide branches. Many festivities revolve around the 'One Book, One Chicago' program, where everyone – including Mayor Daley – reads the same book (past selections have included Elie Wiesel's *Night* and Jane Austen's *Pride & Prejudice*).

CHICAGO INTERNATIONAL FILM FESTIVAL

☎ 312-683-0121; www.chicagofilmfestival.org
This is the city's main film event. It typically shows a few big-name flicks among the myriad not-so-big-name flicks, and brings a few big-name Hollywood stars to town to add a glamorous sheen to the proceedings. It's held during the first two weeks of the month at varying venues.

CHICAGOWEEN

☎ 312-744-3370
From mid-October through Halloween, the city transforms Daley Plaza into Pumpkin Plaza and sets up a Haunted Village for kids.

LASALLE BANK CHICAGO MARATHON

☎ 312-904-9800; www.chicagomarathon.com

More than 45,000 runners from all over the globe compete on the 26-mile course through the city's heart, cheered on by a million spectators. Held on a Sunday in October (when the weather can be pleasant or absolutely freezing), it's considered one of the world's top five marathons.

November

CHICAGO HUMANITIES FESTIVAL

☎ 312-661-1028; www.chfestival.org

Put on your thinking cap: for two weeks in early November, a citywide series of chin-stroking talks, panels, readings, performances, exhibits and screenings take place, all focusing on a single, academic topic (it was climate change in 2007, peace and war in 2006).

MAGNIFICENT MILE LIGHTS FESTIVAL

☎ 312-642-3570; www.themagnificentmile.com

The lighting of all 600,000 tree lights takes place mid-month, after which the little fellas continue to twinkle sweetly through January on Michigan Ave north of the river.

THANKSGIVING PARADE

☎ 312-781-5681; www.chicagofestivals.org

Around 400,000 shivering souls show up to see giant helium balloons, floats, marching bands, and local and national celebrities at the annual turkey day parade. The parade runs along State St from Congress to Randolph Sts.

TREE LIGHTING CEREMONY

☎ 312-744-3370

The mayor flips the switch to light up Chicago's Christmas tree in Daley Plaza on Thanksgiving Day.

December

KWANZAA

☎ 312-744-2400

The increasingly popular African-American holiday adds new events and locations each year. It is celebrated from December 26 through January 1.

NEW YEAR'S EVE FIREWORKS AT BUCKINGHAM FOUNTAIN

☎ 312-744-3370

The city sets off a huge arsenal of fireworks at Chicago's famous fountain – it's an excellent (though chilly) way to ring in the New Year.

COSTS & MONEY

First the good news: it's possible to dine and drink very well in Chicago, without spending an arm and a leg. And thanks to the occasional (though increasingly rare) free days at local museums, coupled with the discounts offered in the *Chicago Guidebook of Special Values* coupon book (available at the Chicago Cultural Center Visitors Center; see p263), there's a good chance you'll be getting into most attractions without having to pay full price.

Now the bad news: your hotel room can cost an awful lot. The rack rates on rooms here are shocking. This is partially because of the 15.4% hotel tax levied by the city, which Chicago depends on to maintain its parks and public buildings. But the city is only partially to blame for the price tags on hotel and motel rooms. Business travelers are the other culprits. Because of the huge number of conventioneers in Chicago at any given moment, hotel rooms are almost always at a premium. And unlike leisure travelers, the business travelers 1) have to come here whether they want to or not, and 2) get reimbursed for their lodging costs.

The high demand and looser purse strings of conventioneers have put hotels and motels in a position where they can charge whatever

HOW MUCH?

Gallon of gas $3.30

Liter of water $1.50

Bottle of Old Style beer $2.50-3

Souvenir T-shirt from the Hideout $10

Italian beef sandwich $5

El fare $2

Green Mill martini $7.50

Near North hotel room $159 approx

Blues club cover charge $15

Small bag of Garrett's caramel popcorn $2.35

the market will bear. And with the city getting a substantial cut of the revenues, there's little incentive for anyone to bring down the prices.

Given the facts, there *are* things you can do to save money on lodgings in town. First and foremost, shop around as much as possible on the internet before committing to anything – sometimes the room price listed on a discount travel website can be $100 lower than the price quoted by the hotel reservation agent (for tips on bidding for rooms, see the boxed text p220). Otherwise, start wooing those long-lost family members you have in Chicago. Aunt Bertha may be annoying, but her foldout couch is crucial to your wallet's plumpness. For additional lodging-related tips and tricks, see Saving Strategies (p216).

Once you conquer the accommodation issue, you're looking at a reasonably priced holiday in the Windy City. Those on dirt-cheap budgets can save further by eating at the choc-a-bloc hot dog and burger joints and *taquerias* (taco eateries). And you don't have to pay a dime for entertainment in summer, thanks to the free music and cultural festivals in Grant and Millennium parks.

INTERNET RESOURCES

Chicago Reader (www.chicagoreader.com) The website for the city's free alternative newspaper has comprehensive arts, eating and entertainment listings, plus thoughtful blogs on local politics, music and media by its staff writers.

Craigslist Chicago (www.chicago.craigslist.org) Looking for a kinky date? Job in accounting? Darth Vader guitar? This all-encompassing site has you covered.

Gaper's Block (www.gapersblock.com) Hip, playful reports on the latest news, cultural happenings and political shenanigans afoot in the Windy City.

Hot Rooms (www.hotrooms.com) Peruse this Chicago-centric hotel room consolidator to save a few bucks (if nothing else, you can take the prices you find here and try to beat 'em on Hotwire or Priceline).

LTH Forum (www.lthforum.com) Foodies, this one's for you: wide-ranging talk about the local restaurant scene from a dedicated community of food lovers. More chow-related sites are listed on p162.

Metromix (www.metromix.com) *Chicago Tribune*–owned website with restaurant, bar, entertainment and gym reviews.

Vegchicago (www.vegchicago.com) Guide to local vegetarian and vegan restaurants and markets; it also lists monthly meet-ups where like-minded individuals can break bread together.

SUSTAINABLE CHICAGO

You can tread gently on the earth and still have a first-class visit to the Windy City. You're spoiled for choice if you wish to avoid flying here. Chicago is an Amtrak, Megabus and Greyhound hub, so take your pick of these lower-impact modes of travel (contact details are in the Transportation chapter, p249). Once in town, ditch the car. Public transportation goes to most visitor-oriented places; taking the train or bus not only cuts down on emissions, but allows you to avoid

ADVANCE PLANNING

It pays – literally – to do a bit of advance planning before arriving in the Windy City. First and foremost, book your lodging ahead of time. Not only will this help avoid unpleasant surprises like the International Screwdriver Association taking up every room in town, but you'll cut costs off the outrageous rack rates. See p216 for detailed advice on saving strategies.

Shopaholics should sign up ahead of time for *Chicago Magazine*'s e-newsletter that tells when and where special sales are taking place each week; instructions are on p120.

While you can get half-price theater tickets on the day of performances from Hot Tix (www.hottix.org), popular shows often sell out. If you have your heart set on a particular performance, keep an eye on the Hot Tix website the week before your arrival and see if your show has a pattern of available tickets. If not, book ahead.

Lollapalooza fans can save money by buying tickets in advance; see p15. Those coming for this music event or any other big summer fest should definitely secure lodging in advance.

You'll save more time than money by ordering your CTA train passes (p253) in advance, but didn't someone once say 'time *is* money'?

Finally, folks who enjoy DIY walking tours should download the several audio excursions the city has to offer. The MP3s cover everything from Loop architecture to blues sights; see p261 for a list of what's on offer.

the mega-hassle of trying to find parking (and paying the absurd price for it).

Heck, if you really want to do it right, buy a recycled two-wheeler from Working Bikes Cooperative (p206) for $40 or so. The cost will be less than a daily bike rental, plus when you're finished, you can donate it back to the group.

Meat-loving Chicago doesn't overflow with organic eateries, but there are certainly enough to keep you from starving, plus several farmers' markets; see 'Straight from the Farm' (p140) for recommended options.

The city's lodgings do the usual by asking visitors to re-use towels and sheets, and some places serve organic coffee; few go beyond these novel ideas. See p217 for the green lodging low-down.

Good resources to check for further ideas:

Chicago Sustainable Business Alliance (www.sustainablechicago.biz) Lists local green businesses; note that it's a self-selected group – members pay to join.

A Fresh Squeeze (www.afreshsqueeze.com) Local e-newsletter that provides tips on how to live a greener life in Chicago; it covers shopping, eating and transportation issues, among others.

Green Maps (www.artic.edu/webspaces/greenmap/) Lists sustainability hotspots by neighborhood, from parks to organic restaurants, fair-trade shops to recycling centers; also lists bad boys like water pollutant sources.

HISTORY

ONIONS, FORTS AND MASSACRES

The Potawatomi Indians were the first folks in town, and they gave the name 'Checaugou' – or wild onions – to the area around the Chicago River's mouth. Needless to say, they weren't particularly pleased when the first settlers arrived in 1803. The newcomers built Fort Dearborn on the river's south bank, on marshy ground under what is today's Michigan Ave Bridge (look for plaques in the sidewalk marking the spot at the corner of Michigan Ave and Wacker Dr).

The Potawatomi's resentment mounted, Dr Phil wasn't around at the time to intervene, and bad things ensued. In 1812, the natives – in cahoots with the British (their allies in the War of 1812) – slaughtered 52 settlers fleeing the fort. The massacre took place near what is today Hillary Rodham Clinton Women's Park (p111). During the war this had been a strategy employed throughout the frontier: the British bought the allegiance of various Indian tribes through trade and other deals, and the Indians paid them back by killing American settlers. The people killed in Chicago had simply waited too long to flee the rising tension and found themselves caught.

After the war ended, everyone let bygones be bygones and hugged it out for the sake of the fur trade.

REAL ESTATE BOOM

Chicago was incorporated as a town in 1833, with a population of 340. Within three years land speculation rocked the local real estate market; lots that sold for $33 in 1829 now went for $100,000. Construction on the Illinois & Michigan Canal – a state project linking the Great Lakes to the Illinois River and thus to the Mississippi River and Atlantic coast – fueled the boom. Swarms of laborers swelled the population to more than 4100 by 1837, and Chicago became a city.

Within 10 years, more than 20,000 people lived in what had become the region's dominant city. The rich Illinois soil supported thousands of farmers, and industrialist Cyrus Hall McCormick moved his reaper factory to the city to serve them. He would soon control one of the Midwest's major fortunes and have a big mansion on Astor St (see p72).

In 1848 the canal opened; shipping flowed through the area and had a marked economic effect on the city. A great financial institution, the Chicago Board of Trade, opened to handle the sale of grain by Illinois farmers, who now had greatly improved access to Eastern markets.

Railroad construction began soon thereafter, and tracks radiated out from Chicago. The city quickly became the hub of America's freight and passenger trains, a position it would hold for the next 100 years.

TIMELINE

Late 1600s

The Potawatomi Indians have the land to themselves – plenty of space to cruise around in their birchbark canoes, fish and ponder what sort of entertainment (Peter Frampton?) they'll have in their future casino.

1779

Jean Baptiste Pointe du Sable, an enterprising gent of African and Caribbean descent, sails down from Québec and sets up a fur-trading post on the Chicago River. He is the city's first settler.

1803

More settlers arrive and build Fort Dearborn at the river's mouth. The Potawatomi locals do not send a fruit basket to their new neighbors. Rather, they massacre the settlers nine years later.

BRING ON THE BACON

By the end of the 1850s, immigrants had poured into the city, drawn by jobs on the railroads that served the ever-growing agricultural trade. Twenty million bushels of produce were shipped through Chicago annually by then. The population topped 100,000.

The city's location smack dab in the middle of the country made it a favorite meeting spot, a legacy that continues to this day (which is why you're paying out the nose for your hotel room). In 1860 the Republican Party held its national political convention in Chicago and selected Abraham Lincoln, a lawyer from Springfield, Illinois, as its presidential candidate.

Like other northern cities, Chicago profited from the Civil War, which boosted business in the burgeoning steel and toolmaking industries, and provided plenty of freight for the railroads and canal. In 1865, the year the war ended, what took place profoundly affected the city for the next century: the Union Stockyards opened on the South Side.

Chicago's rail network and the invention of the iced refrigerator car meant that meat could be shipped for long distances, satiating hungry carnivores all the way east to New York and beyond. The stockyards soon became the major meat supplier to the nation. But besides bringing great wealth to a few and jobs to many, the yards were also a source of water pollution (see the boxed text, p117).

STOP THE BACON!

The stockyard effluvia polluted not only the Chicago River but also Lake Michigan. Flowing into the lake, the fouled waters spoiled the city's source of fresh water and caused cholera and other epidemics that killed thousands. In 1869 the Water Tower and Pumping Station built a two-mile tunnel into Lake Michigan and began bringing water into the city from there; they hoped this set-up would skirt the contaminated areas. Alas, the idea proved resoundingly inadequate, and outbreaks of illness continued.

Two years later, engineers deepened the Illinois & Michigan Canal so they could alter the Chicago River's course and make it flow south, away from the city. Sending waste and sewage down the reversed river provided relief for Chicago residents and helped ease lake pollution, but it was not a welcome change for those living near what had become the city's drainpipe. A resident of Morris, about 60 miles downstream, wrote: 'What right has Chicago to pour its filth down into what was before a sweet and clean river, pollute its waters, and materially reduce the value of property on both sides of the river and canal, and bring sickness and death to the citizens?' The guy had a point.

The river occasionally still flowed into the lake after heavy rains; it wasn't permanently reversed until 1900, when the huge Chicago Sanitary & Ship Canal opened.

BURN BABY BURN – CHICAGO INFERNO

On October 8, 1871, the Chicago fire started just southwest of downtown. For more than 125 years, legend has had it that a cow owned by a certain Mrs O'Leary kicked over a lantern, which ignited some hay, which ignited some lumber, which ignited the whole town. The image of the hapless heifer has endured despite evidence that the fire was actually the fault of Daniel 'Peg Leg' Sullivan, who dropped by the barn on an errand, accidentally started the fire himself and then tried to blame it on the bovine. (The Chicago City Council officially passed a resolution in 1997 absolving the O'Leary family of blame.)

1837

Chicago incorporates as a city (pop: 4170). It's a happenin' place, having skyrocketed from just 340 people four years earlier. And it continues to boom – within 10 years 16,000 folks call the city 'home.'

1865

The Union Stockyards open, and millions of cows get the axe. Thanks to new train tracks and refrigerated railcars, Chicago can send its bacon afar and becomes 'hog butcher for the world' (per poet Carl Sandburg).

1871

The Great Fire torches the entire inner city. Mrs O'Leary's cow takes the blame, though it's eventually determined that Daniel 'Peg Leg' Sullivan kicked over the lantern that started the blaze.

However it started, the results of the Chicago fire were devastating. It burned for three days, killing 300 people, destroying 18,000 buildings and leaving 90,000 people homeless. 'By morning 100,000 people will be without food and shelter. Can you help us?' was the message sent East by Mayor Roswell B Mason as Chicago and City Hall literally burned down around him.

The dry conditions and mostly wood buildings set the stage for a runaway conflagration, as a hot wind carried flaming embers to unburned areas which quickly caught fire. The primitive, horse-drawn fire fighting equipment could do little to keep up with the spreading blaze. Almost every structure was destroyed or gutted in the area bounded by the river on the west, what's now Roosevelt Rd to the south and Fullerton Ave to the north.

Mayor Mason did earn kudos for his skilful handling of Chicago's recovery. His best move was to prevent the aldermen on the city council from getting their hands on the millions of dollars in relief funds that Easterners had donated after the mayor's fireside plea, thus ensuring that the money actually reached the rabble living in the rubble.

MAKE BIG PLANS

Despite the human tragedy, the fire taught the city some valuable lessons – namely, don't build everything from wood. Chicago reconstructed with modern materials, and created space for new industrial and commercial buildings.

The world's best architects poured into the city during the 1880s and 90s to take advantage of the situation. They had a blank canvas to work with, a city giving them lots of dough, and pretty much the green light to use their imagination to its fullest. The world's first skyscraper soon popped up in 1885. Several other important buildings (see p57) also rose during the era, spawning the 'Chicago Style' of architecture. Daniel Burnham was one of the premier designers running the show, and he summed up the city's credo best: 'Make no little plans,' he counseled Chicago's leaders in 1909, 'for they have no magic to stir men's blood… Make big plans.'

top picks

BOOKS ON CHICAGO'S HISTORY

Beyond the history classics (*Chicago: City on the Make* by Nelson Algren, 1951; *Boss: Richard J Daley of Chicago* by Mike Royko, 1971; and *Working: What People do all Day and How They Feel About What They Do* by Studs Terkel, 1974), here are some recent additions to the Chicago bookshelf:

- **Sin in the Second City** (2007, Karen Abbott) In the early 1900s, sisters Minna and Ada Everleigh opened a brothel called the Everleigh Club in Chicago's notorious Levee district. Their courtesans entertained Prince Henry of Prussia and author Theodore Dreiser, plus moguls and senators; the ladies dined on gourmet food, read Balzac and started a culture war that rocked the nation.
- **Murder City: The Bloody History of Chicago in the Twenties** (2007, Michael Lesy) Chicago in the 1920s was America's murder capital – professionals and amateurs alike snuffed each other out with reckless abandon. The book shows that these crimes of loot and love may be the progenitors of our modern age.
- **Richard Nickels' Chicago, Photographs of a Lost City** (2006, Richard Cahan & Michael Williams) Nickels was a photographer and preservationist. He snapped buildings in Chicago in the 1950s and 1960s, at a point when big construction was really starting to take hold and change the city.
- **Encyclopedia of Chicago** (2004) The Newberry Library and Chicago History Museum put together this all-encompassing guide to Windy City history.
- **The Devil in the White City: Murder, Magic, and Madness at the Fair that Changed America** (2003, Erik Larson) This riveting book focuses on the 1893 World's Expo and a gruesome killer who preyed on its attendees.

1880s

People start calling Chicago the 'Windy City' – not because of its blustery weather, but because of its big-mouthed local citizenry who constantly brag about the town's greatness.

1885

The world's first steel-frame 'skyscraper,' the Home Insurance Building, rises up on the skyline. It's 10 stories (138ft) tall and paves the way for big things to come.

1886

Workers fight for their right to an eight-hour workday and decent pay by holding a rally at Haymarket Square. The cops came, bombs exploded, anarchists took the blame and the modern labor movement was born.

GIMME A BREAK

Labor unrest had been brewing in the city for a few years. In 1876, organized strikes began in the railroad yards as workers demanded an eight-hour workday and rest breaks. The turbulence spread to the McCormick Reaper Works, which was then Chicago's largest factory. The police and federal troops broke up the strikes, killing 18 civilians and injuring hundreds more.

By then, May 1 had become the official day of protest for labor groups in Chicago. On that day in 1886, 60,000 workers went on strike, once again demanding an eight-hour workday. As usual, police attacked the strikers at locations throughout the city. Three days later, self-described 'anarchists' staged a protest in Haymarket Square; out of nowhere a bomb exploded, killing seven police officers. The government reacted strongly to what became known as 'the Haymarket Riot.' Eight anarchists were convicted of 'general conspiracy to murder' and four were hanged, although only two had been present at the incident and the bomber was never identified. A sculpture marks the square today (see p100 for details).

FIVE FIGURES WHO CHANGED CHICAGO HISTORY

Daniel Burnham Designer of 'The Chicago Plan,' Burnham played a principal role in developing the Chicago School of architecture and oversaw the beaux arts buildings of the 1893 World's Expo.

Chess Brothers Leonard and Phil are the dudes who brought the electric blues – and ultimately rock and roll – to the world from their Near South Side studio

Richard J Daley Chicago politics have never been the same since Mayor Daley #1 ruled the roost from 1955 to 1976.

Oprah Winfrey She reads Elie Wiesel, America reads Elie Wiesel. She eats lavender applesauce, America eats lavender applesauce. She journals, America journals. She leads the country from her West Loop studio.

Mrs O'Leary's cow When it kicked over the lantern that burned down the city, it created the blank canvas that allowed Chicago's sky-scraping architecture to flourish.

THE WHITE CITY DEBUTS

The 1893 World Expo marked Chicago's showy debut on the international stage. The event centered on a grand complex of specially built structures lying just south of Hyde Park. They were painted white and were brilliantly lit by electric searchlights, which is how the 'White City' tag came to be. Designed by architectural luminaries such as Daniel Burnham, Louis Sullivan and Frederick Law Olmsted, the fairgrounds were meant to show how parks, streets and buildings could be designed in a harmonious manner that would enrich the chaotic urban environment.

Open for only five months, the exposition attracted 27 million visitors, many of whom rode the newly built El train to and from the Loop. The fair offered wonders heretofore unknown to the world: long-distance phone calls, the first moving pictures (courtesy of Thomas Alva Edison's Kinetoscope), the first Ferris wheel and the first zipper. Businessmen were in awe of the first vertical file (invented by Melvil Dewey, of Dewey Decimal System fame) and children were taken with a new gum called 'Juicy Fruit.' It was at this fair that Pabst beer won the blue ribbon that has been part of its name ever since.

The entire assemblage made a huge impact worldwide, and the fair's architects were deluged with commissions to redesign cities. The buildings themselves, despite their grandeur, were short

1893

The World Expo opens near Hyde Park, and Chicago grabs the global spotlight for the wonders it unveils, including the Ferris wheel, movies, Cracker Jack, Pabst beer and the vertical filing cabinet.

1900

In an engineering feat, Chicago reverses the flow of Chicago River, forever ingratiating itself with its downstate neighbors.

1908

Chicago Cubs win the World Series. 'Let's do this again soon,' the team says. But curses involving goats, fans named Bartman and general all-round crappy teams keep them winless for the next 100 years. And counting....

lived, having been built out of a rough equivalent of plaster of Paris that barely lasted through the fair. The only survivor was the Fine Arts Building, which was revamped to become the Museum of Science & Industry (p113).

Around this time, society legend Bertha Palmer was following the lead of other Chicago elite by touring Paris. A prescient art collector, she nabbed Monets, Renoirs and other impressionist works before they had achieved acclaim. Her collection later formed the core of the Art Institute (p52).

THE GREAT MIGRATION

In 1910 eight out of 10 blacks still lived in the southern states of the old Confederacy. Over the next decade a variety of factors combined to change that, as more than two million African Americans moved north in what came to be known as the 'Great Migration'.

Chicago played a pivotal role in this massive population shift, both as an impetus and as a destination. Articles in the black-owned and nationally circulated *Chicago Defender* proclaimed the city a worker's paradise and a place free from the horrors of Southern racism. Ads from Chicago employers also promised jobs to anyone willing to work.

These lures, coupled with glitzy images of thriving neighborhoods like Bronzeville (p116), inspired thousands to take the bait. Chicago's black population zoomed from 44,103 in 1910 to 109,458 in 1920 and continued growing. The migrants, often poorly educated sharecroppers with big dreams, found a reality not as rosy as promised. Chicago did not welcome them with open arms. In 1919 white gangs from Bridgeport led days of rioting that killed 23 local black residents and 15 white ones. Employers were ready with the promised jobs, but many hoped to rid their factories of white unionized workers by replacing them with blacks, which further exacerbated racial tensions. Blacks were also restricted to living in South Side ghettos by openly prejudicial real-estate practices that kept them from buying or renting homes elsewhere in the city. The South Side remains predominately black to this day.

BOOZE FUELS THE MACHINE

Efforts to make the United States 'dry' had never found great favor in Chicago; the city's vast numbers of German and Irish immigrants were never ready to forsake their favored libations. During the 20th century's first two decades, the political party that could portray itself as the 'wettest' would win the local elections. Thus the nationwide enactment of Prohibition in 1920 (the federal constitutional amendment making alcohol consumption illegal) was destined to meet resistance in Chicago, where voters had gone six to one against the law in an advisory referendum. However, few could have predicted how efforts to flout Prohibition would forever mark Chicago's image on a global scale, thanks to a gent named Al Capone (see the boxed text, p79).

WINDY CITY INGENUITY

Chicago has wowed the world with inventions and discoveries such as:

- roller skates (1884)
- the cafeteria (1895)
- Hostess Twinkies (1930)
- pinball (1930)
- Oscar Mayer 'Wienermobile' (1936)
- controlled atomic reaction (1942)
- Peter Cetera (1944)
- daytime TV soap operas (1949)
- Weber Grill (1951)
- Lava Lite 'Lava Lamps' (1965)
- house music (1977)

1915

The *Eastland* steamboat, filled with picnickers, capsizes in the Chicago River while still tied to the dock by LaSalle St Bridge; 844 people die, though the water there is only 20ft deep.

1929

Prohibition conflict comes to a head when seven people are killed in a gang shoot-out between Capone and Bugs Moran. The day becomes known as the St Valentine's Day Massacre.

1931

After years of running the murderous 'Chicago Outfit' and supplying the nation with illegal booze during Prohibition, gangster Al Capone goes to jail for tax evasion. There he's called 'the wop with the mop.'

An important year for the city, 1933 saw Prohibition repealed and a thirsty populace return openly to the bars. Another world's fair, this time called the Century of Progress, opened on the lakefront south of Grant Park and promised a bright future filled with modern conveniences. Then, in the same year, Ed Kelly became mayor. With the help of party boss Pat Nash, he strengthened Chicago's Democratic Party, creating the legendary 'machine' that would control local politics for the next 50 years. Politicians doled out thousands of city jobs to people who worked hard to make sure their patrons were reelected. The same was true for city vendors and contractors, whose continued prosperity was tied to their donations.

DA MAYOR #1: RICHIE J DALEY

The zenith of the machine's power began with the election of Richard J Daley in 1955. Initially thought to be a mere party functionary, Daley was reelected mayor five times before dying while still in office in 1976. With an uncanny understanding of machine politics and how to use it to squelch dissent, he dominated the city in a way no mayor had before. His word was law, and a docile city council routinely approved all his actions, lest a dissenter find his or her ward deprived of vital city services.

Under 'the Boss's' rule, corruption was rampant. A 1957 *Life* magazine report called Chicago's cops the most corrupt in the nation. Although Daley and the machine howled with indignation over the article, further exposés by the press revealed that some cops and politicians were in cahoots with various crime rings. None of this was news to the average Chicagoan.

Chicago's voting practices were also highly suspect, never more so than in 1960, when John F Kennedy ran for president of the United States against Richard Nixon, then vice president. The night of the election, the results were so close nationwide that the outcome hinged on the vote in Illinois.

Mayor Daley called up Kennedy and assured him that 'with a little bit of luck and the help of a few close friends, you're going to carry Illinois.' Kennedy did win Illinois, by 10,000 votes, and that granted him the presidency. For many, that was the perfect embodiment of electoral politics in Chicago, a city where the slogan has long been 'Vote early and vote often,' and voters have been known to rise from the grave to cast ballots.

HIPPIES & RIOTS COME TO TOWN

The year 1968 proved an explosive one for Chicago. When Martin Luther King Jr was assassinated in Memphis, Tennessee, the Chicago's West Side exploded in riots and went up in smoke. Whole stretches of the city were laid to waste, and Daley and the many black politicians in the machine were helpless to stop the violence. Worse yet, the city's hosting of the Democratic National Convention in August degenerated into a fiasco of such proportions that its legacy dogged Chicago for decades.

With the war in Vietnam escalating and general unrest quickly spreading through the US, the convention became a focal point for protest groups of all stripes. However, regardless of the tempest brewing, conservative old Mayor Daley – the personification of a 'square' if there ever was one – was planning a grand convention. Word leaked out that protesters would converge on Chicago, sparking authorities' plans to crack the head of anybody who got in the way of Daley's show. Local officials shot down all of the protesters' requests for

1942

The first nuclear chain reaction occurs on a University of Chicago squash court. Enrico Fermi and his Manhattan Project pals high-five each other for pulling off the feat – and not blowing up the city in the process.

1955

Mayor Daley #1 takes office and fires up the Chicago Machine, ie the Democratic Party's rule of the city based on 'I'll scratch your back if you scratch mine' patronage. He remains mayor for the next 21 years.

1960

McCormick Place opens and is immediately hailed as the 'mistake by the lake'.

parade permits, despite calls from the press and other politicians to uphold the civil right of free assembly.

Enter Abbie Hoffman, Jerry Rubin, Rennie Davis, Tom Hayden, Bobby Seale and David Dellinger – members of the soon-to-become 'Chicago Seven.' They called for a mobilization of 500,000 protesters to converge on Chicago. As the odds of confrontation became high, many moderate protesters decided not to attend. When the convention opened, there were just a few thousand young protesters in the city. But Daley and his cronies spread rumors to the media to bolster the case for their warlike preparations. Some of these whoppers included claims that hippie girls would pose as prostitutes to give the delegates venereal diseases and that LSD would be dumped into the city's water supply.

top picks

HISTORIC SITES

- **St Valentine's Day Massacre Site** (p79)
- **Water Tower** (p70)
- **Haymarket Square** (p100)
- **Graceland Cemetery** (p87)
- **Nuclear Energy sculpture** (p115)

The first few nights of the August 25–30 convention saw police staging midnight raids on hippies and protesters attempting to camp in Lincoln Park. The cops went on massive beating sprees, singling out some individuals for savage attacks. Teenage girls were assaulted by cops who shouted, 'You want free love? Try this!'. Journalists, ministers and federal Justice Department officials were appalled.

The action then shifted to Grant Park, across from the Conrad Hilton (now the Chicago Hilton & Towers), where the main presidential candidates were staying. A few thousand protesters held a rally, which was met by an overwhelming force of 16,000 Chicago police officers, 4000 state police officers and 4000 members of the National Guard armed with tear-gas grenades, nightsticks and machine guns. When some protesters attacked a few officers, the assembled law enforcers staged what investigators later termed a police riot. Among the lowlights: cops shoved bystanders through plate-glass windows and then went on to beat them as they lay bleeding amid the shards; police on motorcycles ran over protesters; police chanted 'Kill, kill, kill!,' swarmed journalists and attempted to do just that; and when some wounded conventioneers were taken to the hotel suite of presidential candidate Gene McCarthy, cops burst through the door and beat everybody in sight.

The long-term effects of the riots were far greater that anyone could have guessed. The Democratic candidate for president, Hubert Humphrey, was left without liberal backing after his tacit support of Daley's tactics, and as a result, Republican Richard Nixon was elected president. Chicago was left with a huge black eye for decades.

POLISHING THE RUST

Meanwhile, the city's economy was hitting the skids. In 1971 financial pressures caused the last of the Chicago stockyards to close, marking the end of one of the city's most infamous enterprises. Factories and steel mills were also shutting down as companies moved to the suburbs or the southern US, where taxes and wages were lower. Chicago and much of the Midwest earned the moniker 'Rust Belt,' describing the area's shrunken economies and rusting factories.

1964

The Rolling Stones come to town for a blues lesson with Muddy Waters and the guys at Chess Records. Keith Richards calls the place 'Mecca.' The band has to haul their own equipment upstairs.

1968

Chicago law enforcement goes nuts at the Democratic National Convention; 24,000 cops and National Guardsmen beat the crap out of a few thousand hippie protestors at the Hilton hotel downtown.

1974

Chicago pops the last girder into the Sears Tower, which becomes the world's tallest building at 110 stories (1454ft) and remains the record-holder for the next quarter century.

But two events happened in the 1970s that were harbingers of the city's more promising future. The world's tallest building (at the time), the Sears Tower, opened in the Loop in 1974, beginning a development trend that would spur the creation of thousands of high-paying white-collar jobs. And in 1975, the Water Tower Place shopping mall brought new life to N Michigan Ave.

The city's first and only female mayor – the colorful Jane Byrne – took the helm in 1979. She opened Chicago up to filmmakers, allowing the producers of *The Blues Brothers* to demolish part of the Daley Center. Moviemaking remains an important city revenue generator today.

Byrne's reign was followed by that of Harold Washington, Chicago's first black mayor, in 1983. His legacy was the success of the African American politicians who followed him. Democrat Carol Moseley-Braun's election to the US senate in 1992 can be credited in part to Washington's political trailblazing. Jesse Jackson Jr and Barack Obama are a couple of other names that come to mind.

DA MAYOR #2: RICHIE M DALEY

In 1989 Chicago elected Richard M Daley, the son of Richard J Daley, to finish the remaining two years of Harold Washington's mayoral term (Washington died in office).

Like his father, Daley had an uncanny instinct for city politics. First, he made nice with state officials, who handed over hundreds of millions of public dollars. Among the projects that bore fruit were an O'Hare airport expansion, a huge addition to the McCormick Place Convention Center and the reconstruction of Navy Pier. He also restructured old, semi-independent bureaucracies such as the Park District and Department of Education. And he entertained the city as well. Daley proved himself prone to amusing verbal blabber, such as this classic, his explanation for why city health inspectors had closed down so many local restaurants: 'Whadda ya want? A rat in yer sandwich or a mouse in yer salad?'

Despite falling to the third-largest US city, population-wise, in the 1990 census (behind New York and LA), the '90s were a good decade for Chicago. In 1991 the Chicago Bulls won the first of six national basketball championships. The 1994 World Cup soccer opening ceremony focused international attention on the city. And in 1996 a 28-year-old demon was exorcised when the Democratic National Convention returned to Chicago. City officials spent millions of dollars spiffing up the city, and thousands of cops underwent sensitivity training on how to deal with protestors. The convention went off like a dream and left Chicagoans believing they were on a roll.

And when you're on a roll, who else do you thank but the guy who seems to have made it all possible? Daley won his re-election bids in 1991, 1995, 1999, 2003 and 2007, pretty much by a landslide every time. If he finishes out his current term through 2010, he'll become Chicago's longest-running mayor. The previous record holder? His dad, who was Chicago's mayor for 21 years.

That's not to say the guy doesn't have issues. In 2003 he bulldozed the lakefront commuter airport of Meigs Field in an autocratic show of power (see Northerly Island, p108, for details). In 2005, the 'Hired Truck scandal' cast an awkward shadow over his administration, when it was discovered that city staff had been accepting bribes in exchange for giving lucrative trucking contracts to companies that never actually did any work. The investigation later widened to include more aspects of the city's patronage system.

1989

Mayor Daley #2 takes office, continuing the Machine legacy of his dad. His reign is highlighted by midnight bulldozings and shiny park unveilings. He's on pace to rule the city even longer than his pa.

2005

Chicago White Sox win the World Series. It's the first baseball championship in almost a century. The city holds a ticker-tape parade and invites Steve Perry from Journey to sing 'Don't Stop Believin'.

2007

Taking Steve Perry at his word (see above), Chicago embarks on a couple of new projects to ensure it stays on the 'world's greatest city' radar: Chicago Spire (another record-breaking skyscraper) and the 2016 Olympics bid.

2016 OR BUST

In 2007, Chicago beat out Los Angeles to become the USA's entry in the Olympic Games hosting contest for summer 2016. The city was stoked, although it now faces stiff competition on the international front from Prague, Rome, Rio de Janeiro, Madrid and Tokyo.

How will Chicago raise the money to accommodate such a massive event? That plan is in the making. The city is in pretty good shape as far as venues go, since it already has several sports stadiums, plus McCormick Place, the world's biggest convention center. But the money, oy! It's estimated Chicago will need $5 billion; the new lakeside Olympic Village alone will supposedly cost $1.1 billion. Will it come from higher taxes? Private funds? Government funds? Chicagoans are waiting for the answer.

Chicago tried and failed to host the games in 1904, 1952 and 1956, and Mayor Daley wants them badly this time around. It's become his pet project, and he's tasked his big-business buddies with finding the dough to make it happen. But he's not alone: the bid is generally well supported throughout town, especially on the South Side, which might get some new venues out of the deal (ie Washington Park is proposed for the Olympic Stadium).

So is it all just an expensive dream? Could it ever really happen in the Windy City? The International Olympic Committee makes its final decision in October 2009. Stay tuned.

SHINY HAPPY CITY

A lot of Chicagoans sigh when they hear about the shenanigans at City Hall. Then they point out all the flowers planted along the streets downtown, and how the once-trashed sidewalks are now clean. What's a little graft when the city looks so *good*?

Take Millennium Park for example. Sure it was four years late in opening and hundreds of millions of dollars over the original cost estimate. And a buddy of the mayor's held the contract to build it, until he had to be fired for not getting the job done properly. But damn, look at that gleaming park now. It's sensational and the whole world agrees.

Uber-buildings like the Chicago Spire are once again soaring above the clouds, and the city is ambitiously planning for the 2016 Olympics (see boxed text above).

As a wise man named Burnham once said, 'Make big plans. Aim high in hope and work.' Apparently the city continues to take his advice

ARTS

There's no greater summation of Chicago's devotedly earnest, if slightly awkward, embrace of the arts than a column by Mike Royko that was written after the unveiling of Picasso's *Untitled*. City politicos hoped that the unpainted, three-dimensional hunk of cubist steel would symbolize the city's cultural rebirth. Royko, the voice of Chicago's working class, saw it differently – first, as merely 'a long stupid face [that] looks like some giant insect that is about to eat a smaller, weaker insect' and then, after some reflection, the spirit of Chicago's sometimes brutal devotion to progress. Both perspectives were correct; such juxtapositions of class, convention and perspective make the city's artistic landscape so deeply, inexhaustibly stimulating.

These contrasts fuel Chicago's creative engine by way of high-concept installations that occupy erstwhile warehouses, challenging symphonic works played for picnicking families in the park and poetry readings that are nearly a contact sport. The dedication to populist artistic ideals – most visible in numerous free summer festivals and ubiquitous public art – lend Chicago artists a unique relationship to their spectators. By pushing boundaries in front of broad audiences, Chicago has shaped one major international movement after another, from beat poetry to house music to modern dance.

While both high-minded and casual artistic hallmarks of blues and ballet soldier on, no area of Chicago arts has seen a greater recent explosion than the theater scene. The stages here have drawn international attention, exemplified by the twinkling marquees and gilded palaces of the Loop, residencies by celebrated dramatists like John Malkovich, and the sheer volume of makeshift productions that defy every convention. Major names in theater, like Goodman and Steppenwolf, routinely stage premieres by world-famous playwrights while small companies like the House Theater and Redmoon represent the amusing vanguard of the form. Even though the buildings that house Steppenwolf and Looking Glass are some of Chicago's newest cultural landmarks, other of the city's smaller theater companies and music ensembles are somewhat transient, setting up productions in whatever space they can get their hands on. If you encounter a company that does not have an address in the following chapters, check local papers to see where they've set up shop.

The visual arts are just steps behind. The city's largest concentration of galleries has outgrown the River North district, migrating west of the Loop and south to the rapidly-gentrifying Latino neighborhood of Pilsen. Art students and upstarts who can't get their creations on walls have a tendency to take matters into their own hands, skirting through the night streets will all variety of guerilla expressions, plastering up political posters and elevating that much-maligned Chicago invention, spray paint, to a highly stylized form.

There are few cities in the United States that can boast such engaging, affordable options for art lovers, and none that can do so with such little pretension. Find a copy of that Royko column and read it in the shadow of the Picasso; you'll have all the inspiration you'll need.

PAINTING & VISUAL ARTS

Nowhere is it easier to see the great chasms and curious bridges of the city's artistic efforts than in the visual arts. While galleries and critics might still highlight the divide between Chicago's various niches, the creators themselves muddle the lines. Take the recent work of painter Kerry James Marshall, who plays with comics and superheroes, or an artist like Chris Ware (p194), who draws comics with architectural perfectionism. Photographer Rashid Johnson evokes 19th-century photographic techniques and elements of hip-hop, while muralist Dzine (pronounced 'design') draws inspiration from Chicago's hip-hop graffiti movement to create outdoor works on the large scale of 19th century muralists.

All of these juxtapositions may well have rankled the fat cat industrialists who raised marble halls and funded collections of old and new European art 100 years ago, but Chicago's public has always embraced pioneering forms. Consider society matron Bertha Palmer, who fostered the city's artistic edge back then as a key collector of the Art Institute's impressionist paintings.

Since then, local artists have contributed to every major international movement – from Archibald Motley Jr portraits of roaring South Side jazz clubs in the 1920s to today's big local names like textile artist Ai Kijima, mosaic artist Juan Chavez and multimedia provocateurs like Matthew Hoffman and Sabrina Raaf.

Taking in works from any of Chicago's younger artists demonstrates that the modern art community has few discernable commonalities. If there is such a thing as a 'Chicago style,' the man with the best idea of its definition might be former gallery owner and writer Paul Klein, who launched a movement in 2005 to open a modern art museum devoted exclusively to Chicago art. Though that gallery is still a pipe dream, Klein's website (www.artletter.com) is an illuminating look at the city's art scene, and hosts a discussion board with rich banter from Chicago's art community.

The most eagerly anticipated development for those interested in modern art is the 2009 opening of the Art Institute of Chicago's Modern Art Wing. This will finally give a proper space to the Institute's vast modern collection, which has too long been given cursory attention by the stamping crowds on the way to see 'American Gothic.'

Gallery Districts & Festivals

The best place to see these younger artists and Chicago's stars of tomorrow will be in one of Chicago's three gallery-dense neighborhoods. The first and most illustrious of these is the River North neighborhood (p66). These galleries sell major works by both local and international artists, and host a busy scene of openings and events. It makes a fun afternoon of browsing, but if you have to ask, you probably can't afford it.

More recently developed gallery districts in the West Loop (p97) and Pilsen (p102) are good options as well. The former brings Chicago edgier works of younger artists, including many painters, photographers and mixed media artists of modest renown. Taking something home still won't be cheap – anywhere from $500 to $5000 – but most of the galleries are a bit more exciting than their vetted neighbors north of the river. Pilsen is the youngest and most casual gallery district in town and work here is largely by Chicago locals. To spend an afternoon strolling past works from the next generation of Chicago's artistic notables see West Loop Gallery tour (p103). A round-up of local gallery happenings can be found through the Chicago Art Dealers Association (CADA; www.chicagoartdealers.org) website or by browsing though Chicago Gallery News (www.chicagogallerynews.org).

If you're after festivals, the CADA sponsors the annual two-week VISION art festival, which draws collectors, gallery owners and artists from all over the world each July. The biggest annual event in Chicago arts is Art Chicago (www.artchicago.com), an international contemporary art fair at the end of April that has recently taken a home in the Merchandise Mart (222 Merchandise Mart Plaza; www.merchandisemart.com).

top picks

ART SPACES

- Art Institute of Chicago (p52) You already own the calendar, now see it for yourself.
- Smith Museum of Stained Glass Windows (p67) Sounds boring right? Wrong. One of the true highlights of the tourist-fest of Navy Pier.
- National Museum of Mexican Arts (p101) This ambitious museum is home to some of the nation's most exciting Mexican and Mexican-American artists.
- Museum of Contemporary Art (p71) The challenging collection at MCA continues to push boundaries.
- Museum of Contemporary Photography (p108) Tidy and engaging, this is a great stop in the South Loop.

PUBLIC ART

Chicago has a standard-setting public policy that has made the city an international center for public art: in 1978, the city council approved an ordinance stipulating that a percentage of costs for constructing or renovating municipal buildings be set aside for the commission or purchase of artworks. The result finds downtown riddled with gaping art lovers taking in a collection that's as much a part of the city's character as its ground-breaking architecture.

The most prominent of these public works go well beyond the staring eyes of the Picasso and Millennium Park's 'Bean.' Alexander Calder has two major works in the city, both completed in 1974. The most visible of these is the arching red 'Flamingo' that sits in front of the Federal Center Plaza at Dearborn and Adams Streets. The other, 'The Universe,' is hardly out of the way for most travelers to the city – its colorful, moving shapes grace the lobby of the Sears Tower. Joan Miró's 'Chicago' – original titled 'The Sun, The Moon and One Star' – is within a short walk, as is an expansive mosaic by Chagall. As for the 'Bean,' its just one of the monumental works of art that have been crammed into Millennium Park (p53), which itself should count as an elegant masterpiece that mirrors the city's pragmatic approach to the arts.

The city's public art program also oversees special projects that have gotten a lot of attention. Among the most successful to date was the 1999 *Cows on Parade* exhibition, a series of brightly painted bovines that has been spun off in major cities around the country. For the most renowned must-sees in the Loop, turn to Public Art (p58).

MUSIC

Its hard to tell what sounds more sincere – Frank Sinatra swinging about 'one town that won't let you down' or Wilco ruing being 'far, far away from those city lights,' hip-hop chart-topper Kanye West rhyming about watching the 'fireworks over Lake Michigan' or Magic Sam wanting to get back to his 'sweet home Chicago.' No foolin': every single facet of American music has the grubby fingerprints of Chicago music makers all over it. The birthplace of electric blues and house music, Chicago also fosters a vibrant independent rock scene, boundary-leaping jazzers and several world-class orchestras. From top to bottom Chicago's music embodies the noblest characteristics of the city itself: musicians are resourceful and hard-working, sweating it out in muggy blues clubs, long orchestra seasons, DIY punk shows and every sound in-between.

Chicago Blues

The most iconoclastic of Chicago forms comes in one color: blue. Bluesmen set up in the open-air markets of Maxwell St in the 1930s, and by 1936 Chicago had become a regional hub of the genre when Delta bluesman Robert Johnson first recorded 'Sweet Home Chicago.' But what distinguishes Chicago blues from Johnson's original ode is simple: volume. Chicago blues is defined by the plugged-in, electric guitars typified by genre fathers Muddy Waters and Howlin' Wolf. Fifties and '60s bluesmen like Willie Dixon, Jimmy Reed and Elmore James and later champions like Buddy Guy and Koko Taylor became national stars. These days, Chicago's blues are still playing much the same song they were 40 years ago, but it's a proud one – synonymous with screaming guitars, rolling bass and R&B-inflected rhythms. You can still shake it to blues at clubs all over town (p182).

House History

Finding the roots of the city's other taste-making musical export is relatively easy: it began in the early '80s at a now-defunct West Side nightclub called the Warehouse where DJ Frankie Knuckles got tired of spinning disco and added samples of European electronic music and beats from this new-fangled invention, the stand-alone drum machine. Uninterested in commercial radio the tracks used deep, pounding bass beats and instrumental samples made for dancing. DJs like Derrick Carter and Larry Heard revolutionized the form and huge second-wave stars like Felix Da Housecat and DJ Sneak took Chicago's thump world-wide. The club scene was all about big beats, wild parties and drugged-out dancing until the late '90s, when police cracked down and the trend boiled over. In the years since, the scene has matured – no more pacifiers and glow sticks – while continuing to innovate. For the skinny on today's best clubs, see the Nightlife's Clubs section (p186).

25 ESSENTIAL CHICAGO SONGS

This sampling of great songs about Chicago and by Chicago musicians is not for the narrow-minded, but neither are the city's wildly eclectic music makers. Load this on the ole iPod, and you'll hear a bit of the whole of the city's music spectrum – from the scrappy punks who ramble through the city's dive bars, to the iconic vocalists of Chicago blues. At 25 songs, this list is woefully abbreviated; it'd be just as easy to list 25,000.

- 'Champagne & Reefer' by Muddy Waters
- 'Sister Havana' by Urge Overkill
- 'Ten-Day Interval' by Tortoise
- 'That's All I Need' by Magic Sam
- 'Plutonian Nights' by Sun Ra
- 'The Superbowl Shuffle' by the 1985 Chicago Bears
- 'Boogie Chillin' by John Lee Hooker
- 'Oh Messy Life' by Cap'n Jazz
- 'Via Chicago' by Wilco
- 'Dolphins' by the Sea and Cake
- 'Rocket Ride' by Felix Da Housecat
- 'We Should Have Never Lived Like We Were Skyscrapers' by Chin Up Chin Up
- 'Wang Dang Doodle' by Koko Taylor
- 'Fever' by Buddy Guy
- 'In The Ghetto' by Elvis Presley
- 'Let's Groove' by Earth Wind and Fire
- 'Champion' by Kanye West
- 'Hold On, Hold On' by Neko Case
- 'Suitcase (For Ray Charles, Elvin Jones and Steve Lacy)' by Vandermark 5
- 'Goin' To Chicago' by Kurt Elling
- 'Sweet Home Chicago' by Robert Johnson (The Blues Brothers)
- 'Tonight, Tonight' by Smashing Pumpkins
- 'My Kinda Town' by Frank Sinatra
- 'Can You Feel It' by Mr Fingers
- 'Three Hundred Pounds Of Joy' by Howlin' Wolf

Jazz, Rock, Hip-hop and Gospel

The many other musical forms of the city are no less noble, but slightly less idiosyncratic on the national stage. The Green Mill (p183) is ground zero of jazz in the city and *Downbeat* award-winning male vocalist Kurt Elling gigs there every Wednesday night. For more cutting-edge jazz, the name to know is AACM, a Chicago-based organization that formed in the 1960s and was a big inspiration for recent scenemakers like Peter Brotzmann, and Ken Vandermark, a MacArthur 'genius' grant recipient

Chicago's underground rock community has filled an important niche during the past two decades through established indie labels like Drag City and Touch & Go, and younger feisty upstarts like Flameshovel Records. The reigning kings of Chicago rock are still Wilco, though after years of keeping MFA candidates enraptured, their star is beginning to fade.

For hip-hop, the heavyweight champ is Kanye 'George Bush doesn't care about black people' West, son of the head of Chicago State University's English department. West put Chicago on the hip-hop map, opening the door for fresh underground names like Lupe Fiasco and Twista.

Folk and gospel in the city are destination-oriented genres: troubadours hold down open mics on weeknights and play the Old Town School of Folk Music (p185; ☎ 773-728-6000; www.oldtownschool.org; 4544 N Lincoln Ave) and South Side gospel churches raising the roof on Sunday morning. Two worthy destinations for old school gospel are on the South Side: Greater Salem Missionary Baptist Church (p116; ☎ 773-874-2325; 215 W 71st St), where famed gospel matron Mahalia Jackson was a member, and Pilgrim Baptist Church (p116; ☎ 312-842-4417; 3301 S Indiana Ave). If you plan on raising the roof with the holy rollers at Pilgrim Baptist, call ahead; a fire gutted their original location in 2006, and during the rebuilding they've held services in a temporary location across the street at the Thomas A Dorsey Center.

FIVE CHICAGO RECORD LABELS THAT CHANGED THE WORLD

From Chess Records in the '40s and '50s to Thrill Jockey today, Chicago labels have long been the trailblazing leaders in new music. Five labels deserve special credit in making Chicago such a musical hotbed over the past five decades.

Bloodshot (www.bloodshotrecords.com) For over a decade this record label has put out some of the best records in the left-of-center American genre 'No Depression' that fuses punk rock and old-school country, alt-country or (the label's preferred moniker) insurgent country.

Chess Records When the blues left the Delta and migrated north, its home in Chicago was Chess Records. Run by two brothers, Leonard and Phil Chess, the label helped launch the careers of Muddy Waters, Howlin' Wolf and legendary harmonica player Little Walter. Chess engineered its records to match the tone of its artists, creating an aggressive, redlining blues sound that remains synonymous with Chicago. The label also served as a catalyst for early rock and roll, recording sessions by Chuck Berry and Bo Diddley.

Delmark Records (www.delmark.com) The oldest independent jazz and blues label in the country, Delmark Records has inspired countless small startups around the world determined to promote the pioneers and mavericks of the two genres. Delmark was founded in 1953 by a 21-year-old music fan named Bob Koester, who, before his leap into the music recording business, had been selling out-of-print blues and jazz records from his dorm room. Over its 50-year life, the label has released blues works by artists like Junior Wells, Otis Rush, Little Walter and Sunnyland Slim, and jazz records by Art Ensemble of Chicago, Sun Ra and Dinah Washington. Koester also runs the Jazz Record Mart (p123), a wax junkie's heaven in Near North.

Thrill Jockey (www.thrilljockey.com) When indie rock began to incorporate elements of jazz in the mid-1990s, Thrill Jockey documented the moment. Started by New York transplant Bettina Richards, the independent label has been the celebrated home of local bands like Tortoise, and the Sea and Cake. The label isn't limited to the 'post-rock' bands that made it famous, however, with signings from local countryish acts like Freakwater and Califone to abstract European electronica artists like Mouse on Mars. Thanks to its consistently solid output and stratospherically high cachet, Thrill Jockey has opened the minds of indie music fans worldwide to new genres and styles.

Wax Trax! It's hard to say what would have happened to industrial music in the '80s without the tireless work of local label Wax Trax!. Along with bringing the raw, electronic mayhem of European artists like KMFDM and Front 242 to the US, Wax Trax! issued works by fledgling domestic acts such as Ministry and Meat Beat Manifesto. Though the label is now defunct, you can hear highlights in the extensive 3-CD box set *Black Box: Wax Trax! Records, The First 13 Years*.

THEATER

Since the London *Guardian* named Chicago the theater capital of the US in 2004, the city has vigorously defended the title with a greater number of productions and more enthusiastic audiences. The Broadway blockbusters in the Loop and Near North continue to draw hordes, but the more intimate dramatic performances happen at Steppenwolf (p196), Lincoln Park's landmark stage. Since 1976 Steppenwolf's matchless reputation has been earned by stunning talent and groundbreaking programming. Known heavyweights like Joan Allen, John Malkovich and Gary Sinise are alums, and they exemplify Chicago's bare-knuckled, physical style of acting. It feels particularly raw when you take in a smaller production by any one of the city's DIY companies that mostly operate in the further-out regions of the city.

But back in the Loop, you'll hardly be victim to another dreary performance of *Phantom*. The new millennium saw numerous renovations and openings including the gorgeous Cadillac Palace Theater and the Chicago Theater, and the Loop is often a pre-Broadway proving ground.

COMEDY & IMPROV

Your sitting in the back of a darkened theater, when suddenly, the man behind you screams in a shrill, ear-piercing falsetto, 'Blow up doll!' This startles the woman to your left, who promptly, cupping her hands around her mouth, yells 'Alpaca! Alpaca! Alpaca!'

'Did someone say "runny eggs?",' says the man on the stage. 'Let's go with runny eggs.' For a moment things seem pretty odd…and then the man on stage starts to sing Wagnerian opera about getting marital counseling with a plate of runny eggs.

Along with Wonder Bread, spray paint and house music, add improvised comedy to the heap of Chicago's wide reaching cultural contributions. Were it not for Chicago's Second City comedy troupe – a performance of intentionally unstructured skits by the Compass Players in a Hyde Park bar in 1955 – the proverbial chicken might still be crossing the road of American comedy. Since 1959, the Compass Players' original gag incorporating audience suggestions into quick-witted comedy became standard fare at The Second City Theater (p190), and made Chicago comedy synonymous with audience participation. The company has produced some of the country's most capable funny bone ticklers in John Belushi, Eugene Levy, Mike Myers, Chris Farley and Tina Fey.

It's a good idea to double check newspaper listings before you go rolling into Second City with the hope of offering your hill-arious suggestion though. Second City stages a surprisingly large variety of shows – some of which are scripted and nearly serious. If you find the offering at Second City and its sundry training stages unappealing or a bit too expensive, there are other places to catch improv all over town, including IO (p189) – which was called ImprovOlympic until a run-in with the International Olympic Committee – or ComedySportz (p189).

For those of you who are not content to simply witness the tomfoolery, there are opportunities that go well beyond just screaming out suggestions from the back row. For information about improv classes, check out the websites for both Second City (www.secondcity.com) and iO (www.iochicago.net).

LITERATURE

'Yet once you've come to be part of this particular patch, you'll never love another,' wrote Chicago literary illuminati Nelson Algen about his hometown. 'Like loving a woman with a broken nose, you may well find lovelier lovelies. But never a lovely so real.'

In the past two years, the Chicago writers have started to love that woman with a broken nose a whole lot, and though the lit scene may be outshined by lovelier lovelies in the US, the attention to and activity within the community has dramatically flourished in the past few years. It might not be too evident at the sometimes scrappy events that are just as likely to take place in a bar as a bookstore, but the number of new blogs and monthly events that have sprung up are a good indication of how quickly the scene is blossoming.

A new meeting place for Chicago's hipster writers who want to give something back to the community is 826 Chicago. Modeled after Dave Eggers' successful 826 Valencia tutoring center

CHICAGO BOOKS

- *Middlesex* (2003, Jeffrey Eugenides) – Set across the lake in Detroit, this novel is a hermaphrodites' coming of age story. It won the Pulitzer in 2003 and, more surprisingly, was selected for Oprah's book club in 2007.
- *Working: What People do all Day and How They Feel About What They Do* (1974, Studs Turkel) – This exploration into the meaning of work from people in all walks of life is a seminal text for 'the city that works.'
- *Presumed Innocent* (1987, Scott Turow) – The seminal work of crime fiction by Chicago's smartest genre novelist.
- *Freakonomics* (2005, Steven Levitt) – The University of Chicago economics professor stayed atop bestseller lists for a long time with this shrewd analysis of the 'hidden side of everything.'
- *The Jungle* (1906, Upton Sinclair) – This epic from 1906 is set on the brutal, blood-soaked floors of Chicago's South Side meatpacking plants. It cast a bright light on the inhumane working conditions of Chicago immigrant communities and was a catalyst for reform.
- *The Man With the Golden Arm* (1949, Nelson Algrens) – A tale of a drug-addicted kid on Division Street, this won the National Book Award in 1950. These days a walk down the same stretch of Division is more likely to get you addicted to clothes from Urban Outfitters.
- *The Adventures of Augie March* (1953, Saul Bellow) – Often listed among the best American novels, this book is an engaging portrayal of a destitute Chicago boy's experiences growing up during the Depression. Bellow died in 2005 but he is still one of the celebrated fathers of the city's fiction world.
- *Annie Allen* (1949, Gwendolyn Brooks) – This collection of poems made Brooks the first African American writer ever to receive a Pulitzer Prize.
- *One More Time: The Best of Mike Royko* (1999, Mike Royko) – Few give you a better introduction to the city's socio-political landscape than this child of Polish and Ukrainian origins and voice of the city's working class. His view on dirty politics and daily life in Chicago at the now-defunct *Daily News* won him a Pulitzer in 1972. This compiles earnest, snappy, often poignant vignettes of Chicago life.
- *Windy City Blues* (1996, Sara Paretsky) – A collection of sharp short stores starring Partersky's beloved character VI Warshawski.
- *I Sailed With Magellan* (2004, Stuart Dybek) – First recognized for 1990's *The Coast of Chicago*, Dybek's second major collection of stories adds an impressive twist on the down-and-out narratives of Nelson Algren.
- *The Devil In White City* (2004, Eric Larson) – A gripping bit of nonfiction about when the World's Columbian Exposition, which was held in Chicago in 1893 and inadvertency became the playground of one of America's first serial killers.
- *The House on Mango Street* (1984, Sandra Cisneros) – This set of interconnected vignettes is set in a Mexican-American Chicago barrio.
- *Sister Carrie* (1900, Theodore Dreiser) – Once a larger-than-life figure in Chicago's literary world, this story by Dreiser tells the story of a small town girl seduced by the city.
- *The City in Which I Love You* (1990, Li-Young Lee) – This, the composed verse of this contemporary Asian-American voice, evokes traditional Chinese poets like Li Bo.

in San Francisco, this store front on Milwaukee Ave has a facetious retail section called 'The Boring Store' (p133) in front – worth a trip in its own right for their wacky, 'boring' supplies for spies – and a tutoring center out back.

The annual Chicago Humanities Festival (www.chfestival.org), makes the end of October a great time of year for book lovers. The two-week schedule of readings, lectures and discussions features an interesting roster of fiction writers and poets. The newcoming literature and publisher's festival, Printers' Ball (www.printersball.org), is a bit more underground, but it offers a meeting of the minds for poets, publishers and fiction writers, and events with a multimedia bash. Year-round, you can become acquainted with the work of Chicago writers in literary magazines like *Other Voices*, *Make* (www.makemag.com) and *ACM*, whose full self-effacing title, *Another Chicago Magazine*, perfectly exemplifies the literary scene's underdog spirit.

For a list of heavy volumes in Chicago's literary history, see the boxed text above.

Poetry & Spoken Word

Chicago is home to the nation's gold-standard of poetic journals, *Poetry*. Long a bellwether for the academic establishment, the attractive little journal got a nice financial boost in 2002 when pharmaceutical heiress and longtime amateur poet Ruth Lilly bequeathed $100 million to its publisher, Chicago's Modern Poetry Association. Since then, former Wall St investment banker John Barr has taken over as president of the organization, creating a number of lucrative poetry prizes (which include the prestigious Ruth Lily prize, naturally) and the 'American Life in Poetry' project (www.americanlifeinpoetry.org), which provides a free weekly column for print and online publications about poetry.

Nothing could be more unlike the quietly scholarly verse of *Poetry* than spending a night at the venerated Uptown Poetry Slam (p200) held at the Green Mill. For a paltry admission fee, The Uptown Poetry Slam features guest performers from around the country, an open mic for newcomers, and their famous slam competition, widely considered to be the birthplace of performance-oriented verse.

For a list of regular readings in the city, see Readings & Spoken Word (p199) or visit the excellent site maintained by the Chicago Poetry Center at www.poetrycenter.org

DANCE

Like many of the city's other expressive hallmarks, jazz dance is an art form based on jarring contradictions; at its core it relies on both exceedingly controlled, and fluidly expressive motion. The invention of the style is credited to legendary Chicago dance teacher Gus Giordano, and the exhilarating performances by his namesake company (these days overseen by his daughter) will quickly annihilate any unsavory associations with campy 'jazz hands' or show-stopping 'razzle dazzle.'

Though Giordano's name tops the list of innovators, it's but one in Chicago's crowded landscape of A-list companies. The Joffrey Ballet settled in Chicago in 1995 to revive the city's awareness of ballet and modern companies like Hubbard Street Dance Chicago and keeps the attention of an international community. Additionally, the dance program at Columbia College supplies dancers and choreographers to the innovative fledgling companies that set up shop in performance spaces around the city. Aside from listings in the *Reader*, the best resource about dance in the city is the newly minted site of See Chicago Dance (www.seechicagodance.com).

CINEMA & TELEVISION

Now for the question that's been weighing on everyone's mind: 'What about Oprah?' Seeing Chicago's media mogul, Oprah Winfrey, firsthand (and maybe even winning a car!) is motivation enough for many out-of-towners to visit. Though Chicagoans themselves aren't too willing to flutter at celebrity sightings, hardly a tour of the city goes by without someone pointing to

CHICAGO, COMICS CAPITAL

The city's long history as a capital for comics goes *waaay* back, to an ambitious tyke named Walt Disney who studied art at a school on Michigan Ave that would one day become the Art Institute. His Mickey Mouse keeps good company with classic fish wrap heroes like Brenda Star and Dick Tracy, both of whom were born in Chicago. Today, illustrator Dick Locher has taken over the Dick Tracy strip – he's also the Pulitzer Prize-winning editorial cartoonist whose work appears in *Tribune*.

The edgier side of the comic world these days can be seen in the work of Oak Park artist Chris Ware and Jeffrey Brown. Ware's amazingly distinct catalogue of work has graced the pages of the *Reader*, *New Yorker* and *New York Times* and has been compiled in many hardback editions including the recent *Best American Comics 2007*. Wares has eclectic influences, but shows great attention to 20th century American aesthetics in both cartooning and graphic design, and precise, geometrical layouts.

Brown is know for a pair of coming-of-age graphic novels, *Clumsy* and *Unlikely*, that generated great local acclaim. He's part of a collective of talented young graphic novelists called the Holy Consumption (www.theholyconsumption.com), which also includes Anders Nilsen, John Hankiewicz and Paul Hornschemeier. The Holy Consumption catalogues some five years of autobiographical whimsy – not the kind of thing to discover if you want to have a productive day at work.

A selection of other local artists and graphic novelists can be found at Quimby's (p131) and Chicago Comics (p127), two great emporiums for comics and graphic novels.

her apartment on Lake Shore Dr and saying, with hushed, due reverence and a hint of wonder, 'That's where Oprah lives.'

You can catch a taping of the Oprah Winfrey Show (Map pp98–9; ☎ 312-591-9222; www.oprah.com; 110 N Carpenter) at her own Harpo Studios (Why Harpo? Spell it backward!). The wildly popular talk-show wheels out celebrities and shrinks before busload of euphoric Midwestern stay-at-homes. The good news is that tickets to join her studio audience are free. The bad news? The chances of getting them are slimmer than the results of her dieting tips. Reservations can only be secured a month in advance, and you have to call between 9am and 5pm Monday to Friday. Expect a busy signal – Oprah's website recommends calling between 1:30pm and 3pm, Chicago time. Alternatively the show's site sometimes announces last-minute openings, request tickets by email.

For some lowbrow TV thrills, travelers might also consider being in the studio audience of the Jerry Springer Show (☎ 312-321-5365; www.jerryspringertv.com; 2nd fl, 454 N Columbus) which is also taped in the Near North. The easiest way to get tickets to the show is through the show's website.

An equally memorable, but perhaps less syndicated taping, can be seen at the city's inimitable public access kids dance party, Chic-A-Go-Go (www.roctober.com/chicagogo; #617, 507 E 53rd St; 🚌 6). No cars and no hair-pulling adulterers, but its pretty fun to watch little tykes cavort around the room to of-the-minute rock bands. The show is hosted by the deliriously chipper Miss Mia and her little buddy Ratso, a puppet. It airs on cable channel 19.

Now that Oprah, Jerry and Ratso out of the way (you can sort out the similarities and differences for yourself), its worth noting that Chicago's much-varied presence on the big screen

CHICAGO FILM & TELEVISION

- *Oprah* – The unchallenged queen of media has no peers. And, she gives away cars!
- *Candyman* (1992, director Bernard Rose) – Yeah, its campy, gory and pretty stupid, but soon this slasher flick will be the best memento of the demolished Cabrini-Green slums. Plus, its scored by Philip Glass!
- *The Fugitive* (1993, director Andrew Davis) – The dramatic pissing contest between smarmy Tommy Lee Jones and growling Harrison Ford is one long, great chase sequence.
- *Jerry Springer Show* – The former Cincinnati mayor is unlikely to give you a car, but, if you're lucky, you might get caught up in a tussle involving the nefarious sexual hi-jinks of inarticulate, poorly-scripted rednecks.
- *The Untouchables* (1987, director Brian De Palma) – Chicago playwright David Mamet wrote the screenplay for this edge-of-the-seat drama about Eliot Ness' takedown of Al Capone.
- *Hoop Dreams* (1994, director Steve James) – This stirring documentary follows the high school basketball careers of two African American teenagers from the South Side. The filmmakers interview the young men and their families, coaches, teachers and friends over several years, showing how the dream of playing college and pro ball – and escaping the ghetto – influences their life choices.
- *Check Please!* – The everyman diners of Chicago pull no punches on this popular dining show, which is constantly the talk of the dining community.
- *High Fidelity* (2000, director Stephen Frears) – This Chicago version of Nick Hornby's classic paean to music nerds stars Chicagoan John Cusack as a man uncommitted about commitment. The record-store set for the film was located at Milwaukee Ave and Honore St in Wicker Park.
- *Ferris Bueller's Day Off* (1986, director John Hughes) – A cinematic ode to Chicago from the director who set almost all of his movies, from *Breakfast Club* to *Home Alone,* in and around the Windy City. This one revolves around a rich North Shore teen discovering the joys of Chicago
- *Chic-A-Go-Go* – Indie rock bands, a little rat puppet and gyrating sugar-high youngsters make this Chicago's best cable access staple.
- *The Blues Brothers* (1980, director John Landis) – In the best-known Chicago movie, Second City alums John Belushi and Dan Aykroyd tear up the city, including City Hall.
- *ER* – This popular TV update of General Hospital was set in Chicago, and sometimes its even filmed there.
- *The Breakfast Club* (1985, director John Hughes) – Sure, it's set in a fictional suburb, but this is Molly in all her mopey brilliance.
- *The Sting* (1973, director George Roy Hill) – A good-natured heist movie staring Paul Newman *and* Robert Redford? Daughters, lock up your mothers!
- *Chicago* (2002, director Rob Marshall) – All the razzle-dazzle nods to the city's jazz dance legacy in this sturdy theatrical adaptation.

has only gotten more prevalent in the past decade. For a list of Chicago cinematic classics see the boxed text on the topic (see opposite).

One reason that Chicago has been so convivial to those shiny faced Hollywood types is that the film industry brings money to the city's coffers. In 2005, Illinois governor Rod Blagojevich extended tax breaks to production companies filming in the state (while conveniently standing on the set of Jennifer Aniston vehicle, *The Breakup*). Blagojevich's insistent, if ham-fisted, recruitment of Hollywood producers has worked pretty well, and you can read all about it in local gossip blogs that buzz with news about Brad and Angelina dining atop the Four Seasons.

ARCHITECTURE

In 2011 Chicago will have another jewel in the well-encrusted skyline – Chicago Spire, North America's tallest free-standing structure. Bulldozers broke ground on the 150-story structure in 2007 after overcoming political, design and financial dilemmas. The futuristic drawings of designer Santiago Calatrava are well-known to residents who will spend the next few years in the growing shadow of a twisting building that resembles the horn of a gargantuan unicorn. The landmark will be the most recent, but hardly the most historically significant on the banks of Lake Michigan.

Ever since the Great Fire of 1871 made the city a blank canvas, Chicago has been home to some of the nation's most exciting architecture. For residents, the skyline is more a part of daily life than a backdrop, and the buildings are both tenderly adored and vehemently hated.

The Chicago Spire might be the boldest reminder of Chicago's architectural boom, but it's hardly alone. The past decade has been marked by great triumphs like Millennium Park, and great controversies, like the colossal South Loop developments.

CHICAGO SCHOOL (1872–99) & PRAIRIE SCHOOL (1895–1915)

Though the 1871 fire didn't seem like an opportunity at the time, it made Chicago what it is today. The opportunity to reshape the burned downtown drew young, ambitious architects like Dankmar Adler, Daniel Burnham, John Root and Louis Sullivan. These men saw the scorched Loop as a sandbox for innovation, and they rapidly built bigger, better commercial structures over the low roughshod buildings that immediately went up after the fire. These men and their colleagues made up the 'Chicago School' (who some say practiced the 'Commercial Style'), which stressed economy, simplicity and function. Using steel framing and high-speed elevators, they created their pinnacle achievement: the modern skyscraper.

The earliest buildings of the Chicago School, like the **Auditorium** (Map pp54–5; 430 S Michigan Ave) and original Monadnock Building (p57) used thick-bases to support the towering walls above. William Le Baron Jenney, the architect who constructed the world's first iron-and-steel-framed building in the 1880s, soon had a studio in Chicago, where he trained a crop of architects who pushed the city skyward through internal frames. The Monadnock itself is a good starting place to get a practical sense of how quickly these innovations were catching on: the original northern half of the building consists of more traditional, load-bearing walls that are six feet thick at the bottom, while the southern half, constructed only two years later, uses the then-revolutionary metal frame for drastically thinner walls that go just as high.

No matter how pragmatic these builders were in inspiration, the steel-framed boxes they erected never suffered from lack of adornment. Maverick firms like Alder & Sullivan and Burnham & Root used a simple, bold geometric language to rebuild downtown in style. Look for strong vertical lines crossed by horizontal bands, contrasted with the sweeping lines of bay windows, curved corners and grand entrances. For more low-down on the city's 'Chicago School' buildings and their locations, see Famous Loop Architecture on p57.

It was the protégé of Louis Sullivan, Frank Lloyd Wright, who would endow Chicago with its most distinctive style, the Prairie School. Wright, a spottily-educated ladies' man from Oak Park was the residential designer for the Alder & Sullivan firm until 1893, when his commissions outside the firm led to his dismissal. Forced into his own practice, he set up a small studio in Oak Park and by 1901 had built 50 structures in the area (see p236 for details on visiting the area).

In the next 15 years Wrights' 'Prairie Houses' contrasted the grand edifices of the Chicago School with their modest charms. The buildings stress low-slung structures with dominant horizon lines, flat roofs, overhanging eaves and an unadorned open space that hoped to mirror the Midwestern landscape. To blend visually, they used natural, neutral materials like brick, limestone and copper. Of all the Prairie Style homes from Wright's hand, the Robie House (p113) is the most dramatic and successful. It's a measuring stick by which all other buildings in the style are often compared and is alone worth the trip to Hyde Park. A bit of Wright's early work is nearer to the city center – the 1894 Robert W Roloson Houses (p116) in Bronzeville, which were designed while Wright still worked for Alder & Sullivan and are his only set of row houses. Wright's notable colleagues in the Prairie Style include Walter Burley Griffin, Marion Mahony Griffin, George W Maher and Robert C Spencer.

BEAUX ARTS (1893–1920) & ART DECO (1920–1939)

While the Chicago and Prairie Schools were forward-looking inventions that grew from the marshy shore of Lake Michigan, 'beaux arts,' named for the École des Beaux-Arts in Paris, took after a French fad that stressed antiquity. Proud local builders like Louis Sullivan hated the style, and he didn't mince words claiming that it set the course of American architecture back 'for half a century from its date, if not longer.' Sullivan aside, these buildings are pleasing today for their eclectic mixed bag of Classical Roman and Greek elements: stately columns, cornices and facades crowded with statuary. The popularity of the style was spurred by Daniel Burnham's colossal, classical-influenced buildings, like the 'White City', at the 1893 Worlds Expo. After Burnham's smash hit there, it became a dominant paradigm for the next two decades and a welcome contrast to the dirty, overcrowded slums that came with Chicago's urban explosion.

The impressive echoes of the White City are seen in some of the city's civic landmarks, like the Art Institute (p52) and the Chicago Cultural Center (p58). The later was born in 1897 as the Chicago Public Library and housed a donated collection of some 8000 books sent by British citizens after the Great Fire. (Many were even autographed by the donors, such as Thomas Carlyle, Lord Tennyson and Benjamin Disraeli). While the books have since moved to the Harold Washington Library, the magnificent public gilded ceilings and classical details remain.

After the decline in popularity of beaux arts, Chicago designers found inspiration from another French movement: art deco. The style may have been as ornamental as beaux arts, but instead of columns and statures, the style took on sharp angles, reflective surfaces and a modern palette of blacks, silvers and greens in more geometric elements. Sadly there are few remaining buildings in the Loop that characterize this style, and the one that does, the **Carbide and Carbon Building** (230 N Michigan Ave), has now become a Hard Rock Hotel Chicago (p216). If you can pull yourself away from the Sammy Hagar memorabilia, check out the building's polished black granite, green terra-cotta and gold crown – all colorful signals of the deco palate, which is rumored to be designed to look like a champagne bottle.

The Carbide and Carbon Building was one of the city's last structures in the style, which withered during WWII.

CHICAGO ARCHITECTURE TODAY

'No More Ugly Buildings' screamed the headline of the *Sun-Times*. The front-page op-ed by Mayor Daley took local architects and developers to task for betraying Chicago with a crop of unsightly condos and townhouse developments. For this, we can blame the big, bad '80s, when real estate prices in the Loop went sky-high and development sprawled in the Near North, South Loop and Near South.

The last time Chicago led the architectural world was when Ludwig Mies van der Rohe pioneered the new 'International Style' in the decades after WWII. The steel frame which once revolutionized the Chicago skyline was again seminal, though now no longer hidden on the inside of walls – the International Style was all about exposed metal and glass, and represents most peoples' image of the modern skyscraper. From 1950 through 1980, the Chicago architectural partnership of Skidmore, Owings & Merrill dominated the skyline by further developing Mies' ideas.

The decades between Mies's work and post-modernity is a mixed bag. The more recent work of note includes a number of playful experiments from Chicago architects like Jeannie Gang,

NOTABLE CHICAGO BUILDINGS

Some of the city's most talked about architectural treasures, these buildings wowed the world when they were first built.

- Chicago Cultural Center (p58) – Exemplifying the beaux arts style, this is a must for travelers who will stand agape at the gilded details.
- Marine City (p66) – Wilco fans aside, these giant corn cobs are strangely charming, especially when they light up at Christmas.
- Chicago Federal Center (p57) – If all the imitators of Ludwig Mies van der Rohe made such attractive office buildings, the modern skyline would be a better place.
- Chicago Board of Trade (p59) – Alvin Meyer's art deco masterpiece is topped by a 31-ft statue of a Roman goddess.
- Rookery (p57) – Frank Lloyd Wright's Prairie School-styled atrium is the perfect place to view the city's structural innovations.
- Jay Pritzker Pavilion (p56) – This performance space is ideal for an afternoon in the park.
- Robie House (p113) – The low eves and graceful lines of this Frank Lloyd Wright building were emulated around the world.
- The Tribune Tower (p62) – The lower level of this building has a wall with stones from the Taj Mahal, Notre Dame, the Great Pyramid, the Alamo, Lincoln's Tomb, the Great Wall of China and the Berlin Wall.
- Chicago Spire (Map pp64–5; 233 S Wacker Dr) – At press time it's not even built yet, but Chicago's newest triumph takes the skyline to artistic (and physical) heights.
- Auditorium Theater (Map pp54–5; 430 S Michigan Ave) – A glimpse inside the bejeweled theater is worth the trip, and certainly achieved the goal of showing Chicago had grown into a cultural magnate.

Brad Lynch and Doug Garofalo. Even more recently comes the success story of Millennium Park, which has again made Chicago the architectural envy of America.

ENVIRONMENT & PLANNING

THE LAND

Chicago's dominant feature is green-glinting Lake Michigan, which laps the city's entire eastern edge. Its ugly stepsibling is the Chicago River, which flows through downtown and has been rerouted, polluted and abused for most of the city's history.

To understand what kind of respect the river gets, consider the 2004 Dave Matthews Band incident: the driver of the group's tour bus decided to dump its septic tanks into the river while driving across the Kinzie St Bridge. He missed his watery target, but managed to score a direct hit on a Chicago Architecture Foundation tour boat that happened to be passing underneath.

Happily, the dumping was an isolated episode in the river's otherwise-upward trajectory since the 1980s. After monitoring and remediation efforts, the levels of toxic chemicals in the river have declined. Bass fishing has actually become a popular pastime on the upper reaches of the river. The city has also started putting in a series of public river walkways, and mandating that developers working along the riverfront to do the same. You won't see Chicagoans swimming in it any time soon, but a lot of them are kayaking down it, signifying the river is finally making a comeback.

Also thriving is the city's population of wild animals. Coyote and deer both live in the large parks on the city's outskirts, and have been known to wander into the Loop. For instance, in 2007 a coyote sauntered into a downtown Quizno's sandwich shop during the lunch-time rush; he sat in a chair by the window until animal control workers were able to catch and release him back into the woods several hours later. Raccoons are also plentiful, and if you drive through suburban neighborhoods like Oak Park at night, your car headlights are likely to catch them as they bound across the road.

No animal species does better in Chicago than rats. Walk through any alley and you'll see the 'Target: Rats' sign that explains when the most recent dose of poison was laid out for the wee beasties. A pet peeve of Mayor Daley's, the rats have met a formicable foe in the city's Department of Streets & Sanitation. One brigade of agents actually patrols the alleys of infested neighborhoods, attacking the rodents with golf clubs. 'We work as a team,' one employee reported to the *Sun-Times*. 'One will whack, while the other one will get the final kill.'

Visitors to Chicago in the summer should be sure to keep an eye out for an infestation of a more beautiful sort. Lightning bugs – a flying beetle with a phosphorescent abdomen – are prevalent in Chicago in July and August. A park full of their twinkling lights is one of the most beautiful things you'll see in the Windy City.

HANDS ON CHICAGO

Want to lend a hand to the environment while you're in town? Check out these groups for their occasional volunteering events:

- Alliance for the Great Lakes (www.greatlakesadopt.org) Holds 'adopt a beach' cleanups along Lake Michigan.
- Friends of the Parks (www.fotp.org) Help pick up trash and plant flowers in Chicago's parks.
- Friends of the Chicago River (www.chicagoriver.org) Work on projects to stop erosion, reduce flooding and remove pollutants.

GREEN CHICAGO

Mayor Daley has pledged to make Chicago 'the greenest city in the US.' He has a way to go at this point, but he has taken a couple of eco-steps that are admirable. The one he blabs about most is his 'green roof' on City Hall. In 2001 he planted a giant garden atop the building, complete with honeybees; it's been quite an energy-saving success, and many other buildings downtown have since followed suit.

The city has also planted thousands of trees throughout Chicago's neighborhoods and parks. It has solar panels on buildings such as the Field Museum, Art Institute and National Museum of Mexican Art, and the transportation department has put 20 diesel-electric buses into service, with more to come.

Oddly, one of the most common green initiatives – recycling – lags in Chicago. The inconvenient 'blue bag' system the city has in place is just too much bother for most locals, and the absence of a deposit on bottles or cans further lowers the incentive to recycle. News reports about disreputable recycling companies simply throwing the recyclables away after collection has further eroded the program's allure. The city does have a facility where residents can drop off hazardous materials (computers, batteries, paint etc), but nothing workable yet for everyday paper, glass and plastic.

Most city initiatives come out of the Department of the Environment. A great resource for individuals is the city's Center for Green Technology (☎ 312-746-9642; www.cityofchicago.org/Environment/GreenTech), with helpful hints and equipment for everything from building a greenhouse to composting, to installing a rain barrel.

URBAN PLANNING & DEVELOPMENT

Chicago isn't building all those downtown condos and offices willy-nilly. No sir, Chicago has a plan. And that plan is called the 'Chicago Metropolis 2020 Plan,' which states things like any new major construction must have a green roof and must adhere to new energy and zoning codes that include sustainable principles, amongst other things.

So the city is trying. Unfortunately, it dug itself a large hole back in its younger days. Chicago's highway system is inadequate and can't handle the exhaustive amount of vehicle traffic between downtown and the city's far-flung neighborhoods and suburbs. Public transportation could help, but only if you happen to live on the predominately white and moneyed North Side. Suburban residents don't have a lot to choose from besides Metra trains (which aren't very frequent), and residents in the lower-income west and south side neighborhoods are limited to irregular buses. The latter areas don't even have good highway access, a remnant of the days of segregation when blacks were isolated in certain pockets of the city.

GOVERNMENT & POLITICS

Chicago's official motto is 'City in a Garden,' but the late *Tribune* columnist Mike Royko wrote that it would be more appropriate to change it to 'Where's mine?' because that's pretty much how things work around here. The entire system of city politics is based on one hand washing the other, with Mayor Daley and his council of 50 alderman (each elected every four years) leading the way.

Maintaining so many politicians and their related offices and staffs is expensive, but proposals to shrink the city council always run aground for the simple reason that the voters like things as they are. Certainly, this amount of bureaucracy is ripe for abuse and corruption (more on that later), but for the average Chicagoan it works well. You got a pothole in front of your house? Somebody stole your trash can? The neighbor's leaving banana peels all over your stoop? Mundane as they are, these are the kinds of matters that directly affect people's lives, and they can be taken care of with a call to the alderman.

With the districts so small in size, the politicians and their staffs can't afford to anger any voters – angry voters start voting for somebody else. Because of this, the aldermen (the term refers to both men and women) are constantly trying to put themselves in a position to do someone a favor. During your visit to Chicago, you'll likely see traces of this mercenary friendliness on billboards and bus shelter ads – aldermen rent them out to help spread their phone numbers and offers of help to their constituents.

Politics is a popular spectator sport in Chicago, in part because of the ongoing scandals associated with the aldermen and other elected officials. As an example, let's look at the Hired Truck scandal, which sparked in 2005. That's when it was discovered that various city staff had been accepting bribes in exchange for giving lucrative trucking contracts to companies that never actually did any work. Imagine that! The investigation got wider and wider, eventually looking into City Hall hiring practices overall, and went higher and higher up the political ladder. As of August 2007, 49 people had been charged in the investigation and 45 have been convicted. The Mayor has remained out of the fire so far, though there are certainly questions about his knowledge of the tit-for-tat patronage system at work in his administration. And while he still won his post-scandal election handily, some of his long-time alderman cronies suffered from the scandal's fallout and got booted in the 2007 elections.

Above Mayor Daley and the pack of aldermen is Illinois governor Rod Blagojevich, a Democrat who replaced incumbent George Ryan in 2003. (Ryan was later convicted on federal racketeering charges as part of the Hired Truck scandal.) Blagojevich (aka 'Blago') immediately made enemies in the Windy City by rejecting a proposal to allow city-sponsored gambling. And he continues to remain in the Chicago news for his acrimonious public disagreements with his father-in-law, Richard Mell, a Chicago alderman. Mell accused Blagojevich's chief fundraiser of offering campaign donors positions on state boards in exchange for contributions. Luckily, all this fun will continue at least through 2010, since Blago was re-elected until then.

Ah, politics.

OBAMA-RAMA

Barack Obama is one of the country's most recognizable figures. Which is amazing, because not so long ago he couldn't even win a congressional election in his own South Side community. After he lost that bid in 2000 (against a highly entrenched local politician), he regrouped and ran for a vacant US Senate seat. Bingo – he won in the largest landslide victory in Illinois history.

His career picked up steam from there big-time. First came 'the speech' – a stirring oration Obama gave at the Democratic National Convention in Boston in 2004. Afterward, more than one pundit commented on Obama's presidential bearing; CNN called him a 'rock star.' Public opinion was so high he decided to run for the White House.

And so here we are, watching the skinny, 46-year-old Chicago lawyer of mixed African and American heritage in a bid that's more quixotic than the city's Olympic one. But remember, this is the guy who titled his 2006 book *The Audacity of Hope*. The pros for Obama, according to polls: he represents change and fresh ideas. The cons: he's inexperienced.

At press time, he was trailing another Chicagoan – Hillary Clinton (she was born in the 'burbs) – by a 20-point margin. Will they eventually join forces and offer a Clinton/Obama double bill, as many people think? Could Chicagoans be ruling the country come November 2008? Who knows. One thing's for certain: the guy with the funny name will be bringing a Windy City perspective to national politics for a long time to come.

MEDIA

NEWSPAPERS

Chicago is a newspaper town, one of the few cities in the country to support two competing dailies, the *Chicago Tribune* and the *Sun-Times*. The *Chicago Tribune* (www.chicagotribune.com) is the more highbrow of the two, and excels at arts and culture coverage; its writers tend to be articulate experts. The newspaper also produces a digest version for 20-something readers titled *Red Eye*. And it doesn't stop there: the Tribune Company conglomerate counts the local WGN TV and radio stations and the Chicago Cubs baseball team (the cash cow) among its holdings. At press time, the whole shebang was up for sale. There's no buyer yet, and it's likely the pieces will be sold off separately, altering Chicago's mediascape in a big way.

The *Sun-Times* (www.suntimes.com) is a tabloid and, true to its format, favors sensationalized stories that play up sex, violence and scandal. Frankly, it's a lot more fun to read than the Trib. It's most famous scribe is movie reviewer Roger Ebert.

The best weekly publication in the city is the free *Chicago Reader* (www.chicagoreader.com). The fat entertainment paper offers good, independent politics and media coverage, plus a catalog of virtually everything going on in town, from theater to live music to offbeat films to performance art. The behemoth also brims with cool comics and popular advice columns, and reading it can take up the better part of a very pleasurable morning. In 2007, the *Reader* was bought by a media company that owns several southern alt-weeklies; Chicagoans are anxiously waiting to see if coverage takes a turn for the conservative.

Other arts papers include *New City* (www.newcitychicago.com), a slim weekly that is a little edgier than the *Reader;* the *Onion* satirical news weekly, which features Chicago-specific entertainment listings in its 'AV Club' section; and the monthly UR, which offers extensive coverage of DJ and club culture. The *Chicago Free Press* (www.chicagofreepress.com) and *Windy City Times* (www.windycitymediagroup.com) are the main gay weeklies, with local, national and entertainment news.

MAGAZINES

The weekly *Time Out Chicago* (www.timeout.com/chicago) launched in 2005, much to the displeasure of the *Reader*. The magazine eschews the *Reader*'s deeper journalism for short, colorful articles and a week's worth of the best entertainment events, shopping sales, museum and gallery exhibits, restaurants, and gay and lesbian goings-on. If you're planning on staying more than a couple of days in the Windy City, *Time Out Chicago* is a worthwhile investment.

Monthly *Chicago Magazine* (www.chicagomag.com) features articles and culture coverage slanted towards upscale readers. For visitors it offers good restaurant listings (indexed by food type, location, cost and more). Its Sales Check e-newsletter is a must for hard-core shoppers looking for the latest sales and events; see the Shopping chapter (p120) for sign-up information.

Moguls and would-be moguls consult *Crain's Chicago Business* (www.chicagobusiness.com), a business tabloid that regularly scoops the dailies despite being a weekly.

Venus Magazine (www.venuszine.com) is a hip, arts-oriented quarterly 'zine for women that's produced in Chicago. You can pick up it, as well as other offbeat publications, at Quimby's (p131).

RADIO

Thanks to the time they spend driving to and from work, most Chicagoans listen to at least an hour of radio a day.

WGN (720AM) broadcasts many of its shows from its street-level studio in the Tribune Tower on N Michigan Ave. You can press your nose up against the glass and make faces at hosts such as the duo of Kathy O'Malley and Judy Markey, two irreverent delights who dish with Chicago's womenfolk.

WBEZ (91.5FM), the National Public Radio affiliate, is well funded and ever-expanding. It's the home station for the hit NPR shows *This American Life* and *Wait, Wait Don't Tell Me.* The studios are located on Navy Pier; the website (www.chicagopublicradio.org) is a great source for local news. And if you happen to be listening at 6:59pm on Saturdays you're in for a special

CHICAGO BLOGS

- Chicagoist (http://chicagoist.com) – Covers the city in all its quirky glory. Topics range from how to neuter feral alley cats to local microbrews to hot bands and festivals around town; it's written from a snarky, 20-something viewpoint.
- Second City Cop (http://secondcitycop.blogspot.com) – Day job: gun-totin' Chicago law man. Secondary job: blogger who lets loose on the mayor, gang-bangers and police department honchos. It's a conservative, frontline look at what cops face, both on the streets and inside the department walls. Check it for the latest scandals afoot.
- Bad at Sports (http://badatsports.com/blog) – 'Bad-assed art review from Chicago,' the tagline says. Three emerging artists interview their brethren as well as curators and critics for the low-down on the local visual arts scene.
- Clout City (http://blogs.chicagoreader.com/politics) – The *Reader's* political beat reporter provides the scoop on the antics at City Hall.
- Chicago Bloggers (www.chicagobloggers.com) – Still looking for more? Try this round-up of local bloggers. They're organized by location, so you can find the one who lives nearest you and see what he or she is saying about that raccoon stalking the neighborhood.

treat: *The Annoying Music Show* presents 'the most awful music ever recorded.' Because it's so harmful to the ears, the show only runs for one minute.

WBBM (780AM) blares news headlines all day long, with traffic reports every 10 minutes. The left-wing Air America network can be found on WCPT (850AM). Its right-wing counterpoint is located nearby at WLS (890AM). And if you're just hungry for the latest sports scores, tune into the ESPN-run WMVP (1000AM) or the local WSCR (670AM).

You'll find the most interesting music on WXRT (93.1FM), a rock station that aggressively avoids falling into any canned format trap. Other notables include the eclectic college stations for the University of Chicago (WHPK, 88.5FM), Loyola (WLUW, 88.7FM) and Northwestern (WNUR, 89.3FM).

TELEVISION

Chicagoans love their TVs, though DVD subscription companies like Netflix have definitely reduced the amount of aimless channel surfing that goes on in the Windy City. Chicago's local network affiliates are little different from their counterparts in other large cities. WLS (channel 7, the ABC affiliate) is generally the ratings leader for newscasts, covering the latest murders and mayhem from the streets. WMAQ (channel 5, the NBC affiliate) is a ratings loser after years of being adrift. WFLD (channel 32, the Fox affiliate) features the usual Fox neon effects.

Other stations in town have their own niches. WGN (channel 9) is owned – at least for now – by the Tribune Company. Its meteorologist, Tom Skilling, is something of a cult figure in Chicago TV for his scientific, incredibly technical weather forecasts. He won't just tell you that it's hailing, but *why* it's hailing. WGN also shows many of the baseball games played by fellow Tribune-empire denizens, the Cubs, and carries Bulls games as well. WTTW (channel 11) is a good public broadcasting station, home of the beloved restaurant-review show *Check Please!*, as well as *Chicago Tonight* at 7pm weekdays, which takes an in-depth look at one of the day's news stories

FASHION

Chicago is a casual town. The apex of fashion for most men is a pair of khakis and a Gap button-down shirt. Women's dress is similarly low-key, valuing comfort over high fashion. In the scorching summer, much of the population looks like they're heading off for a lifeguard shift at the local pool – flip-flops, shorts and T-shirts are acceptable attire most everywhere in the city. (Though arctic-cold air-conditioning in shops and movie theaters can sometimes make tank tops a regrettable choice.) In winter, fashion disappears entirely beneath layers of Thinsulate, Gore-Tex and North Face merchandise.

But if you want a pair of hoity-toity Jimmy Choo shoes, Chicago's got 'em. All the big-name designers are here and prance their wares around Oak St. So you too can be like a Gold Coast matron and accessorize those shoes with a Chanel suit, Prada purse and Hermés scarf. Much more popular for urban fashionistas are the boutiques of Wicker Park and Ukrainian Village, where hip, international labels mix it up on the racks with high-concept, high-priced outfits from local designers. These sleek little stores have virtually eliminated the lag between Milan runways and Chicago shop displays, allowing Chicagoans to spend $200 on a belt just like they do in New York.

Chicago even boasts its own underground fashion scene. Hipsters proudly sport the latest creations from local button-maker Busy Beaver, and attend ramshackle, box-wine fashion shows where works by XNX Designs and fashion artist Cat Chow debut before making their way to Ukrainian Village resale shops.

If you plan on hitting the clubs while you're in town, tight black clothing is the rule for both men and women. Some clubs don't allow blue jeans, tennis shoes or baseball caps; if you only brought Levi's and Adidas and still want to go dancing, do yourself a favor and call ahead to make sure there won't be a problem.

LANGUAGE

As elsewhere in the US, English is the major language spoken in Chicago. In the heart of the ethnic enclaves you'll hear Spanish, Polish, Chinese or Russian, but almost all business is conducted in English. Midwestern accents tend to be a bit flat with just a touch of nasal twang, but compared to other parts of the US, most of the English you'll hear is pretty standard – the middle of the country has always produced a large share of plainspoken TV announcers.

Chicagoans do have their own, special accent. Remember the old *Saturday Night Live* skit where heavy-set Chicago sports fans sat around eating 'sassages' and 'sammiches' and referring to their football team as 'Dah Bears' and their city leader as 'Dah Mare'? It's for real, though limited to south-side enclaves around US Cellular Field and Midway Airport.

CHICAGOESE 101

Use this list to help decipher the local lingo you may encounter:

Downstate Used dismissively by Windy City residents to refer to all the backwards areas in Illinois (ie everywhere outside of Chicago city limits).

The Drive Lake Shore Drive (also referred to as 'LSD').

The Ike The Eisenhower Expressway (aka I-290).

A Polish Short for a Polish sausage sandwich (or sammich, as the case may be).

Wet How to order extra juice on your Italian beef sandwich.

Stoopin' Socializing on the front porch of a home or apartment, usually with friends and beers.

BLUELIST[1] (blu,list) *v.*
to recommend a travel experience.
What's your recommendation? www.lonelyplanet.com/bluelist

NEIGHBORHOODS

top picks

- **Millennium Park** (p53)
  Shiny sculptures, human-gargoyle fountains, music and ice-skating.
- **Art Institute** (p52)
  Home of a quarter million artworks, especially big-time Impressionists.
- **Wrigley Field** (p81)
  Baseball's most historic, cursed and ivy-walled park.
- **John Hancock Center** (p69)
  Sky-high tower with sparkling views enjoyed over cocktails.
- **12th Street Beach** (p108)
  Secret sand-crescent behind the Museum Campus.
- **Chinatown** (p109)
  Shops brim with chestnut cakes, jasmine tea and Hello Kitty trinkets.
- **Willie Dixon's Blues Heaven** (p110)
  Birthplace of Chicago blues and ultimately rock and roll.
- **Navy Pier** (p66)
  Fireworks, a Ferris wheel and flotilla of boats on the waterfront.
- **Field Museum of Natural History** (p104)
  Houses everything but the kitchen sink: dinosaurs, mummies, gemstones and stuffed apes.
- **Lincoln Park** (p75)
  Lakes, leafy paths, paddleboats and a free zoo in their midst.

NEIGHBORHOODS

Chicago prides itself on being a 'city of neighborhoods,' each one marked by its own look, feel and culinary treats. Ethnicity characterizes many areas, and vibrant Mexican, Polish, Chinese, Puerto Rican, Vietnamese and Indian communities waft their flavors from varied home grounds.

'Moving beyond downtown there is a wealth of galleries, historical sights and architectural wonders to see.'

Most draws for visitors are clustered in Chicago's geographic center. The bull's eye is the Loop, the city's historic and business core circled by train tracks (hence the name). Its hubbub spills over into the Near North. Together, these two sight-heavy, shop-and-hotel-laden areas could occupy an entire week. But don't give in to the temptation to spend your whole trip here. Moving beyond downtown there is a wealth of galleries, historical sights and architectural wonders to see and, most importantly, encounters to be had with everyday Chicagoans in the neighborhoods where they live, drink, eat and watch sports.

Take the gilded Gold Coast, for instance, where you can gaze longingly at mansions inhabited by folks living the high life, same as they've been doing for 120 years. Further north is historic Old Town, home of Second City improv, and Lincoln Park, where college students and yuppies enjoy beautiful parklands and hot restaurants.

Keep moving north and you'll find Lake View – a hub for bars and shops, both gay and straight, as well as the Cathedral of Baseball, Wrigley Field. Above Lake View is the jazzy destination of Uptown and European-feeling Andersonville. From there, swing to the southwest to explore trendy Wicker Park and Bucktown, as well as the boutique bloom afoot in abutting Ukrainian Village. Logan Square and Humboldt Park carry on the trendiness, though in a less crowded, more relaxed manner.

A quick ride west of downtown, the Near West Side has galleries, creative eateries, Oprah and holograms. Nearby Pilsen also comprises some odd bedfellows, with Czech homes housing Hispanic residents who go to hip gallery shows. In the museum-rich South Loop and Near South Side, the skyline changes every week as more and more urbanites move into the newly rising condos. And down on the South Side, Hyde Park provides a leafy, bookish retreat.

It's easy to find your way around once you understand the orderly city plan. Chicago's streets are laid out on a grid and numbered; Madison and State Sts in the Loop are the grid's center. As you go north, south, east or west from here, each increase of 800 in street numbers corresponds to one mile. At every increase of 400, there is a major arterial street. For instance, Division St (1200 N) is followed by North Ave (1600 N) and Armitage Ave (2000 N), at which point you're 2.5 miles north of downtown.

Got it? Good. Now let's get moving.

Lakewood-Balmoral
Andersonville
ANDERSONVILLE & UPTOWN (p85)
Wrigleyville
LAKE VIEW & WRIGLEYVILLE (pp82–3)
Lake View
LINCOLN PARK & OLD TOWN (pp76–7)
Bucktown
Old Town
LOGAN SQUARE & HUMBOLDT PARK (p95)
Wicker Park
GOLD COAST (pp70–1)
WICKER PARK, BUCKTOWN & UKRAINIAN VILLAGE (pp90–1)
River North Gallery District
Near North
Ukrainian Village
NEAR NORTH & NAVY PIER (pp64–5)
Streeterville
Illinois Center
THE LOOP (pp54–5)
Greek Town
Lake Michigan
Printer's Row
NEAR WEST SIDE & PILSEN (pp98–9)
Little Italy
Dearborn Park
Central Station
Museum Campus
SOUTH LOOP & NEAR SOUTH SIDE (pp106–7)
Prairie Avenue Historic District
Pilsen
Bronzeville
Bridgeport
Kenwood
HYDE PARK & SOUTH SIDE (p114)
0
3 km
0
2.0 miles

ITINERARY BUILDER

Mix and match your own Chicago adventure: Take your pick of recommended sights, shops, eateries, nightlife and entertainment in Chicago's key neighborhoods in our Itinerary Builder.

AREA / ACTIVITIES	Sights	Shopping	Eating
The Loop	**Millennium Park** (p53) **Art Institute** (p52) **Famous Loop Architecture** (p57)	**Poster Plus** (p121) **Chicago Architecture Foundation Shop** (p121) **Illinois Artisans Shop** (p121)	**Bombon 4** (p141) **Taza** (p141) **The Gage** (p141)
Near North & Navy Pier	**Navy Pier** (p66) **Tribune Tower** (p62) **Smith Museum of Stained Glass Windows** (p67)	**Garrett Popcorn** (p122) **Levi's Store** (p122) **Jazz Record Mart** (p123)	**Frontera Grill** (p144) **Kendall College Dining Room** (p145) **Giordano's** (p144)
Gold Coast	**John Hancock Center** (p69) **Museum of Contemporary Art** (p71) **Astor St** (p72)	**Jimmy Choo** (p125) **City of Chicago Store** (p125) **Water Tower Place** (p125)	**Tempo Café** (p145) **Signature Room at the 95th** (p146) **PJ Clarke's** (p146)
Lincoln Park & Old Town	**Lincoln Park Zoo** (p78) **Lincoln Park Conservatory** (p78) **Biograph Theater** (p78)	**Nau** (p127) **Sam's Wine & Spirits** (p126)	**Alinea** (p147) **Wiener Circle** (p149) **Bourgeois Pig** (p149)
Lake View & Wrigleyville	**Wrigley Field** (p81)	**Threadless** (p128) **Chicago Comics** (p127) **Strange Cargo** (p128)	**Mia Francesca** (p151) **Victory's Banner** (p153) **Tango Sur** (p151)
Wicker Park, Bucktown & Ukrainian Village	**Polish Museum of America** (p89) **Nelson Algren House** (p89)	**Renegade Handmade** (p131) **Tommy's Rock & Roll Café** (p132) **Free People** (p131)	**Handlebar** (p156) **Feed** (p161) **Hot Chocolate** (p157)
South Loop & Near South Side	**Field Museum of Natural History** (p104) **Shedd Aquarium** (p105) **Willie Dixon's Blues Heaven** (p110)	**Giftland** (p135) **Ten Ren Tea & Ginseng Company** (p135) **Aji Ichiban** (p135)	**Yolk** (p165) **Joy Yee's Noodle Shop** (p166) **Wan Shi Da Bakery** (p166)

HOW TO USE THIS TABLE

The table below allows you to plan a day's worth of activities in any area of the city. Simply select which area you wish to explore, and then mix and match from the corresponding listings to build your day. The first item in each cell represents a well-known highlight of the area while the other items are more off-the-beaten track gems.

Drinking & nightlife	Sports & activities	Arts
Cal's Bar (p171) **17 West at the Berghoff** (p171)	**Millennium Park Workouts** (p204) **Millennium Park Ice Skating** (p207) **Critical Mass** (p206)	**Grant Park Music Festival** (p193) **Chicago Symphony Orchestra** (p193) **Goodman Theatre** (p195)
Billy Goat Tavern (p145) **Clark St Ale House** (p172) **Vision** (p189)	**Bike Chicago** (p206)	**Chicago Shakespeare Theater** (p195)
Coq d'Or (p186) **Underground Wonder Bar** (p184) **Gibson's** (p172)	**Oak St Beach** (p209)	**Lookingglass Theatre Company** (p196)
Second City (p190) **Olde Town Ale House** (p173) **Delilah's** (p172)	**North Ave Beach** (p209) **Wateriders** (p209)	**Steppenwolf Theatre** (p196) **Facets Multimedia** (p199)
Hungry Brain (p183) **Metro** (p185) **Gingerman** (p174)	**Chicago Cubs** (p210) **Moksha Yoga** (p205) **Diversey-River Bowl** (p206)	**Music Box Theatre** (p199)
Hideout (p185) **Matchbox** (p176) **Violet Hour** (p177)	**Bikram Yoga** (p205) **Ruby Room** (p204) **Midnight Bike Ride** (p208)	**Danny's Reading Series** (p200) **Dollar Store** (p200) **Elastic Arts Foundation** (p197)
Velvet Lounge (p184) **Richard's Bar** (p176)	**12 St Beach** (p209) **Sledding at Soldier Field** (p207) **Chicago White Sox** (p211)	**Dance Center at Columbia College** (p197)

GREATER CHICAGO

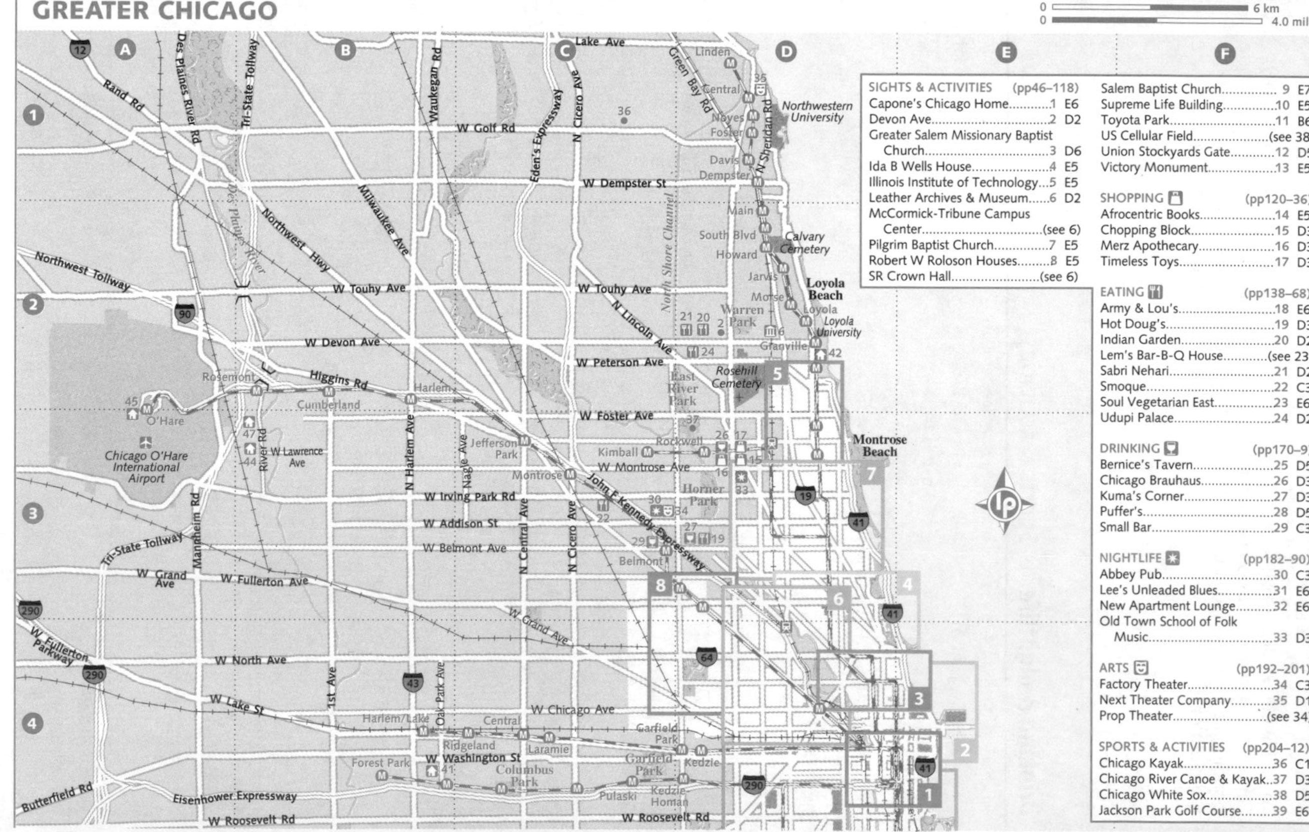

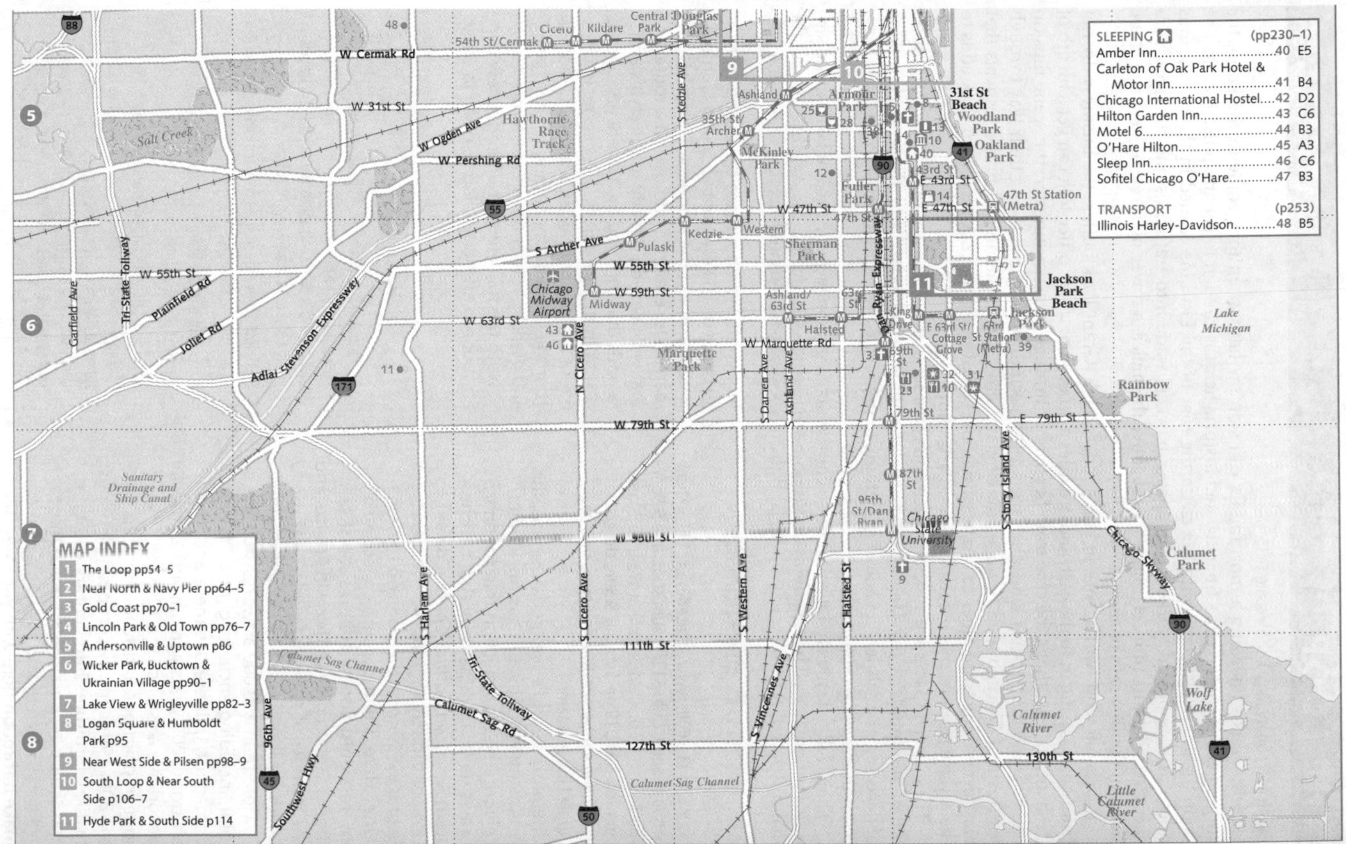
SLEEPING (pp230–1)
Amber Inn......40 E5
Carleton of Oak Park Hotel & Motor Inn......41 B4
Chicago International Hostel......42 D2
Hilton Garden Inn......43 C6
Motel 6......44 B3
O'Hare Hilton......45 A3
Sleep Inn......46 C6
Sofitel Chicago O'Hare......47 B3
TRANSPORT (p253)
Illinois Harley-Davidson......48 B5
MAP INDEX
1 The Loop pp54–5
2 Near North & Navy Pier pp64–5
3 Gold Coast pp70–1
4 Lincoln Park & Old Town pp76–7
5 Andersonville & Uptown p86
6 Wicker Park, Bucktown & Ukrainian Village pp90–1
7 Lake View & Wrigleyville pp82–3
8 Logan Square & Humboldt Park p95
9 Near West Side & Pilsen pp98–9
10 South Loop & Near South Side p106–7
11 Hyde Park & South Side p114
Lake Michigan
Jackson Park Beach
31st St Beach
Woodland Park
Oakland Park
Rainbow Park
Calumet Park
Wolf Lake
Calumet River
Little Calumet River
Chicago Skyway
Dan Ryan Expressway
Adlai Stevenson Expressway
Tri-State Tollway
Southwest Hwy
Calumet Sag Rd
Calumet Sag Channel
Sanitary Drainage and Ship Canal
Salt Creek
Hawthorne Race Track
Chicago Midway Airport
Chicago State University
Sherman Park
McKinley Park
Armour Park
Fuller Park
Marquette Park
Jackson Park
W Cermak Rd
W 31st St
W Ogden Ave
W Pershing Rd
S Archer Ave
W 47th St
W 55th St
W 59th St
W 63rd St
W Marquette Rd
W 79th St
W 95th St
111th St
127th St
130th St
E 79th St
E 43rd St
E 47th St
S Kedzie Ave
S Western Ave
S Ashland Ave
S Damen Ave
S Halsted St
S Vincennes Ave
S Stony Island Ave
N Cicero Ave
S Cicero Ave
S Harlem Ave
96th Ave
Garfield Ave
Joliet Rd
Plainfield Rd
54th St/Cermak
Cicero
Kildare
Central Park
Douglas Park
Kedzie
Pulaski
Midway
Western
35th St/Archer
Ashland
Ashland/63rd St
Halsted
63rd St
69th St
79th St
87th St
95th St/Dan Ryan
King Drive
E 63rd St/Cottage Grove
43rd St
47th St
47th St Station (Metra)
63rd St Station (Metra)

THE LOOP

Eating p140; Shopping p120; Sleeping p215

Caffeine junkies needing a morning fix can skip the latte when they come to the Loop; the surging energy of the city's financial and historic heart is enough to get any pulse racing. The Loop breathes electricity, with the clattering roar of the El trains echoed in the tumultuous tides of office-bound workers. Newspaper hawkers wade into traffic, fishing for sales from executives barking into cell phones. And above the melee, a towering forest of steel and stone soaks in the first rays of sun.

It's not all work-work-work in the 'hood, though. Grant Park buffers the business district from Lake Michigan to the east, and provides a quiet zone where office folk can get a breath of fresh air. At least that's the case from September through May. In summer, the scene flips on its head, and the park is mobbed with tens of thousands of people gnawing their way through the Taste of Chicago food fiesta, or moving and grooving to the myriad music festivals that blast everything from blues to progressive house out over the water. Millennium Park adds to the revelry from its mod perch in Grant Park's northwest corner.

These green spaces are amazing when you consider that the area was once a marshy landfill full of 'dumphills' where 'dog fights alternated with wrestling bouts' and 'the winter's residue of deceased animals lent an added something to the vernal breezes,' as the *Chicago Daily News* put it in the early 1900s.

Thankfully, it smells a lot rosier these days, which is good news since visitors will spend significant time here. The neighborhood is home to big-ticket sights like the Art Institute; all the major theaters, festivals and parades; and the city's world-famous architecture and public art.

ART INSTITUTE OF CHICAGO

Map pp54–5

☎ 312-443-3600; www.artic.edu/aic; 111 S Michigan Ave; adult/child $12/7, admission free 5-9pm Thu & Fri; 🕑 10:30am-5pm Mon-Wed, 10:30am-9pm Thu & Fri, 10am-5pm Sat & Sun, closed Fri evening in winter; Ⓜ Brown, Green, Orange, Purple Line to Adams

One of the world's premier museums, the Art Institute of Chicago has the kind of celebrity-heavy collection that routinely draws gasps from patrons. Grant Wood's stern *American Gothic*? Check. Edward Hopper's lonely *Nighthawks*? Yep. Georges Seurat's *A Sunday Afternoon on La Grand Jatte*? Here. The museum's collection of impressionist and postimpressionist paintings is second only to those in France, and the number of surrealist works – especially boxes by Joseph Cornell – is tremendous.

More than 250,000 artworks stuff the joint, including ancient Egyptian, Greek and Roman art; Chinese, Japanese and Korean art from 5000 years ago onward; European decorative arts since the 12th century; European paintings and sculpture from 1400 to 1800; 19th-century European paintings; textiles; furniture; 20th-century paintings and sculpture; and ever-so-much more.

Friend, you're going to need a plan to make it through here with your feet still intact. While we can get you to a few of the highlights in an hour (see the boxed text, opposite), you'll likely want to spend far more time absorbing the wonders. Grab a free map at the entrance and design a route that will take you directly to the styles and periods that turn you on. Or rent an audio tour ($6) from the front desk. They come in different lengths and styles, with the Director's Tour the standout for cutting to the chase and guiding you to 40 top masterpieces.

Note the museum is building a new wing for modern art, scheduled to open in 2009.

TRANSPORTATION – THE LOOP

Bus Number 56 runs along Milwaukee Ave from Wicker Park into the Loop; 151 comes down Michigan Ave from the lakefront in the north; 156 travels along LaSalle St from River North.

El All lines converge in the Loop; find your destination and take your pick.

Metra Millennium Station for the north loop; Van Buren St Station for the south.

Parking There is an underground pay lot on Michigan Ave at Washington St, and another at Van Buren St. Warning: if you park at a meter along S Columbus Dr, be aware that each meter covers two spaces. If there's no meter at your spot, it's likely you need to feed the closest one. Lots cost about $25 per day.

THE ART INSTITUTE EXPRESS

You could easily spend several days meandering through the Art Institute's millennia-spanning collection. But since the human body can only take so much oohing and aahing before aesthetic overload kicks in, we've narrowed down the treasures into a sprinter's hour of artistic highlights.

Start at the beautiful Grand Staircase in the lobby. Climb up, enjoying being bathed in sunlight, and walk straight ahead into Room 201. The room's main attraction is Paris Street; Rainy Day by Gustave Caillebotte. Caillebotte, an engineer by training, straddled the line between the realism that dominated the established art world of his day and the looser, more experimental approach of his impressionist contemporaries.

Exit right to Room 205, where you'll find Van Gogh's The Bedroom, a painting picturing the sleeping quarters of the artist's house in Arles. It's the second of three versions of the painting executed during Van Gogh's 1889 stay at an asylum. In the same room is Seurat's pointillist masterpiece of 1884, A Sunday Afternoon on La Grande Jatte. Get close enough for the painting to break down into its component dots, and you'll see why it took Seurat two long years to complete it. Next door, in Room 206, the cavalcade of famous impressionists continues with Monet's Stack of Wheat painting. The 15ft-tall stacks, located on the artist's farmhouse grounds in Giverny, were part of a series that effectively launched Monet's career when they sold like hotcakes at a show he organized in 1891.

Continue straight ahead through the Gauguin-filled Room 234B, pausing to admire his Tahitian fixation. Picasso's The Old Guitarist hangs toward the back. The elongated figure is from his 'blue period,' reflecting not only Picasso's color scheme but his mindset as a poor, lonely artist in Paris in the early years. He goes cubist in the next space to the left (Room 233).

Now zigzag to the right through a few rooms, then head back, and back some more, to Room 244. Welcome to the surreal life, crowned by Salvador Dali's nightmarish Inventions of the Monsters. The artist's profile is visible in the lower left corner, along with that of his wife, Gala. Painted in Austria immediately before the Nazi annexation, the title refers to a Nostradamus prediction that the apparition of monsters presages the outbreak of war.

Other must-sees include Grant Wood's 1930 American Gothic. The artist, a lifelong resident of Iowa, used his sister and his dentist as models for the two stern-faced farmers. Edward Hopper's Nighthawks, a poignant snapshot of four solitary souls at a neon-lit diner, was inspired by a Greenwich Ave restaurant in Manhattan. Marc Chagall's blue stained glass America Windows awes, as do Joseph Cornell's works such as Untitled (Soap Bubble Set). We'd love to tell you where they're all hanging, but with renovations going on, they keep moving. Ask at one of the visitor desks for their current whereabouts.

In the interim, some of the modern works are disappearing from view. You might want to call or check the website to avoid disappointment if there's something in this genre that you're dying to see.

And don't forget: more artwork awaits outside. Edward Kemeys' bronze lions have become Chicago icons since they began flanking the entrance to the Art Institute in 1894. The Stock Exchange Arch, located on the museum's northeast side, is not so much a statue as it is a relic amputated from the great Stock Exchange building when it was demolished in 1972. The *AIA Guide to Chicago* calls it the 'Wailing Wall of Chicago's preservation movement.' On the museum's southeast side, Augustus Saint-Gaudens' Sitting Lincoln shows lonely 'Honest Abe' in his office chair. Feel his isolation?

The museum's main entrance is on Michigan Ave (where it meets Adams St). The School of the Art Institute is accessed via the Columbus Dr entrance.

There are a couple of things to check out at the main entrance. Curators often give lectures on various artists and artworks. Many talks are free with admission; inquire at the desk to see if anything sparks your interest. Also, be sure to stop in the museum store, which carries an awesome poster selection of the Warhols, Picassos and other famous paintings inside.

MILLENNIUM PARK Map pp54–5

☎ 312-742-1168; www.millenniumpark.org; Welcome Center, 201 E Randolph St; 🕑 6am-11pm; Ⓜ Brown, Green, Orange, Purple Line to Randolph or Madison

Rising up boldly from Grant Park's northwest corner (between Monroe and Randolph Sts), Millennium Park is Chicago's newest mega-sight. Frank Gehry's 120ft-high swooping silver band shell anchors what is, in essence, an outdoor modern design gallery. It includes Jaume Plensa's 50ft-high Crown Fountain that projects video images of locals spitting out water gargoyle-style; the Gehry-designed BP Bridge that spans Columbus Dr and offers great

THE LOOP

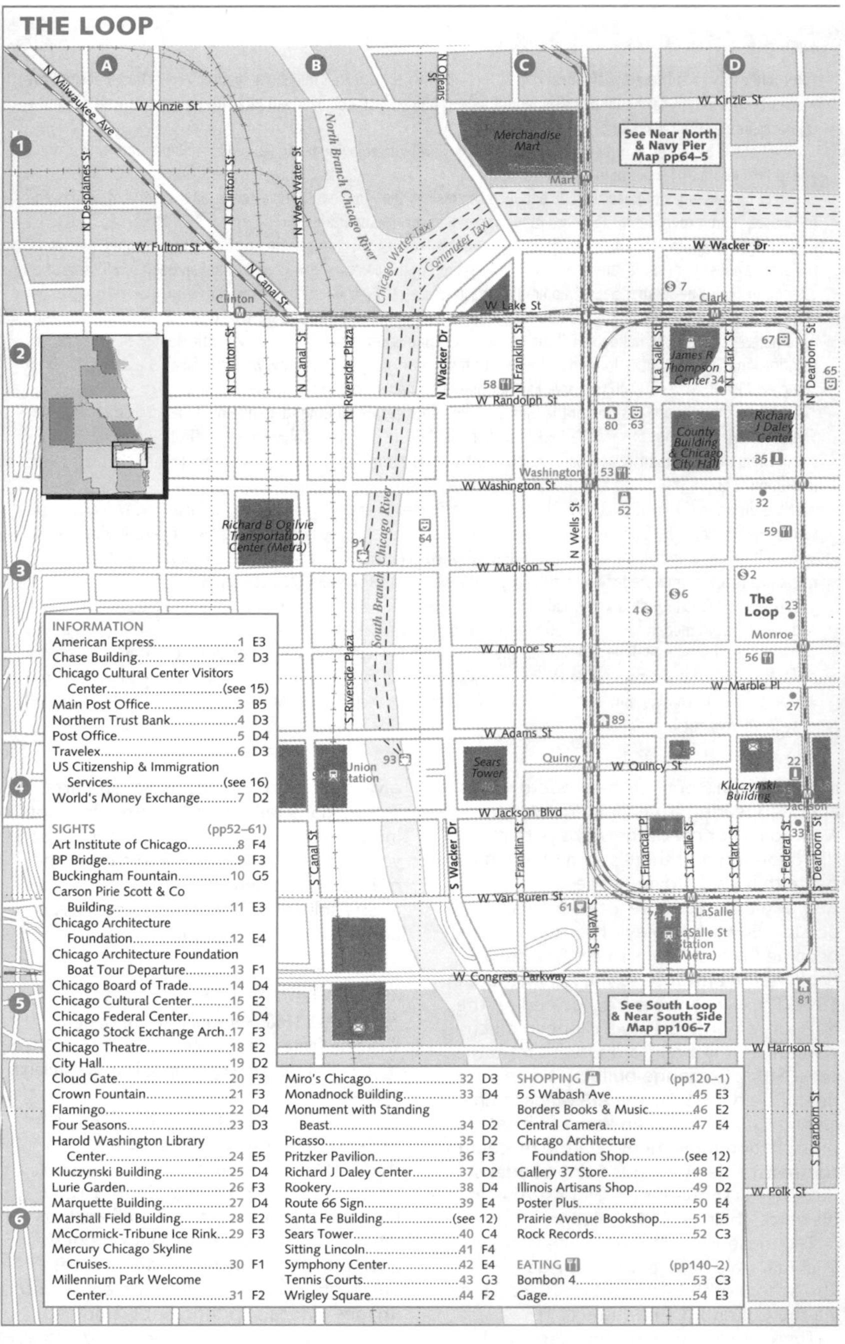
A
B
C
D
1
2
3
4
5
6
N Milwaukee Ave
W Kinzie St
N Orleans St
N Desplaines St
N Clinton St
N West Water St
North Branch Chicago River
Merchandise Mart
Merchandise Mart
See Near North & Navy Pier Map pp64–5
W Fulton St
N Canal St
Chicago Water Taxi
Commuter Taxi
W Wacker Dr
Clinton
W Lake St
Clark
N Clinton St
N Canal St
N Riverside Plaza
N Wacker Dr
N Franklin St
N La Salle St
N Clark St
N Dearborn St
James R Thompson Center
W Randolph St
County Building & Chicago City Hall
Richard J Daley Center
Washington
W Washington St
Richard B Ogilvie Transportation Center (Metra)
South Branch Chicago River
N Wells St
W Madison St
The Loop
Monroe
W Monroe St
W Marble Pl
S Riverside Plaza
W Adams St
Quincy
W Quincy St
Union Station
Sears Tower
Kluczynski Building
Jackson
W Jackson Blvd
S Canal St
S Wacker Dr
S Franklin St
S Financial Pl
S La Salle St
S Clark St
S Federal St
S Dearborn St
W Van Buren St
S Wells St
LaSalle
LaSalle St Station (Metra)
W Congress Parkway
See South Loop & Near South Side Map pp106–7
W Harrison St
S Dearborn St
W Polk St
INFORMATION
American Express....1 E3
Chase Building....2 D3
Chicago Cultural Center Visitors Center....(see 15)
Main Post Office....3 B5
Northern Trust Bank....4 D3
Post Office....5 D4
Travelex....6 D3
US Citizenship & Immigration Services....(see 16)
World's Money Exchange....7 D2
SIGHTS (pp52–61)
Art Institute of Chicago....8 F4
BP Bridge....9 F3
Buckingham Fountain....10 G5
Carson Pirie Scott & Co Building....11 E3
Chicago Architecture Foundation....12 E4
Chicago Architecture Foundation Boat Tour Departure....13 F1
Chicago Board of Trade....14 D4
Chicago Cultural Center....15 E2
Chicago Federal Center....16 D4
Chicago Stock Exchange Arch....17 F3
Chicago Theatre....18 E2
City Hall....19 D2
Cloud Gate....20 F3
Crown Fountain....21 F3
Flamingo....22 D4
Four Seasons....23 D3
Harold Washington Library Center....24 E5
Kluczynski Building....25 D4
Lurie Garden....26 F3
Marquette Building....27 D4
Marshall Field Building....28 E2
McCormick-Tribune Ice Rink....29 F3
Mercury Chicago Skyline Cruises....30 F1
Millennium Park Welcome Center....31 F2
Miro's Chicago....32 D3
Monadnock Building....33 D4
Monument with Standing Beast....34 D2
Picasso....35 D2
Pritzker Pavilion....36 F3
Richard J Daley Center....37 D2
Rookery....38 D4
Route 66 Sign....39 E4
Santa Fe Building....(see 12)
Sears Tower....40 C4
Sitting Lincoln....41 F4
Symphony Center....42 E4
Tennis Courts....43 G3
Wrigley Square....44 F2
SHOPPING (pp120–1)
5 S Wabash Ave....45 E3
Borders Books & Music....46 E2
Central Camera....47 E4
Chicago Architecture Foundation Shop....(see 12)
Gallery 37 Store....48 E2
Illinois Artisans Shop....49 D2
Poster Plus....50 E4
Prairie Avenue Bookshop....51 E5
Rock Records....52 C3
EATING (pp140–2)
Bombon 4....53 C3
Gage....54 E3

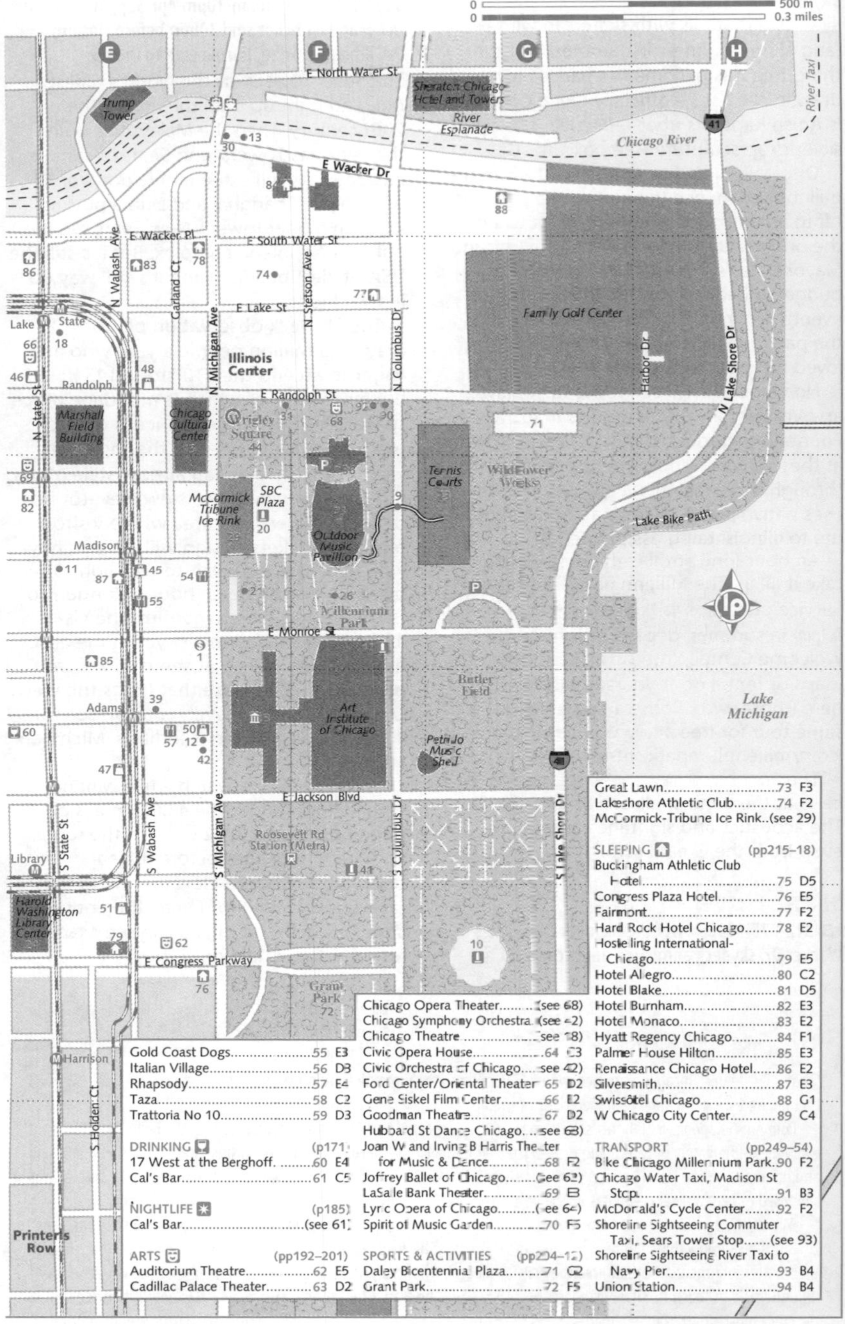
0 500 m
0 0.3 miles
E
F
G
H
E North Water St
Trump Tower
Sheraton Chicago Hotel and Towers
River Esplanade
River Taxi
Chicago River
E Wacker Dr
E Wacker Pl
E South Water St
N Wabash Ave
Garland Ct
N Michigan Ave
N Stetson Ave
N Columbus Dr
E Lake St
Lake
State
Illinois Center
Family Golf Center
Harbor Dr
N Lake Shore Dr
Randolph
E Randolph St
N State St
Marshall Field Building
Chicago Cultural Center
Wrigley Square
Tennis Courts
Wildflower Works
McCormick Tribune Ice Rink
SBC Plaza
Outdoor Music Pavillion
Lake Bike Path
Madison
Millennium Park
E Monroe St
Butler Field
Lake Michigan
Adams
Art Institute of Chicago
Petrillo Music Shell
E Jackson Blvd
S Wabash Ave
S Michigan Ave
Roosevelt Rd Station (Metra)
S Columbus Dr
S Lake Shore Dr
S State St
Library
Harold Washington Library Center
E Congress Parkway
Grant Park
Harrison
S Holden Ct
Printers Row
Gold Coast Dogs....55 E3
Italian Village....56 D3
Rhapsody....57 E4
Taza....58 C2
Trattoria No 10....59 D3
DRINKING (p171)
17 West at the Berghoff....60 E4
Cal's Bar....61 C5
NIGHTLIFE (p185)
Cal's Bar....(see 61)
ARTS (pp192–201)
Auditorium Theatre....62 E5
Cadillac Palace Theater....63 D2
Chicago Opera Theater....(see 68)
Chicago Symphony Orchestra....(see 42)
Chicago Theatre....(see 18)
Civic Opera House....64 C3
Civic Orchestra of Chicago....(see 42)
Ford Center/Oriental Theater....65 D2
Gene Siskel Film Center....66 E2
Goodman Theatre....67 D2
Hubbard St Dance Chicago....(see 68)
Joan W and Irving B Harris Theater for Music & Dance....68 F2
Joffrey Ballet of Chicago....(see 62)
LaSalle Bank Theater....69 E3
Lyric Opera of Chicago....(see 64)
Spirit of Music Garden....70 F5
SPORTS & ACTIVITIES (pp204–12)
Daley Bicentennial Plaza....71 G2
Grant Park....72 F5
Great Lawn....73 F3
Lakeshore Athletic Club....74 F2
McCormick-Tribune Ice Rink....(see 29)
SLEEPING (pp215–18)
Buckingham Athletic Club Hotel....75 D5
Congress Plaza Hotel....76 E5
Fairmont....77 F2
Hard Rock Hotel Chicago....78 E2
Hostelling International-Chicago....79 E5
Hotel Allegro....80 C2
Hotel Blake....81 D5
Hotel Burnham....82 E3
Hotel Monaco....83 E2
Hyatt Regency Chicago....84 F1
Palmer House Hilton....85 E3
Renaissance Chicago Hotel....86 E2
Silversmith....87 E3
Swissôtel Chicago....88 G1
W Chicago City Center....89 C4
TRANSPORT (pp249–54)
Bike Chicago Millennium Park....90 F2
Chicago Water Taxi, Madison St Stop....91 B3
McDonald's Cycle Center....92 F2
Shoreline Sightseeing Commuter Taxi, Sears Tower Stop....(see 93)
Shoreline Sightseeing River Taxi to Navy Pier....93 B4
Union Station....94 B4

skyline views; and the McCormick-Tribune Ice Rink (p207) that fills with skaters in winter (and al fresco diners in summer). But the thing that has become the park's biggest draw is 'the Bean' – officially *Cloud Gate,* this is Anish Kapoor's uber-reflective, 110-ton, silver-drop sculpture (see box, below).

Originally slated to open in 2000 with the millennium (hence the name), the park got off to an embarrassingly slow start when the original contractor – a chum of Chicago Mayor Daley's – went $100 million over budget, missed various deadlines and was eventually fired. But all was forgiven when the park opened in 2004, and Chicagoans loved the sight ever since.

No wonder. Who can resist such playful art? Visitors can splash around in Crown Fountain and touch the Bean. If the crowds at these favorite spots are too much, walk through the peaceful Lurie Garden, which uses native plants to form a botanical tribute to Illinois' tall-grass prairie.

An hour-long stroll is the best way to take it all in. The Millennium Park Greeter Service offers free walking tours (11:30am & 1pm) in summer; departure is from the Welcome Center. You can also pick up free maps or rent a do-it-yourself audio tour ($5) here (those with iPods can download the same tour for free at www.antennaaudio.com/millenniumpark.shtml).

The Grant Park Orchestra (p193) plays free concerts at the band shell, aka Pritzker Pavilion. The acoustics and sightlines are superb, even from the Great Lawn.

SEARS TOWER Map pp54–5

☎ 312-875-9696; www.the-skydeck.com; 233 S Wacker Dr; skydeck admission adult/child 3-11yr $12.95/9.50; 10am-10pm Apr-Sep, 10am-8pm Oct-Mar, last ticket sold 30min before closing; M Brown, Orange, Purple Line to Quincy

The Sears Tower was the world's tallest building right up until the end of the 20th century. Then the Malaysians built the Petronas Towers, and Sears became a has-been. Its self esteem only got worse with Taipei, Shanghai and Dubai putting up even higher towers. Now Sears has an outright Napoleon complex. But it's still the USA's tallest building, and it's still way up in the clouds.

The Skydeck observation platform draws 1.5 million people a year who are eager to ascend the 110-story, 1454ft building (most of which is mundane office space). The Skydeck entrance is off Jackson Blvd. Your journey to the top starts with a walk through an airport-style metal detector, followed by a slow elevator ride down to the waiting area where visitors queue for tickets. A sign will tell you how long you'll have to wait to get high. On busy days it can be an hour or longer, so this is a good time to confirm the visibility – before you invest your time and money. Even days that seem sunny can have upper-level haze that limits the view. On good days, however, you can see for 40 to 50 miles, as far as Indiana, Michigan and Wisconsin.

There's a film to watch while waiting with factoids about the 43,000 miles of phone cable and 2232 steps to the roof, and then more lines before the ear-popping, 70-second elevator ride to the 103rd floor deck. From here, the entire city stretches below, and you can see exactly how Chicago is laid out.

THE MAGIC BEAN

'That's it?' Many Chicagoans fumed when Millennium Park's premier sculpture was unveiled in 2004. 'We pay $23 million, and we get a kidney-shaped hunk of metal?'

Poor Anish Kapoor. First, the artist loftily named his piece *Cloud Gate,* but that degenerated into 'the Bean,' which is what everyone immediately began calling it. Next, he had to unveil the piece before it was finished. Kapoor was still polishing and grinding the 168 stainless steel plates that comprise the Bean when the city showed it to the public. The surface was supposed to be seamless – and it is now. But it wasn't in 2004, and so soon after its debut it went back under wraps.

'We pay $23 million, get a hunk of metal, and now *we can't even see it?*' The locals were more incensed than ever.

But then a funny thing happened. When the Bean came back out again in 2006, people began to marvel at it, despite their better judgment. They admired the way it reflects both the sky and the skyline. They liked that you could get right up under it and touch its silvery smoothness. They liked the way it looked in pictures, which is how it became one of the city's most-photographed images. Soon the Bean was a symbol of Chicago, of the city's hip, cutting-edge mentality. And the locals couldn't be more proud. Didn't they say it was fabulous all along?

For those who prefer a drink with their vertigo – er, view – the John Hancock Center (p69) is a better choice.

FAMOUS LOOP ARCHITECTURE

Map pp54–5

Sure, there's the Sears Tower (see opposite). But it's just one in a long line of high-flying buildings in Chicago. Ever since the city presented the world with the first skyscraper in 1885, it has thought big with its architecture and pushed the envelope of modern design. The Loop is ground-zero for gawking.

The buildings below represent the pioneering 'Chicago School' style, stressing economy, simplicity and function. Daniel Burnham and Louis Sullivan were the era's ideas men. For details, see p37.

Architecture buffs on a pilgrimage bow down first to the Monadnock Building (53 W Jackson Blvd), two buildings in one that depict a crucial juncture in skyscraper development. The north half is the older, traditional design from 1891 (with thick, load-bearing walls), while the south is the newer, mod half (with a metal frame that allows for jazzier-looking walls and bigger windows). See the difference?

The 1888 Rookery (209 S LaSalle St) looks hulking and fortresslike outside, but it's light and airy inside thanks to Frank Lloyd Wright's atrium overhaul. Step inside and have a look. Pigeons used to roost here, hence the name.

Weep all you want over the old Marshall Field's (111 N State St) becoming Macy's; the building remains a classic no matter who's in it. The iconic bronze corner clocks on the outside have given busy Loop workers the time for over 100 years now. Inside, a 6000-sq-ft dome designed by Louis Comfort Tiffany caps the north-side atrium; 50 artists toiled for 18 months to make it. The best view is from Ladies Lingerie, on the 5th floor.

Carson Pirie Scott & Co (1 S State St) was originally criticized as being too ornamental to serve as a retail building. You be the judge, as you admire Louis Sullivan's superb metalwork around the main entrance at State and Madison Sts. Though Sullivan insisted that 'form follows function,' it's hard to see his theory at work in this lavishly flowing cast iron. Amid the flowing botanical and geometric forms, look for Sullivan's initials, LHS. The century-old department store recently vacated the building, and it has become office space.

The architects behind the Marquette Building (140 S Dearborn St) made natural light and ventilation vital components. While that's nice, the most impressive features are the sculptured panels that recall the exploits of French explorer Jacques Marquette; look for them above the entrance and in the lobby.

With its 16 stories of shimmering glass, framed by brilliant white terra-cotta details, the Reliance Building (1 W Washington St) is a breath of fresh air. The structure's lightweight internal metal frame – much of which was erected in only 15 days – supports a glass facade that gives it a feeling of lightness, a style that didn't become universal until after WWII. Today the Reliance houses the chic Hotel Burnham (p217). Added historical bonus: Al Capone's dentist drilled teeth in what's now room 809.

Another terra-cotta beauty is the 1904 Santa Fe Building (224 S Michigan Ave), where architect Daniel Burnham kept his offices. Enter the lobby and look upward at the vast light well Burnham placed in the center – he gave this same feature to the Rookery.

Architecture lovers can delve much deeper into the scene, and the Chicago Architecture Foundation – which happens to be in the Santa Fe Building – is the place to start. The group runs fantastic tours (p262) that explain the aforementioned sights and more. The foundation's shop (p121) sells top-quality books about local buildings and architects if you prefer to do it yourself.

And last, but certainly not least, no discussion of famed Loop architecture is complete without mentioning the boxy, metal-and-glass 'International Style' of Ludwig Mies van der Rohe. His Kluczynski Building (230 S Dearborn St), part of the Chicago Federal Center, is a prime example; he designed many more buildings at the Illinois Institute of Technology (p116).

BUCKINGHAM FOUNTAIN Map pp54–5

🕑 10am-11pm mid-Apr–mid-Oct; Ⓜ Red Line to Jackson

This is one of the world's largest squirters, with a 1.5 million gallon capacity and a 15-story-high spray. Wealthy widow Kate Sturges Buckingham gave the magnificent

WHAT THE EL WAS THAT NOISE?

Novelist Nelson Algren called them Chicago's 'rusty iron heart.' And Chicago's El trains – short for elevated trains – definitely occupy a prized place in the popular consciousness of the city. From El-related blogs (see www.ctatattler.com) to locals wearing T-shirts emblazoned with their favorite transit lines, the El trains have been both a mode of transportation and a mover of souls since they made their debut in the Loop in 1897.

Back then (as now) the Union Loop El trains ran on electricity rather than cables or steam. The whole electric train thing was still a new idea at the time, and the Union Loop was viewed with skepticism and more than a little fear by some residents. The medical profession didn't exactly help matters, either. The New York Academy of Medicine published a paper that year claiming that the elevated trains 'prevented the normal development of children, threw convalescing patients into relapses, and caused insomnia, exhaustion, hysteria, paralysis, meningitis, deafness and death.'

Though the case for meningitis might have been a *little* overstated, visitors to Chicago who stand under one of the trains as they pass will attest to the risk of deafness. In fact, a group of students from Columbia College conducted a study in 2005 that found the screeching from the train cars exceeded legal levels on several of the tracks. Most Chicagoans, though, just shrug off any attempts to make changes to the system that has been rattling Loop windows and sending cars screeching overhead for over 100 years. It may be rusty, but it's their heart all the same.

The tourism office runs free, 40-minute, history-filled El tours twice daily on Saturdays from May to September; pick up tickets at the Chicago Cultural Center Visitors Center (see p263 for details).

structure to the city in 1927 in memory of her brother, Clarence. She also wisely left an endowment to maintain and operate it. The central fountain symbolizes Lake Michigan, with the four water-spouting sea creatures representing the surrounding states.

The fountain lets loose on the hour. Like so much in life, the spray begins small. Each successive basin fills, stimulating more jets, then it climaxes as the central fountain spurts up to its full 150ft. The crowd sighs in awe and is thankful that smoking is allowed. At night (8pm and thereafter) multicolored lights and music accompany the show.

CHICAGO CULTURAL CENTER

Map pp54–5

☎ 312-744-6630; www.chicagoculturalcenter.org; 78 E Washington St; admission free; 🕑 8am-7pm Mon-Thu, 8am-6pm Fri, 9am-6pm Sat, 10am-6pm Sun; Ⓜ Brown, Green, Orange, Purple Line to Randolph

Think you're just going to swing into the Visitors Center here and grab some free maps? Think again. Exhibitions, beautiful interior design and lunchtime concerts and arts lectures (admission free; 12:15pm Mon-Fri) make the block-long Chicago Cultural Center a worthy destination in its own right. Take a moment as you enter on either Randolph or Washington Sts to find the schedule of events (usually posted just inside the doors).

The exquisite beaux arts building began its life as the Chicago Public Library back in 1897, and the Gilded Age interior mixes white Carrara and green Connemara marble throughout. The building also contains two domes by Louis Comfort Tiffany, including the world's largest stained glass Tiffany dome on the 3rd floor (where the circulation desk for the library used to be). The splendor of the building was meant to inspire the rabble toward loftier goals.

Excellent building tours (☎ 312-742-1190; admission free; 🕑 1:15pm Wed, Fri & Sat) leave from the Randolph St lobby. There's also a café on the Randolph side (beside the Visitors Center), and free wi-fi throughout the building.

PUBLIC ART Map pp54–5

Chicago has commissioned several puzzling public artworks throughout the decades. The granddaddy is Pablo Picasso's work, known to everyone as 'the Picasso' (50 W Washington St). The artist was 82 when the work was commissioned. The US Steel Works in Gary, Indiana, made it to Picasso's specifications and erected it in 1967. When Chicago tried to pay Picasso for the work, he refused the money, saying the sculpture was meant as a gift to the city. At the time, many locals thought it was hideous and should be torn down and replaced with a statue of Cubs great Ernie Banks.

Joan Miró's work *The Sun, The Moon and One Star,* known by everyone as Miro's Chicago (69 W Washington St), is across the street. Miró hoped to evoke the 'mystical force of a great earth mother' with this 40ft sculpture, made of various metals, cement and tile in 1981.

French sculptor Jean Dubuffet created Monument with Standing Beast (100 W Randolph St), which everyone just calls 'Snoopy in a Blender,' at around the same time. The white fiberglass work looks a little like inflated puzzle pieces and has a definite Keith Haring-esque feel to it. As you can see by the large number of kids crawling around inside, it's definitely a hands-on piece of art.

Russian-born artist Marc Chagall loved Chicago, and in 1974 he donated a grand mosaic called the Four Seasons (plaza at Dearborn and Monroe Sts) to the city. Using thousands of bits of glass and stone, the artist portrayed six scenes of the city in hues reminiscent of the Mediterranean coast of France, where he kept his studio. Chagall continued to make adjustments, such as updating the skyline, after the work arrived in Chicago.

A few blocks south on Dearborn, Alexander Calder's soaring red-pink sculpture Flamingo (plaza at Dearborn and Adams Sts) provides some much-needed relief from the stark facades of the federal buildings around it. Calder dedicated the sculpture in October 1974 by riding into the Loop on a bandwagon pulled by 40 horses, accompanied by a circus parade.

For the locations of more public artworks stashed around the city, pick up a copy of the highly useful *Chicago Public Art Guide* at any visitors center, or check the website www.cityofchicago.org/publicart. And don't forget to visit the Bean (p56), the current reigning Loop fave.

PEDWAY

Come wintertime, when the going gets tough and icy sleet knifes your face, head down to the Pedway. Chicago has a 40-block labyrinth of underground walkways, built in conjunction with the subway trains. The system isn't entirely connected (ie it would be difficult to walk from one end of the Loop to the other entirely underground), and you'll find that you rise to the surface in the oddest places, say an apartment building, a hotel lobby, Macy's or City Hall. The walkways are also hit-or-miss for amenities: some have coffee shops and fast-food outlets tucked along the way, some have urine smells. The city posts 'Pedway' signs above ground at points of entry.

CHICAGO BOARD OF TRADE

Map pp54–5

141 W Jackson Blvd; Ⓜ Brown, Orange, Purple Line to LaSalle

The Board of Trade is a 1930 art deco gem. Inside, manic traders swap futures and options. No one really knows what those are, other than it has something to do with corn. Or maybe it's wheat. A small visitors center (☎ 312-435-3590; admission free; 🕑 8am-4pm Mon-Fri) tries to explain it all. Or just stay outside and gaze up at the mondo statue of Ceres, the goddess of agriculture, that tops the building.

The Board of Trade merged with the Chicago Mercantile Exchange in 2007, and most operations are now in this building so security is tight.

CHICAGO THEATRE Map pp54–5

☎ 312-462-6363; www.thechicagotheatre.com; 175 N State St; Ⓜ Red Line to Lake

Everyone from Duke Ellington to Frank Sinatra to Prince has taken the stage here over the years (and left their signature on the famous backstage walls). The real show-stopper, though, is the opulent French baroque architecture, including the lobby modeled on the Palace of Versailles. Opened in 1921 the theater originally screened silent movies with a full orchestra and white-gloved ushers leading patrons to their seats. Tickets cost just 50 cents, so rich and poor alike could revel in the splendor. Today it's a concert venue. Tours ($5) are available Tuesdays year-round, Thursdays in summer, and every third Saturday monthly. If nothing else, take a gander at the six-story sign out front; it's an official landmark.

CITY HALL Map pp54–5

121 N LaSalle St; Ⓜ Brown, Orange, Purple, Blue Line to Washington

Da Mayor rules Chicago from mighty City Hall. He also tends garden and keeps bees here. To make a point a few years ago about how the city could conserve energy, he planted City Hall's roof with prairie flowers. Then he let loose 200,000 honey bees among them. By all measures, the nature experiment was a success – other 'green' roofs have blossomed throughout the city, and the bees' sweet wares are sold to make money for kids' art programs. Plus City Hall earns a lot of street cred for letting the Blues Brothers drive their car through the building.

HAROLD WASHINGTON LIBRARY CENTER Map pp54–5

☎ 312-747-4300; www.chicagopubliclibrary.org; 400 S State St; admission free; 9am-9pm Mon-Thu, 9am-5pm Fri & Sat, 1-5pm Sun; M Brown, Orange, Purple Line to Library

This grand, art-filled building with free internet and wi-fi (get a temporary 'guest' card for access) is Chicago's whopping main library. Major authors give readings here, and exhibits constantly show in the galleries. The light-drenched, top-floor Winter Garden is a sweet hideaway for reading, writing or just taking a load off, though you'll have to hike to get there. Take escalators to the 3rd floor, transfer to another set of escalators for five more floors, then take a third escalator up for the final assault. And those green-copper creatures staring down from the exterior roof? They're wise old owls.

ROUTE 66 SIGN Map pp54–5

Adams St btwn Michigan & Wabash Aves; M Brown, Green, Orange, Purple Line to Adams

Attention Route 66 buffs: the Mother Road's starting point is here. Look for the sign that marks the spot on Adams St's north side as you head west toward Wabash Ave. For further details on the nostalgic, corn-dog-laden highway, see p243.

UNION STATION Map pp54–5

☎ 312-655-2385; 225 S Canal St; M Brown, Orange, Purple Line to Quincy

This wonderfully restored 1925 building, designed by Graham, Burnham & Company (Daniel Burnham's successors), looks like it stepped right out of a gangster movie. In fact, it's been used to great effect in exactly this way. Remember director Brian de Palma's classic *The Untouchables,* when Elliott Ness loses his grip on the baby carriage during the shoot-out with Al Capone's henchmen? And the carriage bounces down the stairs in slow motion? Those steps are right here, baby; they're the north ones from Canal St to the waiting room. Come during the day when Amtrak and Metra riders stride through the space, which is dappled with bright shafts of sunlight from the banks of windows.

A POSTCARD PERSPECTIVE

Walking Tour

Why buy postcards when you can make your own? A camera, comfortable shoes, a day spent clicking away at Loop sights and you'll have your own picture postcard perspective of the city. Now you just need a printer…

1 Picasso It's a baboon, it's a babe, it's a babe's private parts. The artist never would say what the 1967 iron sculpture represents. Nevertheless, the untitled Picasso (p58) has become a well-known Chi-town symbol. The most intriguing perspective may just be laying face-up, camera angled, looking at the nose of the beast.

2 Miró's Chicago For more landmark public art, cross the street to Miró's Chicago (p58). Spanish artist Joan Miró unveiled his robot/pagan fertility goddesslike sculpture in 1981. Today a full picture includes societal commentary – nearby office workers use the statue's base as a smoker's lounge; feel free to crop.

3 Chicago Theatre What could be more postcard perfect than a six-story-high lighted sign spelling the town's name? Any time is fine to capture the 1920s marquee for the Chicago Theatre (p59). But if your tour falls on a cloudy day, that would eliminate harsh shadows.

4 Old Marshall Field's Clock 'Meeting under the clock' has been a Chicago tradition since 1897 when Marshall Field installed the elaborate timepiece at Washington & State. (Before that patrons stuck notes for rendezvous-ing friends on the building.) A photo beneath the clock (now Macy's, p57) is a must.

5 Chicago Cultural Center The 38ft diameter Tiffany dome at the Chicago Cultural Center (p58), reputed to be the world's largest, is well worth photographing (as is the 1897 building's hodgepodge of Greek, Roman and European architectural styles). But you're really here to get inspiration from the architectural photos in the Landmark Chicago Gallery.

6 Cloud Gate Plenty of Kodak moments happen at the 24-acre Millennium Park; your first stop, the sculpture Chicagoans call the Bean (officially known as *Cloud Gate,* p56). Stand on

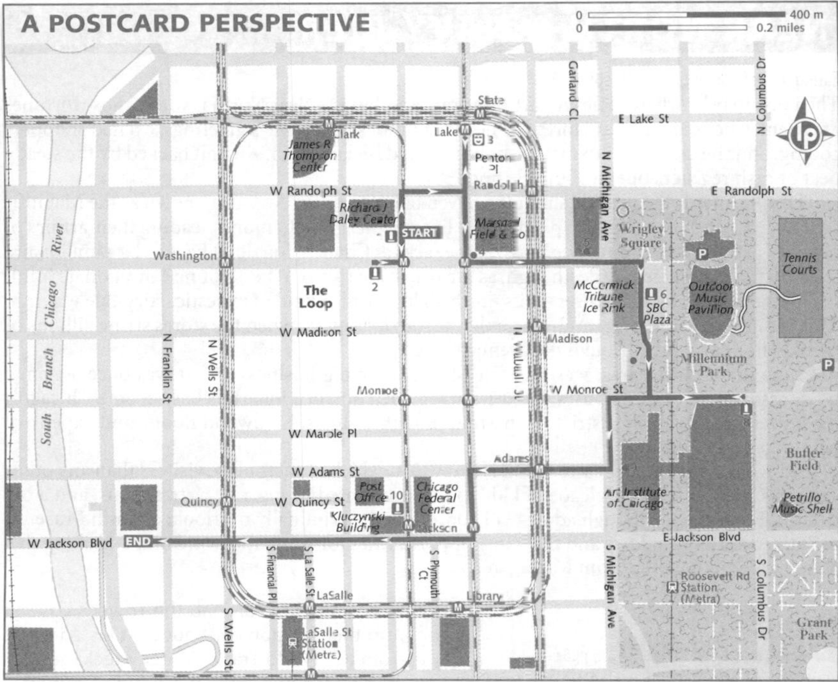

WALK FACTS

Start Picasso
Finish Sears Tower
Duration Four to six hours (more with extended museum time)
Fuel Stop Frontera Fresco, Rick Bayless' 7th floor food court outlet at old Marshall Field's (p57), now Macy's

the west side of the giant mirrored blob, hold the camera waist level and you can take a self-portrait with a skyline background.

7 Crown Fountain Geysers spout from the ground in front of two 50ft LED screens projecting images of peoples' faces. When an open-mouthed guy/gal appears, the Crown Fountain (p53) spouts water as if spitting. Use a fast shutter speed, and stick to a side view unless you've got a waterproof camera.

8 Chicago Stock Exchange Arch Many of renowned early-20th-century architect Louis Sullivan's buildings have been demolished. But you can get up close to his exquisite terracotta ornamentation at the Chicago Stock Exchange Arch, which was rescued and placed outside the Art Institute (p52). A telephoto can isolate the detail.

9 Art Institute Lions Around the front of the Art Institute (p52) stand two 1894 bronze lions – city mascots of sorts. They wore helmets when the Bears won the 1985 Superbowl and a White Sox cap during the 2005 pennant. Zoom in for a striking profile shot silhouetted against city buildings.

10 Flamingo Alexander Calder's Flamingo (p59) is another monumental piece of public art easily recognized in Chicago. That bright red paint job should photograph well, especially if you frame it against Mies van der Rohe's ground-breaking 1974 glass-and-steel Kluczynski Building (p57) in the Chicago Federal Center.

11 Sears Tower Aligning the building's edge on a slight diagonal will add dynamism to a shot of the 1454ft-tall Sears Tower (p56), the tallest US building (pre- and post-World Trade Center). A final photo from the 103rd floor Skydeck sums it up: high-rises galore, lake beyond – that's the Loop.

NEAR NORTH & NAVY PIER

Eating p142; Shopping p122; Sleeping p218

The Loop may be where Chicago fortunes are made, but the Near North is where those fortunes are spent. The song of Near North is a heady choir of salespeople's greetings, excited shoppers cooing, and the crackle of luxury goods being swaddled in paper. All of it backed by the steady beat of cash registers opening and closing.

The epicenter is the upscale shopping haven of N Michigan Ave, also known as the Magnificent Mile (Mag Mile). This is a prime place to see Chicago's old money leading their armies of personal assistants in commando raids on the racks at Chanel. You don't have to be a millionaire to enjoy the Magnificent Mile, though, as the whole area – from the Tribune Tower on its south end to the historic Water Tower on its north – glows with a kind of majestic, fairy-tale warmth. This is especially true from mid-November through January, when the stores string zillions of twinkly holiday lights through the avenue's trees.

In the River North area, west of State St, art is the big business. What was once a grimy, noisy assortment of warehouses, factories and association headquarters has become Chicago's most prestigious gallery district – a bastion of high ceilings, hardwood floors, and expensive paintings and sculpture.

Jutting off Near North's eastern end is Navy Pier, which attracts more visitors than any other sight in Chicago. It's a cavalcade of kid- and teen-oriented shops, rides, attractions, and a big freakin' Ferris wheel, though adults will appreciate the criminally overlooked Smith Museum of Stained Glass Windows and the many opportunities for romantic, windswept strolling. It's about a 15-minute hoof from Michigan Ave.

NEAR NORTH

MAGNIFICENT MILE Map pp64–5

www.themagnificentmile.com; Michigan Ave from the Chicago River north to Oak St; Ⓜ Red Line to Grand

The city likes to claim that the Magnificent Mile, or 'Mag Mile' as it's widely known, is one of the top five shopping streets in the world. It's a bit of a boast, because most of the retailers here are just high-end department stores and national chains that are available throughout the country. Granted, the Mag Mile versions are more slicked up than usual, and their vacuum-packed proximity on Michigan Ave between the river and Oak St is handy. Probably what's most magnificent is the amount of dough they ring up – one billion bucks annually. The road does go all out in December with a festive spread of tree lights and holiday adornments.

TRIBUNE TOWER Map pp64–5

435 N Michigan Ave; Ⓜ Red Line to Grand

Colonel Robert McCormick, eccentric owner of the *Chicago Tribune,* collected – and asked his reporters to send – rocks from famous buildings and monuments around the world. He stockpiled pieces of the Taj Mahal, Westminster Abbey, the Great Pyramid and 120 or so others, which are now embedded around the Tower's base. And the tradition continues: a twisted piece from the World Trade Center wreckage was added recently, and a piece from Sydney's Opera House hit the bricks in 2006.

MCCORMICK TRIBUNE FREEDOM MUSEUM Map pp64–5

☎ 312-222-4860; www.freedommuseum.us; 445 N Michigan Ave; admission $5; 🕒 10am-6pm, closed Tue; Ⓜ Red Line to Grand

Next door to the Tribune Tower, this small museum provokes thought. Hear once-banned music at the listening exhibits,

TRANSPORTATION – NEAR NORTH & NAVY PIER

Bus Number 151 runs along N Michigan Ave; 156 is a good north–south bet through River North; 65 travels along Grand Ave to Navy Pier.

El Red Line to Grand for the Magnificent Mile's south end and River North; Red Line to Chicago for the Mag Mile's north end.

Parking The further you get away from the Mag Mile, the more common the metered parking. Parking at Navy Pier is costly – $15 an hour. Instead, look for signed lots west of Lake Shore Dr near the pier and take a free shuttle to the pier.

or interact with computer exhibits that present actual cases testing free speech rights (ie, can the Ku Klux Klan hold a rally on the community square?).

WRIGLEY BUILDING Map pp64–5

400 N Michigan Ave; (M) Red Line to Grand

The Wrigley Building glows as white as the Doublemint Twins' teeth day or night. Chewing-gum-guy William Wrigley built it that way on purpose, because he wanted it to be attention-grabbing like a billboard. More than 250,000 glazed terra-cotta tiles make up the facade; a computer database tracks each one and when each needs to be cleaned and polished. Banks of mega-watt lamps on the river's south side light the tiles up each night.

RIVER ESPLANADE Map pp64–5

Chicago River waterfront, btwn N Michigan Ave & N McClurg Ct; (bus) 124

The developers looking to cash in on River East Center were given a mandate by the city: for the proposed shopping area to be approved, the company would have to leave the River Esplanade to the Chicago Park District. It was a good deal for both parties, and the River Esplanade makes an excellent place to take a break from your hectic shopping/sightseeing schedule. Beginning with the oddly proportioned curving staircase at the northeast tower of the Michigan Ave Bridge, the landscaped walkway extends east along the river past the Sheraton Hotel.

Every hour on the hour, from 10am to 2pm and again from 5pm to midnight, the esplanade's Centennial Fountain shoots a massive arc of water across the river for 10 minutes. The entire exercise is meant to commemorate the labor-intensive reversal of the Chicago River in 1900, which tidily began sending all of the city's wastes downriver rather than into the lake. (Chicago's neighbors downstate, as you can imagine, do not go out of their way to celebrate this feat of civil engineering; see p21).

HOLY NAME CATHEDRAL Map pp64–5

(tel) 312-787-8040; www.holynamecathedral.com; 735 N State St; admission free; (hours) 7am-7pm; (M) Red Line to Chicago

Holy Name Cathedral is the seat of Chicago's Catholic Church and where its powerful cardinals do their preaching. Built in 1875 to a design by the unheralded Patrick Keeley, the cathedral has twice been remodeled in attempts to spruce it up. The latter effort covered up bullet holes left over from a Capone-era hit across the street (see the boxed text, p79).

The cathedral provides a quiet place for contemplation, unless the excellent choirs are practicing, in which case it's an entertaining respite. Open most of the day, the cathedral holds frequent services. Check out the sanctuary's ceiling while you're inside. The red hats hanging way up there are for deceased cardinals from the cathedral; the hats remain until they turn to dust.

MERCHANDISE MART Map pp64–5

(tel) 800-677-6278; www.merchandisemart.com; 222 Merchandise Mart Plaza; admission free; (hours) 9am-6pm Mon-Fri, 10am-3pm Sat; (M) Brown, Purple Line to Merchandise Mart

The Merchandise Mart is the world's third-largest building (the Pentagon and a Dutch flower market are bigger). Spanning two city blocks, the 1931 monster has its own zip code and gives most of its copious space to wholesale showrooms for home furnishing and design professionals. Technically off-limits to nonindustry types, the showrooms are reachable by any civilian brave enough to hop on one of the many elevators. Unless you can fake a wholesaler license, you won't be allowed to actually buy anything in the rooms. Everyone, though, is welcome to explore the mall on the 1st two floors. The Merchandise Mart also hosts occasional sales that are open to the public; check the 'consumer events' section of the website for details. Tours ($12) are available by appointment.

Outdoors on the mart's river side, a collection of heads on poles rise up like giant Pez dispensers. This is the Merchant's Hall of Fame, and the creepy busts depict famous local retailers such as Marshall Field and Frank Woolworth.

MUSEUM OF BROADCAST COMMUNICATIONS Map pp64–5

(tel) 312-245-8200; www.museum.tv; 360 N State St; (M) Red Line to Grand

The Museum of Broadcast Communications, filled with radio and TV nostalgia, is

NEAR NORTH & NAVY PIER

A
B
C
D
INFORMATION
Fort Dearborn Station Post Office......1 C4
Kinko's......2 B5
Northwestern Memorial Hospital......3 D4
Police Station......4 C3
Walgreens......5 D3
Walgreens......6 D5
SIGHTS & ACTIVITIES (pp62–8)
Carousel......7 G4
Catherine Edelman Gallery......8 B3
Centennial Fountain......9 E5
Chicago Children's Museum......10 G4
Chicago Shakespeare Theater......(see 77)
Chicago Spire......11 F4
Chopping Block......(see 18)
Ferris Wheel......12 G4
Grand Ballroom......13 H4
Holy Name Cathedral......14 C3
IMAX Theater......(see 79)
Jean Albano Gallery......15 B4
Marina City......16 C5
McCormick Tribune Freedom Museum......17 D5
Merchandise Mart......18 B5
Moody Church......19 C3
Museum of Broadcast Communications......20 C5
Mystic Blue Cruises......21 H5
Ohio St Beach......22 F4
River Esplanade......23 E5
Robert Henry Adams Fine Art......24 B4
Shoreline Sightseeing......25 G5
Smith Museum of Stained Glass Windows......26 H4
Tribune Tower......27 D5
USS Chicago Anchor......28 H4
W Chicago-Lakeshore......(see 108)
WBEZ......29 G4
Weird Chicago Tours......30 C4
Wendella Sightseeing Boats......31 D5
Windy......32 G5
Wrigley Building......33 D5
Zolla-Lieberman Gallery......34 B4
SHOPPING (pp122–4)
Abraham Lincoln Book Shop......35 B3
American Girl Place......36 D3
Apple Store......37 D4
Chicago Place Mall......38 D4
Chicago Tribune Store......(see 27)
CompUSA......39 D3
Crate & Barrel......40 D4
Garrett Popcorn......41 D4
Jazz Record Mart......42 D5
Levi's Store......43 D4
Merchandise Mart......(see 18)
Niketown......44 D4
Shops at North Bridge......45 D5
Sports Authority......46 C4
EATING (pp142–6)
Bandera......47 D4
Billy Goat Tavern......(see 66)
Brasserie Jo......48 C5
Cafe Iberico......49 C3
Chicago Chop House......(see 72)
Cabrini-Green
W Oak St
E Walton St
Washington Square
W Locust St
W Chestnut St
E Chestnut St
W Institute Pl
See Gold Coast Map pp70–1
Seneca Park
River North Gallery District
W Chicago Ave
E Chicago Ave
Chicago
W Superior St
E Superior St
Near North
W Huron St
E Huron St
W Erie St
E Erie St
W Ontario St
E Ontario St
W Ohio St
W Grand Ave
Grand
W Illinois St
E Illinois St
W Hubbard St
E Hubbard St
W Kinzie St
Trump Tower
Merchandise Mart
Chicago Water Taxi
Commuter Taxi
E South Water St
Clinton
W Lake St
Lake
State
E Lake St
Illinois Center
W Randolph St
Randolph
Wrigley Square
Millennium Park
Washington
The Loop
McCormick Tribune Ice Rink
SBC Plaza
N Crosby St
N Kingsbury St
N Larrabee St
N Mohawk St
N Cleveland Ave
N Sedgwick St
N Wells St
N Clark St
N State St
N Rush St
N Michigan Ave
N Orleans St
N Franklin St
N La Salle St
N Dearborn St
N Wabash Ave
Magnificent Mile
N St Clair St
N Milwaukee Ave
N Clinton St
N West Water St
N Jefferson St
Canal St
N Riverside Plaza
W Wacker Dr
Garland Ct
N Stetson Ave

0 — 500 m
0 — 0.3 miles

E F G H

Cyrano's Bistrot....................50 B4
Fox & Obel's....................51 E5
Frontera Grill....................(see 62)
Gene and Georgetti....................52 B5
Gino's East....................53 B4
Giordano's....................54 D3
Green Door Tavern....................55 B4
Le Lan....................56 C3
Mr Beef....................57 B4
Nacional 27....................(see 34)
NoMi....................58 D3
Peninsula....................(see 104)
Pizzeria Uno....................59 D4
Portillo's....................60 C4
Shaw's Crab House....................61 C5
Topolobampo....................62 C5
Tru....................63 D4
Whole Foods....................64 C4
Wildfire....................65 B4

DRINKING (pp171–2)
Billy Goat Tavern....................66 D5
Blue Frog Bar & Grill....................67 B4
Brehon Pub....................68 B3
Clark St Ale House....................69 C3

NIGHTLIFE (pp182–90)
Andy's....................70 C5
Blue Chicago....................71 C4
Excalibur....................72 C4
Howl At the Moon....................73 C5
Ontourage....................(see 53)
Sound-Bar....................74 B4

ARTS (pp192–201)
600 N Michigan Theaters....................75 D4
AMC River East....................76 E4
Chicago Shakespeare Theater....................77 C4
House of Blues....................78 C5
IMAX Theater....................79 G4
Skyline Stage....................80 G4
Vision....................81 C4

SPORTS & ACTIVITIES (pp204–12)
Crunch Fitness....................82 D4
Ohio St Beach....................(see 22)

SLEEPING (pp218–23)
Affinia Chicago....................83 D3
Allerton Hotel....................84 D4
Amalfi Hotel Chicago....................85 C5
Best Western River North....................86 C4
Chicago City Centre Hotel & Athletic Club....................87 E4
Chicago Marriott Hotel....................88 D4
Comfort Inn & Suites Downtown....................89 C4
Conrad Chicago....................90 D5
Embassy Suites Chicago-Downtown....................91 C4
Embassy Suites Chicago-River East....................92 E5
Four Points Chicago Downtown....................93 D4
Hampton Inn & Suites-Chicago Downtown....................94 C5
Hilton Garden Inn....................95 C4
Hotel Cass....................96 D4
Hotel Inter-Continental Chicago....................97 D5
Hotel Sax....................98 C5
Howard Johnson Inn....................99 C4
Inn of Chicago....................100 D4
James....................101 D4
Ohio House Motel....................102 C4
Omni Chicago Hotel....................103 D4
Peninsula....................104 D3
Radisson Hotel & Suites....................105 D4
Red Roof Inn....................106 D4
Sheraton Chicago Hotel & Towers....................107 E5
W Chicago-Lakeshore....................108 F4
Westin River North....................109 C5
Wyndham Chicago....................110 D4

TRANSPORT (pp249–54)
Bike Chicago Navy Pier....................111 G5
Chicago Water Taxi, La Salle St Stop....................112 C5
Chicago Water Taxi, Michigan Ave Stop....................113 D5
Currency Exchange....................114 D3
Shoreline Sightseeing Commuter Taxi, Michigan Ave Stop....................115 D5
Shoreline Sightseeing Lake Taxi to Shedd Aquarium....................116 G5
Shoreline Sightseeing River Taxi to Sears Tower....................117 F5

E Pearson St
Lake Shore Park
N Lake Shore Dr
Northwestern University Chicago Campus
Streeterville
Ohio St Beach
Olive Park
Water Filtration Plant
N Fairbanks Ct
N McClurg Ct
E Ohio St
E Grand Ave
Navy Pier
E North Water St
River Esplanade
Chicago River
River Taxi
E Wacker Dr
N Columbus Dr
See The Loop Map p54–5
Family Golf Center
N Lake Shore Dr
E Randolph St
Daley Bicentennial Plaza
Grant Park
Tennis Courts
Wildflower Works
Lake Michigan

a newbie in the 'hood (a smaller incarnation once dwelled in the Chicago Cultural Center). After three-plus years of restructuring, the new museum still had not opened at press time. Call for admission prices and hours.

RIVER NORTH GALLERIES Map pp64–5

near intersection of W Superior & N Franklin Sts; Ⓜ Brown, Purple Line to Chicago

Unlike the ragtag galleries of Pilsen or the up-and-comers in the West Loop, River North galleries tend to show money artists for a money clientele. The atmosphere here is still welcoming, though, and the gallery owners are happy to let normal folk wander through their showrooms. Pick up a gallery map at any of the venues to help find artwork to your liking.

Some of our favorites:

Catherine Edelman Gallery (☎ 312-266-2350; www.edelmangallery.com; 300 W Superior St; 🕑 10am-5:30pm Tue-Sat) If you love photography, drop by this place where artworks range from traditional landscapes to mixed-media photo-based collages.

Jean Albano Gallery (☎ 312-440-0770; www.jeanalbano-artgallery.com; 215 W Superior St; 🕑 10am-5pm Tue-Fri, 11am-5pm Sat) The contemporary art here includes paintings, drawings and interesting textile works.

Robert Henry Adams Fine Art (☎ 312-642-8700; www.adamsfineart.com; 715 N Franklin St; 🕑 10am-5pm Tue-Fri, from noon Sat) A friendly, two-floor gallery specializing in works by pre-WWII American impressionist, regionalist and modernist painters.

Zolla-Lieberman Gallery (☎ 312-944-1990; www.zollaliebermangallery.com; 325 W Huron St; 🕑 10am-5:30pm Tue-Fri, 11am-5:30pm Sat) The first gallery to arrive in River North back in the mid-'70s (when it looked more like the West Loop does today), it continues to show cool, contemporary art by established and emerging artists.

MARINA CITY Map pp64–5

300 N State St; Ⓜ Blue, Orange, Green, Brown, Purple Line to Clark & Lake

For some postmodern fun, check out the twin 'corncob' towers of the 1962 mixed-use Marina City. Designed by Bertrand Goldberg, it has become an iconic part of the Chicago skyline, showing up on the cover of the Wilco CD *Yankee Hotel Foxtrot*. The condos that top the spiraling parking garages are especially picturesque at Christmas, when owners decorate the balconies with a profusion of lights.

NAVY PIER

NAVY PIER Map pp64–5

☎ 312-595-7437; www.navypier.com; 600 E Grand Ave; admission free; 🕑 10am-10pm Sun-Thu, to midnight Fri & Sat, earlier closing times Sep-May; 🚍 124

Chicago's most-visited tourist attraction, half-mile-long Navy Pier, induces groans from locals about its commercialization. But even they can't refute the brilliant lakefront views, cool breezes and whopping fireworks displays on Wednesdays (9:30pm) and Saturdays (10:15pm).

The place will certainly blow the minds of children under 12. The pier's collection of high-tech rides, hands-on fountains, kid-focused educational exhibits, fast-food restaurants and trinket vendors will transport your child into the kind of overstimulated, joyful state you haven't witnessed since you finally gave in and got them a puppy for their birthday last year.

For the childless, Navy Pier's charms revolve around the views and the stomach-curdling ride on the gigantic, 150ft Ferris wheel (per ride $6). It's much more exciting than any Ferris wheel has a right to be, partly because of the dizzying heights of the thing, but also because of the almost nonexistent security precautions (make sure the small gate separating you from the tarmac far below is properly shut!). Nevertheless, as long as you don't suffer from acrophobia, the ride will be one of your best memories of Chicago. The carousel (per ride $5) is another classic, with bobbing, carved horses and organ music. In addition, a flotilla of competing tour boats departs from the pier's southern side; see p260 for details.

Navy Pier isn't all about rides and cotton candy, though. Many of the seven million visitors to the pier each year actually come here on business – the eastern end of the structure consists of exposition space managed in conjunction with McCormick Place. It's a hoot to watch the crowds of laminated-badge-toting conventioneers fighting surly suburban preteens for a table in the pier's McDonalds.

A variety of acts appear through the summer at the Skyline Stage (☎ 312-595-7437), a 1500-seat rooftop venue with a glistening white canopy. An IMAX Theater and the Chicago Shakespeare Theater (p195) also call the pier home.

In summer Shoreline Sightseeing (☎ 312-222-9328; www.shorelinesightseeing.com; adult/child $7/3) runs a handy water taxi between Navy Pier, the river near the Sears Tower and the Shedd Aquarium.

CHICAGO CHILDREN'S MUSEUM

Map pp64–5

☎ 312-527-1000; www.chichildrensmuseum.org; Navy Pier; admission $8, free Thu after 5pm; 10am-5pm Sun-Wed & Fri, to 8pm Thu & Sat; 124

The target audience of this attraction will love the place. Designed to challenge the imaginations of toddlers through to 10-year-olds, the colorful and lively museum near the main entrance to Navy Pier gives its wee visitors enough hands-on exhibits to keep them climbing and creating for hours.

Among the favorite exhibits, Dinosaur Expedition explores the world of paleontology. The game show 'Face to Face' teaches the young ones how not to grow up to be jerks by cautioning against prejudice and discrimination. Designing your own flight of fancy is the goal at the build-your-own-airplane Inventing Lab. And Waterways lets kids get wet just when they've finally dried out from the Navy Pier fountains. Hint: come in the afternoon to avoid the crowds.

The museum is planning a move to larger, specially built digs in a few years; the proposed site is in Grant Park, though at press time nearby condo owners were pressuring Mayor Daley to veto it.

SMITH MUSEUM OF STAINED GLASS WINDOWS Map pp64–5

☎ 312-595-5024; Navy Pier; admission free; 10am-10pm Sun-Thu, to midnight Fri & Sat, earlier closing times Sep-May; 124

The owners of Navy Pier don't promote this free, impressive attraction very well, but visitors who wander along the lower-level terraces of Festival Hall will discover the country's first museum dedicated entirely to stained glass. Many of the 150 pieces on display were made in Chicago (a stained-glass hub in the late 1800s, thanks to the influx of European immigrants), and most hung at one point in Chicago churches, homes and office buildings. Even if you think stained glass is something for blue-haired grandmas, you should make a point of coming by; the articulately explained collection ranges from typical Victorian religious themes to far-out political designs (the Martin Luther King Jr one is especially noteworthy). And fans of Louis Comfort Tiffany will rejoice to find 13 of his works hanging here.

top picks

FOR CHILDREN

Chicago is a kid's kind of town. Here are the top sights that will have the wee ones screaming (in a positive way). A good resource is the free publication *Chicago Parent* (www.chicagoparent.com), available at the Children's Museum and libraries.

- Chicago Children's Museum (left) The only problem you'll face at this educational playland on Navy Pier is making your kids leave come closing time.
- Chicago's beaches (p209) The pint-sized waves are perfect for pint-sized swimmers.
- Crown Fountain at Millennium Park (p53) It's like swimming in art.
- Field Museum of Natural History (p104) Dinosaurs! Need we say more?
- Shedd Aquarium (p105) The top-notch collection of fish and marine mammals makes for a whale of a good time.
- Lincoln Park Zoo (p78) The African exhibit and farm-in-the-zoo are always young crowd pleasers.
- Sears Tower Skydeck (p56) Fantastic views and special kid-friendly history exhibits make this a sky-high treat.
- Adler Planetarium (p105) Where little astronomers are stars.
- Museum of Science & Industry (p113) This huge museum will leave even the most energetic child happily spent after a few educational hours.
- Navy Pier fountains and rides (p63) A Ferris wheel, a carousel and a thousand joyful ways to get soaked.

ABOVE, ON & IN THE WATER

Walking Tour

Recreational playground, drinking water source, transportation lane – Lake Michigan is the watery lifeblood of the city. There's no better place to experience its numerous facets than around Navy Pier.

ABOVE, ON & IN THE WATER

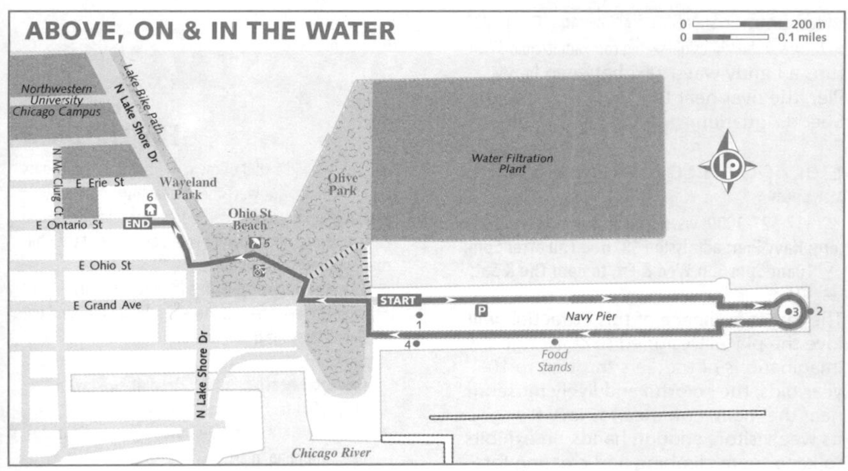

WALK FACTS

Start Navy Pier entrance
Finish W Chicago-Lakeshore hotel
Duration Two hours
Fuel stop Any of the numerous food stands (or Beer Garden) on Navy Pier

1 Navy Pier Opened in 1914, Navy Pier (p66) has seen use as a busy inland port, a naval installment, a university campus, a convention center and today's entertainment complex. Despite the amusement rides, food and shops you still get a real sense of the water walking along the pier's 3000ft expanse.

2 USS Chicago Anchor Follow the quieter northern path to the pier's east end for the best views. The WWII-era *USS Chicago* anchor reminds us of the nearly 200 planes that met a watery end training here in the 1940s. (On a calm day you can see them underwater from the John Hancock observatory.)

3 Grand Ballroom One of the few remaining 1916 buildings, the rotund Grand Ballroom still has 30,000 lights tracing the dome's arcs. With 180 degrees of water views out the windows, wouldn't a party here be grand? The historic buildings adjacent (now meeting spaces) held a military mess hall, and then the University of Illinois cafeteria.

4 Boat Rides Enough history already, you want to get on the water. No problem. Power boats, sightseeing or dinner-dance cruises, and a sail-powered tall ship all dock along the southside of the pier (see p262). The best deal is the water taxi (p252) that takes you to Museum Campus for $7.

5 Ohio St Beach If you want to brave the cool water (about 70°F/21°C in August) you can do so at Ohio St Beach (p209). Just as many people sit on the concrete steps and look at the waves lapping the north shore as those that sink their toes in the sand.

6 W Chicago-Lakeshore If you're loaded, you've booked a high-floor junior suite at the W (p219) for an unbeatable private lake lookout. Otherwise, take the elevator up to the 33rd floor bar, Whisky Sky. (Note: Navy Pier hosts fireworks Saturdays and Wednesdays in summer.)

GOLD COAST

Eating p146; Shopping p124; Sleeping p223

In its most pristine reaches, the Gold Coast outshines even its gilded name, the well-heeled historic mansions glinting with an unselfconscious wealth. When you stroll through the neighborhood, especially the Astor St area, you'll take in some of the most beautiful old homes in Chicago, if not the country. With a little imagination, you can almost see the late-19th-century moguls who settled the area brandishing diamond-tipped canes at each other, and cradling their tiny dogs on the carriage rides into their Loop offices.

Today those magnates would have to fight their way to the curb through the throngs of *House and Garden* devotees clinging to the iron gates and drooling. This being Chicago, though, the Gold Coast's historic enclaves like Astor St weren't always so revered. A great number of the beautiful old mansions disappeared 50 years ago to make room for the high-rise, high-cost apartments lining the lakefront.

Despite the area's upper-class leanings, the atmosphere is anything but sedate. Teens on gas-powered scooters zoom up the paths along Lake Shore Dr past crowds of beach volleyball players gathering for a lunchtime match. At night, young professionals mingle at Museum of Contemporary Art (MCA) socials, shifting the party to the singles bars around Rush and Division Sts as the hour grows later. Businessmen carve into porterhouses and martinis at the old-school steakhouses, and ogle the action.

The further you move away from the lake, the less rarefied the Gold Coast's air. At one time, the Cabrini-Green housing project, one of the city's most bleak, sat at the western edge of the neighborhood. Today it's being demolished, and its residents relocated far away to the Chicago suburbs. True to Gold Coast form, developers have drawn up plans for luxury townhomes that will eventually sweep across the valuable 70-acre plot of land.

JOHN HANCOCK CENTER Map pp70–1

☎ 312-751-3681; www.hancock-observatory.com; 875 N Michigan Ave; adult/child 5-12yr $11.30/7.15; 9am-11pm; M Red Line to Chicago

The world's tallest 'mixed-use' building (meaning that it contains both residential and commercial space), the Hancock is the third-tallest building in Chicago, at 1127ft. Much less popular than the Sears Tower's Skydeck, the Hancock's viewing platform benefits from having shorter lines and no sappy film. The friendly employees guide you to the fast – 23mph – elevators for the 40-second ride to the 94th floor. In many ways the view here surpasses the one at Sears Tower – the Hancock is closer to the lake and a little further north.

However pleasant that view from the platform, locals shake their heads sadly at the suckers who pay to make the ascent. The elevator ride to the Hancock's 96th-floor Signature Lounge, they're quick to point out, is free. Why shell out $11 to go stand around on some windblown viewing deck when the same money could get you a glass of wine, a comfy seat, and almost identical views a few floors higher? They've got a point. The lounge's elevators are to the right of the cashier's desk for the observatory. Time your sips to coincide with Navy Pier's fireworks (p69) and you're stylin'.

Strange factoids: a stuntman in a Spider-Man costume set out to climb to the top of the Hancock Center using suction cups in 1981. The man in question, 'Spider Dan' Goodwin, succeeded despite a questionable intervention attempt by the Chicago Fire Department, who tried to discourage the climb by spraying him with water from their fire hoses. Also, Chicago comedian Chris Farley lived here, and was found dead from a drug overdose in his 60th-floor apartment in 1997.

TRANSPORTATION – GOLD COAST

Bus Number 151 runs along N Michigan Ave; 70 runs along Division St before swooping south to the Newberry Library; 66 swings by the Museum of Contemporary Art.

El Red Line to Clark/Division for the northern reaches; Red Line to Chicago for the southern areas.

Parking Resident-only streets stymie street parking. Try LaSalle St for unmetered parking, or let a restaurant valet find you a spot for around $10.

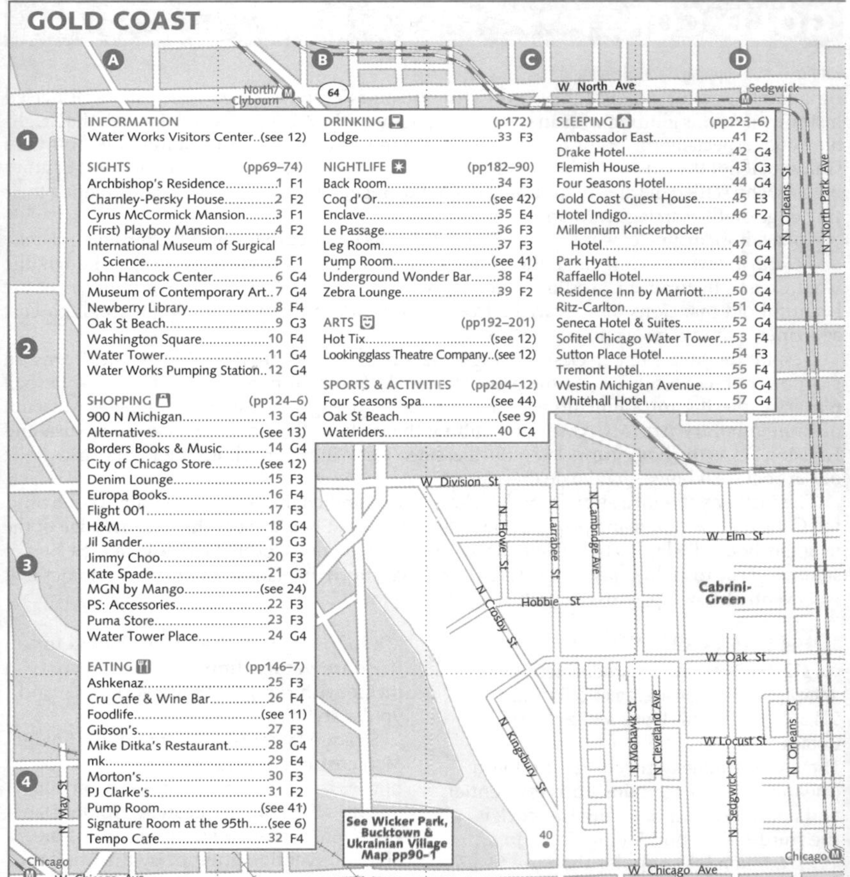

WATER TOWER Map pp70–1

806 N Michigan Ave; Ⓜ Red Line to Chicago

Believe it or not, the 154ft Water Tower, a city icon and focal point of the Mag Mile, once dwarfed all the surrounding buildings. Built in 1869, the Water Tower and its associated building, the Pumping Station (aka the Water Works) across the street, were constructed with local yellow limestone in a Gothic style popular at the time. This stone construction and lack of flammable interiors saved them in 1871, when the Great Chicago Fire roared through town; they're the only downtown buildings that survived.

The Water Tower was the great hope of Chicago when it first opened, one part of a great technological breakthrough that was going to provide fresh, clean water for the city from intake cribs set far out in Lake Michigan. Before then, the city's drinking water had come from shore-side collection basins that sucked in sewage-laden water and industrial runoff from the Chicago River. Garnished with the occasional school of small fish, it all ended up in the sinks and bathtubs of unhappy Chicago residents.

Though the fish problem was solved by the new system, the plan was ultimately a failure. Sewage from the river, propelled by spring rains, made its way out to the new intake bins. The whole smelly situation didn't abate until the Chicago River was reversed in the 1890s (when engineers used canals and locks to send sewage *away* from Lake Michigan). By 1906, the Water Tower was obsolete, and only public outcry saved it from demolition three times.

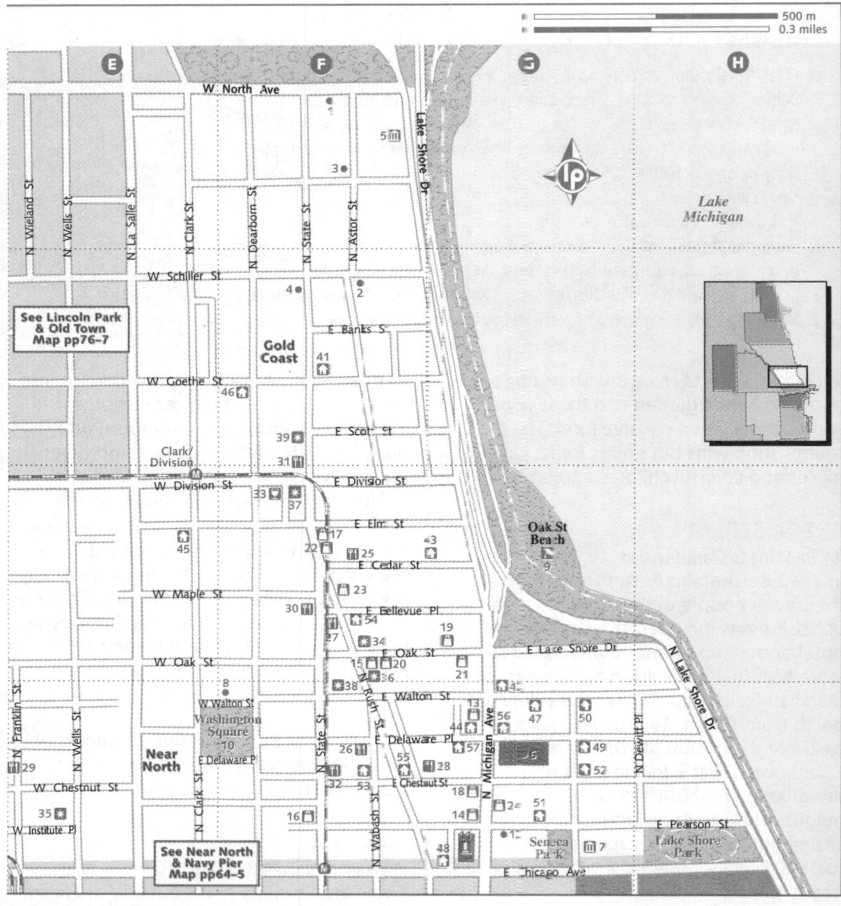

Whether Oscar Wilde would have joined the preservationists is debatable: when he visited Chicago in 1881, he called the Water Tower 'a castellated monstrosity with salt and pepper boxes stuck all over it.' Restoration in 1962 ensured the tower's survival, and today it houses the City Gallery (☎ 312-742-0808; admission free; 🕑 10am-6:30pm Mon-Sat, 10am-5pm Sun), showcasing Chicago-themed works by local photographers. The Pumping Station across the street houses a visitor information center (p263).

MUSEUM OF CONTEMPORARY ART (MCA) Map pp70–1

☎ 312-280-2660; www.mcachicago.org; 220 E Chicago Ave; adult/student 12-18yr $10/6, admission free Tue; 🕑 10am-8pm Tue, 10am-5pm Wed-Sun; Ⓜ Red Line to Chicago

Covering art from 1945 forward, the MCA uses extensive piece descriptions to alleviate a lot of the head-scratching, 'what the hell is it?' befuddlement that often accompanies encounters with modern art. The museum boasts an especially strong minimalist, surrealist and book arts collection, but the works here span the modern art gamut, from Jenny Holzer's LED *Truisms* to Joseph Beuys' austere *Felt Suit*. The permanent collection includes art by Franz Kline, René Magritte, Cindy Sherman and Andy Warhol, with displays arranged to highlight the blurring of the boundaries between painting, photography, sculpture, video and other media. The MCA also regularly hosts dance, film and speaking events from an international array of contemporary artists. Puck's at the MCA, a café overlooking Lake

THINGS TO DO WHEN THE WEATHER BLOWS

Don't let the rain, snow and sleet spoil your fun. When the weather sucks, try the following:

- Burrow into the Art Institute (p52) and its vast collection of masterworks.
- Smell the flowers at Lincoln Park Conservatory (p78) or Garfield Park Conservatory (p101).
- Imbibe with locals in a bar – an activity to which we've devoted an entire chapter (p170).
- Brush up on your batting skills at Sluggers (p205).
- Sip tea in Chinatown (p109).
- Visit the whales and dolphins at Shedd Aquarium (p105).
- Unsheathe the credit card and commence shopping at Water Tower Place (p125).
- Hear world music, ogle stained glass and use the free wi-fi at the Chicago Cultural Center (p58).
- Examine the mummies, dinosaurs, gemstones and Bushman the stuffed ape, at the Field Museum (p104).
- Stop being a wimp – put on your parka and go outside to ice skate or sled ride (p207).

Michigan, attracts crowds with its fine views of the sculpture garden and the lake beyond, as well as its creative food. The museum's shop wins big points for its jewelry pieces and colorful children's toys.

ASTOR STREET Map pp70–1

Ⓜ Red Line to Clark/Division

In 1882 Bertha and Potter Palmer were the power couple of Chicago. His web of businesses included the city's best hotel and a huge general merchandise store that he later sold to a clerk named Marshall Field. When they later relocated north from Prairie Ave to a crenellated castle of a mansion at what is now 1350 N Lake Shore Dr, the Palmers set off a lemminglike rush of Chicago's wealthy to the neighborhood around them. The mansions sitting along Astor St, especially the 1300 to 1500 blocks, reflect the grandeur of that heady period.

While he was still working for Louis Sullivan, Frank Lloyd Wright (who was 19 at the time) designed the large but only 11-room Charnley-Persky House (☎ 312-915-0105; www.charnleyhouse.org; 1365 N Astor St; tours $5-10; 🕒 Wed & Sat, call for times), and proclaimed with his soon-to-be-trademarked bombast that it was the 'first modern building.' Why? Simply because it did away with Victorian gaudiness in favor of plain, abstract forms that went on to become the modern style. It was completed in 1892 and now houses the Society of Architectural Historians.

The Cyrus McCormick Mansion (1500 N Astor St) is one of the neighborhood standouts. The 1893 neoclassical home was designed by New York architect Stanford White. McCormick and his family had the whole place to themselves, but it's now divided up into condos. It's still the high-rent district – a three-bedroom, three-bathroom unit goes for $1.75 million (washer and dryer included).

The 1885 mansion that serves as the Archbishop's Residence (1555 N State St) spans the entire block to Astor. The sweet crib, complete with 19 chimneys, is one of the many perks that comes with leading the Chicago Catholic Archdiocese. Seven archbishops have lived here, and world leaders from Franklin D Roosevelt to Pope John Paul II have crashed at the residence while in town.

Don't forgot to check out another special house in the 'hood: Hugh Hefner's first Playboy Mansion is nearby (see opposite).

OAK ST BEACH Map pp70–1

🕒 dusk-dawn; Ⓜ Red Line to Clark/Division

There aren't many cities outside of Florida that offer such an abundance of sand and (miniaturized) surf this close to their major business districts. Oak St Beach makes for a wonderful respite and offers a lower-key experience than certain beaches further north, where you're likely to get a volleyball spiked on your head if you're not paying attention. The 'beachstro' provides nourishment.

INTERNATIONAL MUSEUM OF SURGICAL SCIENCE Map pp70–1

☎ 312-642-6502; www.imss.org; 1524 N Lake Shore Dr; adult/student $8/4, admission free Tue; 🕒 10am-4pm Tue-Sun May-Sep, closed Sun Oct-Apr; Ⓜ Red Line to Clark/Division, 🚌 151

Home to an eclectic collection of surgery-related items, the Museum of Surgical

Science features such a poorly marked assortment of medical items that at first it seems like nothing more than a place to escape a vicious lake squall. But start exploring and you'll soon be rewarded with fascinating thematic displays, like the one on bloodletting – the act of bleeding patients to 'cure' them. The undeniable gems of the collection are the 'stones,' as in 'kidney stone' and 'gallstone.' All of the spectacularly large specimens were passed by patients who may have wished instead for a good bloodletting.

NEWBERRY LIBRARY Map pp70–1

☎ 312-943-9090; www.newberry.org; 60 W Walton St; admission free, must be 16 or older; 🕑 10am-6pm Tue-Thu, 9am-5pm Fri & Sat; Ⓜ Red Line to Chicago

Humanities nerds and those trying to document far-flung branches of their family tree will have a field day at this research library. Entry requires a library card, but one-day passes are available for curious browsers. Once inside, you can pester the patient librarians with requests for help in tracking down all manner of historical ephemera. (The collection is non-circulating, though, so don't expect to take that 1st edition of the King James Bible home with you.) The Newberry also often features interesting special exhibits, and has a bookstore where you can pick up such treatises as *Buffy the Vampire Slayer and Philosophy,* and cool vintage Chicago travel posters. Free tours of the impressive building take place at 3pm Thursday and 10:30am Saturday.

THE (FIRST) PLAYBOY MANSION Map pp70–1

1340 N State St; Ⓜ Red Line to Clark/Division

The sexual revolution pretty much started in the basement 'grotto' of this 1899 mansion. Chicago magazine impresario Hugh Hefner bought it in 1959 and dubbed it the first Playboy Mansion, even hanging a brass plate over the door warning 'If You Don't Swing, Don't Ring.' Alas, Chicago became too square for Hef by the mid '70s, so he packed up and built a new Playboy Mansion in LA, which is where he remains today, in his pajamas.

After he left, he donated the State St building to the School of the Art Institute for a dorm (imagine the pick-up lines!). It was gutted in 1993 and turned into four very staid but very expensive condos.

Playboy, now run by Hugh's daughter Christine, maintains its corporate headquarters in Chicago, and Walton St (at Michigan Ave) has been named 'Honorary Hugh M Hefner Way' in an official tip of the hat to Hef.

WASHINGTON SQUARE Map pp70–1

btwn N Clark St, N Dearborn St, W Delaware Pl, W Walton St; Ⓜ Red Line to Chicago

This plain-looking park across from the Newberry Library has had both a colorful and a tragic history. In the 1920s it was known as 'Bughouse Sq' because of the communists, socialists, anarchists and other -ists who gave soapbox orations here. Clarence Darrow and Carl Sandburg are among the respected speakers who climbed up and shouted.

In the 1970s, when it was a gathering place for young male prostitutes, it gained tragic infamy as the preferred pick-up spot of mass-murderer John Wayne Gacy. Gacy took his victims back to his suburban home, where he killed them and buried their bodies in the basement. Convicted on 33 counts of murder (although the actual tally may be higher), he was executed in 1994.

Today the square bears little trace of its past lives – except for one weekend a year in late July. That's when the Bughouse Debates occur, and orators return to holler at each other.

LIVING WELL
Walking Tour

Wish you had a lifestyle of the rich and famous? Live it up for a day on the Gold Coast.

1 Four Seasons Hotel OK, so you may not be able to afford $500 a night at the Four Seasons (p223), but you can at least start your afternoon tour in style. Book a vanilla sugar exfoliating rub, then relax in the serene spa lounge. Or pop by for tea in the palm-laden, lobby-level Conservatory.

2 John Hancock Center Meander across the street to the John Hancock Center (p69) and take the elevator up to the 96th-floor Signature Lounge. Order a glass of sparkling Rheinland cuvée and the artisanal cheese plate to go with your million-dollar view.

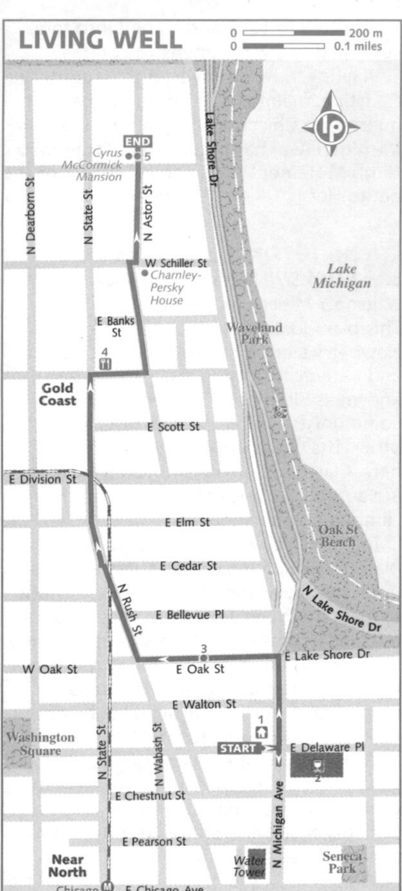

WALK FACTS

Start Four Seasons Hotel
Finish Cyrus McCormick Mansion
Duration Three or more hours (with meals and massage)

3 Oak St Boutiques Next, peruse the window displays of the tony Oak St boutiques, between N Michigan and N Rush Sts (see Shopping p124). What can't you live without? That hand-folded Hermés tie, a Prada purse, the perfect pair of Jimmy Choo pumps, a Chanel suit? They're all here and more.

4 Pump Room Maybe one of the celebrities whose photos line the entryway walls will be there when you get to the Pump Room (p146) at the Ambassador East. If not, sink into a rear booth and console yourself with a chilled lobster salad or steak tartare appetizers and cocktails.

5 Astor St Mansions Stroll north on leafy Astor St to ogle the fine 19th-century homes built by Chicago's elite. The Charnley-Perskey House (p72), designed by both Louis Sullivan and Frank Lloyd Wright, and the Cyrus McCormick Mansion (p72), onetime home to a local industrialist, are just two of the many on show. Can't you just see yourself living here?

LINCOLN PARK & OLD TOWN

Eating p147; Shopping p126; Sleeping p226

If you've lost track of a Midwestern fraternity brother or sorority sister, chances are you'll find them living happily in Lincoln Park. Ground zero for Chicago's yuppie population, the neighborhood bustles with Banana Republic–wearing residents walking dogs, Rollerblading and pushing babies around in $300 strollers. Local curmudgeons will grouse about Lincoln Park being a soulless victim of gentrification, but the area has some undeniable charms, including many great restaurants, cute boutiques, a couple of gangster sights, and the Clark St record-store corridor, where the city's music illuminati pick up tomorrow's hits. The yuppieness (and prices) are further tempered by DePaul University and its large student population near the Lincoln/Fullerton Ave intersection.

Lincoln Park also has the park itself, a well-loved playland. Almost 50% larger than Central Park in New York, the park offers Chicagoans a chance to celebrate summer with an oasis of ponds and paths, plus roaring lions, fidgety monkeys and an ark's worth of other critters hanging out in the park's free zoo. North Ave Beach washes up to the south side; it's one of the biggest and most active sandlots in the city.

South of Lincoln Park, Old Town was free-spirited in the 1960s as the epicenter of Chicago's hippie culture. Artists, long-hairs and other freaks flocked to Old Town to tune in, turn on and drop their money on cool black-light posters and bongs from head shops on Wells St. Falling into disrepair in the 1970s, Old Town made a comeback in the 1980s and now is one of the North Side's most expensive places to buy property. Visitors won't find too much in the way of sights, but Old Town outranks its more lively neighbors when it comes to comedy – improv bastion Second City is here.

LINCOLN PARK Map pp76–7

151

The neighborhood gets its name from this park, Chicago's largest. Its 1200 acres stretch for 6 miles, from North Ave north to Diversey Pkwy, where it narrows along the lake and continues until the end of Lake Shore Dr. The park's many lakes, trails and paths make it an excellent place for recreation. Cross-country skiing in the winter and sunbathing in warmer months are just two of the activities Chicagoans enjoy in Lincoln Park. Many buy picnic vittles from the markets on Clark St and Diversey Pkwy.

Most of Lincoln Park's pleasures are natural, though one of its joys is sculptor Augustus Saint-Gaudens' Standing Lincoln, which shows the 16th president deep in contemplation right before he delivers a great speech. Saint-Gaudens based the work on casts made of Lincoln's face and hands while Lincoln was alive. The statue stands in its own garden east of the Chicago History Museum. The artist also sculpted a Sitting Lincoln (p53) that rests its rump by the Art Institute.

Near the southeast corner of LaSalle Dr and Clark St, the Mausoleum is the sole reminder of the land's pre-1864 use: the entire area was a municipal cemetery. Many of the graves contained hundreds of dead prisoners from Camp Douglas, a horrific prisoner-of-war stockade on the city's South Side during the Civil War. Removing the bodies from the designated park area proved a greater undertaking than the city could stomach and, today, if you start digging at the south end of the park, you're liable to make some ghoulish discoveries.

From a little dock in front of pretty Café Brauer, a 1908 Prairie School architectural creation, you can rent two-person paddleboats and cruise the South Pond, south of the zoo. The rental season is roughly May through September.

TRANSPORTATION – LINCOLN PARK & OLD TOWN

Bus Number 76 runs along Diversey Pkwy; 74 spans Fullerton; 72 runs through Old Town along North Ave.

El Brown, Purple or Red Line to Fullerton or the Brown or Purple Line to Armitage for Lincoln Park; Brown or Purple Line to Sedgwick, or the Red Line to Clark/Division for Old Town.

Parking Lincoln Park is a headache. If you're stuck for a spot, consider heading out to the meters along Diversey Harbor. Old Town has plenty of cars competing for its plentiful meters. Try the pay garage at Piper's Alley, at North Ave and Wells St.

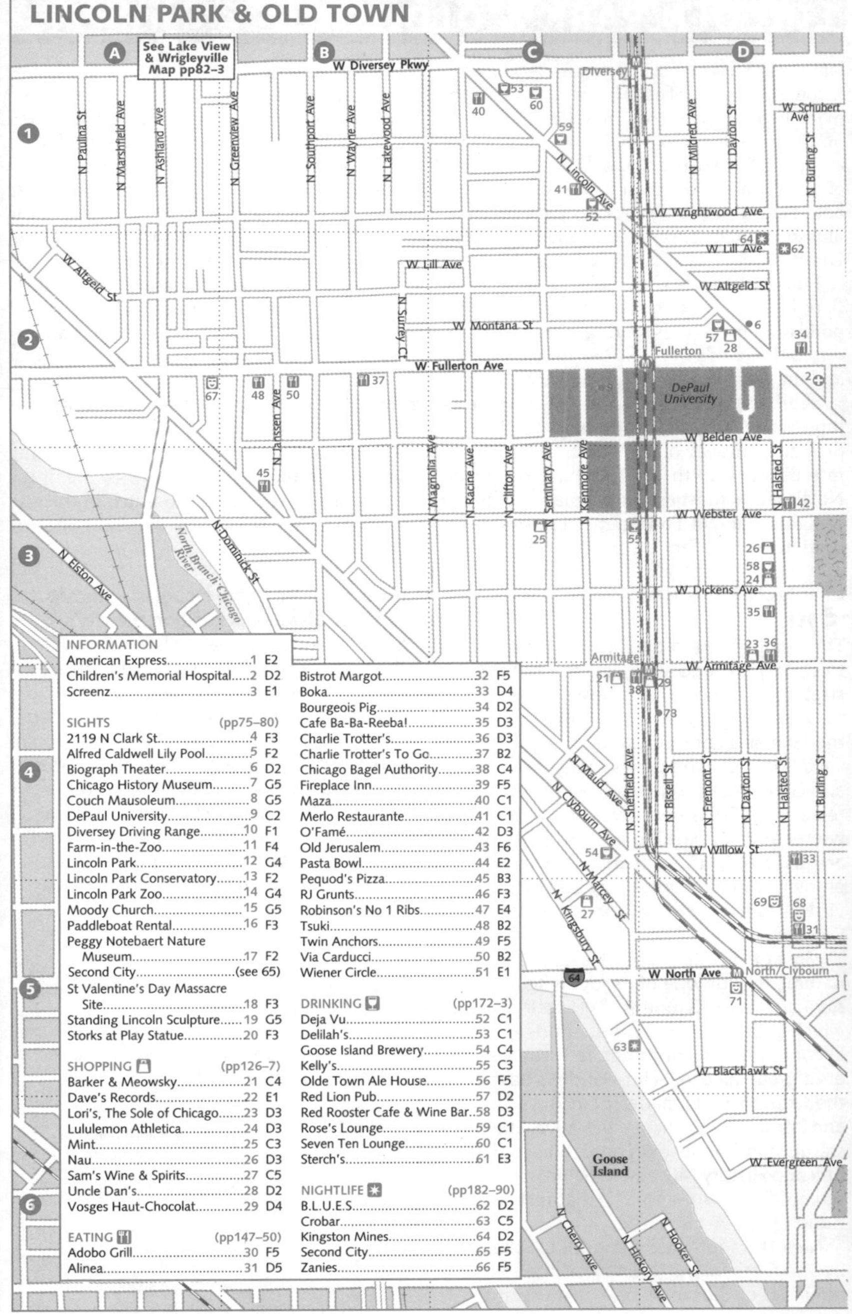
LINCOLN PARK & OLD TOWN
See Lake View & Wrigleyville Map pp82–3
W Diversey Pkwy
Diversey
N Paulina St
N Marshfield Ave
N Ashland Ave
N Greenview Ave
N Southport Ave
N Wayne Ave
N Lakewood Ave
N Lincoln Ave
N Mildred Ave
N Dayton St
N Burling St
W Schubert Ave
W Wrightwood Ave
W Lill Ave
W Altgeld St
N Surrey Ct
W Montana St
Fullerton
W Fullerton Ave
DePaul University
W Belden Ave
N Janssen Ave
N Magnolia Ave
N Racine Ave
N Clifton Ave
N Seminary Ave
N Kenmore Ave
N Halsted St
W Webster Ave
N Dominick St
North Branch Chicago River
N Elston Ave
W Dickens Ave
Armitage
W Armitage Ave
N Maud Ave
N Clybourn Ave
N Sheffield Ave
N Bissell St
N Fremont St
W Willow St
N Marcey St
N Kingsbury St
W North Ave
North/Clybourn
W Blackhawk St
Goose Island
W Evergreen Ave
N Cherry Ave
N Hickory Ave
N Hooker St
INFORMATION
American Express 1 E2
Children's Memorial Hospital 2 D2
Screenz 3 E1
SIGHTS (pp75–80)
2119 N Clark St 4 F3
Alfred Caldwell Lily Pool 5 F2
Biograph Theater 6 D2
Chicago History Museum 7 G5
Couch Mausoleum 8 G5
DePaul University 9 C2
Diversey Driving Range 10 F1
Farm-in-the-Zoo 11 F4
Lincoln Park 12 G4
Lincoln Park Conservatory 13 F2
Lincoln Park Zoo 14 G4
Moody Church 15 G5
Paddleboat Rental 16 F3
Peggy Notebaert Nature Museum 17 F2
Second City (see 65)
St Valentine's Day Massacre Site 18 F3
Standing Lincoln Sculpture 19 G5
Storks at Play Statue 20 F3
SHOPPING (pp126–7)
Barker & Meowsky 21 C4
Dave's Records 22 E1
Lori's, The Sole of Chicago 23 D3
Lululemon Athletica 24 D3
Mint 25 C3
Nau 26 D3
Sam's Wine & Spirits 27 C5
Uncle Dan's 28 D2
Vosges Haut-Chocolat 29 D4
EATING (pp147–50)
Adobo Grill 30 F5
Alinea 31 D5
Bistrot Margot 32 F5
Boka 33 D4
Bourgeois Pig 34 D2
Cafe Ba-Ba-Reeba! 35 D3
Charlie Trotter's 36 D3
Charlie Trotter's To Go 37 B2
Chicago Bagel Authority 38 C4
Fireplace Inn 39 F5
Maza 40 C1
Merlo Restaurante 41 C1
O'Famé 42 D3
Old Jerusalem 43 F6
Pasta Bowl 44 E2
Pequod's Pizza 45 B3
RJ Grunts 46 F3
Robinson's No 1 Ribs 47 E4
Tsuki 48 B2
Twin Anchors 49 F5
Via Carducci 50 B2
Wiener Circle 51 E1
DRINKING (pp172–3)
Deja Vu 52 C1
Delilah's 53 C1
Goose Island Brewery 54 C4
Kelly's 55 C3
Olde Town Ale House 56 F5
Red Lion Pub 57 D2
Red Rooster Cafe & Wine Bar 58 D3
Rose's Lounge 59 C1
Seven Ten Lounge 60 C1
Sterch's 61 E3
NIGHTLIFE (pp182–90)
B.L.U.E.S. 62 D2
Crobar 63 C5
Kingston Mines 64 D2
Second City 65 F5
Zanies 66 F5

0 500 m
0 0.3 miles
ARTS (pp192–201)
Facets Multimedia....67 A2
Royal George Theatre....68 D5
Steppenwolf Theater....69 D5
Victory Gardens Theater....70 E3
Weed's Poetry Night....71 D5
SPORTS & ACTIVITIES (pp204–12)
Fullerton Beach....72 G2
Harmony Mind Body Fitness....73 D4
North Ave Beach....74 H4
SLEEPING (pp226–7)
Arlington House....75 E2
Belden-Stratford Hotel....76 F2
Days Inn Lincoln Park North....77 E1
Inn at Lincoln Park....78 E1
TRANSPORT (p252)
Bike Chicago North Ave Beach..79 H4
W Diversey Pkwy
Diversey Harbor
Waveland Park
North Pond
Fullerton Beach
W Fullerton Parkway
Lincoln Park
Lincoln Park Zoo
South Pond
Old Town
North Ave Beach
N North Ave
Sedgwick
See Gold Coast Map pp78–1
Clark/Division
Gold Coast
Cabrini-Green
Lake Shore Dr
Lake Bike Path

LINCOLN PARK ZOO Map pp76–7

☎ 312-742-2000; www.lpzoo.com; 2200 N Cannon Dr; admission free; ⌚ 10am-4:30pm Nov-Mar, 10am-5pm Apr-Oct, 10am-6:30pm Sat & Sun Jun-Aug; 🚌 151

The free zoo is one of Chicago's most popular attractions. The naturalistic Regenstein African Journey is top of the exhibit heap. The walk-through lets you get surprisingly close to animals who swim, hop and crawl in remarkably lifelike environments. Adults will love the cuddly, perpetually puzzled-looking meerkat, and kids will scream with disgusted glee at the entire room filled with hissing cockroaches. The Primate House also pleases customers with its swingin' monkeys.

The rest of the zoo – which opened in 1868 – is fairly typical. Farm-in-the-Zoo (where many urbanites first learn that milk doesn't come from cardboard containers), features a full range of barnyard animals in a faux farm setting just south of the zoo. Frequent demonstrations of cow milking, horse grooming, butter churning and other chores take place.

The exhibits for the lions and other big cats, elephants and sea lions are fine but unremarkable. And the cramped penguin habitat borders on the depressing. Still, free is a good price, and if you come during colder months, you'll have many of the exhibits to yourself.

You can easily reach the zoo from most parts of the park; there are entrances on all sides. The Gateway Pavilion is the main one, and is where you can pick up a free map that provides times and locations for feeding times, training demonstrations and free talks about various animals by zookeepers. Drivers be warned: parking is among the worst in the city.

LINCOLN PARK CONSERVATORY Map pp76–7

☎ 312-742-7736; 2391 N Stockton Dr; admission free; ⌚ 9am-5pm; 🚌 151

The glass-bedecked conservatory features three acres of lush gardens from a variety of ecosystems, and hosts a rotating array of annual flower shows. Just south of the conservatory, the 1887 statue Storks at Play has enchanted generations of Chicagoans. And speaking of plants and birds, the Alfred Caldwell Lily Pool, immediately northeast of the conservatory, is an important stopover for migrating birds. The stonework here resembles the stratified canyons of the Wisconsin Dells. When not overrun with people, the pool is a magical setting, especially in winter.

NORTH AVENUE BEACH Map pp76–7

⌚ dawn-dusk; 🚌 151

Chicago's most popular beach gives off a southern California vibe. Countless volleyball nets draw scores of skimpy-suited beautiful people to the sand. Dodgeball and roller hockey leagues go at it in the beachside rinks. The steamship-inspired beach house contains a seasonal café. A short walk on the curving breakwater anytime of year yields postcard city views from a spot that seems almost a world apart. Lifeguards watch the beach throughout summer.

BIOGRAPH THEATER Map pp76–7

2433 N Lincoln Ave; Ⓜ Red, Brown, Purple Line to Fullerton

In 1934, the 'lady in red' betrayed gangster John Dillinger at this theater, which used to show movies. It started out as a date – Dillinger took new girlfriend Polly Hamilton to the show, and Polly's roommate Anna Sage tagged along, wearing a red dress. Alas, Dillinger was a notorious bank robber and the FBI's very first 'Public Enemy Number One.' Sage also had troubles with the law, and was about to be deported. To avoid it, she agreed to set Dillinger up. FBI agents shot him in the alley beside the theater. The venue now hosts plays by the Victory Gardens Theater (p196).

PEGGY NOTEBAERT NATURE MUSEUM Map pp76–7

☎ 773-755-5100; www.naturemuseum.org; 2430 N Cannon Dr; adult/child 3-12yr $7/4, admission free Thu; ⌚ 9am-4:30pm Mon-Fri, 10am-5pm Sat & Sun; 🚌 151

This hands-on museum allows you to do everything from walking among fluttering butterflies to engineering your own river system. Other exhibits show how many different wild animals live in urban Chicago, both inside and out. A computer lab allows visitors to solve environmental problems, and kids are given free rein to explore, scamper and climb while they learn.

CHICAGO HISTORY MUSEUM Map pp76–7

☎ 312-642-4600; www.chicagohs.org; 1601 N Clark St; adult/child 12-18yr $12/10, admission free Mon; ⌚ 9:30am-4:30pm Mon-Sat, to 8pm Thu, noon-5pm Sun; Ⓜ Brown, Purple Line to Sedgwick, 🚌 22

The Chicago History Museum is the new, less-fusty-sounding name for the entity formerly known as the Chicago Historical

CAPONE'S CHICAGO

Chicagoans traveling the world often experience an unusual phenomenon when others ask where they're from. When they answer 'Chicago,' the local drops into a crouch and yells something along the lines of 'Rat-a-tat-a-tat, Al Capone!' Although civic boosters bemoan Chicago's long association with a scar-faced hoodlum, it's an image that has been burned into the public consciousness by movies such as *The Untouchables*, and other aspects of pop culture.

Capone was the mob boss in Chicago from 1924 to 1931, when he was brought down on tax evasion charges by Elliot Ness, the federal agent whose task force earned the name 'The Untouchables' because its members were supposedly impervious to bribes. (This wasn't a small claim, given that thousands of Chicago police and other officials were on the take, some of them raking in more than $1000 a week.)

Capone came to Chicago from New York in 1919. He quickly moved up the ranks to take control of the city's South Side in 1924, expanding his empire by making 'hits' on his rivals. These acts, which usually involved bullets shot out of submachine guns, were carried out by Capone's lieutenants. Incidentally, Capone earned the nickname 'Scarface' not because he ended up on the wrong side of a bullet but because a dance-hall fight left him with a large scar on his left cheek.

The success of the Chicago mob was fueled by Prohibition. Not surprisingly, the citizens' thirst for booze wasn't eliminated by government mandate, and gangs made fortunes dealing in illegal beer, gin and other intoxicants. Clubs called 'speakeasies' were highly popular and were only marginally hidden from the law, an unnecessary precaution given that crooked cops were usually the ones working the doors. Commenting on the hypocrisy of a society that would ban booze and then pay him a fortune to sell it, Capone said: 'When I sell liquor, they call it bootlegging. When my patrons serve it on silver trays on Lake Shore Dr, they call it hospitality.'

It's a challenge to find traces of the Capone era in Chicago. The city and the Chicago History Museum take dim views of Chicago's gangland past, with nary a brochure or exhibit on Capone or his cronies (though the CHM bookstore does have a good selection of books on the topic). Many of the actual sites have been torn down – some of the more notable survivors:

Capone's Chicago Home (Map p50; 7244 S Prairie Ave) This South Side home was built by Capone and mostly used by his wife Mae, son Sonny and other relatives. Al preferred to stay where his vices were. The house looks almost the same today.

City Hall (Map pp54–5; 121 N La Salle St) This building was the workplace of some of Capone's best pals. During William 'Big Bill' Thompson's successful campaign for mayor in 1927, Al donated well over $100,000.

Green Mill (Map p86; 4802 N Broadway St) This tavern was one of Capone's favorite nightspots. During the mid-1920s the cover for the speakeasy in the basement was $10. You can still listen to jazz in its swank setting today (see p183).

Holy Name Cathedral (Map pp64–5; 735 N State St) Two gangland murders took place near this church. In 1924 North Side boss Dion O'Banion was gunned down in his floral shop (738 N State St) after he crossed Capone. In 1926 his successor, Hymie Weiss, died en route to church in a hail of Capone-ordered bullets emanating from a window at 740 N State.

Maxwell St Police Station (Map pp98–9; 943 W Maxwell St) This station, two blocks west of Halsted St, exemplified the corruption rife in the Chicago Police Department in the 1920s. At one time, five captains and about 400 uniformed police were on the take here.

Mt Carmel Cemetery (Map p50; cnr Roosevelt & S Wolf Rds, Hillside) Capone is now buried in this cemetery in Hillside, west of Chicago. He and his relatives were moved here in 1950. Al's simple gray gravestone, which has been stolen and replaced twice, is concealed by a hedge. It reads 'Alphonse Capone, 1899-1947. My Jesus Mercy.' Capone's neighbors include old rivals Dion O'Banion and Hymie Weiss. Both tried to rub out Capone, who returned the favor in a far more effective manner.

St Valentine's Day Massacre Site (Map pp76–7; 2122 N Clark St) In perhaps the most infamous event of the Capone era, seven members of the Bugs Moran gang were lined up against a garage wall and gunned down by mobsters dressed as cops. After that, Moran cut his losses and Capone gained control of Chicago's North Side vice. The garage was torn down in 1967 to make way for a retirement home, and residents there claim they sometimes hear ghostly noises at night. A house (2119 N Clark St) used as a lookout by the killers stands across the street.

Society. Opened late 2006 after a $27.5 million rehaul, the museum has blown the dust off its relics and fired up multimedia displays that cover the Great Fire and 1968 Democratic Convention, among other storied events. The 'City on the Make' exhibit recreates Fort Dearborn, Chicago's first settlement; the fire and Haymarket riots get their close-up in 'City in Crisis'; and 'Second to None' details local ingenuity in developing the skyscraper and nuclear chain reaction. Cool textiles and costumes (George

Washington's suit, anyone?) also make appearances. The on-site bookstore stocks hard-to-find local history tomes, including some scholarly looks at the city's gangsters.

MOODY CHURCH Map pp76–7

☎ 312-943-0466; www.moodychurch.org; 1630 N Clark St; Ⓜ Brown, Purple Line to Sedgwick, 🚌 22

Directly across from the Chicago History Museum stands the hulking nondenominational Moody Church, which 19th-century missionary Dwight Moody started. He also founded the Moody Bible Institute in the Gold Coast, and was basically the Billy Graham of his age – a charismatic preacher who took his literal interpretations of the Bible to audiences around the world. During the 1893 World's Expo, Moody organized huge Christian revivalist events under enormous tents in Jackson Park, hoping to warn fair-goers away from the moral ruin awaiting them on the Midway and in Chicago's infamous Levee District. This Clark St structure, which can hold almost 4000 worshippers, was built in 1925. Tours are available by request.

THE ZOO & BEYOND

Walking Tour

Looking to entertain the little ones? A day in Lincoln Park will keep you busy without breaking the budget. Generations of Chicagoans (like this writer) remember their grandparents bringing them here to what's now one of the last free zoos in the country.

1 Lincoln Park Zoo Stroll through recreated regions in the African Journey and watch Primate House monkeys play at the two best exhibits at the zoo (p78). See if your kids can identify the following: the smallest member of the bear family? The big beast prized for its horns? The panda of a different color?

2 RJ Grunts Moving fast, you can hit the highlights of the zoo in two hours or so, before heading to RJ Grunts (p148) for lunch. The hostess will store your stroller while you order a chocolate-peanut-butter-banana milkshake and burgers. The menu, and the hubbub, are entirely kid-friendly.

3 Café Brauer Paddleboat Rental To work off any sugar-fueled energy head to the paddleboat rental (p75) next to the 1908, Prairie School–style Café Brauer (snacks available). A plain two-paddler (four person capacity) costs $12, or two of you can power a giant white swan around the South Pond for a few bucks more.

WALK FACTS

Start Lincoln Park Zoo
Finish North Ave Beach
Duration Four to five hours (or as long as your kids hold out)
Fuel Stop Ice-cream stand at Café Brauer

THE ZOO & BEYOND

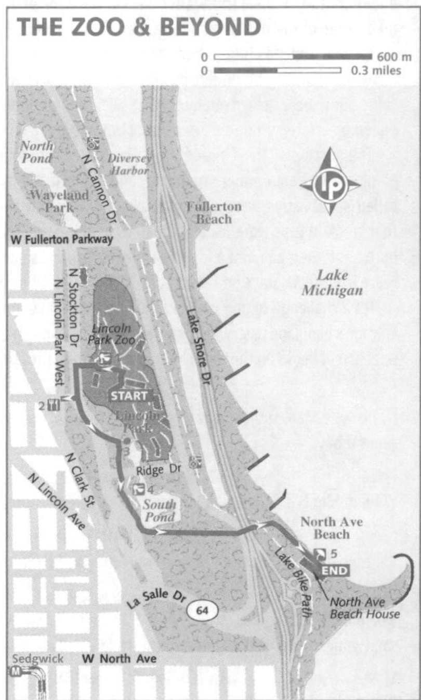

4 Farm-in-the-Zoo Next it's the big ol' barn and the Farm-in-the-Zoo (p78). Little ones seem to love petting sheep, watching chicks hatch and learning how to milk a cow. Parents like that this, too, is free. By now you've spent more than four hours in the park. If you have enough energy to continue…

5 North Ave Beach Walk south along the pond and turn east past ballfields before you cross the bridge to North Ave Beach (p78). Grab a refreshment, rent a beach chair and watch your kids construct castles in the sand. The point's city skyline view is an ideal background for a family photo.

LAKE VIEW & WRIGLEYVILLE

Eating p150; Shopping p127; Sleeping p227

Lake View is the overarching name of this good-time neighborhood, inhabited by 20- and 30-somethings. Wrigleyville is the pocket that surrounds star attraction Wrigley Field. The neighborhood has become a magnet for singles, who frolic and cruise in the ridiculous number of bars and restaurants lining Clark St and Southport Ave. It's usually well-mannered by day with an impish dose of carousing by night. But when the Cubs play at Wrigley, look out: 40,000 fans descend on the 'hood, and the party kicks into high gear.

Either the rainbow flags or the abundance of hot, well-dressed men will tip you off to the fact that you've arrived in Boystown. The well-heeled hub of Chicago's gay community, it bustles on Broadway St during the day and gets hedonistic on Halsted St at night. It's also the place to come if you accidentally left those fur-lined handcuffs at home; the shops here are known for their quirky, fun and sex-friendly vibe.

Though the crowds may be straighter, the shopping scene is equally wild in Belmont, just west of Boystown. This is the youngest-feeling of Lake View's pockets, and the stores here cater to the lifestyle whims of local goths, punks and hipsters. Whether you need hair dye, a Fender Telecaster, or a vintage Morrissey T-shirt, you can count on the endearingly attitude-heavy emporiums here to come through for you.

The Southport Corridor, along Southport Ave between Belmont Ave and Irving Park Rd, is more staid; it's for those who outgrew their Belmont lifestyle and now need a designer wardrobe for their toddler.

For all its copious energy, Lake View has little in the way of historic sights or cultural attractions beyond the ballpark. Just bring your credit cards, walking shoes and festive attitude, and you'll be set.

WRIGLEY FIELD Map pp82–3

☎ 773-404-2827; 1060 W Addison St; Ⓜ Red Line to Addison

Built in 1914 and named for the chewing-gum guy, Wrigley Field – aka The Friendly Confines – is the second-oldest baseball park in the major leagues. It's filled with legendary traditions and curses (see the box, p210), as well as a team that suffers from the longest dry spell in US sports history. The hapless Cubbies haven't won a championship since 1908, a sad record unmatched in pro football, hockey or basketball.

If they're playing a home game, you can peep through the 'knothole,' a garage-door-sized opening on Sheffield Ave and watch the action for free. Baseball fanatics can take a 90-minute stadium tour (☎ 773-404-2827; tours $25) that goes through the clubhouse, dugouts and press box. Tours take place on selected weekends when the Cubs are out of town. Reservations are required.

BOYSTOWN Map pp82–3

btwn Halsted & Broadway Sts, Belmont Ave & Addison St; Ⓜ Red Line to Addison

What the Castro is to San Francisco, Boystown is to the Windy City. The mecca of queer Chicago (especially for men), the streets of Boystown are full of rainbow flags and packed with bars, shops and restaurants catering to the residents of the gay neighborhood. For more info on gay Chicago, see the boxed text, p186.

ALTA VISTA TERRACE Map pp82–3

btwn Byron & Grace Sts; Ⓜ Red Line to Sheridan

Chicago's first designated historic district is worthy of the honor. Developer Samuel Eberly Gross re-created a block of London row houses on Alta Vista Tce in 1904. The 20 exquisitely detailed homes on either side of the street mirror each other diagonally,

TRANSPORTATION – LAKE VIEW & WRIGLEYVILLE

Bus Number 152 traces Addison St; 22 follows Clark St; 8 runs along Halsted St.

El Red Line Addison stop for Wrigleyville; Brown and Red Line Belmont stop for Belmont and Boystown.

Parking In a word: nightmare. Especially in Wrigleyville, where side streets are resident-only. Take the train or bring a really good book-on-tape to listen to as you try to find parking.

LAKE VIEW & WRIGLEYVILLE

A
B
C
D
1
2
3
4
5
6
See Andersonville & Uptown Map p86
N Beacon St
N Malden St
W Montrose Ave
Montrose
W Cullom Ave
W Berteau Ave
W Belle Plaine Ave
N Clark St
N Ravenswood Ave
N Hermitage Ave
N Paulina St
N Ashland Ave
Irving Park
W Irving Park Rd
W Byron St
W Grace St
N Lincoln Ave
N Western Ave
W Waveland Ave
N Damen Ave
N Marshfield Ave
N Southport Ave
N Lakewood Ave
Addison
W Addison St
W Cornelia Ave
W Roscoe St
Paulina
Southport
W Henderson St
W School St
W Melrose St
W Belmont Ave
W Fletcher St
W Barry Ave
W Nelson St
W Diversey Ave
INFORMATION
Advocate Illinois Masonic Medical Center......1 F6
Chicago Area Gay & Lesbian Chamber of Commerce......2 F3
Kinko's......3 D4
SIGHTS (pp81–4)
Alta Vista Terrace......4 E3
Wrigley Field......5 E3
SHOPPING (pp127–9)
A OK Official......6 F5
Alley......7 F5
Architectural Artifacts......8 C1
Army Navy Surplus USA......9 D5
Borders Books & Music......10 G6
Chicago Comics......11 F5
Fourth World Artisans......12 D3
Gay Mart......13 F4
Gramaphone Records......14 G6
Medusa's Circle......15 F5
Midwest Stereo......16 G6
Sports World......17 E4
Strange Cargo......18 E4
Threadless......19 G5
Uncle Fun......20 D5
Windward Sports......21 F4
Yesterday......22 E4

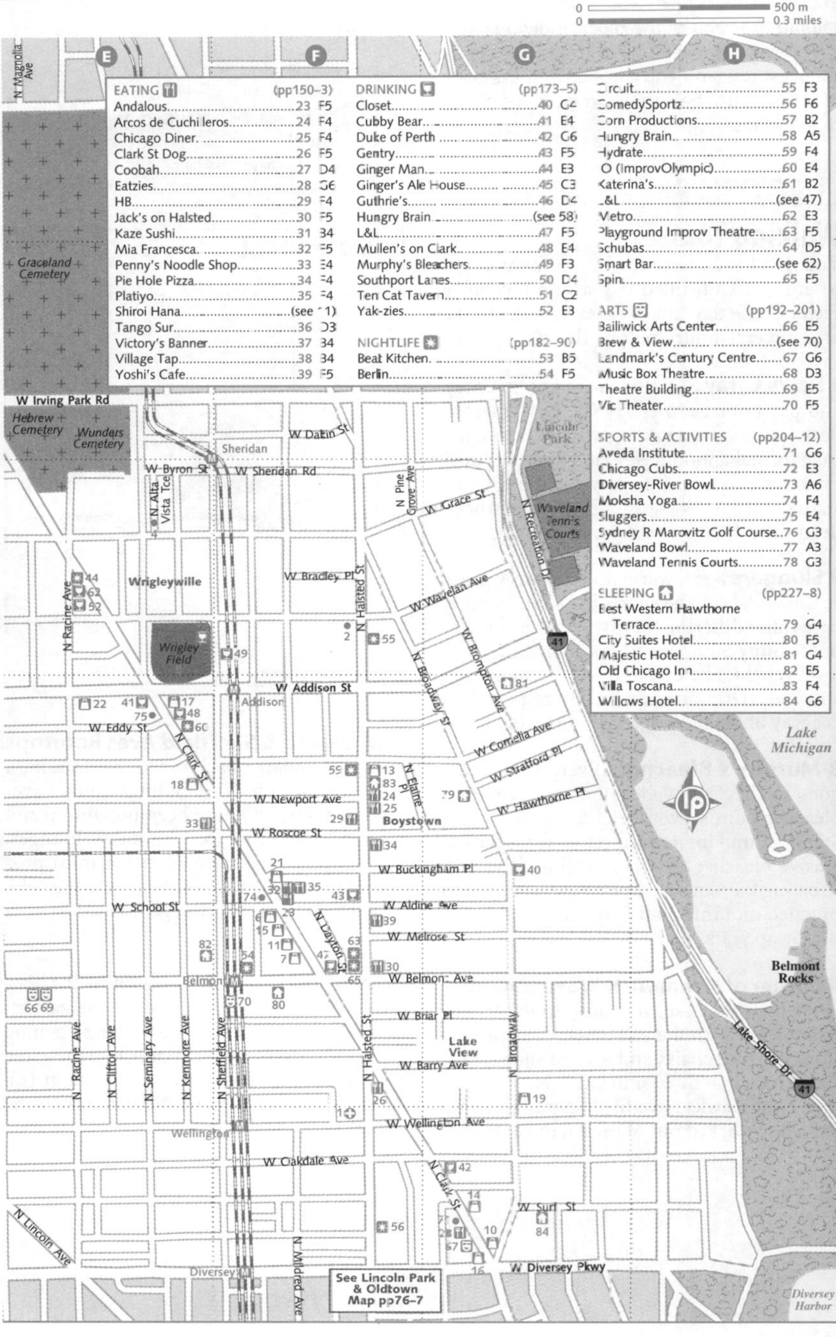
0 500 m
0 0.3 miles
EATING (pp150–3)
Andalous 23 F5
Arcos de Cuchilleros 24 F4
Chicago Diner 25 F4
Clark St Dog 26 F5
Coobah 27 D4
Eatzies 28 G6
HB 29 F4
Jack's on Halsted 30 F5
Kaze Sushi 31 B4
Mia Francesca 32 F5
Penny's Noodle Shop 33 E4
Pie Hole Pizza 34 F4
Platiyo 35 F4
Shiroi Hana (see 11)
Tango Sur 36 D3
Victory's Banner 37 B4
Village Tap 38 B4
Yoshi's Cafe 39 F5
DRINKING (pp173–5)
Closet 40 G4
Cubby Bear 41 E4
Duke of Perth 42 G6
Gentry 43 F5
Ginger Man 44 E3
Ginger's Ale House 45 C3
Guthrie's 46 D4
Hungry Brain (see 58)
L&L 47 F5
Mullen's on Clark 48 E4
Murphy's Bleachers 49 F3
Southport Lanes 50 D4
Ten Cat Tavern 51 C2
Yak-zies 52 E3
NIGHTLIFE (pp182–90)
Beat Kitchen 53 B5
Berlin 54 F5
Circuit 55 F3
ComedySportz 56 F6
Corn Productions 57 B2
Hungry Brain 58 A5
Hydrate 59 F4
IO (ImprovOlympic) 60 E4
Katerina's 61 B2
L&L (see 47)
Metro 62 E3
Playground Improv Theatre 63 F5
Schubas 64 D5
Smart Bar (see 62)
Spin 65 F5
ARTS (pp192–201)
Bailiwick Arts Center 66 E5
Brew & View (see 70)
Landmark's Century Centre 67 G6
Music Box Theatre 68 D3
Theatre Building 69 E5
Vic Theater 70 F5
SPORTS & ACTIVITIES (pp204–12)
Aveda Institute 71 G6
Chicago Cubs 72 E3
Diversey-River Bowl 73 A6
Moksha Yoga 74 F4
Sluggers 75 E4
Sydney R Marovitz Golf Course 76 G3
Waveland Bowl 77 A3
Waveland Tennis Courts 78 G3
SLEEPING (pp227–8)
Best Western Hawthorne Terrace 79 G4
City Suites Hotel 80 F5
Majestic Hotel 81 G4
Old Chicago Inn 82 E5
Villa Toscana 83 F4
Willows Hotel 84 G6
N Magnolia Ave
Graceland Cemetery
W Irving Park Rd
Hebrew Cemetery
Wunders Cemetery
Sheridan
W Byron St
W Sheridan Rd
W Dakin St
N Alta Vista Tce
N Pine Grove Ave
W Grace St
Wrigleyville
W Bradley Pl
N Halsted St
W Waveland Ave
Wrigley Field
N Broadway St
W Brompton Ave
W Addison St
Addison
W Eddy St
N Clark St
W Cornelia Ave
W Stratford Pl
W Hawthorne Pl
N Racine Ave
N Elaine Pl
W Newport Ave
Boystown
W Roscoe St
W Buckingham Pl
W School St
W Aldine Ave
N Dayton St
W Melrose St
Belmont
W Belmont Ave
W Briar Pl
Lake View
W Barry Ave
N Clifton Ave
N Seminary Ave
N Kenmore Ave
N Sheffield Ave
N Broadway
W Wellington Ave
Wellington
W Oakdale Ave
W Surf St
N Lincoln Ave
N Mildred Ave
Diversey
W Diversey Pkwy
See Lincoln Park & Oldtown Map pp76–7
Lincoln Park
N Recreation Dr
Waveland Tennis Courts
Lake Michigan
Belmont Rocks
Lake Shore Dr
41
Diversey Harbor

and the owners have worked hard at maintaining the spirit of the block. Individuality isn't dead, however – head to the back of the west row and you'll notice that the back of every house has grown in dramatically different fashions.

CUBBYVILLE
Walking Tour

You don't even have to go into the stadium to enjoy a Cub-filled day around Wrigley Field. Game day fun starts early – get to the area several hours before the first pitch.

1 Harry Caray Statue First things first. Stop and pay homage to Harry Caray, the legendary sports commentator who was more fan than formal announcer. ('Holy Cow!') You'll likely have to line up to get a picture with his statue at Wrigley Field (p81) – though he's been dead since 1998 he's still quite popular.

2 Sluggers Next, warm up for your A-game at Sluggers (p205). The sports bar's four batting cages offer differing speeds. So, even if you're not Sammy Sosa, you've got a shot. Maybe a few brewskies beforehand will warm up that stiff body. Drinking heavily (but responsibly) is a way of life in Wrigleyville. Moving on…

3 Murphy's Bleachers Every Joe Shmoe goes to the Cubby Bear bar, but you're a bleacher bum so you head to Murphy's (p174). Stand around in the yard across from the exclusive bleacher entrance swilling beer and debating the Cubs chances. You may want to practice mouthing off – rowdiness rules in the cheap seats.

4 Corner of Kenmore & Waveland Aves Once the game's started, head to the corner to hang out with the ball hawks. The professionals set up chairs and wait to snag errant home runs that fly over the wall. No kid-stuff this – ball hawks have filed lawsuits when a ball was knocked out of their hands.

WALK FACTS

Start Harry Caray Statue
Finish Knothole, Wrigley Field
Duration An hour and a half (more depending how long you drink)
Fuel Stop Murphey's Bleachers (176)

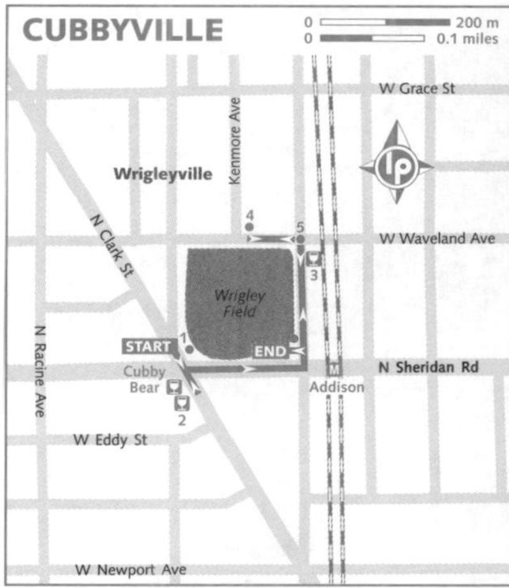

5 Waveland & Sheffield Aves Rooftops As you're walking back to the main stadium entrance, look up. The buildings along Waveland and Sheffield have been bought up and turned into corporate hospitality lounges. Rooftop seats (see p210 for ticket info) provide a unique perspective down onto the field. Watch from here and you get food and drink included.

6 Knothole A 2006 expansion of the Wrigley Field (p81) bleachers beefed up the eastern wall. The franchise left a 20-ft long opening (with iron bars) so you can peek into the game field-level. The right-field vantage point is a bit skewed – but it's free. Now go watch the game.

ANDERSONVILLE, LINCOLN SQUARE & UPTOWN

Eating p153; Shopping p129; Sleeping p228

The vibe in Andersonville is continental with a friendly, European pace. Locals linger at cafés and bars long after they should be on their way, and dinners at Andersonville's collection of middle- and highbrow restaurants are hours-long events meant to be savored and recounted later.

You can blame some of that Euro-feel on the Swedes, who started building homes here when Andersonville was little more than a cherry orchard. Their legacy continues today in many of the stores, like the butter-lovin' Swedish Bakery.

But the Swedes are only partly responsible for the district flavor of Andersonville. The blocks surrounding Clark St from Argyle St through Bryn Mawr Ave have become popular with young professionals. The once-low rents attracted creative types in the 1980s and '90s. Many lesbians found a home among the widely varied residents, and rainbow flags commonly flutter alongside the blue-and-yellow flags of Sweden. The shopkeepers and condo owners may still routinely sweep their sidewalks each day, as per Swedish tradition, but these broom-wielding businesspeople are as likely to be Lebanese or gay, as they are to be the stolid older Nordic residents.

Uptown, the scrappy neighborhood to the south of Andersonville, has a fascinating history of its own. Al Capone often drank here at his favorite speakeasy, the Green Mill (still a jazz venue today; see p183). It's also where his gang stored their bootleg booze (in tunnels under the club) after it came off boats in nearby Lake Michigan. Circa 1915, the neighborhood was the epicenter of moviemaking in the United States. Yep, before there was Hollywood, there was Uptown, cranking out the country's silent films and harboring contract players like Charlie Chaplin and WC Fields.

Uptown's most recent cultural contributions are the kind you eat with chopsticks. Hole-in-the-wall Asian eateries along Argyle St have earned this area the name 'Little Saigon' and made it a mecca for fans of Vietnamese food.

West of Uptown lies Lincoln Square, an old German enclave that's blossoming into an eating/drinking/shopping destination with a Euro-vibe reminiscent of Andersonville.

ANDERSONVILLE

SWEDISH AMERICAN MUSEUM CENTER Map p86

☎ 773-728-8111; www.samac.org; 5211 N Clark St; adult/child $4/3; ⏲ 10am-4pm Tue-Fri, 11am-4pm Sat & Sun; Ⓜ Red Line to Berwyn

The permanent collection at this small storefront museum focuses on the lives of the Swedes who originally settled Chicago. In that sense it reflects the dreams and aspirations of many of the groups who have poured into the city since it was founded. At the museum, you can check out some of the items people felt were important to bring with them on their journey to America. Butter churns, traditional bedroom furniture, religious relics and more are all included in the collection.

ROSEHILL CEMETERY Map p86

☎ 773-561-5940; 5800 N Ravenswood Ave; ⏲ 8am-5pm Mon-Sat, 10am-4pm Sun; 🚌 84 to Ravenswood

The entrance gate to Chicago's largest cemetery is worth the trip alone. Designed by WW Boyington (the architect who created the old Water Tower on Michigan Ave) the entry looks like a cross between high Gothic and low Disney. Through the gates, you'll see the graves of plenty of Chicago bigwigs, from Chicago mayors and a US vice president to meat man Oscar Mayer. You'll also find some of the weirdest grave monuments in the city, including a postal train and an huge carved boulder from a

TRANSPORTATION – ANDERSONVILLE, LINCOLN SQUARE & UPTOWN

Bus The bus 151 runs along Sheridan Rd; 22 travels on Clark St; 80 on Park Rd; and 78 on Montrose Ave.

El Take the Red Line to Berwyn, six blocks east of Clark St, for Andersonville; take the Red Line to Argyle for Argyle St; the Red Line's Lawrence Ave is good for trips to lower Uptown; Red Line to Sheridan for Graceland Cemetery and around. For Lincoln Sq, take the Brown Line to Western.

Parking Meter and on-street parking available in Andersonville and Uptown, though big concerts at Uptown's music venues can make things hairy.

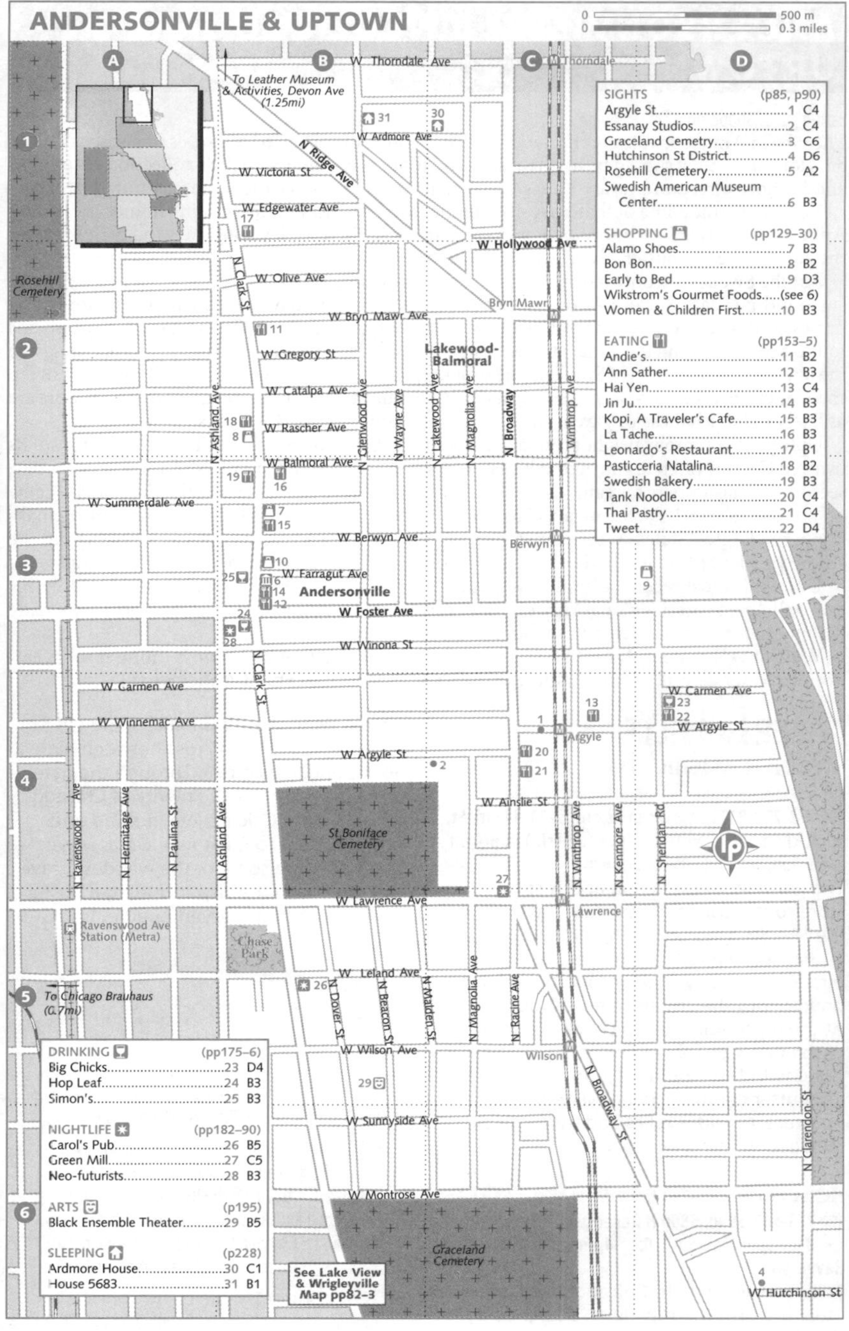

ANDERSONVILLE & UPTOWN
0 500 m
0 0.3 miles
A
B
C
D
1
2
3
4
5
6
SIGHTS (p85, p90)
Argyle St....1 C4
Essanay Studios....2 C4
Graceland Cemetery....3 C6
Hutchinson St District....4 D6
Rosehill Cemetery....5 A2
Swedish American Museum Center....6 B3
SHOPPING (pp129–30)
Alamo Shoes....7 B3
Bon Bon....8 B2
Early to Bed....9 D3
Wikstrom's Gourmet Foods....(see 6)
Women & Children First....10 B3
EATING (pp153–5)
Andie's....11 B2
Ann Sather....12 B3
Hai Yen....13 C4
Jin Ju....14 B3
Kopi, A Traveler's Cafe....15 B3
La Tache....16 B3
Leonardo's Restaurant....17 B1
Pasticceria Natalina....18 B2
Swedish Bakery....19 B3
Tank Noodle....20 C4
Thai Pastry....21 C4
Tweet....22 D4
DRINKING (pp175–6)
Big Chicks....23 D4
Hop Leaf....24 B3
Simon's....25 B3
NIGHTLIFE (pp182–90)
Carol's Pub....26 B5
Green Mill....27 C5
Neo-futurists....28 B3
ARTS (p195)
Black Ensemble Theater....29 B5
SLEEPING (p228)
Ardmore House....30 C1
House 5683....31 B1
To Leather Museum & Activities, Devon Ave (1.25mi)
W Thorndale Ave
Thorndale
W Ardmore Ave
N Ridge Ave
W Victoria St
W Edgewater Ave
W Hollywood Ave
W Olive Ave
N Clark St
Rosehill Cemetery
Bryn Mawr
W Bryn Mawr Ave
W Gregory St
Lakewood-Balmoral
W Catalpa Ave
W Rascher Ave
W Balmoral Ave
N Ashland Ave
N Glenwood Ave
N Wayne Ave
N Lakewood Ave
N Magnolia Ave
N Broadway
N Winthrop Ave
W Summerdale Ave
W Berwyn Ave
Berwyn
W Farragut Ave
Andersonville
W Foster Ave
W Winona St
W Carmen Ave
W Winnemac Ave
W Argyle St
Argyle
W Ainslie St
St Boniface Cemetery
N Ravenswood Ave
N Hermitage Ave
N Paulina St
N Kenmore Ave
N Sheridan Rd
W Lawrence Ave
Lawrence
Ravenswood Ave Station (Metra)
Chase Park
W Leland Ave
To Chicago Brauhaus (0.7mi)
N Dover St
N Beacon St
N Malden St
N Racine Ave
W Wilson Ave
Wilson
N Broadway St
W Sunnyside Ave
N Clarendon St
W Montrose Ave
Graceland Cemetery
See Lake View & Wrigleyville Map pp82–3
W Hutchinson St

top picks

PLACES TO ESCAPE THE CROWDS

- Graceland Cemetery (below)
- Harold Washington Winter Garden (p60)
- 12th St Beach (p108)
- Art Institute in the Ancient Egyptian or Southeast Asian galleries (p52)
- Garfield Park Conservatory (p101)

Civil War battlefield in Georgia. More than one ghost story started here; keep an eye out for vapors as night falls.

UPTOWN

GRACELAND CEMETERY Map p86

☎ 773-525-1105; 4001 N Clark St; 8am-4:30pm; M Red Line to Sheridan

Graceland Cemetery is the final resting place for some of the biggest names in Chicago history. Most of the notable tombs lie around the lake, in the northern half of the 121 acres. Pick up a free map at the entrance to navigate the swirl of paths and streets.

Many of the memorials relate to the lives of the dead in symbolic and touching ways: National League founder William Hulbert lies under a baseball; hotelier Dexter Graves lies under a work titled *Eternal Silence;* and George Pullman, the railroad car magnate who sparked so much labor unrest, lies under a hidden fortress designed to prevent angry union members from digging him up.

Daniel Burnham, who did so much to design Chicago, gets his own island. Photographer Richard Nickel, who helped form Chicago's budding preservation movement and was killed during the demolition of his beloved Chicago Stock Exchange Building, has a stone designed by admiring architects. Other notables interred here include architects John Wellborn Root, Louis Sullivan and Ludwig Mies van der Rohe, plus retail magnate Marshall Field and power couple Potter and Bertha Palmer.

ARGYLE STREET Map p86

btwn Broadway Ave & Sheridan Rd; M Red Line to Argyle

As you round the corner from Broadway Ave onto Argyle St, whoa! Everything from the stores to the restaurants to the car-detailing shops is decked out in Laotian, Vietnamese and Cambodian script. Even the El train station is topped with a pagoda and painted in the auspicious colors of green and red. Many of the area's residents came here as refugees from the Vietnam war, and their presence has solved city planners' worries about how to reverse the declining fortunes of this Uptown enclave. The storefronts are all filled now (though the area still looks a little scuffy). The several blocks of Argyle St make a good stopover for lunch, or for a half hour's wandering and window-shopping.

ESSANAY STUDIOS Map p86

1333-1345 W Argyle St; M Red Line to Argyle

Back before the talkies made silent film obsolete, Chicago reigned supreme as the number one producer of movie magic in the US. Essanay churned out silent films with soon-to-be household names like WC Fields, Charlie Chaplin and Gilbert M Anderson (aka 'Bronco Billy,' the trailblazing star of the brand-new Western genre and co-founder of Essanay). Filming took place at the studio, but also in the surrounding neighborhoods. Getting the product out the door and into theaters was more important than producing artful, well-made films, so editing was viewed somewhat circumspectly. As a result, it was common in the early Essanay films to see local children performing unintentional cameos, or bits of familiar neighborhoods poking into the edge of 'California' mesas. Essanay folded in 1917, about the time that many of its actors were being lured to the bright lights of a still-nascent Hollywood. These days, the building belongs to a local college but the company's terra-cotta Indian head logo remains above the door at 1345.

HUTCHINSON STREET DISTRICT Map p86

M Red Line to Sheridan

In marked contrast to some of Uptown's seedier areas, the Hutchinson St District is a well-maintained area perfect for a genteel promenade. Homes here were built in the early 1900s and represent some of the best examples of Prairie School residences in Chicago. Several of the homes along Hutchinson St – including the one at 839 Hutchinson St – are the work of George W Maher, a famous student of Frank Lloyd Wright. Also of note are 817 Hutchinson St and 4243 Hazel St.

LEATHER ARCHIVES & MUSEUM
Map p50

☎ 773-761-9200; www.leatherarchives.org; 6418 N Greenview Ave; admission $5; noon-8pm Thu & Fri, noon-5pm Sat & Sun; 22

Who knew? Ben Franklin liked to be flogged, and Egypt's Queen Hatshepsut had a foot fetish. The Leather Archives & Museum reveals this and more in its displays of leather, fetish and S&M subcultures. The on-site shop sells posters, pins and other 'pervertibles.'

DEVON AVENUE Map p50

intersection of Devon & Western Aves; M Brown Line to Western, transfer to 49B

OK, it's technically not in Andersonville or Uptown, but rather about a mile and a half north. Often called Chicago's 'International Marketplace,' Devon Ave is an ethnic mash-up where Indian women in jewel-toned saris glide by Muslim men in white skullcaps, and Nigerian women in bright print robes shop beside Orthodox men in black yarmulkes. It's a fun destination for shopping (see p130) and serial grazing on the samosas, kabobs, kosher doughnuts and other snack-shop items. Or get curried away with a full meal (p167).

SWEET TREATS
Walking Tour

Who knows why the combination of Swedish heritage, old neighborhood buildings and upscale gay and lesbian culture has attracted so many pastry shops, and who cares – enjoy!

1 Ann Sather Start your tempting tour at Ann Sather (p154), with the café's gigantic hot cinnamon rolls that have vanilla icing slathered on top (Swedish pancakes aren't bad either). Wall murals tell the Swedish tale of misbehaving young Nils who's turned into an elf and the adventures he has trying to redeem himself.

2 Swedish American Museum Center Next door at the shop for the Swedish American Museum Center (p85), pick up a baking cookbook and some ligonberry jam so you can make your own goodies (they also sell cookies). Upstairs in the museum, letters and belongings shed light on the lives of the neighborhood's first immigrants.

3 Swedish Bakery Allergy-sufferers beware, almonds are very popular in Swedish pastries; they're infused in the majority of cakes, cookies and confections at the landmark Swedish Bakery (p155). Take a number and wait to order your chocolate-almond-buttercream macaroons or frog-shaped almond cake.

4 Pasticceria Natalina Shortly after opening in 2007, Pasticceria Natalina (p154) was already drawing comments like 'best bakery in Chicago.' The flaky pastry of the cannoli, stuffed with imported fresh sheep's milk ricotta, is the star at this Sicilian bakery. But there's the chocolate-hazelnut biscotti and the tiramisu to try…

5 Bon Bon Finally, we get to the serious chocolate. Bon Bon (p129) specializes in exotic flavors (and shapes, like the Kama Sutra). Sit at one of the two tiny tables and nibble dark chocolate infused with Chinese five-spice or rose petals mixed into white chocolate ganache.

WALK FACTS
Start Ann Sather
Finish Bon Bon
Duration An hour and a half (unless you're too full to move)

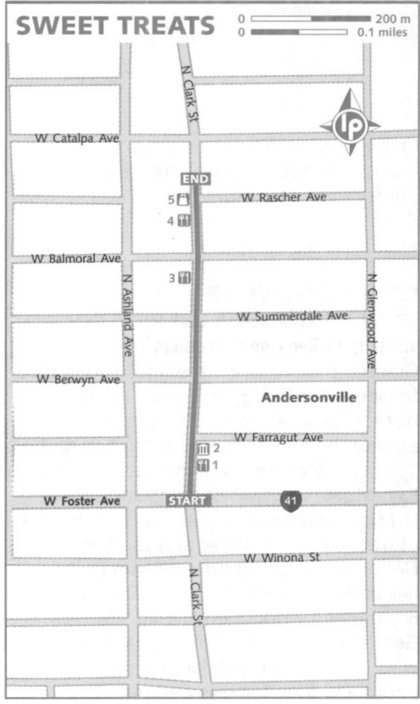

WICKER PARK, BUCKTOWN & UKRAINIAN VILLAGE

Eating p155; Shopping p130; Sleeping p228

Just try to make your way along Milwaukee Ave near Damen Ave on a Friday night, and you'll get a sense of the riotous popularity of the Wicker Park/Bucktown neighborhood. Clubs, bars and restaurants here are packed, and during the weekend indie rock concerts, underground author readings and beading classes all happen within 30ft of each other. On any given day, dozens of hip shoe stores, boutiques, bookstores, restaurants and salons hold court, providing Chicagoans with the necessary fuel for the modern urban lifestyle.

The hubbub would have been slightly bewildering to the Central European butchers, bakers and candlestick-makers who lived here originally. They would have been surprised, too, by the era through the early 1990s when prostitution, gangs and drive-by shootings were the norm. And their jaw would have hit the floor had they known their simple wood-frame houses would be ripped down to make way for row after row of break-the-bank condos in the new millennium. But that's gentrification, baby, and it took care of this neighborhood in a big way.

The action keeps moving south, with Division St the most recent block to feel the love. Its organic restaurants, crafty shops and low-lit lounges are quite a change from the road's former glory as 'Polish Broadway' (a name that came from all the polka bars that once lined the road). Luckily, a few of the era's dive bars remain to keep it real. Ukrainian Village is next in line, as development swoops down toward Chicago Ave, dropping cool cafés and shops in its path.

You can visit the neighborhoods' ethnic museums and art galleries, as well as swing by Nelson Algren's pad, but what you're really here for is the food, drink and window browsing.

WICKER PARK & BUCKTOWN

WICKER PARK Map pp90–1

btwn N Damen Ave, W Schiller St & N Wicker Park Ave; Ⓜ Blue Line to Damen

Sure, Chicago invented the zipper and a handful of other useless bric-a-brac. The city's true legacy, though, will be in a strange softball game invented here. Aptly named, 16-Inch Softball uses the same rules as normal softball, but with shorter games, a bigger, squishier ball and a complete lack of gloves or mitts on the fielders. They've been playing it in Chicago for over 75 years, and Wicker Park is a prime place to see the uniquely Chicago sport played by die-hard fanatics. And for travelers suffering withdrawal from the pooch left at home, Wicker Park's dog park is a great way to get in some quality canine time.

NELSON ALGREN HOUSE Map pp90–1

1958 W Evergreen Ave; Ⓜ Blue Line to Damen

In a three-flat, one block south of the park, writer Nelson Algren created some of his greatest works about gritty life in the neighborhood. Algren won the 1950 National Book Award for his novel *The Man with the Golden Arm,* set on Division St near Milwaukee Ave. You can't go into the house, but you can admire it from the street.

FLAT IRON BUILDING Map pp90–1

1579 N Milwaukee Ave; Ⓜ Blue Line to Damen

The warren of galleries, studios and workshops in this landmark building has been responsible for a sizable percentage of the artistic zaniness that has long made Wicker Park such a magnet for creative types. Keep an eye on telephone poles around the area for flyers detailing the latest shows and gallery open-houses. For information on the annual Around the Coyote Arts Festival, see p16.

POLISH MUSEUM OF AMERICA Map pp90–1

☎ 773-384-3352; 984 N Milwaukee Ave; adult/senior & student $5/4; 🕒 11am-4pm, closed Thu; Ⓜ Blue Line to Division

If you don't know Pulaski from a *pierogi,* this is the place to get the scoop on Polish culture. The museum is the oldest ethnic museum in the USA, and while you won't find high-tech 3D virtual roller-coaster rides or IMAX screens, you will get a chance to learn about some of the Poles who helped shape Chicago's history. (Pulaski, by the way, was a Polish hero in the American Revolution.) The collection of traditional Polish costumes, WWII artifacts and oddball, amateur food displays feel like they were all lovingly created by Polish retirees

WICKER PARK, BUCKTOWN & UKRAINIAN VILLAGE

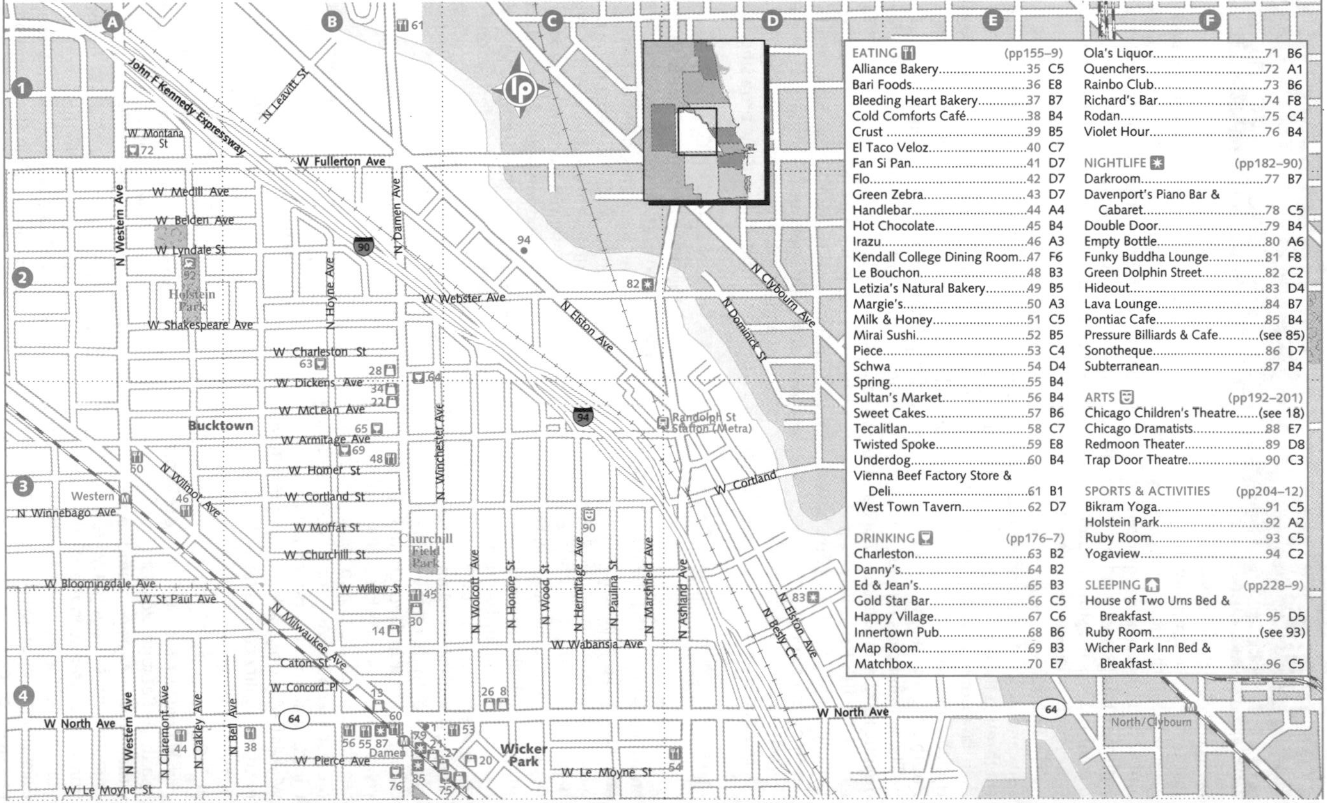

0 500 m
0 0.3 miles

EATING (pp155–9)

Name	No.	Grid
Alliance Bakery	35	C5
Bari Foods	36	E8
Bleeding Heart Bakery	37	B7
Cold Comforts Café	38	B4
Crust	39	B5
El Taco Veloz	40	C7
Fan Si Pan	41	D7
Flo	42	D7
Green Zebra	43	D7
Handlebar	44	A4
Hot Chocolate	45	B4
Irazu	46	A3
Kendall College Dining Room	47	F6
Le Bouchon	48	B3
Letizia's Natural Bakery	49	B5
Margie's	50	A3
Milk & Honey	51	C5
Mirai Sushi	52	B5
Piece	53	C4
Schwa	54	D4
Spring	55	B4
Sultan's Market	56	B4
Sweet Cakes	57	B6
Tecalitlan	58	C7
Twisted Spoke	59	E8
Underdog	60	B4
Vienna Beef Factory Store & Deli	61	B1
West Town Tavern	62	D7

DRINKING (pp176–7)

Name	No.	Grid
Charleston	63	B2
Danny's	64	B2
Ed & Jean's	65	B3
Gold Star Bar	66	C5
Happy Village	67	C6
Innertown Pub	68	B6
Map Room	69	B3
Matchbox	70	E7
Ola's Liquor	71	B6
Quenchers	72	A1
Rainbo Club	73	B6
Richard's Bar	74	F8
Rodan	75	C4
Violet Hour	76	B4

NIGHTLIFE (pp182–90)

Name	No.	Grid
Darkroom	77	B7
Davenport's Piano Bar & Cabaret	78	C5
Double Door	79	B4
Empty Bottle	80	A6
Funky Buddha Lounge	81	F8
Green Dolphin Street	82	C2
Hideout	83	D4
Lava Lounge	84	B7
Pontiac Cafe	85	B4
Pressure Billiards & Cafe	(see 85)	
Sonotheque	86	D7
Subterranean	87	B4

ARTS (pp192–201)

Name	No.	Grid
Chicago Children's Theatre	(see 18)	
Chicago Dramatists	88	E7
Redmoon Theater	89	D8
Trap Door Theatre	90	C3

SPORTS & ACTIVITIES (pp204–12)

Name	No.	Grid
Bikram Yoga	91	C5
Holstein Park	92	A2
Ruby Room	93	C5
Yogaview	94	C2

SLEEPING (pp228–9)

Name	No.	Grid
House of Two Urns Bed & Breakfast	95	D5
Ruby Room	(see 93)	
Wicher Park Inn Bed & Breakfast	96	C5

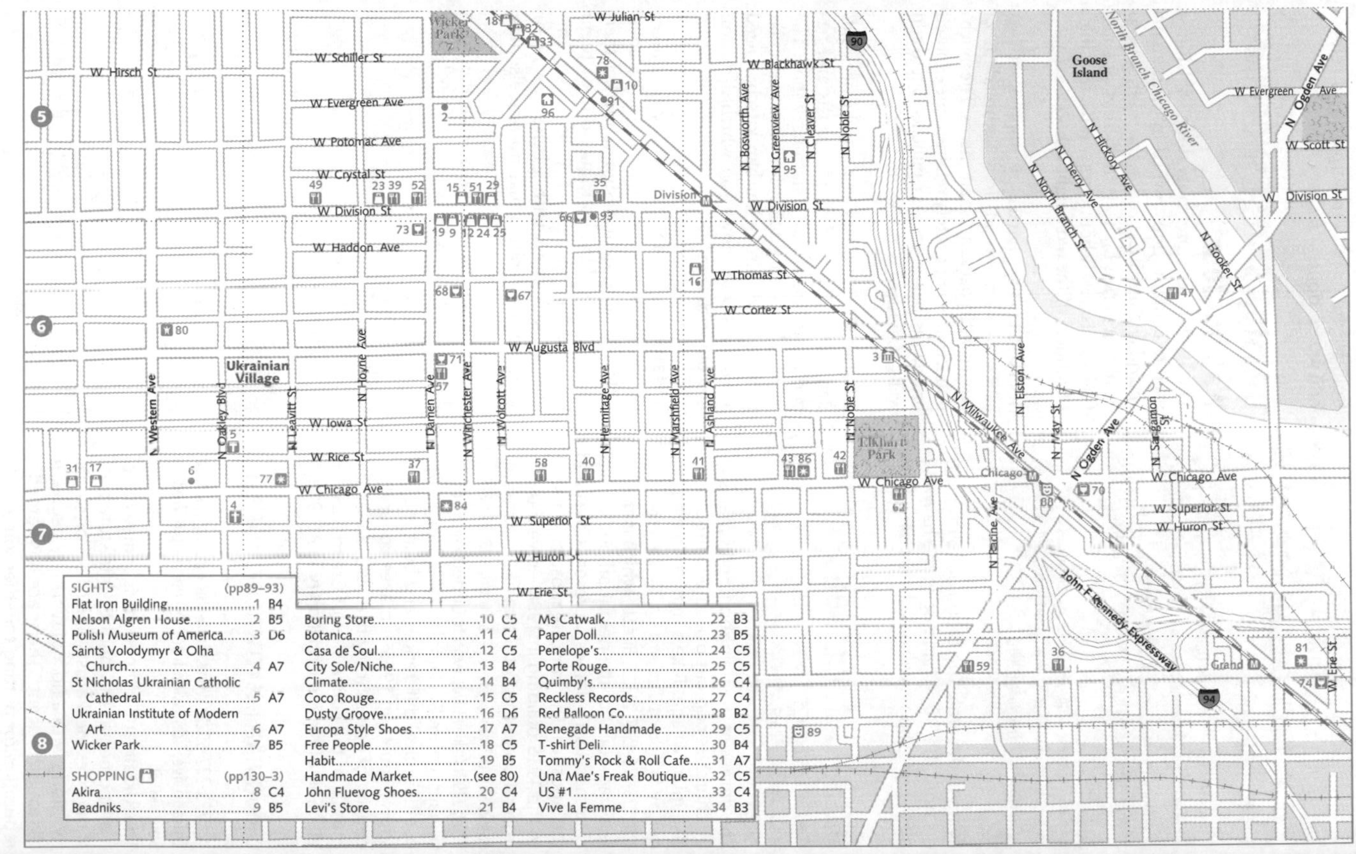
Goose Island
North Branch Chicago River
Wicker Park
Ukrainian Village
Elkhart Park
W Julian St
W Schiller St
W Hirsch St
W Evergreen Ave
W Potomac Ave
W Crystal St
W Division St
W Haddon Ave
W Blackhawk St
W Thomas St
W Cortez St
W Augusta Blvd
W Iowa St
W Rice St
W Chicago Ave
W Superior St
W Huron St
W Erie St
W Scott St
N Western Ave
N Oakley Blvd
N Leavitt St
N Hoyne Ave
N Damen Ave
N Winchester Ave
N Wolcott Ave
N Hermitage Ave
N Marshfield Ave
N Ashland Ave
N Noble St
N Bosworth Ave
N Greenview Ave
N Cleaver St
N Milwaukee Ave
N Elston Ave
N May St
N Ogden Ave
N Sangamon St
N Racine Ave
N Hickory Ave
N Cherry Ave
N North Branch St
N Hooker St
John F Kennedy Expressway
Division
Chicago
Grand
90
94
5
6
7
8
SIGHTS (pp89–93)
Flat Iron Building 1 B4
Nelson Algren House 2 B5
Polish Museum of America 3 D6
Saints Volodymyr & Olha Church 4 A7
St Nicholas Ukrainian Catholic Cathedral 5 A7
Ukrainian Institute of Modern Art 6 A7
Wicker Park 7 B5
SHOPPING (pp130–3)
Akira 8 C4
Beadniks 9 B5
Boring Store 10 C5
Botanica 11 C4
Casa de Soul 12 C5
City Sole/Niche 13 B4
Climate 14 B4
Coco Rouge 15 C5
Dusty Groove 16 D6
Europa Style Shoes 17 A7
Free People 18 C5
Habit 19 B5
Handmade Market (see 80)
John Fluevog Shoes 20 C4
Levi's Store 21 B4
Ms Catwalk 22 B3
Paper Doll 23 B5
Penelope's 24 C5
Porte Rouge 25 C5
Quimby's 26 C4
Reckless Records 27 C4
Red Balloon Co 28 B2
Renegade Handmade 29 C5
T-shirt Deli 30 B4
Tommy's Rock & Roll Cafe 31 A7
Una Mae's Freak Boutique 32 C5
US #1 33 C4
Vive la Femme 34 B3

TRANSPORTATION – WICKER PARK, BUCKTOWN & UKRAINIAN VILLAGE

Bus Number 50 runs up Damen Ave; 72 runs along North Ave; 70 travels along Division St.

El Blue Line to Damen Ave for Wicker Park and Bucktown; Blue Line to Division for Ukrainian Village.

Parking Meter and free on-street parking at a premium in Wicker Park and Bucktown; widely available in Ukrainian Village.

living in the area. The group of Polish posters from the '30s – hanging in the hallway by the gift shop – will delight art deco fans.

UKRAINIAN VILLAGE

CHURCHES OF UKRAINIAN VILLAGE Map pp90–1

66

The domes of the neighborhood's majestic churches pop out over the treetops in Ukrainian Village. Take a minute to wander by St Nicholas Ukrainian Catholic Cathedral (773-276-4537; 2238 W Rice St), which is the less traditional of the neighborhood's main churches. Its 13 domes represent Christ and the Apostles. The intricate mosaics – added to the 1915 building in 1988 – owe their inspiration to the Cathedral of St Sophia in Kiev. Saints Volodymyr & Olha Church (312-829-5209; 739 N Oakley Blvd) was founded by traditionalists from St Nicholas, who broke away over liturgical differences and built this showy church in 1975. It makes up for its paucity of domes (only five) with a massive mosaic of the conversion of Grand Duke Vladimir of Kiev to Christianity in AD 988.

UKRAINIAN INSTITUTE OF MODERN ART Map pp90–1

773-227-5522; www.uima-chicago.org; 2320 W Chicago Ave; admission free; noon-4pm Wed-Sun; 66

The 'Ukrainian' in the name is somewhat of a misnomer, as this bright white storefront showcases local artists regardless of ethnicity (along with a host of works by people of Ukrainian descent). The space has earned a reputation for putting together some of the best exhibits in Chicago. Shows here range from playfully pretty to perplexingly cerebral works, done in a host of media.

DIVISION STREET SHOPPING

Walking Tour

The 1990s brick storefronts along Division St used to contain shops owned by Ukrainians and other ethnicities. Today, the southern end of Wicker Park is highly gentrified; what you'll find now is trendy boutiques – and a few small reminders of the old neighborhood.

1 Crust Fortify yourself by stopping at Crust (p156) for some wood-fired flatbread pizza topped with goat's cheese and herbs. The much-publicized organic eatery retains some exposed brick walls, but others were punched out to add walls of modern windows and light.

2 Paper Doll Look for ethnic influences hidden among the bold graphic cards and papers at the Paper Doll (p132) stationary shop. The *matroyska* nesting doll cards are a particular favorite. They also sell urban kitsch – need a compass that shows you which direction Lincoln Park is in?

3 Habit Immigrant tailors may no longer sew clothing to order, but Habit (p131) does. Fifteen independent designers market their wares at this sleek boutique; one of them takes custom orders. Try on a streamlined deep-V dress with a belted waste, or snag that little purse that no one else has.

4 Beadniks Incense wafts from the open door as you pass Beadniks (p130). They'll help

WALK FACTS

Start Crust restaurant
Finish Coco Rouge chocolate shop
Duration Ten minutes to walk, two hours to eat and browse

DIVISION STREET SHOPPING

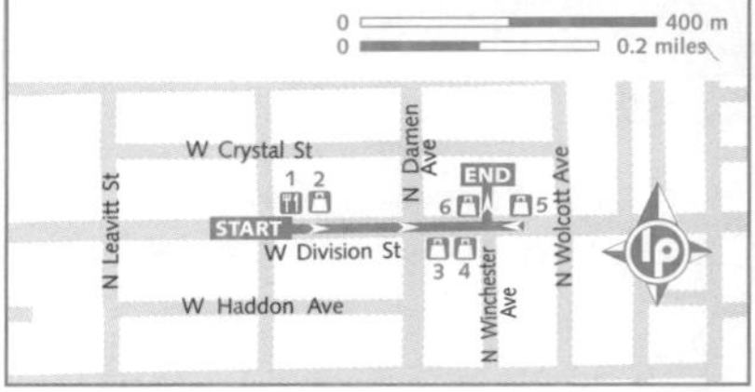

you string together beads from all over the world – including those from the Old Country (well, the Czech Republic anyway). Pick up supplies, or make a necklace in-store.

5 Renegade Handmade Continue down and across the street; you pass several clothing boutiques, trendy kidswear, a gorgeous European homewares shop and the 1906 Russian Bath building. Crafts sold at an annual local arts fair – pillows, prints, toys, paper goods – were so popular that they spawned the Renegade Handmade (p131) store.

6 Coco Rouge The elegantly minimalist room is like an empty theater with only a few handfuls of truffles taking center stage in a glass case. Your babushka would love the decadent chocolate at Coco Rouge (p134), though she might be put off by the prices.

LOGAN SQUARE & HUMBOLDT PARK

Eating p160; Shopping p133

When the Bucktown, Wicker Park and Ukrainian Village hipsters could no longer afford rent in those neighborhoods, they moved west to Logan Sq. The mostly Latino neighborhood had a lot to offer, especially around the square itself (a sort of island formed by strangely intersecting roads). There were old buildings with huge amounts of living space, decent transportation via the Blue Line, tree-shaded boulevards, and cheap eats at the myriad *taquerias* (taco eateries). It took awhile, but stylish restaurants, bars and shops finally caught up with the crowd, and provide the main impetus for visiting. Today the scene is well established, but since the neighborhood remains primarily residential, and spread out over a large area, it feels much more relaxed and off the beaten path than the Bucktown/Wicker Park/Ukrainian Village chaos. Despite gentrification's relentless push, Logan Sq has somehow held on to its dignity.

Humboldt Park, to the south, is where the hipsters priced out of Logan Square ended up. The neighborhood definitely has a rough-around-the-edges feel. It's still heavily Puerto Rican, and is the birthplace of the heart-stopping *jibarito* sandwich (garlic mayo–slathered steak served between sliced-plantain 'bread'). The eponymous park is the area's focal point.

Both neighborhoods have big old houses, boulevards and unexpectedly grand monuments like the column in Logan Sq and the boathouse in Humboldt Park. Their eating and drinking options make them ideal for a low-key evening.

HUMBOLDT PARK Map p95

1359 N Humboldt Blvd (also called N Sacramento Ave); 🚌 70

This 207-acre park, which lends its name to the surrounding neighborhood, comes out of nowhere and gob-smacks you with Mother Nature. A lagoon edged with irises, bulrushes and other native plants takes up much of the green space. Red-winged blackbirds and even the occasional blue heron fly overhead. The Prairie School boathouse rises up from the lagoon's edge and serves as the park's showpiece. Built in 1907, it was a hot spot at the time for picnicking, fishing, boating and concerts. A gravel path takes off from here and circles the water, where you'll sometimes see people casting lines.

Across the street from the boathouse, on the northwest corner of Humboldt Blvd and Division St, lies the Formal Garden, rich with jelly-bean-colored flower beds and a walk-through fountain. It's a fine place to sit and smell the roses (or whatever those flowers may be).

The park has gone through some rough times since German naturalist Alexander von Humboldt built it in 1869. It has really only come into its own again in the past five years. While it's family-filled by day, it's still pretty rough, and best avoided, at night.

The annual *Fiestas Puertorriqueñas* (Puerto Rican party) takes over the park in mid-June (see p14).

PASEO BORICUA Map p95

Division St btwn Western Ave & Mozart Ave; 🚌 70

Paseo Boricua, aka the Puerto Rican Passage, is a mile-long stretch of Division St stuffed with Puerto Rican shops and restaurants. It's marked at either end by a 45-ton, steel Puerto Rican flag sculpture that arches over the road; the eastern flag stands at Western Ave, while the western one is at Mozart Ave. This area has long been the epicenter of Chicago's 113,000-strong Puerto Rican community.

ILLINOIS CENTENNIAL MEMORIAL COLUMN Map p95

intersection of Kedzie Blvd, Logan Blvd & Milwaukee Ave; Ⓜ Blue Line to Logan Sq

What's that giant, phallic thing in the middle of the road, causing traffic to swerve every which way? Excellent question. Most locals

TRANSPORTATION – LOGAN SQUARE & HUMBOLDT PARK

Bus Number 70 travels along Division St to Humboldt Park's heart. Other useful buses are 77 along Belmont Ave and 72 along North Ave.

El Blue Line to Logan Sq puts you at the epicenter for that 'hood; Blue Line to California or Western puts you at its fringe.

Parking Street parking isn't bad compared with other neighborhoods, although it can get tight around Logan Sq near Lula Café.

LOGAN SQUARE & HUMBOLDT PARK

SIGHTS	(pp94–6)
Boathouse	1 C5
Formal Garden	2 B5
Humboldt Park	3 C5
Illinois Centennial Memorial Column	4 B1
Puerto Rican Flag Sculpture	5 C5
Puerto Rican Flag Sculpture	6 D5
SHOPPING	(p133)
Wolfbait & B-girls	7 B1
EATING	(pp160–1)
Borinquen Restaurant	8 C4
El Cid 2	9 B1
Feed	10 C6
Lazo's Tacos	11 D3
Lula Café	12 B1
DRINKING	(pp177–8)
Fireside Bowl	13 D2
Whirlaway Lounge	14 B2
NIGHTLIFE	(pp182–90)
Logan Square Auditorium	15 B1
Rosa's Lounge	16 A3
ARTS	(pp192–201)
California Clipper	17 C6
Elastic Arts Foundation	18 A1

have no idea. Turns out it's a monument commemorating the 100th anniversary of Illinois' statehood, by a gent named Henry Bacon – the same architect who created the Lincoln Memorial in Washington DC. The eagle atop the column echoes that on the Illinois state flag. The reliefs of Native Americans, explorers, farmers and laborers represent the great changes the state experienced during its first century.

LOGAN SQUARE

Walking Tour

Once a predominately Latino neighborhood, with a large Puerto Rican population, Logan Square has morphed into a hip residential area for young urbanites.

1 El Cid 2 A mango margarita and a fish taco await you at El Cid (p160), a Mexican restaurant and bar. The back patio garden is an excellent place to start your tour. Saturdays and some Wednesdays, live Latin jazz or Spanish guitar entertains.

2 N Milwaukee Ave Rent and real estate prices have already risen, and gentrification set in around the square. But you can still get a look at the Latin side of life. Walk north along Milwaukee to check out the little *taquerias* and trinket shops where they *hablo Español.*

3 Illinois Centennial Memorial Column Dead center in Logan Sq stands a 70ft column erected (OK, bad pun) in 1918 to celebrate 100 years of Illinois statehood. The architect, Henry Bacon, is better known for Washington DC's Lincoln Memorial. The square is a part of a boulevard system that connects northwestern neighborhoods via green space–filled parkways.

4 Wolfbait & B-girls You know a neighborhood's gone trendy when it has a store like Wolfbait & B-girls (p133). As many as 50 local

WALK FACTS

Start El Cid 2
Finish Logan Square Auditorium
Duration An hour

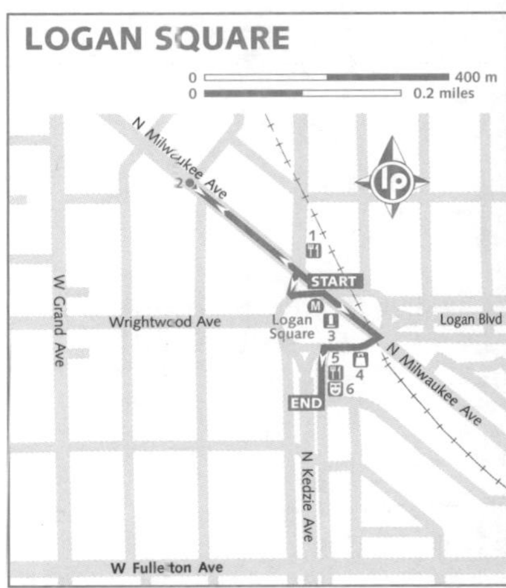

designers vend their funky women's wear and accessories at this energetic boutique. Weren't you looking for a hand-dyed repurposed mini-dress made from men's boxer shorts?

5 Lula Café Local foodies flock to Lula (p160) for the worldly-wise artisan dishes. Grab a sidewalk table and order a tofu-peanut satay while your tablemate tries the duck leg with potato puree. The dinner menu changes nightly, but what stays the same is the laid-back attitude and lack of pretense.

6 Logan Square Auditorium If you're lucky, afterwards, you can catch a live local music concert upstairs – raves to retro – at Logan Square Auditorium (p185). Get up close to the sounds in this ballroom that resembles an old gymnasium (thin wood-plank floors and all). Otherwise, it's back to El Cid for more margaritas…

NEAR WEST SIDE & PILSEN

Eating p161; Shopping p134; Sleeping p229

You rub your eyes and look again. Are those two black-clad guys in punishing German eyewear discussing post-minimalism next to a rubber-booted man hosing beef off a forklift?

Ah, meat and art, together at last. At least they are in the West Loop. Akin to New York City's Meatpacking District, the West Loop's up-and-coming restaurants, clubs and galleries poke out between meat-processing plants left over from the area's industrial days. Of all people, Oprah was one of the first to see the potential here, and she plunked down her studio on Washington Blvd years ago.

In addition to the West Loop, the Near West Side includes the ethnic neighborhoods of Greektown (along Halsted St) and Little Italy (along Taylor St). Neither has much in the way of sights, but gustatory tourists will revel in the tavernas and *tzatzikis* (yogurt dip) of the former, and the pastas and lemon ice of the latter. The University of Illinois at Chicago (UIC) lies between the two, and has been on a development rampage that's remaking the neighborhood, mostly for the better.

To the southwest lies Pilsen, the center of Chicago's Mexican community. A trip to this convenient neighborhood really is like stepping into the streets of a foreign country. It thumps with *tejano* (music that's a mix of Mexican and American styles) and brassy mariachi music, and the streets flow with the sounds of Spanish. The salsas here scald, the moles soothe, and the sidewalks are filled with umbrella'd food carts that tempt passers-by with a rainbow array of cold, pulpy *agua frescas* (fruit-flavored waters) and spicy-sweet *verduras* (thin slices of melon or cucumber dusted with a chili-powder kick).

Chicago's hipster underground has also been quietly relocating to Pilsen for the last decade or so. The area around 18th and Halsted Sts is a hub for storefront art galleries and painter's spaces. Even the taste-making record label Thrill Jockey has its offices here. And take a gander at the architecture: the original Czechoslovakian settlers not only named the 'hood after their homeland, but modeled their three-flats and storefronts on the world they'd left behind. Note, too, how many houses have their front yards several feet below sidewalk level; this is because the city later raised the streets for sewer construction.

While Pilsen is easy to reach by train, the Near West Side isn't as accessible; taking a cab will save you lots of time and hassle.

NEAR WEST SIDE

HARPO STUDIOS Map pp98–9

☎ studio 312-633-1000, tickets 312-591-9222; www.oprah.com; 1058 W Washington Blvd; Ⓜ Green Line to Clinton

Accept it: tickets to *The Oprah Winfrey Show* are freakin' hard to obtain (to try, see p35). So the odds on getting a Tyra Banks makeover or a brand new Pontiac are slim. But hey, the 'Harpo Studios' sign is a classic Chicago photo op. And who knows who might be arriving in that white limo coming up the street?

MUSEUM OF HOLOGRAPHY Map pp98–9

☎ 312-226-1007; www.holographiccenter.com; 1134 W Washington Blvd; admission $5; 🕑 12:30-4:30pm Wed-Sun; Ⓜ Green Line to Clinton

This trippy museum contains the world's largest collection of holograms. Giant tarantulas, naked women and Michael Jordan are among the three-dimensional images. Top pick goes to the 'binocular' hologram you look through to see 'birds' (more holograms). There's a school and laboratory dedicated to the science on-site, too.

WEST LOOP GALLERIES Map pp98–9

near intersection of Peoria & Washington Sts; Ⓜ Green Line to Clinton

Tucked between meatpacking plants and warehouses, the galleries of the West Loop are the beachhead for contemporary art in Chicago. Though less entrenched than their River North peers, the lower rents here mean larger showrooms. Generally speaking, the galleries also take bigger chances on up-and-coming and controversial artists. Most venues are located about three-quarters of a mile from the Green Line's Clinton stop, and are awkward to reach via public transportation; consider a cab. Gallery hours run from 11am to 5pm, Tuesday to Saturday; admission is

NEAR WEST SIDE & PILSEN

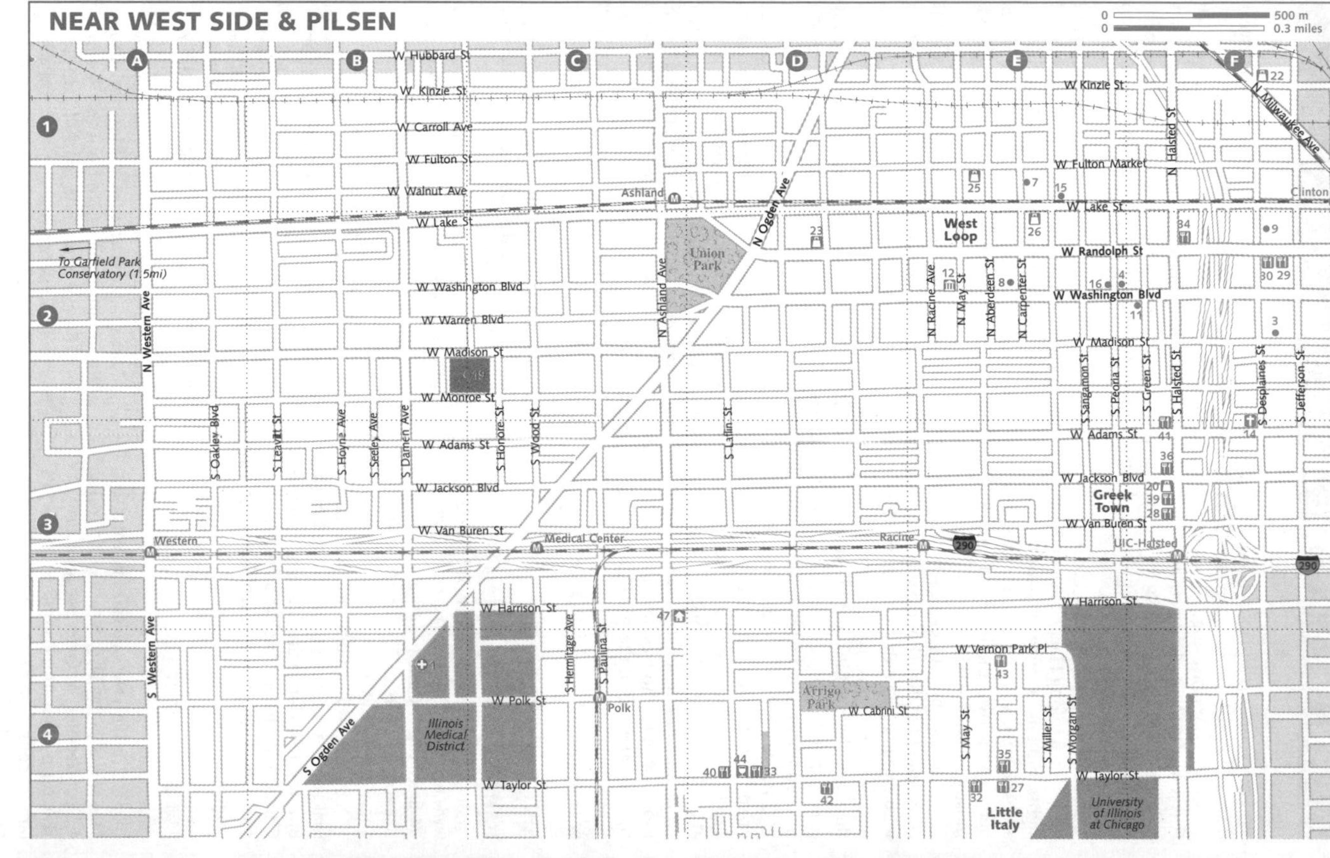

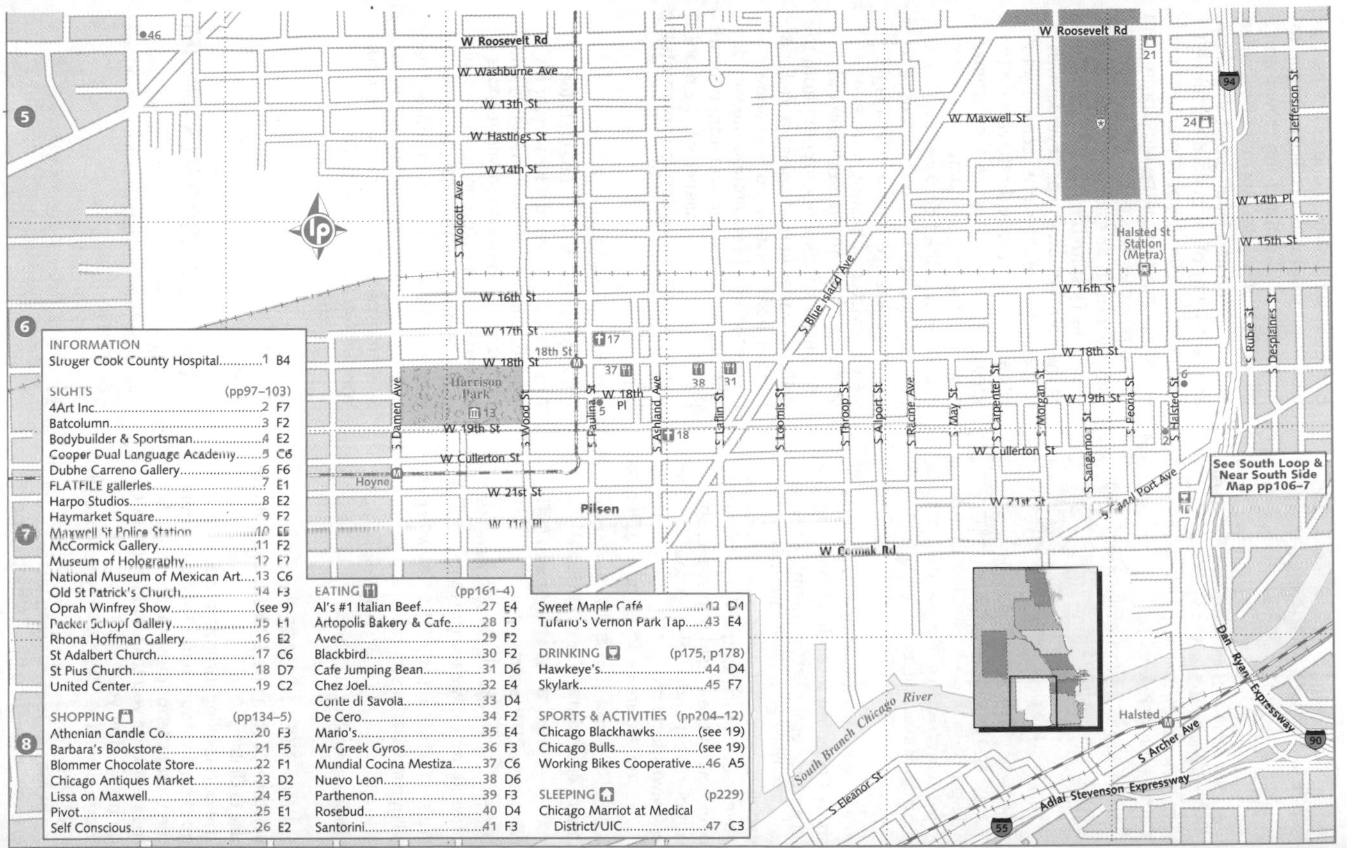

INFORMATION
Stroger Cook County Hospital............1 B4
SIGHTS (pp97–103)
4Art Inc..............................2 F7
Batcolumn.............................3 F2
Bodybuilder & Sportsman...............4 E2
Cooper Dual Language Academy..........5 C6
Dubhe Carreno Gallery.................6 F6
FLATFILE galleries....................7 E1
Harpo Studios.........................8 E2
Haymarket Square......................9 F2
Maxwell St Police Station.............10 E5
McCormick Gallery.....................11 F2
Museum of Holography..................12 F2
National Museum of Mexican Art........13 C6
Old St Patrick's Church...............14 F3
Oprah Winfrey Show....................(see 9)
Packer Schopf Gallery.................15 E1
Rhona Hoffman Gallery.................16 E2
St Adalbert Church....................17 C6
St Pius Church........................18 D7
United Center.........................19 C2
SHOPPING (pp134–5)
Athenian Candle Co....................20 F3
Barbara's Bookstore...................21 F5
Blommer Chocolate Store...............22 F1
Chicago Antiques Market...............23 D2
Lissa on Maxwell......................24 F5
Pivot.................................25 E1
Self Conscious........................26 E2
EATING (pp161–4)
Al's #1 Italian Beef..................27 E4
Artopolis Bakery & Cafe...............28 F3
Avec..................................29 F2
Blackbird.............................30 F2
Cafe Jumping Bean.....................31 D6
Chez Joel.............................32 E4
Conte di Savola.......................33 D4
De Cero...............................34 F2
Mario's...............................35 E4
Mr Greek Gyros........................36 F3
Mundial Cocina Mestiza................37 C6
Nuevo Leon............................38 D6
Parthenon.............................39 F3
Rosebud...............................40 D4
Santorini.............................41 F3
Sweet Maple Café......................42 D4
Tufano's Vernon Park Tap..............43 E4
DRINKING (p175, p178)
Hawkeye's.............................44 D4
Skylark...............................45 F7
SPORTS & ACTIVITIES (pp204–12)
Chicago Blackhawks....................(see 19)
Chicago Bulls.........................(see 19)
Working Bikes Cooperative.............46 A5
SLEEPING (p229)
Chicago Marriot at Medical District/UIC..47 C3
See South Loop & Near South Side Map pp106–7
W Roosevelt Rd
W Washburne Ave
W 13th St
W Hastings St
W 14th St
W 16th St
W 17th St
W 18th St
18th St
W 18th Pl
W 19th St
W Cullerton St
W 21st St
W 21st Pl
W Cermak Rd
W Maxwell St
W 14th Pl
W 15th St
S Wolcott Ave
S Damen Ave
S Wood St
S Paulina St
S Ashland Ave
S Laflin St
S Loomis St
S Throop St
S Allport St
S Racine Ave
S May St
S Carpenter St
S Morgan St
S Sangamon St
S Peoria St
S Halsted St
S Rube St
S Desplaines St
S Jefferson St
S Blue Island Ave
S Canal Port Ave
S Archer Ave
S Eleanor St
Harrison Park
Hoyne
Halsted
Halsted St Station (Metra)
Pilsen
South Branch Chicago River
Dan Ryan Expressway
Adlai Stevenson Expressway

TRANSPORTATION – NEAR WEST SIDE & PILSEN

Bus Number 20 runs Loop-bound along Washington St, returns along Madison St; 8 travels along Halsted St; 9 travels north–south on Ashland Ave between Pilsen and Irving Park Rd.

El Green Line to Clinton for the West Loop; Blue Line to UIC-Halsted for Greektown; Blue Line to Polk for Little Italy; Green Line to Conservatory for Garfield Park Conservatory; Blue Line to 18th St for Pilsen.

Parking West Loop free parking is plentiful, especially in the afternoon; Greektown parking can be tough to find but valets abound; Little Italy is fine for free on-street parking. Pilsen has plentiful parking on its side streets.

free. The best time to come is during a show's opening reception (check the gallery websites for lists of them), when wine and like-minded individuals enliven the evening. Note that owners often take off a week or two in August. For a thorough overview of the West Loop scene, check out our West Loop Galleries tour (p103) or www.westloop.org.

Among the area's dozen or so galleries:

Bodybuilder & Sportsman (☎ 312-492-7261; www.bodybuilderandsportsman.com; 119 N Peoria)

FLATFILE galleries (☎ 312-491-1190; www.flatfilegalleries.com; 217 N Carpenter St)

McCormick Gallery (☎ 312-226-6800; www.thomasmccormick.com; 835 W Washington Blvd)

Packer Schopf Gallery (☎ 312-226-8984; www.packergallery.com; 942 W Lake St)

Rhona Hoffman Gallery (☎ 312-455-1990; www.rhoffmangallery.com; 118 N Peoria)

HAYMARKET SQUARE Map pp98–9

Desplaines St btwn Lake & Randolph Sts; Ⓜ Green Line to Clinton

The odd-looking, bronze statue of some guys on a wagon marks the spot where the world's labor movement began. So the next time you take a lunch break or go home after your eight-hour work day, thank Haymarket Sq, which you're standing upon.

On May 4, 1886, striking factory workers held a meeting here. A mob of police appeared toward the end of the meeting, which quickly degenerated into chaos – a bomb exploded, killing one policeman and wounding several others. Police began to fire shots into the dispersing crowd, and by the end of the day, six more policemen had been shot and killed (most shot down accidentally by other policemen) and 60 others were injured. Eight anarchist leaders, including some of the most prominent speakers and writers of the movement, were eventually arrested and accused of the crime. Despite the fact that the identity of the bomb-thrower was never known, that only two of the eight accused actually attended the rally (both were on the speaker's platform – which the current bronze statue commemorates – in view of police when the bomb went off), and that no evidence linking the accused to the crime was ever produced, all eight were convicted of inciting murder and sentenced to hang. Four of them did soon thereafter. Before dropping from the gallows, leader August Spies uttered the famous words that would later appear on posters and flyers around the world: 'The day will come,' he said from beneath his hood, 'when our silence will be more powerful than the voices you are throttling today.'

BATCOLUMN Map pp98–9

600 W Madison St; Ⓜ Green Line to Clinton

Artist Claes Oldenburg – known for his gigantic shuttlecocks in Kansas City and oversized cherry-spoon in Minneapolis – delivered this simple, controversial sculpture to Chicago in 1977. The artist mused that the 96ft bat 'seemed to connect earth and sky the way a tornado does.' Hmm… See it for yourself in front of the Harold Washington Social Security Center.

top picks

CHICAGO PHOTO OPPORTUNITIES

In addition to the sights we've listed in our 'Postcard Perspective' tour (p60), get your camera ready for these classic shots:

- Mr Beef sign (p145)
- Wrigley Field front entrance sign (p81)
- Chicago skyline from North Ave Beach (p78)
- 'Chicago' sign at the Brown Line El station
- Harpo Studios sign (p97)

CHICAGO FIRE DEPARTMENT ACADEMY Map pp98–9

☎ 312-747-7239; 558 W DeKoven St; 🚌 8

Rarely has a public building been placed in a more appropriate place: the fire department's school stands on the very spot where the 1871 fire began – between Clinton and Jefferson Sts. Although there's no word on whether junk mail still shows up for Mrs O'Leary, the academy trains firefighters so they'll be ready the next time somebody, or some critter, kicks over a lantern (see p21).

OLD ST PATRICK'S CHURCH Map pp98–9

☎ 312-648-1021; www.oldstpats.org; 700 W Adams St; Ⓜ Blue Line to UIC-Halsted

A Chicago fire survivor, this 1852 church is not only the city's oldest but also one of its fastest-growing, thanks to the strategies of its politically connected former pastor, Father Jack Wall. Old St Pat's is best known for its year-round calendar of social events for singles, including the enormously popular World's Largest Block Party; this is a weekend-long party with big-name rock bands where Catholic singles can flirt. (No less an authority than Oprah has proclaimed the block party the best place to meet one's match.) The social programs have certainly boosted Old St Pat's membership, which has gone from four (yes, four) in 1983 to thousands two decades later. The domed steeple signifies the Eastern Church; the spire signifies the Western Church. Call to find out when the church is open so you can see the beautifully restored Celtic-patterned interior.

UNITED CENTER Map pp98–9

☎ 312-455-4650; www.unitedcenter.com; 1901 W Madison St; 🚌 19

Built for $175 million and opened in 1992, the United Center arena is home to the Bulls and the Blackhawks (see p211), and is the venue for special events such as the circus. The statue of an airborne Michael Jordan in front of the east entrance pays a lively tribute to the man whose talents financed the edifice. The center, surrounded by parking lots, is OK by day but gets pretty edgy at night – unless there's a game, in which case squads of cops are everywhere in order to ensure public safety.

GARFIELD PARK CONSERVATORY Map pp98–9

☎ 312-746-5100; www.garfield-conservatory.org; 300 N Central Park Blvd; admission free; 🕒 9am-5pm Fri-Wed, to 8pm Thu; Ⓜ Green Line to Conservatory

With 4.5 acres under glass, the Park District's pride and joy, built in 1907, seemed like a lost cause in 1994. Located far away from the heart of the city, in a neighborhood that tended to scare away visitors, the conservatory nevertheless began a multimillion-dollar restoration campaign. By 2000 it was completed, and the crowds have been pouring in ever since. One of the original designers, Jens Jensen, intended for the 5000 palms, ferns and other plants to re-create what Chicago looked like during prehistoric times. Today the effect continues – all that's missing is a rampaging stegosaurus. The Economic House features a fascinating range of plants that are used for food, medicine and shelter. New halls contain displays of seasonal plants, which are especially spectacular in the weeks before Easter. A children's garden lets kids play with plants that aren't rare or irreplaceable, and a Demonstration Garden was added in 2002 to help answer the questions of the wide-eyed urban gardeners who come here. If you drive, note that the neighborhood is still not the safest.

PILSEN

NATIONAL MUSEUM OF MEXICAN ART Map pp98–9

☎ 312-738-1503; www.nationalmuseumofmexicanart.org; 1852 W 19th St; admission free; 🕒 10am-5pm Tue-Sun; Ⓜ Blue Line to 18th St

Founded in 1982, this vibrant museum has become one of the best in the city. Housed in a renovated field house in Harrison Park, the gleaming exhibit space tackles a bewilderingly complex task (summing up 1000 years of Mexican art and culture), and pulls it off beautifully. The art here ranges from classical-themed portraits to piles of carved minibus tires. The turbulent politics and revolutionary leaders of Mexican history are well represented, including works about Cesar Chavez and Emiliano Zapata. The museum also sponsors readings by top authors and performances by musicians and artists. And if you are in town during the fall, be sure to check out the exhibits and celebrations relating to November 1,

IT'S FREE

Heck, we'd pay for the following sights and activities; luckily we don't have to. Don't forget, too, about the blues, jazz and other free music fests in Grant Park all summer long, as well as the museum free days listed throughout this chapter.

- There are so many freebies on offer at Millennium Park (p53) it's hard to keep track: free tours of the avant-garde park grounds, free concerts by the Grant Park orchestra (p193) and free yoga and workouts on Saturday mornings (p204).
- You think stained glass is for squares? We did too, until we came upon the Smith Museum of Stained Glass Windows (p67), stuck in a hallway of Navy Pier.
- You'll find unlimited access to aardvarks and elephants at Lincoln Park Zoo (p78) – all day long!
- Your views on Mexican art will never be the same once you've visited the National Museum of Mexican Art (p101) – it's that good.
- There's something about seeing Cary Grant and Ingrid Bergman smooch under the stars at the Outdoor Film Festival (p14) that you just don't get at home watching them on your DVD player.

the Day of the Dead, a traditional Mexican holiday that combines the festive with the religious. The events take place for a month on either side of the day. The on-site store is a winner, with brightly painted Mexican handicrafts filling its shelves.

PILSEN MURALS Map pp98–9

Ⓜ Blue Line to 18th St

Murals are a traditional Mexican art form, and they're splashed all over Pilsen's buildings. Check out the exterior wall of the Cooper Dual Language Academy (1645 W 18th Pl), the canvas for a 1990s tile mosaic that shows a diverse range of Mexican images, from a portrait of farmworker advocate Dolores Huerta to the Virgin of Guadalupe. Each summer, art students add more panels.

Local artist Jose Guerrero leads the highly recommended Pilsen Mural Tours (☎ 773-342-4191; 1½hr tour $100) where you can learn more about the neighborhood's images; call to arrange an excursion.

PILSEN GALLERIES Map pp98–9

near intersection of Halsted & 18th Sts; Ⓜ Blue Line to 18th St

Seven years ago the Pilsen galleries were the punk rockers of the Chicago art world. Few of them had phone numbers, most were only open on Saturday, and many were located in the 'curator's' living room. The galleries were run by 20-somethings, showcasing art by 20-somethings, and the rules that governed the commercially oriented 'white cubes' of River North and West Loop galleries didn't apply here.

Since then, though, the scene has matured, and seeing art in Pilsen no longer requires stepping over upended furniture (or upended artists) sprawled out from a party the night before. A great time to come here is on Second Fridays, when the dozen or so Pilsen galleries – known collectively as the Chicago Arts District (www.chicagoartsdistrict.org) – all stay open late on the second Friday of each month to welcome throngs of wandering art patrons with wine, snacks, and freshly hung paintings, ceramics and photos. The galleries, with a few notable exceptions, are located on S Halsted St, just south of 18th St.

Some of the best bets in Pilsen include the eclectic Parts Unknown Gallery (☎ 312-492-9058; www.partsunknown.org; 645 W 18th St; 🕑 11am-5pm Tue-Sat), the ceramics-oriented Dubhe Carreno Gallery (☎ 312-666-3150; www.dubhecarrenogallery.com; 1841 S Halsted St; 🕑 11am-5pm Tue-Sat) and 4Art Inc (☎ 312-850-1816; www.4artinc.com; #100, 1932 S Halsted St; 🕑 10am-6pm Tue-Sat), which specializes in large-scale group shows.

PILSEN CHURCHES Map pp98–9

Ⓜ Blue Line to 18th St

Some wonderful European-influenced churches remain throughout Pilsen. The 1914 St Adalbert Church (1650 W 17th St) features 185ft steeples and is a good example of the soaring religious structures built by Chicago's ethnic populations through thousands of small donations from parishioners, who would cut family budgets to the bone to make their weekly contribution. The rich ornamentation in the interior of this Catholic church glorifies Polish saints and religious figures. The Poles had St Adalbert's; the Irish had St Pius (1901 S Ashland Ave), a Romanesque revival edifice built between 1885 and 1892. Its smooth masonry contrasts with the rough stones of its contemporaries. Catholics of one ethnic group never attended the churches of the others, which explains why this part of town, with its concentration of Catholic immigrants, is thick with steeples.

WEST LOOP GALLERIES

Walking Tour

The West Loop galleries may be less well known that those in River North, but this is contemporary art central.

1 FLATFILE galleries Stepping into FLATFILE (p100) is like visiting several galleries in one. Cavernous rooms upstairs host contemporary, often abstract, painting. And downstairs look for international and Chicago-based photography – from slickly futuristic fashion shoots to strange Central European nudes. Staff members here are young and friendly.

2 Packer Schopf Gallery Ring the buzzer and find your way up the narrow old stairs (if they answer) to Packer Schopf Gallery (p100). Artists in all media exhibit here, but it's the 'outsider art' that has the sharpest edge. Some exhibits are not for the easily offended.

3 W Randolph St Eateries Before you have an art overload, take time out for reflection at one of the trendy eateries that keep popping up along W Randolph St. The north side of the street, between N Peoria and N Green Sts, is chockablock full of 'em.

4 Rhona Hoffman Gallery At 118 N Peoria St, you'll find one of the several West Loop buildings that contain a veritable warren of galleries. This one includes the Rhona Hoffman Gallery (p100), which has been showing contemporary art from all media since 1976. Both emerging and established artists are represented.

WALK FACTS

Start FLATFILE galleries
Finish McCormick Gallery
Duration Two hours
Fuel Stop W Randolph St eateries

5 Bodybuilder & Sportsman Across the street, ring the doorbell to get into Bodybuilder & Sportsman (p100). Run by School of the Art Institute of Chicago grad Tony Wight, the space stole the name from the onetime sporting goods shop it used to occupy. Paintings, drawings and video works tend to poke holes in the over-inflated art world.

6 McCormick Gallery Abstract expressionism and mid-century modern art are the specialties of the McCormick Gallery (p100). Other galleries at the same 835 W Washington address host minishows, and 30-something contemporary artists, many of them from the Chicago area.

SOUTH LOOP & NEAR SOUTH SIDE

Eating p164; Shopping p135; Sleeping p229

High-rise lofts and luxury condos have sprouted up everywhere in the South Loop. It seems Chicagoans can't resist this prime real estate that includes the lower ends of downtown and Grant Park, plus the lakefront Museum Campus and Soldier Field. The students of Columbia College add an artsy veneer to the proceedings. And guess what? Developers decided to keep on building; condos and townhomes now spread all the way down through the Near South Side.

Visitors will certainly experience all this shiny new-ness firsthand, as it's impossible not to make your way here during a Chicago stay. The South Loop is where the Big Three – the Field Museum, Shedd Aquarium and Adler Planetarium – sit side-by-side on the lakeshore, alongside forgotten 12th St Beach. Cafés and restaurants have finally colonized the area, so you no longer have to starve while museum-going.

Blues fans will want to make the pilgrimage further south to the old Chess Records site, a humble building where Muddy Waters and Howlin' Wolf plugged in their amps and paved the way for rock 'n' roll. History buffs will appreciate mansion-full Prairie Ave between 16th and 20th Sts, where the millionaires lived before the opium dens and hookers moved in from the Levee District four blocks west.

And finally, to top off the wealth of neighborhood offerings, there's Chinatown. It's a brilliant place to stuff your face with dim sum, bubble teas and heaping bowls of spicy noodles.

SOUTH LOOP

FIELD MUSEUM OF NATURAL HISTORY Map pp106–7

☎ 312-922-9410; www.fieldmuseum.org; 1400 S Lake Shore Dr; adult/child 4-11yr $12/7, some exhibits extra, admission discounted selected Mon & Tue Sep-Feb; 9am-5pm, last admission 4pm; 146

With over 70 PhD-wielding scientists and 20 million artifacts, you know things are going to be hopping at the Field Museum. The big attraction is the *Tyrannosaurus rex* named Sue, a 13ft-tall, 41ft-long beast who menaces the grand space with ferocious aplomb. Sue, the most complete *T rex* ever discovered, takes its name from Sue Hendrickson, the fossil-hunter who found the 90%-complete skeleton in South Dakota in 1990.

The head honchos at the Field know how large dinosaurs loom large in the grade-school imagination, which is why Sue is just one of many dinosaur-related exhibits here. 'Evolving Planet' has more of the big guys and gals. You can also watch staff paleontologists clean up fossils, learn about the evolution of the massive reptiles, and even learn about *Homo sapiens*' evolutionary ties to the extinct beasts.

A clever blend of the fanciful with a large amount of Field artifacts, the 'Inside Ancient Egypt' exhibit re-creates an Egyptian burial chamber on three levels. The mastaba (tomb) contains 23 actual mummies and is a reconstruction of the one built for Unis-ankh, the son of the last pharaoh of the Fifth dynasty, who died at age 21 in 2407 BC. The bottom level, with its twisting caverns, is especially worthwhile. Those reeds growing in the stream are real.

Other displays worth your time include 'Underground Adventure,' a vast exhibit exploring the habitats of animals and insects that live underground, and the 'Pawnee Earth Lodge,' which allows visitors to explore a complete dwelling of the Great Plains tribe.

If there's a dinosaur lover in your life, drop by one of the on-site stores (Sue actu-

TRANSPORTATION: SOUTH LOOP & NEAR SOUTH SIDE

Bus Number 146 to the Museum Campus/Soldier Field; 1 to Prairie Ave and sights on S Michigan Ave.

El Red, Green, Orange Lines to Roosevelt for Museum Campus/Soldier Field; Red Line to Harrison for Printer's Row and photography museum; Red Line to Cermak-Chinatown for Chinatown.

Metra Roosevelt Rd stop for Museum Campus/Soldier Field; 18th St for Prairie Ave Historic District; 23rd St for McCormick Place.

Parking The Museum Campus boasts plenty of lot parking; meter parking is available but scarce in the South Loop, and readily available in Near South Side.

VOICES: MIKI GREENBERG

Miki has lived in Chicago for more than 25 years. During that time, he's been a musician with innumerable bands and Ira Glass' 'tape guy' (ie he duplicated cassette tapes for listeners who wanted copies of *This American Life* – this was in the days before podcasts). Miki is currently the café manager at the Old Town School of Folk Music.

What's your favorite museum? The Shedd Aquarium. When else do you get the chance to stand 10ft away from beluga whales? When you're finished, you can walk through all the rooms of colored fish. And outside you can have a picnic by the lake.

Any other favorites? The Lincoln Park Conservatory. It's a half hour of heaven. The smells, the feeling in the air – there's desert, jungle, orchids – you tour the world through plants. It makes you forget everything, like you've just gone on a vacation. And it's free.

What's your favorite activity? Bike riding at sunrise along the lakefront. It's not crowded, and it looks different every day you go. It's the most romantic date you can take someone on. Bring a blanket, and some cereal and juice.

Where's the top place you'd take a visitor to town? Millennium Park's Crown Fountain. No matter where you're from, you've never seen anything like it. There are always people having fun in it, kids running around in an inch of water, all these people getting soaking wet without planning for it. It's so spontaneous.

ally has her very own store, near where she stands).

SHEDD AQUARIUM Map pp106–7

☎ 312-939-2438; www.sheddaquarium.org; 1200 S Lake Shore Dr; pass to all exhibits adult/child 3-11yr $27.50/20.50, aquarium-only ticket adult/child 3-11yr $8/6; 9am-6pm Jun-Aug, to 10pm some Thu, reduced hr Sep-May; 146

The world's largest assortment of finned, gilled, amphibious and other aquatic creatures swims within the marble-clad confines of the John G Shedd Aquarium. Though it could simply rest on its superlative exhibits – say, beluga whales in a 4-million-gallon aquarium – the Shedd makes a point of trying to tie concepts of ecosystems, food webs and marine biology into its presentation of supercool animals. Permanent exhibits include the multilevel oceanarium, which mimics ocean conditions off the northwest coast of North America. The beluga whales inside are remarkably cute creatures that come from the pint-sized end of the whale scale. Their humped heads and natural 'smiles' make them look eerily human. You'll also see Pacific white-sided dolphins, harbor seals and sea otters. Don't linger only on the main floor – you can go underneath the cement seats and watch the mammals from below through viewing windows. The 'Wild Reef' exhibit will have sharkophiles and sharkophobes equally entranced; over a dozen sharks cut through the waters in a simulation of a Philippines reef ecosystem. And the 'Amazon Rising' exhibits offer a captivating look at a year in the Amazon River and rain forest. Some of the newer and special exhibits sell out early in the morning; consider buying tickets on the website beforehand to ensure entry.

The stretch of grass on the lake between the Shedd and the Adler begs for your camera. One look toward the skyline will show you why: the view is good year-round; on clear winter days, when the lake partially freezes and steam rises off the Loop buildings, it verges on the sensational.

ADLER PLANETARIUM & ASTRONOMY MUSEUM Map pp106–7

☎ 312-922-7827; www.adlerplanetarium.org; 1300 S Lake Shore Dr; adult/child 4-17yr $10/6, plus $13 for sky show, admission free selected Mon & Tue Sep-Feb; 9:30am-6pm Jun-Aug, 9:30am-4:30pm Sep-May; 146

The first planetarium built in the western hemisphere, the Adler has seen visitor numbers soar in recent years. From the entrance, visitors descend below the 1930's building, which has 12 sides, one for each sign of the zodiac. In the newest wing, a digital sky show re-creates such cataclysmic phenomena as supernovas. Interactive exhibits allow you to simulate cosmic events such as a meteor hitting the earth (this one is especially cool). The original planetarium does a good job planning special events around celestial occurrences, be they eclipses or National Aeronautics & Space Administration (NASA) missions. In the Sky Theater a mechanical Zeiss projector can create a huge variety of nighttime sky effects.

SOUTH LOOP & NEAR SOUTH SIDE

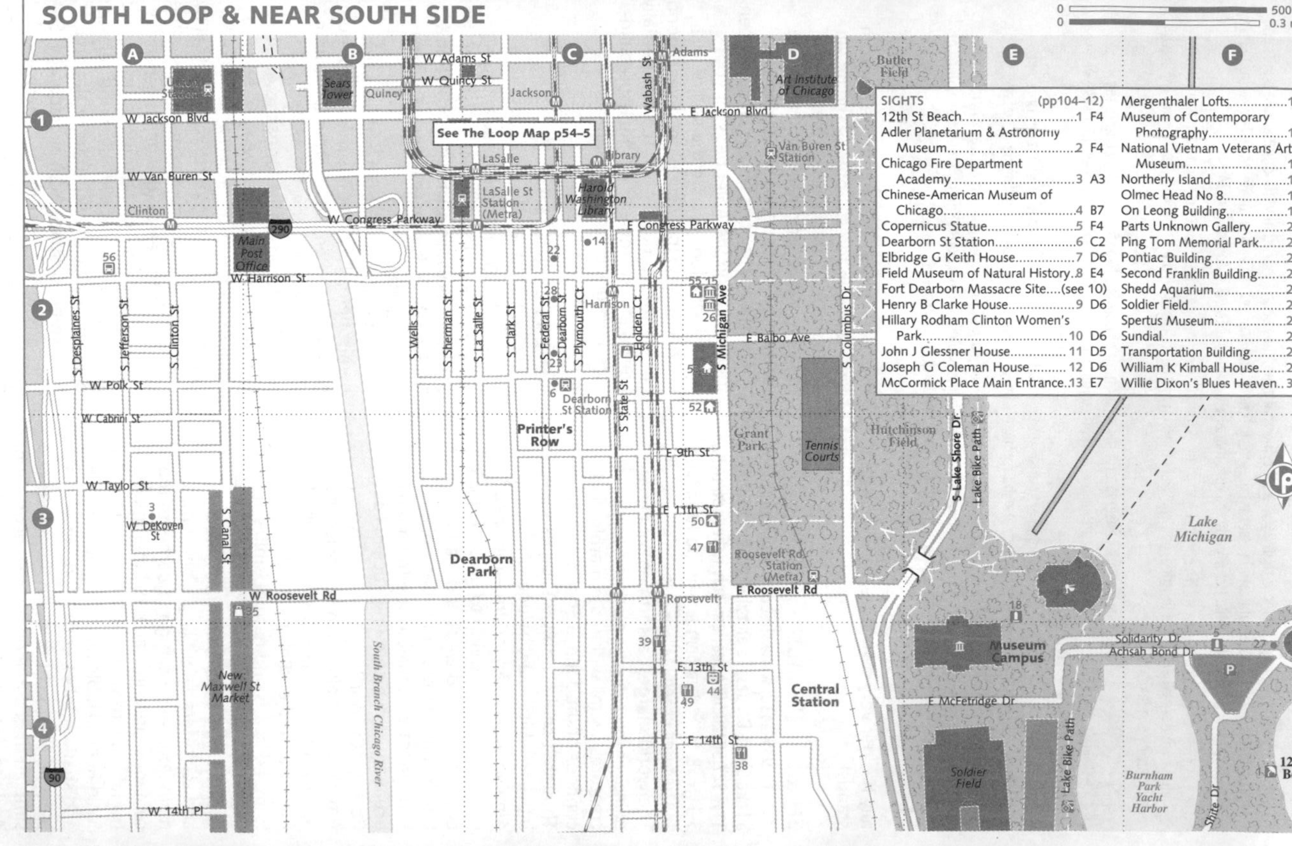

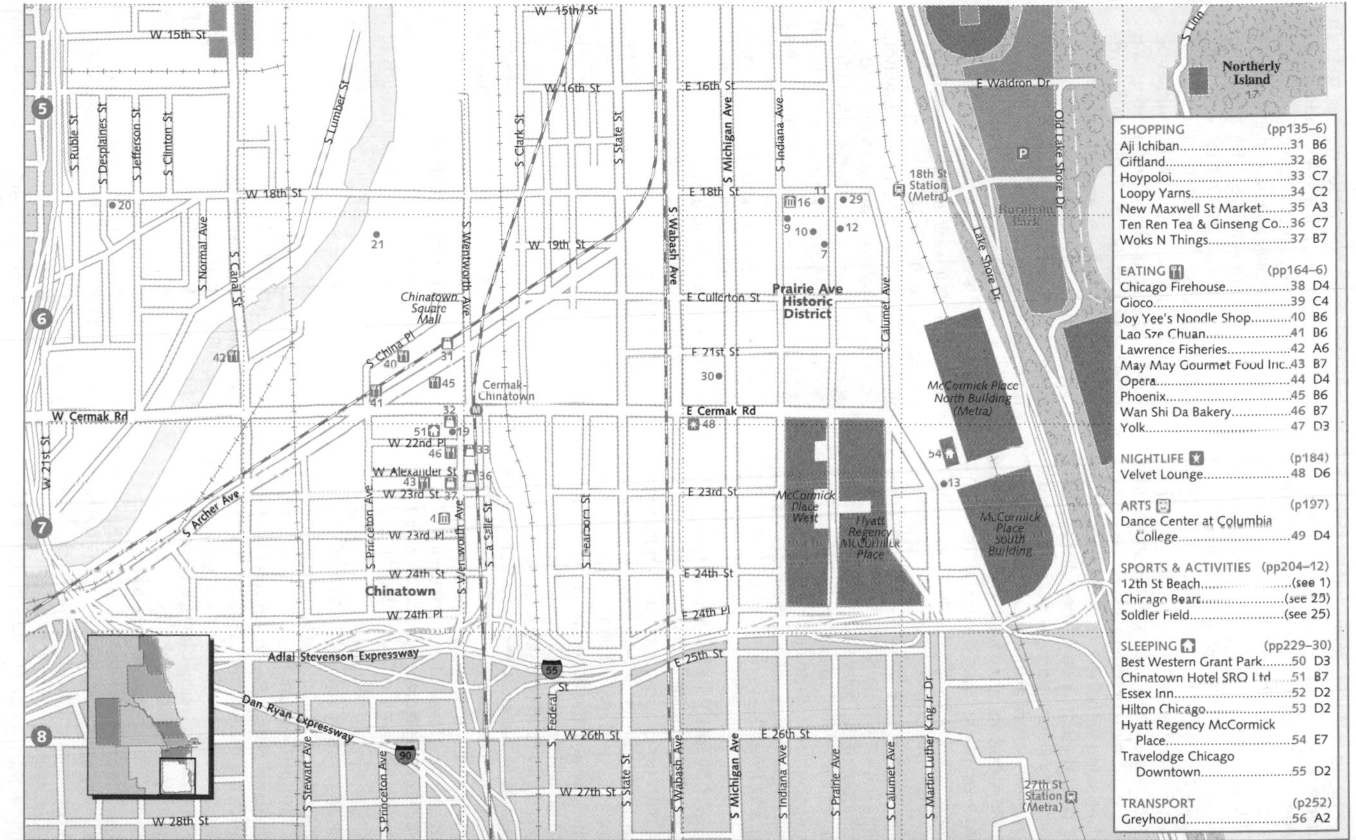
SHOPPING (pp135–6)
Aji Ichiban....31 B6
Giftland....32 B6
Hoypoloi....33 C7
Loopy Yarns....34 C2
New Maxwell St Market....35 A3
Ten Ren Tea & Ginseng Co....36 C7
Woks N Things....37 B7
EATING (pp164–6)
Chicago Firehouse....38 D4
Gioco....39 C4
Joy Yee's Noodle Shop....40 B6
Lao Sze Chuan....41 B6
Lawrence Fisheries....42 A6
May May Gourmet Food Inc....43 B7
Opera....44 D4
Phoenix....45 B6
Wan Shi Da Bakery....46 B7
Yolk....47 D3
NIGHTLIFE (p184)
Velvet Lounge....48 D6
ARTS (p197)
Dance Center at Columbia College....49 D4
SPORTS & ACTIVITIES (pp204–12)
12th St Beach....(see 1)
Chicago Bears....(see 25)
Soldier Field....(see 25)
SLEEPING (pp229–30)
Best Western Grant Park....50 D3
Chinatown Hotel SRO Ltd....51 B7
Essex Inn....52 D2
Hilton Chicago....53 D2
Hyatt Regency McCormick Place....54 E7
Travelodge Chicago Downtown....55 D2
TRANSPORT (p252)
Greyhound....56 A2
Northerly Island
S Linn
E Waldron Dr
Old Lake Shore Dr
Lake Shore Dr
Burnham Park
18th St Station (Metra)
27th St Station (Metra)
McCormick Place North Building (Metra)
McCormick Place South Building
McCormick Place West
Hyatt Regency McCormick Place
Prairie Ave Historic District
Chinatown
Chinatown Square Mall
Cermak-Chinatown
Adlai Stevenson Expressway
Dan Ryan Expressway
S Archer Ave
W Cermak Rd
E Cermak Rd
W 15th St
W 16th St
E 16th St
W 18th St
E 18th St
W 19th St
E Cullerton St
E 21st St
W 21st St
W 22nd Pl
W Alexander St
W 23rd St
E 23rd St
W 23rd Pl
W 24th St
E 24th St
W 24th Pl
E 24th Pl
E 25th St
W 26th St
E 26th St
W 27th St
W 28th St
S Ruble St
S Desplaines St
S Jefferson St
S Clinton St
S Normal Ave
S Canal St
S Lumber St
S China Pl
S Wentworth Ave
S Clark St
S La Salle St
S State St
S Dearborn St
S Federal St
S Wabash Ave
S Michigan Ave
S Indiana Ave
S Prairie Ave
S Calumet Ave
S Martin Luther King Jr Dr
S Princeton Ave
S Stewart Ave

The Adler does a commendable job of involving visitors in astronomy, with live video links to telescopes around the world and research facilities that are totally accessible to visitors. The sky show programs last about 50 minutes. The whole place can be easily covered in less than two hours. On the first Friday night of every month – aka Far Out Fridays – the Adler's astronomers bring out their telescopes and let you view the skies along with them (adult/child $20/17).

Near the entrance to the Adler, a 12ft sundial by Henry Moore is dedicated to the golden years of astronomy, from 1930 to 1980, when so many fundamental discoveries were made using the first generation of huge telescopes. About 100yd west, in the median, the bronze Copernicus statue shows the 16th-century Polish astronomer Nicolaus Copernicus holding a compass and a model of the solar system. But the best thing about the Adler's entrance? Its front steps, which are the city's most renowned make-out spot (perhaps the romance sparks from the sexy city view).

12TH STREET BEACH Map pp106–7

1200 S Lake Shore Dr; 🚌 146

A path runs south from the planetarium to 12th St Beach, where you can climb the rocks to the breakwater for good views of the lake and the fishermen who are likely to be casting there. Despite the beach's proximity to the Museum Campus and its zillions of visitors, the crescent-shaped sand sliver remains bizarrely (but happily) secluded. Beach bonus: if you can't get tickets to see your favorite band at Charter One Pavilion (see Northerly Island, below), you can sit here and still hear the tunes.

NORTHERLY ISLAND Map pp106–7

1400 S Linn White Dr; 🚌 146

A bit further south from the Adler Planetarium and 12th St Beach, Northerly Island was once the busy commuter airport known as Meigs Field. Now it's a prairie-grassed park with walking trails, fishing, bird-watching and the (allegedly temporary) Charter One Pavilion (☎ 312-540-2668; www.charteronepavilion.com) outdoor concert venue. The shift from runway to willowy grasses has its root in a controversial incident that reads a little like a municipal spy thriller, complete with midnight operatives and surprise bulldozings. To sum it up: Mayor Daley wanted the land for a park; businesses wanted to keep it for their private planes. A standoff ensued. Then, one dark night in March 2003, Daley fired up the heavy machinery and razed the airfield while the city slept. His reasoning? Terrorists could attack Chicago with tiny planes launched from Meigs; the airfield was a security liability. Why it couldn't be jackhammered during daylight hours was never answered. But by 2005, the controversy had died down, and Chicagoans were out in force, happily exploring this beautiful piece of lakefront that had been off-limits for a half century.

SOLDIER FIELD Map pp106–7

☎ 312-235-7000; www.soldierfield.net; 1410 S Museum Campus Dr; 🚌 146

Built between 1922 and 1926 to pay homage to WWI soldiers, the oft-renovated edifice has been home to everything from civil rights speeches by Martin Luther King Jr to Brazilian soccer games. It got its latest UFO-landing-upon-a-Greek-ruin look in a controversial 2003 makeover. Prior to that, the stadium's architecture was so noteworthy it was named a National Historic Landmark. Unfortunately, the landmark lacked corporate skyboxes and giant bathrooms, so the city (the venue is owned by the park district) decided it was time for a change. The new look met almost unanimous derision when it was unveiled; critics quickly dubbed it 'the Mistake on the Lake.' The landmark folks agreed and whacked it from their list, saying it jeopardized the national landmark integrity. And that was that. The Bears play football here in the fall and early winter; see p212 for ticket details. Stadium tours are available for groups of 10 or more; call ☎ 312-235-7244 for details. Advance booking is required.

MUSEUM OF CONTEMPORARY PHOTOGRAPHY Map pp106–7

☎ 312-663-5554; www.mocp.org; Columbia College, 600 S Michigan Ave; admission free; 🕓 10am-5pm Mon-Sat, to 8pm Thu, noon-5pm Sun; Ⓜ Red Line to Harrison

This museum focuses on American photography since 1937, and is the only institution of its kind between the coasts. The permanent collection includes the works of Debbie Fleming Caffery, Mark Klett, Catherine Wagner, Patrick Nagatani and 500 more of the best photographers working today.

Special exhibitions augment the rotating permanent collection.

SPERTUS MUSEUM Map pp106–7

☎ 312-322-1700; www.spertus.edu; 610 S Michigan Ave; call for admission price; 🕑 10am-5pm Sun-Wed, to 7pm Thu, to 3pm Fri; Ⓜ Red Line to Harrison

Located in a mod, brand-spanking-new facility, Spertus explores 5000 years of Jewish faith and culture. The Zell Holocaust Memorial – the country's first permanent museum exhibition of its kind – features oral histories from survivors who emigrated to Chicago, as well as the names of Chicagoans' relatives who died.

The museum mounts well-curated special exhibitions that cover topics as diverse as Biblical images in classical art and Jewish humor in the US. The basement is devoted to a children's area called the ARTiFACT Center, where kids can conduct their own archeological dig for artifacts of Jewish life.

OLMEC HEAD NO 8 Map pp106–7

🚌 146

Near the Field Museum, the city has installed Olmec Head No 8. Over 7ft tall, it's a copy of one of the many amazing stone carvings done by the Olmec people more than 3500 years ago in what is now the Veracruz state of Mexico. No one has been able to figure out how the Olmec carved the hard volcanic rock.

PRINTER'S ROW Map pp106–7

Dearborn St btwn Congress Pkwy & Polk St; Ⓜ Red Line to Harrison

Chicago was a center for printing at the turn of the 20th century, and the rows of buildings on S Dearborn St from W Congress Pkwy south to W Polk St housed the heart of the city's publishing industry. By the 1970s the printers had left for more-economical quarters elsewhere, and the buildings had been largely emptied out, some of them barely getting by on the feeble rents of obscure nonprofit groups.

In the late 1970s savvy developers saw the potential in these derelicts, and one of the most successful gentrification projects in Chicago began. The following describes some of the notable buildings in the area as you travel from north to south.

A snazzy renovation of the Mergenthaler Lofts (531 S Plymouth Ct), the 1886 headquarters for the legendary linotype company, included the artful preservation of a diner storefront. The Pontiac Building (542 S Dearborn St), a classic 1891 design by Holabird & Roche, features the same flowing masonry surfaces as the firm's Monadnock Building, to the north.

A massive and once-windowless wreck, the 1911 Transportation Building (600 S Dearborn St) enjoyed a 1980 restoration that assured the neighborhood had arrived. The Second Franklin Building (720 S Dearborn St), a 1912 factory, shows the history of printing in its tiled facade. The roof slopes to allow for a huge skylight over the top floor where books were hand-bound; this building existed long before fluorescent lights or high-intensity lamps. The large windows on many of the other buildings in the area serve the same purpose.

Once the Chicago terminal of the Santa Fe Railroad, the 1885 Dearborn St Station (47 W Polk St) used to be the premier station for trains to and from California. Today it merely sees the trains of parent-propelled strollers from the Dearborn Park neighborhood, built on the site of the tracks to the south.

NEAR SOUTH SIDE

CHINATOWN Map pp106–7

intersection of Cermak Rd & Wentworth Ave; Ⓜ Red Line to Cermak-Chinatown

Chinatown's charm is best enjoyed by going from bakery to bakery, nibbling chestnut cakes and almond cookies, then shopping for Hello Kitty trinkets and tea in the small shops. Old Chinatown stretches along Wentworth Ave south of Cermak, and is the neighborhood's traditional retail heart (and a good place to purchase a turtle). Chinatown Square, along Archer Ave north of Cermak, is the newer commerce district; it's filled with restaurants and at its wonderful noisiest on weekends.

When you're not stuffing your face, you can check out a couple of sights. Ping Tom Memorial Park (300 W 19th St), behind the square, offers dramatic city-railroad-bridge views. The On Leong Building (Pui Tak Center; 2216 S Wentworth Ave) stands out in old Chinatown. It once housed neighborhood service organizations and some illegal gambling operations that led to spectacular police raids. It now houses the Chinese Merchants Association. Built in 1928, the grand structure is a fantasy of Chinese architecture that makes good use of glazed terra-cotta details. Note how the lions guarding the door have twisted their heads so they don't have to risk bad luck by turning their backs to each other. The small Chinese-American Museum of Chicago (☎ 312-949-1000; www.ccamuseum.org; 238 W 23rd St; adult/child $2/1; 9:30am-1:30pm Fri, 10am-5pm Sat & Sun) is a couple of blocks south. Along with displays of historical artifacts donated by the community, the museum hosts interesting cultural lectures such as 'Chop Suey: The American Passion for non-Chinese Chinese Food.'

The neighborhood keeps growing, with its affluent residents developing land in all directions even as more immigrants arrive.

WILLIE DIXON'S BLUES HEAVEN

Map pp106–7

☎ 312-808-1286; www.bluesheaven.com; 2120 S Michigan Ave; tours $10; noon-3pm Mon-Fri, to 2pm Sat, reservations required; 1

From 1957 to 1967, this humble building was the home of the legendary Chess Records, a temple of blues and a spawning ground of rock 'n' roll. The Chess brothers, two Polish Jews, ran the recording studio that saw – and heard – the likes of Muddy Waters, Bo Diddley, Koko Taylor and others. Chuck Berry recorded four 'Top 10' singles here, and the Rolling Stones named a song '2120 S Michigan Ave' after a recording session at this spot in 1964. (Rock trivia buffs will know that the Stones named themselves after the Muddy Waters song 'Rolling Stone.')

Today the building belongs to Willie Dixon's Blues Heaven, a nonprofit group, set up by the late blues great who often recorded at the studios, to promote blues and preserve its legacy. A gift store is open in front, while the old studios are upstairs. There are many artifacts on hand as well.

More often than not visitors will meet AJ Tribble, Blues Heaven docent and Willie Dixon's nephew. Dixon, by the way, was the guy who wrote most of Chess' hits and the one who summed up the genre best: 'Blues is the roots, and everything else is the fruits.'

NATIONAL VIETNAM VETERANS ART MUSEUM

Map pp106–7

☎ 312-326-0270; www.nvvam.org; 1801 S Indiana Ave; adult/student $10/7; 11am-6pm Tue-Fri, 10am-5pm Sat; 1

Opened in 1996, the National Vietnam Veterans Art Museum displays the art of Americans who served in the military during the war in Vietnam. Spread over three floors in an old commercial building, it features a large and growing collection of haunting, angry, mournful and powerful works by veterans.

Cleveland Wright's *We Regret to Inform You* is a heartbreaking look at a mother in her kitchen at the moment she learns of her son's death. Joseph Fornelli's sculpture *Dressed to Kill* comments on the role of the average grunt in Vietnam. Some 58,000 dog tags hang from the ceiling, a haunting reminder of the Americans who died in the war. There's also a small café here that serves snacks.

The museum has run into financial troubles recently, and was pondering a takeover by the park district and subsequent move. Call before making the trip.

PRAIRIE AVENUE HISTORIC DISTRICT

pp106–7

1

By 1900 Chicago's crème de la crème had had enough of the scum de la scum in the nearby neighborhoods. Potter Palmer led a procession of millionaires north to new mansions on the Gold Coast. The once-pristine neighborhood, which lined Prairie Ave for several blocks south of 16th St, fell into quick decline as one mansion after another gave way to warehouses and industry, hookers and gin. Thanks to the efforts of the Chicago Architecture Foundation, a few of the prime homes from the area have also been carefully restored. Streets have been closed off, making the neighborhood a good place to stroll. A footbridge over the train tracks links the area to Burnham Park and the Museum Campus.

The John J Glessner House (☎ 312-326-1480; www.glessnerhouse.org; 1800 S Prairie Ave; tours adult/child $10/5, admission free Wed; tours 1pm & 3pm Wed-Sun) is the premier survivor of the neighborhood. Famed American architect Henry Hobson Richardson took full advantage of the corner site for this beautiful composition of rusticated granite. Built from 1885 to 1887, the L-shaped house, which surrounds a sunny southern courtyard, got a 100-year jump on the modern craze for interior courtyards. Much of the house's interior is reminiscent of an English manor house, with heavy wooden beams and other English-style details. Additionally, more than 80% of the current furnishings are authentic, thanks to the Glessner family's penchant for family photos.

The nearby Henry B Clarke House (☎ 312-326-1480; 1827 S Indiana Ave; tours adult/child $10/5, admission free Wed; ⌚ tours noon & 2pm Wed-Sun) is the oldest structure in the city. When Caroline and Henry Clarke built this imposing Greek revival home in 1836, log cabins were still the rage in Chicago residential architecture. The sturdy frame paid off – during the past 160 years the house has been moved twice to escape demolition. The present address is about as close as researchers can get to its somewhat undefined original location. The interior has been restored to the period of the Clarkes' occupation, which ended in 1872. A combination ticket (adult/child $15/8) to tour both the Clarke and Glessner houses is available.

Unfortunately, it's not possible for you to visit the following houses, but you still can admire them from the outside. Modeled after 15th-century French châteaus, the William K Kimball House (1801 S Prairie Ave) dates from 1890 to 1892. Both it and the Romanesque Joseph G Coleman House (1811 S Prairie Ave) now serve as the incongruous headquarters for the US Soccer Federation. Limestone puts a glitzy facade on the brick Elbridge G Keith House (1900 S Prairie Ave), an early 1870 home.

HILLARY RODHAM CLINTON WOMEN'S PARK Map pp106–7

🚌 1

Fronting on Prairie Ave, with the Glessner House to the north and the Clarke House to the west (see Prairie Ave Historic District, opposite), the 4-acre park is named for former first lady, now US Senator, Hillary Rodham Clinton, who grew up in suburban Park Ridge. Since she dedicated the park in 1997, landscapers have added a French garden, fountain and winding paths. As bright as its future looks, the park has a notorious past. The Fort Dearborn massacre, in which a group of local Native Americans rebelled against the incursion of white settlers, is thought to have occurred on this very spot on August 15, 1812.

MCCORMICK PLACE Map pp106–7

☎ 312-791-7000; www.mccormickplace.com; 2301 S Lake Shore Dr, main entrance on S Martin Luther King Jr Dr; Ⓜ Metra to 23rd St

Called the 'mistake by the lake' before the Soldier Field renovation stole the title, the McCormick Place convention center is an economic engine that drives up profits for the city's hotels, restaurants, shops and airlines. 'Vast' isn't big enough to describe it, nor 'huge,' and 'enormous' doesn't work, so settle for whatever word describes the biggest thing you've ever seen. The 2.7 million sq ft of meeting space spreads out over four halls, making this the largest convention center in the country.

UNEXPECTED MUSEUM CAMPUS

Walking Tour

Museum Campus is visited by millions of tourists every year, but the museums and sights still hold some surprises.

1 Field Museum of Natural History So you've heard of Sue, the *Tyrannosaurus rex* who resides at the Field Museum (p104). But did you know that the museum has hundreds of totem poles from the American northwest? Many of them were shipped to Chicago for the 1893 World Expo.

2 Shedd Aquarium Most everyone who comes to Shedd Aquarium (p105) wants to see the beluga whales. But did you know the players change? Seven North American aquariums cooperate in a breeding program that occasionally relocates members of the 40-strong population. Six calves have been born here since 1998.

3 Adler Planetarium & Astronomy Museum You knew you could explore black holes and see stars at the Adler Planetarium (p105). But did you realize that from out here, at the end of a peninsula jutting into Lake Michigan, you get some of the most complete city skyline views?

4 12th Street Beach Beaches are for sand and swimming, and 12th Street Beach (p108) is less populated than most. But did you know it's a concert venue as well? If you take your tour when there's a concert at Charter One

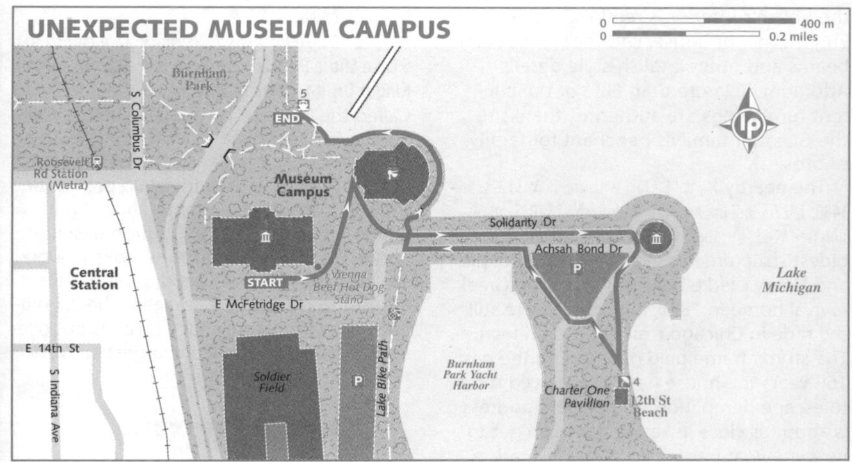

WALK FACTS

Start Field Museum of Natural History
Finish Water taxi to Navy Pier
Duration Six hours
Fuel stop Vienna Beef hot dog cart outside Field Museum

Pavilion, you can listen for free from the beach.

5 Water Taxi You planned on taking a bus, or schlepping all the way back to your Near North hotel. But why, when you can take a water taxi (p252) ride from here all the way to Navy Pier for $7. The sightseeing is thrown in gratis.

HYDE PARK & SOUTH SIDE

Eating p166; Shopping p136; Sleeping p230

The University of Chicago dominates Hyde Park and offers two things in great abundance: gargoyles atop its Gothic buildings, and Nobel Laureates in its hallowed halls (the school has more of the brainiacs per square inch than any other place on Earth). The neighborhood isn't everyone's cup of tea due to its distance from downtown, but it does have some worthy sights if you're willing to make the trip.

Two huge parks flank the neighborhood: Washington Park in the west and Jackson Park to the east. The latter is where the city held the 1893 World Expo, when the global spotlight swung this way and Chicago introduced the world to wonders such as the Ferris wheel, moving pictures and the zipper. The Museum of Science and Industry is a remnant of the grand structures built for the event, and it's really the area's main attraction today. Lagoons and Japanese gardens fill in the rest of the space. A long green strip of land called the Midway Plaisance connects Jackson and Washington parks; it's home to an ice rink and college students kicking around soccer balls. Stately Jackson Park Beach and rocky Promontory Point lie along Hyde Park's shoreline and offer cool breezes on hot days.

The intersection of 57th St and S University Ave is a great place to start your campus explorations. That'll put you close to the cool bookstores, Frank Lloyd Wright's Robie House and the site where the atomic age began.

The South Side is the generic term applied to Chicago's myriad neighborhoods (such as Hyde Park) to the south of roughly 25th St. Most of the area has had a tough time since WWII. Housing projects created impoverished neighborhoods where community ties were broken and gangs held sway. The landscape is still pretty bleak, but intrepid visitors will be rewarded with authentic soul food, blues and jazz, especially around 74th and 75th Sts. You'll need a car to get here.

HYDE PARK

MUSEUM OF SCIENCE & INDUSTRY

Map p114

☎ 773-684-1414; www.msichicago.org; cnr 57th St & S Lake Shore Dr; adult/child 3-11yr $11/7; 🕒 9:30am-4pm Mon-Sat, 11am-4pm Sun, to 5:30pm Jun-Aug; 🚍 6, Ⓜ Metra to 55th-56th-57th

This overstimulating museum will defeat even the most rambunctious six-year-old. (If you're older than six, give in now – you don't stand a chance.) Nine permanent exhibits thoroughly examine everything on Earth, from cerebral concepts like the passage of time to basic questions about the origins of breakfast cereal. Visitors can climb through a German U-boat ($5 extra to tour it) captured during WWII and press their noses against the window of the Apollo 8 command module. Some of the museum's most famous exhibits are also its simplest. The 'Human Body Slices' exhibit consists of a man and a woman who died in the 1940s – their bodies were cut in half-inch sections, then pressed between pieces of glass. Eeew, we know. But amazing all the same.

The main building of the museum served as the Palace of Fine Arts at the landmark 1893 World Expo, which was set in the surrounding Jackson Park. When you've had your fill of space capsules, coalmines and Zephyrs at the museum, the park makes an excellent setting to recuperate.

ROBIE HOUSE Map p114

☎ 773-834-1847; www.wrightplus.org; 5757 S Woodlawn Ave; adult/child 11-18yr $12/10; 🕒 tours 11am, 1pm & 3pm Mon-Fri, continuous tours 11am-3:30pm Sat & Sun; 🚍 6, Ⓜ Metra to 55th-56th-57th

This masterpiece is the ultimate expression of Frank Lloyd Wright's Prairie School style; it makes the otherwise charming surrounding houses look like dowdy old aunts. The long, thin Roman bricks and limestone trim mirror the same basic shape of the entire house. The long and low lines, which reflect Midwest topography, are ornamented solely by the exquisite stained- and leaded-glass doors and windows.

Tours take in only a portion of the interior, as it's currently undergoing renovation. In fact, it's pretty empty inside, though still worth checking out as the docents are incredibly knowledgeable about architecture. A gift shop with books and other mementos operates in the garage.

HYDE PARK & SOUTH SIDE

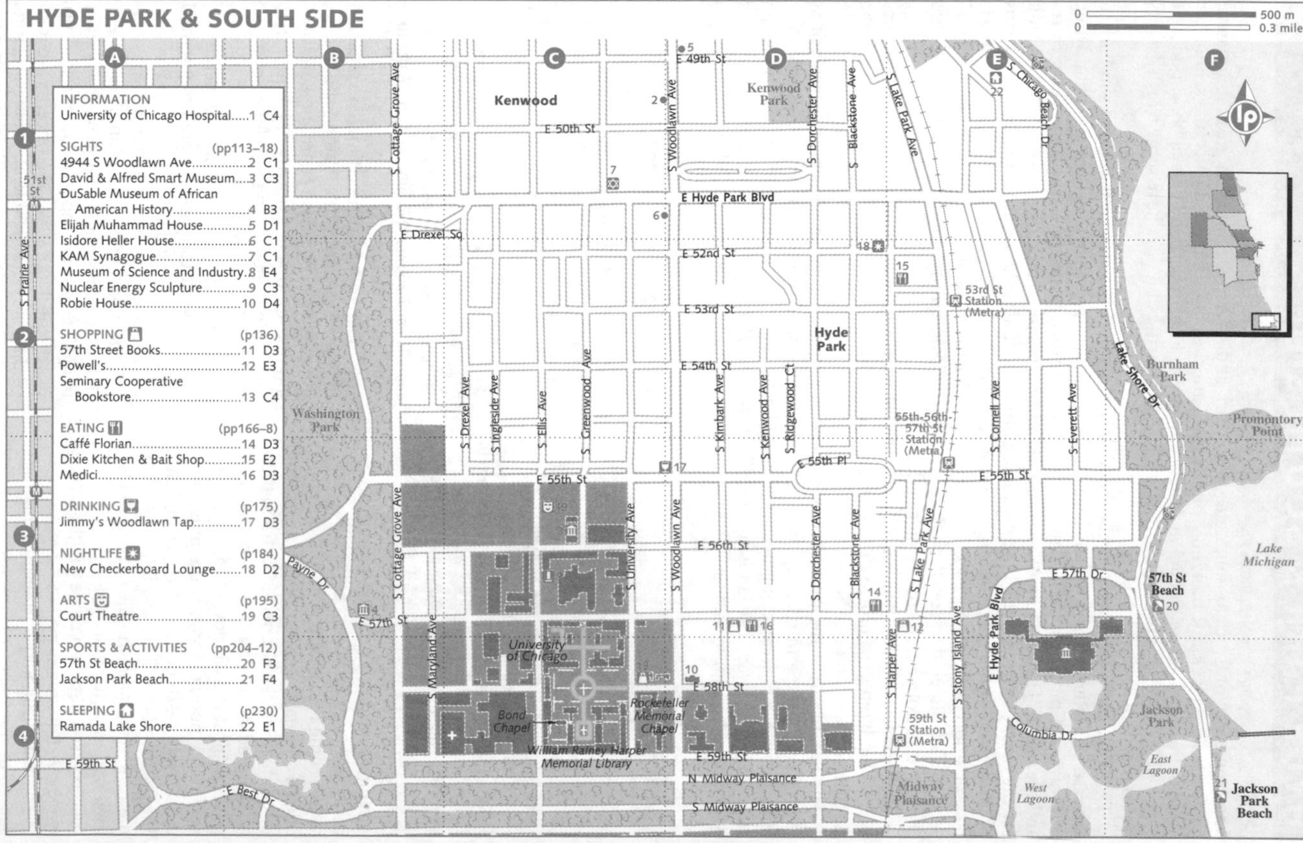

UNIVERSITY OF CHICAGO Map p114

☎ 773-702-1234; www.uchicago.edu; 5801 S Ellis Ave; 🚌 6, Ⓜ Metra to 55th-56th-57th

Some universities collect football championships. The University of Chicago collects Nobel Prizes – 80 so far and counting. In particular, the economics department has been a regular winner, with faculty and former students pulling in 23 prizes since the first Nobel for economics was awarded in 1969. Merton Miller, a University of Chicago economics faculty member and a Nobel Prize winner, explained the string of wins to the *Sun-Times:* 'It must be the water; it certainly can't be the coffee.'

The university's classes first met on October 1, 1892. John D Rockefeller was a major contributor to the institution, donating more than $35 million, calling it 'the best investment I ever made in my life.' The original campus was constructed in an English Gothic style. Highlights of a campus tour include the Rockefeller Memorial Chapel (5850 S Woodlawn), the exterior of which will send sculpture-lovers into paroxysms of joy – the facade bears 24 life-sized and 53 smaller religious figures, with even more inside. The William Rainey Harper Memorial Library (1116 E 59th St) is another must-see. The long row of arched, two-story windows bathes the 3rd-floor reading room with light and an almost medieval sense of calm. The Bond Chapel (1050 E 59th St) is equally serene. Built in 1926, the exquisite 300-seat chapel is the harmonious creation of the architects, sculptors, woodcarvers and glassmakers who worked together on the project.

On Ellis Ave, between 56th and 57th, sits the 1968 Henry Moore bronze sculpture, Nuclear Energy, marking the spot where Enrico Fermi and company started the nuclear age (see the boxed text, p116).

DAVID & ALFRED SMART MUSEUM OF ART Map p114

☎ 773-702-0200; http://smartmuseum.uchicago.edu; 5550 S Greenwood Ave; admission free; 🕑 10am-4pm Tue-Fri, to 8pm Thu, 11am-5pm Sat & Sun; 🚌 6, Ⓜ Metra to 55th-56th-57th

Named after the founders of *Esquire* magazine, who contributed the money to get it started, the official fine arts museum of the university opened in 1974 and expanded in 1999. The 8000 items in the collection include some excellent works from ancient China and Japan, and a colorful and detailed Syrian mosaic from about AD 600. The strength of the collection lies in the paintings and sculpture contemporary to the university's existence, including works by Arthur Davies, Jean Arp, Henry Moore and many others.

TRANSPORTATION: HYDE PARK & SOUTH SIDE

Bus Number 6 runs from State St in the Loop to 57th St in Hyde Park.

El Green Line to 35th St/Bronzeville/IIT is useful for Bronzeville and the Illinois Institute of Technology sights.

Metra 55th-56th-57th St station for Hyde Park, 53rd St station for Kenwood.

Parking Hyde Park can be tight. Free parking is available on the street and in university parking lots after 4pm weekdays and all day on weekends. If you're really stumped, look south of the Midway Plaisance. Other South Side neighborhoods shouldn't be a problem.

DUSABLE MUSEUM OF AFRICAN AMERICAN HISTORY Map p114

☎ 773-947-0600; www.dusablemuseum.org; 740 E 56th Pl; adult/child 6-13yr $3/1, admission free Sun; 🕑 10am-5pm Tue-Sat, noon-5pm Sun; 🚌 4

In a peaceful part of Washington Park, this newly expanded museum features more than 100 works of African American art and permanent exhibits that cover African Americans' experiences from slavery through the Civil Rights movement. The museum, housed in a 1910 building, takes its name from Chicago's first permanent settler, Jean Baptiste Pointe du Sable, a French Canadian of Haitian descent.

SOUTH SIDE

Keep an eye out for the Chicago Blues Museum (☎ 773-828-8118; chicagobluesmuseum@att.net). It had closed its Bronzeville facility at press time, but was promising to re-open somewhere in the neighborhood. Call or email for current details.

A BOMB IS BORN

At 3:53pm on December 2, 1942, Enrico Fermi looked at a small crowd of men around him and said, 'The reaction is self-sustaining.' The scene was a dank squash court under the abandoned football stadium in the heart of the University of Chicago. With great secrecy, the gathered scientists had just achieved the world's first controlled release of nuclear energy. More than one sigh of relief was heard amid the ensuing rounds of congratulations. The nuclear reactor was supposed to have been built in a remote corner of a forest preserve 20 miles away, but a labor strike had stopped work. The impatient scientists went ahead on campus, despite the objections of many who thought the thing might blow up and take a good part of the city with it. Places such as Los Alamos in New Mexico and Hiroshima and Nagasaki in Japan are more closely linked to the nuclear era, but Chicago is where it began.

BRONZEVILLE HISTORIC BUILDINGS

Map p50

Ⓜ Green Line to 35th-Bronzeville-IIT

Once home to Louis Armstrong and other notables, Bronzeville thrived as the vibrant center of black life in the city from 1920 to 1950, boasting an economic and cultural strength akin to New York's Harlem. Shifting populations, urban decay and the construction of a wall of public housing along State St led to Bronzeville's decline. A few years ago it started its comeback. Many young urban professionals have moved back to the neighborhood, and South Loop development stretches all the way here. Still, be careful at night; it's not a good place to be walking around after dark.

Examples of stylish architecture from the past can be found throughout Bronzeville, but some of the buildings are in miserable shape and aren't worthy of more than an inspection of the exterior. You can see some fine homes along two blocks of Calumet Ave between 31st and 33rd Sts, an area known as 'the Gap.' The buildings here include Frank Lloyd Wright's only row houses, the Robert W Roloson Houses (3213-3219 S Calumet Ave).

One of scores of Romanesque houses that date from the 1880s, the Ida B Wells House (3624 S Martin Luther King Jr Dr) is named for its 1920s resident. Wells was a crusading journalist who investigated lynchings and other racially motivated crimes. She coined the line: 'Eternal vigilance is the price of liberty.'

Gospel music got its start at Pilgrim Baptist Church (☎ 312-842-5830; 3301 S Indiana Ave), originally built as a synagogue from 1890 to 1891. Unfortunately, the opulent structure burned to the ground (barring these few exterior walls) in 2006 when a roof repairman lost control of his blowtorch. Gospel fans can make a pilgrimage to two more places further south where the music still soars on Sundays. The Greater Salem Missionary Baptist Church (☎ 773-874-2325; 215 W 71st St) is where gospel great Mahalia Jackson was a lifelong member. Still further south, modern Salem Baptist Church (☎ 773-371-2300; 11800 S Indiana Ave) boasts one the city's top choral ensembles, and is helmed by the charismatic state senator Reverend James Meeks.

The Supreme Life Building (3501 S Martin Luther King Jr Dr), a 1930s office building, was the spot where John H Johnson Jr, the publishing mogul who founded *Ebony* magazine, got the idea for his empire, which includes *Jet* and other important titles serving African Americans. In 2005 the building was renovated after falling into disrepair, a good sign for the rising Bronzeville neighborhood.

In the median at 35th St and Martin Luther King Jr Dr, the Victory Monument was erected in 1928 in honor of the black soldiers who fought in WWI. The figures include a soldier, a mother and Columbia, the mythical figure meant to symbolize the New World.

ILLINOIS INSTITUTE OF TECHNOLOGY

Map p50

☎ 312-567-5014; www.mies.iit.edu; 3300 S Federal St; Ⓜ Green Line to 35th-Bronzeville-IIT

A world-class leader in technology, industrial design and architecture, Illinois Institute of Technology (IIT) owes much of its look to legendary architect Ludwig Mies van der Rohe, who fled the Nazis in Germany for Chicago in 1938. From 1940 until his retirement in 1958, Mies designed 22 IIT buildings that reflected his tenets of architecture, combining simple, black metal frames with glass and brick infills. The look became known as the 'International Style.' The star of the campus and Mies' undisputed masterpiece is SR Crown Hall (3360 S State St), appropriately home to the College of Architecture. The building, close to the center of campus, appears to be a transparent glass box floating between its translucent base and suspended roof. At night it glows from within like an illuminated jewel.

Mies isn't the only architectural hero whose works are on display at IIT. In 2003 the campus opened two other buzz-worthy buildings by world-renowned architects. Dutch architect Rem Koolhaas designed the McCormick Tribune Campus Center (3201 S State St, cnr 33rd) with its simple lines and striking en-tubing of the El tracks that run overhead. This is Koolhaas' only building in the US. Just south of the Campus Center is the Helmut Jahn–designed State Street Village (cnr 33rd & State Sts). Jahn studied at IIT in his younger days, and his strip of rounded glass-and-steel residence halls is a natural progression from the works of the modernist bigwigs he learned from while here.

You can take a 90-minute, docent-led tour ($5; 10am & 1pm) that covers all architectural highlights; it departs from the information center in the McCormick Tribune Campus Center. The center also rents audio tours.

BRIDGEPORT & UNION STOCKYARDS GATE Map p50

The community of Bridgeport is more important for its historical role than for its ability to draw tourists. The stockyards were once a major attraction, but they have long since been closed and the land is being rapidly covered by new warehouses. The traditional home of Chicago's Irish mayors (this is where the Daley dynasty grew up), Bridgeport remains an enclave of descendants of Irish settlers. Chinese and Hispanic groups have moved in, but many African Americans, who live to the south and east, feel that they're not welcome. While some residents say Bridgeport is more tolerant now, it will probably never live down its role in the 1919 race riots, when thugs went on a killing spree after a black youth on a raft floated too close to a 'white' beach.

Halsted St, from 31st St south to 43rd St, is Bridgeport's rather uninteresting main drag. Most of the neighborhood lies west of the huge train embankment that itself is west of US Cellular Field. However, Bridgeport extends north of the park all the way to Chinatown and makes for a good walk after a game if you're in a group and don't stray east of the Dan Ryan Expressway.

A tiny vestige of the stockyards lies a block west of the 4100 block of S Halsted St. The Union Stockyards Gate (850 W Exchange Ave) was once the main entrance to the vast stockyards where millions of cows and almost as many hogs met their ends each year. During the 1893 World Expo the stockyards were a popular tourist draw, with nearly 10,000 people a day making the trek here to stare, awestruck, as the butchering machine took in animals and spat out blood and meat.

The value of those slaughtered in 1910 was an enormous $225 million. While sanitary conditions eventually improved from the hideous levels documented by Upton Sinclair (see the boxed text, below), during the Spanish-American war, American soldiers suffered more casualties because of bad cans of meat from the Chicago packing houses than because of enemy fire.

HOG-SQUEAL OF THE UNIVERSE

In *The Jungle,* Upton Sinclair described the Chicago stockyards this way: 'One could not stand and watch very long without becoming philosophical, without beginning to deal in symbols and similes, and to hear the hog-squeal of the universe.'

These were slaughterhouses beyond compare. By the early 1870s they processed more than one million hogs a year and almost as many cattle, plus scores of unlucky sheep, horses and other critters. All of them trundled through the still-standing Union Stockyards Gate (850 W Exchange Ave), one of the first commissions of Burnham & Root's young architecture company.

It was a coldly efficient operation. The old saying – that once the animals were in the packinghouses, everything was used but the squeal – was almost true. Some bits of pig debris for which no other use could be found were fed to scavenger pigs, who turned the waste into valuable meat. But a vast amount of waste was simply flushed into the south branch of the Chicago River, flowing into the lake. Beyond the aesthetic and health problems that ensued, the packers had to contend with other consequences of their pollution.

Meat processed in Chicago was shipped in ice-packed railroad cars to the huge markets in the East. The ice was harvested from lakes and rivers each winter and then stored for use all year long. But ice that was taken from the Chicago River returned to its stinky liquid state as it thawed over the meat on the journey east, thus rendering the carcasses unpalatable. The packers finally had to resort to harvesting their ice in huge operations in unpolluted Wisconsin.

KENWOOD HISTORIC ARCHITECTURE Map p114

172, Metra to 53rd

Historic homes fill this neighborhood abutting Hyde Park. Among the treasures is the Kehilath Anshe Ma'ariv-Isaiah Israel Temple (KAM Synagogue; ☎ 773-924-1234; 1100 E Hyde Park Blvd). It's a domed masterpiece in the Byzantine style with acoustics that are said to be perfect. Call for opening times. Many classic homes line shaded Woodlawn Ave, including the Isidore Heller House (5132 S Woodlawn Ave), an 1897 Frank Lloyd Wright house with the characteristic side entrance. The house at 4944 S Woodlawn Ave was once home to Muhammad Ali. Bodyguards around the 1971 Elijah Muhammad House (4855 S Woodlawn Ave) indicate that Nation of Islam leader Louis Farrakhan currently lives here.

HIGHER LEARNING

Walking Tour

You can learn a lot walking around the University of Chicago's Hyde Park campus and beyond.

WALK FACTS

Start Smart Museum of Art
Finish Museum of Science & Industry
Duration Five hours
Fuel Stop Pizza at Medici (p167)

1 David & Alfred Smart Museum of Art Brush up on your art acumen at the Smart Museum (p115). Exhibits here explore 'the struggle between realist and abstract.' Learn about artists from Europe and the Americas from the 19th to the mid-20th century, including Mexican painter Diego Riviera.

2 Nuclear Energy Sculpture Under Stagg Field Stadium on the University of Chicago campus, in secret, scientists initiated the first self-sustaining controlled nuclear reaction on December 2, 1942 – the precursor to the atomic bomb (see p118). Today, the spot is marked by a bronze, skull-like sculpture flanking a tennis court. What can we learn from this?

3 Robie House Frank Lloyd Wright's Robie House (p115) is an excellent opportunity to educate yourself on Prairie School architecture. Notice that by painting out the vertical mortar in the brick facade, and leaving the white horizontal mortar, Wright emphasized the low-lying flatness so essential to his vision.

4 Powell's Between Kimbark and Harper Aves on E 57th St, there are several new and used bookstores. No matter what subject you want to study – astronomy, architecture, rocket science – you're likely to find a second-hand book about it at Powell's (p136).

5 Museum of Science & Industry Delve into WWII sea warfare history at the Museum of Science & Industry (p113). The only German U-505 on US soil is part of a multimedia, multi-million dollar exhibit. You can also explore a full scale coal mine or walk through a giant heart here.

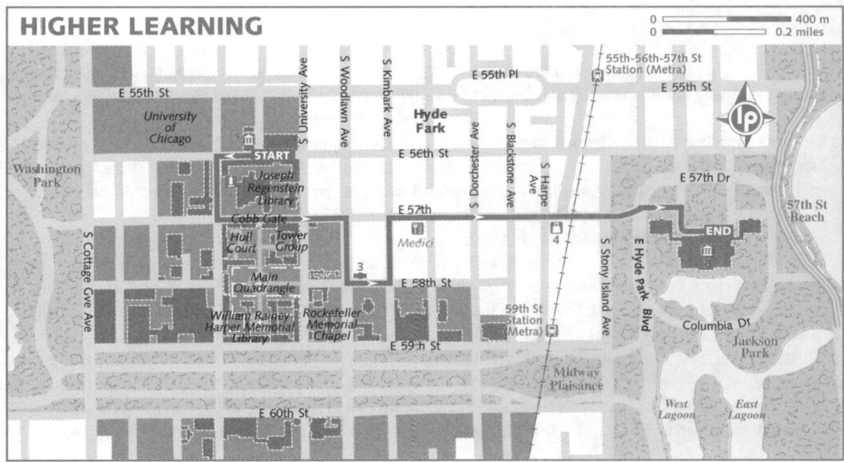

BLUELIST[1] (blu,list) *v.*
to recommend a travel experience.
What's your recommendation? www.lonelyplanet.com/bluelist

SHOPPING

top picks

SHOPPING

From the glossy department stores of the Magnificent Mile to the gay, goth and comics shops of Lake View to the indie designers of Wicker Park, Chicago is a shopper's destination. The entire family can abuse the credit card here, and an afternoon spent browsing might result in a Crate & Barrel cappuccino maker for mom, a Cubs ball cap for dad, a nipple ring and Darth Vader guitar for the teenage son in a band, a corn-polyester blend jacket for vegetarian sis, and a lucky bingo candle for grandma.

Shopping is in Chicago's blood. The city birthed national retail giants such as Sears, Montgomery Ward, Marshall Field's and Woolworth's. True, three of the four companies no longer exist, victims of big-box retailers and overseas trade. But Chicago is still at its happiest filling shopping bags, and you'll feel the love across town.

Though chains like Old Navy and Target sit on practically every street corner, Chicago has managed to maintain a thriving culture of independent and family-run stores. A friendly Midwestern atmosphere prevails, even among the high-end stores on the Magnificent Mile.

Music, new and retro fashions, art and architecture-related items and ethnic goods are the city's shopping strengths. For a list of easy-to-obtain local souvenirs, see p122.

Note to serious shoppers: sign up for Chicago Magazine's 'Sales Check' e-newsletter (www.chicagomag@salescheck_subscribe) or check the archived version online (www.chicagomag.com – click the 'Shopping' tab). It's published weekly and lists sales during the upcoming days, as well as new store openings and events. It's an invaluable tool for guidance about where to unsheathe your credit card and how to save a few bucks.

SHOPPING AREAS

The shoppers' siren song emanates from Michigan Ave in the Near North, along what's called the Magnificent Mile. It's stuffed with vertical malls and high-end chains and is the busiest shopping area in town. It's particularly festive around the winter holidays. Next door in the Gold Coast, ritzy designers from Paris, Milan and Manhattan mix it up on Oak St.

Moving north and west of downtown, you'll find boutiques filling Wicker Park and Bucktown (mod), Lincoln Park (tony), Lake View (countercultural) and Andersonville (all three).

top picks

SHOPPING STREETS

- Clark St (p127) Shops on this eclectic strip sell everything from human-sized dog collars to humanities tomes.
- Damen Ave (p130) Fashionistas revel in the swath of mid- to high-end boutiques.
- Michigan Ave, aka the Magnificent Mile (p122) Big-city shopping at its best, with sky-high malls and glossy large-scale retailers.
- Armitage Ave (p126) Classy yoga togs, haute chocolates and sassy shoes are among the urban accoutrements.
- Division St (p130) It explodes with crafters and newbie designers offering locally made, one-of-a-kind wares.

OPENING HOURS

Typical retail shopping hours are 11am to 7pm Monday to Saturday and noon to 6pm Sunday, though it varies depending on the season, the neighborhood and the amount of foot traffic. Prime shopping areas and malls may stay open until 9pm.

The following listings note stores' hours that stray from these rough standards, as well as any closed days.

CONSUMER TAXES

Chicago's sales tax on goods (excluding food) is 9%, though it could be more by the time you're reading this – the city government was threatening to raise taxes at press time.

THE LOOP

Shopping in the Loop, filled with iconic department stores in grand old buildings, used to be a legendary experience. Marshall

Field's had its flagship store here for 100-plus years, where it invented traditions such as the money-back guarantee, bridal registry and the bargain basement. Around the corner, Carson Pirie Scott was once so prominent it got rock-star architect Louis Sullivan to design its space in the 1890s (see p57 for details). Alas, between 2006 and 2007, both stores went kaput. While the Loop still has plenty of mondo retailers, they're mostly national chains that have moved in to serve the enormous population of office workers trying to squeeze shopping into their lunch hours.

GALLERY 37 STORE

Map pp54–5 Arts & Crafts

☎ 312-744-7274; 66 E Randolph St; closed Sun; M Brown, Green, Orange, Purple Line to Randolph

It's a win-win proposition at this nonprofit entity: painters, sculptors and other artists get paid for creating their wares while teaching inner-city teens – who serve as apprentices – to do the same. Their artworks, including paintings, mosaic tables, puppets and carved-wood walking sticks, are sold in the gallery here. Profits return to the organization.

ILLINOIS ARTISANS SHOP

Map pp54–5 Arts & Crafts

☎ 312-814-5321; 2nd level, James R Thompson Center, 100 W Randolph St; closed Sat & Sun; M Brown, Green, Orange, Purple, Blue Line to Clark

The best work of artisans from throughout the state are sold here, including ceramics, glass and wood coaxed into jewelry, wine jugs, glassware, mobiles and toys – prices verge on cheap. The enthusiastic staff will tell you all about the people who created the various pieces. The Illinois Art Gallery next door sells paintings and sculptures under the same arrangement.

PRAIRIE AVENUE BOOKSHOP

Map pp54–5 Bookstore

☎ 312-922-8311; 418 S Wabash Ave; closed Sun; M Brown, Orange, Purple Line to Library

This is easily the classiest and most lavishly decorated bookstore in the city. The beautiful architectural tomes – including many hard-to-find titles – rest on hardwood shelves, and the thick carpet muffles the noise of customers. Soon you'll want to don a smoking jacket, stoke a pipe and curl up in a corner leather chair.

CENTRAL CAMERA

Map pp54–5 Computers & Electronics

☎ 312-427-5580; 230 S Wabash Ave; M Red Line to Jackson

Whatever your photos needs, Central Camera has the answer. If you're traveling with a shutterbug, be sure to avoid this place until the very end of your trip, lest you risk seeing the sights all by yourself. Once photo-holics step inside the long, narrow store, it will be days before they surface again.

POSTER PLUS Map pp54–5 Fine Arts

☎ 312-461-9277; 200 S Michigan Ave; M Brown, Green, Orange, Purple Line to Adams

Located across from the Art Institute, this superlative poster store carries reproductions of many of the museum's best-known works, along with a number of fun, Chicago-specific historical prints dating from the late 19th century. Upstairs in the vintage room, European and American poster originals can go for as much as $30,000.

5 S WABASH AVE Map pp54–5 Jewelry

5 S Wabash Ave; closed Sun; M Brown, Green, Orange, Purple Line to Madison

This old building, located on a block commonly referred to as 'Jewelers Row,' is the center of Chicago's family jeweler trade. Hundreds of shops in here sell every kind of watch, ring, gemstone and bauble imaginable. Most are quick to promise, 'I can get it for you wholesale!'

ROCK RECORDS Map pp54–5 Music Store

☎ 312-346-3489; 175 W Washington St; closed Sun; M Brown, Orange, Purple Line to Washington

Don't let the sometimes surly staff scare you away from this well-stocked independent record store, which has a good number of listening stations and a wide selection of pop, indie rock, hip-hop and country.

CHICAGO ARCHITECTURE FOUNDATION SHOP

Map pp54–5 Souvenirs

☎ 312-922-3432; 224 S Michigan Ave; M Brown, Green, Orange, Purple Line to Adams

Skyscraper playing cards, Frank Lloyd Wright notecards and heaps of books and posters celebrate local architecture at this haven for anyone with an edifice complex. The items make excellent only-in-Chicago type souvenirs.

NEAR NORTH & NAVY PIER

The Magnificent Mile, or 'Mag Mile' as it's widely known, encompasses the sleek high-end department stores and national chains on Michigan Ave between the river and Oak St. The little stretch sells $1 billion worth of goods annually; it's at its frenzied peak during December.

ABRAHAM LINCOLN BOOK SHOP

Map pp64–5 Bookstore

☎ 312-944-3085; 357 W Chicago Ave; closed Sun; M Brown, Purple Line to Chicago

This hushed, museum-like shop carries new, used and antiquarian books about Honest Abe, the Civil War and the presidency in general. If you want a real, Lincoln-signed White House memo – and have $30,000 to drop on it – you'll walk out of here a satisfied customer. The knowledgeable staff regularly hold open round-table discussions with Civil War scholars.

LEVI'S STORE

Map pp64–5 Clothing & Accessories

☎ 312-642-9613; 600 N Michigan Ave; M Red Line to Grand

Welcome to denim's mecca. The sheer volume of Levi's for sale here will spin your head: skinny cut? boot-cut? flare 501s? petite? dark-washed? They're all in the stacks, and in every combination imaginable. Prices span the gamut, from basics as low as $45 to fashion-forward styles costing upward of $245.

APPLE STORE

Map pp64–5 Computers & Electronics

☎ 312-981-4104; 679 N Michigan Ave; M Red Line to Chicago

Powerbooks, iPods and everything else for Mac enthusiasts are splayed across butcher-block tables in this bright, airy store. The user-friendly setup comes with plenty of clued-up staff to answer product questions, a 'genius bar' on the 2nd floor to sort out equipment issues and free internet access on machines throughout the store.

COMPUSA Map pp64–5 Computers & Electronics

☎ 312-787-6776; 101 E Chicago Ave; M Red Line to Chicago

A convenient superstore for those looking to pick up laptop supplies, CompUSA offers unbeatable prices on things like wireless cards and hand-held computing devices. Come with a clear idea of what you want – the teenage 'help' rarely knows more than the customers.

top picks

CLASSIC SOUVENIRS

The ultimate memento from Chicago is a deep-dish pizza. A couple of chains pack pies on dry ice and ship them anywhere in the US. Try Giordano's (☎ 800-982-1756; www.giordanos.com) or Gino's East (☎ 800-344-5455; www.ginoseast.com). The pie itself costs roughly $25, plus about $25 more for shipping. Suggestions for lighter, less perishable keepsakes include:

- A mini Sears Tower replica from the City of Chicago Store (p125)
- Impressionist art posters selected from the Art Institute (p52)
- A Cubs-logoed ball cap or T-shirt from the Chicago Tribune Store (opposite)
- Jazz or blues CDs found at Jazz Record Mart (opposite)
- Popcorn bought from Garrett Popcorn (below)

GARRETT POPCORN

Map pp64–5 Food & Drink

☎ 312-944-2630; 670 N Michigan Ave; M Red Line to Grand

Like lemmings drawn to a cliff, people form long lines outside this kernel-sized store on the Mag Mile. Granted, the caramel corn is heavenly and the cheese popcorn decadent, but is it worth waiting in the whipping snow for a chance to buy some? Actually, it is. There's a rumor this store may soon close. If so, try the store in the Loop (Map pp54–5; ☎ 312-630-0127; 26 W Randolph St), where the lines are usually shorter anyway.

CRATE & BARREL

Map pp64–5 Housewares

☎ 312-787-5900; 646 N Michigan Ave; M Red Line to Grand

The handsome housewares purveyor started right here in Chicago, and this glassy, sassy uber-store is the flagship. Inside, suburban soccer moms fill their carts with hip but functional lamps, wine goblets, casserole dishes and brass beds, same as the downtown loft-nesters shopping beside them.

JAZZ RECORD MART

Map pp64–5 Music Store

☎ 312-222-1467; 27 E Illinois St; Ⓜ Red Line to Grand

Musicians, serious jazz and blues aficionados, and vintage album collectors flock to this store, which is thoroughly stocked-up on the jazz and blues genres. Bob Koester and his dedicated staff can find just about anything your heart desires, no matter how obscure. If you're looking to complete your Bix Beiderbecke collection, the Jazz Record Mart will certainly help you get it done.

CHICAGO PLACE MALL

Map pp64–5 Shopping Mall

☎ 312-642-4811; 700 N Michigan Ave; Ⓜ Red Line to Chicago

This eight-story mall is occupied mostly by big chain stores such as Saks Fifth Ave and Talbots. Smaller stores that fill the gaps between the large retailers feel a little bit thrown-together, though **Love From Chicago** (☎ 312-787-0838; 8th fl) is one of the best places to get gifts and souvenirs, including the elusive Al Capone shot glass. Chicago Place Mall also boasts one of the most dramatic food courts in the city – the plant- and fountain-filled area has wonderful views.

MERCHANDISE MART

Map pp64–5 Shopping Mall

☎ 312-527-4141; 222 Merchandise Mart Plaza, W Kinzie & N Well Sts; 🕑 most stores closed Sun; Ⓜ Brown, Purple Line to Merchandise Mart

Beautifully restored in the early 1990s, the Mart contains a modest collection of chain stores on its lower floors. But the real allure lies on the upper floors devoted to distributor showrooms for home furnishings and other interior fittings. As you prowl the halls, you can find next year's hot trends on display today. Technically, only retailers and buyers can shop on most of these floors, though LuxeHome, with its 100,000 sq ft of kitchen and bathroom fixtures, is open to the public. See above for further information on the Mart, including tours.

CLOTHING SIZES

Women's clothing

Aus/UK	8	10	12	14	16	18
Europe	36	38	40	42	44	46
Japan	5	7	9	11	13	15
USA	6	8	10	12	14	16

Women's shoes

Aus/USA	5	6	7	8	9	10
Europe	35	36	37	38	39	40
France only	35	36	38	39	40	42
Japan	22	23	24	25	26	27
UK	3½	4½	5½	6½	7½	8½

Men's clothing

Aus	92	96	100	104	108	112
Europe	46	48	50	52	54	56
Japan	S		M	M		L
UK/USA	35	36	37	38	39	40

Men's shirts (collar sizes)

Aus/Japan	38	39	40	41	42	43
Europe	38	39	40	41	42	43
UK/USA	15	15½	16	16½	17	17½

Men's shoes

Aus/UK	7	8	9	10	11	12
Europe	41	42	43	44½	46	47
Japan	26	27	27½	28	29	30
USA	7½	8½	9½	10½	11½	12½

Measurements approximate only, try before you buy

SHOPS AT NORTH BRIDGE

Map pp64–5 Shopping Mall

☎ 312-327-2300; 520 N Michigan Ave; Ⓜ Red Line to Grand

The newest of the classy Michigan Ave malls, Shops at North Bridge appeals to a less aggressively froufrou demographic with stores like the Body Shop, Ann Taylor Loft and the LEGO Store. The multilevel mall connects anchor department store Nordstrom to Michigan Ave via a gracefully curving, shop-lined atrium.

CHICAGO TRIBUNE STORE

Map pp64–5 Souvenirs

☎ 312-222-3080; Tribune Tower, 435 N Michigan Ave; 🕑 closed Sun; Ⓜ Red Line to Grand

While this small store doesn't have the selection of other souvenir places in Chicago, it does outdo its competitors in *Tribune*-related merchandise. Cubs hats and jerseys, and books by noted Chicago authors, are also available.

NIKETOWN Map pp64–5 Sportswear

☎ 312-642-6363; 669 N Michigan Ave; Ⓜ Red Line to Grand

It's no longer the unique, museum-ish store it once was (outlets have cropped up in many other cities), but this Nike temple has all the flash and sparkle you'd expect from the shoe giant. It remains hugely popular, with every swooshed T-shirt, sweatshirt, jersey and hi-top imaginable.

SPORTS AUTHORITY

Map pp64–5 Sportswear

☎ 312-337-6151; 620 N LaSalle St; Ⓜ Red Line to Grand

In a classic rags-to-riches story, Morrie Mages got his start in his family's store in the old Maxwell St Jewish ghetto, where some of the city's leading retailers launched their careers by selling clothes between WWI and WWII. Mages built this into the world's largest sporting goods store, eventually moving it from Maxwell St into its own renovated eight-story warehouse here. Though Morrie sold the company for a fortune back in 1994, and the store is now owned by national chain Sports Authority, it still continues his discounting philosophy. Check out Mages' *Chicago Sports Hall of Fame,* on the Ontario St exterior wall.

AMERICAN GIRL PLACE

Map pp64–5 Toy Shop

☎ 877-247-5223; 111 E Chicago Ave; Ⓜ Red Line to Chicago

You know the red shopping bags you see every female under the age of 12 carrying on Michigan Ave? They come from American Girl Place, a three-story doll store so bizarre you must see it to believe it. Dolls are treated as real people here: the 'hospital' admits them and takes them away in a wheelchair if they need repair; the café seats and treats them as part of the family, including offering them their own tea service. You can even order a doll made to look just like you. The store is scheduled to move across the street to new digs Water Tower Place sometime in 2008.

GOLD COAST

Uber-designer boutiques pop up like mushrooms on the tiny blocks just west of Michigan Ave, particularly in the single block of Oak St between Michigan Ave and Rush St. Note that Oak St is the one place in town where visitors might experience haughty attitudes from shopkeepers.

BORDERS BOOKS & MUSIC

Map pp70–1 Bookstore

☎ 312-573-0564; 830 N Michigan Ave; Ⓜ Red Line to Chicago

This humungous Borders, right across from the Water Tower, is always crowded. Thousands of books, including lots of special-interest titles, are spread out over four floors. You'll find a good selection of magazines and newspapers near the main entrance. Borders also has opened a much-needed branch in the Loop (Map pp54–5; ☎ 312-606-0750; 150 N State St) and a less attractive store in Lake View (Map pp82–3; ☎ 773-935-3909; 2817 N Clark St).

EUROPA BOOKS Map pp70–1 Bookstore

☎ 312-335-9677; 832 N State St; Ⓜ Red Line to Chicago

As the name promises, this store carries newspapers, magazines and books, primarily in European languages.

DENIM LOUNGE

Map pp70–1 Clothing & Accessories

☎ 312-642-6403; 43 E Oaks St; Ⓜ Red Line to Clark/Division

The entire family can get outfitted in jeans here, from the kiddies on up to mom and dad. It's all cool, easily wearable designer brands, and the four-dimensional fitting station lets you check out the look from every angle in high definition (not always a rewarding feature). The lounge is attached to a hip kids clothing shop called Madison & Friends.

H&M Map pp70–1 Clothing & Accessories

☎ 312-640-0060; 840 N Michigan Ave; Ⓜ Red Line to Chicago

This Swedish-based purveyor of trendy togs is usually packed with customers clawing the racks for high fashion at low prices. Men and women will find a variety of European-cut styles ranging from business suits to bathing suits. There's another outlet at 22 N State St, but this one is bigger.

JIL SANDER Map pp70–1 Clothing & Accessories

☎ 312-335-0006; 48 E Oak St; 🕑 closed Sun; Ⓜ Red Line to Clark/Division

Jil Sander's minimalist colors and simple designs somehow manage to remain fashionable long after other trendsetters have disappeared from the scene.

KATE SPADE Map pp70–1 Clothing & Accessories

☎ 312-654-8853; 101 E Oak St; Ⓜ Red Line to Clark/Division

Beloved by the women of Lincoln Park, Kate Spade specializes in bags constructed with clean lines. This store also offers jewelry, shoes and sunglasses by a host of designers.

MNG BY MANGO

Map pp70–1 Clothing & Accessories

☎ 312-397-9800; 4th fl, Water Tower Place, 835 N Michigan Ave; Ⓜ Red Line to Chicago

This Barcelona-based company offers trendy women's clothing for justifiable prices. It's geared mostly to 20- and 30-something urbanites – think Penelope Cruz, who is the company's spokesperson, as well as one of its designers. New shipments arrive twice a week; it's located in Water Tower Place.

ALTERNATIVES Map pp70–1 Shoes

☎ 312-266-1545; 5th fl, 900 N Michigan Ave; Ⓜ Red Line to Chicago

The kinds of shoes that delight the eye and appall the feet are the specialty at this store, located in the 900 N Michigan mall. Featuring one of the most cutting-edge collections in town, its prices will gladden the hearts of budding Imelda Marcoses everywhere.

JIMMY CHOO Map pp70–1 Shoes

☎ 312-255-1170; 63 E Oak St; Ⓜ Red Line to Clark/Division

The prices are almost as high as the stiletto heels at Jimmy Choo, revered foot stylist to the rich and famous. Oh go ahead – be like J Lo and Beyonce. All it takes is a toss of the head, the willingness to drop $800 on a pair of kicks and the attitude that footwear doesn't make the outfit, it is the outfit.

PS: ACCESSORIES Map pp70–1 Shoes

☎ 312-932-0077; 1127 N State St; Ⓜ Red Line to Clark/Division

As the name implies, this shop features shoes, jewelry, purses and belts. It's more laid back than many Gold Coast shops, ie you grab your own shoes from the boxes stacked on the floor. The relaxed attitude shows up in the decent prices, too.

900 N MICHIGAN

Map pp70–1 Shopping Mall

☎ 312-915-3916; 900 N Michigan Ave; Ⓜ Red Line to Chicago

This huge mall is home to an upscale collection of stores including Diesel, Gucci and J Crew, among many others. Water Tower Place (see below) is under the same management, and they simply placed all the really expensive stores over here.

WATER TOWER PLACE

Map pp70–1 Shopping Mall

☎ 312-440-3166; 835 N Michigan Ave; Ⓜ Red Line to Chicago

Featuring the coolest fountain in all of Chicago mall-land (you'll see it on your ride up the main escalator), Water Tower Place launched the city's love affair with vertical shopping centers. Many locals swear this first one remains the best one. The mall houses 100 stores on seven levels, including Abercrombie & Fitch, Sharper Image, the Limited, Express and Macy's.

CITY OF CHICAGO STORE

Map pp70–1 Souvenirs

☎ 312-742-8811; Water Works Visitor Information Center, 163 E Pearson St; Ⓜ Red Line to Chicago

This city-run store is a mecca for those wise enough not to try to steal their own 'official' souvenirs. Cheerful city workers will sell you anything from a decommissioned city parking meter ($175) to street signs for famous local streets ($50). The usual array of Chicago books, shot glasses and pint-sized metal replicas of the city's tallest buildings are also available.

PUMA STORE Map pp70–1 Sportswear

☎ 312-751-8574; 1051 N Rush St; Ⓜ Red Line to Clark/Division

Visiting Puma's minimalist, white-walled store has been described as daytime clubbing. DJs spin tunes (mostly on weekends), and buff young bodies bounce to the beat while checking out men's and women's shoes that are impossible to find anywhere else. The first floor is devoted to the brand's sporty urban clothing line.

FLIGHT 001 Map pp70–1 Travel

☎ 312-944-1001; 1133 N State St; Ⓜ Red Line to Clark/Division

Pick out sassy new luggage or mini iPod speakers or maybe a game of travel Scrabble, then take it to the retro airline ticket counter to make the purchase. Whatever your travel needs, it's likely Flight 001 can accommodate it in jet-set style.

LINCOLN PARK & OLD TOWN

Lincoln Park contains plenty of tony shops, many of which bunch near the intersection of Halsted St and Armitage Ave. Clark St is also choc-a-block, though offers more casual options. The area around North and Clybourn Aves is thick with Pottery Barn, J Crew and other urban-living chains.

MINT Map pp76–7 Arts & Crafts

☎ 773-322-2944; 1450 W Webster Ave; closed Mon; M Red, Brown, Purple Line to Fullerton

Mint's teensy showroom displays handmade handbags, scented candles, jewelry, soaps, greeting cards and other crafty creations by Midwestern artists. Designers rotate in and out, so there's always something new on the shelves.

SAM'S WINE & SPIRITS

Map pp76–7 Food & Drink

☎ 312-664-4394; 1720 N Marcey St; M Red Line to North/Clybourn

Cavernous Sam's carries Chicago's largest selection of imported vino. It's easy to spend hours chatting with the informative staff and loading up for future dinner parties. Tastings occur a few times each month, usually on Tuesday or Wednesday evenings. Beer, spirits, champagne and cheese are sold en masse, too.

VOSGES HAUT-CHOCOLAT

Map pp76–7 Food & Drink

☎ 773-296-9866; 951 W Armitage Ave; M Brown, Purple Line to Armitage

Owner/chocolatier Katrina Markoff is making a huge name for herself by whipping up truffles, ice cream and candy bars with exotic ingredients like curry powder, chilies and wasabi. They sounds weird but taste great, as the abundant samples laid out along the back counter prove (though the simplest concoction of the bunch – the dark-milk-chocolate-and-sea-salt Barcelona Bar – remains the sweet to beat).

DAVE'S RECORDS Map pp76–7 Music Store

☎ 773-929-6325; 2604 N Clark St; M Brown, Purple Line to Diversey

Dave's is an all-vinyl shop that feels a little like the setting of Nick Hornby's music-nerd classic, *High Fidelity*. Whether or not that's a good thing probably depends on your level of music nerddom. You'll find everything from vocal jazz to techno.

UNCLE DAN'S Map pp76–7 Outdoor Gear

☎ 773-477-1918; 2440 N Lincoln Ave; M Red, Brown, Purple Line to Fullerton

The smell of leather hits you in the face as you walk into this outdoor gear store, offering a big selection of hiking boots and equipment, plus camping supplies and many brands of backpacks. It's a relaxed place to buy outdoor gear, without the derisive looks of lurking sales dudes who consider anything less than a frontal assault on K2 to be for wimps.

BARKER & MEOWSKY

Map pp76–7 Pet Supplies

☎ 773-868-0200; 1003 W Armitage Ave; M Brown Line to Armitage

Fido and Fluffy get their due here. Sales staff welcomes four-legged visitors with a treat from the all-natural pet food stash, and then the critters are allowed to commence sniffing up and over the fun apparel, beds and carriers. Top wags go to the Chewy Vuitton purse-shaped squeak-toys and Cubs ball caps, the shop's best sellers.

LORI'S, THE SOLE OF CHICAGO

Map pp76–7 Shoes

☎ 773-281-5655; 824 W Armitage Ave; M Brown, Purple Line to Armitage

Lori's caters to shoe junkies who tear through boxes and tissue paper to get at Franco Sarto, Apepazza and other European brands. The general frenzy morphs into a true gorge-fest during season-ending sales in July/August and January/February; lines can form out the door during these sales.

LULULEMON ATHLETICA

Map pp76–7 Sportswear

☎ 773-883-8860; 2104 N Halsted St; M Brown Line to Armitage

Canada's famous yoga-wear maker opened shop in Chicago recently, giving locals access to its colorful togs made of organic cotton, hemp and bamboo. They're flattering, too: the Boogie Pants and Groove Pants 'give every girl a great-looking butt,' swears one devoted customer. Bonus: the shop offers free, one-hour yoga classes at 10am Sundays; call ahead to register, and bring your own mat.

NAU Map pp76–7 Sportswear

☎ 773-281-1363; 2118 N Halsted St; Ⓜ Brown Line to Armitage

The wares at Nau (it means 'welcome' in Maori) are similar to Lululemon, only the outdoor clothing ratchets up a notch in cleverness (for instance, a skirt you can wear while riding your bike to work, and a dress designed to enable its wearer to bust out a karate kick, should the need arise). The eco-conscious fabrics include organic cotton, recycled polyester and a corn-polyester blend.

LAKE VIEW & WRIGLEYVILLE

Stuff that's never worn – let alone sold – on Michigan Ave is de rigueur on Halsted and Clark Sts in Lake View. Even if you're not buying, the browsing is entertainment in itself. Near Belmont Ave several stores serve the rebellious needs of full-on punks and teenagers. On weekend days the sidewalks attract a throng of characters – rich teens from the North Shore, black-clad punks with blond roots and the rest of Lake View's diverse tribes. If you'd prefer a classic designer dress and other apparel to a nipple ring and PVC bikini, head to Southport Ave, where a string of clothing boutiques have laid down roots.

ARCHITECTURAL ARTIFACTS

Map pp82–3 Antiques

☎ 773-348-0622; 4325 N Ravenswood Ave; Ⓜ Brown Line to Montrose

This mammoth, 80,000 sq ft salvage warehouse, located a bit northwest of Lake View proper, is a treasure trove that prompts continual mutterings of 'Where on earth did they find *that*?' Italian marionettes, 1920s French mannequins and Argentinian cast-iron mailboxes rest alongside decorative doors, tiles, stained-glass windows, fireplace mantels and garden furnishings. Be sure to step into the free, attached Museum of Historic Chicago Architecture.

FOURTH WORLD ARTISANS

Map pp82–3 Arts & Crafts

☎ 773-404-5200; 3727 N Southport Ave; Ⓜ Brown Line to Southport

This exotic bazaar provides local artisans, recent immigrants and small importers a market for their handicrafts, and assistance in learning entrepreneurial skills. Reasonably priced folk art, textiles, masks, musical instruments and jewelry from Vietnam, Ghana, Pakistan and other far-flung countries fill the shelves.

CHICAGO COMICS Map pp82–3 Bookstore

☎ 773-528-1983; 3244 N Clark St; Ⓜ Red, Brown, Purple Line to Belmont

This comic emporium has won the 'best comic book store in the US' honor from all sorts of people who should know. Old Marvel *Superman* back issues share shelf space with hand-drawn works by cutting-edge local artists like Chris Ware, Ivan Brunetti and Dan Clowes (who lived here during his early *Eightball* days). *Simpsons* fanatics will 'd'oh!' with joy at the huge toy selection.

ALLEY Map pp82–3 Clothing & Accessories

☎ 773-525-3180; 3228 N Clark St; Ⓜ Red, Brown, Purple Line to Belmont

A vast emporium based on counterculture and pop trends, the Alley offers everything from pot pipes to band posters to human-sized dog collars. Loud, obnoxious punk-rock tees ('I've got the biggest dick in the band' etc) are a specialty of the house. The labyrinth of rooms includes one devoted to the Alley's 'Architectural Revolution' store, which sells plaster reproductions of gargoyles, Ionic pillars and other items that have found a mainstream market with non-dog-collar-wearing interior designers.

MEDUSA'S CIRCLE

Map pp82–3 Clothing & Accessories

☎ 773-935-5950; 3268 N Clark St; 🕓 closed Mon & Tue; Ⓜ Red, Brown, Purple Line to Belmont

Not sweating enough? Medusa's carries everything for raven-haired folk who like to wear dark velvet clothes on hot days. It's mostly girly tough stuff, like T-shirts of kittens armed with guns, and purses decorated with skulls wearing pink bows.

STRANGE CARGO

Map pp82–3 Clothing & Accessories

☎ 773-327-8090; 3448 N Clark St; Ⓜ Red Line to Addison

One of the coolest stores in Chicago for retro T-shirts and thrift-store-esque hipster wear, Strange Cargo also sells wigs, clunky shoes and leather jackets. Buy a vintage-style T-shirt, then use the iron-on machine to enliven it with a message or decal of your choice. There's an excellent selection of kitschy ones featuring Mike Ditka, Harry Caray and other local sports heroes, which make top souvenirs.

THREADLESS

Map pp82–3 Clothing & Accessories

☎ 773-525-8640; 3011 N Broadway Ave; Ⓜ Brown, Purple Line to Wellington

Threadless has a unique business plan. First, it runs an ongoing T-shirt design competition on its website (www.threadless.com) in which designers submit ideas and consumers cast votes (750,000 weekly). The company then releases the seven winning styles in limited quantities of 1500, and they're only available for two weeks. The new designs appear in-store on Fridays, before they're posted online on Mondays. Prices range from about $15 to $25. Bring back your shopping bag and get $1 off your next purchase.

MIDWEST STEREO

Map pp82–3 Computers & Electronics

☎ 773-929-5523; 2806 N Clark St; Ⓜ Red, Brown, Purple Line to Belmont

This is a hub for DJ gear, both used and new. If you're looking for a basic mixer or a Technics turntable (or a PA system that will quickly make you the talk of your neighborhood), this is your store.

GRAMAPHONE RECORDS

Map pp82–3 Music Store

☎ 773-472-3683; 2843 N Clark St; Ⓜ Brown, Purple Line to Diversey

Gramaphone is the hippest record store in Chicago – you'd have to either be a DJ or be dating a DJ to have heard of most of the hip-hop and electronic music sold here. Along with its collection of trendsetting sounds, Gramaphone offers record needles and DJ supplies, and a host of info on upcoming parties.

ARMY NAVY SURPLUS USA

Map pp82–3 Outdoor Gear

☎ 773-348-8930; 3100 N Lincoln Ave; 🕒 closed Sun; Ⓜ Brown Line to Southport

The merchandise area here would send a drill sergeant into a conniption. The place is a huge mess. But among the torn boxes and shambles of merchandise there are actual military surplus items of the highest quality the taxpayer can afford.

SPORTS WORLD

Map pp82–3 Souvenirs

☎ 312-472-7701; 3555 N Clark St; Ⓜ Red Line to Addison

This store across from Wrigley Field overflows with – that's right, Sherlock – Cubs sportswear. It carries all shapes and sizes of jerseys, T-shirts, sweatshirts and ball caps,

RETRO CHIC CHICAGO

Much to the chagrin of fashion-forward metropolises New York City and Los Angeles, Chicago is fashion-backward, and proud of it. Place the blame – or praise, as the case may be – on its denizens' thrifty, Midwestern sensibilities. Folks here don't throw out their old bowling shirts, pillbox hats, faux-fur coats and costume jewelry. Instead, they deposit used duds at vintage or secondhand stores, of which there are hundreds. These places provide a shopping bonanza for bargain seekers patient enough to comb through the racks. The payoff is when you find that perfect 'My Name is Bob' gas station attendant work shirt or chestnut-colored fake mouton coat – both for $5.

For those less patient, several stores have popped up that offer retro-style clothes, but you'll be the first one to wear them.

Lake View and Wicker Park/Bucktown present the most fertile hunting grounds for retro chic styles: We recommend:

Strange Cargo (above)

T-Shirt Deli (p131)

Una Mae's Freak Boutique (p132)

US #1 (p132)

plus baby clothes and drink flasks. Surprisingly, the prices aren't bad given the attraction-side location.

A OK OFFICIAL Map pp82–3 Sportswear

☎ 773-248-4547; 3270 N Clark St; Ⓜ Red, Brown, Purple Line to Belmont

Local artists design and customize sneakers, which are sold here alongside weird vinyl toys. It's all very hip and urban, with sneakerheads clamoring for the limited-edition goods (which typically cost upward of $100).

WINDWARD SPORTS
Map pp82–3 Sportswear

☎ 773-472-6868; 3317 N Clark St; 🕑 closed Tue; Ⓜ Red, Brown, Purple Line to Belmont

One-stop shopping for sporty gear, whether you're into windsurfing, in-line skating, snowboarding or the see-it-to-believe-it 'flowboarding' (kind of like a cross between skateboarding and snowboarding). Ask at the store about various beach rentals of windsurfing equipment during the summer.

GAY MART Map pp82–3 Toy Shop

☎ 773-929-4272; 3457 N Halsted St; Ⓜ Red Line to Addison

The Woolworth's of the strip sells toys, novelties, calendars, souvenirs, you name it. One of the top sellers is Billy, the heroically endowed 'world's first out and proud gay doll.' Ken would just wilt in Billy's presence – that is, if Ken had anything to wilt.

UNCLE FUN Map pp82–3 Toy Shop

☎ 773-477-8223; 1338 W Belmont Ave; 🕑 closed Mon; Ⓜ Red, Brown, Purple Line to Belmont

This weird toy and novelty shop is one of the best spots in Chicago for goofy gifts, kitschy postcards and vintage games. The shelves are overflowing with strange finds like fake moustache kits, 3-D Jesus postcards and Chinese-made tapestries of the US lunar landing (just $5, baby).

YESTERDAY Map pp82–3 Toy Shop

☎ 773-248-8087; 1143 W Addison St; 🕑 closed Sun; Ⓜ Red Line to Addison

If you've ever actually lived through the classic 'mom's thrown out all of my baseball cards' tale, you can come here to find out what a fortune you've lost. Old sports memorabilia is the specialty of this shop, which is even older than some of the goods on sale.

ANDERSONVILLE & UPTOWN

Clark St, north of Foster Ave, is the main commercial drag, hosting fashion and furnishing stores with reasonable prices. The Swedish-goods shops that are sprinkled between attest to the neighborhood's former inhabitants.

WOMEN & CHILDREN FIRST
Map p86 Bookstore

☎ 773-769-9299; 5233 N Clark St; Ⓜ Red Line to Berwyn

Hillary Clinton caused a mob scene when she came to this Andersonville feminist mainstay for her 2003 reading. High-profile book-signings and author events happen every week at the welcoming shop, which features fiction and nonfiction by and about women, along with children's books.

BON BON Map p86 Food & Drink

☎ 773-784-9882; 5110 N Clark St; 🕑 closed Mon & Tue; Ⓜ Red Line to Berwyn

A mother-daughter team infuses the handmade chocolates with exotic, heady ingredients like rose petals, chilies and chai tea. As if that wasn't sensuous enough, they then mold the pieces into figures from the Kama Sutra (as well as into little Buddhas and King Tuts, who are still kind of sexy). Serve the rich concoctions to the object of your affection, and you'll be ripping each others' clothes off in no time.

WIKSTROM'S GOURMET FOODS
Map p86 Food & Drink

☎ 773-275-6100; 5217 N Clark St; Ⓜ Red Line to Berwyn

Scandinavians from all over Illinois flock here for homemade limpa, herring and lutefisk. It sells over 4000lb of Swedish meatballs around Christmas time.

EARLY TO BED Map p86 Sex & Fetish

🕑 773-271-1219; 5232 N Sheridan Rd; 🕑 closed Mon; Ⓜ Red Line to Berwyn

This low-key, women-owned sex shop is good for novices – it provides easy to understand explanatory pages and customer reviews throughout the store, so you'll be able to know your anal beads from cock

WORTH THE TRIP: LINCOLN SQUARE & DEVON AVE

The old German neighborhood of Lincoln Square has been gentrified, yet it retains strong European roots that flavor its deserving-of-a-visit shops. It's located between Andersonville and Lake View, to the west; the shopping district is at the intersection of Lincoln, Lawrence and Western Aves. Take the Brown Line to Western.

Chopping Block (Map pp50-1; www.thechoppingblock.net; 4747 N Lincoln Ave; M Brown Line to Western) Let's say your recipe calls for Hungarian cinnamon, gray sea salt and Balinese long pepper. Instead of throwing up your hands in despair after searching the local grocery, and then calling for a pizza delivery, stop in here for specialty foods, high-end cookware and hard-to-find utensils. Chopping Block also offers cooking classes; see p255 for details.

Merz Apothecary (Map pp50-1; ☎ 773-989-0900; 4716 N Lincoln Ave; closed Sun) Merz is a true, turn-of-the-century European apothecary. Antique pharmacy jars contain herbs, homeopathic remedies, vitamins and supplements, and the shelves are stacked high with skin care, personal care, bath and aromatherapy products from around the world.

Timeless Toys (Map pp50-1; ☎ 773-334-4445; 4749 N Lincoln Ave) This charming independent shop is better described for what it does *not* carry – no Barbies, Harry Potter books or trendy kiddie togs. Instead you'll find high-quality, old-fashioned toys, many of which are made in Germany and other European countries. Have fun playing with the bug magnifier, microscopes, glitter balls and wooden spinning tops.

Hell, now that you're this far north, why not keep going? Devon Ave is two miles up the road and the only place in town to pick up a cell phone, kosher doughnut and sari in one fell swoop. Known as Chicago's 'International Marketplace,' Devon Ave is where worlds collide – Indian, Pakastani, Georgian, Russian, Nigerian, Hindu, Muslim, Orthodox Jewish – you name the ethnicity, and someone from the group has set up a shop or eatery here.

Devon at Western Ave is the main intersection. Indian sari and jewelry shops start near 2600 W Devon; to the west they give way to Jewish and Islamic goods stores, while to the east they trickle out into a gaggle of electronics and dollar stores. It's a good place to stock up on low-cost cell phone necessities, over-the-counter medicines, luggage and other travel goods. Or just buy an armful of jangly bangles. If you want to stay for a meal – and you should – see p167 for recommended options. Take the Brown Line to Western and transfer to bus 49B.

rings from bullet vibes. Also on hand are feather boas, bondage tapes and vegan condoms (made with casein-free latex; casein is a milk-derived product usually used in latex production). Videos and books round out the offerings; the latter includes serious resources like sex manuals for rape victims.

ALAMO SHOES Map p86 Shoes

☎ 773-784-8936; 5321 N Clark St; M Red Line to Berwyn

This throwback to the 1960s focuses on comfortable Swedish shoes and Birkenstocks for both men and women, all at really good prices. The enthusiastic staffers hop off to the back room and emerge with stacks of boxes until you find what you want or you're entirely walled in by the possibilities.

WICKER PARK, BUCKTOWN & UKRAINIAN VILLAGE

Damen and Milwaukee Aves in Wicker Park are two of the city's best shopping drags. You'll find the more oddball and youth-oriented resale shops residing on Milwaukee, while Damen holds a wealth of women's clothing boutiques. Division St is honing in fast on this territory with its young designer, home-furnishing and crafters' stores.

BEADNIKS Map pp90–1 Arts & Crafts

☎ 773-276-2323; 1937 W Division St; M Blue Line to Division

Incense envelops you at the door, and you know right away you're in for a hippie treat. Mounds of worldly beads heaped on tables. African trade beads and Thai silver-dipped beads? Got 'em. Bright-hued stone beads, ceramic beads, glass beads? All present. For $3 the kindly staff will help you string your choices into a necklace. Or take a workshop (two to three hours, $20-60) and learn to wield the pliers yourself; classes usually take place on Tuesday evenings and Sunday afternoons, but call for further information.

HANDMADE MARKET

Map pp90–1 Arts & Crafts

☎ 773-276-3600; 1035 N Western Ave; noon-4:30pm; M Blue Line to Damen

Held the second Saturday of every month at the Empty Bottle (p185), this event showcases Chicago crafters who make funky glass pendants, knitted items, handbags, scarves, journals and greeting cards. The bar serves drinks throughout the event, for those who enjoy sipping while shopping.

RENEGADE HANDMADE

Map pp90–1 Arts & Crafts

☎ 773-227-2707; 1924 W Division St; Ⓜ Blue Line to Division

This store sprung up out of a popular local craft fair. Rather than just selling their goods for two days per year, participants thought it would be a swell idea to have an outlet to sell from year-round. Bravo! The reasonably priced merchandise veers toward mod, such as bo-ho tops, graphic-print guitar straps, journals reconstructed from vintage hardback cookbooks and shadow puppets (why not, eh?).

QUIMBY'S

Map pp90–1 Bookstore

☎ 773-342-0910; 1854 W North Ave; Ⓜ Blue Line to Damen

The epicenter of Chicago's comic and zine worlds, Quimby's is one of the linchpins of underground culture in the city. You can find everything here from crayon-powered punk-rock manifestos to slickly produced graphic novels.

AKIRA

Map pp90–1 Clothing & Accessories

☎ 773-489-0818; 1814 W North Ave; Ⓜ Blue Line to Damen

Several fashion design students work here, manning (or woman-ing, to be precise) the denim bar, stocked with 20-plus different brands of jeans. There's a focus on up-and-coming and newly popular lines. This particular location is women-oriented, but three other Akira shops – one for men's clothing, one for shoes, and one for accessories – hover on the same block.

CASA DE SOUL

Map pp90–1 Clothing & Accessories

☎ 773-252-2520; 1919 W Division St; Ⓜ Blue Line to Division

While the turntable in front blasts groovy tunes, check out the shell-inlaid coin purses, beaded handbags, unique clothing and earrings, and African wood-carved items (from the owner's homeland).

FREE PEOPLE

Map pp90–1 Clothing & Accessories

☎ 773-227-4871; 1464 N Milwaukee Ave; Ⓜ Blue Line to Damen

Owned by the same parent company as Urban Outfitters (young hipster styles) and Anthropologie (older feminine styles), Free People lands in the middle with boho-chic tank tops, cardigan sweaters, herringbone jackets and patterned dresses.

HABIT

Map pp90–1 Clothing & Accessories

☎ 773-342-0093; 1951 W Division St; 🕒 closed Mon; Ⓜ Blue Line to Division

Despite the name, this wee woman's clothing boutique definitely doesn't sell outfits to nuns. Rather, its space is devoted to 15 indie designers – many of whom are local – who showcase their simple-but-chic dresses and purses. The look is upscale, though the prices are affordable (many pieces cost around $100).

MS CATWALK

Map pp90–1 Clothing & Accessories

☎ 773-235-2750; 2042 N Damen Ave; 🕒 closed Mon; Ⓜ Blue Line to Damen

Ms Catwalk stocks fun, flirty clothing and garnishes for women. T-shirts feature images from Buddha to Supergirl to Junior Mints candies; hoodies, low-rise corduroy pants and big silvery bags to accessorize your selection.

PENELOPE'S

Map pp90–1 Clothing & Accessories

☎ 773-395-2351; 1913 W Division St; Ⓜ Blue Line to Division

Named after the owners' ridiculously cute pug, Penelope's is a warm boutique for 20- and 30-somethings. Offering both men's and women's fashions (they're new but look thrift-store-bought) along with nifty gifty things, Penelope's further ups the ante by providing an arcade-style stand-up Ms Pac-Man game to keep significant others occupied while loved ones try on clothes.

T-SHIRT DELI

Map pp90–1 Clothing & Accessories

☎ 773-276-6266; 1739 N Damen Ave; Ⓜ Blue Line to Damen

They take the 'deli' part seriously: after they cook (aka iron a retro design on) your T-shirt, they wrap it in butcher paper and serve it to you with potato chips. Choose from heaps of shirt styles and decals, of which Mao, Sean Connery, Patty Hearst and a red-white-and-blue bong are but the beginning.

UNA MAE'S FREAK BOUTIQUE

Map pp90–1 Clothing & Accessories

☎ 773-276-7002; 1422 N Milwaukee Ave; Ⓜ Blue Line to Damen

It's unlikely that the solid suburban women who once wore the pillbox hats and fine Republican cloth coats on sale here would ever have thought of themselves as freaks. Along with the vintage wear, Una Mae's has a growing collection of new accessories like scarves, hats and cosmetics.

US #1 Map pp90–1 Clothing & Accessories

☎ 773-489-9428; 1460 N Milwaukee Ave; Ⓜ Blue Line to Damen

From the outside this place looks like a dump. Inside, however, you'll find rack after rack of affordable, vintage '70s bowling, Hawaiian and western-wear shirts, as well as towers of old Levis jeans.

VIVE LA FEMME

Map pp90–1 Clothing & Accessories

☎ 773-772-7429; 2048 N Damen Ave; closed Mon; Ⓜ Blue Line to Damen

Plus-size shops for women are often woefully lacking in style. Not so at Vive La Femme, where larger women can find sassy and classy designs in sizes 12 to 24.

COCO ROUGE Map pp90–1 Food & Drink

☎ 773-772-2626; 1940 W Divsion St; closed Mon; Ⓜ Blue Line to Division

You're probably sensing a pattern in the embarrassing number of chocolate shops we've listed so far. But you need to keep your energy up, right? So here we go again, this time at Coco Rouge. Behind the velvet drapes lies a tiny glass-case counter, and inside the counter lie the sweetest truffles you've ever laid lips on. Point at your fancy, then the staff whisks it to the back room and genteely wraps it. It's all quite a production.

CLIMATE Map pp90–1 Gifts

☎ 773-862-7075; 1702 N Damen Ave; Ⓜ Blue Line to Damen

'Eclectic' doesn't do justice to the array of items packed into this small store, including cocktail party kits, sassy dating guides and other tongue-in-cheek essentials for urban living.

PAPER DOLL Map pp90–1 Gifts

☎ 773-227-6950; 2048 W Division St; closed Mon; Ⓜ Blue Line to Division

Stationery rules the house at Paper Doll, and many a Wicker Park thriftster has ordered her wedding cards from the mod assortment on hand. Then, a few years later, she orders her baby announcements from the same spot. Kitschy gifts round out the inventory, and eventually that same woman returns to buy a book like *The Three Martini Play Date*.

PORTE ROUGE Map pp90–1 Housewares

☎ 773-269-2800; 1911 W Division St; Ⓜ Blue Line to Division

This sunny, French-kissed shop offers hand-painted crockery and chic kitchen accessories that make even the most marginal, grilled cheese-burning cooks among us look gourmet.

DUSTY GROOVE Map pp90–1 Music Store

☎ 773-342-5800; 1120 N Ashland; Ⓜ Blue Line to Division

A mecca for soul, jazz and electronica, Dusty Groove stocks a fine (and hard-to-find) selection of battery-powered record players among the hot tunes.

RECKLESS RECORDS

Map pp90–1 Music Store

☎ 773-235-3727; 1532 N Milwaukee Ave; Ⓜ Blue Line to Damen

Chicago's best indie-rock record and CD emporium allows you to listen to everything before you buy. If you're looking for CDs by local bands like Tortoise or Gastro del Sol, come here first.

TOMMY'S ROCK & ROLL CAFÉ

Map pp90–1 Music Store

☎ 773-486-6768; 2500 W Chicago Ave; closed Sun; 66

Located at the edge of Ukrainian Village, Tommy's is hands-down the most rawkin' guitar store in town. So grab a doughnut or a Polish sausage at the tiny front café, then strum (after you wash your hands!) the vintage axes in all their polka-dotted, snake-skinned, heart-shaped and Darth

Vader-painted glory. Elvis impersonator photos, letters from Tom Petty, big-ass amps and a whole lot of handcuffs ratchet up the entertainment.

BOTANICA Map pp90–1 Religious Items

☎ 773-486-5894; 1524 N Milwaukee Ave; closed Sun; Ⓜ Blue Line to Damen

This slightly spooky, old-world storefront sells sacred candles, tarot cards, herbal remedies and devotional paraphernalia amid the dust and clutter.

CITY SOLE/NICHE Map pp90–1 Shoes

☎ 773-489-2001; 2001 W North Ave; Ⓜ Blue Line to Damen

One of the hippest men's and women's shoe stores in Chicago is divided into two sections. Niche is where high-priced designs dwell, and City Sole is its more down-to-earth cousin. Together they service the neighborhood: punks, young housewives and old Polish women alike.

EUROPA STYLE SHOES Map pp90–1 Shoes

☎ 773-235-2325; 2456 W Chicago Ave; 66

More than 800 styles of footwear travel across the pond from Italy, Spain and Russia searching for feet that appreciate great Euro-brand style for prices hovering between $60 and $120. About three-quarters of the stock is for women, from leopard-print girly kicks to waffle-stomping boots.

JOHN FLUEVOG SHOES Map pp90–1 Shoes

☎ 773-772-1983; 1539-1541 N Milwaukee Ave; Ⓜ Blue Line to Damen

Bold and colorful shoes by the eccentric designer are the order of the day at this close-out haven. They come as tough-girl chunky or sex-kitten pointy as you like, with equally hip selections for men.

BORING STORE Map pp90–1 Toy Shop

☎ 773-772-8108; 1331 N Milwaukee Ave; Ⓜ Blue Line to Damen

The big orange sign out front will have you scratching your head, but do yourself a favor and step inside (don't worry, those 25 surveillance camera pointed at you are harmless). The place sells crazy-ass spy gear! Mustache disguise kits, underwater voice amplifiers, banana-shaped cases to hide your cell phone in – it's genius. And better yet: profits from sales go toward supporting the after-school writing and tutoring programs that take place on-site at nonprofit group 826CHI.

top picks

MUSIC STORES

Independent record stores flood Chicago's neighborhoods, supported by the thriving live-music scene in town (see p182). Vinyl geeks will discover heaps of stacks to flip through, while jazz, blues and hip-hop lovers are well positioned for obscure finds. And memo to future rock stars: your star-making axe awaits at Tommy's.

- Dusty Groove (opposite)
- Gramaphone Records (p128)
- Jazz Record Mart (p123)
- Reckless Records (opposite)
- Tommy's Rock & Roll Café (opposite)

RED BALLOON CO Map pp90–1 Toy Shop

☎ 773-489-9800; 2060 N Damen Ave; Ⓜ Blue Line to Damen

When hipsters get good jobs and start having kids, this is where they outfit the li'l pups. Adorable clothes, classic children's books and '50s-ish toys prevail in the cozy space.

LOGAN SQUARE & HUMBOLDT PARK

There's not a lot of shops in these neighborhoods quantity-wise, but those stores that are here make up for it in fashionable quality.

WOLFBAIT & B-GIRLS Map p95 Arts & Crafts

☎ 312-698-8685; 3131 W Logan Blvd; closed Mon; Ⓜ Blue Line to Logan Sq

Old ironing boards serve as display tables; tape measures, scissors and other designers' tools hang from vintage hooks. You get that crafting feeling as soon as you walk in, and indeed, Wolfbait & B-girls both sells the wares (tops, dresses, handbags and jewelry) of local indie designers and serves as a working studio for them. Take a fabric printing workshop (two hours, $30, materials and drinks included), and who knows? Maybe your stuff will be for sale soon, too.

CRAFTY CHICAGO

A wave of craftiness has washed over the city, thanks to the success of the Indie Designer Fashion Market (inside the massive Chicago Antique Market, below). Now everyone is opening a store/studio proffering handbags, pendants, scarves and journals that they've stitched, sewed, beaded and glue-gunned themselves. It's great news for shoppers, as the items are locally made, often using recycled materials, and they're 100% unique. What's more, many crafters teach how to do-it-yourself (DIY) via low-key, low-cost workshops on fabric printing, knitting and the like.

Wicker Park is ground zero for the DIY explosion, particularly Division St. Good shops citywide include:

Beadniks (p130)

Handmade Market (p130)

Loopy Yarns (opposite)

Renegade Handmade (p131)

Wolfbait & B-Girls (p133)

NEAR WEST SIDE & PILSEN

Ethnic shops and used-goods and antique markets are percolating in the Near West Side neighborhood. Gallery lovers should check out the West Loop's scene (see p97). Pilsen also has galleries (see p102), as well as scores of small Mexican shops selling devotional candles and *tejano* CDs around 18th St.

CHICAGO ANTIQUE MARKET

Map pp98–9 Antiques

☎ 312-951-9939; 1350 W Randolph St; admission $8; 9am-5pm last Sat & Sun of the month May-Oct; 20 or free trolley hourly from Tribune Tower, 435 N Michigan Ave

This market has become quite the ta-do in town. It takes place inside the beaux arts Plumbers Hall, where more than 200 dealers hock collectibles, costume jewelry, furniture, books, Turkish rugs and pinball machines. One of the coolest facets is the Indie Designer Fashion Market, where the city's fledgling designers sell their one-of-a-kind skirts, shawls, handbags and other pieces. Hard-core antique hounds can pay $20 and get first crack at the goods from 7:30am to 9am on Saturday.

BARBARA'S BOOKSTORE

Map pp98–9 Bookstore

☎ 312-413-2665; www.barabarabookstore.com; 1218 S Halsted St; 8

For serious fiction, you can't touch this locally owned store. Staff members have read what they sell, and touring authors regularly give readings.

LISSA ON MAXWELL

Map pp98–9 Clothing & Accessories

☎ 312-563-9470; 729 W Maxwell St; 8

This women's boutique can be pricey (most items cost between $200 and $400), but the owner does a nice job handpicking designers on the rise, and you'll likely be the only one wearing in town their floaty dresses, fitted trousers and stylish jeans. The pieces are usually structured and long-lined so they'll look good on most body types.

PIVOT

Map pp98–9 Clothing & Accessories

☎ 312-243-4754; 1101 W Fulton Market; closed Mon; M Green Line to Clinton

About as opposite as you can get from neighboring Self Conscious (opposite), Pivot goes green instead of gangsta. All items are made from eco-friendly fabrics, such as the soft bamboo T-shirts. Even the shopping bags (50% recycled content) and clothing racks (made of reclaimed wood and steel) were created according to sustainable principles.

BLOMMER CHOCOLATE STORE

Map pp98–9 Food & Drink

☎ 312-492-1336; 600 W Kinzie St; closed Sun; M Blue Line to Grand

Often in the Loop, a smell wafts through that's so enticing you'd shoot your own mother in the kneecaps to get to it. It comes from Blommer Chocolate Factory, which provides the sweet stuff to big-time manufacturers like Fannie May and Nabisco. Luckily, the wee outlet store sells a line of Blommer's own goodies straight to consumers at cut-rate prices. The dark chocolate, especially with covered almonds, reigns supreme.

ATHENIAN CANDLE CO

Map pp98–9 Religious Items

☎ 312-332-6988; 300 S Halsted St; closed Wed & Sun; M Blue Line to UIC/Halsted

Whether you're hoping to get lucky at bingo, remove a jinx or fall in love, this store promises to help with its array of candles, incense, love potions and miracle oils. Though they've been making candles for the city's Orthodox churches on-site since 1919, the owners aren't devoted to one religion: you'll find Buddha statues, Pope holograms, Turkish evil eye stones, tarot cards and door *mezuzahs* (parchment inscribed with Hebrew verses from the Torah). Unlike other stores of the ilk, which can be creepy, Athenian is tidy and the staff amiable.

SELF CONSCIOUS

Map pp98–9 Sportswear

☎ 312-633-4000; 1021 W Lake St; Ⓜ Green Line to Clinton

Chicago Bears players, Bulls players and rappers browse through the hoodies, track jackets and T-shirts in this converted West Loop warehouse. The bling-y, limited edition Adidas and Nike shoes are the main attraction, such as the $2000 crocodile-and-Italian-leather Nike Air Force Ones, complete with an 18-karat gold shoelace bauble.

SOUTH LOOP & NEAR SOUTH SIDE

Most of the neighborhood's cool shopping options are in Chinatown, which sells the same things as every other Chinatown the world over: inexpensive groceries and housewares, Hello Kitty trinkets and all the Buddhist altar goods the ancestors require. It makes an entertaining shopping spree post dim sum or other noodle-y meal.

LOOPY YARNS Map pp106–7 Arts & Crafts

☎ 312-583-9276; 719 S State St; Ⓜ Red Line to Harrison

This isn't your grandma's knitting shop. Loopy Yarns caters mostly to students from the nearby Art Institute, so the books, patterns, needles, hooks and designer yarns are about as hip as they come. Beginners can learn to knit or crochet in a workshop (two hours, $60-110, materials included), while advanced practitioners can learn more complex techniques while making a reverse-cable scarf or argyle vest (two hours, $20-60, materials not included). Check the website (www.loopyyarns.com) for the schedule.

WORTH THE TRIP: KANE COUNTY FLEA MARKET

True antique-o-philes will want to make the pilgrimage to suburban St Charles, about 45 miles west of Chicago, to the Kane County Flea Market (☎ 630-377-2252; www.kanecountyfleamarket.com; 525 S Randall Rd, btwn Rtes 64 & 38 in St Charles; admission $5; ⏲ noon-5pm Sat, 7am-4pm Sun 1st weekend every month), where hundreds of dealers sell everything from junk to books to rare curios.

AJI ICHIBAN Map pp106–7 Food & Drink

☎ 312-328-9998; 2117-A S China Pl (in Chinatown Sq Mall); Ⓜ Red Line to Cermak-Chinatown

The front sign at this Asian snack and candy store says 'Munchies Paradise,' and so it is. Sweet and salty treats fill the bulk bins, from dried salted plum to chocolate wafer cookies, roasted fish crisps to fruity hard candies. It's all packaged in cool, cartoon-y wrappers, with plenty of samples out for grabs.

TEN REN TEA & GINSENG CO

Map pp106–7 Food & Drink

☎ 312-842-1171; 2247 S Wentworth Ave; Ⓜ Red Line to Cermak-Chinatown

Ten Ren is *the* place to buy green, red, white and black teas, plus the teacups and teapots to serve them in. They also sell thirst-quenching bubble teas at the counter.

GIFTLAND Map pp106–7 Gifts

☎ 312-225-0088; 2212 S Wentworth Ave; Ⓜ Red Line to Cermak-Chinatown

After you see it, you'll wonder how you've lived without it: a toast-scented Hello Kitty eraser. Giftland stocks a swell supply of pens, stationery, coin purses and backpacks donning the images of Kitty as well as Mashi Maro, Pucca, Doraemon and other Asian cartoon characters.

HOYPOLOI Map pp106–7 Housewares

☎ 312-225-6477; 2235 S Wentworth Ave; Ⓜ Red Line to Cermak-Chinatown

Hoypoloi is more upscale than most Chinatown stores – almost like a gallery – filled with Asian artwork, glassware, funky lamps and other interior items. The wind-chime selection wins kudos.

WOKS N THINGS Map pp106–7 Housewares

☎ 312-842-0701; 2234 S Wentworth Ave; Ⓜ Red Line to Cermak-Chinatown

This busy store carries every kind of utensil and cookware you could want – pots, pans, wok brushes, knives. Don't miss the baseball-bat-shaped chopstick holders.

NEW MAXWELL ST MARKET

Map pp106–7 Market

S Canal St btwn Taylor St & roughly 16th St; 7am-3pm Sun; Ⓜ Blue Line to Clinton

Every Sunday morning hundreds of vendors set up stalls that sell everything from Cubs jerseys in the wrong colors to tube-sock 10-packs to tacos for $1. Don't let the name mislead you: the market is not actually on Maxwell St, though it was for decades until the ever-sprawling University of Illinois at Chicago campus forced it to relocate. Also, it's not really 'new' anymore, since the move happened in 1994. Still, it's an entertaining place to nosh with abandon, pick up a new stereo or buy hubcaps (legitimately obtained, versus the days of yore, when odds were they'd be fresh from your own car).

HYDE PARK & SOUTH SIDE

Bibliophiles should hop on the next Metra train to Hyde Park to check out the great selection of bookstores around the University of Chicago campus.

57TH STREET BOOKS

Map p114 Bookstore

☎ 773-684-1300; 1301 E 57th St; Ⓜ Metra to 55th-56th-57th

A vast selection of general-interest titles fills the basements of two buildings. It's the kind of old-fashioned bookstore that makes you want to own a bookstore. Luckily, it's for sale. Or at least a $10 share is – it's a co-op. The travel section features a commendable choice of Lonely Planet guides, a table and chairs for careful choosing and a chilled-water dispenser. Seminary Co-op (below) is the sister shop selling academic tomes.

AFROCENTRIC BOOKSTORE

Map pp50-1 Bookstore

☎ 773-924-3966; 4655 S Martin Luther King Dr; 3

'Seeing the world through an Afrikan point of view' is the slogan at this store, where big-name black authors give readings.

POWELL'S Map p114 Bookstore

☎ 773-955-7780; 1501 E 57th St; to 11pm; Ⓜ Metra to 55th-56th-57th

This leading store for used-books can get you just about any book ever published. Shelf after heaving shelf prop up the well-arranged stock. Another outlet is located in Lake View (Map pp82–3; ☎ 773-248-1444; 2850 N Lincoln Ave).

SEMINARY COOPERATIVE BOOKSTORE

Map p114 Bookstore

☎ 773-752-4381; 5757 S University Ave; Ⓜ Metra to 55th-56th-57th

This is the bookstore of choice for several University of Chicago Nobel Prize winners, including Robert Fogel, who says, 'For a scholar, it's one of the great bookstores of the world.' The shop is owned by the same folks as 57th St Books, listed above.

EATING

top picks

- **Avec** (p161)
- **Kuma's Corner** (p160)
- **Frontera Grill** (p144)
- **Billy Goat Tavern** (p145)
- **Borinquen** Restaurant (p160)
- **Charlie Trotters** (p142)
- **Smoque** (p160)
- **Sweet Maple Cafe** (p164)

EATING

Even though Chicago's immigrants import global tastes, and innovative stars of the city can go knife-to-knife with chefs from any other cosmopolitan metropolis, there's no escaping Chicago's lasting culinary legacy: meat.

Tasty reminders of Chicago's historical meat-packing epicenter are immediate – from the first snap of a Vienna dog, laden with peppers and pickles (though under no circumstances ketchup!) to the soggy finale of a sandwich from Al's #1 Italian Beef (p164). Equally palpable? The sticky-handed mess of BBQ from Smoque (p160) and buttery tenderness of an aged porterhouse from Chicago Chop House (p142). Eating in this city is a largely carnivorous activity.

And it can be an exhausting one as well. Just stare down a heavy-metal-themed, half-pound angus burger smothered in cheddar, pulled pork and pickles (the 'Led Zepplin') at Kuma's Corner (p160) or a cheese-and-sausage-filled slice from Giordano's that's as thick as a Gutenberg bible, and you'll be downright awestruck. In the 'city that works,' diners simultaneously stretch their dollars and their beltlines by demanding brawny serving sizes.

That's certainly not to say that the hulking plates of meat haven't spawned a discernable backlash. Vegans and vegetarians have staked out their own turf in cultishly popular destinations like Victory's Banner (p153) and the Chicago Diner (p152). In 2006 the City Council made Chicago the first city in the US to prohibit the sale of foie gras, the fatty livers of force-fed geese and ducks considered a French delicacy but derided as a product of inhumane animal treatment. Hot Doug's (p161) received the first ticket in 2007 for disregarding the ban – appropriately in the form of a foie gras hot dog.

Foie gras weenies are tame compared to the dynamic vanguard of Chicago chefs leading the growing 'molecular gastronomy' trend – a catch-all term for the exciting approach to meal preparation that's more like a science experiment. The refined tasting menu of Alinea (p147) and visionary plates at Charlie Trotter's Diner (p140) are short-listed among the most inspiring dinner destinations in the world.

But Chicago's immigrants still cook the city's most exciting, affordable fare. Once you get out of heavily traveled precincts like Greek Town and Little Italy, Chicago offers plenty of innovative ethnic cuisine. Try a *jibirito*, a pork sandwich covered in garlicky mayo, served between two thick, crispy slices of plantain. While this popular concept at Borinquen Restaurant (p160) may be making its way to Puerto Rican lunch menus around Chicago, you're unlikely to find one as good elsewhere.

With all the competition, the wild array of eateries have to earn their stripes – Chicago's discriminating diners aren't likely to jump on trendy food bandwagons that swoop in from the coasts, or steer you the wrong way when you ask for advice. Also, if you're interested in bringing along that dusty bottle of Bordeaux – or washing down the pizza with something *other* than Old Style suds – congratulations, many Chicago restaurants have a bring your own beverage (BYOB) policy.

PIZZA & BRUNCH: THE GREAT CIVIC DEBATES

Chicago-style pizza often tops the traveler's edible agenda, but don't be surprised if locals tend to point you in different directions for the ambassadorial deep-dish…and do so emphatically. These behemoths are nothing like the flat circular disks known by the same name in the rest of the world; they're made in a special pan – kind of like a frying pan without a handle – so the dough, which encases a molten bed of American-style mozzarella cheese and other typical ingredients, is oven-fried. The flagship Pizzeria Uno (p144) claims to have invented it in the '40s, but this, like many other fanatical conversations about pizza in the Windy City, will inspire debate. For better or worse, Pizzeria Uno is a worthy tourist warhorse, although those who want their gooey deep dish without a side of screaming children should try Pequod's Pizza (p149).

Just as much debate is saved for brunch – more of a reverently-regarded social event in the city than a mere hybrid of breakfast and lunch. Lula Café (p160) and Hot Chocolate (p157)

top picks

EAT STREETS

Good restaurants in Chicago have a magnetic ability to attract other quality eateries. Here are five streets with an embarrassment of dining riches.

- **Clark St, Lake View** (Map pp82–3) Between the buffalo-sized burgers, top-notch Thai and supreme sashimi, if your mouths not watering here, you must not be hungry.
- **Damen Avenue, Bucktown** (Map pp90–1) The boutique street does dining right.
- **Devon Avenue, Far North** (p167) It's a trip, but the brightly lit Indian and Pakistani eateries are worth it.
- **Division St, Ukrainian Village** (Map pp90–1) This hipster's dining paradise features copious sidewalk seating.
- **Randolph Street, West Loop** (Map pp54–5) Some of Chicago's best and brightest restaurateurs have set up shop here.

dish out upscale comfort food to ascendant young hipsters, though Nuevo Leon (p164) in Pilsen has less people-watching and more fun, providing free surprise appetizers with their excellent Mexican breakfasts. The most lovingly made breakfast in the city belongs to Sweet Maple Café (p164) who, by serving until 2pm, can qualify as way more than just brunch.

THE CITY OF CHAINS

It's strangely fitting that Ray Kroc opened the first McDonald's franchise restaurant in a Chicago burb: even top-flight Chicago restaurateurs love to expand their turf into multiple locations. Although the following chapter avoids soulless chain fast-food restaurants like the McPlague, a few quality Windy City staples outside of the ubiquitous Pizzera Uno (p144) can be spotted around town. Sometimes – as is the case with Giordano's (p144) and the high class Taylor Street pasta shop Rosebud (p162) – it's a good thing. Cookie-cutter franchise locals like the Billy Goat Tavern (p144) – including one at the airport! – are more like the unfortunate sequel to a great movie. None of these Windy City staples are likely to enjoy the culinary colonization of Micky D's, or even local Pizzeria Uno – when possible, try to stick with the original location.

FOOD MEDIA

For a place so unimpressed by snooty food trends, it follows that Chicagoans are a self-reliant bunch when it comes to picking where to eat. Case in point? The oft-discussed *Check Please!*, a local channel 11 TV program that sends dining citizens to restaurants across the spectrum, to get their straightforward critiques. The show has been flooded with applications from would-be food critics by the tens of thousands – not shocking in a city where a discussion about pizza can end in fisticuffs.

The same instinct has yielded a number of successful websites that feature user reviews. See the box Bites & Bytes (p162) for some of the best blogs, review sites and message boards to study before your visit.

PRACTICALITIES

Opening Hours

Most places that serve lunch open around 11am and stay open until 10pm, with fast-food chains and coffee shops opening about 7am and staying open until midnight. The busiest dinner hours are between 6:30pm and 8:30pm, the lunch rush is usually between 11:30am and 2pm, and breakfast tends to be served from 8am to 10am. On weekends you can get brunch until about 3pm. High-end restaurants in town might not serve lunch and are often closed on Sunday or Monday.

The following listings note venues' hours that stray from these rough standards, as well as any closed days. Chicago is a late-night diners' paradise, especially on weekends, so see the Midnight Munchies (p143) for places to get a bite after last call.

How Much?

The following restaurants are grouped by neighborhood and listed in descending price order, with the most expensive options first. If a restaurant has a listing for 'mains $6-25' it represents both the lunch and dinner menu with the cheapest main dish at $6, and the most expensive at $25.

A sit-down lunch in Chicago will be about $15 per person, including a drink and tip. For dinner, expect to pay around $25 per person, including a drink and a tip. If you're watching your budget, eat ethnic. The excellent options for Indian, Thai, Chinese

STRAIGHT FROM THE FARM

Always a bit unwilling to jump on culinary band wagons, Chicago has come late to sustainable and macrobiotic eating trends that have swept though other American cities. A pizzeria, Crust (p156), is the city's first certified organic eatery, Bleeding Heart Bakery (p159) is a pioneering bake shop, praised for their organic ingredients, and Lula Café (p160) is another excellent option for sustainable eats. For something fresher – as in straight from the farm – try some of a farmers' markets around town. They mostly operate from May to October, and are open between 7am and 3pm. For a complete list of markets in the city, visit www.cityofchicago.org/specialevents, or try Green City Market (www.chicagogreencitymarket.org) for additional info on the sustainable local scene.

Daley Plaza Farmers' Market At Washington & Dearborn, every Thursday.

Federal Plaza Farmers' Market At Adams & Dearborn, every Tuesday.

Lincoln Park Farmers' Market At Armitage & Orchard, every Saturday.

Near North Farmers' Market At Division & Dearborn, every Saturday.

Wicker Park & Bucktown Farmers' Market In Wicker Park, every Sunday.

or Ethiopian will save you money, as will sticking to Chicago's humble favorite: the hot dog.

Booking Tables

The rule here is simple: when in doubt, call ahead. This is especially true of fancier places, but most of Chicago's restaurants get busy on the weekends. Certain places won't take a reservation for parties of less than four, and some take none at all. Call ahead if your evening plans are contingent on dining at a certain hour or place.

Tipping

Adding a tip of 15% to the pre-tax bill has long been standard for adequate service, though outstanding service might call for as much as 20%. If the service made the meal worse, express your displeasure with a smaller tip; truly awful service warrants no tip and a discussion with the manager, which might be awkward, but may bring a reduced bill. If you're dining with parties of six or more, the gratuity, often as high as 18%, will be added automatically.

For counter service, like inexpensive cafés or *taquerias,* there are no hard and fast rules, even with the tip jar prominently displayed. If someone delivers food to the table, its kind to leave 10% in the tip jar, though takeout orders don't require a tip.

Valet parkers should get anywhere from $2 to $5 when they return your car.

PRICE GUIDE

The following is a guide to the pricing system in this chapter.

$$$	over $25 for a main dish
$$	$10-25 for a main dish
$	under $10 for a main dish

Self-Catering

A nice summer day in Chicago begs for a picnic. For simple supplies of lunch meat and Wonder Bread (a Chicago original, by the way) find a ubiquitous Jewel (☎ 800-539-3561); though those with a slightly healthier bent might seek out a Whole Foods (Map pp64–5; ☎ 312-932-9600; 30 W Huron St). Deli counters at Bari Foods (p159), Eatzies (Map pp82–3; ☎ 773-832-9063; 2828 N Clark St) or Fox & Obel's (p145) are all first-rate, as are the precooked delicacies at Charlie Trotter's To Go (Map pp76–7; 1337 W Fullerton Ave).

For fresher eats, try the city-sponsored farmers' markets that are common between May and October. Complete schedules can be found on the Chicago farmers' markets website (www.cityofchicago.org/specialevents).

THE LOOP

The Loop's dining scene closely mirrors the different groups you'll elbow past on the sidewalk – early morning coffee shops and lunch counters for office jockeys, non-descript chain restaurants for the less adventurous conventioneers and tourists, and high-dollar supper clubs that help ease executives through their thick expense accounts. Theatergoers who want to make it through dessert before the curtain rises should call ahead and inform wait staff about the timeframe as soon as they sit down.

ITALIAN VILLAGE

Map pp54–5 Italian $$$

☎ 312-332-7005; 71 W Monroe St; mains $15-35; ⌚ La Cantina Enoteca & Vivere closed Sun; Ⓜ Blue Line to Monroe

Of the three restaurants under the one roof, two are worth your while: the namesake Village, and Vivere. The former is decorated with the facades and twinkling lights of an Italian hill town – campy but cute – and has a menu of time-honored pasta and meat dishes that come soaked in traditional sauces. Vivere is the more creative cousin downstairs, offering a wide-ranging wine list that's some 1500 bottles strong, with bold flavors and bigger price tags.

TRATTORIA NO 10

Map pp54–5 Italian $$$

☎ 312-984-1718; www.trattoriaten.com; 10 N Dearborn; mains $14-34; ⌚ closed lunch Sat, closed Sun; Ⓜ Blue Line to Washington

An ideal stop for ticket holders, this lively bistro is just steps from the Loop theater district. The straightforward menu provides exceptionally flavorful takes on familiar items like ravioli (try the one filled with asparagus tip, *bufala* cheese, and sun-dried tomatoes) and risotto with skirt steak.

GAGE Map pp54–5 American $$

☎ 312-372-4243; www.thegagechicago.com; 24 S Michigan Ave; mains $10-35; Ⓜ Brown, Orange, Purple, Green Line to Adams

It's clear from the formidable Scotch Egg – a sausage-encased, deep-fried, hard-boiled egg the girth of a softball – that this elegant Loop newcomer approaches their Brit-bent bar grub with whimsical execution. Standards like the $14 (but worth it) Gage burger and delightful fish and chips plate are perfect washed down with one of the wide selection of pints, while upscale choices, like the duck confit in huckleberry reduction or saddle of elk with junipers, reward the more discriminating palate.

RHAPSODY

Map pp54–5 American $$

☎ 312-786-9911; 65 E Adams St; mains $11-28; Ⓜ Brown, Green, Orange, Purple Line to Adams

Tucked inside Symphony Center, Rhapsody's dining room opens to a lovely garden

top picks

THE LOOP

- Savoring the symphonic flavors at Rhapsody (left).
- Breaking into the juicy Scotch Egg at high-class pub newcomer, Gage (left).
- Choosing a crusty, delicious *torta* or sweet pastry at Bombon 4 (below).
- Feeling the heat of the spicy falafel from Taza (below).
- Relishing pre-theater eats at Trattoria No 10 (left).

– perfect for regaining your strength after a visit to the Art Institute, or dining early before some Mahler. Menu highlights include the halibut with roasted artichokes and little neck clams and succulent beef tenderloin. Some of the top-notch desserts even feature chocolate bits cleverly etched with gilded musical notes.

BOMBON 4 Map pp54–5 Mexican $

☎ 312-781-2788; www.bomboncafe.com; 170 W Washington St; mains $6-9; Ⓜ Brown, Orange, Purple Line to Washington

An offshoot of their revered Pilsen flagship, this bright Mexican café and bakery draws mobs of lunching cubicle workers for the array of *tortas* (Mexican sandwiches on thick, crusty bread). The die-hard sweet tooth should consider heading straight to the bakery case, as the pastries are also renowned.

TAZA

Map pp54–5 Mediterranean $

☎ 312-201-9885; 176 N Franklin St; mains $4-7; ⌚ lunch only; Ⓜ Brown, Orange Line to Washington

The tiled floor and undressed tables don't overwhelm with ambience, but when it comes to the holy trinity of cheapie Mediterranean pita-wrapped staples – falafel (spiced chickpea patties), *shawarma* (marinated meat with tomatoes and garnish) and gyro (spit-roasted lamb) – this humble lunch joint is awe-inspiring. The balance of lip-warming spice and cool cucumber, lettuce and tomato make the crispy falafel a particular triumph.

GOLD COAST DOGS

Map pp54–5 American $

☎ 312-578-1133; 17 S Wabash Ave; mains $3-6; ⏰ to 6pm; Ⓜ Brown, Green, Orange, Purple Line to Madison

A good place in the Loop to sample the classic 'Chicago dog,' this humble café serves the handheld tubed pork with the city's elaborate dressing: onions, relish, mustard, hot peppers, celery salt and a pickle spear. The atmosphere is unsightly – it shares a space with a fast-food chain – but when the weather permits, better environs are a short walk away at Millennium Park.

NEAR NORTH & NAVY PIER

Above the north bank of the Chicago River are some of the best dining options, and the concentration of quality eateries is great enough to simply follow your nose. You'll catch a whiff of Chicago's acclaimed pizza on nearly every block, but other options abound; upscale ethnic eateries are everywhere, as is the city's best steakhouse.

Unfortunately, Navy Pier is quite the opposite. Visitors to Chicago's most popular tourist destination will likely leave with a stomach full of McDonald's and the wrong impression of Chicago's culinary capacity. Bring a picnic from Fox & Obel's (p145), an amazing grocer/café only a few blocks away, and skip the Pier's food altogether.

TRU Map pp64–5 French $$$

☎ 312-202-0001; 676 N St Clair St; dinner $95-250; ⏰ dinner, closed Sun; Ⓜ Red Line to Grand

When Gale Gand (of the Food Network's *Sweet Dreams*) and Rick Tramonto opened Tru in 1999, it was instantly heralded among the city's best, featuring a French prix fixe that is equally artful and whimsical. The eclectic, highly seasonal menu features a renowned cheese course and brilliant desserts. Menus include an all-vegetarian version and the decadent deluxe version ($250). As you might expect by the price, the service is ace and a jacket is suggested. Getting a nibble doesn't have to break the bank though; all prix fixe items are available à la carte in the adjoining lounge.

CHICAGO CHOP HOUSE

Map pp64–5 Steakhouse $$$

☎ 312-787-7100; 60 W Ontario St; mains $21-99; Ⓜ Red Line to Grand

In the proud tradition of Chicago chops, this comfortable, upscale, independently-owned steakhouse is king. Look forward to perfectly-cured meats butchered on site, and an atmosphere befitting of the city's famous politicos and mob bosses – many of whom look down from framed portraits lining the walls.

MORTON'S Map pp64–5 Steakhouse $$$

☎ 312-266-4820; 1050 N State St; mains $19-75; ⏰ dinner; Ⓜ Red Line to Clark/Division

The meat here is aged to perfection and displayed tableside before cooking. See that half a cow? It's the 48oz double porterhouse. Smaller – but still quite dangerous if dropped on your toe – are the fillets, strip steaks and other cuts. The immense baked potatoes could prop up church foundations or try the hash browns, a superb version of a side dish all too often ignored. Expensive reds anchor the wine list.

NOMI Map pp64–5 French $$$

☎ 312-239-4030; www.nomirestaurant.com; 800 N Michigan Ave; mains $10-55; Ⓜ Red Line to Chicago

NoMi is perched on the 7th floor of the Park Hyatt hotel, offering a sleek, minimalist interior and spectacular views over the Magnificent Mile. Acclaimed Chef Sandro Gamba's knack for combining French fare with Asian flair is evident in the dishes,

top picks

NEAR NORTH & NAVY PIER

- Getting a bite-sized peek at the innovative fare at Tru by ordering à la carte at the lounge (left).
- Tasting tomorrow's culinary stars at the Kendall College Dining Room (p145).
- Enduring the scorn of cooks and mobs of tourists for a 'cheezeborger' at the Billy Goat Tavern (p145).
- Rediscovering south-of-the-border flavors at the Frontera Grill (p144).
- Making a picnic for Navy Pier at Fox & Obel's (p145).

MIDNIGHT MUNCHIES

Chicago is a town that treats midnight snacking with diligence. You can get a burger at any hour in the wealth of old-school, 24-hour family restaurants like the Golden Spike or Golden Apple. Or you can try one of the following:

- Handlebar (p156) Where you can eat and drink 'til midnight weekdays and 2am on weekends.
- Lazo's Tacos (Map p95; ☎ 773-486-3303; 2009 N Western Ave; mains $3-16; Ⓜ Blue Line to Damen) The quintessential taco stop after a night of long drinking.
- El Taco Veloz (Map pp90–1; ☎ 312-738-0363; 1745 W Chicago Ave; mains $3-10; Ⓜ Blue Line to Chicago) The other quintessential taco stop after a night of long drinking, with occasional karaoke.
- Tempo Cafe (p145) Serving eggs and such around the clock.
- Pie Hole Pizza (p155) Sassy staff and big slices are the perfect night cap after partying in Boystown.

ranging from caramelized Maine scallops to langoustine risotto. Reserve a window table around sunset – it's one of the most romantic experiences that Chicago has to offer. Reservations are required.

SHAW'S CRAB HOUSE

Map pp64–5 Seafood $$$

☎ 312-527-2722; 21 E Hubbard St; mains $10-50; ⏲ closed lunch Sat & Sun; Ⓜ Red Line to Grand

Shaw's beautiful old dining room and adjoining lounge has an elegant, historic feel, complimented by dark woods and the occasional jazz combo. To find out what selections on the menu are freshest, ask one of the friendly and efficient servers. A crab-cake appetizer and key lime pie dessert make faultless bookends to the meal.

LE LAN

Map pp64–5 French-Vietnamese $$$

☎ 312-280-9100; www.lelanrestaurant.com; 749 N Clark St; mains $23-36; ⏲ closed Sun; Ⓜ Red Line to Chicago

A joint venture of two of Chicago's most respected chefs – Roland Liccioni (of Les Nomades) and Arun Sampanthavivat (of Arun's) – yields Chicago's most venerated Asian fusion. Enjoy the exquisite marriage of French and Vietnamese cuisine in a brick-walled setting.

MK Map pp64–5 New American $$$

☎ 312-482-9719; www.mkchicago.com; 868 N Franklin St; mains $12-36; Ⓜ Brown Line to Chicago

Chef Michael Kornick (who was nominated for a James Beard award in 2005) wows the mostly business crowds with artfully presented dishes like ahi tuna, roast rack of lamb and sautéed veal sweetbreads. The desserts are equally scrumptious.

GENE & GEORGETTI

Map pp64–5 American $$$

☎ 312-527-3718; 500 N Franklin St; mains $15-35; ⏲ closed Sun; Ⓜ Brown Line to Merchandise Mart

For once, a place touting itself as one of Frank Sinatra's favorite restaurants can back it up – a fact evidenced in the framed pic of Ol' Blue Eyes by the door. Old-timers, politicos and crusty regulars are seated downstairs. New-timers, conventioneers and tourists are seated upstairs. The steaks are the same on both levels: thick, well aged and well priced.

TOPOLOBAMPO Map pp64–5 Mexican $$

☎ 312-661-1434; 445 N Clark St; mains $16-33; ⏲ closed Sun, Mon; Ⓜ Red Line to Grand

Part of the same operation as Frontera Grill (p144), this is where Chef Rick Bayless unleashes his creativity, unfettered by cost restrictions. Compared with its rollicking neighbor, Topolobampo's mood seems downright severe, as diners sample flavor combinations most people never knew existed. The menu changes nightly; be prepared for a memorable experience. Reservations required.

CAFE IBERICO Map pp64–5 Spanish $$

☎ 312-573-1510; 739 N La Salle St; mains $15-30; Ⓜ Brown Line to Chicago

The creative tapas burst with flavor. Among the standouts: *salpicon de marisco* (seafood salad with shrimp, octopus and squid), *croquetas de pollo* (chicken and ham puffs with garlic sauce) and *vieiras a la plancha* (grilled scallops with saffron). Most of the small dishes average $5. Iberico's heady sangria draws wearied Loop workers by the dozens in the summer.

BRASSERIE JO Map pp64–5 French $$

☎ 312-595-0800; 59 W Hubbard St; mains $9-30; ⏲ dinner; Ⓜ Blue Line to Merchandise Mart

This huge, open place serves wonderful food from Alsace, where owner Jean Joho was born. From the signature beer specially brewed by a local microbrewery to the hot, fresh baguettes, all the details are right. Try the great *choucroute* (smoked meats and sausages on sauerkraut) or the shrimp in a bag. Wear a fancy hat on Thursday and get a free *chapeau au chocolat* (chocolate hat) dessert.

BANDERA

Map pp64–5 American $$

☎ 312-644-3524; 535 N Michigan Ave; mains $10-27; Ⓜ Red Line to Grand

Looking up at the entry to this 2nd-story restaurant on Michigan Ave, you'd have no idea of the gem that waits inside. The red-bedecked Bandera has the comfortable, retro feel of an expensive supper club, without the snooty waiters (and at half the price). American classics – meat loaf, grilled fish and rotisserie chicken – predominate here. When you've shopped till you've dropped, this is the place to come pick yourself back up again.

GIORDANO'S

Map pp64–5 Pizza $$

☎ 312-951-0747; 730 N Rush St; mains $8-26; Ⓜ Red Line to Chicago

The founders of Giordano's, Efren and Joseph Boglio, claim that they got their winning recipe for stuffed pizza from – aww – their mother back in Italy. If you want a slice of heaven, order the 'special,' a stuffed pizza containing sausage, mushroom, green pepper and onions. We think it's the best deep-dish pizza in Chicago.

PIZZERIA UNO

Map pp64–5 Pizza $$

☎ 312-321-1000; 29 E Ohio St; mains $8-26; Ⓜ Red Line to Grand

Ike Sewell supposedly invented Chicago-style pizza here on December 3, 1943, although his claim to fame is hotly disputed. A light, flaky crust holds piles of cheese and a herb-laced tomato sauce. The pizzas take a while, but stick to the pitchers of beer and cheap red wine to kill time and avoid the salad and other distractions so you can save room for the main event. The $18 classic lands on the table with a resounding thud and can feed a family of four.

FRONTERA GRILL

Map pp64–5 Mexican $$

☎ 312-661-1434; 445 N Clark St; mains $14-25; ⏲ closed Sun; Ⓜ Red Line to Grand

Rated in the top three casual restaurants in the world by critic and author Patricia Wells, the Fontera Grill makes it impossible to stomach the so-so stuff most places pass off as high Mexican cuisine. Chef-owner Rick Bayless has achieved celebrity status with fresh south-of-the-border inspirations, including remarkable pepper sauces that can be savored like a fine wine. Of course, warm tortillas are made on-site for tacos *al carbón,* filled with charred beef and grilled green onions. The place is always mobbed, so expect to wait; reservations are only taken for five or more. See also the listing for Topolobampo (p143).

GINO'S EAST

Map pp64–5 Pizza $$

☎ 312-943-1124; 633 N Wells St; mains $7-25; Ⓜ Brown Line to Chicago

In the great deep-dish pizza wars going on in Chicago, Gino's is easily one of the top three heavies. And it encourages its customers to do something neither Pizzeria Uno nor Giordano's would allow: cover every available surface (except for the actual food) with graffiti. The pizza is something you'll write home about: the classic stuffed cheese-and-sausage pie oozes countless pounds of cheese over its crispy cornmeal crust.

NACIONAL 27

Map pp64–5 Latin American $$

☎ 312-664-2727; 325 W Huron St; mains $12-23; Ⓜ Brown, Purple Line to Chicago

Latin-American flavors aren't limited to the menu – salsa dancing breaks out here after 11pm on weekends. Chef Randy Zweiban mixes things up with a savory Pan-American menu; the seviche (raw fish marinated in citrus juice) is some of the best you'll find in Chicago.

KENDALL COLLEGE DINING ROOM

Map pp64–5 New American & French $$

☎ 312-752-2328; 900 N North Branch St; mains $8-22; closed lunch Sat & dinner Mon, closed Sun; 66

The School of Culinary Arts at Kendall College has turned out a host of local cooking luminaries, and this classy space with river and skyline views is where they honed their chops. Inventive French and New American cuisine comes at a fantastic value. The Dining Room is only open during the school term; call ahead for reservations.

WILDFIRE Map pp64–5 American $$

☎ 312-787-9000; 159 W Erie St; mains $11-23; dinner; M Brown Line to Chicago

A rotisserie and wood-burning oven roast shrimp, prime rib, steak and ribs at this haven for barbecuers. Prices for the generous portions average about $19 – not bad for this comfortable and welcoming place. In the best tradition of Chicago's smoke-filled rooms (where dubious political deals are cut), you'll emerge smelling of smoke, but at least it's barbecue rather than cigar.

CYRANO'S BISTROT

Map pp64–5 French $$

☎ 312-467-0546; 546 N Wells St; mains $9-19; closed Sun; M Blue Line to Merchandise Mart

This popular, casual French restaurant is named for the famous Cyrano of Bergerac, who shares his hometown with chef and owner Didier Durand. A very cheerful place, Cyrano's serves a menu of southern French favorites, including numerous roasted meats. A few tables line the street and make a good place to sip one of the many wines while watching the after-work hordes march home. The $15 lunch special is a four-course marvel that's served all at once.

FOX & OBEL'S Map pp64–5 American $$

☎ 312-379-0112; www.foxandobel.com; 401 E Illinois St; mains $6-15; lunch; M Red Line to Grand

A short stroll from Navy Pier, this bustling café has a boon of options for those looking to avoid dodgy, overpriced carnival food. Early in the day, the egg dishes are excellent; later, try sandwich options ranging from upscale (roast beef and blue brie) to classic (grilled cheese), or one of the well-executed comfort-centric large plate options, like the roasted salmon over succotash. If you can't find anything you like, the adjoining store is packed with supplies for an idyllic picnic on the pier.

GREEN DOOR TAVERN

Map pp64–5 American $$

☎ 312-664-5496; 678 N Orleans St; mains $6-14; closed Sun; M Brown Line to Chicago

The 1872 building housing this veteran bar and grill is one of the oldest structures north of the river and the Green Door Tavern has long served great burgers, sandwiches, salads and a few pasta dishes. The walls here are completely covered with ancient photos, signs and memorabilia. For simple but well-cooked food in a lively old-Chicago setting, this is the place.

TEMPO CAFE Map pp64–5 American $

☎ 312-943-3929; 6 E Chestnut St; mains $6-13; 24hr; M Red Line to Chicago

Bright and cheery, this upscale diner brings most of its meals to the table the way they're meant to be served – in a skillet. Its omelette-centric menu includes all manner of fresh veggies and meat, as well as sandwiches, soups and salads. After the bars close the scene here is chaotic and fun.

MR BEEF Map pp64–5 American $

☎ 312-337-8500; 660 N Orleans St; mains $4-7; lunch, closed Sun; M Brown Line to Chicago

At this local classic, the $5 Italian beef sandwiches come with long, spongy white buns that rapidly go soggy after a load of the spicy beef and cooking juices has been ladled on. Past a sign marked 'Elegant Dining Room,' you'll find a decidedly inelegant porch with picnic tables and an odd selection of movie posters on the wall.

BILLY GOAT TAVERN

Map pp64–5 American $

☎ 312-222-1525; www.billygoattavern.com; lower level, 430 N Michigan Ave; mains $3-6; M Red Line to Grand

Literally beneath the pie-eyed mobs on the Magnificent Mile, the subterranean Billy Goat, which enjoyed the fame of John Belushi's SNL skit ('Cheezborger! Cheezborger! No fries! Cheeps!'), remains a deserving tourist magnate. Skip the franchise locations for the original – a windowless haunt with an entire wall dedicated to former Tribune columnist

Mike Royko, famously cantankerous Greeks at the grill and scads of old-Chicago charm. Greasy-spoon fare is the only option, and you'll have to order a double cheeseburger if you're interested in tasting meat amongst the substantial bun. Most importantly remember – No fries, chips! No Pepsi, Coke!

PORTILLO'S

Map pp64–5 American $

☎ **312-587-8910; 100 W Ontario St; mains $2-6; Ⓜ Red Line to Grand**

Die-hard hot dog purists might bemoan the lack of true Chicago dogs in the vicinity of tourist hotspots, but this outpost of the local Portillo's chain – gussied up in a *nearly* corny '20s, '30s and '40s gangster theme – is the place to get one. Try one of their famous dogs and a slice of the heavenly chocolate cake: far and away the best inexpensive meal in the neighborhood.

GOLD COAST

Many of the most time-honored Gold Coast eateries are populated by 40-something gents in power suits who like their steaks rare and their handshakes firm. Luckily there is a crop of exciting neighborhood restaurants that cater to slightly younger singles who are well dressed, well heeled and inclined to enjoy a cocktail or three in the adjoining lounge while they wait for a table. The small, triangular park between Chicago, State and Rush Streets is the heart of the action, but the neighborhood is packed with good dining options and worth a stroll. If you have to wait a bit for a table during rush hour, all the better; the people watching is excellent.

GIBSON'S

Map pp70–1 Steakhouse $$$

☎ **312-266-8999; 1028 N Rush St; mains $20-80; 🕑 closed lunch Mon-Thu; Ⓜ Red Line to Clark/Division**

There is a scene nightly at this local original. Politicians, movers, shakers and the shaken-down compete for prime table space in the buzzing dining area. The bar is a prime stalking place for available millionaires. As for the meat on the plates, the steaks are as good as they come, and the seafood is fresh and expensive.

SIGNATURE ROOM AT THE 95TH

Map pp70–1 American $$$

☎ **312-787-9596; John Hancock Center, 875 N Michigan Ave; mains $12-39; Ⓜ Red Line to Chicago**

Given that diners spend most of the meal gaping at the stunning views, you'd think the kitchen atop the Hancock wouldn't trouble itself with the food, but the fish, steak and pasta dishes are yum. The lunch buffet ($14, served Monday to Saturday) is the best deal for the view, since the price of lunch is comparable to a foodless ticket to the observation deck. Families come for Sunday brunch; cheapskates get the same soul-stirring views for the price of a (costly) beer, one flight up in the Signature Lounge.

PUMP ROOM

Map pp70–1 American $$

☎ **312-266-0360; 1301 N State St, Ambassador East; mains $11-38; Ⓜ Red Line to Clark/Division**

Famous since the 1940s, the Pump Room continues its tradition of understated elegance. Real VIPs, or just lucky poseurs, sit in the dining room's legendary Booth One, a see-and-be-seen throwback to a previous, glamorous era. The dress code insures you'll be well attired for the cheek-to-cheek dancing that begins most nights after dinner. Veal porterhouse and grilled sea bass head up the American menu.

CRU CAFE & WINE BAR

Map pp70–1 French $$

☎ **312-337-4001; www.cruawinebar.com; 25 E Deleware; mains $12-24; 🕑 to 1am; Ⓜ Red Line to Chicago**

With no less than 300 bottles at this sleek wine bar, food gets less attention than the oenophiliac delights, though creative offerings like the 'surf and turf club' with lobster and beef tenderloin, and shared small plates are well-executed.

PJ CLARKE'S

Map pp70–1 American $$

☎ **312-664-1650; 1204 N State St; mains $8-23; Ⓜ Red Line to Clark/Division**

Chicago's straight, 30-something singles come to eyeball one another at this upscale restaurant-pub. Classy and cozy, PJ Clarke's specializes in comfort foods with high-end twists, like the béarnaise burger and teriyaki skirt steak sandwich.

MIKE DITKA'S RESTAURANT

Map pp70–1 American $$

☎ 312-587-8989; 100 E Chestnut St; mains $9-22; Ⓜ Red Line to Chicago

When it's too cold for a tailgate party, come to this Near North spot owned by the famously cantankerous former coach of the Chicago Bears. The menu is as meaty as you'd expect (the Fridge burger could feed a family for weeks), and fans will love the memorabilia-filled display cases.

ASHKENAZ Map pp70–1 Deli $$

☎ 312- 944-5006; 12 E Cedar St; mains $8-15; Ⓜ Red Line to Chicago

There aren't that many kosher delis in Chicago, but the thick stacks of corned beef and pastrami that come from Ashkenaz would stand out anywhere east of New York. Also, amongst the pricey options and chain restaurants of the Gold Coast, they offer the best quick lunch in the neighborhood.

FOODLIFE Map pp70–1 Eclectic $

☎ 312-787-7100; www.foodlifechicago.com; 835 N Michigan Ave; mains $5-10; 🕑 7:30am-8pm Mon-Fri, 11am-9pm Sat & Sun; Ⓜ Red Line to Chicago

'Call it a restaurant. Call it an eatery. Just don't call it a food court!' demands the mantra of Foodlife – a place with over a dozen different globally-themed kitchens featuring fresh, gourmet, à la carte options in a sleek atmosphere. Even if you call it a you-know-what, it might be the most wondrous one you've ever visited. Situated inside the Water Tower Place shopping center, it's ideal for gangs of shoppers who are so overwhelmed by the Magnificent Mile that they can't come to a consensus.

LINCOLN PARK & OLD TOWN

Once a bit rougher around the edges, the restaurant scene in Lincoln Park these days is hip, catering to legions of 20- and 30-somethings who unwind after long days at the office at trendy joints that have come with the neighborhood's gentrification. The sprawl makes it a bit less manageable on foot, but Halsted and Lincoln are busy with options, as is the slightly cheaper district surrounding DePaul.

A bit to the south, Old Town is quieter and quainter, run through by Wells Street and populated by older diners.

LINCOLN PARK

ALINEA Map pp76–7 Tapas $$$

☎ 312-867-0110; www.alinea-restaurant.com; 1723 N Halsted St; mains $135-195; 🕑 dinner, closed Mon & Tue; Ⓜ Red Line to North/Clybourn

Helmed by superstar chef and James Beard-Award winner Grant Achatz, the small

LOCAL VOICES: GRANT ACHATZ

By creating food that exists at the cutting edge of edible, nearly scientific innovation Grant Achatz has made his restaurant, Alinea, an embodiment of the city's young, hip and creative culinary landscape; this could certainly be the credo of Alinea's menu.

How do you think the character of Chicago's culinary world is distinctive from the food on the coasts? We are lucky to have the energy and youthful spirit that is conducive to creative concepts here in Chicago. With restaurants like Green Zebra, Moto, Schwa, and Alinea providing exciting alternatives in their own categories...and restaurants that have been around for years establishing themselves as the pillars of the community, we have managed to build a gastronomic city right here in the Midwest. Twenty years ago, who would have ever thought the national press would be hinting that Chicago's restaurants are better than New York's and San Francisco's?

What do you think a characteristically 'Chicago' meal is? There are too many dining experiences that are quintessentially Chicago to list only one. For somebody, a dog at the Bears game might be 'the Chicago meal.' Someone could also argue an experience at Charlie Trotter's is just as iconic Chicago.

What are your favorite three meals in Chicago, at any price range? Avenues at the Peninsula Hotel, Potbelly's Sandwich Works, and Schwa.

After all the success and recognition of Alinea, what continues to inspire you? The same things that inspired me before all of the success and recognition: food, cooking, ingredients, art, life.

You're known for bold culinary experiments. Have there been any over the years that have failed? Nothing ever fails.

dining room at Alinea is widely regarded as Chicago's most exciting space for foodies, where giddy, awestruck culinary cognoscenti document each course with a digital photo before eating it. The options are limited to a 12-course 'tasting' for $135, and a 20-plus-course 'tour' for $195, bringing an artistic carnival of strange pairings served in steel and glass contraptions, created especially for each dish. Expect otherworldly single-bite dishes and futuristic delights like the duck served with 'pillow of lavender air.' The once-in-a-lifetime meal can take upwards of four hours, and you can add a note-perfect wine pairing for an additional $75.

MERLO RESTAURANTE

Map pp76–7 Italian $$$

☎ 773-529-0747; 2638 N Lincoln Ave, mains $16-39; 🚌 9 to Ashland & Webster

Bolognese regional fare is the forte of this cozy family-operated slow food bistro and wine bar, where steaming dishes of risotto-of-the-day and hand-rolled pastas dominate the menu, offering particular comfort when the weather turns cold. This is one place where an otherwise conservative choice of the *tagliatelle bolognese* brings a plate of perfectly sweet and savory meat sauce and ribbons of homemade pasta that would delight any Italian grandmother.

CAFE BA-BA-REEBA!

Map pp76–7 Tapas $$

☎ 773-935-5000; www.cafebabareeba.com; 2024 N Halsted St; mains $12-30; Ⓜ Brown, Red Line to Armitage

At this delightfully ersatz tapas joint, the garlic-laced sauces may have you surreptitiously licking the plates. The menu changes daily but always includes some spicy meats, marinated fish and the city's most renowned small plates. For a main event, order one of the nine paellas ($12 a person) as soon as you get seated – they take a while to prepare.

BOKA

Map pp76–7 New American $$

☎ 312-337-6070; 1729 N Halsted St; mains $9-34; 🕑 dinner; Ⓜ Red Line to North/Clybourn

A hip restaurant-lounge hybrid with a seafood-leaning menu, Boka has become the pre- and post-theater stomping ground *du jour* for younger Steppenwolf patrons. Order a cocktail at the bar, or slip into one of the booths for small-plate dishes like grilled Santa Barbara prawns and a radicchio and portobello mushroom salad with a hazelnut bacon vinaigrette.

MAZA Map pp76–7 Middle Eastern $$

☎ 773-929-9600; 2748 N Lincoln Ave; mains $9-20; Ⓜ Brown, Purple, Red Lines to Fullerton

Romantic yet unpretentious, this Lebanese favorite even has menu items for couples, including the wide-ranging Maza Deluxe, a tasting of hot and cold appetizers that includes marinated meats and stuffed grape leaves, and the fanciful Maza's Signature Entree, which offers a stuffed crown of lamb, served flambé. For a more platonic and less pricey experience, go with baked *kibbeh* (a traditional ball of cracked wheat, stuffed with spiced sirloin) or a broiled kebob. Afterwards, try the hearty Lebanese coffee and a slice of gooey homemade baklava. Be warned, the place can get packed on the weekends.

VIA CARDUCCI Map pp76–7 Italian $$

☎ 773-665-1981; 1419 W Fullerton Ave; mains $7-20; 🕑 dinner; Brown, Red Line to Fullerton

The simple, southern Italian dishes regularly draw moans of delight from diners at this small Lincoln Park gem. Red-checkered tablecloths complement the baroque murals on the walls, and the food leans toward thick tomato-based sauces and amazing sausages.

O'FAMÉ Map pp76–7 American $$

☎ 773-929-5111; www.ofame.com; 750 W Webster Ave; mains $6-18; Ⓜ Brown, Red Line to Armitage

This sit-down restaurant serves thin-crust pizza and ribs that are popular with the neighborhood diners and Steppenwolf theatergoers. You can get picnic versions of everything from the gleaming white-tile takeout area to enjoy in Oz Park, across the street.

RJ GRUNTS Map pp76–7 American $$

☎ 773-929-5363; 2056 N Lincoln Park West; mains $7-14; 🚌 22

The very first of the now-ubiquitous Lettuce Entertain You stable of restaurants, RJ Grunts came on to the scene in the 1970s, when Lincoln Park emerged as the young

top picks

LINCOLN PARK & OLD TOWN

- Pondering the world's tastiest science experiment at Alinea (p147).
- Digging deep dish sans tourists at Pequod's Pizza (below).
- Sushi before Steppenwolf at Tsuki (below).
- Going miles beyond the typical south-of-the-border flavors at Adobo Grill (p150)
- Rediscovering the art of pasta Merlo Restaurante (opposite)

singles' neighborhood of choice. Now, as then, the huge fruit and vegetable bar and burgers are the mainstays. This is a fun post-zoo lunch spot; even the pickiest kids (and parents) will find something to love.

PASTA BOWL Map pp76–7 Italian $$

☎ 773-525-2695; 2434 N Clark St; mains $6-13; 🚌 22

You get more than you pay for at this affordable neighborhood pasta joint. The sauces are top-notch; the pesto reeks of garlic and the bolognese is redolent with basil. The meatball sub is also excellent, and the prices are just a fraction higher than you'd pay across the street at Subway.

PEQUOD'S PIZZA Map pp76–7 Pizza $

☎ 731-327-1512; 2207 N Clybourn Ave, mains $7-10; 🚌 9 to Ashland & Webster

Like the ship in *Moby Dick*, from which this neighborhood restaurant takes it's name, Pequod's deep-dish is the thing of legend – head and shoulders above chain competitors because of its caramelized cheese, generous toppings and sweetly flavored sauce. The atmosphere is affably rugged too, with surly waitrons and graffiti-covered walls.

TSUKI

Map pp76–7 Japanese $

☎ 773-883-8722; www.tsuki.us; 1441 W Fullerton Ave; sushi $3-12; 🕑 dinner; Ⓜ Brown, Red Line to Fullerton

This large, urbane sushi destination opened in 2004 and quickly became beloved for its fresh sashimi and playful approach to traditional rolls. Top picks include the smoked duck *nigiri* and the intriguing pistachio-salmon teriyaki. Soba and *udon* noodles and tempura round out the menu, which also includes some vegetarian selections. Most selections on the simple, late-night lounge menu are $5 or less, making for the best nighttime eats around.

BOURGEOIS PIG

Map pp76–7 Coffee Shop $

☎ 773-883-5282; 738 W Fullerton Parkway; mains $5-9; Ⓜ Brown, Purple, Red Line to Fullerton

A coffee shop whose powerful brew is only matched by the heartiness of its sandwiches and salads, the Bourgeois Pig is a convivial place to have a bite to eat while working through the *Reader* or chatting with friends. Tea drinkers and vegetarians will find many options on offer.

WIENER CIRCLE

Map pp76–7 American $

☎ 773-477-7444; 2622 N Clark St; mains $3-6; 🕑 24hr; Ⓜ Brown, Red Line to Diversey

'Order now or get the f*** out!' screams the apron-clad man behind the counter while an addled patron tries to comply. It's 4:30am at this Lincoln Park equivalent of a roadhouse, and the scene has reached its frenetic peak. Wiener Circle is both infamous and revered in Chicago; the charred hot dogs are good and the verbal berating is a cheerful sport.

CHICAGO BAGEL AUTHORITY

Map pp76–7 American $

☎ 773-248-9606; 953 W Armitage Ave; mains $2-6; Ⓜ Brown, Red Line to Armitage

This plucky little spot has managed to fight off the commercial developments which surround them, catering to DePaul students who drop in for fast breakfast bagels and sandwiches at lunch. There's free wi-fi, a staff of friendly neighborhood experts, and quality tunes on the stereo.

OLD TOWN

FIREPLACE INN

Map pp76–7 American $$

☎ 312-664-5264; 1448 N Wells St; mains $12-27; 🕑 to 1:30am Fri & Sat; Ⓜ Brown Line to Sedgwick

This local legend has been serving up Chicago-style baby-back ribs and perfect steak fries for over 35 years. The two-level dining room is heavy with wood – almost as much as the namesake fireplace burns up in a night. When the snow is blowing off the lake and the sidewalks are piling up with drifts, you can warm your cockles here – or you can air them out in the summer at the garden tables.

BISTROT MARGOT

Map pp76–7 French $$

☎ 312-587-3660; 1437 N Wells St; mains $7-20; Ⓜ Brown Line to Sedgwick

A visit to Bistrot Margot is like a visit to a little Parisian corner bistro in one of the remoter districts. Roast chicken, steak and *frites,* mussels and other coastal shellfish highlight the classic menu. The interior decor mixes dark wood with bright tiles and red booths, and the busy crowd adds to the atmosphere. It's a good idea to make reservations for the popular Sunday brunch.

ADOBO GRILL

Map pp76–7 Mexican $$

☎ 312-266-7999; 1610 N Wells; mains $10-19; closed lunch Mon-Fri; Ⓜ Brown Line to Sedgwick

Like Rick Bayless at Topolobampo, Adobo Chef Paul LoDuca takes Mexican food and flavors to another dimension at his lively eatery near Second City. The yummy guacamole appetizer is made tableside, and the dishes that follow are no less extraordinary. Try the trout steamed in cornhusk or the tender chicken breast in an Oaxacan black mole sauce. Thirsty? The margaritas are predictably good, but Adobo also has over 80 sipping tequilas on hand.

TWIN ANCHORS

Map pp76–7 American $$

☎ 312-266-1616; 1655 N Sedgwick St; mains $8-18; Ⓜ Brown Line to Sedgwick

Twin Anchors is synonymous with ribs, and Chicagoans can get violent if you leave their city without sampling some of Twin Anchors' baby-backs. The meat drops from the ribs as soon as you lift them. Choose fries, onion rings and baked potatoes for sides. This spot doesn't take reservations, so you'll have to wait outside or around the neon-lit 1950s bar, which sets the tone for the place. An almost all-Sinatra jukebox completes the '50s supper-club ambience.

OLD JERUSALEM

Map pp76–7 Middle Eastern $

☎ 312-944-0459; 1411 N Wells; mains $5-9; Ⓜ Brown Line to Sedgwick

The Middle Eastern pita sandwiches and falafel are fantastic at this friendly, 30-year-old Old Town joint. Looking for something leafy? Try the Greek salad, served with Lebanese flatbread. The atmosphere is bare bones; get it to go and have a feast in Lincoln Park.

ROBINSON'S NO 1 RIBS

Map pp76–7 BBQ $

☎ 312-337-1399; www.rib1.com; 655 Armitage Ave; mains $3-8; closed lunch Sat & Sun, closed Mon; Ⓜ Brown Line to Armitage

In the fierce battle to produce the city's best ribs, this tiny shop is a mighty contender. Smoky, meaty ribs in a tangy sauce make napkins silly at Robinson's (why waste all that perfectly good flavor on a dumb napkin?). The chicken is also good, and lunch specials run under five bucks for your pick of a meat, french fries and soda.

LAKE VIEW & WRIGLEYVILLE

It's best to eat your way through Lake View and Wrigleyville with broad expectations and a big appetite. Hungry wanderers will navigate chic bistros, ultra-late-night gay-friendly pizzerias and Clark Street's seemingly endless stretch of inexpensive ethnic eateries. On foot, there are three different, distinctive areas to explore: Halsted St north of Belmont Ave in Boystown, the long stretch of Clark on both sides of Wrigley Field and the dense restaurant row on Southport Ave north of Addison. Dining in Wrigleyville before or after a Cubs games is a nightmare for those in search of a quiet dinner.

An up-and-coming dining neighborhood is Roscoe Village, just east of the corner of Roscoe St and Damen, where a number of recent openings have gotten a lot of attention.

YOSHI'S CAFE

Map pp82–3 Japanese $$

☎ 773-248-6160; 3257 N Halsted St; mains $16-26; closed Mon; Ⓜ Brown, Red Line to Diversey

Yoshi and Nobuko Katsumura preside over one of the most innovative casual places in town. The changing menu focuses on low-

top picks

LAKE VIEW & WRIGLEYVILLE

- Cut beef with a butter knife at Tango Sur (below).
- Taste the tangine at Andalous (right).
- Discover another of Chicago's best-pizza contenders at Mia Francesca (below).
- Nod along to new age music over brunch at Victory's Banner (p153).
- Rethink the meatless Ruben at Chicago Diner (p152).

fat dishes with a Japanese flair. The kitchen treats all ingredients with the utmost respect, from the salmon to the tofu in the vegetarian dishes. Try to save room for the group dessert, which includes a little bit of everything on the menu. The service is every bit as good as the food.

JACK'S ON HALSTED

Map pp82–3 New American $$

☎ 773-244-9191; 3201 N Halsted St; mains $13-25; closed lunch Mon-Sat; M Brown, Red Line to Belmont

The menu hops around the world, juxtaposing American steak and Cajun fare with capable Italian, French and Asian dishes. You can wash down every course with the many fine American wines. Be sure to save room for dessert. Sunday brunch is worthy of special occasions.

TANGO SUR

Map pp82–3 Steakhouse $$

☎ 773-477-5466; 3763 N Southport Ave; mains $11-27; closed lunch Mon-Sat; 80

This candlelit BYOB Argentine steakhouse makes an idyllic date location, serving classic skirt steaks and other tender, grass-fed options. In addition to the traditional cuts, the chef's special is 'bife Vesuvio,' a prime strip stuffed with garlic spinach, cheese – it's a triumph. In summer, tables outside expand the seating from the small and spare interior.

MIA FRANCESCA

Map pp82–3 Italian $$

☎ 773-281-3310; 3311 N Clark St; mains $10-25; M Brown, Red Line to Belmont

Diners quickly fill up the dining room at one of the most popular small, family-run Italian bistros in the city. A buzz of energy swirls among the closely spaced tables, topped with white tablecloths and fresh flowers. The frequently changing handwritten menu features earthy standards with aggressive seasoning from southern Italy. Other treats include wafer-thin pizzas and the often-overlooked staple of Italian kitchens: polenta. Service can be harried because of the clamoring crowds.

ANDALOUS Map pp82–3 Moroccan $$

☎ 773-281-6885; www.andalous.com; 3307 N Clark St; mains $11-18; 4-10pm Mon-Thu, to midnight Fri, 11am-midnight Sat, to 10pm Sun; M Brown, Purple, Red to Belmont

Artifacts and pictures of the homeland color the atmosphere at Chicago's best Moroccan joint, where the tangines (a North African dish prepared in a clay pot) are remarkable. The Meknes tangine – filled with marinated chicken, and accented with red olives and lemon zest – was among the highlights, as was the *hareera,* a savory lentil soup with a keen blend of chili-powder, cilantro, cumin and chickpeas.

PLATIYO Map pp82–3 Mexican $$

☎ 773-477-6700; 3313 N Clark St; mains $9-18; M Brown, Red Line to Belmont

The warm dining room of this creative Mexican restaurant is packed with locals who come for the upbeat atmosphere and dishes like mahi-mahi tacos and the excellent shrimp fajitas. The chef of Platiyo learned his chops working at the superlative Frontera Grill (p144), and you can taste the mastery – at least until you've imbibed too many items from its inventive margarita menu.

KAZE SUSHI Map pp82–3 Japanese $$

☎ 733-327-4860; www.kazesushi.com; 2032 W Roscoe; mains $6-15; M Brown Line to Paulina

The most refined option on the Roscoe St strip, Kaze's Tuesday night tasting menu features their signature specialties: inventive sushi and Japanese dishes with a French inflection. The seasonal menu has much to offer in the way of large plates, though sushi aficionados will delight in the creative rolls – like the Blue Fin tuna dressed with pickled onions, burdock root, chives and truffle oil – and simple *nigiri* cuts, ideal to accent with the house-made soy sauce.

ARCOS DE CUCHILLEROS

Map pp82–3 Spanish $$

☎ **773-296-6046; 3445 N Halsted St; mains $7-17; closed Mon; Ⓜ Red Line to Addison**

The owners come from Madrid, and they have faithfully replicated a traditional Madrid family café, with a long bar, narrow room, dark wood furniture and small plates of classics like sautéed lima beans, chickpea croquettes and tortilla *española* (a cold egg and potato omelette) at about $7 each. Don't bother keeping track of how many pitchers of tangy sangria you drink; just keep ordering.

COOBAH Map pp82–3 Latin American $$

☎ **773-528-2220; www.coobah.com; 3423 N Southport Ave; mains $7-16; closed lunch Mon-Fri; Ⓜ Brown Line to Southport**

This hopping Latin restaurant and bar in the hot Southport corridor serves up spicy tamales and sweet plantains along with some ace mojitos. Despite the fever pitch of energy that the place reaches on weekend nights (DJs start spinning at 10pm), servers remain attentive and friendly. Try the Coobah pancakes (buttermilk pancakes with cinnamon butter and rum maple syrup) at the weekend brunch.

HB

Map pp82–3 American $$

☎ **773-661-0299; 3404 N Halsted St; mains $8-14; closed lunch Tue-Fri, closed Mon; Ⓜ Brown, Purple, Red Line to Belmont**

The owners of this friendly café-turned-restaurant won *The Next Food Network Star* reality TV show in 2005, but the real star is the food. Come by on weekends for the justly famous brunch, or drop in at night for an array of comfort foods – from pork chops to pan-fried crabs. HB is BYOB.

VILLAGE TAP

Map pp82–3 American $

☎ **773-883-0817; 2055 W Roscoe St; mains $6-12; 50**

Even though it can get overly packed on the weekends, this neighborhood tavern does everything well: food, drink and atmosphere. The friendly bartenders give out free samples of the ever-changing and carefully chosen lineup of Midwestern microbrews. The kitchen turns out some great burgers, veggie burgers and chicken sandwiches, served with a side of spiced pita chips. Out back the beer garden contains a fountain; inside the tables enjoy good views of the TVs for ball games.

SHIROI HANA

Map pp82–3 Japanese $

☎ **773-477-1652; 3242 N Clark St; mains $5-12; closed lunch Sun; Ⓜ Brown, Red Line to Belmont**

Every large city, if it's lucky, has its Shiroi Hana – the dirt-cheap sushi place where the food is consistently good, if not overwhelming. Lunch is a particularly sweet deal, with most sushi costing just $1.20 per piece.

CHICAGO DINER

Map pp82–3 Vegetarian $

☎ **773-935-6696; 3411 N Halsted St; mains $5-11; Ⓜ Red Line to Belmont**

The gold standard for Chicago vegetarians, this place has been serving barbecue *seitan* (a meat substitute), wheatmeat and tofu stroganoff for over 20 years. The hipster staff members are friendly, and will guide you to the best stuff on the menu, including the peanut butter vegan 'supershakes' and 'Radical Ruben,' a lunch plate that truly earns its name. Vegans take note: even the pesto for the pasta can be had without a lick of cheese.

CLARK STREET DOG

Map pp82–3 American $

☎ **773-281-6690; 3040 N Clark St; mains $5-10; to 3am Sun-Thu, to 4am Fri & Sat; Ⓜ Red Line to Chicago**

top picks

VEGGIE DELIGHTS

Some suggestions for when Chicago's bacon fixation gets a little old:

- Chicago Diner (above) The all-vegetarian diner.
- Victory's Banner (opposite) New Age, meat-free bliss (and a great brunch) awaits.
- Green Zebra (p158) Where Chicago's beloved Chef Shawn McClain veges out.
- Lula Café (p160) Smart, delicious food in cozy surroundings.
- Sultan's Market (p157) A place where chickpeas trump chickens.

Clark Dog is the brighter, friendlier version of the brash Weiner Circle with only a smidgeon of the confrontational attitude. Apart from hot dogs, other carnivorous delights include the hearty combo – which marries Italian beef *and* Italian sausage on a single soggy bun – and the chili cheese fries. If all the salty dogs make you thirsty, head to the supremely divey adjoining Clark Street Bar for some cheap cold ones.

VICTORY'S BANNER

Map pp82–3 Vegetarian $

☎ 733-665-0227; iwww.victorysbanner.com; 2100 W Roscoe; mains $6-9; M Brown Line to Paulina

The tough decision at this revered breakfast house is between the fresh, free-range egg omelets and the legendary French toast, cooked in rich cream batter and sided with peach butter. New Age tunes and muted colors give it a soothing vibe, even when the place is mobbed on weekend mornings.

PENNY'S NOODLE SHOP

Map pp82–3 Asian $

☎ 773-281-8222; 3400 N Sheffield Ave; mains $5-9; M Brown, Red Line to Belmont

Despite the presence of several other excellent Asian choices within a few blocks, this place attracts crowds most hours of the day and night. You'll see people waiting outside in all kinds of weather, good and bad. Maybe these hapless hordes are drawn by the place's minimalist decor, low prices or – no doubt – the cheap, tasty noodle soups ($6 average). Penny's is BYOB, so stock up on drinks before you get here.

PIE HOLE PIZZA

Map pp82–3 Pizza $

☎ 773-525-8888; 737 W Roscoe St; mains $4-7; 5pm-3am Mon-Thu, 5pm-5am Fri, 11am-4am Sat, 11am-3am Sun; M Red Line to Belmont

Closing when the sun comes up, the yummy gourmet slices and cheeky humor ('Point of reference,' reads a note on the menu, 'This menu is fourteen inches long.') make Pie Hole Pizza the final chance to troll for phone numbers and soak up the booze after a night of Boystown clubbing. A playful staff and laid-back atmosphere accompany the evening hours, giving way to an affably rowdy all male pick-up scene after last call.

ANDERSONVILLE & UPTOWN

Getting to Andersonville is a hike, so if you don't take a car or cab, exit the Red Line at the Berwyn stop. Luckily you'll know you're there when you look skyward and see the big yellow and blue flag painted on a water tower above the neighborhood's main drag. It's a nod to the district's Swedish history, which lives on proudly at the marvelous Swedish Bakery, though Andersonville also includes some excellent options from other corners of the globe.

The relatively cheap rent in Uptown has ensured that it, too, boasts strong immigrant enclaves, though these days most immigrants come by way of Southeast Asia, rather than Scandinavia. Look for rows of affordable and excellent noodle houses and Asian bakeries on Argyle St, the adjoining stretch found on Broadway, located three blocks east on Sheridan Rd.

If you're interested in letting your nose lead you to a place for dinner, head to Lincoln Sq, where a stroll up N Lincoln Ave will reveal something to suit a wide spectrum of tastes and budgets.

ANDERSONVILLE

LA TACHE Map p86 French $$

☎ 773-334-7168; 1475 W Balmoral Ave; mains $12-27; dinner; M Red Line to Berwyn

With its deco finish, La Tache offers sweet elegance and reasonably priced, high-end bistro fare to a rapidly growing fan base. The veal cheeks here are wonderful, as is Napoleon's favorite postbattle meal,

> **top picks**
>
> **ANDERSONVILLE & UPTOWN**
>
> - Going for the whole boneless chicken at Leonardo's Restaurant (p156).
> - Romancing the night away at La Tache (above).
> - Playing cookie monster at the Swedish Bakery (p155).
> - Tasting the love in every crumbling bite of a pastry from Pasticceria Natalina (p156).
> - Washing down the kimchi with a *soju*-tini at Jin Ju (p154).

EATING CHICAGO STYLE – BY THE BOOK

Books by Chicago chefs and about the city's culinary history are a good way to bring the city's culinary character home. Here are some recent favorites:

- *Raw* (Ten Speed Press, 2007) – Luminary Chicago chef Charlie Trotter turns his attentions to the raw food craze with his latest collection of meticulous recipes.
- *Talk with Your Mouth Full: The Hearty Boys Cookbook* (Stewart, Tabori and Chang, 2007) Local Food Network personalities and HB owners offer recipes for the sophisticated party host.
- *Mexican Everyday* (WW Norton & Company, 2005) – Rick Bayless, celebrated mind behind Frontera, writes euphoric prose to accompany his brilliant recipes.
- *Tru: A Cookbook from the Legendary Chicago Restaurant* (Random House, 2004) – The elaborate creations in this collection come from the team of chefs at one of the city's best restaurant, and are predictably intricate. Even so, it offers a way to enjoy a Tru dinner, without the heavy price tag.

chicken Marengo – this version has chicken served with garlicky crawfish, mushrooms and a poached egg. Looking for a romantic restaurant on the North Side? Look no further.

LEONARDO'S RESTAURANT

Map p86 Italian $$

☎ 773-561-5028; 5657 N Clark St; mains $8-25; closed Monday; Ⓜ Red Line to Berwyn

A sleek-yet-quaint atmosphere and delicious traditional Tuscan fare make this a fiercely-guarded local neighborhood favorite. No yawnish pasta and meatballs; the 18 Hour Ravioli – stuffed with a mouth watering combination of braised osso bucco & goat cheese, covered in caramelized pearl onions, sage and a succulent demi glaze – is the champion of the menu, and a whole boneless chicken tops the meat mains.

JIN JU Map p86 Asian $$

☎ 773-334-6377; 5203 N Clark St; mains $7-17; dinner; Ⓜ Red Line to Berwyn

One of only a handful of 'nouveau Korean' restaurants in town, Jin Ju throws a culinary curveball by tempering Korean food to Western tastes. The minimalist, candlelit interior of Jin Ju echoes softly with downbeat techno, and the stylish 30-somethings who come here enjoy entrees like *haemul pajon* (a fried pancake stuffed with seafood) and *kalbi* (beef short ribs). The drink menu must is the *'soju*-tini', a cocktail made with *soju,* a Korean spirit that is distilled from sweet potatoes.

ANDIE'S

Map p86 Mediterranean $$

☎ 773-784-8616; 5253 N Clark St; mains $6-14; Ⓜ Red Line to Berwyn

The larger Reza's next door may draw the yuppie hordes, but discerning Andersonville locals flock to Andie's for smooth hummus and much more. A recent remodeling has transformed the dining room into a Mediterranean showplace.

ANN SATHER

Map p86 American $

☎ 773-271-6677; 5207 N Clark; mains $6-13; Ⓜ Red Line to Berwyn

The cinnamon rolls are the marquee item at the flagship of this small, friendly local chain that offers Swedish standards in a pleasant café environment. Filling, familiar Nordic offerings like meatballs and potato sausage join selections of American comfort food on the dinner menu.

KOPI, A TRAVELER'S CAFE

Map p86 Coffee Shop $

☎ 773-989-5674; 5317 N Clark St; mains $5-8; Ⓜ Red Line to Berwyn

An extremely casual coffee shop with a pile of pillows on the floor in the window, Kopi stocks travel books and serves sandwiches and desserts to its lefty clientele. On the bulletin board you'll find ads from people looking for trekking partners to Kazakhstan or looking to unload last year's rock-climbing gear.

PASTICCERIA NATALINA

Map p86 Bakery $

☎ 773-989-5674; 5317 N Clark St; mains $5-8; 7am-6pm Tue-Fri, 8am-5pm Sat- Sun; Ⓜ Red Line to Berwyn

The bright green awning announces the friendly little bakery of Natalie and Nick

Zarzour, who achieve the most authentic, lovingly-made Italian sweets in the city by importing the hard-to-find ingredients (pistachios, rosewater, Sicilian sheep's milk ricotta, etc) from the motherland. The creations change daily, though all are made with unfailing attentiveness. The luckiest (or most watchful) visitors pick up *cassata*, an Italian liqueur-soaked cake filled with sweet ricotta cream, covered in marzipan and candied fruit. Don't leave the neighborhood without a box of the old fashioned Sicilian lemon cookies – bites of buttery crumbly goodness.

SWEDISH BAKERY

Map p86 Bakery $

☎ 773-561-8919; 5348 N Clark St; cookies $1; closed Sun; Ⓜ Red Line to Berwyn

You get free coffee in amazingly small cups here, but that's the only minimalist thing about the place, with its stock of butter-laden breads, cookies and pastries that have fattened up Andersonville for 75 years. Everything is good, but the princess cake and semla buns require a bit of extra attention.

UPTOWN

HAI YEN

Map p86 Vietnamese/Chinese $$

☎ 773-989-0712; 1007 W Argyle St; mains $5-25; closed Wed; Ⓜ Red Line to Argyle

Many of the dishes at this warm Argyle St eatery require some assembly, pairing shrimp, beef or squid with rice crepes, mint, Thai basil and lettuce. For an appetizer, try the *goi cuon*, fresh rolls of vermicelli rice noodles along with shrimp, pork and carrots. The *bo bay mon* consists of seven (yes, seven) different kinds of beef. Order sparingly, or ask for some help from your server – like the *bo bay mon*, many of the dishes are large enough to feed an army.

TWEET Map p86

Breakfast $$

☎ 773-728-5576; 5020 N Sheridan Rd; mains $7-15; 9am-3pm Mon, Wed-Sun; Ⓜ Red Line to Argyle

A dish of perfect biscuits and gravy is a surprise just steps from the city's northern Asian enclave, but so are many of the re-imagined breakfast standards made by former Charlie Trotters chefs at this cozy morning spot. The 'Country Benedict' adds two poached eggs and a thick slab of sausage for a decadent opening meal. For something lighter, try the corn arepas, corn pancakes with eggs, avocado and crème fraîche.

TANK NOODLE

Map p86 Vietnamese $$

☎ 773-878-2253; www.tanknoodle.com; 4953 N Broadway; mains $5-15; closed Wed; Ⓜ Red Line to Argyle

The servers wear camouflage aprons at this spacious corner eatery, a quirky touch in an otherwise utilitarian restaurant. The crowds come for *bahn mi* (Vietnamese sandwiches), served on crunchy fresh baguette rolls and the *pho* (noodle soup), which is regarded as the city's best. More adventurous palates should try the marinated squid, item #203 on the sprawling menu.

THAI PASTRY Map p86

Asian

☎ 773-784-5399; 4925 N Broadway; mains $5-10; Red Line to Argyle

A lunchtime favorite with workers from both Uptown and Andersonville, this Thai restaurant has a window filled with accolades and awards, and the food to back it up. The pad thai is excellent, and the spot-on curries arrive still simmering in a clay pot. For a quick, cheap snack, visit the counter for a baked pastry.

WICKER PARK, BUCKTOWN & UKRAINIAN VILLAGE

Exiting the Blue Line at the Damen stop at the adjoining neighborhoods of Wicker Park and Bucktown, you'll find yourself amid Chicago's most exciting eating and drinking opportunities, with restaurants representing every facet of the city's culinary scene: the spectrum includes elegant, expensive newcomers and reliable familiar street food. The disorienting angular intersection of Damen, North and Milwaukee Avenues is the center of the bustle, and is surrounded by places to tie one on after dinner (p176).

A short stroll south is Ukrainian Village, where slightly lower rents bring bigger risks and younger crowds. The city's first organic eatery – serving pizza, of course – opened at the corner of Division St near Damen at the center of the neighborhood's dining hub. Further south and east, near Chicago Ave and Halsted St you'll find some of the best of all, but, since they're more widespread and the neighborhood is a bit rougher, a cab or car might be best after dark.

WICKER PARK & BUCKTOWN

SCHWA Map pp90–1 Vietnamese $$$

☎ 773-252-1466; www.schwarestaurant.com; 1466 N Ashland; three course menu from $55; closed Wed; M Blue line to Division

Exceedingly popular, reservations for Chef Michael Carlson's masterful restaurant should be booked around the same time as your airline ticket. The fact that Carlson worked at Alinea is apparent in an avant garde three- or nine-course menu ($55 and $105 respectively) that redefines American comfort food.

LE BOUCHON Map pp90–1 French $$

☎ 773-862-6600; 1958 N Damen Ave; mains $12-23; dinner, closed Sun; M Blue Line to Damen

Classic French defines the menu at this quaint spot, a favorite for neighborhood types seeking a good deal and romantic environs. The lyonnaise salad is a winner, and other faves on the short menu range from escargot to chocolate *marquisse* (chocolate mousse without the egg whites).

SPRING

Map pp90–1 New American $$

☎ 773-395-7100; 2039 W North Ave; mains $15-28; dinner, closed Mon; M Blue Line to Damen

The seafood mains at this award-winning place come to your plate by way of Asia, with Chef Shawn McClain lovingly dressing up dishes of lobster, grouper, halibut and scallops in mouthwatering soy glazes, hot and sour broth, and fresh wasabi. The restaurant – which was a bathhouse in a former life – looks a little like an Ikea showroom: simple, modern lines and muted greens set the tone.

MIRAI SUSHI

Map pp90–1 Japanese $$

☎ 773-862-8500; 2020 W Division St; mains $9-19; dinner; M Blue Line to Damen

top picks

WICKER PARK, BUCKTOWN & UKRAINIAN VILLAGE

- Experiencing a whole new level of doughnut at Hot Chocolate (opposite).
- Having it cheap and chunky with a Costa Rican burrito and oatmeal shake at Irazu (opposite).
- Going green at Green Zebra (p160).
- Savoring the divine mac 'n' cheese at Milk & Honey (opposite).
- Grabbing a quick *fettia* (dough with egg and cheese baked over it) for the road from Sultan's Market (opposite).

This high-energy restaurant has an even higher-energy lounge upstairs; both are packed with happy, shiny Wicker Park residents enjoying some of the freshest sushi in the area. From the trance-hop electronic music to the young, black-clad staff, Mirai is where true connoisseurs of sashimi and *maki* (rolled sushi) gather to throw back a few cocktails between savoury morsels of yellowtail and shiitake tempura lightly fried to perfection.

CRUST

Map pp90–1 Pizza $$

☎ 773-235-5511; 2056 W Division St; mains $8-14; Blue Line to Division

Mind your semantics when you step into the first certified organic restaurant in the Midwest: that's no pizza, it's flatbread! The seemingly minor distinction allows for more sophisticated, global flavors (including Mexican- and Asian-themed pies, which outshine their conventional counterparts), with tender wood-fired crust. If you choose your patio seat wisely, you can even pick your own fresh herbs for garnish. For those more thirsty than hungry, explore the excellent house-infused vodka selection.

HANDLEBAR Map pp90–1 Fusion $

☎ 773-384-9546; www.handlebarchicago.com; 2311 W North Ave; mains $7-12; 11am-midnight Mon-Wed, to 2am Thu-Fri, 10am-2am Sat, to midnight Sun; M Blue Line to Damen

The cult of the bike messenger runs strong in Chicago, and this bicycle-themed restaurant and bar is a way station for the tattooed couriers and locals who come for the interesting beer list, vegetarian-friendly menu, and back beer garden. Bike messengers with ID get special deals on some nights.

HOT CHOCOLATE

Map pp90–1 Dessert $

☎ 773-489-1747; 1747 N Damen Ave; mains $7-19; closed Mon; M Blue Line to Damen

'Come for dessert, stay for dinner' might be the motto at this buzz-heavy Bucktown upstart. Run by renowned pastry Chef Mindy Segal, the cute place feels exactly like the irresistible, upscale chocolate desserts it peddles. With five different kinds of hot chocolate available, along with mini brioche doughnuts, you may forget to order any of the other food on offer, such as Kobe beef skirt steak and mussels.

PIECE Map pp90–1 Pizza $

☎ 773-772-4422; www.piecechicago.com; 1927 W North Ave; mains $6-12 11:30am-1:30am Mon-Thu, to 2am Fri, to 3am Sat; M Blue Line to Damen

After hefting enough gooey bricks of deep-dish, the thin, flour-dusted crust of 'New Haven-style' pizza at this spacious Wicker Park pizzeria and microbrewery offers a welcome reprieve. The best is the white variety – a sauceless pie dressed simply in olive oil, garlic and mozzarella – that makes a clean pairing with brewer Jon Cutler's award-winning beer. The easygoing, sky-lit ambience changes after dark, when ball games beam down from ubiquitous flat-screens, an occasional band plugs-in, and the 30-something patrons get a bit more boisterous.

MARGIE'S Map pp90–1 Dessert $

☎ 773-384-1035; 1960 N Western Ave; mains $6-11; to 1am; M Blue Line to Western

This ice-cream parlor on the outer northwest edge of Wicker Park has been making and selling its own, piled-high on sundaes, splits and cones since 1921. It's been almost as long since the crowded place was redecorated; the tables are few and a half hour wait is common. Once you get a seat, you can forestall the inevitable with a burger or sandwich, or just throw yourself into the cold, creamy main course.

MILK & HONEY Map pp90–1 American $

☎ 773-395-9434; 1920 W Division; mains $6-10; lunch; M Blue Line to Division

A bright, stylish space for an excellent breakfast or lunch, Milk & Honey has become the hangout *du jour* for discerning Ukrainian Village socialites. Most of the dishes are prepared from scratch by co-owner Carol Watson (don't miss the mac 'n' cheese) and the menu includes a long list of salads.

IRAZU Map pp90–1 Costa Rican $

☎ 773-252-5687; 1865 N Milwaukee; mains $4-10; closed Sun; M Blue Line to Western

This unbelievably cheap hole-in-the-wall would be one of Chicago's best value places at three times the price. The Costa Rican burritos are plump with chicken, black beans and fresh avocado, and the sandwiches contain a Costa Rican 'mystery sauce' that should be patented. Try the oatmeal shake; it's like drinking a cold, delicious oatmeal cookie. Cash only.

SULTAN'S MARKET

Map pp90–1 Middle Eastern $

☎ 773-235-3072; 2057 W North Ave; mains $5-9; closed Sun; M Blue Line to Damen

Steps from the Blue Line, this Middle Eastern spot has meat-free delights like falafel sandwiches, spinach pies and a sizable salad bar. Especially recommended: the $3 egg *fettia*, an egg sandwich with two kinds of cheese baked over it.

ALLIANCE BAKERY

Map pp90–1 Bakery $

☎ 773-278-0366; 1736 W Division; mains $5-7; M Blue Line to Division

Staff members are friendly and the sandwiches awesome at this independent bakery. Best of all, if you get lunch here, a dessert bar item comes with your meal. In 2005 the bakery doubled its space, opening a large, comfy room next door where café patrons can sit and enjoy their goodies (with free wireless to boot!).

LETIZIA'S NATURAL BAKERY

Map pp90–1 Bakery $

☎ 773-342-1011; 2144 W Division St; mains $4-7; M Red Line to Clark/Division

Early risers can get their fix of fantastic baked goods here starting at 6:30am, and everyone else can swing by at a more reasonable hour for their crunchy, toasty panini, slices of gourmet pizza and some mind-expanding coffee. Salads are good too.

UNDERDOG Map pp90–1 Mexican $

☎ 773-772-1997; 1570 1/2 N Damen Ave; mains $1-7; Ⓜ Blue Line to Damen

This subterranean late-night hot dog stop is a drunkard's paradise after a long night on Wicker Park bar stools. Inebriated or not, the hot dogs and gyros are on par with the city's high standard. For more booze fueled mayhem and Mexican, try a couple of *al pastor* (grilled pork with pineapple) tacos upstairs.

VIENNA BEEF FACTORY STORE & DELI Map pp90–1 American $

☎ 773-235-6652; 2501 N Damen; mains $3-6; lunch, closed Sun; 50

After eating them all over town, it's worth a trip to the source. The Vienna Beef Factory makes the majority of hot dogs sold in Chicago, and the factory's workers' deli is one of the freshest places to try the famous creations. Hot-dog haters can nosh on corned-beef sandwiches or potato pancakes. And Vienna diehards can pick up a case of the dogs at the on-site store to bring back home.

UKRAINIAN VILLAGE

WEST TOWN TAVERN

Map pp90–1 New American $$

☎ 312-666-6175; 1329 W Chicago Ave; mains $14-20; dinner, closed Sun; 66

The owners of the West Town Tavern hoped to create a neighborhood restaurant that evoked Chicago of the '40s, and the exposed brick walls and tin ceiling in the handsome dining area do just that. The atmosphere – casual, ebullient and unpretentious – mirrors the outstanding cuisine, and the beef, chicken, and pork mains are all crafted with care.

GREEN ZEBRA

Map pp90–1 New American $$

☎ 312-243-7100; 1460 W Chicago Ave; mains $8-15; dinner, closed Mon; 66

Chicken breast might be a rarity on the menu of typical vegetarian restaurants, but Chef Shawn McClain's veggie haven is anything but conventional. With a few nods to the meatily inclined, most of the menu is focused on amazing odes to meatless meals. The seasonal menu at Green Zebra is heavy on arty infusions (black-truffle essence, anyone?) and rich broths.

GONE TO THE DOGS

Like Elvis sightings and fishing stories, the invention of the classic Chicago hot dog is the subject of lore and legend, a long evolution that is much more than the story of wiener-meets-bun. A real-deal Chicago dog requires a litany of toppings and a sophisticated construction that seems perfectly designed to defy easy consumption.

For the record, a Chicago hot dog begins with an all-beef hot dog, preferably a local Vienna brand. The variation in cooking method is wide – some places steam, others boil and a few grill – but the poppy-seed bun and toppings are musts, as is the strict censure of ketchup. A traditional dog covers most of the essential food groups through the following toppings, although local variations exist:

- diced onions, white or yellow
- diced tomatoes
- sliced cucumbers, possibly slightly pickled
- shredded iceberg lettuce
- diced green bell pepper
- pepperoncini (Italian hot and pickled peppers)
- sweet relish, usually a virulent shade of green
- bright yellow mustard
- celery salt

The result? Part salad, part hot dog. It's not hard to find one either. A great Near North option is Portillo's (p146), which started in a Chicago suburb in the '50s. If you like a little theater with your dog, try Wiener Circle(p149) in Lincoln Park. For everything from a straight-up Chicago dog to one made with alligator, try Hot Doug's (p161), just north of Logan Sq.

FLO Map pp90–1 Mexican $$

☎ 312-243-0477; www.eatatflo.com; 1434 W Chicago Ave; mains $5-14; ⏲ closed Mon; Ⓜ Blue Line to Chicago

Think you've had a good breakfast burrito before? Not until you've eaten here. The southwestern-bent dishes and jovial staff at this brunch hotspot draw hordes of late-rising neighborhood hipsters on the weekend, though tart, potent mojitos and an elegant menu take over after dark.

TWISTED SPOKE

Map pp90–1 American $

☎ 312-666-1500; www.twistedspoke.com; 501 N Ogden Ave, mains $7-10; Ⓜ Blue Line to Grand

Don't let the motorcycle theme, burly burgers and steel finishing intimidate you: behind the macho facade at this popular brunch spot are artful dishes better calibrated for nesting yuppies than hard-scrabble Hell's Angels. If the smoky-sweet BBQ Kobe Brisket isn't tough enough for you, order their famous, though unfortunately named, 'Road Rash' bloody mary extra spicy, and chomp your way through its accompanying array of harpooned veggies.

TECALITLAN Map pp90–1 Mexican $

☎ 312-384-4285; 1814 W Chicago Ave; mains $4-12; Ⓜ Blue Line to Chicago

Weighing in at more than a pound and costing less than $5, the *carne asada* (roast meat) burrito with cheese is not just one of the city's best food values, it's one of the city's best foods. Add the optional avocado and you'll have a full day's worth of food groups wrapped in a huge flour tortilla. The *horchata* (a rice-based beverage made with water, sugar, cinnamon, vanilla and lime) is creamy and refreshing.

SWEET CAKES Map pp90–1 Bakery $

☎ 773-772-5771; 935 N Damen Ave; mains $5-10; ⏲ 8am-6pm Tue-Sun; Ⓜ Blue Line to Division

Try 'the egg' – a hard-boiled egg baked into a corn muffin – at this Ukrainian Village newcomer, where baked goods for breakfast, a spacious, shady patio and free wi-fi entice travelers to grab a quick bite and plan their day. When you head out, pick from the array of bite-sized cupcakes.

COLD COMFORTS CAFÉ

Map pp90–1 Deli $

☎ 773-772-4552; 2211 W North Ave; mains $6-8; ⏲ 8am-4pm Tue-Sat, 9am-3pm Sun; Ⓜ Blue Line to Damen

Sure, Cold Comforts does begrudgingly cater to unadventurous souls with smoked turkey, and ham and cheese, but the magic in their nearly 50 choices are the ones that push boring deli definitions to the limit. With one called 'Who Is Che Guevara?' (a hot turkey pastrami, feta, tomato and spinach delight on ciabatta) or the amazing 'Torta de Kosher Salchicha,' (strips of kosher dogs, lettuce, tomato, mozzarella and chipotle sauce), they're easily Wicker Park's most creative deli.

BLEEDING HEART BAKERY

Map pp90–1 Bakery $

☎ 773-278-3638; www.thebleedingheartbakery.com; 2018 W Chicago; mains $5-8; ⏲ 7am-7pm Tue-Sat, 8am-6pm Sun; 🚌 66

With cuddly punk-rock decor (think: hot pink walls and fuzzy bakery case), the relentless Sex Pistols soundtrack and tattooed counter staff, owners Michelle and Valentin Garcia have opened the country's first wholly organic bakery. The 'punk rock pastries' are the draw, but smaller treats (many of which are vegan) and lunch sandwiches are pulled off with flamboyant flare.

BARI FOODS

Map pp90–1 Deli $

☎ 312-666-0730; 1120 W Grand Ave; mains $4-7; ⏲ lunch; Ⓜ Blue Line to Grand

You'll find the best meats Chicago has to offer in this Italian grocery. If you have a car and plan to picnic, drop by Bari and pick up a sub or two (the Italian meatball is particularly scrumptious) and a nice bottle of Italian red.

FAN SI PAN Map pp90–1 Vietnamese $

☎ 312-738-1405; 1618 W Chicago Ave; mains $3-6; 🚌 66

This cute, bright-green box with the eye-catching sign has got some cooking muscle behind it: the chef worked in upscale kitchens such as the Four Seasons before opening this tiny 'fast-food' joint specializing in minty, Vietnamese spring rolls, served alone or over noodles.

LOGAN SQUARE & HUMBOLDT PARK

If the greedy forces of gentrification are gobbling up affordable real estate in Logan Sq & Humboldt Park at an alarming rate, it's already apparent in the broad array of restaurants; prices are slowly ballooning to capitalize on the deep pockets of newcomers. A glimpse into the future of Logan Sq can be had at Lula Café, where hipster intelligentsia ponder the Sunday *Times* over plates of comfort food that's creative enough to warrant the high price tag. The neighborhood's past is just as visible though in the affordable menus of Borinquen and El Cid 2, local restaurants in the flavors of the old neighborhood.

top picks

LOGAN SQUARE & HUMBOLDT PARK

- Downing margaritas and listing to the minstrel at El Cid 2(below).
- Biting into Chicago's unique Puerto Rican sammy, the *jibarito*, at Borinquen Restaurant (left).
- Head banging to monstrous heavy metal-themed burgers at Kuma's Corner (left).
- Eyeing the hipsters and inventive egg dishes at Lula Café (left).
- Ordering the mouth watering BBQ at Smoque (below).

LULA CAFÉ Map p95 — New American $$

☎ 773-489-9554; 2573 N Kedzie Ave; mains $8-22; closed Tue; Ⓜ Blue Line to Logan Sq

Located in the up-and-coming neighborhood of Logan Sq (to the northwest of Wicker Park), this friendly, upmarket café is where hipsters come when they have something to celebrate. Even the muffins here are something to drool over, and that goes double for lunch items like pasta *yiayia* (bucatini pasta with Moroccan cinnamon, feta and garlic) and dinners such as marinated rib-eye with braised kale.

BORINQUEN RESTAURANT Map p95 — Puerto Rican $$

☎ 773-442-8001; 1720 N California Ave; mains $6-20; Ⓜ Brown Line to Western

The story goes that Borinquen owner Juan 'Peter' Figueroa created his signature dish after reading an article in a Puerto Rican newspaper about a sandwich that subbed plantains for bread – a flash of inspiration that birthed the *jibarito,* an auspiciously popular dish that piles steak, lettuce, tomato and garlic mayo between two thick, crisply fried plantain slices. The remarkably delicious dish is all the rage within Chicago food circles and has since started popping up at other Puerto Rican eateries. It's the marquee item at Borinquen, though more traditional Puerto Rican fare is also available at this homey family spot.

KUMA'S CORNER Map pp50-1 — American $$

☎ 773-604-8769; www.kumascorner.com; 2900 W Belmont; mains $10; 11:30am-2am Mon-Fri, to 3am Sat, 10am-11pm Sun; 77 to Elston

Kuma's Corner might be a dark corner of heaven, where a soundtrack of thrashing rock compliments a roster of burgers themed after heavy metal icons. The results can be straightforward (Black Sabbath comes blackened with chili and pepper jack), esoteric (Led Zeppelin is piled with pulled pork, bacon, cheddar and pickles) or whimsical (Judas Priest has bacon, blue cheese, fruit and nuts), but the concept has earned an emphatic cult following. More combative diners should try the Slayer, served sans-bun atop a pile of fries, with ingredients including chili, Andouille sausage and 'anger.'

EL CID 2 Map p95 — Mexican $

☎ 773-395-0505; 2645 N Kedzie Ave; mains $6-14; Ⓜ Blue Line to Logan Sq

The tart, fresh margaritas and fish tacos (not batter-fried, simply grilled) steal the show at this bright, friendly Mexican eatery, which is a stone's throw from the Logan Sq El stop. On busy nights an acoustic minstrel sets up indoors, and when its warm, patrons head out back to the romantic patio to dine under strings of lights.

SMOQUE Map p95 — BBQ $

☎ 773-545-7427; www.smoquebbq.com; 3800 N Pulaski Rd; mains $7-10; Ⓜ Blue Line to Irving Park

There are no linens or candles, but the restaurant's spelling is a hint: with slow-smoked meats and homemade sauces, this worthy destination is a sight more refined than many of its BBQ-slinging brethren. Here, the mac 'n cheese comes with a cornmeal crust, and the salads are crunchy and fresh. But it's the St Louis-style BBQ that lines 'em up: brisket, pulled pork and hot link dishes soaked in rich, smoky and slightly sweet sauce. The squeaky-clean, family friendly environment and efficient staff are bonuses. BYOB.

FEED Map p95 Southern $

☎ 773-489-4600; 2803 W Chicago; mains $5-10; 11am-10pm Mon-Sat, 9am-3pm Sun; 66

With red-checked tablecloths, a free-play jukebox piled with classic rock and country, and a menu of southern home cookin' with a Tex-Mex inflection, this west Ukrainian Villiage destination has the chipper feel of a lost *Hee Haw* set. All the framed portraits of poultry allude to the house specialty – juicy, tender rotisserie chicken that falls off the bone – but the sides, including hand-cut fries, mashed potatoes, corn pudding and mac 'n' cheese are equally stellar. It's cash only, but they have an ATM on hand.

HOT DOUG'S Map pp50-1 American $

☎ 773-279-9550; 3324 N California; mains $2-5; lunch, closed Sun; bus 77

The gourmet sausages served here by the owner, Doug, may be at the forefront of a Chicago hot-dog revolution. With specialties ranging from blueberry-merlot-venison to sesame-ginger-duck, the food at this friendly place has reviewers dragging out their superlatives. On Friday and Saturday, Doug offers fries cooked in thick duck fat (you have to ask for them).

NEAR WEST SIDE & PILSEN

The West Side is vast, though our focus is on three relatively close neighborhoods: the West Loop, Little Italy and Greektown. Of these, the West Loop offers creative cuisine and hip atmospheres that outshine the sturdy stalwarts of the other two districts. Most options are along the Randolf St corridor, which will require a cab or car, since the closest El stops on the Green and Blue lines are far afield.

There are few surprises in Little Italy and Greektown, but those seeking a heaping plate of pasta or hollers of 'Opa!' to accompany a flaming plate of *saganaki* will have plenty of options.

South of Little Italy, Pilsen is Chicago's most densely populated Latino community, where vendors sling watermelon pops and butter-slathered cobs of corn. The 18th St stop on the Blue Line puts you at the strip's west end of.

WEST LOOP

BLACKBIRD Map pp98–9 New American $$$

☎ 312-715-0708; www.blackbirdrestaurant.com; 619 W Randolph; mains $26-32; closed lunch Sat, closed Sun; M Green Line to Clinton

One of the most talked-about restaurants in Chicago, this chic dining destination for Chicago's young and wealthy perches atop best-of lists for its exciting, notably seasonal menu. The warm-ups – like the confit of suckling pig with concord grape, roasted chiogga beets, and house made prosciutto – are a perfect introduction to the visionary entrees, which pairs well with the short, but careful wine list.

AVEC Map pp98–9 New American $$

☎ 312-377-2002; 615 W Randolph; mains $8-18; closed lunch; M Green Line to Clinton

Feeling social? This casual cousin to neighboring Blackbird gives diners a chance to rub elbows at eight-person communal tables. Dishes are meant for sharing (though you only have to share with people you know), and the food from Chef Koren Grieveson is exceptional.

DE CERO Map pp98–9 Mexican $$

☎ 312-455-8114; 814 W Randolph; mains $3-17; closed lunch Sat, closed Sun; M Green Line to Clinton

top picks

NEAR WEST SIDE & PILSEN

- Getting cozy with the neighbors at Avec (above).
- Getting a little surprise appetizer with breakfast at Nuevo Leon (p164).
- Disregarding all concerns about cholesterol with the 'Bacon, Egg and Cheeser' at the Sweet Maple Café (p164).
- Sampling fancy tequila and tacos at De Cero (above).
- Cooling off with a fresh fruit-filled popsicle from a Pilsen street vendor.

This *taquería* offers a high-end, culinary riff on traditional Mexican cuisine, turning out familiar items such as fajitas with home-made tortillas and spicy chorizo tacos, along with novelties like duck nachos. De Cero's drink list includes several dozen tequilas, along with one-of-a-kind concoctions such as the locally famous raspberry-basil daiquiri.

GREEKTOWN

SANTORINI Map pp98–9 Greek $$

☎ 312-829-8820; 800 W Adams St; mains $10-20; M Blue Line to UIC-Halsted

Fish, both shelled and finned, honor the legacies of Greek fishermen at this popular spot, where fresh whole fish can be prepared and served tableside. The boisterous room manages to seem cozy, thanks in part to the large Aegean fireplace. Everything from the bread to the baklava is well made, arriving in portions huge enough to encourage convivial sharing.

PARTHENON Map pp98–9 Greek $$

☎ 312-726-2407; 314 S Halsted St; mains $8-17; M Blue Line to UIC-Halsted

This veteran has anchored Greektown for three decades, hearing countless yells of 'Opa' to accompany the flaming *saganaki* (sharp, hard cheese cut into wedges or squares and fried). Greeks returning to the city from their suburban retreats have made this place a favorite. A plus for drivers: there's free valet service.

ARTOPOLIS BAKERY & CAFE

Map pp98–9 Greek $$

☎ 312-559-9000; 306 S Halsted St; mains $6-14; M Blue Line to UIC-Halsted

Like a good Greek salad, this place has many ingredients: one of the city's top bakeries – many of the nearby Randolph St joints get their bread here – which sells oozing baklava for $1.50; a café-bar that opens on to the street, with tables along the front; and a food bar with classics like spinach pie, which you can eat in or get to go.

MR GREEK GYROS Map pp98–9 Greek $

☎ 312-906-8731; 234 S Halsted St; mains $4-7; 🕑 24hr; M Blue Line to UIC-Halsted

Although there's no sign of Mrs, Ms or Mr Greek, 'the Mr' is a classic gyros joint with good prices. While the fluorescent lighting and plastic decor may lack a little in charm, the gyros have a beauty of their own. A full meal comes at just over $5, and they're open 24 hours a day.

LITTLE ITALY

CHEZ JOEL Map pp98–9 French $$

☎ 312-226-6479; www.chezjoelbistro.com; 1119 W Taylor St; mains $15-24; M Blue Line to Racine

Whether dining outside under the big oak tree, or tucked in a cozy corner, atmosphere and exceptional French fare make Chez Joel – the renowned namesake of Chef Joel Kazouini's – a romantic favorite, though an odd duck amongst the predominantly Italian stretch of Taylor Street. The menu is anchored by bistro favorites like duck leg *confit* and *coq au vin,* and is complemented by an extensive wine list.

ROSEBUD Map pp98–9 Italian $$

☎ 312-942-1117; www.rosebudrestaurants.com; 1500 W Taylor St; mains $14-22; M Blue Line to Polk

BITES & BYTES

Even though the original Chicago food blog, www.ChicagoEats.net, is recently dormant, there are scores of other websites, blogs and discussion boards that focus, often obsessively, on eating in the city. The following are some places where Chicagoans and Windy City visitors share reviews, get advice and offer recommendations.

www.chicagobites.com A blog that has well-categorized information, reviews and links to a related podcast about food in the Windy City.

www.gapersblock.com/drivethru An entertaining blog dedicated to 'Chicago bite by bite.'

www.lthforum.com Wide-ranging, friendly talk about the restaurant scene from a dedicated community of local-minded food-lovers. This is the place to get breaking news and the latest buzz.

www.yelp.com/chicago This persevering dot com based on user generated reviews has finally taken off with Chicagoans, who pull no punches in their starred reviews.

CHICAGO'S CULINARY SUPERSTARS

Square footage in Chicago is a bit less pricey than other American food cities like New York and San Francisco, allowing exciting young culinary stars to really go for it, opening boldly innovative restaurants and taking big risks. This has not gone unnoticed by diners outside the city's borders, bringing the Second City a disproportionate number of prestigious Mobil Stars and recognition from the James Beard Foundation – a kind of Pulitzer for cooking. It takes a well-heeled, broad-minded eater to sample the work of the following A-List chefs, but here are some names on every foodie's lips.

Grant Achatz of Alinea

In a nutshell Achatz was named the 'Rising Star Chef of the Year' by the James Beard Foundation in 2003, and has since made 'molecular gastronomy' a culinary buzz word and earned his renowned Alinea (p147; prix-fixe menu from $135) five Mobil stars in 2007 (a distinction shared with only 15 other restaurants in the US). The food is as cutting edge as it gets, served in 12 to 24 courses, and often seeming more like a delicious science experiment.

One dish to try The famous PB&J, a single grape covered in homemade peanut butter and brioche.

Charlie Trotter of Charlie Trotter's

In a nutshell It's no overstatement: Charlie Trotter is king of Chicago cooking and rightful father of the 'nouvelle' standards exemplified at Alinea. Trotter's eponymous restaurant (Map pp76–7; ☎ 773-248-6228; 86 W Armitage Ave; average meal for 1 person $200) in Lincoln Park is the flagship, though his to-go locations have begun to spring up elsewhere. His outspoken opposition to foie gras led to a public skirmish with Tru chef Rick Tramato, and, eventually, the city ban. Trotter will open a new restaurant atop the Elysian tower in late 2008.

One dish to try He's never served the same menu twice, but it's all excellent.

Rick Tramanto of Tru

In a nutshell Tramanto has piled up a couple James Beard awards since opening his landmark restaurant, Tru (p142; prix-fixe menu from $95), in 1999. His menus know no bounds, blending French, American, Italian and Asian flavors and techniques in the most artfully presented dishes in the city

One dish to try The whimsical caviar staircase, featuring little fish egg's waltzing down the stairs.

Graham Elliot Bowles of Avenues

In a nutshell Inspired to move to Chicago by a book by Charlie Trotter, Bowles' spent time in the kitchen at Tru before working atop the Peninsula Hotel at Avenues (Map pp64–5; ☎ 312-573-6754; at the Peninsula, 108 East Superior; from $90 per person). His prix-fixe menu, including the 20-course Chef's Palate menu that runs over $250, has created quite a stir and earned him a place next to his former role model.

One dish to try Dry cured tuna loin with saffron tapioca, his signature.

This location in Little Italy is the first branch of an empire of quality Italian restaurants that spread throughout the city. It is popular with politicos and old-school Taylor St Italians who slurp down colossal piles of pasta and spinach gnocchi soaked in red sauces. Bring a big appetite.

TUFANO'S VERNON PARK TAP

Map pp98–9 Italian $$

☎ 312-733-3393; 1073 W Vernon Park Pl; mains $8-14; ⌚ closed lunch Sat & Sun, closed Mon; Ⓜ Blue Line to Polk

Still family-run after three generations, Tufano's serves old-fashioned, hearty Italian fare for modest prices. The blackboards carry a long list of daily specials, which can include such wonderful items as pasta with garlic-crusted broccoli. Amid the usual celebrity photos on the wall you'll see some really nice shots of Joey Di Buono and his family and their patrons through the decades.

CONTE DI SAVOIA Map pp98–9 Italian $

☎ 312-666-3471; 1438 W Taylor St; mains $4-8; Ⓜ Blue Line to Polk

This large grocery sells everything an Italian cook could hope for, including scores of imported rarities and fine wines. The deli counter, which sells various lunch items you can eat at simple tables inside and out, will make visiting Italians feel right at home.

AL'S #1 ITALIAN BEEF

Map pp98–9 Italian $

☎ 312-226-4017; www.alsbeef.com; 1079 W Taylor St; mains $3-5; Ⓜ Blue Line to Racine

The original location of this local chain might not be the place to grab lunch if you want to get off your feet – there are no tables, only a stand-up counter – but the legendary namesake sandwich is a favorite of Hillary Clinton (who ordered them for her 50th birthday party). Piled high with savory beef that soaks through the thick bun, the inexpensive treat is one of the city's culinary hallmarks.

MARIO'S Map pp98–9 Italian $

1068 W Taylor St; drinks $2-4; ⏲ May-Oct; Ⓜ Blue Line to UIC-Halsted

At this cheerful box-front store super Italian ice comes loaded with big chunks of fresh fruit – keeps crowds coming in the summer.

PILSEN

MUNDIAL COCINA MESTIZA

Map pp98–9 Mexican/Fusion $$

☎ 312-491-9908; 1640 W 18th St; mains $7-21; Ⓜ Blue Line to 18th St

With a menu that blends Mediterranean and Mexican cuisine, Mundial is a good escape from the traditional staples of Pilsen. Goat-cheese ravioli and roasted corn risotto represent the Mediterranean influence and the excellent *mojarra empapelada* – a whole baked tilapia, wrapped in foil, stuffed with chorizo, pungent epazote and jalapeño-mayo – is an example of their broad-minded approach to traditional Mexican flavors.

NUEVO LEON

Map pp98–9 Mexican $$

☎ 312-421-1517; 1515 W 18th St; mains $7-14; Blue Line to 18th St

Tour buses line up, disgorging dozens of gringo tourists to sample the famed cuisine of Pilsen's most celebrated restaurant. Sounds horrible, right? Wrong. This huge place is a well deserved tour stop, and tourists are well outnumbered by the Latino families who fill up the tables. Outstanding tacos, tamales and enchiladas are available, though the dish most likely to blow any meat-eater's taste buds is the *assado de puerco* – tender roast pork served with homemade flour tortillas. The breakfast is also excellent.

SWEET MAPLE CAFÉ

Map pp98–9 Southern/Breakfast $

☎ 312-243-8908; 1339 W Taylor St; mains $7-11; ⏲ 7am-2pm Mon-Sun; Ⓜ Blue Line to Racine

The creaking floorboards, matronly staff and soulful home cookin' lend the Sweet Maple Café the bucolic appeal of a roadside southern diner. The signature dishes – inch-thick banana (or, seasonally, peaches and cream) pancakes, cheddar grits and fluffy, fresh-baked biscuits that come smothered in spicy sausage gravy or as a part of a fried 'Chick'n Egg and Cheeser' – earn the superlatives of locals, but the egg dishes, sturdy muffins and lunch sandwiches are done with equal aplomb. If you only have time for one breakfast in the city, this is the place.

CAFE JUMPING BEAN

Map pp98–9 Coffee Shop $

☎ 312-455-0019; 1439 W 18th St; mains $4-9; Ⓜ Blue Line to 18th St

This ramshackle café will make you feel like a regular as soon as you step through the door, serving excellent, hot focaccia sandwiches, baked goods and strong coffee to the 20- and 30-something crowd of MFA-wielding local bohemians. Chess and domino games are always breaking out here, and the comfy confines make it an excellent spot for whiling away a couple of hours with a mocha, soaking up Pilsen's colorful surroundings.

SOUTH LOOP & NEAR SOUTH SIDE

The bulldozers of progress have brought 'luxury' townhouse developments to the South Loop in recent years, bringing with them a handful of pioneering restaurants along Wabash and Michigan Aves. Though the eating scene here is likely to blossom as new condo dwellers move in, the best eats in this area are still in Chinatown, even if the divided neighborhood can be a little disorienting. The Cermak-Chinatown stop of the Red Line drops you off between Chinatown's two distinct parts – with the more touristy Chinatown Sq (basically an enormous bi-level strip mall) to the north and the slightly grittier, more authentic stretch of shops along Wentworth to the south.

CHICAGO FIREHOUSE

Map pp106–7 American $$$

☎ 312-786-1401; www.chicagofirehouse.com 1401 S Michigan Ave; mains $20-54; 🕑 closed lunch Sat & Sun; Ⓜ Red Line to Roosevelt

Situated in a carefully restored turn-of-the-century firehouse, this place offers traditional American cuisine in the South Loop. Ribs and steaks headline the show here, although they're pushed out of the spotlight when local resident Mayor Richard M Daley drops in.

GIOCO Map pp106–7 Italian $$$

☎ 312-939-3870; www.gioco-chicago.com; 1312 S Wabash Ave; mains $13-34; 🕑 closed lunch Sat & Sun; Ⓜ Red Line to Roosevelt

Restaurateurs Jerry Kleiner and Howard Davis made Randolph St on the West Side one of Chicago's hottest dining areas in the 1990s. Their whimsical Italian restaurant opened a few years ago in a desolate stretch of the Near South featuring a menu laden with classic Chicago-Italian dishes including delicate pizzas from a wood-burning oven. Surprises abound, such as the tasty lobster gnocchi.

OPERA Map pp106–7 Chinese $$

☎ 312-461-0161; 1301 S Wabash Ave; mains $14-25; 🕑 closed lunch; Ⓜ Red Line to Roosevelt

Owned by the same folks behind Gioco, this upmarket Chinese restaurant is easy on the eyes, exuding a quirky, cinematic pan-Asian ambience (heightened by the intimate 'vault' seating constructed from old film-reel vaults). You'll find familiar dishes on the menu – Peking duck, Kung Pao beef, general's chicken, etc – remade with boutique meats, sharp spices and a light touch.

YOLK Map pp106–7 Breakfast $

☎ 312-789-9655; 1120 S Michigan Ave; mains $5-11; 🕑 closed dinner; Ⓜ Red Line to Roosevelt

Slinking into one of the custom booths at this cheerful diner is worth the long wait – you'll dig into the best traditional breakfast

> **top picks**
>
> **SOUTH LOOP & NEAR SOUTH SIDE**
>
> - Slurping down a banana tapioca smoothie at Joy Yee's Noodle Shop (p166).
> - Scanning da room for da mayor at Chicago Firehouse (left).
> - Going south for gumbo at Dixie Kitchen & Bait Shop (p167).

in the South Loop. The omelets range from healthy options (the Iron Man has egg whites and comes loaded with veggies and avocado) to heart-stoppers (the meaty Butcher Shop) and there are scores of big salads and burgers for those inclined to order lunch.

LAWRENCE FISHERIES

Map pp106–7 Southern $

☎ 312-225-2113; www.lawrencesfisheries.com; 2120 S Canal St; mains $4-11; 🕑 24hrs; Ⓜ Red Line to Chinatown/Cermak

There's not much to look at inside this 24-hr fish-and-chips joint, but the window at the end of the long dining room frames a stunning scene of the Sear's Tower over the Chicago River. Not that you have much option but to stand agape once your order arrives – delicious treats like popcorn shrimp, oysters and fish chips are stalwarts, but frog legs and scallops round out the menu of batter-crusted goodies from the sea. At night the parking lot outside of this typically family-oriented joint is a primo location for locals to sit on car hoods and shop for suspiciously current DVDs.

LOU MITCHELL'S Map pp106–7 Breakfast $

☎ 312-939-3111; www.loumitchellsrestaurant.com; 565 W Jackson Blvd; mains $5-9; 🕑 lunch; Ⓜ Blue Line to Clinton

Immediately west of the Loop and close to Union Station, this popular coffee shop brings in elbow-to-elbow tourists for their breakfasts. The omelettes hang off the plates, and the fluffy flapjacks and crisp waffles are prepared with practiced perfection. Cups of coffee are bottomless, just like the charm of the staff members who hand out free treats to young and old alike.

THAT'S AMORE

When pizza first arrived in Chicago it was a scrawny, sickly specimen, and it took about a half century before an enterprising restaurateur named Ike Sewell finally made it well.

Ike, the owner of Pizzeria Uno, rolled out the first 'deep-dish' pizza in 1943. His creation had a flakier crust than the Neapolitan-style pizza, and the thing was *deep* – it had a full inch of red sauce, chopped plum tomatoes, shredded American-style mozzarella cheese and a number of optional toppings.

You may have tried Chicago-style pizza at restaurants in your hometown. But until you've hefted a slice of cheesy Chicago pie in the 312 (or 773) area code, you can't say you've fully lived. You can get a heaping helping at any of the following establishments:

Gino's East (p144)

Giordano's (p144)

Pequod's Pizza (p149)

Pizzeria Uno (p144)

CHINATOWN

LAO SZE CHUAN

Map pp106–7 Chinese $$

☎ 312-326-5040; www.laoszechuan.com; 2172 S Archer Ave; mains $8-20; Ⓜ Red Line to Cermak/Chinatown

Lao Sze Chuan is the most authentic option in the heavily-touristy Chinatown Sq. The house special is the special three chili chicken, which is tender and very spicy, though the extensive menu has excellent hotpots next to recipes from the far reaches of the Szechuan province. If the choices are overwhelming, look for advice from watchful chef and owner 'Tony' Xiao Jun Hu.

PHOENIX

Map pp106–7 Chinese $$

☎ 312-328-0848; 2131 S Archer Ave; mains $7-16; Ⓜ Red Line to Cermak-Chinatown

Though better sit-down dinner experiences in Chinatown are abundant, the draw here is their excellent dim sum. Small plates of *char siu bao* (barbecued pork buns), shrimp-filled rice noodles, egg custards and other popular vitals roll around the dining room in a seemingly endless parade of carts. The language barrier can be an issue, so keep in mind that if it looks like chicken feet, it probably is.

JOY YEE'S NOODLE SHOP

Map pp106–7 Asian $

☎ 312-328-0001; 2159 S China Pl (Chinatown Sq); mains $6-12; Ⓜ Red Line to Cermak-Chinatown

Folks line up for bubble teas packed with fresh fruit at this brightly colored, hip café. Do yourself a favor though, and save one of the deliciously sweet drinks for dessert after a bowl of *udon* (a thick, wheat-based noodle), *chow fun* (rice noodles) or chow mein.

MAY MAY GOURMET FOOD INC

Map pp106–7 Chinese $

☎ 312-842-3366; 211 W 23rd; mains $3-10; Ⓜ Red Line to Cermak/Chinatown

Ask a Chinatown local for the most authentic meal in the neighborhood and you'll invariably be directed down a side street to the green-painted exterior of this windowless café, also referred to simply as 'Gourmet Restaurant.' Don't be put off; what it lacks in decor – which is considerable – is made up with the freshness of their made-to-order Cantonese dishes. Expect some degree of language barrier, easily overcome by pointing to the delicious-looking dish on the table next to you.

WAN SHI DA BAKERY

Map pp106–7 Chinese $

☎ 312-225-2113; 2229 S. Wentworth St; mains $1-3; 🕑 6am-10pm, Mon-Fri; Ⓜ Red Line to Cermak/Chinatown

The best, and cheapest à la carte lunch in Chinatown, this bright little bakery has fluffy BBQ pork buns, hot dog buns (a Chinese variation on the pig-in-a-blanket), bite-sized egg custards, coconut and winter melon pastries and some dim-sum fare. It's available to go, or to scarf down by the handful at the no-frills tables in the back. The more weather-beaten sister bakery across the street, Chiu Quon Bakery, has a nearly identical menu and more tourist foot traffic.

HYDE PARK & SOUTH SIDE

Chicago's South Side isn't a heavily traveled dining destination, but if you ask around you'll find excellent African American soul food favorites like collard greens and fried chicken, and some of the city's best BBQ – with or without meat – around the so-called 'BBQ triangle.'

GETTING CURRIED AWAY

The blinking lights, aromatic spice shops and scads of Indian restaurants make Devon Ave west of Western Ave seem like a little side trip to India on the outer stretches of Chicago. The best curry in the city is here, but the El doesn't come close, so you'll have to drive, take a cab or take the Brown Line to Western and then transfer to bus 49B.

Indian Garden (Map pp50-1; ☎ 773-338-2929; 2548 W Devon Ave; mains $6-15; 🚌 155) Items not found on most South Asian menus dominate here. The cooks use wok-like pans and simple iron griddles to prepare a lot of the items. Vegetables go beyond the soggy cauliflower in goopy sauces found at other, less inspired places. Wash it all down with a mango shake.

Sabri Nehari (Map pp50-1; ☎ 773-743-6200; 2511 W Devon Ave; mains $7-16; 🚌 155) Fresh, fresh meat and vegetable dishes, distinctly seasoned, set this Pakistani place apart from its competitors on Devon. Try the 'frontier' chicken, which comes with a plate of fresh-cut onions, tomatoes, cucumber and lemon, and enough perfectly cooked chicken for two. For dessert, check out the *kheer*, a creamy rice pudding.

Udupi Palace (Map pp50-1; ☎ 773-338-2152; 2543 W Devon Ave; mains $5-10; 🚌 155) This bustling all-vegetarian Indian restaurant serves toasty, kite-sized rice crepes stuffed with all manner of vegetables and spices, along with an array of curries. The room gets quite loud once it packs out with 20-something Anglo hipsters and a young Indian crowd.

Hyde Park, which surrounds the University of Chicago, has the requisite college-town fare at similarly low prices. The distances are much too far to walk, so it's best to take a car.

DIXIE KITCHEN & BAIT SHOP

Map p114 Southern $$

☎ 773-363-4943, TK-363-4943; www.dixiekitchenchicago.com; 5225 S Harper; mains $7-16; 🕑 11am-10pm Sun-Thurs, to 11pm Fri-Sat; 🚌 6

After marching through the gothic hallows of the University of Chicago, the hodge-podge of rusting gas station signs and odd-ball Southern memorabilia at this Dixie eatery is an unassuming, homey delight – even if it feels a bit misplaced at the edge of an aging strip mall. Despite the name, there's no fish food here, but service for humans starts with complimentary biscuits and mini loaves of cornbread. Start things on the right foot with fried green tomatoes, crawfish and cornbread fritters, or a cup of gumbo. For more quality southern fare, try an oyster po'boy or reliable country fried steak.

ARMY & LOU'S Map pp50-1 Southern $$

☎ 773-483-3100; 422 E 75th St, near Martin Luther King Dr; mains $6-15; 🕑 closed Tue; 🚌 75

If you've never had soul food before, you've got to start at this warm and welcoming Chicago classic. It rises above the crowd of similar local establishments with its fried chicken, catfish, collard greens, sweet-potato pie and other classics at prices that are good for your soul. Don't be surprised if you see a few famous black politicians, led by Jesse Jackson. And don't be surprised if some white politicians show up for a photo-op.

MEDICI Map p114 American $$

☎ 773-667-7394; 1327 E 57th St; mains $6-14; Ⓜ Metra to 59th St

The menu of thin-crust pizzas, sandwiches and salads draw UC students to this colorful café and bakery. For breakfast, try the 'eggs espresso,' made by steaming eggs in an espresso machine. After your meal, check the vast bulletin board out front. It's the perfect place to size up the character of the community and possibly find the complete works of John Maynard Keynes for sale, cheap.

SOUL VEGETARIAN EAST

Map pp50-1 BBQ $$

☎ 773-224-0104; 203 E 75th St; mains $5-15; Ⓜ Metra to 59th St

Finding soul food that meets the tenants of the vegan diet is such a rarity that the creative BBQ sandwiches and dinner plates at this comfy South Side place have earned a national reputation. Carnivores should head up the street to Lem's Bar-B-Q House (Map pp50-1; ☎ 773-994-2428; 311 E 75th St) for more traditional fare; it sits atop Chicago's 'BBQ Triangle.'

CAFFÉ FLORIAN Map p114 American $

☎ 773-752-4100; 1450 E 57th St; mains $6-11; Ⓜ Metra to 59th St

The menu here traces the cafe's name back to the original Caffé Florian, which opened in Venice in 1720 as a meeting place for 'the intelligentsia, with patrons including the most celebrated artists, poets, dramatists, actors, musicians and philosophers of the time.' The humbler modern version serves lesser mortals, and much of the fare (black-bean nachos, fish-and-chips) has never graced a tabletop in Venice. But a few Italian items do make the menu, which covers much of the world.

DRINKING

top picks

- **Violet Hour** (p177)
- **Billy Goat Tavern**(p171)
- **Happy Village** (p176)
- **Matchbox** (p176)
- **Schaller's Pump** (p180)
- **Yak-zies** (p174)
- **Bernice's Tavern** (p179)
- **Delilah's** (p172)
- **Rainbo Club** (p176)
- **Ola's Liquor** (p178)

DRINKING

A signed portrait of Sinatra looks down over the bar at Gene & Georgetti, an old-world Italian place where the drinks menu bears a simple dedication 'to those merry souls of other days...who, whatever they may drink, prove able to carry it, enjoy it, and remain gentlemen.' The baffling abundance of bars in Chicago makes it clear that residents of the Windy City certainly enjoy drinking as much as those merry souls. The part about remaining gentlemen? Well, aside from the stumbling co-eds in Lincoln Park and the boisterous post-game mobs in Wrigleyville, the city approaches drinking with gentlemanly diligence. From knocking back bottles at a linoleum-floored Ukrainian Village tavern to consulting food pairings with an expert mixologist at a sophisticated speakeasy, Chicago's drinking culture is nothing if not serious, and a widely-cherished civic pastime.

OPENING HOURS

Chicagoans are so serious about drinking that many drinking establishments stay open late on the weekends – some until 5am. If you've got a superhuman liver and enough determination, it's not impossible to find bars that open up again an hour later. Most Chicago bars, however, are catered to slightly more reasonable drinkers, opening at 11am and closing at 2am. The majority are also open seven days a week, though bars tend to close around midnight on Sunday. Seasonally, summer is the best time to drink in Chicago, due to ubiquitous open-air patios where patrons toast the balmy evenings.

HOW MUCH

The good news for spendthrift travelers is that drinking in Chicago can be done on a pittance compared to other big American cities; a bottle of Chicago's rank-and-file favorites, Pabst and Old Style, will set you back about $3. That doesn't mean there's a lack of options on the other end of the spectrum; in swish neighborhoods around the Loop, a $10 cocktail is common. If you've got the means, the newly-opened Violet Hour (p177), which has earned a national buzz since opening in the summer of 2007, has cocktails that actually live up to the $11 price tag. Seriously.

TIPPING

Like elsewhere, the love and devoted attention of a bartender can usually be bought with courteous behavior and cold hard cash, and big tips often result in a heavy pour. Tipping a dollar per drink is the norm, though if you order a round for buddies, a $5 tip should suffice.

DRINKING DESTINATIONS

The heart and soul of the city's culture is found at the omnipresent neighborhood taverns with Old Style signs out front, dedicated patrons warming the stools inside, and open contempt for the mojito craze. But if your thirst for adventure accompanies one for rainbow-colored inebriants, it's easy to hail a cab and find a neighborhood to suit your taste. Lincoln Ave and Halsted St in Lincoln Park draw raging DePaul students, while indie rock jukebox bars on Damen Ave in Wicker Park and Bucktown bring in hordes of post-collegiate hipsters. The Boystown stretch of Broadway in Lake View is an energetic epicenter of gay nightlife, while the posse of single older gents on the make and upscale singles earned the Gold Coast the nickname 'Viagra Triangle.'

PRACTICALITIES

Though a ban on public smoking sailed through city council back in 2005, it wasn't enforced until January 2008, when Chicago joined New York, Boston and Los Angeles by sending smokers outside to light up. No problem in the summer, when open-air patios are aplenty, but a bit harsh during the long winter. Even so, loopholes in the ordinance ensure that indomitable smokers will still be able to find a hazy refuge – just ask around.

Also keep in mind that even though the vast majority of bars will run a tab on your credit card, it's a good idea to have cash on you. This is especially true at small neighborhood bars, some of which accept cash only.

The following listings are establishments where people primarily go to thin their blood and socialize. The Nightlife chapter (p182) has options if you're looking for an active night of dancing or live music, but if the evening's primary activity is lifting a pint glass, these are the best places to belly up.

THE LOOP

Big hotels and office buildings loom over the Loop, which has plenty of options for a three-martini lunch, but limited choices at night. The Loop's wildly eclectic warhorses are exciting outposts amid empty skyscrapers and relatively quiet nighttime streets.

CAL'S BAR Map pp54–5 Bar

☎ 312-922-6392; 400 S Wells St; 7am-8pm Sun-Wed, to 2am Thu-Sat; M Blue Line to La Salle

The bartenders serve plenty of 'tude with the drinks at this family owned dive bar and liquor store, which serves as a lone oasis for scruffy hipsters who find themselves lost amongst suits in the Loop. On weekend nights, punk-rock bands with names like Broadzilla and Johnny Vomit take the stage (see p185 for more).

17 WEST AT THE BERGHOFF Map pp54–5 Café

☎ 312-427-3170; 17 W Adams St; 11am-9pm Mon-Thu, to 9:30pm Fri, 11:30am-10pm Sat; M Blue Line to Jackson

The entire city mourned the closing of the Berghoff Standup Bar, the historic watering hole formerly in this location. Its sleekly remodeled replacement is generally met with a grumble from locals, even though the food is reliable and the atmosphere retains much of the old charm. At lunch you'll probably have to fight your way through desk jockeys craving roast beef.

NEAR NORTH & NAVY PIER

There ain't much by way of character in the watering holes of Navy Pier, but the sheer variety in the adjoining Near North makes it a drunkard's dream. The crowds here tend to be a mix of tourists and office workers on the prowl, neither of which seem to mind much about paying for the relatively pricey drinks.

BILLY GOAT TAVERN Map pp64–5 Café

☎ 312-222-1525; lower level, 430 N Michigan Ave; 6am-2am Mon-Fri, 10am-3am Sat, 11am-2am Sun; M Red Line to Grand

Somehow, despite the steady line of tourists that line up for SNL-famous 'cheezborgers,' and the soulless franchise locations all over town, this subterranean haunt for *Tribune* writers is an enduring, endearing classic. See p145 for details on their solids.

BREHON PUB Map pp64–5 Pub

☎ 312-642-1071; 731 N Wells St; 11am-2am Mon-Fri, noon-3am Sat, noon-2am Sun; M Brown Line to Chicago

This Irish stalwart is a fine example of the corner saloons that once dotted the city.

GAME ON

The balmy, humid summer of patio-hopping keeps patrons moving, but the nasty weather in Chi-town can be a challenge for the active drinker. Though most of the city's bars cater to inebriated inactivity, there are plenty of arenas for time-tested boozy athletics like darts or pool, as well as activities to actually work up a thirst.

There's fierce competition, but the city's best board-game action is at the Blue Frog Bar & Grill (Map pp64–5; ☎ 312-943-8900; 676 N La Salle St; 11:30am-2am Mon-Thu, from noon Fri, 6pm-3am Sat, closed Sun; M Blue Line to LaSalle). This haven for retro games resounds with the shouts of triumph and moans of defeat as players hunch over cardboard battlefields of yesteryear like Sorry! and Operation. Pub quiz contestants should hit Ginger's Ale House (Map pp82–3; ☎ 773-348-2767; 3801 N Ashland Ave; 11am-2am Mon-Fri, from 10am Sat & Sun; M Brown Line to Southport) on Sunday nights. Part of your $5 entry fee goes to cancer charities.

For darts, try Ginger's Ale House, above, or Mullen's on Clark (Map pp82–3; ☎ 773-325-2319; 3527 N Clark St; 5pm-2am Sun-Thu, from 4pm Fri, from 11am Sat; M Red Line to Addison), where foosball warriors give their little troops a whirl. Pool sharks can test their mettle on the two gorgeous, lovingly restored tables at the Ten Cat Tavern (p175), or on one of the six tables at Southport Lanes (p174).

The truly sporty bar-hoppers might opt for activities where you have to put the beer down, like bowling a few frames at the Fireside Bowl (p177) or slightly more yuppified Seven Ten Lounge (Map pp76–7 ☎ 773-549-2695; 2747 N Lincoln Ave; 5pm-2am Sun-Fri, to 3am Sat; 🚌 11). To really work off the beer gut, try a cutthroat ping-pong session at Happy Village (p176).

The ample selection of draft beer in frosted glasses is served to neighborhood crowds perched on the high stools.

CLARK ST ALE HOUSE Map pp64–5 Pub

☎ 312-642-9253; 742 N Clark St; 4pm-4am Mon-Thu, to 5am Fri & Sat, to 2am Sun; M Red Line to Chicago

Doubtlessly the Loop's best beer selection, the rotating assortment frequently features some of the best Midwestern microbreweries. Work up a thirst on the free pretzels and cool off in the beer garden out back.

GOLD COAST

When the sun goes down, the bars of the Gold Coast swell with vivacious 30- and 40-somethings who are dressed to the nines and on the prowl. The small, triangular green space formed between Chicago, State and Rush Streets – coyly dubbed the 'Viagra Triangle' by locals – is at the heart of the action. The three-sided catwalk offers unparalleled people watching.

GIBSON'S Map pp70–1 Bar

☎ 312-266-8999; 1028 N Rush St; 11am-1am; M Red Line to Clark/Division

Gibson martinis (served with a cocktail onion) are the namesake item at this lively bar attached to Gibson's steakhouse. See the review on p146 for details on sitting down for a meal. A piano player begins tickling the ivories at 5pm.

LODGE Map pp70–1 Bar

☎ 312-642-4406; 21 W Division St; 5pm-4am Sun-Fri, to 5am Sat; M Red Line to Clark/Division

Dressed up like a misplaced hunting cabin, the Lodge has a bit more polish than most of its neighbors on Division Street. A Wurlitzer jukebox spins oldies, and the bowls of salty peanuts complement the abundant beers on tap. The crowd of mostly 40-somethings drink like they mean it, sometimes until dawn.

LINCOLN PARK & OLD TOWN

The blood-alcohol levels run pretty high in Lincoln Park's bars, where hard-drinking yuppies who used to socialize over fraternity kegs are now sucking down microbrews and Cosmopolitans and flirting to a Coldplay soundtrack. The bars around DePaul University further heighten the party-hearty feel of the place, serving as beer-soaked launching pads for plenty of awkward conversations the following morning. In Old Town, you'll find the pace is slower and quirkier.

DEJA VU

Map pp76–7 Bar

☎ 773-871-0205; 2624 N Lincoln Ave; 9pm-4am Sun-Fri, to 5am Sat; M Brown, Red Line to Fullerton

Open until 5am (!) on Saturdays, Deja offers more than just a deliriously late last call. The decor at this friendly place is a mix of opulent Middle Eastern and garage sale art deco, with free pool thrown into the mix. Between Thursday and Saturday, music is served up by live bands or DJs, sometimes asking a modest cover.

DELILAH'S

Map pp76–7 Bar

☎ 773-472-2771; 2771 N Lincoln Ave; 4pm-2am Sun-Fri, to 3am Sat; M Brown Line to Diversey

A bartender rightfully referred to this bad-ass black sheep of the neighborhood as the 'pride of Lincoln Avenue,' a title earned by its underground rockers for the heavy pours and best whiskey selection in the city. Among their discerning roster of single-malts is one of their own making: Delilah's 13th Anniversary Single Malt Scotch. If the first floor gets too rowdy, take things upstairs, where it's a bit quieter.

top picks

BOOZING BLOCKS

- Rowdy night owls: Clark St in Lake View (Map pp82–3).
- Thirty-something hipsters: Division St in Ukrainian Village (Map pp90–1).
- Collegiate beer-chuggers: Lincoln Ave in Lincoln Park (Map pp76–7).
- Patio-hopping boozehounds: Damen Ave in Bucktown (Map pp90–1).
- Pan-genre bar-hoppers: Milwaukee Ave in Wicker Park (Map pp90–1).

GOOSE ISLAND BREWERY

Map pp76–7 Bar

☎ 773-915-0071; 1800 N Clybourn Ave; 🕑 11am-1am Mon-Fri, to 2am Sat, to midnight Sun; Ⓜ Red Line to North/Clybourn

Get to the source at this local brewery, where the hoppy Honker's Ale and potent XXX Porter are fresher than other taps around town. The TVs tune to the Bulls and Cubs games. The outdoor area is nice in summer, especially with their tasty summer ale.

KELLY'S Map pp76–7 Bar

☎ 773-281-0656; 949 W Webster Ave; 🕑 11am-2am Sun-Fri, 11am-3am Sat; Ⓜ Brown, Red Line to Fullerton

DePaul students and fans can get elbow to elbow at this classic pub that's been family owned and operated since the day after Prohibition ended. It's directly under the El, so hold onto your glass when a train goes by.

RED ROOSTER CAFE & WINE BAR

Map pp76–7 Bar

☎ 773-871-2100; 2100 N Halsted St; 🕑 5-10:30pm Mon-Thu, to 11:30pm Fri & Sat, to 10pm Sun; Ⓜ Brown, Red Line to Armitage

Connected to Cafe Bernard, this funky little wine bar makes a great stop before or after meals or the theater. Choose from plenty of wines by the glass.

ROSE'S LOUNGE Map pp76–7 Bar

☎ 773-327-4000; 2656 N Lincoln Ave; 🕑 4pm-2am; Ⓜ Brown Line to Diversey

Once your eyes adjust to the dark of Rose's, the eclectic bric-a-brac, drop ceiling and dollar brews make it an odd duck amongst Lincoln Park's yuppie lounges. The ultra-cheap beers are the big draw, bringing in a motley set of spendthrift regulars.

STERCH'S Map pp76–7 Bar

☎ 773-281-2653; 2238 N Lincoln Ave; 🕑 3:30pm-2am Sun-Fri, to 3am Sat; Ⓜ Brown, Red Line to Fullerton

'No Corona. No foolish drinks. Limited dancing,' reads the sign in the window at this otherwise convivial dive. Those rules invite a genial older crowd of writers and grizzled neighborhood types, as does a jukebox stocked with Coltrane and the Stones.

top picks

CHICAGO BAR MOMENTS

- Deceptively potent ginger gimlets and cocktails from scratch at the Matchbox (p176).
- Slurping mussels and creamy Belgian beer at Hop Leaf (p176).
- Getting aced by cheerful locals in the Happy Village (p176) ping-pong room
- Picking up the illusive 7-10 split at the Southport Lanes (p174).

WEED'S Map pp76–7 Bar

☎ 312-943-7815; 1555 N Dayton St; 🕑 4pm-2am Mon-Sat; Ⓜ Red Line to North/Clybourn

Bras hang like animal pelts at this bar where beatnik meets bohemia. If the walls of Weed's could talk, you'd hear some strange yarns, most of them courtesy of dada-esque owner Sergio Mayora, whose name has motivated an unsuccessful bid for mayor.

OLDE TOWN ALE HOUSE

Map pp76–7 Pub

☎ 312-944-7020; 219 W North Ave; 🕑 noon-4am Sun-Fri, noon-5am Sat; Ⓜ Brown Line to Sedgwick

This Old Town neighborhood staple has been the scene of late-night musings since the 1960s – the last time paint was applied. Grab a book from the lending library, put some classic jazz on the jukebox and settle in for atmospheric merriment under salacious paintings and portraits of past regulars created by the owner, Bruce.

RED LION PUB Map pp76–7 Pub

☎ 773-348-2695; 2446 N Lincoln Ave; 🕑 2pm-2am; Ⓜ Brown, Red Line to Fullerton

A British-style pub run by gen-u-ine Brits, this cozy spot features UK brews, the best onion rings in the city and regular literary events. The fish-and-chips were a favorite of film critic Gene Siskel.

LAKE VIEW & WRIGLEYVILLE

The bars of Lake View flaunt the distinct characteristics of the neighborhoods that surround them; there are bars full of high-fiving Cubs fans in Wrigleyville, high-stakes pool players near the Southport corridor, and high-energy gay clubs in Boystown. Unless you come to toast the Cubs, avoid the traffic snarls and crowds of Wrigleyville like the plague on game day.

CLOSET Map pp82–3 Bar

☎ 773-477-8533; 3325 N Broadway St; 🕑 2pm-4am Mon-Fri, noon-5am Sat, to 4am Sun; M Brown, Red Line to Belmont

One of the very few lesbian-centric bars in Chicago, the Closet changes mood and tempo at 2am, when the crowd becomes more mixed, the music gets louder and things get a little rowdier.

GENTRY Map pp82–3 Bar

☎ 773-348-1053; 3320 N Halsted St; 🕑 4pm-2am Sun-Fri, to 3am Sat; M Brown, Red Line to Belmont

This stately, brick-walled piano bar serves as a welcome respite for 30- and 40-year-old gay men, weary of the pounding house beats of Boystown's clubs. Live cabaret music nightly.

GINGER MAN Map pp82–3 Bar

☎ 773-549-2050; 3740 N Clark St; 🕑 3pm-2am Mon-Fri, noon-3am Sat, to 2am Sun; M Brown, Red Line to Diversey

A splendid place to pass an evening, this spot features a huge and eclectic beer selection that's enjoyed by theater types and other creative folks. They offer respite from the Cubs mania of the rest of the strip by playing classical music and jazz during home games. Pool is free on Sunday.

GUTHRIE'S Map pp82–3 Bar

☎ 773-477-2900; 1300 W Addison St; 🕑 4pm-2am; M Red Line to Addison

A local institution, and the perfect neighborhood hangout, Guthrie's remains true to its mellow roots even as the neighborhood goes manic around it. The glassed-in back porch is fittingly furnished with patio chairs and filled with 30- and 40-somethings, and most tables sport a box of Trivial Pursuit cards. European soccer and rugby fanatics are also dedicated patrons, rewarded when the bar occasionally opens at 6am to show games live via satellite.

HUNGRY BRAIN

Map pp82–3 Bar

☎ 773-935-2118; 2319 W Belmont Ave; 🕑 7pm-4am Sun-Fri, to 5am Sat; 🚌 77

The kind bartenders, roving Tamale vendors and well-worn charm are inviting at this Roscoe Village staple, which hosts sets of free live jazz from some of the city's best young players on Sunday nights, see p183 for more info.

MURPHY'S BLEACHERS

Map pp82–3 Bar

☎ 773-281-5356; 3655 N Sheffield Ave; M Brown, Red Line to Diversey

Getting well lubricated before the big game is the prerogative of Cubs fans at this well-loved, historic watering hole, only steps away from the entrance to Wrigley's bleacher seats. They jam this place like sardines on game day.

SOUTHPORT LANES

Map pp82–3 Bar

☎ 773-472-6600; 3325 N Southport Ave; 🕑 4pm-1am Mon-Fri, noon-2am Sat, to 1am Sun; M Brown Line to Southport

This old-fashioned, local bar has been classily updated under the thoughtful management of some new owners who oversee the bar itself and an annex with four hand-set bowling lanes. The main bar features an inspirational mural of cavorting nymphs and tables sprawl onto the sidewalk in summer.

YAK-ZIES Map pp82–3 Bar

☎ 773-525-9200; 3710 N Clark St; 🕑 11am-4am Sun-Fri, to 5am Sat; M Brown, Red Line to Diversey

The covered outdoor patio and reasonable prices make Yak-zies one of the best places in Wrigleyville to cheer on the Cubs. Many a greasy high-five has been exchanged over heaping piles of chicken wings and Tang Chicken Pizza (a buffalo chicken covered pie). To enter the eye of the hurricane, head down the block and elbow into the famous **Cubby Bear** (Map pp82–3; ☎ 773-327-1662; 1059 W Addison; 🕑 call for opening hours; M Red, Brown Line to Diversey), where the can beer is expensive and the whooping fraternity boys can get downright unruly.

DUKE OF PERTH

Map pp82–3 Pub

☎ 773-477-1741; 2913 N Clark St; ⏲ 5:30pm-2am Mon, 11:30am-2am Tue-Fri, to 3am Sat, noon-2am Sun; 🚌 22

The UK beers and 80+ bottles of single-malt scotch are nearly overwhelming at this cozy, laid-back pub. After enough of them, try the fish-and-chips, which is all-you-can-eat for lunch and dinner for $9 on Wednesday and Friday.

TEN CAT TAVERN

Map pp82–3 Pub

☎ 773-935-5377; 3931 N Ashland Ave; ⏲ 3pm-2am Sun-Fri, to 3am Sat; 🚌 9

Pool is serious business on the two vintage tables that Ten Cat co-owner Richard Vonachen refelts regularly with material from Belgium. The ever-changing, eye-catching art comes courtesy of neighborhood artists, and the furniture is a garage-saler's dream. Regulars (most in their 30s) down leisurely drinks at the bar or, in warm weather, head to the beer garden.

ANDERSONVILLE & UPTOWN

Although Andersonville and Uptown are geared toward quieter outings and unlikely to attract the hard-partying bar hounds, there are a number of worthy destinations, including Chicago's best beer bar and one of the city's favorite gay dance parties.

SIMON'S Map p86 Bar

☎ 773-878-0894; 5210 N Clark St; ⏲ 11am-2am; Ⓜ Red Line to Berwyn

One of Andersonville's few 20-something hangouts, this nautical-themed bar has Clap Your Hands Say Yeah playing on the stereo, and a long bar right out of the '50s. The mural is of the original owner Simon Lundberg and his friends. Lundberg's son now lovingly runs the place.

BIG CHICKS Map p86 Café

☎ 773-728-5511; 5024 N Sheridan Rd; ⏲ 4pm-2am Mon-Fri, to 3am Sat, 3pm-2am Sun; Ⓜ Red Line to Argyle

Uptown's Big Chicks has an enjoyable bipolar disorder. During the week, the bar is a cozily sedate place for gay and straight to socialize beneath the sizable collection of woman-themed art. On weekends, though, gay men pack the stamp-sized dance floor and boogie until all hours. Every Sunday, Big Chicks hosts a legendary free barbecue brunch.

CHICAGO BRAUHAUS Map pp50-1 Café

☎ 773-784-4444; 4732 N Lincoln Ave; ⏲ 4pm-midnight Mon, closed Tue, 4pm-midnight Wed-Fri, 11am-midnight Sat & Sun; Ⓜ Brown Line to Western

Unlikely as it may seem for a bar, the oompah soundtrack, rosy-cheeked staff and early last call give this spacious Bavarian-themed joint the all-ages appeal of a Disney ride. Dinnertime is best, when the 'world-famous' lederhosen-clad Brauhaus Trio starts bumping, and steaming plates of schnitzel seem

WORTH A TRIP

Some of the city's most worthwhile watering holes are off the well-trodden path. This is especially true on Chicago's West and South Sides. Here are some of the standouts:

Hawkeye's (Map pp98–9; ☎ 312-226-3951; 1458 W Taylor St; ⏲ 11am-2am Sun-Fri, to 3am Sat; Ⓜ Blue Line to Polk) This Little Italy institution runs a free shuttle from the United Center to its doorstep when the Bulls or Blackhawks are playing, making it a good place to come to celebrate a victory or agonize over a defeat. Its virtues include a good burger-based menu and fine seasonal tables outside.

Jimmy's Woodlawn Tap (Map p114; ☎ 773-643-5516; 1172 E 55th St; ⏲ 10:30am-2am Mon-Fri, to 3am Sat, 11am-2am Sun; Ⓜ Metra to 55th St) Some of the geniuses of our age have killed plenty of brain cells right here in one of Hyde Park's few worthwhile bars. The place is dark and beery, and a little seedy. But for thousands of University of Chicago students deprived of a thriving bar scene, it's home. Hungry? The Swissburgers are legendary.

Puffer's (Map pp50-1; ☎ 773-927-6073; 3356 S Halsted St; ⏲ 9pm-4am Sun-Fri, to 5am Sat; Ⓜ Red Line to Sox-35th) A cool pub in staid old Bridgeport, Puffer's boasts a bright orange facade and the neighborhood's most amiable clientele, with folks just hanging out and sampling from the excellent beer selection. A good choice after a Sox game, it's a 15-minute walk west from Comiskey Park, er, US Cellular Field.

heaven-sent. Bring your dancing shoes too – there's polka action six nights a week.

HOP LEAF Map p86 Café

☎ 773-334-9851; 5148 N Clark St; 2pm-2am Mon-Fri, 11am-3am Sat, to 2am Sun; M Red Line to Berwyn

Using the name of the national beer from his ancestral Malta, owner Michael Roper operates one of the city's best, classiest beer bars. The overwhelming selection of beers is artfully selected by Roper, with an emphasis on Belgian and American brews. The kitchen serves excellent Belgian *frites* and mussels.

WICKER PARK, BUCKTOWN & UKRAINIAN VILLAGE

Taking the Blue Line to Damen leaves you at the doorstep of some of Chicago's most eclectic nightlife, with cozy neighborhood taverns just around the corner from highfalutin cocktail lounges. A stroll down Damen Ave puts you in the thick of it, amongst a parade of hipsters set on navigating the end of their 20s with oceans of gin and tonic.

CHARLESTON Map pp90–1 Bar

☎ 773-489-4757; 2076 N Hoyne Ave; 3pm-2am Mon-Sat, from noon Sun; 50

The resident cats curl up on your lap at this laid-back favorite of Bucktown locals. When the occasional folk and bluegrass acts set up in the middle of the narrow room, it gets crowded, but it's definitely worth it.

DANNY'S Map pp90–1 Bar

☎ 773-489-6457; 1951 W Dickens Ave; 7pm-2am Sun-Fri, to 3am Sat; 50

Little Danny's is a hipster magnet, featuring a comfortably dim and dog-eared atmosphere and occasional DJ sets of Stax 45s. Blessedly TV-free, Danny's is a great place to come for conversation early in the evening, or to shake a tail feather at an impromptu dance party on the weekend.

GOLD STAR BAR Map pp90–1 Bar

☎ 773-227-8700; 1755 W Division St; 4pm-2am Sun-Fri, to 3am Sat; M Blue Line to Division

Though it's surrounded on all sides by no-frills neighborhood dives, the Gold Star is a cut above, drawing a posse of bike-messengers – and people who dress like them – for cheapie libations and a great jukebox.

HAPPY VILLAGE Map pp90–1 Bar

☎ 773-486-1512; 1059 N Wolcott Ave; 4pm-2am Mon-Fri, to 3am Sat, noon-2am Sun; M Blue Line to Damen

The sign boasting the 'happiest place in the east village' seems like an understatement on a summer evening when a strolling Tamale vendor appears on the vine-covered patio – then it's happiest place on Earth. Don't knock too many back before entering the table tennis room adjoining the bar; the competition is fierce.

INNERTOWN PUB Map pp90–1 Bar

☎ 773-235-9795; 1935 W Thomas St; 4pm-2am Sun-Fri, to 3am Sat; M Blue Line to Damen

A cigar-smoking moose and bronze bust of Elvis overlook the crowd of artsy regulars playing pool and drinking cheap at this lovably divey watering hole. Order a 'Christmas Morning,' a delightful shot of hot espresso and chilled Rumplemintz.

MATCHBOX Map pp90–1 Bar

☎ 312-666-9292; 770 N Milwaukee Ave; 4pm-2am Mon-Fri, 3pm-3am Sat; 3pm-2am Sun; 56

Patrons jam this extremely cozy bar for some of the best (and most potent) cocktails in the city, made entirely from scratch. Favorites include the Pisco Sour and ginger gimlet, ladled from an amber vat of homemade ginger-infused vodka. When the weather is warm, claustrophobics take solace on the sidewalk patio.

RAINBO CLUB Map pp90–1 Bar

☎ 773-489-5999; 1150 N Damen Ave; 4pm-2am Sun-Fri, to 3am Sat; M Blue Line to Damen

Ground zero for indie elite during the week, the boxy, dark-wood Rainbo Club has an impressive semicircular bar and one of the city's best photo booths. The service is slow and the place goes a little suburban on weekends, but otherwise it's an excellent place to hang out with artsy locals.

RICHARD'S BAR Map pp90–1 Bar

☎ 312-421-4597; 725 W Grand Ave; 8am-2am Mon-Fri, from 9am Sat, from noon Sun; M Blue Line to Grand

CANS, CHICAGO STYLE

The red and blue Old Style crest is emblematic of Chicago drinking, whether it hangs on a sign in front of a favored neighborhood tavern or toasts a double play at Wrigley. The beer itself – an inexpensive, unpretentious workingman's pilsner with proud Midwestern immigrant roots – is perfectly suited for the 'city that works.' Every refreshing clack of a pop-top honors the tradition of Gottlieb Heileman, a German-born brewer who set up shop in La Crosse, Wisconsin. Heileman's 'high end' product, Heileman's Old Style Beer, was first brewed in 1902 and quickly found favor with so-called 'flatlanders,' Chicagoans vacationing in the north woods. The beery migration was aided by its partnership with the Cubs, which started in 1950. Heileman Brewing Company survived myriad mergers through the '80s and '90s, until it was taken over by rival Milwaukee brewer Pabst Brewing Company, a kind of Capulet-Montague marriage of inexpensive swills that jointly dominate working class bars throughout the city.

The younger of the two main bartenders in this timeless dive is in his 70s. The bar – with its tall, humming refrigerated coolers for to-go orders and strange mix of Rat Pack and Saturday Night Fever on the jukebox – feels like something out of a Jim Jarmusch movie. Hang around long enough and the owner may bring out a huge platter of food for everyone.

RODAN Map pp90–1 Bar

☎ 773-276-7036; 1530 N Milwaukee Ave; 🕒 6pm-2am Mon-Thu, 5pm-3am Fri & Sat, to 2am Sun; Ⓜ Blue Line to Damen

This sleek, cinematic spot for 30-something slides from restaurant mode to bar mode around 10pm. Arty videos courtesy of Chicago artists are projected on the back wall, and the space often hosts interesting live collaborations between electronic composers and video artists.

VIOLET HOUR Map pp90–1 Café

☎ 773-252-1500; 1520 N Damen Ave; 🕒 8pm-2am Sun-Fri, to 3am on Sat; Ⓜ Blue Line to Damen

The unmarked, poster-covered edifice and sleek interior lend this newcomer the atmosphere of a highbrow speakeasy. So do elaborately-engineered cocktails that use homemade bitters applied with an eyedropper and come shaken or poured over six varieties of ice. After a few, turn to the menu of playfully haughty bar food by hot-handed Avec owner Justin Large.

MAP ROOM Map pp90–1 Pub

☎ 773-252-7636; 1949 N Hoyne Ave; 🕒 6:30am-2am Mon-Fri, 7am-3am Sat, 11am-2am Sun; Ⓜ Blue Line to Damen

You can drink locally and think globally at this friendly corner café–bar that's wallpapered with a world map. Board games and *National Geographics* are within reach and there's free wi-fi, though the shrewd selections on tap are entertainment enough.

QUENCHERS Map pp90–1 Pub

☎ 773-276-9730; W Fullerton Ave; 🕒 11am-2am Mon-Sat, noon-1am Sun; 🚌 74

At the north end of Bucktown, Quenchers peddles a global selection of over 200 beers from more than 40 nations. Locals, artisans, laborers and visiting brew masters enjoy Earle Miller's hospitality. Even when the live music gets loud, the bargain prices are worth the noise.

LOGAN SQUARE & HUMBOLDT PARK

Even though hipsters have begun to flock to Logan Sq for cheap real estate, the professionally ascendant cosmo crowd hasn't taken over yet. The neighborhood's best bars are soaked in the proud legacy of Eastern European tavern owners that don't roll over and gentrify so easily – they're ideal for low-key evenings and low priced swill.

FIRESIDE BOWL Map p95 Bar

☎ 773-486-2700; 3224 W Fullerton; 🕒 6pm-1am Mon-Thu, 6pm-2am Fri-Sun; Ⓜ Blue Line to California

In the not-so-distant past, the Fireside Bowl was a premiere venue for up-and-coming rock, punk and hardcore shows. The punk spirit, and most shows, were ditched in 2004, but the remodeled bar remains a great place to enjoy the time-honored marriage of frosty pints and clattering pins.

GET REAL

In a city that holds drinking in such high regard, it's telling that the highest honor to bestow on a drinking establishment is mystifyingly simple: 'That place,' a local is wont to say with a far-off look, 'is a *real* Chicago bar.' You'll know one when you walk in the door: These 'real Chicago bars' are the kind of family-owned-and-operated, work-a-day joints that were once on every corner of the city. Usually soaked in some kind of proud ethnic proclivity, they're filled with fiercely loyal regulars who gripe about the mayor and cheer whatever baseball club is within closer geographical proximity. There are no hard and fast rules for what makes a bar 'real' and another less so, but here are some things to look out for, and a few favorites.

- The Old Style Sign – A disorienting ubiquity in Chicago, the neon-lit sign advertising the city's favorite everyman beer hangs outside nearly every tavern in the city. One of the best dive bars in the city is under one such sign at Ed & Jean's (Map pp90–1; 2032 W Armitage), where the wood-paneling, kitschy knickknacks and 'shot-ana-beer' orders give the place character. They have no listed phone number and the hours are at Ed and Jean's whim, so good luck.
- Seemingly Illegal To-Go Laws – This classic 'slashie' – a term for bar/liquor store combos hidden around Ukrainian Village – Ola's Liquor (Map pp90–1; ☎ 773-384-7259; 947 N Damen Ave; 🕑 7am-2am Mon-Fri, to 3am Sat, 11am-2am Sun; 🚌 50), has hours catering to third-shift locals and the most indomitable night owls. Order the advertised 'zimne piwo' (Polish for 'cold beer,' of course) and blast some tunes on the juke in the same language.
- Picture of (either) Mayor Daley – Chicagoans alternately toast and scorn their infamous politicos, so it's only natural to hang a portrait over the bar. Try Schaller's Pump (Map pp50-1; ☎ 773-376-6332; 3714 S Halsted; 🕑 11am-9pm Mon-Fri, 5:30pm-11pm Sat, 3-9pm Sun; Ⓜ Orange Line to Archer/Halsted); it's Chicago's oldest continually operating tavern and is conveniently located across the street from the 11th Ward Democratic offices.
- Mysterious Ethnic Liquors – A mystery bottle of foreign spirits is a must for immigrant tavern owners to toast the motherland. Try the Starka (a flavorsome mix of honey and propane) at Bernice's (opposite).
- Scorn of Fruity Drinks – The dim, inviting L&L (Map pp82–3; ☎ 773-528-1303; 3207 N Clark St; 🕑 2pm-2am Mon-Fri, noon-3am Sat, to 2am Sun; Ⓜ Red, Brown, Purple Line to Belmont) is one of the few places on Clark where ordering 'Sex on the Beach' might get you 86ed. Instead, relax with $2 Pabst or a sip from their impressive assortment of Irish Whiskey. Another excellent no-frills option is Sterch's (p173).

WHIRLAWAY LOUNGE

Map p95 — Bar

☎ 773-276-6809; 3224 W Fullerton; 🕑 1pm-1:30am Mon-Sun; Ⓜ Blue Line to Logan Sq

With threadbare couches and broken in board games, this neighborhood fave has the homey charm of your uncle's '70s rumpus room – that is if your uncle had loads of hipster pals with an insatiable thirst for Pabst. Sweetheart owner Maria Jaimes is downright saintly.

KUMA'S CORNER

Map pp50-1 — Café

☎ 773-604-8769; www.kumascorner.com; 2900 W Belmont; 🕑 11:30am-2am Mon-Fri, to 3am Sat, 10am-11pm Sun; 🚌 77 to Elston

'Death to Budweiser…Seriously,' glowers the drink menu at Kuma's. Like formidable heavy-metal themed hamburgers (see p160) the drinks here ain't no joke. Be prepared to do some dancing when you order the one delivered by the little plastic robot.

SMALL BAR Map pp50-1 — Café

☎ 773-509-9888; 2956 N Albany; 🕑 4pm-2am Mon-Fri, 11am-3am Sat, 11am-2am Sun; Ⓜ Blue Line to Logan Sq

Its ace jukebox, affordable food menu and kindly staff make this unpretentious gem an easygoing place to spend an evening in the neighborhood. An interesting fact is that the mirror behind the bar dates back to the 1907 founding.

NEAR WEST SIDE & PILSEN

SKYLARK Map pp98–9 — Bar

☎ 312-948-5275; 2159 S Halsted St; 🚌 8

The Skylark is the place to end a long night after exploring southern reaches of the city; it's a bastion for artsy drunkards, who slouch into big booths sipping on strong drinks and eyeing the long room.

SOUTH LOOP & NEAR SOUTH SIDE

In the South Loop and Near South Side, drinking holes are scattered far away from any major boozing blocks, but they attract a wealth of unique Chicago characters. It can be a long haul to visit on foot and an even longer stumble home, so cabbing is highly recommended.

BERNICE'S TAVERN Map pp50-1 Bar

☎ 312-326-9460; 3238 S Halsted St; 3pm-12am Mon, closed Tue, 3pm-2am Wed-Thu, to 2am Fri, 11am-3am Sat, 11am-12am Sun; 8

A motley assemblage of local artists and neighborhood regulars haunt this work-a-day Bridgeport tavern, where the eclectic calendar includes weekly metal DJs and a folkie open mic. Order a Starka, a honey-flavored liqueur every bit as Lithuanian as the owners.

BLUELIST[1] (blu,list) *v.*
to recommend a travel experience.
What's your recommendation? www.lonelyplanet.com/bluelist

NIGHTLIFE

top picks

- **Empty Bottle** (p185)
- **Pitchfork Music Festival** (p182)
- **Katerina's** (p183)
- **Second City Etc** (p190)
- **Vision** (p189)
- **Hungry Brain** (p183)
- **Rosa's Lounge** (p184)
- **Old Town School of Folk Music** (p185)
- **Abbey Pub** (p184)
- **Sonotheque** (p188)

Finding something to do in Chicago on any given night is effortless, and the spectrum of entertainment that's available every price range is overwhelming. Just heft the voluminous arts and entertainment section of the city's newsweekly, the *Reader,* and Chicagoan's insatiable appetite for nocturnal amusement becomes apparent. Acres of forests fall to supply the pages of club listings, theater openings and concert announcements published every Thursday in the free publication. There's more concise, slightly more manageable, information between the glossy covers of Chicago's newly-minted entertainment mag *Time Out Chicago.*

So name your poison. Wanna bust a gut over edgy, experimental improv comedy or bust your eardrums in front of edgy jazz? No problem. How about dancing in a converted warehouse that birthed house music, or in a rugged beer hall that safeguards traditional Chicago blues? Easy.

Undaunted by the weather, or the work week, Chicagoans turn out en masse for everything from blockbusting hip-hop acts to groundbreaking hucksters; ticket prices for live music and comedy varies wildly by venue. A $5 cover at the door will get front row admittance for a local punk band, while nosebleed seats for a big rock band at United Center might start at $60. Popular concert venues will (reluctantly) offer tickets through the charge-by-phone ticket retailing giant Ticketmaster (☎ 312-559-1212), an automated service which tacks on its own mysteriously expensive fees.

OPENING HOURS

Most nightlife options start the evening's entertainment around 9pm, and stay open until 2am. A few clubs keep things going a bit later on weekends, until 4am or 5am. Opening hours are noted for places that stray from these standards – like piano bars and small jazz or blues clubs. For particulars on start times on other events, it's best to call the venue or check newspaper listings.

LIVE MUSIC

If the family tree of American pop and rock music takes root in the blues, it follows that Chicago's proud heritage as a capitol of electric blues has inspired generation after generation of world-class performers. The good news is that many of the surly, guitar-wielding oldsters who put Chicago on the map are still wailing about what happened after they 'woke up this mornin',' often just blocks away from younger crowds who uphold the city's reputation for musical innovation. If the sound of a distorted guitar doesn't fit your mood, a cab to the city's ethnic strongholds offers a global soundtrack.

If a music lover wants to gorge, visit Chicago during the summer; blankets are spread and corks or cans are popped before a continuous string of outdoor music festivals. These happen on city blocks and parks in every neighborhood, often with sounds reflecting the surrounding community. The band shells at Millennium Park and Grant Park host loads of free concerts to suit every taste.

Festivals requiring admission are also plentiful. The grunge-rocking '90s carnival Lollapalooza (www.lollapalooza.com) quit touring and made Chicago its permanent home in 2005, bringing marquee rock acts for a weekend-long event every August. Another rising star is the Pitchfork Music Festival (www.pitchforkmusicfestival.com), which is run by the widely influential local indie rock tastemakers at *Pitchfork* magazine in July.

For more details on Lolla, Pitchfork and Chicago's many other music fests, see p12 or visit www.chicagofests.com.

BLUES & JAZZ

Chicago's blues icons like Buddy Guy and Koko Taylor are an aging lot, and audiences should savor these treasured performers while they still can. You'll find that Guy's famous bar, Buddy Guy's Legends, is a glaring omission in the following listings. As of fall 2007, Buddy Guy's was still packing 'em in at 754 N Wabash, but when the lease expired, the future of the club was uncertain. Regardless, you'll hardly need a guide book to find out about the latest. It's a citywide hot topic that interests a far wider community than diehard blues fans.

Jazz fans will find that the nightly scene here runs the gamut – from hard bop traditionalists to the most progressive, noisy fusion. For gospel, the majority of action happens, appropriately, on Sunday, when historic South Side churches (p116) raise the roof.

ANDY'S Map pp64–5

☎ 312-642-6805; 11 E Hubbard St; Ⓜ Red Line to Grand

This veteran blues and jazz bar–restaurant doesn't charge a cover for its lunchtime shows, which deliver hard-swinging, though fairly traditional sounds. Just across the river from the Loop, some desk jockeys come for lunch and never quite make it back to the office.

BACK ROOM Map pp70–1

☎ 312-751-2433; www.backroomchicago.com; 1007 N Rush St; Ⓜ Red Line to Clark/Division

This venerated Gold Coast jazz room is so cozy that there isn't a bad view in the house, even when you take in the stage via a long mirror. If the small main floor gets too tight, head up the spiral staircase and take things in from above. Bop purists be warned: the tunes here can get more than a little smooth.

BLUE CHICAGO Map pp64–5

☎ 312-642-6261; www.bluechicago.com; 736 N Clark St; Ⓜ Red Line to Chicago

The talent lives up to the club's name at this mainstream blues club. If you're staying in the neighborhood and don't feel like hitting the road, you won't go wrong here. Admission to Blue Chicago gets you into two nearby branches, Blue Chicago on Clark (Map pp64–5; ☎ 312-661-0100; 536 N Clark) and the Blue Chicago Store (Map pp64–5; ☎ 312-661-0100; 536 N Clark), a combined retail and performance space.

B.L.U.E.S. Map pp76–7

☎ 773-528-1012; www.chicagobluesbar.com; 2519 N Halsted St; Ⓜ Brown Line to Diversey

Long, narrow and crowded, this veteran club, where the slightly older crowd soaks up every crackling, electrified moment. Look for names like Big James & the Chicago Playboys.

HUNGRY BRAIN Map pp82–3

☎ 773- 935-2118; 2319 W Belmont; 🚌 77

The Sunday Transmission series, hosted by the Emerging Improvisers collective, is the best time to get a feel for this unassuming, comfortable dive. On that and other nights, young jazzers drink cheap (see p174) and build their chops, often resulting in inspired sessions.

top picks

LIVE MUSIC VENUES

- **Empty Bottle** (p185) Capture the best evening of Chicago indie rock by taking home a strip of photos from the booth in back.
- **Hungry Brain** (left) The proving ground for tomorrow's jazz improvisers has inexpensive drinks and no pretension.
- **Hideout** (p185) It's in the middle of nowhere, but it feels leagues ahead of other small rock venues.
- **New Apartment Lounge** (p184) Hearing Von Freeman cut loose is the best Tuesday night of music in town.
- **Schubas** (p185) Shh! I can't hear my favorite alt-country singer emote!

GREEN DOLPHIN STREET Map pp90–1

☎ 773-395-0066; www.jazzitup.com; 2200 N Ashland Ave; 🚌 6

This classy venue combines excellent and inventive cuisine with good jazz. It's hard to imagine that this riverside club, which looks like it's been around since the 1940s, used to be a junk-auto dealer before its renovation.

GREEN MILL Map p86

☎ 773-878-5552; www.greenmilljazz.com; 4802 N Broadway; Ⓜ Brown Line to Lawrence

You can sit in Al Capone's favorite spot at the timeless Green Mill, a true cocktail lounge that comes complete with curved leather booths and colorful tales about mob henchmen who owned shares in the place. Little has changed in 70 years – the club still books top local and national jazz acts. On Sunday night it hosts a nationally known poetry slam where would-be poets try out their best work on the openly skeptical crowd.

KATERINA'S Map pp82–3

☎ 773-348-7592; www.katerinas.com; 1920 W Irving Park; Ⓜ Brown Line to Diversey

The swish Southern European finish and soulful pan-ethnic gypsy jazz and blues makes Katerina's a stylish, soulful destination in less-traveled Irving Park. A sophisticated set of 30- and 40-somethings down martinis, dig the good tunes and hang here all night.

KINGSTON MINES Map pp76–7

☎ 773-477-4646; www.kingstonmines.com; 2548 N Halsted St; Ⓜ Brown Line to Diversey
Popular enough to draw big names, it's so hot and sweaty here that blues neophytes will feel like they're having a genuine experience – sort of like a gritty theme park. Two stages ensure somebody's always on.

LEE'S UNLEADED BLUES
Map pp50-1

☎ 773-493-3477; 7401 S South Chicago Ave; 🚌 30
Lee's and Rosa's Lounge (p186) are cut from the same cloth; this is a no-nonsense blues local far from touristy parts of town. The cover is low – when there is one – and live music runs Thursday to Monday.

NEW CHECKERBOARD LOUNGE
Map p114

☎ 773-684-1472; 5201 S Harper Ct; 🚌 15
When the original location of this Bronzeville blues room closed in 2003, enthusiasts mourned – until it reopened in this bigger, better sounding space in Hyde Park. The relocation is more inviting for university kids who often join locals for quality local and national electric blues acts. The cover varies with the reputation of the bluesmen on stage and so does the start time, so call ahead.

NEW APARTMENT LOUNGE Map pp50-1

☎ 773-483-7728; 504 E 75th St; 🚌 3
The only night to come to this storefront venue on the far South Side is Tuesday, when saxophonist Von Freeman leads his long-running, roof-raising jam to rousing calls from the ultra-casual, deep-listening audience. The session starts at 10:30pm, but if you want to get into the tiny room, come early.

ROSA'S LOUNGE Map p96

☎ 773-342-0452; www.rosaslounge.com; 3420 W Armitage Ave; 🚌 73
This is hard-core blues. Top local talents perform at this unadorned West Side club in a neighborhood that's still a few decades away from attracting developers. Take a cab.

UNDERGROUND WONDER BAR
Map pp70–1

☎ 312-266-7761; www.undergroundwonderbar.com; 10 E Walton St; 🕑 4pm-4am Mon-Fri, to 5am Sat, 8pm-4am Sun; Ⓜ Red Line to Chicago
This live-music venue run by musician Lonie Walker features little-known jazz and bluesmen, along with the occasional rock or reggae player. The club is tiny, and Lonie herself takes the stage for her sultry show several nights a week.

VELVET LOUNGE Map pp106–7

☎ 312-791-9050; www.velvetlounge.net; 67 E Cermak Rd; Ⓜ Red Line to Cermak/Chinatown
Tenor saxophonist Fred Anderson (one of the founding members of the Association for the Advancement of Creative Musicians) owns the Velvet, which left its former historic location around the corner and moved here in 2006. Visiting jazz musicians often hang out here late at night. The place rocks during impromptu jam sessions.

ROCK, POP & INDIE

Just as the bossy electrified sound of Chicago shaped fledgling American rock 'n' roll, Chicago's rock scene has a national reputation for brazenly defying conventions and muddling sonic borders. Today, the city's rock scene is inventive, proud and broadly influential, from rootsy folk rock to jarring, jazz-influenced post rock. Chicago's most popular rock exports of the past couple decades, Wilco and the Smashing Pumpkins, both sprung from the city's bustling indie underground, which has been abuzz with creative, challenging independent music makers for years. Rock fans visiting the city have no shortage of options for a big show, but the distinct flavor of the city is better savored at smaller venues like the Hideout (opposite) or Empty Bottle (opposite), where you're certain to catch some great local rock and likely to rub shoulders with Chicago's self-made guitar heroes.

ABBEY PUB Map pp50-1

☎ 773-478-4408; www.abbeypub.com; 3420 W Grace St; Ⓜ Blue Line to Addison
This has gradually become one of the city's best smaller rock venues, often bringing in acts on the cusp of much bigger stages.

This club is located far from the city center, on the northwest side.

BEAT KITCHEN Map pp82–3

☎ 773-281-4444; www.beatkitchen.com; 2100 W Belmont Ave; 🚌 72

Everything you need to know is in the name – entertaining beats traverse a spectrum of sounds and the kitchen turns out better-than-average dinners. Dine early in the front of the house, since service is unhurried. Music in the homely back room can be funky or jammy, but a crop of Chicago's smart, broadly appealing songwriters dominate the calendar.

CAL'S BAR Map pp54–5

☎ 312-922-6392; 400 S Wells St; 🕑 7am-8pm Sun-Wed, to 2am Thu-Sat; Ⓜ Blue Line to LaSalle

Sure, from the outside it looks like a good place to get your butt kicked (see p171 for more), but the facade is perfect for scaring away the suits of the Loop – not that they'd dig the soundtrack of gritty punk and earsplitting rock anyway.

DOUBLE DOOR Map pp90–1

☎ 773-489-3160; www.doubledoor.com; 1572 N Milwaukee Ave; Ⓜ Blue Line to Damen

Edgy, alternative rock that's *just* under the radar finds a home at this former liquor store, which still has the original sign out front and remains a landmark around the Wicker Park bustle. On weekends, popular underground acts of the past (Mudhoney) and future (The Go! Team) pack the room, though four-band local bills take over on weeknights.

EMPTY BOTTLE Map pp90–1

☎ 773-276-3600; www.emptybottle.com; 1035 N Western Ave; Ⓜ Blue Line to Damen

With the photo booth and the parade of Chicago's rock insiders, the Empty Bottle gets its pick of the smaller buzz bands to come through town. The impressive programming here doesn't stick to electric guitars and power chords, however – free-jazz improvisational master Ken Vandermark has been a mainstay of the venue's Chicago Improvisers Series.

HIDEOUT Map pp90–1

☎ 773-227-4433; www.hideoutchiago.com; 1354 W Wabansia; 🚌 72

Maybe it's all the Pabst, the strangely industrial surroundings, or the room of sweaty thrift-store bedecked hipsters grinding to soul records at the post-show dance party, but an evening in this two-room lodge of underground rock can be downright transcendent. On the weekend, the crowd goes every which way, and ultra-late dance parties bring the night to a close.

LOGAN SQUARE AUDITORIUM Map p95

☎ 773-252-6179; www.metrochicago.com; 2539 N Kedzie; Ⓜ Blue Line to Logan Sq

Logan Square's legions of gentrifying scene-makers need some place to catch grimy, DIY, underground rock, and this spacious former ballroom answers the call. The gigs here, like the neighborhood, are a work-in-progress.

METRO Map pp82–3

☎ 773-549-0203; www.metrochicago.com; 3730 N Clark St; Ⓜ Red Line to Addison

After graduating from the Abbey Pub (opposite), acts teetering on the verge of superstardom play this former classic theater, which has the sightlines and sound system to make it among the best venues in Chicago.

FOLK, COUNTRY & REGGAE

While Chicago lies a bit too far north of the Mason-Dixon to have much of a traditional country scene, the city is silly with roots alt-country acts, some of the best of which find a home on the local Bloodshot Records label and take the stage of Schuba's (p186). The traditional folk scene has a very centralized home in the venerated Old Town School of Folk Music (below), where you can see performances or even take some lessons.

CAROL'S PUB Map p86

☎ 773-334-2402; 4659 N Clark St; 🚌 22

The closest thing Chicago has to a honky-tonk, Carol's Pub offers (at times ironic) boot-stompin' Bud-drinkin' good times to patrons, who come out on weekends to dance like crazy to the house country band.

OLD TOWN SCHOOL OF FOLK MUSIC Map pp50–1

☎ 773-728-6000; www.oldtownschool.org; 4544 N Lincoln Ave; Ⓜ Brown Line to Western

You can hear the call of the banjos from the street outside this venue, where major national and local acts like John Gorka, Richard Thompson and Joan Baez sometimes play. Best of all, the space has an educational component that offers classes and clinics. The Old Town School's (Map pp70–1; ☎ 773-525-7793; 909 W Armitage Ave) original location in Old Town offers classes for children.

SCHUBAS Map pp82–3

☎ 773-525-2508; www.schubas.com; 3159 N Southport Ave; Ⓜ Brown, Red Line to Belmont

Something of an alt-country legend, Schubas presents a host of twangy, acoustic artists, and indie rock acts that don't get booked across town at the Empty Bottle. While the bar area itself is friendly and boisterous, the back music room is for serious listening – chatty patrons should expect to be shushed.

PIANO BAR & CABARET

COQ D'OR Map pp70–1

☎ 312-787-2200; Drake Hotel, 140 E Walton St; 🕑 11am-2am Mon-Sat, to 1am Sun; Ⓜ Red Line to Chicago

Cole Porter and Frank Sinatra are just part of the repertoire of highly talented piano players and singers who rotate through this stately lounge. The live music gets going nightly at 7pm.

HOWL AT THE MOON Map pp64–5

☎ 312-863-7427; 26 W Hubbard; 🕑 5pm-2am Mon-Fri, to 3am Sat, 7-2pm Sun; Ⓜ Red Line to Grand

The Guns 'n' Roses covers, dirt cheap happy hour specials and flirty singles scene here could make nearly anyone into a piano bar convert. Billy Joel? Sorry, how about AC/DC?

DAVENPORT'S PIANO BAR & CABARET Map pp90–1

☎ 773-278-1830; 1383 N Milwaukee Ave; 🕑 7pm-midnight Mon, Wed & Thu, to 2am Fri & Sat, to 11pm Sun; Ⓜ Blue Line to Damen

Old standards get new interpretations and new songs are heard for the first time at this swanky place on an up-and-coming stretch of Milwaukee Ave. The front room is a fun, inclusive (read: sing-along) place, with the back reserved for more fancy-pants cabaret events (where singing along will get you thrown out).

ZEBRA LOUNGE Map pp70–1

☎ 312-642-5140; 1220 N State St; 🕑 2pm-2am Sun-Thu, to 3am Fri & Sat; Ⓜ Red Line to Clark/Division

The piano can get as scratchy as the voices of the crowd, which consists mainly of older folks who like to sing along. Regular ivory-stroker Tom Oman is a veteran who knows his stuff.

CLUBS

Let's get the semantics out of the way: the clubs listed below differ from mere bars by putting an emphasis on entertainment, mostly by way of DJ sets, themed nights, and a big dance floor. They also regularly charge a cover that can range from $5 to $20. If you want an evening of simple drinking and socializing, turn back to the Drinking chapter (p170), where there are plenty of low-key options.

Within that rudimentary taxonomy, the distinctions are vast. At the high-end of the spectrum, Chicago clubs are stylish and sleek places where dropping serious coin gains access to cavernous, surreal playgrounds of loud music, and liquored-up, well-dressed clubbers. The of-the-minute mix hip-hop and house tracks serves mostly as a soundtrack for people-watching until the $10 mojitos kick in – the dance floor gets crowded and phone numbers, both real and nearly real, are fluidly exchanged and tomorrow's regrets are born.

top picks

GAY & LESBIAN NIGHTLIFE

- **Circuit** (opposite) This community-oriented, Latin-flavored nightclub is Boystown's best. Live showtunes drive away the Sunday night blues.
- **Berlin** (opposite) Right off the El, this is a great place to get sweaty on the dance floor, no matter your orientation.
- **Closet** (p174) This lesbian-centric hole-in-the-wall is fun and unpretentious.
- **Big Chicks** (p175) The dance floor is perfectly tiny at this mainstay.
- **Spin** (p189) 'Shower Night' makes a raunchy departure from the excellent action on the dance floor.

A smaller number of proud Chicago stalwarts at the other end of the spectrum take the musical element a bit more seriously and shun 'Trixies' and 'Chads' – hipster shorthand for well-groomed scene makers. Here, attire is more casual, crowds come to dance, and DJs are held to a high standard.

Whatever the case, don't expect the glow-stick-and-pills paradise of yore; Chicago cops cracked down on the club drug scene in the late '90s and the club crowd parties a bit more discretely these days.

A copy of the free monthly paper *UR* serves as the most succinct guide to Chicago's club scene, including detailed listings of one-offs and regular DJ engagements. For the more-underground events, look for flyers at hip record stores like Gramaphone Records (p130) or post-raver boutiques along Milwaukee Ave in Wicker Park.

top picks

DANCE CLUBS

- Crobar (left) Better dress to impress, and then get down in the best mega-club in town.
- Darkroom (below) Where DJ Mother Hubbard still holds down the best indie dance party.
- Leg Room (p188) The friendliest place to gawk at the Rush St meat market.
- Smart Bar (p188) Few 'Trixies' and 'Chads' to soil this high-minded subterranean space.
- Lava Lounge (p188) Mostly cover free, the DJs at this near dive have omnivorous tastes.

BERLIN Map pp82–3

☎ 773-348-4975; www.berlinchicago.com; 954 W Belmont Ave; ⌚ 8pm-4am Mon, 5pm-4am Tue-Fri, 5pm-5am Sat, 8pm-4am Sun; Ⓜ Brown, Red Line to Belmont

Stepping off the El at Belmont has long been one of the city's best bets for finding a packed, sweaty dance floor. Berlin caters to a mostly gay crowd midweek, though partiers of all stripes jam the place on the weekends. Monitors flicker through the latest video dispatches from cult pop and electronic acts, while DJs take the dance floor on trancey detours.

CIRCUIT Map pp82–3

☎ 773-325-2233; www. circuitclub.com; 3641 N Halsted St; ⌚ 9pm-4am Thu-Fri, Sun-Mon, to 5am Sat; Ⓜ Red Line to Addison

The classiest of the Boystown nightclub mainstays has a lovely rooftop deck where a highly stylized, sexually mixed, though gay dominated crowd, wile away the summer evenings – the perfect perch to look down their noses at the mobs of shirtless, crotch-grabbing twinks at the club next door, Hydrate (p190). Don't leave without trying the fat-free alcoholic slushies or visiting the Star Trek room.

CROBAR Map pp76–7

☎ 312-266-1900; www.crobar.com; 1543 N Kingsbury; ⌚ 10pm-4am Wed, Fri, to 5am Sat; Ⓜ Red Line to North/Clybourn

If any club harkens back to Chicago's hedonic past it's Crobar, where the industrial space is livened by pastel highlights and mirrors, high-minded techno rules the dance floor, and the mixed crowd is hipper, younger, and here to party…*hard*.

DARKROOM Map pp90–1

☎ 773-276-1411; www.darkroombar.com; 2210 W Chicago Ave; ⌚ 9pm-2am Sun-Fri, to 3am Sat; 🚌 66

Everyone from goths to reggae-heads go to this welcoming, brick-walled bar, which changes personality depending on what comes from its turntables. The Life During Wartime indie dance, led by local DJ Mother Hubbard, takes place on the first Friday of every month; it's a guaranteed good time.

ENCLAVE Map pp64–5

☎ 312-654-0234; www.enclavechicago.com; 220 W Chicago Ave; ⌚ 9pm-2am Thu-Fri, to 3am Sat; 🚌 66

This newcomer to Chicago's club network is *big* – 15,000 square-feet of former warehouse redone with glossy hardwood floors and lively art installations. Even with the platform dancers and coy martini menu, it's fairly classy, bringing in Chicago celebs and a downtown crowd who dance to mainstream pan-genre hits.

EXCALIBUR Map pp64–5

☎ 312-266-1944; www.excaliburchicago.com; 632 N Dearborn St; ⌚ 7pm-4am Sun-Thu, from 5pm Fri & Sat; Ⓜ Red Line to Grand

The building, which once housed the Chicago Historical Society, has been remade, with three levels of dancing to mainstream house, hip-hop and '80s tunes. Other areas of the funhouse include jukeboxes, electronic games, pool and the occasional performance by a spirit-conjuring necromancer. Suburban and touristy crowds adore it.

HYDRATE Map pp82–3

☎ 773-975-9244; www.hydratechicago.com; 3458 N Halsted St; 8pm-4am Mon-Fri, 4pm-5am Sat, 6pm-4am Sun; Ⓜ Red Line to Addison

A wild night on the Boystown club circuit requires a visit to this frenzied spot, which boasts an open-air feel (thanks to retractable windows) and chatty pickup scene (thanks to $1 well drinks). It's not all roses; the service gets rude and the crowds unruly (also thanks to the $1 well drinks), but the weekly martini and a manicure package is clever. Other special events at the club include lube wrestling and female impersonators.

LAVA LOUNGE Map pp90–1

☎ 773-772-3355; www.lavachicago.com; 859 N Damen Ave; 7pm-2am Sun-Fri, to 3am Sat; 50

Serious electronic musicheads love this unpretentious, dim and mostly cover-free club. Well-attended DJ nights dot the week and a different female DJ rocks the club every Wednesday for the long-running Flirt. Better still: the beer supply is wide ranging and the cocktails cheap.

LE PASSAGE Map pp70–1

☎ 312-255-0022; www.lepassage.tv; 937 N Rush St; 7pm-4am Wed-Fri, to 5am Sat; Ⓜ Red Line to Chicago

Take a hint from the faux-French name, this restaurant–nightclub is not without its affected pretensions – once past the doorperson's clipboard though, it's a beautiful club with French-colonial decor. It makes the appropriate backdrop for would-be models and their pursuers, all who try to maintain their poise while sucking down fruity Polynesian concoctions like the 'Scorpion Bowl.'

LEG ROOM Map pp70–1

☎ 312-337-2583; www.legroomchicago.com; 7 W Division St; 9pm-4am Mon-Wed, 7pm-4am Thu-Fri, to 5am Sat; Ⓜ Red Line to Grand

The Leg Room wins few points for originality, with safari-print stools and schmoozing, scantily-dressed singles, but the laid-back vibe and friendly staff make it the most inviting place to gawk at the Rush Street pick up scene.

ONTOURAGE Map pp64–5

☎ 312-573-1470; 157 W Ontario; 9pm-2am Sun-Mon, Thu-Fri, to 3am Sat; Ⓜ Red Line to Grand/State

VIPs get all-access to the exclusive recesses of this neon-lit hip-hop and house club, though it's arguably more fun to hang downstairs with the dressed-up commoners. Newly arrived on the Gold Coast club scene, it has a tough road to hoe: this space has housed a revolving door of defunct flash-in-the-pan clubs.

PUMP ROOM Map pp70–1

☎ 312-266-0360; Ambassador East, 1301 N State St; 6pm-midnight; Ⓜ Red Line to Clark/Division

A certain timelessness prevails at this Gold Coast classic, where vocalists and jazz and dance trios provide slow-dance swing Wednesday through Saturday. The black they insist you wear here should be formal, not grunge. For details on the exquisite food, see p146.

SMART BAR Map pp82–3

☎ 773-549-4140; www.smartbarchicago.com; 3730 N Clark St; 10pm-4am Sun-Fri, 9pm-5am Sat; Ⓜ Red Line to Addison

This downstairs adjunct to the Metro (p185) is a dance and music-lover's dream, and the DJs who spin here often have more renowned reputations than you'd expect the intimate space to accommodate. A who's-who of forward-looking break artists, house and trance DJs have held down the turntables.

SONOTHEQUE Map pp90–1

☎ 312-226-7600; 1444 W Chicago Ave; 8pm-2am Wed-Fri, to 3am Sat; Ⓜ Blue Line to Chicago

The DJs here spin genres of electronic music that are so hip they don't even have names yet, but are perfectly matched with the futuristic space. This kind of bar would be a snooty disaster in New York, but absolutely down-to-earth patrons and reasonable drink prices make it feel like the corner pub of 2015.

SOUND-BAR Map pp64–5

☎ 312-787-4480; www.sound-bar.com; 226 W Ontario St; 9pm-4am Sun-Fri, to 5am Sat; M Red Line to Grand

This 4000 sq ft nightspot rises above the city's other sprawling megaclubs by way of superstar trance and house DJs (John Digweed, Dimitri from Paris etc). There's an amazing sound system and a dramatic setting.

SPIN Map pp82–3

☎ 773-327-7711; www.spin-nightclub.com; 800 W Belmont Ave; 10pm-2am Sun-Fri, to 3am Sat; M Red Line to Belmont

Though its clientele consists mostly of gay men in their 20s, Spin has become a popular destination for hetero men and women on the weekends. Serious dancers hit the floor, while chatty cruisers orbit the large bar by the entrance. Don't miss Spin's shower contest every Friday night, when hopefuls of both genders bare (almost) all.

SUBTERRANEAN Map pp90–1

☎ 773-278-6600; www.subt.net; 2011 W North Ave; 7pm-2am Mon, 6pm-2am Tue-Fri, 7pm-3am Sat, 8pm-2am Sun; M Blue Line to Damen

DJs spin hip-hop and other styles to a trendy crowd at this place, which looks slick inside and out. The cabaret room upstairs draws good indie rock bands and popular open-mic events.

VISION Map pp64–5

☎ 312-266-1944; www.visionnightclub.com; 640 N Dearborn St; 10pm-4am Thu, Fri & Sun, to 5am Sat; M Red Line to Grand

Located next to Excalibur, Vision throws some of the best techno parties in Chicago. Big-name DJs like Sasha, Doc Martin and Derrick Carter have all spun here, and the crowds of 2000-strong visit every weekend to dance (rather than pose) under the laser-lit extravaganza. The recently expanded club also plays hip-hop in the smaller of its two spaces.

IMPROV & COMEDY

Dating back to the Compass Players – the 1950s cabaret that birthed Second City – Chicago has earned its reputation for bleeding edge comedy one snicker at a time. Stand-up takes a backseat to group improv and a sampling of the city's nightlife isn't complete without checking it out. It doesn't have to break the bank either, while Second City is the launching pad for tomorrow's kings and queens of comedy, lower profile training stages and jokesters outside of the Second City empire are less expensive.

Chicago's famous comedic names and ensembles will descend on the city in the spring for the Chicago Improv Festival (☎ 773-935-9810; www.chicagoimprovfestival.org). If you're lucky enough to catch it, it's worth your while and easy to find – it takes over stages around the city.

COMEDYSPORTZ Map pp82–3

☎ 773-549-8080; www.comedysportzchicago.com; 2851 N Halsted St; M Red, Brown Line to Diversey

The gimmick? Two improv teams compete with deadly seriousness to make you laugh hysterically. The audience benefits from this comic capitalism, and all the fun is G-rated. Alcohol is allowed, but it's BYOB.

CORN PRODUCTIONS Map pp82–3

☎ 312-409-6435; www.cornservatory.org; 4210 N Lincoln Ave; M Brown Line to Irving Park

Though they occasionally stage something serious, most of the Corn productions are kitschy and inexpensive. With the 7-year engagement of *Floss!* they lampooned hoity dance programs.

HELL IN A HANDBAG PRODUCTIONS

☎ 312-409-4357; www.handbagproductions.org

This award-winning young group of actors, producers, designers and composers produces hilarious parodies of sundry pop culture staples (a recent Halloween production was a send-up of Hitchcock's *The Birds*), often in musical form. Their Christmastime reviews are an annual hit with Chicago audiences The group takes up residence in spaces that vary depending on the production, so check their website for details.

IO (IMPROVOLYMPIC) Map pp82–3

☎ 773-880-0199; www.improvolympic.com; 3541 N Clark St; M Red Line to Addison

The Olympic Committee forced this comic veteran to change the name to its initials in 2005, a suitably laughable development in a long career of chuckles. ImprovOlympic launched the careers of Mike Myers and MTV's Andy Dick, along with a host of other well-known comics. Shows hinge entirely

YOUR GIG IN CHICAGO

Open mic nights in Chicago aren't much like the navel-gazing mopefests of other cities. Here, you get the sense that songwriters and musicians are in the room to hone their craft, not bare their souls. If you're a visiting musician, there's no better way to get an intimate feel for Chicago's music scene than to get into it first hand. Guitar-picking songwriters or aspiring blues men have it easy – just head to a gig, sign up to play (if it's required) and politely ask around for a loaner axe. Horn-playing jazzers have it harder, since even the friendliest soul won't likely want to share your saliva, but sitting in for a couple songs in the rhythm section usually only requires an inquiry between sets. Just keep in mind Chicagoans take this stuff seriously, so if your chops aren't in the league of the guys on stage, it's best to enjoy the tunes from the sidelines. Here are a few places to tour while you're in town:

Pontiac Cafe (Map pp90–1; ☎ 773-252-7767; 1531 N Damen Ave). Lead the band at the Pontiac. The 'live band karaoke' gigs every Friday night are awesome, and the bands know a million chestnuts from the rock and pop canon.

Uptown Poetry Slam at the Green Mill (p183). This is where slam poetry got started, and you can carve your name into the movement's history during the open session that precedes the slam competition. The open-mic portion of the evening runs from 7pm to 8pm.

Pressure Billiards & Cafe (Map pp64–5; ☎ 773-252-7767; 1531 N Damen) Heard the one about the hapless tourist who got heckled off the stage? It's likely to happen here, where heckling is part of the laughs at Chicago's lewdest comedy open mic.

Gentry (p174) On Sundays, release your closeted affinity for show tunes at this genial Boystown bar where Becky tickles the ivories on cabaret classics for the crowd of mostly older gay gents.

on audience suggestions, and each turn can run 40 minutes or longer. If you're thoroughly motivated by what you see, IO offers a range of courses to suit every budget. Shows tend to be a little bawdier than at ComedySportz.

NEO-FUTURISTS Map p86

☎ 773-275-5255; www.neofuturists.org; 5153 N Ashland Ave; M Red Line to Berwyn

Best known for its long-running, brilliant *Too Much Light Makes the Baby Go Blind,* in which the hyper troupe makes a manic attempt to perform 30 plays in 60 minutes. Admission cost is based on a dice throw.

PLAYGROUND IMPROV THEATER Map pp82–3

☎ 773-871-3793; www.the-playground.com; 3209 N Halsted St; M Brown, Red Line to Belmont

This nonprofit temple of improv hosts irreverent pieces by some of Chicago's emerging improv ensembles. The lineup changes every night, but Sunday's *Big Yellow Bus* show is always a hoot.

SECOND CITY Map pp76–7

☎ 312-337-3992; www.secondcity.com; 1616 N Wells St; M Brown Line to Sedgwick

A Chicago must-see, this club is best symbolized by John Belushi, who emerged from the suburbs in 1970 and earned a place in the Second City improv troupe with his creative, manic, no-holds-barred style. Belushi soon moved to the main stage, and then to *Saturday Night Live,* and then on to fame and fortune. Second City's shows are sharp and biting commentaries on life, politics, love and anything else that falls in the crosshairs of the comedians' rapid-fire, hard-hitting wit.

SECOND CITY ETC Map pp76–7

☎ 312-337-3992; www.secondcity.com; 1608 N Wells St; M Brown Line to Sedgwick

Second City's second company often presents more risky work, as actors try to get noticed and make the main stage. Both theaters offer the city's best comedy value after the last show most nights, when the comics present free improv performances.

ZANIES Map pp76–7

☎ 312-337-4027; www.chicago.zanies.com; 1548 N Wells St; M Brown Line to Sedgwick

The city's main stand-up comedy venue regularly books big-name national acts familiar to anyone with a TV, and also frequently invites comics you're *going to* hear about on TV. The shows last less than two hours and usually include the efforts of a couple of up-and-comers before the main act. The ceiling is low and the seating is cramped, which only adds to the good cheer.

THE ARTS

top picks

- **Printers' Ball** (p199)
- **Grant Park Music Festival** (p193)
- **Giordono Jazz Dance Chicago** (p198)
- **Steppenwolf** (p196)
- **Elastic Arts Foundation** (p197)
- **Redmoon Theater** (p196)
- **Chicago Moving Co** (p197)
- **Ravinia** (p195)
- **Black Ensemble Theater** (p195)
- **Dollar Store** (p200)

THE ARTS

The following chapter casts the spotlight on the city's wealth of high culture – everything from classical music, theater and literature to film and dance. Chicago is a distinguished, world-class destination in all areas. If you're in the mood for a rowdy evening of thundering house music, howling electric blues or uproarious sketch comedy, turn back to the Nightlife chapter (p182) for Chicago's more boisterous hallmarks.

Not that art in Chicago is a buttoned-up, blue-haired affair; audiences embody the city's open-minded, unpretentious spirit, rewarding daring artistic underdogs who take big risks and answering adventuresome programming at civic institutions like the Chicago Symphony with unwavering patronage.

Finally, some of the greatest rewards in Chicago's art scene are reserved for those who know how to find them. If an organization listed below doesn't have a specific street address its likely because they will perform in sundry spaces around the city. Check the *Reader* or *Time Out* for their exact performance location. For more on the topic, see They're Playing Where? (below).

TICKETS

The League of Chicago Theatres (www.chicagoplays.com; ☎ 312-554-9800) has made catching a big show easy by setting up Hot Tix (www.hottix.org) booths at tourist hubs in the Loop (Map pp54–5; 72 E Randolph St) and Gold Coast (Map pp70–1; 163 E Pearson St). There, same-day tickets to participating shows are sold at half-price, and full-price tickets are available for upcoming shows. The league's website, www.chicagoplays.com, is updated daily with details about shows and theater news.

For dance tickets and productions that aren't handled by Hot Tix, call the box office directly.

CLASSICAL MUSIC & OPERA

The Chicago Symphony Orchestra (CSO) has been one of America's best orchestras for a generation, and wrestling seats out of the hands of season ticket holders is difficult. That doesn't mean that seeing an expert orchestral performance is impossible; performances by brilliant younger players of the Civic Orchestra of Chicago and the Grant Park Orchestra are stunning – and free.

Though tickets to Chicago's The Lyric Opera are as competitive as the CSO, there are worthy alternatives at various churches and smaller concert series throughout town.

Many classical performances will be listed in the *Reader*, but the best resource for obtaining tickets and information about all classical events is the Chicago Classical Music website (www.chicagoclassicalmusic.org), which has the latest news, an accurate calendar and a ticket swap. If you're truly desperate to see the CSO or the Lyric Opera, it's worth a try to hanging around the box office before the baton drops. Some generous swell might give you theirs for free.

APOLLO CHORUS OF CHICAGO

☎ 312-427-5620; www.apollochorus.org

A 150-member vocal group founded in 1872, the Apollo usually performs at the Symphony Center (see Chicago Symphony Orchestra opposite). Unless you plan *way* in advance, catching the chorus' Christmas performance of Handel's *Messiah* is impossible.

CHICAGO CHAMBER MUSICIANS

☎ 312-819-5800; www.chicagochambermusic.org

This 15-member ensemble is comprised of world-class soloists and CSO section lead-

THEY'RE PLAYING WHERE?

The more you know Chicago's entertainment venues, the more confused you'll be by who plays where and when. The booking style here involves a lot of club-sharing by wildly different entertainment factions, meaning that the best reggae club in Chicago on Friday is a scooter-filled mod hangout on Saturday...and a gay musical theater group on Sunday. It's a game of musical chairs that keeps different scenes rotating on to and off the same barstools each night. It's part of the fun mixing of cultures that helps make Chicago so exciting, but it also means that you'd do well to check the club listings carefully before you head back to your favorite reggae bar two nights running.

CLASSICAL MUSIC FESTIVALS

Though it was always popular, the Grant Park Music Festival (☎ 312-742-7638; www.grantparkmusicfestival.com) has recently become an indispensable part of summer in Millennium Park – the festival's name is a bit of a misnomer since it's no longer held in Grant Park. The orchestra and chorus are excellent, and though the programming targets populist choices like Bernstein and Beethoven, the directorial board wisely sneaks more challenging slices of orchestral rep on the picnicking laymen.

These free concerts happen around twilight on Wednesday, Friday, Saturday and Sunday evenings throughout the summer, although other big events like the Jazz Festival can alter the schedule. If you can't make the gig, catching a sparsely-attended daytime rehearsal at the park provides an intimate glimpse into the mechanics of the great ensemble.

In the summer the CSO heads to Ravinia (Map pp50-1; ☎ 847-266-5100; www.ravinia.org; Green Bay & Lake Cook Rds), a vast open-air summer series in Highland Park on the North Shore. It's certainly a hike from downtown, but if you go, avoid the traffic and take the 45-minute Metra/Union Pacific North Line train from the Ogilvie Transportation Center to Ravinia Station ($8 round-trip). Trains stop both before and after the concerts right in front of the park gates.

ers, known and revered for educational outreach programs and their two affiliated groups – the Chicago String Quartet and CCM brass.

CHICAGO OPERA THEATER Map pp54–5

☎ 312-704-8414; www.chicagooperatheater.org; Harris Theater for Music & Dance, 205 E Randolph St; Ⓜ Brown, Green, Orange Line to Randolph

Chicago's premiere of John Adam's challenging modern opera *A Flowering Tree* and Mozart's warhorse *Don Giovanni* were offered on their spring 2008 schedule – mere indications of this innovative groups broad range. Under general director Brian Dickie, Chicago Opera Theater has soared to critical acclaim.

CHICAGO SINFONIETTA

☎ 312-236-3681; www.chicagosinfonietta.org

Led by Paul Freeman, this beloved organization is all about knocking down the cultural walls that surround traditional classical ensembles. Expect broad-minded premieres and wide-ranging guest artists, including jazz luminaries and ethnic folk musicians.

CHICAGO SYMPHONY ORCHESTRA

Map pp54–5

☎ 312-294-3000; www.cso.org; Symphony Center, 220 S Michigan Ave; Ⓜ Brown, Green, Orange Line to Adams

This is a period of transition for the Chicago Symphony, who in 2006 saw director Daniel Barenboim depart. No matter who fills his shoes, quality and attendance are unlikely to sag. The CSO is among America's best symphonies, known for fervent subscribers and an untouchable brass section. The season is from September to May, though they play summer engagements at Ravinia (see above).

CIVIC ORCHESTRA OF CHICAGO

Map pp54–5

☎ 312-294-3420; www.cso.org; Symphony Center, 220 S Michigan Ave; Ⓜ Brown, Green, Orange Line to Adams

Founded in 1919, this orchestra is something of the kid sibling to the CSO, made up of younger players who often graduate to the big-time professional symphonic institutions around the world. It's the only training orchestra of its kind in the world, and, amazingly, tickets to performances at Symphony Center are free.

LYRIC OPERA OF CHICAGO Map pp54–5

☎ 312-332-2244; www.lyricopera.org; Civic Opera House, 20 N Wacker Dr; Ⓜ Brown, Orange Line to Washington

By taking on a premiere of William Bolcom's *A Wedding* (an adaptation of a Robert Altman movie) for its 50th anniversary, the Lyric Opera showed its stripes. A truly great modern opera company, the seasons are popular with subscribers, who fill the ornate Civic Opera House (☎ 312-419-0033; www.civicoperahouse.com; 20 N Wacker Dr; Ⓜ Brown Line to Quincy) for a shrewd mix of common classics and daring premiers from September to March. If your Italian isn't up to snuff, don't be put off; much to the horror of purists,

CHICAGO ARTS: THINGS YOU SHOULD KNOW

- Martha Lavey – A vet director and actor of the Goodman and Victory Gardens theater, Lavey's post as Artistic Director of Steppenwolf has helped Chicago's reputation for 'serious' theater surpass even that of New York.
- Ira Glass – The creator and host of *This American Life* is a legend in the city, though these days his show sports a New York address to the chagrin of Chicago fans. *This American Life* documents all facets of our perplexing, disturbing and ultimately lovable nation.
- Studs Terkel – At 93, the oral historian and master conversationalist has put a small library's worth of amazing stories into print.
- Chris Ware – The first comic artist ever to have work in the Whitney Museum's biennial exhibit, Ware has forever raised the bar for the funny pages. Miserable weather? Grab a copy of Ware's *Jimmy Corrigan* at Quimby's and spend a wonderful afternoon under its spell.
- Mary Zimmerman – As the director and ensemble member of Chicago's Lookingglass Theatre, Zimmerman is one of those bright suns around which entire scenes revolve.

the company projects English 'supertitles,' above the proscenium.

MUSIC OF THE BAROQUE

☎ 312-551-1415; www.baroque.org

One of the largest choral and orchestral groups of its kind in the US, Music of the Baroque (MoB) brings the music of the Middle Ages and Renaissance to vibrant life. Its Christmas brass and choral concerts are huge successes.

THEATER

Steppenwolf is Chicago's world-renowned main stage, but the number of smaller curtains that rise in the city casts Chicago in a vigorous supporting role to great American acting cities like New York and Los Angeles. Though the international awareness might be less intense here, Chicago's actors and players are a passionate, busy lot and most productions are first-rate.

The venues below are listed two ways. First, by location: those historic palaces and dramatic houses that always have shows and advertise aggressively to tourists. The second kind of listings are usually more low-key and adventurous, listed by performance organization, not the name of the theater. Some of these organizations set up shop at small theaters throughout the city, and those without regular homes will have only a phone number and web address, not a street address or a permanent location.

These listings represent a small, high-quality fraction of what's going on. Check the local press to find out what's hot, or maybe just ask your waiter.

ABOUT FACE THEATRE

☎ 773-784-8565; www.aboutfacetheatre.com

This itinerant ensemble primarily stages serious plays dealing with gay and lesbian themes at small, but quality Chicago houses. Their three series include the Mainstage Season and a New Works Program.

BAILIWICK ARTS CENTER Map pp82–3

☎ 773-883-1090; www.bailiwick.org; 1229 W Belmont Ave; Ⓜ Brown, Red Line to Belmont

This facility boasts two stages seeing a constant stream of productions of all walks from the resident Bailiwick Repertory. The high quality of performances have won many civic honors, including an induction to Chicago's Gay and Lesbian Hall of Fame.

THEATER FESTIVALS

Fans of musicals should try to make the mid-August Stages Festival, which brings a dozens of tuneful new scores, some from Chicago writers, to the Theatre Building (Map pp82–3; ☎ 773-327-5252; www.theatrebuildingchicago.org; 1225 W Belmont Ave). Around the same time of year, there's a two-week presentation of solo shows called the Single File Festival (☎ 312-498-3369; www.singlefilechicago.com).

The most talked-about festival of late however is the Rhinoceros Theater Festival (www.rhinofest.com), which has been treating Chicago to new, dramatic works for around 20 years, and has enjoyed a recent revival. It runs through the fall at various theaters. Check the website for more information.

BLACK ENSEMBLE THEATRE Map p86

☎ 773-769-4451; www.blackensembletheatre.org; Uptown Center Hull House, 4520 N Beacon St; Ⓜ Red Line to Wilson

This well-established group saw their fledgling production of *The Jackie Wilson Story* attract wide attention and national tours. The focus here has long been on original productions about the African American experience though mostly biographical, historical scripts.

CHICAGO DRAMATISTS Map pp90–1

☎ 312-633-0630; www.chicagodramatists.org; 1105 W Chicago Ave; Ⓜ Blue Line to Chicago

For a visit to the heart of Chicago's dramatic scene, step into this small, functional theater space, a testing ground for Chicago's new playwrights and plays. It's no surprise that this embracing environment has earned stunning results; current resident playwrights are Emmy-nominee Susan Lieberman and Nambi E Kelly.

CHICAGO SHAKESPEARE THEATER

Map pp64–5

☎ 312-595-5600; www.chicagoshakes.com; Navy Pier, 800 E Grand Ave; 🚌 66

Now snuggled into their beautiful, highly visible new home on Navy Pier, this company is currently at the top of their game, presenting works from *the* bard that are fresh, inventive and timeless.

COURT THEATRE Map p114

☎ 773-753-4472; www.courttheatre.org; 5535 S Ellis Ave; Ⓜ Metra to 55th St

A classical company hosted by the University of Chicago, the Court focuses on great works from the Greeks to Shakespeare, and various international plays not often performed in the US. In a marriage of their strong suits, the 2007 season saw British playwright Caryl Churchill's recent translation of Seneca's epic tragedy.

FACTORY THEATER Map pp50-1

☎ 312-409-3247; www.thefactorytheater.com; 3504 N Elston Ave

This company has been staging ridiculous (*Poppin' and Lockdown 2: Dance the Right Thing*) and marginally serious plays for 15 years. It still maintains a nervy, irreverent edge that makes its schedule a must for Chicago theater and comedy fans.

GOODMAN THEATRE Map pp54–5

☎ 312-443-3800; www.goodman-theatre.org; 170 N Dearborn St; Ⓜ Blue, Brown, Green, Orange Line to Clark/Lake

The Goodman, opened in 1925, was named by *Time* magazine in 2003 as one of the best regional theaters in the US, and specializes in new and classic American theater. Its annual production of *A Christmas Carol* has become a local family tradition. Goodman's distinguished Artistic Collective is another great source of new work.

HOUSE THEATRE

☎ 773-251-2195; www.thehousetheatre.com

By throwing out the rule book, 'Chicago's most exciting young theater company' (*Tribune*) presents a mix of quirky, funny, touching shows written by untrained playwrights. Single tickets are around $20 and those interested in the whole season can join a society called 'The Secret Order of the Magic Pearl' for only $65.

KIDS' ART & THEATER

Art Institute of Chicago (see p52) Considered one of the most child-friendly art museums in the US, the bustling calendar of children's' activities makes an impressive day unto themselves.

Chicago Children's Theatre (Map pp82–3; ☎ 773-227-0180; www.chicagochildrenstheatre.org; 2nd fl, 1464 N Milwaukee Avenue; Ⓜ Blue Line to Damen) Check their website for the latest production from this award-winning company dedicated to young audiences.

Emerald City Theatre Company (☎ 773-935-6100; www.emeraldcitytheatre.com) Presenting some of the most innovative plays for children in the country, from blockbusters like *High School Musical* to slightly lesser-known works like *How I Became A Pirate*.

Rascal's Children's Theatre (☎ 773-561-5893; www.roguetheater.com) This venerated branch of the Rogue Theater Company offers favorites like *The Legend of Sleepy Hollow*.

LOOKINGGLASS THEATRE COMPANY
Map pp70–1

☎ 312-337-0665; www.lookingglasstheatre.org; 821 N Michigan Ave; Ⓜ Red Line to Chicago

This company took a step into the big time with the opening of its new, spacious digs on Michigan Ave. The ensemble cast – which includes co-founder David Schwimmer of TV's *Friends* – loves to use physical stunts and acrobatics to enhance its thought-provoking plays.

NEXT THEATRE COMPANY Map pp50-1

☎ 847-475-6763; www.nexttheatre.org; 927 Noyes Street, Evanston; Ⓜ Purple Line to Noyes

Like many of Chicago's most exciting company's Next was founded in the 80s and has grown into one of the regions most dynamic, celebrated performance spaces encouraging local premieres. The recent appointment of executive director Lisa Fulton from Tony Award-winning INTIMAN Theatre in Seattle ensures that their future is just as bright.

PROP THTR Map pp50-1

☎ 773-539-7838; www.propthtr.org; 3502 N Elston Ave; 🚌 152

This long-running troupe presents fresh stage adaptations of literary works by serious writers, from Nabokov to William Burroughs. The productions are typically dark in theme and well executed and they are a big part of the buzzed-about annual Rhinoceros Theater Festival.

REDMOON THEATER Map pp90–1

☎ 312-850-8440; www.redmoon.org; 1463 W Hubbard St; Ⓜ Green Line to Ashland

The interaction of humans and puppets is key to the magical, haunting adaptations of classic works like *Moby Dick* and new commissions like *The Princess Club,* a fairly twisted look at children's fairy-tales. The innovative nonprofit troupe is headed up by performance artists Blair Thomas and Jim Lasko and never fails to mesmerize. Be ready – the puppets can get downright creepy.

ROYAL GEORGE THEATRE Map pp76–7

☎ 312-988-9000; 1641 N Halsted St; Ⓜ Red Line to North/Clybourn

The Royal George is actually three theaters in one building. The cabaret venue presents long-running mainstream productions such as *Late Nite Catechism,* a nun-centered comedy. The main stage presents works with big-name stars, and the gallery hosts various improv and minor works performed by small troupes.

STEPPENWOLF THEATER Map pp76–7

☎ 312-335-1650; www.steppenwolf.org; 1650 N Halsted St; Ⓜ Red Line to North/Clybourn

With 20,000 annual subscribers and productions of the highest quality, this legendary name in Chicago theater was founded by Terry Kinney, Gary Sinise and Jeff Perry. It quickly outgrew one space after another, won a Tony in 1985 for regional theater excellence, and is a leading international destination for dramatic arts. Among the many famous alumns who have gone on to illustrious careers are John Malkovich, Gary Cole and John Mahoney.

TRAP DOOR THEATRE Map pp90–1

☎ 773-384-0494; www.trapdoortheatre.com; 1655 W Cortland Ave; 🚌 9

This ragtag operation once had to hold a fundraiser to purchase a bathroom for its tiny theater, but it is starting to draw bigger audiences for its consistently great productions of European avant-garde plays and originals. A recent production of *The Bitter Tears of Petra Van Kant* won three illustrious local 'After Dark' awards.

VICTORY GARDENS THEATER
Map pp76–7

☎ 773-871-3000; www.victorygardens.org; 2257 N Lincoln Ave; Ⓜ Brown, Red Line to Fullerton

Long established and playwright-friendly, Victory Gardens specializes in world premieres of plays by Chicago authors. The *Wall St Journal* called it 'one of the most important playwright theaters in the US.'

DANCE

With a renowned ballet company and a classical ballet training center, its not hard to see a pirouette while in town, but Chicago's world of dance has far more innovative and eclectic depths for those who seek it.

Millennium Park's **Joan W & Irving B Harris Theater for Music & Dance** (Map pp54–5; ☎ 312-334-7777; www.madtchi.com; 205 E Randolph Dr), has given Chicago's small-but-vibrant modern dance community

THE PALACES OF THE LOOP

Chicago boasts some dreamboat old theaters, all of which have been renovated and reopened in recent years as part of the Loop theater district restoration. Signs are posted in front of each palatial property detailing the zaniness that went on during its heyday. Whether they're showing a Cuban ballet company or a Disney musical, these beauties are worth the price of admission alone.

Auditorium Theater (Map pp54–5; ☎ 312-902-1500; 50 E Congress Pkwy)

Cadillac Palace Theater (Map pp54–5; ☎ 312-902-1400; 151 W Randolph St)

Chicago Theatre (Map pp54–5; ☎ 312-443-1130; 175 N State St)

Ford Center/Oriental Theater (Map pp54–5; ☎ 312-902-1400; 24 W Randolph St)

LaSalle Bank Theatre (Map pp54–5; ☎ 312-977-1700; 22 W Monroe St)

a high-profile home. Long before the center was complete though, jazz dance thrived in Chicago because of local pioneers like Gus Giordano. The Joffrey Ballet has also settled in to the city nicely since its relocation from New York City in 1995.

See Chicago Dance (www.seechicagodance.com) is the well-maintained online hub for information about companies that go far deeper than the marquee names, and though that site is the best resource, you'll find more information in the *Reader* or *Time Out* listings.

BALLET CHICAGO

☎ 312-251-8838; www.balletchicago.org

The repertoire of technician and choreographer George Balanchine, admired as a founding father of American Ballet, makes the foundation of this pre-professional training center. The performance troupe wins wide acclaim.

CHICAGO MOVING CO

☎ 773-880-5402; www.chicagomovingcompany.org

Known for gutsy, energetic performances, this exciting group was founded over 30 years ago by Nana Shineflug, a pioneer of modern dance in Chicago. The works and performers are all local.

DANCE CENTER AT COLUMBIA COLLEGE Map pp106–7

☎ 312-344-8300; www.dancecenter.org; 1306 S Michigan Ave; Ⓜ Green/Orange Line to Roosevelt/Wabash Station

More than an academic institution, one of the most focused collegiate modern dance programs in the country, the Dance Center has carved out a fine reputation by presenting top local and international talent. The center's new state-of-the-art facility within Columbia College helps it to continue attracting quality dance from beyond the city's border.

ELASTIC ARTS FOUNDATION Map p95

☎ 773-880-5402; www.elasticrevolution.com; 2nd fl, 2830 N Milwaukee; Ⓜ Blue Line to Logan Sq

The calendar at Elastic Arts is far-reaching and impossible to pin down – one week the city's most exciting experimental choreographers will fill the space, and the next will see a performance of original art music by cutting edge international ensembles.

DANCE FESTIVALS

Plenty of dance festivals move the city, starting with Chicago SummerDance (☎ 312-742-4007; evenings Thu-Sat & afternoons Sun Jun-Aug), where ordinary Chicagoans get free lessons and hone their ballroom and Latin dance moves to a live orchestra in the Spirit of Music Garden (Map pp54–5).

For spectators, the Jazz Dance World Congress (☎ 847-866-9442; www.jazzdanceworldcongress.org) visits the city for a week in August at the Harris Theater for Music & Dance bringing a set of exciting performances by top jazz dance companies. November holds the city's biggest dance event though, Dance Chicago (☎ 773-989-0698; www.dancechicago.com), which brings dancers from across disciplines to the Athenaeum Theatre (Map pp54–5; 2936 N Southport Ave) for a month-long series.

Regardless, this is at the edge of Chicago's art community.

GIORDANO JAZZ DANCE CHICAGO

☎ 874-866-6779; www.giordanojazzdance.com
This Chicago company was founded by one of the most important people in the history of American dance form, Gus Giordano. Now headed by his daughter Nan, the company is out on the road for much of the year, but still comes back for occasional performances in its hometown.

HUBBARD ST DANCE CHICAGO

Map pp54–5

☎ 312-850-9744; www.hubbardstreetdance.com; Harris Theater for Music & Dance, 205 E Randolph Dr; Ⓜ Brown, Green, Orange Line to Randolph
Hubbard St is the preeminent dance group in the city, with a well-deserved international reputation to match. The group is known for energetic and technically virtuoso performances under the direction of the best choreographers in the world, including founder Lou Conte.

JOFFREY BALLET OF CHICAGO

Map pp54–5

☎ 312-739-0120; www.joffreyballet.org; Auditorium Theatre, 50 E Congress Pkwy; Ⓜ Brown, Orange Line to Library
This famous group has flourished since it relocated from New York in 1995. Noted for its energetic work, the company frequently travels the world and boasts an impressive storehouse of regularly performed repertoire.

MUNTU DANCE THEATER OF CHICAGO

☎ 773-602-1135; www.muntu.com
The word *muntu* means 'the essence of humanity' in Bantu. This company was founded in 1972 to perform African and American dances that draw on ancient and contemporary movement. The fiery performances of traditional dances from West Africa are an essential part of Muntu's signature.

RIVER NORTH DANCE COMPANY

☎ 312-944-2888; www.rivernorthchicago.com
This vibrant young company has quickly become among Chicago's most admired modern companies, bringing a mixed bag of pop culture (including mime) and theatrical modern dance.

FILM

Chicagoans will spend whole weekends in the cool, darkened confines of a movie theater during unbearably humid summer days, but movie houses are scarcely less packed in the winter, as folks will trudge through the snow to catch the latest art-house blockbuster.

Chicago is packed with movie theaters, including the Illinois-based Kerasotes Theatres chain; but the following have been selected with the interests of travelers in mind. Show times are printed in the *Reader* or in either daily paper, or available via multiple online movie sites.

600 N MICHIGAN THEATERS

Map pp64–5

☎ 312-255-9340; 600 N Michigan Ave; Ⓜ Red Line to Chicago
Despite the name, the entrance to these centrally located theaters is off Rush St. This comfortable complex is quiet during the week and features six screens of various sizes, plus a café and concession stand on each of its three floors.

CHICAGO FILM FESTIVALS

The Midwest Independent Film Festival (www.midwestfilm.com) – a monthly event dedicated to showcasing the best indie films from the Midwest – is a great way to catch a flick from Chicago's up-and-coming filmmakers. It happens the first Tuesday of the month at Landmark's Century Centre (opposite).

If you have a shorter attention span, try the Fast Forward Film Festival (www.fastforwardfilmfest.com), which challenges locals to make and edit a three-minute video within 24 hours and occurs a few times a year. The results are shown to giddy, sleep-deprived audiences at DIY spaces around town. Check the website for updates.

In October, the Chicago Film Festival (☎ 312-683-0121; www.chicagofilmfestival.org) is the main event. If your visit coincides, check with the festival website for the complete schedule. For more unique offerings in a festival environment, check out the Chicago Underground Film Festival (www.cuff.org), which runs in late August.

AMC RIVER EAST Map pp64–5

☎ 312-596-0333; 322 E Illinois St; Ⓜ Red Line to Chicago, 🚌 65

The screens are huge and the sound will rumble your dental work loose at this high-tech theater – the perfect place to get out of the humidity, suck down buckets of Coke and take in an explosion-filled, scantily clad, special effects-laden blockbuster. Parking is pricey, so take public transportation.

BREW & VIEW Map pp82–3

☎ 773-929-6713; www.brewview.com; Vic Theater, 3145 N Sheffield Ave; Ⓜ Brown, Red Line to Belmont

Even the worst film gets better when you've got a pizza in front of you and a pitcher of beer at your side. As you watch second-run Hollywood releases, you can behave as badly as you would at home – in fact, the $2 mid-week drink specials encourage it. You must be 18.

FACETS MULTIMEDIA Map pp76–7

☎ 773-281-9075; www.facets.org; 1517 W Fullerton Ave; 🚌 74

Facets' main business is as the country's largest distributor of foreign and cult films, so it follows that their 'cinematheque' movie house shows interesting, obscure movies that would never get booked elsewhere.

GENE SISKEL FILM CENTER Map pp54–5

☎ 312-846-2600; www.siskelfilmcenter.org; 164 N State St; Ⓜ Brown, Green, Orange Line to State

The former Film Center of the School of the Art Institute was renamed for the late *Chicago Tribune* film critic Gene Siskel. It shows everything from amateurish stuff by students to wonderful but unsung gems by Estonian directors. The monthly schedule includes theme nights of forgotten American classics.

LANDMARK'S CENTURY CENTRE Map pp82–3

☎ 773-509-4949; 2828 N Clark St; Ⓜ Brown, Purple Line to Diversey

This seven-screen, high-tech cinema is a big bucket of popcorn better than typically rough shod art houses. They have stadium seating just like the multiplexes and a gourmet snack bar for the fanciest filmgoer.

MUSIC BOX THEATRE Map pp82–3

☎ 773-871-6604; www.musicboxtheatre.com; 3733 N Southport Ave; Ⓜ Brown Line to Southport

The current feature hardly matters; the Music Box itself is worth the visit. This perfectly restored theater dates from 1929 and looks like a Moorish palace with clouds floating across the ceiling, under twinkling stars. The programs are always first-rate, including a midnight roster of cult hits like *The Big Lebowski*. A second, small and serviceable theater shows held-over films.

READINGS & SPOKEN WORD

Chicago's literary scene might be small but it is feisty, featuring locals and out-of-towner readings in comfortable (often boozy) DIY settings. Quimby's (p131), Danny's (p176) and the California Clipper (Map p95; ☎ 773-384-2547; www.californiaclipper.com; 1002 N California) host reliable events, while the Red Lion Pub (p173) is another good bet for beery bookishness.

The more established (and sober) men and women of letters are likely to read at Barbara's Bookstore (p134) where events are frequent. The only event that might bring all these scenes together is the annual Printers' Ball (www.printersball.org), which brings all sorts of

top picks

LITERARY BLOGS

- **Literago** (www.literago.org) This ace blog by Gretchen Kalwinski and Eugenia Williamson was founded to 'show the world Chicago isn't an illerate sinkhole.'
- **Book Slut** (www.bookslut.com) A sharp monthly online lit magazine of reviews headed by Jessa Crispin.
- **Golden Rule Jones** (www.goldenrulejones.com) The title of this blog is a nod to Samuel Milton 'Golden Rule' Jones, literature-loving businessman and progressive politician of the early 20th century. It's been publishing literary criticism and events in the Windy City since 2002.
- **Shoot The Messinger** (www.shootthemessinger.com) A blog about literature and life by Jonathan Messinger, the founder of the Dollar Store Show (p200).

TWO THUMBS UP

They were the most powerful movie reviewers in history. And they were no taller than a stick of gum. Yes, Roger Ebert's and Gene Siskel's thumbs mercilessly ruled film criticism during their 24-year run of televised reviewing. The two Chicago newspaper reporters created their first show on Chicago TV station WTTW in 1975. Eleven years and two networks later, the duo was national, inventing the thumb system – which they eventually trademarked. Rather than simply reviewing the Hollywood movies that Americans were most likely to see, the duo saw themselves as advocates for overlooked cinema as well. For an up-and-coming director, getting a 'two thumbs up' rating could transform their film from an art-house also-ran to a commercial success overnight. Enthusiastic endorsements of offbeat movies like *My Dinner With Andre* and *Hoop Dreams* made them part of the American vernacular, and any time a movie achieved a 'two thumbs up' rating it was sure to be plastered in blockbuster type across posters.

However benevolent they could be for a struggling auteur, Siskel and Ebert had an occasionally venomous on-camera relationship with each other. Viewers tuned in for astute insights on new movies, but the swipes and jabs thrown by the reviewers were also part of the show's draw. 'We would have a fight every taping day over something,' the Pulitzer Prize-winning Ebert recalls in an interview with the Sun-Times, After Siskel's surprise death from surgery complications in 1999, the Film Center of the School of the Art Institute of Chicago was renamed Gene Siskel Film Center (p199) in his honor. Ebert's soldiered on for a few years alongside Siskel's successor, fellow *Sun-Times* critic Richard Roeper, but in 2006 Ebert himself left the program, citing health problems. In 2005 the city of Chicago named July 12th 'Roger Ebert Day,' placing a plaque dedicated to the legendary man and his discerning thumb in front of the Chicago Theatre (p197).

performance and lit-based events to Chicago venues for a month-long literary hootenanny in July. In 2007 it got downright out of hand; the cops busted the closing party.

DANNY'S READING SERIES

☎ 773-489-6457; 1951 W Dickens Ave; 🚌 50

Held the third Wednesday of every month at Danny's (p176), this is one of the city's best places to see young poets from Chicago and abroad. The atmosphere is casual and the roster heady, making it Chicago's quintessential younger poets' event.

DOLLAR STORE

☎ 773-227-4433; www.dollarstoreshow.com; Hideout, 1354 W Wabansia; 🚌 72

This high-concept, low-pretension lit event at Hideout (p185) hands a small group of young novelists, poets, spoken-word artists and other artistic souls a dime-store object – perhaps a tacky souvenir or a box of Monoxodil – and gives them 30 days to write a piece incorporating the object. The resulting story is then performed by the author at the Dollar Store event, held on the first Friday of every month.

GUILD COMPLEX LITERARY COMPLEX

☎ 877-394-5061; www.guildcomplex.org

The prose series and BYOP (P is for 'people,' of course) of this smart nonprofit organization brings together the young, old, hip and square of Chicago's literary scene, for free events at the brilliantly divey California Clipper (Map p95; ☎ 773-384-2547; www.californiaclipper.com; 1002 N California). For Spanish speakers they also organize the bi-lingual Palabra Pura series.

HAROLD WASHINGTON LIBRARY CENTER READINGS

☎ 312-747-4050; www.chipublib.org

Several writers each month come to the country's largest library, the Harold Washington Library Center (p60), and give a talk about their recent projects. Recent guests have included John Irving and *Wicked* author Gregory Maguire. The library's author calendar can be seen on its website, or drop by the library for a flyer.

UPTOWN POETRY SLAM AT THE GREEN MILL

☎ 773-878-5552; www.slampapi.com

This long-running event birthed the national slam fad, and it's still going every Sunday night at the Green Mill (p183). Watch shaky first-timers take to the mic from 7pm to 8pm, then for an hour after that a featured guest has a go and the slam competition begins in earnest. There's a $6 cover.

WEED'S POETRY NIGHT Map pp70–1

☎ 312-943-7815; 1555 N Dayton St; Ⓜ Red Line to North/Clybourn

Verse comes in all shapes and sizes at Weed's weekly night, when a cast of delightfully eccentric poets get on the mic to vent about love, sex, war, booze, urban living and pretty much everything in between. Some of it rhymes, some of it rambles, but the proportions make for a pretty cool scene.

WRITERS ON RECORD RADIO SHOW TAPING

☎ 312-832-6789

Host Victoria Lautman sits down for an hour-long chat with a famous writer – recent guests have included Jonathan Safran Foer, and Susan Orlean – during this taped WFMT program, taped in the Lookingglass Theatre (p196). The tickets are free, but must be reserved in advance.

SPORTS & ACTIVITIES

top picks

- **Chicago Cubs** (p210)
- **Working Bikes Cooperative** (p206)
- **Lakefront Bike Path** (p206)
- **Millennium Park Workouts** (p204)
- **Smelt Fishing** (p207)
- **Baseball Batting Cages** (p207)
- **North Ave Beach** (p209)
- **Ice Skating in Millennium Park** (p207)
- **Moksha Yoga** (p205)
- **Diversey-River Bowl** (p206)

SPORTS & ACTIVITIES

Chicago is the USA's greatest sports town. There – we said it. Listen in at the office watercooler on Monday morning, and the talk is all about the Bears. Eavesdrop on a conversation between neighbors as they tidy their yards, and the chatter revolves around the Cubs or White Sox.

Sports are deeply woven into the local fabric. This is a city that sees no conflict of interest in taking one of its most-revered cultural icons – the Art Institute's lion sculptures – and plopping giant fiberglass Bears helmets on them when the local team is in the Super Bowl. The creatures also donned White Sox ball caps during the 2005 World Series. Even the city's staid skyscrapers get into the spirit, arranging their window lights to spell 'Go Bears' or 'Go Cubs' when the teams make a run for the championship.

It's not all about passively watching sports, though. When the sun peeps out in April after the long, cold winter, everyone busts out of work and makes a dash for the lakefront to jog, skate or ride their bike. Chicago provides plenty of places to get active via its city-spanning shoreline, 33 beaches and 552 parks.

OK, OK, it's true: the bars during a Bears game are still more crowded than a free 9am yoga class in Millennium Park. And statistics show that Chicagoans are not particularly fit as a whole (the city placed in the top five for chubbiness, according to a recent national study). But hey, is it the locals' fault beer and pizza have so many calories?

The point is, Chicago has a sweet array of sports and activity options, so whether you want to open your chakras, fish for smelt or practice your homerun swing, the Windy City has you covered.

HEALTH & FITNESS

For a fun and free exercise session, try Millennium Park Workouts (www.millenniumpark.org/parkevents/fitness.aspx). Every Saturday morning between 8am and 11am, from mid June to late October, the park hosts a workout on the Great Lawn (Map pp54–5). It might be yoga, or Pilates, or maybe even a kids-oriented session that entails chasing bubbles. Exact start times vary, so check the website for the schedule.

Hotels almost always have either their own fitness facilities or agreements with nearby clubs. We've listed some additional options below. Gym day passes cost $20 to $25; yoga drop-in classes cost around $15.

HEALTH & DAY SPAS

AVEDA INSTITUTE Map pp82–3

☎ 773-883-1560; www.avedainstitutechicago.com; 2828 N Clark St; 🕑 9:15am-4:30pm Tue-Fri, 8:30am-5pm Sat; Ⓜ Brown, Purple Line to Diversey

Aveda makes nice-smelling, plant-based beauty products. The Institute teaches future cosmetologists to use those products on people. So what you get here are discounted services by students who use Aveda goodies to beautify you. Haircuts ($14 to $16) are the most popular offering, but you can also get treatments such as the Caribbean seaweed body wrap and mini-massage ($50); a Dead Sea salt exfoliation and massage ($45); and a variety of facials ($30-50), each of which includes a bonus foot soak with hot stones. Attention men: Aveda can remove your back hair (from $30).

FOUR SEASONS SPA Map pp70–1

☎ 312-280-8800; Four Seasons Hotel, 120 E Delaware Pl; 🕑 8am-8pm; Ⓜ Red Line to Chicago

If you really want to do it in style, head to the Four Seasons Spa, where pleasures like the elixir paraffin wrap and the green tea and ginger mud body mask will 'revitalize your energy meridians.' They also feel pretty great. You can do quick 30-minute sessions or have a luxurious all-day affair. Prices start sky high and go up from there.

RUBY ROOM Map pp90–1

☎ 773-235-2323; www.rubyroom.com; 1743-5 W Division St; 🕑 10am-7pm Mon-Fri, 9am-7pm Sat, 10am-6pm Sun; Ⓜ Blue Line to Division

Ruby Room is a spa and 'healing sanctuary' serving up a wild array of services. The 'intuitive numerotherapy' option ($90 for 60 minutes) will help you figure out why you keep dating meat-headed jerks and working at dead-end jobs. Or maybe you just need an energy healing ($90 for 60 minutes) to get your aura back to its proper color. More down-to-earth services – massages, facials, haircuts etc – are also on the menu. You may well need the 30-minute scalp massage ($65 for 30 minutes) after wrestling all those unproductive feelings during your 'intuitive exploration' ($90 for 60 minutes). For details on lodgings here, see p229.

YOGA & PILATES

Chicago has a few option for excercising the body and mind. Call or check the websites for class times.

BIKRAM YOGA Map pp90–1

☎ 773-315-9150; www.bycic.com; 1344 N Milwaukee Ave; Ⓜ Blue Line to Damen
For a great yoga-only experience, try this place in Wicker Park, where classes run daily and cost $15 per 90-minute session. This is 'hot' yoga, in a heated room, so arrive hydrated.

HARMONY MIND BODY FITNESS Map pp76–7

☎ 773-296-0263; www.harmonybody.com; 1962 N Bissell; Ⓜ Brown, Purple Line to Armitage
A staff of fully certified Pilates purists offers classes in Pilates, Gyrotonic, yoga and Feldenkrais techniques. Group-yoga classes and Pilates-mat classes cost $20; private sessions run up to $75.

MOKSHA YOGA Map pp82–3

☎ 773-975-9642; www.mokshayoga.com; 3334 N Clark St; Ⓜ Brown, Purple, Red Line to Belmont
Hatha, vinyasa, ashtanga and tantric-hatha classes happen throughout the day, seven days a week. Drop-in classes cost $10 to $16, depending on their length; students with ID receive a 20% discount. Moksha also offers a free 'community' class from 4pm to 5:30pm on Saturdays; its yoga style varies.

YOGAVIEW Map pp90–1

☎ 773-342-9642; www.yogaview.com; Suite 200, 2211 N Elston Ave; 🚌 6
Most Yogaview instructors teach some type of vinyasa, but individual teachers can lean toward an iyengar or ashtanga approach, too. Drop-in classes cost $10, which is about as low as they go in Chicago.

GYMS

CRUNCH FITNESS Map pp64–5

☎ 312-828-9777; www.crunch.com; 38 E Grand Ave; 🕑 5:30am-10pm Mon-Thu, to 8pm Fri, 8am-6:30pm Sat & Sun; Ⓜ Red Line to Grand
Located in Near North, Crunch offers workout opportunities at the more extreme end of the spectrum, with martial-arts classes, yoga, boxing and Pilates.

FITNESS FORMULA CLUB Map pp82–3

☎ 773-755-3232; www.fitnessformulaclubs.com; 3228 N Halsted St; 🕑 24hr Mon-Thu, to 9:30pm Fri, 7am-9pm Sat, 8am-9pm Sun; Ⓜ Brown, Purple, Red Line to Belmont
This club is particularly well-regarded for its strength training. Along with the usual workout machines, swimming pools and basketball courts the half-dozen locations around town also offer kickboxing, yoga and Pilates classes.

LAKESHORE ATHLETIC CLUB Map pp54–5

☎ 312-644-4880; www.lsac.com; 441 N Wabash Ave; Ⓜ Red Line to Grand
Lakeshore offers an indoor jogging track, tennis and squash courts, and a full equipment set-up at this location. The outlet at the Illinois Center (Map pp54–5; ☎ 312-616-9000; www.lsac.com; 211 North Stetson Ave; 🕑 5:15am-10pm Mon-Fri, 8am-6pm Sat & Sun; Ⓜ Brown, Green, Orange, Purple Line to State) has an impressive seven-story indoor climbing wall, for which day use and orientation fees cost about $40. General-use gym rates are about $25 per day.

ACTIVITIES

When the weather warms, Chicagoans dash like sun-starved maniacs for the parks and beaches. On the first nice day (there's usually one in April), bikers, joggers and skaters jam the lakefront path – it's worse than anything on the local highways. Winter is quieter, though the hardy bundle up to ice skate and sled-ride.

BASEBALL BATTING CAGES

Tired of watching your favorite Cubs or Sox player strike out, and think you could do better? Give it a try at Sluggers (Map pp82–3; ☎ 773-472-9696; 3540 N Clark St), a popular bar and

CHICAGO'S LUCKY STRIKES

Bowling is a distinctly Midwestern activity. People of all shapes, sizes and ages gather in boisterous groups to send balls crashing into pins. Talent is not a prerequisite, but a willingness to consume copious pitchers of cheap beer is. Bowling alleys draw the most crowds during the cold months.

To try your luck on the lanes, visit:

Diversey-River Bowl (Map pp82–3; ☎ 773-227-5800; 2211 W Diversey Pkwy; 🚌 76) Nicknamed the 'rock n bowl' for its late-night light show, fog machines and loud music.

Southport Lanes (Map pp82–3; ☎ 773-472-6600; 3325 N Southport Ave; Ⓜ Brown Line to Southport) Has old-fashioned, hand-set pins; slip a dollar into the ball when you roll it back, and the pin-setter might knock down a few extra ones on your behalf.

Waveland Bowl (Map pp82–3; ☎ 773-472-5900; 3700 N Western Ave; Ⓜ Brown Line to Addison, transfer to 🚌 152) Open 24/7 baby, so you can roll the ball and wear the spiffy shoes whenever the mood strikes (pun!).

grill across from Wrigley Field. Sidestep the drunk fans and giant screen TVs and head to the second floor, where there are four batting cages. Ten pitches cost $1; you'll begin feeling the pain pretty soon after your efforts.

CYCLING & IN-LINE SKATING

Curbs are the highest mountains you'll find in Chicago, making it ideal for biking and in-line skating. The popular, 18.5-mile Lakefront Path from Hollywood Ave in the north to 71st St in the south is an excellent way to see the city, and in hot weather the lake offers cool breezes. Lincoln Park is another good spot for biking and rolling, with paths snaking around the small lakes and the zoo. Another surprisingly good option for biking is the Loop on Sundays. The traffic clears out of the business district, giving wheeled tourists an exhilarating, stress-free opportunity to roll through the historic architecture of downtown.

The city's Department of Transportation (www.chicagobikes.org) offers a free map of bike-friendly streets, plus info on bike shops, publications, local regulations and a slew of other resources. The advocacy group Chicagoland Bicycle Federation (www.biketraffic.org) is another goldmine for cyclists; it includes details on grassroots events such as 'veggie bike rides,' where enthusiasts get together for a ride and meat-free meal.

Chicago offers a great gift to bikers in the form of the McDonald's Cycle Center (www.chicagobikestation.com) at Millennium Park. The facility offers bike storage, repairs and gymlike features to make bike commuting an appealing option for workers. It's also a convenient place to pick up rental bikes (per hour/day $8/35), including road, hybrid, tandem and children's bikes. Bike Chicago (www.bikechicago.com) is the rental company doing the honors here, as well as from outlets on Navy Pier and North Ave Beach. It offers customers free guided bike tours three times daily (at 10am, 1pm and 6:30pm). In-line skates can also be rented at each of Bike Chicago's outlets for the same price as bikes. For details on opening hours and locations, see p251.

If you're going to need a bike for more than a few days, consider buying a recycled two-wheeler from Working Bikes Cooperative (Map pp98–9; ☎ 312-421-5048; 1125 S Western Ave). The nonprofit group trawls local landfills and scrap yards for junked bikes, then brings them back to its warehouse and refurbishes them. Half get sold in the storefront shop; proceeds enable the group to ship the rest to developing countries. WBC now recycles 10,000 bikes annually this way. It's a great deal – you'll get a sturdy, well-oiled machine for the bargain price of about $40 or so. When you're finished, you can donate the bike back. Note you will have to factor in the cost of a lock and helmet (rental companies provide these for free).

If you're looking for a very big, very slow group ride while you're in town, Chicago Critical Mass (www.chicagocriticalmass.org) organizes rides through the streets on the last Friday of the month. The rides, which are intended to celebrate bike use and disrupt the car-dependent status quo, begin at Daley Plaza (cnr of Dearborn and Washington Sts) at 5:30pm. The mood is lighthearted and routes unfold spontaneously. If you're in town over Memorial Day weekend, Bike the Drive (www.bikethedrive.org) lets riders have Lake Shore Drive all to themselves for one glorious morning; for event details, see p13.

FISHING

Between the fishing derbies organized by the mayor's office, the state-sponsored Urban Fishing Program and, of course, smelt season, fisherfolk cast a lot more lines in the city than you might expect. The waters of Lake Michigan just off Northerly Island (p108) boast good fishing, as does the lagoon in Humboldt Park (p94). If the fish are biting, expect to catch rock bass, smallmouth bass, largemouth bass and the ubiquitous catfish.

In April, it's all about smelt, the wee fish that swarm into Chicago's harbors to spawn. Anglers meet them with nets and deep-fat fryers from piers up and down the lakefront (beers and portable TVs are also part of the deal).

Anglers over 16 years of age will need a license (available online at http://dnr.state.il.us and at any bait shop for $6 per day). Online resources for maps and tips include Windy City Fishing (www.windycityfishing.com) and the Illinois Department of Natural Resources (www.ifishillinois.org).

GOLF

Chicago golfers stretch the season as far as possible in both directions; basically you can play until it snows.

The Chicago Park District has six public golf courses and three driving ranges, all overseen by Kemper Golf Management (☎ 312-245-0909; www.cpdgolf.com). Call or go online to find out more about the courses, as well as to make your tee times.

DIVERSEY DRIVING RANGE

Map pp82–3

☎ 312-742-7929; Diversey Pkwy, Lincoln Park; 7am-10pm; 151

If you just want to knock a bucket of balls around, this driving range in Lincoln Park will let you whack away to your heart's content. Rental clubs are available, and a bucket is about $8.

JACKSON PARK GOLF COURSE

Map pp50-1

☎ 773-667-0524; E 63rd St & Lake Shore Dr; 6, Metra to 63rd

The district's only 18-hole course is moderately challenging. Public fees range from $23 to $26. Reservations are recommended.

SYDNEY R MAROVITZ GOLF COURSE

Map pp32–3

☎ 312-742-7930; 3600 N Recreation Dr (Lake Shore Dr) in Lincoln Park; 151

The nine-hole course enjoys sweeping views of the lake and skyline. The course is very popular, and in order to secure a tee time, golfers cheerfully arrive at 5:30am. You can avoid that sort of lunacy by spending a few dollars extra to get a reservation. Public fees cost $20 to $23 in summer. You can also rent clubs here.

ICE-SKATING & SLEDDING

The Chicago Park District operates a first-class winter rink at Daley Bicentennial Plaza (Map pp54–5; ☎ 312-742-7650; 337 E Randolph St) and at the McCormick-Tribune Ice Rink (Map pp54–5; ☎ 312-742-5222; 55 N Michigan Ave) in Millennium Park. Admission is free to both; skate rental costs $5 to $7. They're open from late November to late February.

The Park District also operates a free, 33ft sledding hill by Soldier Field (Map pp106–7; 425 E McFetridge Dr) in winter; bring your own gear. They fire up a snow-making machine for times when the weather doesn't cooperate.

PICK-UP GAMES

Those looking to put in a little time on the basketball court will be especially excited by Chicago's offerings; casual hoops happen at almost every park in the city. If you're near Wicker Park (the park, not the neighborhood), you can get a game there. Ultimate Frisbee is also big in Chicago. An informative website (www.ultimatechicago.org) dedicated to the sport will keep you informed about start times. A regular Tuesday evening game is held in Montrose Park in the summer and in Clarendon Park in the winter.

RUNNING & WALKING

The lakefront path (opposite) also has a runner's side for those looking to get a little bipedal workout. Runners hit the trail around 5am. If you're looking for a good starting point, try Oak St Beach on the Gold Coast and head north. The path from the beach northward is largely cinder rather than asphalt, which your feet will appreciate.

If you find yourself getting distracted by the great city and park views, you can regain focus on the free cinder oval track at Lake Shore Park (808 N Lake Shore Dr), at the intersection of Chicago Ave and Lake Shore Dr.

OFFBEAT ACTIVITIES

Bet you never expected to go surfing or become a cornhole master in Chicago, did you?

Midnight Bike Riding On the third Saturday of every month, a group of cycling enthusiasts meets at the Handlebar (p156) for a beverage or four, followed by a two-hour ride at 11:30pm through the 'hood. Several of the regulars dress up (one guy always wears a Viking helmet), but that's optional.

Cornhole Get your mind out of the gutter; we're not talking porn here. We're talking *corn,* as in small corn-filled bags (aka beanbags) that participants toss into a sloped box with a hole in it. It started as a bar game but vaulted into the big time in 2007, when the First Annual Windy City Cornhole Classic took over Soldier Field (yes, the football stadium). Bars are still the place to see the game in action; ones like the Cubby Bear (☎ 773-327-1662; 1059 W Addison St) have leagues and tournaments. Check www.chicagocornhole.com for other locations.

Urban Golf A group of folks called the Chicago Urban Devils Golf Enthusiasts' League (CUDGEL; www.cudgel.org) gather to hit balls (usually tennis balls) with clubs through the city's alleyways. The 'hole' is often in a local bar, so be prepared to imbibe. The group has been quiet recently, but keep an eye on the website for future outings.

Kitesurfing Pump up your adrenaline with Chicago Kitesurfing (www.chicagokitesurfing.com). Beginners can sign up for three- to four-hour lessons ($150 to $250, gear included). These take place at beaches outside the city, wherever wind conditions are best (but they're usually no more than an hour away). If you don't want to participate, you can always watch experienced kitesurfers go at it from Montrose Beach.

Surfing You'll have to travel about an hour and a half outside of town to New Buffalo, Michigan (p239), but there you'll see dudes licking some tasty waves.

Any questions about running should be directed to the Chicago Area Runners Association (☎ 312-666-9836; www.cararuns.org), which sponsors training programs and offers free downloadable running maps on its website.

For those looking to move at a more leisurely pace, walking through the city's parks is a great way to get exercise. The Chicago Park District (www.chicagoparkdistrict.com) offers extensive path lists, maps and ratings of its hundreds of city-maintained walking trails on its website. The site even offers a flower and plant finder to help you identify any flora you see en route.

TENNIS

Some of Chicago's public tennis courts require reservations and charge fees (usually around $7 per hour), while others are free and players just queue for their turns on the court. Place your racket by the net and you're next in line. The season runs from mid-April to mid-October.

Good options include:

Daley Bicentennial Plaza (Map pp54–5; ☎ 312-742-7648; 337 E Randolph St; Ⓜ Brown, Green, Orange, Purple Line to Randolph) Charges a fee for its 12 lit courts.

Grant Park (Map pp106–7; 900 S Columbus Dr near E Balbo Dr; 🚌 6) No reservations are taken for the 12 lit courts, but fees are charged at peak times.

Lake Shore Park (Map pp70–1; ☎ 312-742-7891; 808 N Lake Shore Dr; Ⓜ Red Line to Chicago) Two very popular (and free) lit courts near the lake.

Waveland Tennis Courts (Map pp82–3; ☎ 312-742-8515; east side of N Lake Shore Dr where Waveland Ave meets Lincoln Park; 🚌 151) Charges a fee for its 20 courts.

WATERSPORTS

Between Lake Michigan, the Chicago River and Chicago's public pools, there are limitless ways to make a splash in the city.

Lakefront beaches (see the boxed text, opposite) have lifeguards in summer. However, you can swim at your own risk whenever you want, depending on what you think of the temperature. The water in August is usually in the 70°s F (21° to 26°C). If you're looking for chlorinated water, try the large pool at Holstein Park (Map pp90–1; ☎ 312-742-7554; 2200 N Oakley Ave; admission free; 🕐 7am-8pm Mon-Fri, from 9am Sat & Sun) in the heart of Bucktown. You can rent a suit and leave your sweaty duds in a locker. Best of all, the pool has frequent adult-only hours, so there's no fear of squealing kids.

Kayaking has taken off in the city, and several outfitters rent kayaks along the Chicago River. It's not the world's cleanest body of water, but that doesn't seem to be deterring anyone. Note that boat traffic can get heavy as you approach downtown. If you're a beginner, you might want to chat with the outfitter about local conditions to make sure you're up for the task. Rentals cost $15 to $20 per hour.

CHICAGO BEACHES

Visitors often don't realize Chicago is a beach town. In fact, it has 33 sandy stretches along Lake Michigan, all operated by the Park District (☎ 312-742-7529; www.chicagoparkdistrict.com). Call it the Miami of the Midwest – at least for a few months each year. Lifeguards patrol *Baywatch*-style from late May through early September. Our favorites, from north to south, are:

- Loyola Beach (Map pp50-1) – Runs for more than eight blocks from North Shore Ave to Touhy Ave; features an upscale wooden playground for kids. It's fairly close to the Loyola El stop.
- Montrose Beach (Map pp50-1) – A great wide beach with a curving breakwater. The Montrose Harbor bait shop sells ice for coolers. Sometimes you'll see kitesurfers, and there are almost always anglers casting here. There's ample parking, but the walks to the beach can be long. To get there by bus, take 146 or 151.
- Fullerton Beach (Map pp76–7) – Fills with zoo day-trippers and Lincoln Parkers. The narrow beach can get jammed on weekends, but a five-minute walk south from Fullerton yields uncrowded vistas.
- North Ave Beach (Map pp76–7) – Chicago's Southern California-style pocket, with loads of beautiful people, volleyball nets and million-dollar views; for more information, see p78.
- Oak St Beach (Map pp70–1) – Lies at the north end of Michigan Ave, less than five minutes from the Water Tower. The hulking Lake Shore Dr condos cast shadows in the afternoon, but the beach remains packed. See p72 for more information.
- Ohio St Beach (Map pp64–5) – Nestled between Lake Shore Dr and Navy Pier, this beach is convenient for those who want a quick dip or a chance to feel some sand between sweaty toes.
- 12th St Beach (Map pp106–7) – Hidden behind the Adler Planetarium, it makes a great break from the myriad sights of the Museum Campus. Its out-of-the-way location gives the narrow enclave an exclusive feel. See p108 for more details.
- 57th St Beach (Map p114) – Just across Lake Shore Dr from the Museum of Science & Industry, 57th St Beach features an expanse of clean, golden sand.
- Jackson Park Beach (Map p114) – A bit further south from 57th St Beach; contains a stately restored beach house with dramatic breezeways. This beach, next to the yacht harbor, has a charm lacking at the beaches with more modern – and mundane – facilities.

Or opt for a guided paddle, which all of the companies below offer as well.

CHICAGO KAYAK Map pp50-1

☎ 847-425-9925; www.chicagokayak.com; 2738 Noyes St, Evanston

Based in suburban Evanston, this company teaches courses in sea kayaking for the novice to the advanced kayaker. Numerous trips on Lake Michigan and the Chicago River depart from points in the city. Rates start at $75 for a four-hour course.

CHICAGO RIVER CANOE & KAYAK Map pp50-1

☎ 773-704-2663; www.chicagoriverpaddle.com; 3400 N Rockwell Ave; Ⓜ Brown Line to Addison, transfer to 🚌 152

The launch point is about two miles north of downtown, so it's better for beginners (ie away from traffic). Guided trips head downtown, like the Skyscraper Canyon tour ($30 to $40).

WATERIDERS Map pp70–1

☎ 312-953-9287; www.wateriders.com; 900 N Kingsbury St; Ⓜ Brown, Purple Line to Chicago

Wateriders is closest to downtown. If you decide to go with a guide, it offers excellent 'Ghost and Gangster' tours ($45 to $55) on Saturdays and Sundays that glide by notorious downtown sites.

SPECTATOR SPORTS

Almost every Chicagoan declares a firm allegiance to at least one of the city's teams, and the place goes absolutely nuts when one of them hits the big-time. Take the White Sox World Series win in 2005: tens of thousands of people lined the street from US Cellular Field to the Loop for a raucous ticker-tape parade (which included F-16 fighter planes, Journey's Steve Perry and Oprah, all strangely woven together). And when the Bears went to the Super Bowl in 2007, the city couldn't talk about anything else. Businesses with coat-and-tie dress codes were suddenly requiring staff to wear their blue-and-orange jerseys to the office.

There are various ways to procure tickets, which we've described below. All sports teams save the Cubs use Ticketmaster (☎ 312-559-1212; www.ticketmaster.com) as their ticketing outlet.

BASEBALL

Chicago is one of only a few US cities to boast two Major League baseball teams. The Cubs are the lovable losers on the North Side, with record-breaking yuppie attendance year after year despite generally woeful play. The White Sox are the working man's team on the South Side, appalled at all the hoopla across town.

The two ballparks are also a study in contrasts: traditional Wrigley Field (p81) is baseball's second-oldest park and about as charming as it gets in this sport. US Cellular Field is the new breed of stadium with amenities like a chock-full food court (veggie burgers and burritos are among the eats at present) and fireworks if the Sox hit a homerun at night.

The two stadiums are equidistant from the Loop: Wrigley is 4.5 miles north, while The Cell is 4.5 miles south. The Red Line train connects them both. The two teams play catch from early April through September.

top picks

CHICAGO SPORTS SOUVENIRS

- Ditka T-shirt from Strange Cargo (p128)
- Cubs flask, ball cap or mini Wrigley Field street sign from Sports World (p128)
- Ozzie Guillen bobblehead doll from US Cellular Field gift shop (opposite)
- Cubs or Sox jersey for your pooch from Barker & Meowsky (p126)

CHICAGO CUBS Map pp82–3

☎ 773-404-2827; www.cubs.com; Wrigley Field, 1060 W Addison St; Ⓜ Red Line to Addison

By far the local favorite, the Cubs play at Wrigley Field. Tickets are available at the box office, through the team's website, or by calling ☎ 800-843-2827 (within Illinois) or ☎ 866-652-2827 (from out of state). The cheapest tickets (about $18) are the 'upper deck, restricted view' ones, and they're not bad.

But know this: unless you plan waaaay ahead (like in March), the game you want likely will be sold out. No big deal – you still have options. First, try the box office for standing-room tickets ($12). They release these about two hours before the game if it's a sell-out. Next, try the rather frightfully named 'scalpers.' These guys stand across from the ballpark entrance (ie on Clark St's west side and Addison St's south side). They typically charge above face value for tickets – until the 4th inning or so. Then tickets can be yours for a pittance. Private fans also try to unload tickets they can't use, usually at face value. Look for the sad-faced people walking around and asking, 'Anyone need tickets?' Finally, you can enquire about rooftop seats (ie those not in the park, but rather on the rooftops of the surrounding houses on Sheffield and Waveland Aves). They're usually booked out by groups, but not always, and they include food and drinks

A DAY AT THE FRIENDLY CONFINES

Let's assume you've already procured tickets (see above), and let's assume you've already walked our Cubbyville tour (p84) around the environs. Now it's time to enter the pearly gates – after taking a keepsake photo under the main-entrance neon sign, of course.

Ahh. You scan around and see the green-grass field, the hand-operated scoreboard and ivy-covered outfield walls. It looks pretty much the same as when Babe Ruth batted here all those years ago. You order a hot dog and Old Style beer, Wrigley's traditional fare (notice there's no sushi, tofu or other frippery anywhere to be found), and head to your seat.

The Cubs are getting clobbered, and the guy next to you says it's The Curse. You nod, because you know all about Billy Sianis, owner of the Billy Goat Tavern (p145). When he tried to enter Wrigley Field with his pet goat in 1945, ballpark staff refused, saying the goat stank. Sianis threw up his arms, and called down a mighty hex: 'The Cubs will never win a World Series!' And they haven't.

And then – holy smoke – here comes a home-run ball straight at you! Unfortunately, the opposing team slugged it, so you're honor-bound to throw it back onto the field. That's a Wrigley ritual, as is the 7th inning stretch sing-a-long of 'Take Me Out to the Ballgame.'

All too quickly the game ends. Another loss. 'Wait 'til next year,' everyone says. Another tradition – Cubbie hope, despite all odds.

CHICAGO SPORTS HEROES PRIMER

Should you find yourself in a sports bar anywhere in the Windy City, a misty-eyed mention of any of the names below will help bond you to your fellow drinkers. Heck, someone might even buy you an Old Style.

Mike Ditka The Chicago Bears star (and current Chicago restaurateur), Ditka is the only person to have won a Super Bowl as a player, assistant coach and head coach. His mustache is legendary.

Michael Jordan The Chicago Bulls great ended his career of 15 seasons with the highest per-game scoring average in National Basketball Association (NBA) history.

Ryne Sandberg The Cubs second baseman played a record 123 consecutive games without an error, and in 2005 became the fourth Cubs player ever to have his number retired. Recently, he's been coaching the Cubs' minor league team in Peoria.

Dick Butkus Elected to the Pro Football Hall of Fame in 1979, the Bears player recovered 25 fumbles in his career, a record at the time of his retirement.

Walter Payton The Chicago Bears great is ranked second on the National Football League (NFL) all-time rushing list, and seventh in all-time scoring.

Ernie Banks Voted the National League's most valuable player (MVP) twice (1958 and 1959), he was the first baseball player to have his number retired by the Cubs.

Stan Mikita The Czech-born hockey star played his entire career with the Chicago Blackhawks, from 1959 to 1980, retiring with the second-most points of any player.

Bobby Hull Nicknamed Nicknamed 'The Golden Jet,' the Blackhawks left winger is considered one of hockey's all-time greats.

Ozzie Guillen Current White Sox coach and former player, known for his outspoken and politically incorrect comments. Still, many love him since he brought the World Series trophy to Chicago in 2005 – the first big win in almost 100 years.

Scottie Pippen Leading the Bulls through champion seasons throughout the 1990s, Pippen is known for pioneering the point forward position on the basketball court.

as part of the deal; check www.ballparkrooftops.com.

CHICAGO WHITE SOX Map pp50-1

☎ 312-674-1000; www.whitesox.com; US Cellular Field, 333 W 35th St; Ⓜ Red Line to Sox-35th

The White Sox play at US Cellular Field (aka The Cell, though often referred to by its pre-corporate-sponsorship name, Comiskey Park). Less loved than the Cubs despite their 2005 World Series win, the Sox resort to more promotions and cheaper tickets to lure fans to their southerly location. Thus, you might be treated to a pre-game '80s hair band or a free hot dog with admission. Tickets are available through the team's website, at the ballpark box office or at any Ticketmaster outlet. Sell-outs aren't usually an issue. The Cell sports a couple of cool features, such as the Bullpen Bar, where you sip your beer practically right freakin' on the field; and the pet-check, which allows dog owners to bring Fido to the game and drop him off with a babysitter for a fee.

BASKETBALL

The Bulls, once the stuff of legend, haven't posed much of a threat since the 1997–98 season, when Michael Jordan led the team. The controversial owner Jerry Reinsdorf allowed Jordan, Zen coach Phil Jackson, Scottie Pippen and other key parts of the Bulls juggernaut to leave after that championship year, and since then the team has ranged from awful to so-so. They did make it to the playoff semifinals in 2007, so fans see the light beginning to brighten. The Bulls shoot their hoops on the West Side in the cavernous United Center. The season runs from November to April.

CHICAGO BULLS Map pp98–9

☎ 800-462-2849; www.nba.com/bulls; United Center, 1901 W Madison St; 🚌 19

They may not be the mythical champions of yore, but the Bulls are still well loved and draw good crowds. Tickets are available through the United Center box office – located at Gate 4 on the building's east side – and at Ticketmaster outlets. On game days, the Chicago Transit Authority runs a special express bus (No 19) on Madison St that heads west to the stadium.

FOOTBALL

Once upon a time the Chicago Bears were one of the most revered franchises in the National Football League. Owner and coach George Halas epitomized the team's no-nonsense, take-no-prisoners approach. The tradition continued with players such as Walter Payton, Dick Butkus and Mike Singletary and coach Mike Ditka. In 1986 the Bears won the Super Bowl with a splendid collection of misfits and characters, such as Jim McMahon and William 'the Refrigerator' Perry, who enthralled and charmed the entire city. Then came 17 years of mediocrity. Then came the 2007 Super Bowl! The Bears kicked serious ass to get there, then sadly, got their ass handed right back.

Expectations are high these days, and fans are flocking back to silly-looking Soldier Field (see p108 for how it earned its 'Mistake on the Lake' nickname). The season runs from August to December, when you can get snowed on.

CHICAGO BEARS Map pp106–7

☎ 847-615-2327; www.chicagobears.com; Soldier Field, 425 E McFetridge Dr; 🚌 146

Da Bears can be found, sleet, snow or dark of night, at Soldier Field. Since the inauguration of the new stadium in 2003, tickets have been hard to come by, and are available only through Ticketmaster. Arrive early on game days and wander through the parking lots – you won't believe the elaborate tailgate feasts people cook up from the back of their cars. And for crissake, dress warmly.

HOCKEY

The poor Blackhawks. Besides their small core of admittedly rabid fans, no one pays them much attention – least of all, the local media. Go ahead: try finding a hockey game to watch on TV or listen to on the radio. True, the 'Hawks haven't helped their cause by losing loads of games in recent years. And it's been almost a half-century since the Stanley Cup came to town (in 1961). The fervor does pick up when rivals like the Detroit Red Wings or the New York Rangers skate into the United Center (which the Blackhawks share with the Bulls). The season runs October to April.

WINDY CITY ROLLERS

The bang-'em-up sport of roller derby was born in Chicago in 1935, and it's made a comeback in recent years thanks to the battlin' beauties of the Windy City Rollers (www.windycityrollers.com) league. Players boast names like Mob Hit Molley and Annie Maim, and there is a fair amount of campy theater surrounding the bouts. But the action is real (check the injury gallery on the league's website for proof), and the players are dedicated to the derby cause. Matches take place once a month at the Stadium (1909 S Laramie Ave in suburban Cicero), and often feature live rock bands and plenty of booze.

CHICAGO BLACKHAWKS Map pp98–9

☎ 312-455-7000; www.chicagoblackhawks.com; United Center, 1901 W Madison St; 🚌 19

Tickets shouldn't be too difficult to get – the box office and Ticketmaster do the honors – but if you run into trouble, brokers and concierges can usually obtain them for a minimal markup. Transportation information is the same as the Bulls (p211).

SOCCER

Thanks to support from Chicago's large Latino and European communities, the city's soccer team, the Fire, attracts a decent-sized fan base (despite being ignored by the mainstream media). The team has made the Major League Soccer playoffs several times in recent years, and last won the championship in 1998.

The Fire play in their brand-spankin' new stadium – Toyota Park – way the hell southwest of downtown. The regular season runs from April to September, and the finals take place in October.

CHICAGO FIRE Map pp50-1

☎ 708-594-7200, 888-657-3473; www.chicago-fire.com; Toyota Park, 71st & Harlem; 🚌 386

Fire tickets are available through Ticketmaster, and are fairly easy to come by. Less easy is getting to the stadium in suburban Bridgeview. If you get to Midway Airport via the Orange Line, you can catch the suburban Pace Bus No 386 Toyota Park Express, which runs on game days only. The full trip from the Loop will likely take an hour or so.

SLEEPING

top picks

- **The James** (p219)
- **Hotel Monaco** (p216)
- **Hotel Burnham** (p217)
- **Affinia Chicago** (p221)
- **Hotel Indigo** (p224)
- **Peninsula** (p218)
- **Hostelling International-Chicago** (p218)
- **Gold Coast Guest House** (p226)
- **Wicker Park Inn** (p229)
- **Essex Inn** (p230)

SLEEPING

Look out from a wall of windows onto a stunning panorama of Lake Michigan and Navy Pier, submerge yourself in a bubble bath surrounded by rose petals, borrow a goldfish to keep as a pet during your stay… You'll have no problem finding over-the-top-end experiences at Chicago hotels. What's a bit harder to track down is a reasonable rate. This city is convention central, so demand is high year-round. Even 'cheap' motels aren't really. If you're willing to be flexible with your dates, reservation staff can help you work around convention times. Consolidators and online room bookers are another way to go if cost-cutting is your primary objective (for more, see Saving Strategies p216). Because of conventions, there is no easily definable 'high season,' though nonconvention-related rates climb in summer (June to August), especially on weekends.

Though there are a handful of hostels in town, the vast majority of the city's 30,000 rooms are in high-rise hotels. Many of the buildings date from the early 1900s, which can mean some pretty miniscule rooms by today's US standards. If you want space, you'll need to upgrade to a higher class (deluxe, grand deluxe…) in older properties. Boutique hotels abound, mixed in among the newer-construction million-room marvels. Most hotels are affiliated with one chain or other. Of the 3000 or so rooms expected to be built by 2010, it's those in the Trump Tower (www.trumpchicago.com; 401 N Wabash). that really have people talking. The 92-story riverfront building is under construction at the time of writing. Hotel condominiums (with full kitchens) will occupy the 17th to 27th floors only.

With so many choices, picking a place can be daunting. Choosing your neighborhood first helps. Shopping-bag-toting tourists crowd the streets and pack into the high-priced Gold Coast hotels. Just to the south, the ever so slightly more moderate Near North lodgings are close to nightlife and shopping, but at least a step or two removed from the throngs. You feel the shift from pleasure to business as you cross the river south into the Loop. Hotels here are right in the gritty city heart. With an El station every couple of blocks, you can get most anywhere in town easily. Generally speaking, the further south you go, the lower the hotel prices. There are a few good deals in the South Loop and beyond, some overlooking the lakefront.

Less central, but more personal, are area bed-and-breakfasts. A few old town homes – in Wicker Park, Lake View and Andersonville – have been turned into great places to stay. (There are even a couple north in the Gold Coast.) Eat at local haunts, drink at neighborhood bars – sightseeing closer to town is just a train ride away. Pluses like free internet, comfy surrounds and some free parking give B&Bs more bang for the midrange buck. Unless otherwise noted, breakfast is continental (rolls, pastries, fruit, juice, coffee) here and at other places that offer free morning munchies. Most have minimum-stay requirements, and the older buildings do generally let in some street noise. In addition to the B&Bs listed below, you can also check out Bed & Breakfast Chicago (www.chicago-bed-breakfast.com).

LONGER-TERM RENTALS

Staying a week or more? Condos, apartments and corporate rentals often have prime locations. But besides being able to cook your own meals, there's not always a cost advantage. Parking is extra, but internet access is sometimes included. Extended stay hotels, which generally have two rooms and at least a microwave and minifridge, are listed in the appropriate neighborhood section. For more on all types of long-term accommodation check out www.biz-stay.com.

You can occasionally find a bargain online at Sublet.com (www.sublet.com), where apartment owners sublease their place by the week or the month. Only premium listings are free to contact. Otherwise you have to pay $25 to join. Rates run from $450-1500 a week for a one bedroom rental. You can find a bedroom in a shared apartment ($85 night to $700 a month) or whole studio or one-bedroom apartment to sublet (from $575 per month) at Craigslist (www.chicago.craigslist.org).

Some services that usually offer longer term rentals are also available by the night (from

PRICE GUIDE

$$$	over $250 a night
$$	$125-249 a night
$	under $125 a night

$120 to $200 per night for one bedroom). Vacation Rental By Owner (www.vrbo.com) is an excellent online source for high-rise condominiums. You work out all the details with the owner themselves; the website just acts as a clearing house. Check if there's a cleaning fee added, because it can be substantial (from $100). Lake Shore Dr addresses command more money, of course.

At Home in Chicago (☎ 312-640-1050, 800-375-7084; www.athomeinnchicago.com) rents out apartments and B&B rooms around town in neighborhoods like Wrigleyville and Lincoln Park. For lodging that caters to the business traveler, try Habitat Corporate Suites Network (☎ 312-902-2092, 800-833-0331; www.habitatcsn.com), which runs several high-rise properties in Near North. Expect weekly maid service, and business and fitness centers on-site.

ROOM RATES

The rates listed in this chapter are for standard double-occupancy rooms with bathroom (unless otherwise indicated), deluxe rooms are 10-20% more, suites are an additional 30% to 40% or more. The range noted takes into account seasonal fluctuations and the vagaries of weekend versus weekday lodging. The prices are for comparison purposes only, since a large convention of doctors in town can make them laughably off-base. The 15.4% hotel tax tagged on adds up, but that's not the only extra cost.

You'll pay dearly for parking in downtown Chicago, an average of $25 to $41 per night extra (ouch!) If you can leave your car at home, do. Pretty much all hotels have lots in the same building or very nearby. B&B parking is usually on-street. We've used a Ⓟ to indicate the rare and treasured establishment that offers a free home for your car.

Internet access is ubiquitous – unless otherwise noted, lodgings listed have wired and/or wireless in-room access – but it'll cost you, too. Some high-end hotels charge $14.95 a night, but $9.95 per night is more common. Lobbies sometimes serve as free wi-fi zones. If a place has complimentary in-room access or internet terminals you can use (rare outside hostels and B&Bs), it's noted in reviews below.

Every lodging we list has air-conditioning. Check in time is usually around 3pm, check out at 11am.

BOOK ACCOMMODATIONS ONLINE

For more accommodation reviews and recommendations by Lonely Planet authors, check out the online booking service at www.lonelyplanet.com. You'll find the true, insider lowdown on the best places to stay. Reviews are thorough and independent. Best of all, you can book online.

THE LOOP

Fast-walking office workers whisk by you as the clack-clack-clack of an El train reverberates overhead. The business center of town pulses in the daytime, but the further you get from the lake or the river, the more it empties out at night. You know you're in a big city here – grime and all. Every El and train line in the city converges on the Loop, making the boutique hotels and historic properties here super convenient to everywhere. Millennium and Grant Park are just a Frisbee throw away and you're no more than a 15-minute walk to River North dining and South Loop museums.

FAIRMONT Map pp54–5 Hotel $$$

☎ 312-565-8000, 800-527-7544; www.fairmont.com; 200 N Columbus Dr; r $279-499; Ⓜ Brown, Green, Orange line to Randolph;

Millennium Park here you come. All 687 luxury rooms and suites here are as close to the statues and fountains as you can stay. Upgrade above a standard room to get a park or lake view (those near the top of the hotel's 45 stories are the best). Accents like Asian ceramics combine with French empire chairs to create a soft – if a bit stodgy – surrounds.

W CHICAGO CITY CENTER

Map pp54–5 Hotel $$$

☎ 312-332-1200, 877-946-8357; www.whotels.com; 172 W Adams St; r $229-499; Ⓜ Brown, Orange Line to Quincy; ⊠

Employees all wear black at this hip hotel where the soaring 'living room' (lobby/bar) bar feels a little like a dance club, especially when the DJ gets going. Sleek urban rooms, in black and beiges, seem stark to some. Special gay pride packages include W Pride T-shirts and complimentary rainbow-themed cocktails, usually in summertime.

SAVING STRATEGIES

Don't think a $115 motel room qualifies as a budget buy? Neither do we. But that's Chicago. Unless you're willing to stay in a hostel, your low-end options are limited. A few saving strategies to try:

- Look for the (P) – Parking can add $40 a day in Chicago. Aim for places – motels, chains like Best Western and some B&Bs – that offer this service free. We mark them in the listings with a (P).
- Added extras – If you never skip the most important meal of the day, or can't stand to be disconnected, look for properties that give away hot breakfasts (extended stay, some B&Bs) and internet access (which usually costs $10 a day).
- Book online – Large hotels often have discounted net-only rates. You have to pay ahead (and can't cancel), but if your plans are set, why not?
- Shop around – Some chains have low price guarantees on their websites; at others, you'll get a better rate at a booking website like www.hotrooms.com, www.travelocity.com and www.expedia.com.
- Be flexible – Hotel rates in Chicago change by the day. Call ahead and ask when it'd be best to come. The www.hotels.com website also has an excellent rate calendar. Once you click 'Select rooms and rates' for a particular date at a specific property, you're given an 'Flexible dates?' option which pulls up a calendar that shows the prices on different days.
- Take a gamble – When maximizing quality for the price is your main concern, consolidator websites like www.priceline.com and www.hotwire.com are an excellent risk to take. They don't let you see the name of the property before you buy, but you can save up to 50%. The hotel gets to unload their unsold rooms (without sacrificing their rep by advertising it) and you benefit. Pick your neighborhood, the hotel's star rating and how much you're willing to pay. Once you've bought and paid, you're told where you're staying. Note that making changes once you've reserved is harder than crossing Lake Shore Dr at rush hour. See also, Bidding on a Bed (p222).
- Flop out – A few alcohol-soaked, bum-infested flop houses still exist in the city ($60 to $70 per night; cash, plus key deposit). We don't recommend them as safe. If you want to stay in a truly crappy hotel, go find it yourself (hint: they have words in their name like Wacker and Tokyo).

HOTEL MONACO

Map pp54–5 Boutique Hotel $$$

☎ 312-960-8500, 866-610-0081; www.monaco-chicago.com; 225 N Wabash Ave; r $299-379; (M) Brown, Orange Line to State; ⊠

Had to leave your beloved poodle Fifi at home this trip? Pick up a complimentary pet goldfish to keep you company during your stay instead. Hotel Monaco's fun-loving nature comes out in the room decor too. Curvaceous couches offset bold moss-green-and-white stripe wallpaper and raspberry window seat cushions. In the Party Like A Rock Star Suite, a permanently suspended TV appears to have already been 'thrown' through the window. All this posh quirkiness and they have free wi-fi and chair massages during happy hour – wow!

HARD ROCK HOTEL CHICAGO

Map pp54–5 Boutique Hotel $$$

☎ 312-345-1000; 866-966-5166; www.hardrockhotelchicago.com; 230 N Michigan Ave; r $259-359; (M) Red Line to Lake

A giant black-faux-lizard must have died to make the wall covering behind the reception desk – how sad. This whole place tries just a little too hard to be hip. Requisite black covers walls, the bar, even the staff members bodies. Each floor is named after a rocker, with the expected memorabilia scattered about. Despite the price level, standard rooms are just that – standard. And they don't have enough floor space to party like even a D-list star.

HOTEL ALLEGRO

Map pp54–5 Hotel $$$

☎ 312-236-0123, 800-643-1500; www.allegrochicago.com; 171 W Randolph St; r $259-349; (M) Brown, Orange Line to Randolph; ⊠

Boutique bliss. Hotel Allegro is another historic property, part of the fun and flirty Kimpton Hotel chain. Jacuzzi suites come with Mr Bubble for the tub, harmonicas wait in every room and the wine happy hour is complimentary. A scheduled overhaul will close the place down for a few months in 2008, but theme suites (like the Lion King) are likely to still have a theatrical bent. After all, it's next door to the Cadillac Palace Theater. Free wi-fi.

RENAISSANCE CHICAGO HOTEL

Map pp54–5 Hotel $$$

☎ 312-372-7200, 888-236-2427; www.renaissancehotels.com; 1 W Wacker Dr; r $250-359; (M) Brown, Green, Orange Line to State; ⊠

ENVIRONMENTAL STANDARDS

Chicago hotels aren't the greenest on the planet. For the most part, the extent of their effort is asking guests to reuse towels and sheets (which also saves them $$). A few go a bit farther – the Marriott chain has replaced millions of light bulbs nationwide with florescent ones, and the Sofitel Chicago O'Hare (p231) installed energy-efficient appliances and low-flow water devices. But it's the three Kimpton properties – Hotel Allegro (opposite), Hotel Burnham (below) and Hotel Monaco (opposite) – that deserve a green star. In addition to energy-efficient fixtures, every room has a recycling bin, organic tea and coffee are served in the lobby, and the staff only use recycled paper and soy-based inks for correspondence. Ask for the 'green rate,' it includes a $10 donation to the Trust for Public Lands.

Don't be fooled by the bland exterior. Step into the lobby and modern art, sink-right-in couches and lively earth tones exude warmth and style. Rooms are pretty typical contemporary stuff, but those with a water view (about $50 extra) have bay windows overlooking the skyline and the adjacent river.

HOTEL BURNHAM

Map pp54–5 Boutique Hotel $$$

☎ 312-782-1111, 877-294-9712; www.burnhamhotel.com; 1 W Washington St; r $199-319; Ⓜ Red Line to Washington; ☒

Blue velvet headboards and gold-and-blue stripe silk draperies make you feel like you're sleeping in a tufted jewel box at this gem of a boutique hotel. Renowned Chicago architect Daniel Burnham helped design the 1895 Reliance office building that holds the hotel. Its 14-story steel construction, with ornate terracotta-and-glass exterior, was a precursor to today's skyscrapers. History buffs should ask for one of the rooms with original wood-and-glass doors (complete with old brass key). A full mp3 history tour is downloadable from the web. Like other Kimpton Hotels, this one has complimentary wi-fi, wine reception and yoga equipment to borrow.

SWISSÔTEL CHICAGO

Map pp54–5 Hotel $$

☎ 312-565-0565, 800-654-7263; www.chicago.swissotel.com; 323 E Wacker Dr; r $209-259; Ⓜ Brown, Green, Orange Line to Randolph;

Water vistas are just part of the attraction at this triangular-shape, mirrored-glass high-rise at the confluence of river and lake. Families love the oversized layouts, separate shower and tub, and special kid rooms with colorful furnishings and toys. Summer weekends book up fast. No wonder since on-site you can munch on home-made pastries in the café or tackle a heck of a hunk of beef at the Palm steakhouse.

HOTEL BLAKE

Map pp54–5 Boutique Hotel $$

☎ 312-986-1234; www.hotelblake.com; 500 S Dearborn St; r $199-259; Ⓜ Red Line to LaSalle

The old customs house building has found new life as a mod boutique hotel where red leather squares pop out of sleek ebony-colored wood headboards. Unfortunately the ultra-cool surrounds seem to have rubbed off on the staff's attitude – they can be chilly. The Bath & Body Works amenities, free broadband access and proximity to Grant Park help make up for that.

HYATT REGENCY CHICAGO

Map pp54–5 Hotel $$

☎ 312-565-1234, 800-233-1234; www.chicago.hyatt.com; 151 E Wacker Dr; r $179-299; Ⓜ Brown, Green, Orange Line to State

With more than 2019 rooms and five restaurants and bars, the contemporary Hyatt Regency is best known for being big. And kind of blah. Drinkers will rejoice at the fact it makes claim to having the longest freestanding bar in North America. No swimming pool though. Lots of specials keep all those rooms filled in off-peak times.

PALMER HOUSE HILTON

Map pp54–5 Historic Hotel $$

☎ 312-726-7500, 800-445-8667; www.hilton.com; 17 E Monroe St; r $129-279; Ⓜ Brown, Green, Orange Line to Adams;

Chicago legend Potter Palmer set many worldwide hotelier records with his 1873 hotel (first to use electric lighting, first to have in-room telephones, inventor of the brownie…). After a $150 million renovation, today the Palmer House Hilton lobby has an 'Oh my God' opulence – Tiffany chandeliers, ceiling frescos – that make a look-see imperative. The 1600-plus guest rooms give off a more updated vibe: graphic swirl prints on draperies and countertop bowl sinks seem like an updated play on antique design. IPod-ready radios come standard – Potter would be proud.

SILVERSMITH Map pp54–5 Historic Hotel $$

☎ 312-372-7696; www.silversmithchicagohotel.com; 10 S Wabash Ave; r $159-229; Ⓜ Brown, Green, Orange Line to Madison

Another Loop architectural gem, this one was built in 1894. Although the exterior was designed by Daniel Burnham's firm, the hotel's interior recalls Frank Lloyd Wright: the chunky wood furniture has a distinct Prairie School charm. Too bad that windows overlook the El tracks, or face right onto another building.

BUCKINGHAM ATHLETIC CLUB HOTEL Map pp54–5 Boutique Hotel $$

☎ 312-663-8910; www.bac-chicago.com; 440 S LaSalle St; r incl breakfast $165-190; Ⓜ Brown, Green, Orange Line to LaSalle;

Tucked onto the 40th floor of an office building, the 21-room Buckingham Athletic Club Hotel is far from easy to find. The benefit if you do? Quiet (on weekends and evenings especially) and expansive views south of town. Elegant rooms here are so spacious they'd be considered suites elsewhere. Take the elevator down to the namesake gym and dive into the lap pool, or work it out on the racquetball court, before your massage appointment.

CONGRESS PLAZA HOTEL

Map pp54–5 Hotel $$

☎ 312-427-3800, 800-635-3800; www.congressplazahotel.com; 520 S Michigan Ave; r $129-179; Ⓜ Blue, Red Line to Jackson

Ask for a corner room on an upper floor (there are 12) in the north tower, and you get the city's best bargain view – of Buckingham Fountain in Grant Park and the lake beyond. OK, so the wallpaper, with the hotel's emblem, may have been hung in the Eisenhower era and non-corner rooms are a bit dark. The furniture is perfectly respectable and the price and location are right.

top picks

PET FRIENDLY

- **Palmer House Hilton** (p219)
- **Hotel Burnham** (p217)
- **W Hotel Chicago-Lakeshore** (opposite)
- **Peninsula** (below)
- **Hotel Monaco** (p216)

HOSTELLING INTERNATIONAL-CHICAGO

Map pp54–5 Hostel $

☎ 312-360-0300; www.hichicago.org; 24 E Congress Pkwy; dm $35-45; Ⓜ Blue, Red Line to Jackson

By far the best hostelling option in town. Kick back in the giant common room with free wi-fi (the computer room has 10 terminals for rent, too), ping-pong, tons of sofas and chairs – and a concierge. Sign up for daily field-trips to interesting neighborhoods, bar-hopping or sight-seeing. In the morning, toast, cereal and pastries await in the enormous dining room and kitchen. Throughout, a clean, dorm-like feel pervades. That's probably because half of the 500 beds go to Columbia College students during the school year. Some of the single-sex, six-bed rooms have bathrooms en suite. Linens included.

NEAR NORTH & NAVY PIER

A little bit nicer than the Loop and slightly less mobbed than the Gold Coast (but walking distance to both), Near North is a good compromise – especially if you bid on a room and got a great price (see Bidding on a Bed p220). Art galleries are to the east, Navy Pier to the west. Bars and restaurants are everywhere.

PENINSULA Map pp64–5 Hotel $$$

☎ 312-337-2888, 866-288-8889; www.peninsula.com; 108 E Superior St; r $505-635; Ⓜ Red Line to Chicago;

Talk about over-the-top. Friday evenings the lobby bar offers a sumptuous chocolate buffet – truffles, pots de crème, ice cream, tortes – for $32. You'd expect no less from the premier lodging in town. Nestled into the neoclassical rooms, among the equestrian statues and marquetry furnishings, are five phones. Lighting and electronics tie into impressively complicated high-tech systems. Two-story walls of glass enclose the pool where you can swim after your essence-of-rubies spa facial. How's the service? Buttoned down. Staff members are even required to take personal grooming classes.

HOTEL SAX Map pp64–5 Hotel $$$

☎ 312-245-0333, 877-569-3742; www.hotelsaxchicago.com; 333 N Dearborn St; r $249-409; Ⓜ Red Line to Grand

Fluff up your best feather boa and head for the bar – the crystal-drenched chandeliers and deep-tufted red velvet sofas would make any high-class madam feel right at home. An odd lighting-related theme continues throughout. The reception desk looks like a crystal shop, faux chandelier shadows are painted on guest room walls and flickering lights illuminate (sort of) the dark corridors. This former House of Blues hotel (redesigned in 2007) is still highly theatric.

W CHICAGO-LAKESHORE

Map pp64–5 Hotel $$$

☎ 312-943-9200, 877-946-8357; www.whotels.com; 644 N Lake Shore Dr; r $239-379; 🚌 66; 🅿

Lobby chairs appear to be carved out of tree trunks and river rocks fill a public bathroom trough-like sink… The earthy aesthetic feels entirely appropriate here on the lake front. You can see the water from telescopes by windows in the elevator bays, from 'spectacular' rooms and 'magnificent' suites. Navy Pier and ocean-like expanses stretch before you while running on the treadmill or laying on the pool deck. It's just too bad that the round glass room at the building's apex is a banquet hall; the adjacent Whisky Sky's windows are too smoky to see through.

CONRAD CHICAGO Map pp64–5 Hotel $$$

☎ 312-645-1500; 800-445-8667; http://conradhotels1.hilton.com; 520 N Michigan Ave (main entrance on N Rush St); r $230-365; Ⓜ Red Line to Grand

Euro sleek, urban chic. Slide into 500-thread count Italian linens and put your favorite CD on the Bose surround-sound stereo. That is if you're not too busy watching the 42in plasma TV or docking your iPod – these rooms are wired. Adding to the discrete sense of luxury, the lobby is hiding on the sixth floor of Michigan Ave's North Bridge Shops. Lounging alfresco on the padded rattan sofas at the terrace bar is surpassed only by splurging on the grand suite, with 1000 sq ft of terrace all to yourself.

JAMES Map pp64–5 Boutique Hotel $$$

☎ 312-337-1000, 877-526-3755; www.jameshotels.com; 616 N Rush St; r $259-499; Ⓜ Red Line to Grand

Low and loungey chairs sidle up to oversized tripod lamps. Strings of silver beads act as a dividing curtain between the platform bed and living room. Porthole windows allow you to peep through sliding bathroom doors. Fans of mid-century modern design must stay here. But everyone can appreciate the little luxuries: Kiehl's bath products, Turkish cotton towels, a bar that has half bottles instead of minis… You can tell from the gym and spa that the co-owner created Equinox fitness centers. An overwhelmingly gracious staff help work out any service kinks, like rooms not being ready on time. Free wi-fi.

OMNI CHICAGO HOTEL

Map pp64–5 Hotel $$$

☎ 312-944-6664, 800-444-6664; www.omnihotels.com; 676 N Michigan Ave (entrance on Huron St); r $179-479; Ⓜ Red Line to Chicago; 🅿

Each room is really two. French doors connect the bedroom with the sitting area;

top picks

OVER-THE-TOP AMENITIES

- A $60,000 proposal package – with ring – at the James (above).
- A goldfish (and bowl) you can borrow during your stay at the Hotel Monaco (p218).
- The sound pillow with harmonic sleep CD at Affinia Chicago (p221).
- A butler to walk your dog at the Peninsula (opposite).
- A Bose surround-sound home theater with 42in flat-screen plasma TV at the Conrad Chicago (left).

both are decked out in rich colors and cherry wood. Girl's night packages come with chick flick DVDs, wine and chocolate; guy's nights include sports DVDs, beer and chips. Ask ahead and kids receive suitcases full of games to keep them entertained – if they aren't swimming in the pool or watching the plasma TV.

WESTIN RIVER NORTH

Map pp64–5 Hotel $$

☎ 312-744-1900, 877-866-9216; www.westinrivernorth.com; 320 N Dearborn St; r $189-369; M Brown, Green, Orange Line to State;

Yet another riverfront chain hotel. At least this one has a decent sushi bar and vaguely Asian decor – a rock garden, lots of orchids – to set it apart. Frequent travelers chose the Westin chain for the 'heavenly bed,' with superthick mattresses and high thread-count sheets. Sorry, no pool here, but the showers have dual spa heads – does that help?

HOTEL CASS

Map pp64–5 Boutique Hotel $$

☎ 312-787-4030, 800-799-4030; www.casshotel.com; 640 N Wabash Ave; r incl breakfast $199-350; M Red Line to Grand

It's hard to imagine that this property was a bare bones budget option not too long ago. In late 2007 expensive hardwoods, Kohler fixtures and other upscale treatments transformed what was an aging 1920s hotel into a Holiday Inn Express-affiliated boutique. Small room spaces are maximized with modern flair: hanging flat-screen TVs, mod C-shaped tables and armless couches.

EMBASSY SUITES CHICAGO-RIVER EAST

Map pp64–5 Extended Stay $$

☎ 312-836-5900, 866-866-8095; www.chicagoembassy.com; 511 N Columbus Dr; ste incl breakfast $209-245; 66;

Peer out through the shutters of your living room window into the forest of beach trees growing in the atrium; an outside-in arrangement that's quite interesting. The bedroom of each suite (with microwave and refrigerator) fronts the street, away from the noisy hubbub of the monumental hot breakfast buffet that takes over the courtyard each morning. Lines form early.

AMALFI HOTEL CHICAGO

Map pp64–5 Boutique Hotel $$

☎ 312-395-9000; 877-262-5341; www.amalfihotelchicago.com; 20 W Kinzie St; r $149-299; M Red Line to Grand

The Amalfi lobby blooms like a bird of paradise: vivid oranges contrast with deep turquoise hues on thoroughly mod furnishings. Upstairs, the rooms are a bit more subdued, in jewel tones, but the whole hotel is clearly high-end, and modern-design driven. The receptionists that sit behind free-standing desks assess you with a glance. Once you convince them you belong, they warm right up. Each floor has a sumptuous spread of pastries and bagels laid out every morning and you can borrow CDs and DVDs for free.

HILTON GARDEN INN Map pp64–5 Hotel $$

☎ 312-595-0000, 800-774-1500; www.hiltongardeninn.com; 10 E Grand Ave; r $117-329; M Red Line to Grand;

BIDDING ON A BED

In the interest of totally non-scientific study, and because this author loves room service but hates paying a lot for a hotel room, she undertook to test the two main consolidator booking sites. The hypothesis: Is it possible to get a three-star hotel in Near North for less than $110 in high summer season? The answer: absolutely.

- Test 1 – Bid $80 for a three-star room in 'North Michigan Ave – River North' with the Name Your Own Price option from www.priceline.com. Got it! Three nights at the Chicago City Centre Hotel with a sliver of a lake view, huge pools and fitness center, free lobby wi-fi, two eating outlets – all three blocks from Michigan Ave. Called the front desk to see how much it'd be to stay an extra night at hotel rate – $199.
- Test 2 – Agreed to a $109 rate for a three-star, 'Magnificent Mile – Streeterville area' hotel at www.hotwire.com. It showed having breakfast, internet access, pool, laundry, business center. Turned out to be the Embassy Suites Chicago-River East. A huge, two-room suite overlooking the lake, super close to Navy Pier The hot breakfast was colossal. A night at the hotel rate? $331.
- Test 3 – Bid $96 for a three star River North hotel at www.priceline.com. Rejected. Instead booked a $106 room at a 3½-star Mag Mile hotel on www.hotwire.com. The Wyndham Chicago room was plush and palatial. No view, limited TV channels, but only two blocks from Mag Mile. Regular rate? $279.

Lather up with Neutrogena products in the shower before you head down to the Weber Grill restaurant for an evening cook-out, hang-on make that a cook-in. If your honey thinks you smell too good to leave the room, that's OK; area restaurants deliver to this up-to-date 23-story hotel. And you can keep the leftovers in the fridge and nuke them in-room the next day. Rates vary wildly, so you may get a steal.

EMBASSY SUITES CHICAGO-DOWNTOWN

Map pp64–5 Extended Stay $$

☎ 312-943-3800, 800-362-2779; www.embassysuiteschicago.com; 600 N State St; ste incl breakfast $162-279; Ⓜ Red Line to Grand;

Cooked-to-order eggs, and pancakes, and waffles, and, and… An enormous breakfast buffet comes standard with the two-room suites. Families know it, too; boy, do they mob the place. The pool's hardly big enough to hold all the little ones. Good thing that they usually head out to nearby River North shopping for the day. Eighteen suites have special equipment like knock detectors and vibrating bed alarms for the disabled.

HOTEL INTER-CONTINENTAL CHICAGO

Map pp64–5 Hotel $$

☎ 312-944-4100, 800-327-0200; www.icchicagohotel.com; 505 N Michigan Ave; r $179-259; Ⓜ Red Line to Grand;

Once the Medina Athletic Club, the ornate original tower (c 1929) retains many of the eclectic details meant for rich men's eyes only. Thank goodness now everyone can float by the Neptune fountain in the mosaic-tile indoor swimming pool area. Historic rooms have a similar elegant, heavily draped look, with thick brocades and sumptuous silks. A more conservative, masculine feel – angular lines, neutral earth tones – characterizes the main building rooms. Moorish-inspired lamps add a touch of whimsy. After all, it's not a man's hotel anymore.

CHICAGO MARRIOTT HOTEL

Map pp64–5 Hotel $$

☎ 312-836-0100, 800-228-9290; www.marriott.com; 540 N Michigan Ave; r $159-269; Ⓜ Red Line to Grand; ⊠

A Magnificent Mile address is the primary draw card at this 46-story behemoth. You have to upgrade to a 'studio' room to get the size (320 sq ft) most people expect at these rates. The downy duvets and flat-screen TVs will do though. Packages include everything from museum tickets to American Girl shopping discounts.

SHERATON CHICAGO HOTEL & TOWERS

Map pp64–5 Hotel $$

☎ 312-464-1000, 877-242-2558; www.sheratonchicago.com; 301 E North Water St; r $199-219; 56;

From this riverfront location, you can stroll along the esplanade to catch a water taxi or architectural tour. River view upgrades are worth the $50 or so, but dark accent walls and contemporary corporate decor make all the rooms acceptable. Be warned, you may be the only person staying at this 1204-room hotel that's not part of a group.

AFFINIA CHICAGO

Map pp64–5 Boutique Hotel $$

☎ 312-787-6000; 866-246-2203; www.affinia.com; 166 E Superior St; r $149-259; Ⓜ Red Line to Grand; ⊠

Dreamed of belonging to an every-whim-catered for private urban club? Affinia Chicago is poised to fulfill your wishes. By the time you read this, rooms will be swank and the lobby new and shiny. The staff – in cabana-like shirts – already have the enthusiastic 'what can I do for you?' down. A pillow menu (buckwheat, memory foam…), a personal shopper and free 3oz 'airline restriction relief' amenities (contact solution, polish remover, etc) are a few things they've thought of already.

ALLERTON HOTEL

Map pp64–5 Historic Hotel $$

☎ 312-440-1500; www.theallertonhotel.com; 701 N Michigan Ave; r $99-309; Ⓜ Red Line to Grand

High atop the Italianate red-brick facade shines the red neon Allerton Tip Top sign, a reminder of the hotel's past. In the 1920s–50s, the penthouse Tip Top Club (now a ballroom space) was a happening place. All the big bands and early radio stars played here. Because of the building's age, space varies from room to room. Standard rooms are by no means large (they even call them 'petite classics'), but they can be a tremendous bargain off-peak.

COMFORT INN & SUITES DOWNTOWN Map pp64–5 Hotel $$

☎ 312-894-0900, 888-775-4111; www.chicagocomfortinn.com; 15 E Ohio St; r $159-249; Ⓜ Red Line to Grand

Can a hotel be schizophrenic? It would explain the convergence of an art deco-style 1920s building, a Tudoresque dark wood lobby and the contemporary dusty blue-and-beige guest rooms. Though classier than the typical Comfort Inn, prices are over-inflated. (The street level liquor store caters to all the city's finest, not). Free wi-fi.

WYNDHAM CHICAGO Map pp64–5 Hotel $$

☎ 312-573-0300, 877-999-3223; www.wyndham.com; 633 N St Clair St; r $129-260; Ⓜ Red Line to Grand;

You and 15 of your closest friends could sack out on the floor for a slumber party, the space in a base level room is so great. Cushy beds and soft neutrals, like beige and cream, are far too refined for that. Several energetic concierges field travel requests deftly, all day and evening long. But why ask about restaurants when the Capital Grill Steakhouse is downstairs?

FOUR POINTS CHICAGO DOWNTOWN Map pp64–5 Extended Stay $$

☎ 312-981-6600, 800-368-7764; www.fourpointschicago.com; 630 N Rush St; ste $149-239; Ⓜ Red Line to Grand;

Constructed in 2005, this Sheraton-affiliated hotel has more sound-proofing and less wear than many of the other big name chains in town. Setting it apart style-wise are renowned artist Dale Chihuly's six abstract paintings and the small glass 'Amethyst' sculpture in the lobby. Every room has microwaves, minifridges, coffee makers and free wi-fi that come standard. (Balconies and whirlpool tubs extra.)

HAMPTON INN & SUITES-CHICAGO DOWNTOWN Map pp64–5 Hotel $$

☎ 312-832-0330, 800-426-7866; www.hamptonsuiteschicago.com; 33 W Illinois St; r incl breakfast $119-249; Ⓜ Red Line to Grand;

Thick oak desks and angular leaded-glass lamps give the two-story lobby a Prairie School feel, and historic Chicago photos line the hallways. But the Frank Lloyd Wright influence is less apparent once you get to the contemporary rooms. Nearly half are studio and one-bedroom suites, some with full kitchens. The roominess, and a big, hot breakfast, attract families and business travelers.

RADISSON HOTEL & SUITES Map pp64–5 Hotel $$

☎ 312-787-2900, 800-333-3333; www.radisson.com/chicagoil; 160 E Huron St; r $140-210; Ⓜ Red Line to Chicago;

A small heated rooftop pool and sundeck help elevate this midrange hotel. You won't sweat the minuscule exercise room, once you see its 40th floor view. Rooms are pretty unexceptional, but suites come with two rooms, a microwave and mini-fridge.

CHICAGO CITY CENTRE HOTEL & ATHLETIC CLUB Map pp64–5 Hotel $$

☎ 312-787-6100; www.chicc.com; 300 E Ohio St; r $129-199; 66;

Relax on your window seat and look out at the sliver of a lake view many rooms have here in Streeterville, near Navy Pier. If you're not looking for anything fancy, you've found it. Floral bedspreads and traditional furniture are entirely generic. But there is a 50,000 sq ft athletic club, two pools, a café and a restaurant, and free wi-fi in the lobby. This three-star property pops up at lower rates on discount booking websites quite often.

BEST WESTERN RIVER NORTH Map pp64–5 Hotel $$

☎ 312-467-0800, 800-727-8088; www.bestwestern.com/rivernorthhotel; 125 W Ohio St; r $109-199; Ⓜ Red Line to Grand; Ⓟ

Think seven-story motel. Surprisingly cheery, well-maintained rooms with maple veneer beds and desks make this a River North value. Free parking and broadband access seal the deal. Oh, and did we mention the giant indoor pool and attached Italian restaurant?

INN OF CHICAGO Map pp64–5 Boutique Hotel $$

☎ 312-787-3100, 800-557-2378; www.innofchicago.com; 162 E Ohio St; r $99-199; Ⓜ Red Line to Grand

The Inn has shed it's Best Western skin and emerged more boutiquelike than ever. Zebra stripe ottomans prowl the lobby; lime-green-and-chocolate color schemes look delicious. And prices are right – it's just too bad the rooms are so darn 1920s-era small. Don't try to take two steps in the stylish bathroom, one is all there's room for.

HOWARD JOHNSON INN

Map pp64–5 Motel $

☎ 312-664-8100, 800-446-4656; www.hojo.com; 720 N LaSalle St; r $99-169; Ⓜ Brown Line to Chicago; Ⓟ

Ah, the outdated charm of a cheap motel. At least this one's in the city, on the edge of respectable, in far west River North. Sure the rooms could use a serious re-do. If you care about furniture more than free parking, look elsewhere. Complimentary wi-fi in the lobby, no room internet.

RED ROOF INN Map pp64–5 Hotel $

☎ 312-787-3580, 800-466-8356; www.redroof.com; 162 E Ontario St; r $90-140; Ⓜ Red Line to Grand

If you snag one of the lower rates, it might be worth your while to stay here, steps from the Michigan Ave shopping bonanza. But just how much money are you willing to pay for stained couches, faded wallpaper and barely enough space to walk around two beds?

OHIO HOUSE MOTEL Map pp64–5 Motel $

☎ 312-943-6000; www.ohiohousemotel.com; 600 N LaSalle Dr; r $85-120; Ⓜ Red Line to Grand; Ⓟ

The retro stylings of Ohio House (ie a diamond-shape marquee, the diner in the parking lot and more) are by no means put on. This place really is from the 1960s. Given the dingy cement-block detailing on the outside, it's a pleasant surprise to find the rooms within are modern (if a bit basic) and quite clean. The neighborhood to the west near the highway feels a bit ragged, but you're still in River North so you're close to transport and loads of restaurants to the east.

GOLD COAST

Many of the truly top-end digs in town are in the chi-chi Gold Coast, where the sidewalks have small garden islands with art installations. Michigan Ave and Magnificent Mile shopping and dining are outside your door, and the lake is rarely more than five blocks away. Don't expect to be alone here though, even the sidewalks have traffic jams.

FOUR SEASONS HOTEL

Map pp70–1 Hotel $$$

☎ 312-280-8800, 800-332-3442; www.fourseasons.com/chicagofs; 120 E Delaware Pl; r $445-560; Ⓜ Red Line to Chicago;

Service is taken seriously here. Call for food day or night and they'll attempt to fulfill any request, on the menu or not. Even the little ones are pampered – with munchkin-sized bathrobes and a special teen-interest concierge in summer. Slip into the spa for a four-seasons aromatherapy treatment with scents from winter, spring, summer and fall. Then relax further, dipping into the pool beneath the Romanesque domes. The elegantly tailored rooms are scheduled for an update in '08, so expect even more amenities to come.

RITZ-CARLTON Map pp70–1 Hotel $$$

☎ 312-266-1000, 800-621-6906; www.fourseasons.com/chicagorc; 160 E Pearson St; r $385-560; Ⓜ Red Line to Chicago;

Just think of all the shopping you can do without leaving the building if you stay in one of the 32 stories above Water Tower Place. High-back tapestry chairs, Renaissance paintings and porcelain vases containing stunning floral displays characterize the Franco-Asian elegance of the lobby. Guest rooms follow suit with antique armoires and expensive fabrics in fine print. (Non-feather duvets and anti-irritant cleaners are used in 'allergy sensitive' rooms.) The Dining Room, also French in flavor, serves prix-fixe and degustation menus for after your exhausting day burning up the credit cards.

PARK HYATT Map pp70–1 Hotel $$$

☎ 312-335-1234, 800-633-7313; www.parkchicago.hyatt.com; 800 N Michigan Ave; r $405-505; Ⓜ Red Line to Chicago;

Want every inch of your suite covered in rose petals, candles lit and your bath water run? They've done it before at this ask-and-it-be-granted luxury flagship of the locally based Hyatt chain. From the miniature TVs in the bathroom to the butler and courtesy car service, no expense has been spared. Bow-shaped tubs hide behind rolling window shades in some rooms so you can soak and still admire the view. Terrace kings have small balconies looking out across the street to the Water Tower and the lake beyond. Several years after opening, NoMi restaurant, on-site, is still receiving rave reviews.

DRAKE HOTEL Map pp70–1 Historic Hotel $$$

☎ 312-787-2200, 800-553-7253; www.thedrakehotel.com; 140 E Walton St; r $259-329; Ⓜ Red Line to Chicago

Queen Elizabeth, Winston Churchill, Charles Lindbergh, Dean Martin, Princess Di…the Reagans, the Bushes, the Clintons… Who hasn't stayed at the elegant Drake Hotel since it opened in 1920? The grande dame commands a striking location at the north end of Michigan Ave, near Oak St Beach. Embroidered gold silk coverlets and Grecian urn lamps are almost as impressive as the water views from the junior suites. Whether enjoying lobster in the Cape Cod Room (like Marilyn Monroe did) or having a drink accompanied by a local jazz artist in the Palm Court, you'll feel like somebody special too.

WESTIN MICHIGAN AVENUE

Map pp70–1 Hotel $$$

☎ 312-943-7200, 888-625-5144; www.westin.com/michiganave; 909 N Michigan Ave (entrance on E Delaware Pl); r $189-399; Ⓜ Red Line to Chicago; ⊠

Bloomingdales, the 900 Shops, Oak St boutiques: they're all within easy pouncing distance, about a block from this Michigan Ave address. After a hectic day of walking and spending, stepping into the soft contemporary lobby is a calming relief – low-profile brown leather sofas and retro armchairs wait to embrace you. Crisp bed linens offset moss green loungers in the smoke-free rooms. Lake views available.

SUTTON PLACE HOTEL

Map pp70–1 Boutique Hotel $$

☎ 312-266-2100, 800-606-8188; www.chicago.suttonplace.com; 21 E Bellevue Pl; r $171-329; Ⓜ Red Line to Clark/Division

Walking into one of the all-business guest rooms might just remind you of a man's suit: oversized gray stripes on the wall, a tailored grayish bedspread, and marine blue on singular accent pillows, which could easily be the color of a tie or an ascot. The contemporary decor is accented by Robert Mapplethorpe's floral photos (the controversial stuff is over at the Museum of Contemporary Art.) Plush robes and Gilchrist & Soames bath products do at least seem to have been chosen with a woman in mind. On-site Whiskey Bar and MEXX Kitchen have a local following.

top picks

LAKE VIEWS

- W Chicago-Lakeshore (p219)
- Park Hyatt (p223)
- Drake Hotel (left)
- Congress Plaza Hotel (p218)
- Swissôtel Chicago (p217)

SOFITEL CHICAGO WATER TOWER

Map pp70–1 Hotel $$

☎ 312-324-4000, 800-763-4835; www.sofitel-chicago-watertower.com; 20 E Chestnut St; r $179-310; Ⓜ Red Line to Chicago

The Sofitel looks a little like some state-of-the-art Mac computing device from the outside, its triangular glass tower leaning gracefully forward into space. Inside, stylish staff members tend to stylish 30- and 40-something guests, who come here for the minimalist vibe (think blond-wood and rectangular lines). CDA (Café des Architectes) restaurant, with its sculptural food served in a striking red-and-black dining room, fits right in.

RESIDENCE INN BY MARRIOTT

Map pp70–1 Extended Stay $$

☎ 312-943-9800; 888-236-2427; www.marriott.com; 201 E Walton St; r incl breakfast $159-309; Ⓜ Red line to Chicago; ⊠

What to say about a totally generic extended-stay hotel…Well, it's got all the extras families crave – weekday happy hour, kitchens, laundry facilities, free wi-fi, pantry shop. They'll even run out and buy groceries for you. Studios, one and two bedrooms available. No pool though – sorry, kids.

HOTEL INDIGO Map pp70–1 Boutique Hotel $$

☎ 312-787-4980, 866-246-3446; www.hotelindigo.com; 1244 N Dearborn; r $189-259; Ⓜ Red Line to Clark/Division

A pile of blueberries, a hyacinth bush, sea glass or a cable knit sweater: any of these may be the subject of your room's macro photo wall mural – as long as they're indigo in color. Hardwood floors and neon green, orange and sunny yellow accent fabrics perk up the rooms further. Boring and bland the Hotel Indigo ain't. Oversized Adirondack sofas in the lobby double as the restaurant chairs. There's free wi-fi, and spa services available.

RAFFAELLO HOTEL
Map pp70–1 Boutique Hotel $$

☎ 312-943-5000; 888-560-4977; www.chicagoraffaello.com; 201 E Delaware Pl; r $149-295; Ⓜ Red Line to Chicago; ☒

If only you could live in the silk-draped modernity of these guest rooms. Oh, wait, you can – they're condominiums, too. Smart suites have micro-and-minifridge marble cook centers in addition to roomy seating areas or separate living rooms. Double rooms are smaller, but they have similar upscale amenities, like rain forest shower heads and high thread-count linens. No restaurant here yet, but it's in the works.

TREMONT HOTEL Map pp70–1 Hotel $$

☎ 312-751-1900, 800-621-8133; www.tremontchicago.com; 100 E Chestnut St; r $129-289; Ⓜ Red Line to Chicago

The tasseled-loafer lawyer set feels right at home among the leather wing-back chairs and forest green walls of the library parlor. In the winter you may linger by the fireplace, or check email with the free wi-fi there (some rooms have paid access, some don't). Light yellow florals keep things bright, if old-fashioned, upstairs. The former Bears coach, Mike Ditka, has his meaty restaurant on-site. Need a full kitchen? Ask for one of the studio, one- or two-bedroom suites the hotel runs next door. Starwood Hotels-affiliated.

MILLENNIUM KNICKERBOCKER HOTEL Map pp70–1 Historic Hotel $$

☎ 312-751-8100; www.chicagoraffaello.com; 163 E Walton Pl; r $139-259; Ⓜ Red Line to Chicago

Built in 1927, the Knickerbocker Hotel has quite a notorious history. The 14th floor once contained a casino (now it's banquet space). Al Capone slipped out more than once through the secret passageway from there down to the street. Then in the 1970s, this became the Playboy hotel. You'd never suspect anything from the public space elegance (peek into the lobby-level ballroom) and the neo-traditional guest rooms.

FLEMISH HOUSE Map pp70–1 B&B $$

☎ 312-664-9981; www.innchicago.com; 68 E Cedar St; r incl breakfast $145-225; 🚌 151; ☒

A wall full of framed line drawings, coffered panels and rosette woodwork, an exquisite porcelain collection atop the armoire: indeed, you can tell that one of the co-owners of this 1892 row house is an architect. Travelers check into these self-service apartments (with full kitchens) for the quiet remove. Don't expect the typical B&B socializing; breakfast supplies are stocked in the fridge before you arrive. Free wi-fi; the closest parking is a lot a couple blocks away. No children under 6.

AMBASSADOR EAST
Map pp70–1 Historic Hotel $$

☎ 312-787-7200, 888-506-3471; www.theambassadoreasthotel.com; 1301 N State St; r $99-269; Ⓜ Red Line to Clark/Division

For many, the 1926 Ambassador East and its Pump Room restaurant are synonymous with Chicago. In Hitchcock's *North by Northwest*, Cary Grant got to hang out at this hotel with Eva Marie Saint before he meets that crop-duster in the Indiana cornfield. Today people still come to admire the celebrity photos, grab a round booth and dig into golden-age classics at the restaurant. Tired, traditional rooms, with Louis-the-something-esque furniture, will hopefully be renovated soon.

WHITEHALL HOTEL
Map pp70–1 Historic Hotel $$

☎ 312-944-6300; www.thewhitehallhotel.com; 105 E Delaware Pl; r $109-259; Ⓜ Red Line to Chicago

Tally-ho, my good chap, we're off to the fox hunt. Cozy rooms, hunting-dog paintings and clubby furniture: this old Chicago hotel speaks with a decidedly British accent. Extremely popular with wedding parties, you'll often see gown-clad beauties flowing by. Families who belong to the Disney Vacation Club, of which the hotel is a part, stay here, too. Town car service will shuttle you within a few miles radius from the door, but why bother? Michigan Ave is supremely close. Note: only 'pinnacle' rooms have internet access, but then it's included in the price.

SENECA HOTEL & SUITES

Map pp70–1 Boutique Hotel $$

☎ 312-787-8900, 800-800-6261; www.senecahotel.com; 200 E Chestnut St; r $109-229; Ⓜ Red Line to Chicago; ⊠

Sigh, it's the rare street in Chicago that's quiet and tree-lined, but you'll find the Seneca on one. A middle-aged and older cliental seems to favor this serene spot. Ornate brass drawer-pulls on the dressers and carved finial headboards are decidedly colonial. Two-room suites have full kitchens and discounted rates for extended stay. Long-term guests love the laundry facilities and free wired internet access.

GOLD COAST GUEST HOUSE

Map pp70–1 B&B $$

☎ 312-337-0361; www.bbchicago.com; 113 W Elm St; r incl breakfast $129-229; Ⓜ Red Line to Clark/Division

Innkeeper Sally Baker has been making stays memorable for more than 15 years. She'll lead you to a happy hour bargain on lobster, make a discounted tour reservation or even procure an international phone card if yours doesn't work. Her 1873 classic three-story town house has a delightful secret garden, and rooms made light and airy by muted taupes, blues and creams. Single-serve coffee, juices, breads and cheeses are among breakfast choices. Help yourself to sodas and snacks round the clock. Wi-fi and computer use are free, parking (on-street with permit) is $25. She also rents apartments nearby. No children under 10.

LINCOLN PARK & OLD TOWN

Staying here, you're close to some great neighborhood nightlife. Town houses are more common than high-rises and dog-walkers outnumber business suits on the street two-to-one. You may be able to walk to the zoo and beach from area lodgings, and museums and such in the Loop are a 15-minute or so El or bus ride south.

BELDEN-STRATFORD HOTEL

Map pp76–7 Extended Stay $$

☎ 773-281-2900, 800-800-8301; www.beldenstratfordhotel.com; 2300 N Lincoln Park W; ste $112-223; 🚍 22, 151; ⊠

Count yourself lucky if you get to walk beneath the trompe l'oeil sky past French bistro Mon Ami Gabi to check in. Out of the 300 rooms at the stately 1924 apartment house, only 35 are for rent. A few of the larger full-kitchen suites front Lincoln Park and the lake beyond. Free wi-fi.

INN AT LINCOLN PARK

Map pp76–7 Hotel $$

☎ 773-348-2810, 866-774-7275; www.innlp.com; 601 W Diversey Pkwy; r $124-169; Ⓜ Brown, Purple Line to Diversey

The fine oak moldings, burgundy walls and antique lighting in the lobby seem to promise a level of sophistication that the 1920s-era hotel doesn't deliver. Motel-quality rooms are nothing special (the economy size is just 10ft by 10ft) and air-con is from window units. The free morning muffins, coffee service all day, $12 parking and pleasant staff are what make it tolerable.

DAYS INN LINCOLN PARK NORTH

Map pp76–7 Hotel $$

☎ 773-525-7010, 888-576-3297; www.lpndaysinn.com; 644 W Diversey Pkwy; r incl breakfast $91-189; Ⓜ Brown, Purple Line to Diversey

This is a busy hotel on a busy intersection. The Days Inn caters to the budget-minded with value added punches like free wi-fi, lobby computer use and hot waffle breakfasts. Avoid the standard doubles if you're claustrophobic; kings are much roomier. The whistling air-con window units and worn carpet unfortunately give away the building's age.

ARLINGTON HOUSE

Map pp76–7 Hostel $

☎ 773-929-5380, 800-467-8355; www.arlingtonhouse.com; 616 W Arlington Pl; dm $29-31, r $64-78; 🚍 22, Ⓜ Red, Brown, Purple Line to Fullerton; ⊠

Primed for a night out? Stay equidistant from neighborhood bars, restaurants and buses on Clark St and those on Halsted, near the El. Though the building's old, rooms are fairly freshly painted: choose between six-bed dorms with no air-con or one 30-bed room with cooling capabilities. Private doubles (no air-con) either have a full bathroom, half a bathroom or share one down the hall. With all the college-age travelers waiting, getting on one of the two computers can be tough (no

LOCAL VOICES: MARK TUNNEY

For nearly 20 years Mark Tunney has worked on the marketing end of the hospitality industry. The last four he's spent as the Managing Director of Convention Sales for the Chicago Convention and Tourism Bureau.

Hotel rates in Chicago seem hugely tied to conventions. Everyone says watch out when the radiologists are in town. Why? Quite frankly, there are shows that sell out every hotel room in the city, every year. The Radiological Society of North America convention, usually the Friday and Saturday after Thanksgiving, is one of them.

So, what months should leisure travelers avoid convention-wise? Spring and fall are the busiest, but it changes by the week. The restaurant show is usually around the third weekend in May, but Mother's Day, the week before, is pretty quiet. The best thing to do is call the hotel and ask what dates are the least expensive.

When are there the fewest groups in town? Holidays are always a good time to come. December and January are slow. People think they should avoid Chicago in the winter, but it's not actually a bad time. We get snow, but not the arctic temperatures. And there's the ice rink at Millennium Park and lots of Broadway-quality shows to see.

What do hotel trends in Chicago travel indicate? Leisure travel is strong in Chicago. There are 3000 hotel rooms in the pipeline and a lot more that are in the proposal stage. Real estate prices are high, so expect a lot more boutique hotels carving out their own niche. Everyone wants to be a trendsetter.

wi-fi). There are numerous rules, like no standing outside the building after 11pm, but the place is open 24/7. Now where's that party?

LAKE VIEW & WRIGLEYVILLE

The beer-pounding, bar-hopping parade that is Wrigleyville makes up just part of this prime area. Bunches of shops and eateries provide services for all the locals that live in area condos. Boystown gay nightlife is near. And frequent buses and trains provide easy access to the Loop, 20 minutes south. Streets still bustle, but here you've escaped the high-rise jungle.

BEST WESTERN HAWTHORNE TERRACE Map pp82–3 Hotel $$

☎ 773-244-3434, 888-675-2378; www.hawthorneterrace.com; 3434 N Broadway St; r incl breakfast $159-209; 🚌 36

As part of the daily breakfast, they bring in Ann Sather's famous muffins from the nearby restaurant – just one of the out-of-the-ordinary extras here. A microwave-minifridge combo comes standard. There's free wired internet (and lobby computer for your use). The fitness room has sauna and whirlpool and parking's only $20. Deluxe rooms have a private terrace and whirlpool tub. The 1920s Federal-style apartment building retains a not-the-newest but classic appeal inside and out.

OLD CHICAGO INN Map pp82–3 B&B $$

☎ 773-816-2465; www.oldchicagoinn.com; 3222 N Sheffield Ave; r incl breakfast $99-250; Ⓜ Brown, Red, Purple Line to Belmont; ⊠

Locals love living in this high-energy neighborhood, so close to nightlife. Sure the street din may seep into the turn-of-the-20th-century townhouse, but that's the price you pay. For quiet, ask for the cozy room in the rear (hardly big enough to stretch your arms out). Much bigger is the Wrigleyville basement suite, where you could organize a decent game of catch. Ballpark pics and a neon sign get you in the mood. You also get a $10 gift certificate for food at the owner's pub, Trader Todd's, two doors down. Free wi-fi, on-street parking nearby.

CITY SUITES HOTEL Map pp82–3 Hotel $$

☎ 773-404-3400, 800-248-9108; www.cityinns.com; 933 W Belmont Ave; r incl breakfast $109-221; Ⓜ Brown, Red, Purple Line to Belmont

City Suites Hotel, one of three Neighborhood Inns, may remind European visitors pleasantly of home. The 1920s building facade has an Old World influence and staff members speak with Eastern European accents. Art deco-tinged rooms are a good bit more modern than the building's shell. You won't go hungry or thirsty – not here in the middle of a neighborhood bustling with business. Free wi-fi.

MAJESTIC HOTEL Map pp82–3 Hotel $$

☎ 773-404-3499, 800-727-5108; www.cityinns.com; 528 W Brompton Ave; r incl breakfast $109-209; 🚌 151

Nestled into a row of residential housing, the Majestic is still close to both Wrigley Field and Halsted St neighborhood. From the lobby fireplace and dark-wood furnishings to the Laura Ashley-like floral decor, the interior has the cozy feel of an English manor. Rooms are slightly larger than those of the other two Neighborhood Inns properties, while all have free wi-fi.

VILLA TOSCANA Map pp82–3 B&B $$

☎ 773-404-2643, 800-404-2643; www.thevillatoscana.com; 3447 N Halsted St; r incl breakfast $99-139; 🚌 8

A 1890s Victorian home seems a bit out of place set next to Gay Mart on the busiest of Boystown streets. Wander through the leafy front garden and you're transported. Purple silks evoke Morocco in one room, toile reminds of France in another. All eight diminutive lodgings (five with private bathroom) are often booked, so plan ahead. Enjoy breakfast pastries on the rear sundeck in nice weather. Free wi-fi and broadband.

WILLOWS HOTEL Map pp82–3 Hotel $$

☎ 773-528-8400, 800-787-3108; www.cityinns.com; 555 W Surf St; r $119-242; 🚌 22

The architectural pick of the Neighborhood Inns of Chicago trio, the Willows puts forth a detailed Italianate. Curl up by the chateaux-esque oversized fireplace in the lobby. Even in the busiest times the hotel remains blessedly quiet. At the south end of Lake View, near Clark St, you're not far from Lincoln Park and the lakefront. Free wi-fi, breakfast breads and afternoon cookies.

ANDERSONVILLE & UPTOWN

Traveling north through non-descript neighborhoods, Andersonville's cute, old town buildings come as a surprise. Once a Swedish ethnic enclave, today the homey hood has some restaurants, a lot of places to live, and a large lesbian and gay community. What you trade in access (the Loop is 30 minutes south by El or bus), you gain in leafy tranquility.

top picks

GAY STAYS

- **Villa Toscana** (left)
- **Ardmore House** (below)
- **House 5683** (below)
- **Flemish House** (p225)
- **W Chicago City Center** (p215)

HOUSE 5683 Map p86 B&B $$

☎ 773-994-5555; www.house5863.com; 5683 N Glenwood Ave; r $99-179; Ⓜ Red line to Thorndale; ⊠

Hip and urban, sleek and sophisticated: House 5683 is a thoroughly modern B&B. You'll find no frilly ruffles here, just clean-lined furnishings and abstract art in an old apartment house. Lounge on the black leather sofa in the common living room and watch the plasma TV, or surf the wireless web in your room for free. Adirondack chairs invite lolling about in the backyard. Neither N Broadway nor N Clark St are far, but a party place this neighborhood ain't. Garage parking available ($20).

ARDMORE HOUSE Map p86 B&B $$

☎ 773-728-5414; www.ardmorehousebb.com; 1248 W Ardmore Ave; r $99-179; Ⓜ Red line to Thorndale; ⊠

Originally marketed as a gay-stay destination, today's clientele includes a lot of European travelers and grown families too. The Victorian cottage is a bit more homey than sister property House 5683. The manager says they're going for the Restoration Hardware look of an upscale classic – they're succeeding. Soak in the hot tub or lay out on the sundeck in the roomy backyard. Free wi-fi and snacks. No children under 17.

WICKER PARK, BUCKTOWN & UKRAINIAN VILLAGE

Eclectic shopping and plenty of trendy places to eat make Wicker Park, Bucktown and Ukrainian Village great places to live. But unless you have a friend with a fold-out couch, you have to stay at a B&B in these mostly residential northwest neighborhoods. No hotels here.

RUBY ROOM Map pp90–1 B&B $$

☎ 773-235-2323; www.rubyroom.com; 1743-5 W Division St; r $155-185; Ⓜ Blue Line to Division; ⊠

Take an Anusara yoga class, go on a guided intuitive journey or get your chakra massaged. Ruby Room is primarily a spa and a 'healing sanctuary.' Eight simplified rooms are boiled down to the essence of comfort. No TVs, no telephones, no elevator, no breakfast. Instead, expect 500-thread count sheets, pristine white interiors, pillow-top mattresses and Aveda products. Free wi-fi is the only thing that may spoil your peace. No children under 12.

WICKER PARK INN BED & BREAKFAST Map pp90–1 B&B $$

☎ 773-486-2743; www.wickerparkinn.com; 1329 N Wicker Park Ave; r incl breakfast $125-185; Ⓜ Blue Line to Damen; Ⓟ ⊠

Choose the Wicker Park, the most romantic room in this row house, for its exposed brick, wood-burning fireplace and canopy bed. Accommodations aren't huge, but all have hardwood floors, terry cloth robes and small desk spaces where you can use the free wi-fi. Across the street, the two kitchen apartments have refrigerators stocked with similar goodies. Park streetside for free and head out to the hipster Wicker Park scene just beyond your door.

HOUSE OF TWO URNS BED & BREAKFAST Map pp90–1 B&B $$

☎ 773-235-1408, 877-896-8767; www.twourns.com; 1239 N Greenview Ave; r incl breakfast $109-185; Ⓜ Blue Line to Division; Ⓟ ⊠

Old cameras, cobalt glass and other collections help make this former Polish bakery building more lively than a quaint B&B. Four rooms (two with shared bath) are in the main brownstone; two apartment-like digs are across the street (full kitchens, Jacuzzi tubs). Guests all gather in the main dining room for a hot, home-cooked breakfast; banana French toast, for example. Your helpful hosts lend out umbrellas, provide free snacks, share their 200+ DVDs. They also rent several three-bedroom, self-service apartments nearby. Free on-street parking, free wi-fi and a public computer access. Cribs available.

NEAR WEST SIDE & PILSEN

Unless you're visiting the University of Illinois at Chicago, or just really love the town's little-Little Italy, there's no compelling reason to stay on the West Side, near the highway and warehouses.

CHICAGO MARRIOTT AT MEDICAL DISTRICT/UIC Map pp98–9 Hotel $$

☎ 312-491-1234, 800-356-3641; www.marriott.com; 625 S Ashland Ave; r $189-269; Ⓜ Blue Line to Racine

Jaunty striped curtains and cobalt blue coverlets pep up the otherwise plain-Jane Marriott. Most guests are visiting friends and family at the huge medical center complex nearby. A complimentary bus shuttles you to the hospital door, to the University or to Little Italy – anywhere within a mile radius.

SOUTH LOOP & NEAR SOUTH SIDE

Proximity to the Museum Campus, and potential lake views along S Michigan Ave, attract sightseers to the South Loop hotels. That and also a desire for a bargain. In general, prices here are less than that of Near North, but that's because you're a 15-minute train or bus ride from its action. Outside the hotels there are few restaurants around here.

HYATT REGENCY MCCORMICK PLACE Map pp106–7 Hotel $$

☎ 312-567-1234, 800-633-7313; www.mccormickplace.hyatt.com; 2233 S Martin Luther King Jr Dr; r $139-359; Ⓜ Metra to McCormick Place; ♿

If you're manning a show booth at McCormick Place, you can't beat the short walk to your bed in this attached hotel. Lobby monitors help you keep track of meeting schedules, and the business center computers are free to use. However, if you're not a conventioneer, even the skyline views may not be reason enough to stay in one of these 800 modern rooms, 2 miles south of the Loop.

HILTON CHICAGO Map pp106–7 Hotel $$

☎ **312-922-4400, 800-445-8667; www.hilton.com; 720 S Michigan Ave; r $126-270; Ⓜ Red Line to Harrison;**

When built in 1927 (for $30 mil), this was the world's largest hotel, having close to 3000 rooms (and a hospital, and a theater…). Renovations brought that total down to a mere 1544, but the gilt grandeur and crystal-dripping class have remained. Anecdotes abound at the Hilton: in the 1940s, it served as an army barracks. The police tossed protesters through the plate-glass windows here at the height of the 1968 Democratic National Convention riots. And the TV show ER often films helicopter landing scenes on the roof. Make sure to upgrade to a lake view.

BEST WESTERN GRANT PARK
Map pp106–7 Hotel $$

☎ **312-922-2900, 800-780-7234; www.bestwestern.com; 1100 S Michigan Ave; r $110-199; Ⓜ Green, Orange Line to Roosevelt;**

Outside convention time, the Best Western can be a bargain. Check one of the booking sites, like www.hotels.com; you'll often get a lower rate there than on the hotel's website. Free wi-fi and $24 parking increase the attraction. Though the lobby's gone modern, rooms are still pretty standard oak-bed-and-floral spread stuff.

ESSEX INN Map pp106–7 Hotel $

☎ **312-939-2800, 800-621-6909; www.essexinn.com; 800 S Michigan Ave; r $79-189; Ⓜ Red Line to Harrison;**

Walk out to the fourth floor rooftop garden and soak in the sun, or swim protected in the giant glass-enclosed pool, which looks like a bit like an Olympic pavilion. Both are a pleasant surprise at this low-end price. Plus, a free shuttle takes you north to the Mag Mile, the business center has free internet (wi-fi $4 per stay) and the staff is effusive. Bright colored pendant lights and low-slung lobby leather say mod. By early 2008 all rooms are to be renovated with furnishings and fixtures in a similar up-to-date style. Prices aren't expected to change much.

TRAVELODGE CHICAGO DOWNTOWN Map pp106–7 Hotel $

☎ **312-427-8000, 800-211-6706; www.travelodgehoteldowntown.com; 65 E Harrison St; r $109-139; Ⓜ Red Line to Harrison**

The nearby Best Western is a better quality chain hotel, with more amenities, but the Travelodge's prices are more consistently low. What do you say about totally lackluster motellike rooms? Um, they're there. Small car parking is $20, wi-fi free.

CHINATOWN HOTEL SRO LTD
Map pp106–7 Hotel $

☎ **312-225-8888; 214 W 22nd Pl; r $65-95; Ⓜ Red Line to Cermak-Chinatown**

No ice machines, the lobby internet terminal doesn't always work (neither does the free wi-fi), rooms are small and shabby…but this hotel is one of the few safe dirt-cheap options. Intrepid travelers love all the eating options here in Chinatown (think of the dim sum!) and ignore the beggars a couple of blocks away at the El stop. You might try the bidding sites first before staying here (see Saving Strategies p216)

HYDE PARK & SOUTH SIDE

RAMADA LAKE SHORE Map p114 Motel $

☎ **773-288-5800, 800-272-6232; www.ramada-chicago.com; 4900 S Lake Shore Dr; r $79-129; 6; Ⓟ**

Rooms at this two-story motel may not be the freshest and the door jambs may be scuffed. But who cares when you're across from the lake, parking is free and you're paying under $100? A free shuttle takes you up to Michigan Ave, or you can hop on the bus for the 15-minute ride. The outdoor pool is open summers only. Free wi-fi.

GREATER CHICAGO

Chicago's an old town by US standards, which means there isn't room for shiny new strip mall motels close to the El. Avid Frank Lloyd Wright fans should think about staying out in Oak Park (p238), about a 20 minute ride from the Loop, but walking distance to area Prairie School homes. The El travels through some iffy neighborhoods to get there, but it's fine in the daytime, and there are Oak Park restaurants and bars galore for evening entertainment.

AMBER INN Map pp50-1 Motel $

☎ 773-285-1000; www.amberinn4u.com; 3900 S Michigan Ave; r $69-89; Ⓜ Green line to Indiana, 🚌 1; Ⓟ

Accessing this Bronzeville motel is easy – the No 1 bus, running up Michigan Ave, stops right outside the building at 39th St and there's a green line El stop around back. Rooms are early dumpy motel style – far more dated furniture than necessary is crammed into each. The real highlight here is Pearl's Place soul food restaurant, where even smelling the superb fried chicken can cause weight gain. The predominately African American neighborhood is not bad exactly, but it's on the cusp at night. Single females, consider seriously.

CARLETON OF OAK PARK HOTEL & MOTOR INN

Map pp50-1 Hotel/Motel $$

☎ 708-848-5000, 888-227-5866; www.carletonhotel.com; 1110 Pleasant St, Oak Park; hotel r $139-179, motel r $94-104; Ⓜ Green Line to Oak Park; Ⓟ

Two buildings, one from 1928 and one dating to 1892, make up the historic hotel. Each individually-decorated room has period details – pencil post beds and curvaceous carved desks – and free wireless. Adjacent, the exterior-access motel rooms are smaller, less recently renovated, and have no in-room heating and air-con controls. You also have to schlep over to the hotel lobby for the free wi-fi. The Carleton is a block from the El, among old town restaurants and shops. But there's also a dry-aged-beef steakhouse and a cozy neighborhood pub – serving live music and seafood – on-site.

CHICAGO INTERNATIONAL HOSTEL

Map pp50-1 Hostel $

☎ 773-262-1011; www.hostelinchicago.com; 6318 N Winthrop Ave; dm $25, r $40-78; Ⓜ Red Line to Loyola

Groovy blueberry, lime and gold walls add character to this comfortably shabby hostel. The full kitchen comes complete with mix-and-match chairs just like at home. Not enough lockers and abrupt staff responses turn a lot of hostellers off. As does the 45 minute El ride to Chicago Ave. (The Loyola college campus area does offer some nightlife.) Internet access here sucks – both the wi-fi (free) and internet terminal only work occasionally.

AIRPORT ACCOMMODATIONS

Got an early flight to catch? Given the crazy Chicago traffic, or long El commute (45 minutes from the Loop), resting your head at one of the dozens of airport hotels may be your best bet. The vast majority run free 24-hour airport shuttles.

O'Hare

O'Hare Hilton (Map pp50-1; ☎ 773-686-8000, 800-445-8667; www.hilton.com; O'Hare International Airport; r $139-279; Ⓜ Blue Line to O'Hare;) Attached to the airport via an underground tunnel. Relax in the sauna, take a refreshing dip in the indoor pool and then retire to your soundproofed contemporary room.

Sofitel Chicago O'Hare (Map pp50-1; ☎ 847-678-4488, 800-763-4835; www.sofitel.com; 5550 N River Rd, Rosemont; r $89-199; Ⓜ Blue Line to Rosemont) Winner of a three-leaf rating from Audubon for environmental friendliness. The organic food offerings and commitment to recycling are as attractive as the honey-oak guest rooms here.

Motel 6 (Map pp50-1; ☎ 847-671-4282, 800-466-8356; www.motel6.com; 9408 W Lawrence Ave, Schiller Park; r $53-62; Ⓜ Blue Line to Rosemont; Ⓟ) No frills motel with free parking. There's no shuttle, but you can walk the 1.25 miles from the Rosemont El stop, or take a cab for $5.

Midway

Hilton Garden Inn (Map pp50-1; ☎ 708-496-2700, 800-445-8667; www.hiltongardeninn.com; 6530 S Cicero Ave, Bedford Park; r incl breakfast $159-219; Ⓜ Orange line to Midway; Ⓟ) One of the newest in the Midway Hotel Center complex of seven hotels. A big, hot, cooked-to-order breakfast, free broadband access and parking are included.

Sleep Inn (Map pp50-1; ☎ 708-594-0001, 877-424-6423; www.choicehotels.com; 6550 S Cicero Ave, Bedford Park; r $79-149; Ⓜ Orange line to Midway; Ⓟ) Slightly cheaper, but in the same complex. Modern modular rooms are perfectly acceptable. The whirlpool and workout room are nice touches. Free wi-fi.

DAY TRIPS & EXCURSIONS

DAY TRIPS & EXCURSIONS

Certainly Chicago has enough sky-high buildings, rockin' live-music clubs, beaches, boozers and ballparks to keep you occupied for weeks. But let's say you want to scale sand dunes, go surfing or nibble a hunk of freshly made cheese – you're out of luck in the city limits. Which means you'll have to hit the road to broaden your experience. The destinations in this chapter range from 20-minute jaunts to 3½-hour journeys, many reachable by bus or train for those without a car, and they fan out beyond Illinois into Wisconsin, Indiana and Michigan.

Oak Park is a short El ride from downtown, though it seems a world away with its huge old houses, wrap-around porches and sprawling green yards. Frank Lloyd Wright designed many of the town's buildings and had his studio here. Ernest Hemingway was born a few blocks away, and his home is now a museum.

Beach bums will want to proceed east to Indiana Dunes, where heaps of sand provide opportunities for shoreside lounging or dune hiking. Just beyond in New Buffalo, adventure seekers can surf or skimboard over Lake Michigan's waves.

Turning the wheel north to Wisconsin rewards the road-tripper with two worthy cities: down-to-earth Milwaukee, which admirably balances Harleys and beer with world-class art and cultural festivals; and liberal, leafy Madison, the small state capital loaded with coffee shops, bookstores, farmers markets and cheap, international places to grab a bite. And, of course, there's no escaping the Dairy State without cheese, so we provide a jaunt to the nation's densest cheese-making area.

Back in Illinois, Route 66, the nostalgic 'Mother Road', starts in downtown Chicago in front of the Art Institute, and carries travelers south through a trail of kitschy roadside attractions, drive-in movie theaters and scattered shrines to local hero Abe Lincoln. Genteel Galena, a B&B-stuffed, Civil War-era town near the Mississippi River, transports visitors back to a slower, horse-drawn age.

And finally, Michigan's Gold Coast provides sand, antiques and mango-colored sunsets.

The prices listed here are for peak season, which runs from late May to early September. During the off-season, many places reduce their hours and some even close entirely.

ACTIVE ENDEAVORS

C'mon, haul your buns off the couch and get out there. The region offers activities to match a variety of weather moods and personal tastes, and the scenery will knock your socks off. Visitors can kayak and bicycle in Madison (p241); hike, swim and cross-country ski in Indiana Dunes (p237); and tramp over rugged, wooded sandbanks in the parks along Michigan's Gold Coast (p245). And get this: visitors can surf or skimboard, as well as bike and swim, in New Buffalo (p239). Woo-hoo!

FOODIE FORAGES

Make sure to wear expandable trousers when you embark. Crane's Pie Pantry (p248) near Saugatuck is famed for its fruit pies; the blueberries, raspberries and other fillings come straight from the surrounding orchard. Beer, cheese and bratwursts are Wisconsin specialties; the state even produces a guide that'll take you straight to the local sources. Madison's Dane County Farmers' Market (p241) is one place to indulge with its beer-cooked brats and artisanal cheeses. Or travel south to Monroe (p242), where more cheesemakers reside than anywhere else in the country. Don't dare leave the state without knocking back a frozen custard at Kopp's (p240) in Milwaukee. Favorite restaurants include Café Soleil & L'Etoile (p242) in Madison, where the chefs have been doing the slow food thing for 30-plus years; and Miller Bakery Café (p239) near Indiana Dunes, fusing French, Asian and contemporary American flavors.

ART & HISTORY

Impress your friends by returning from your Midwest excursion more knowledgeable about art, architecture and history. Architecture buffs can be unleashed in Oak Park to view Frank Lloyd Wright's studio (p236) and a couple of streets' worth of homes he designed; Taliesin (p242), outside Madison,

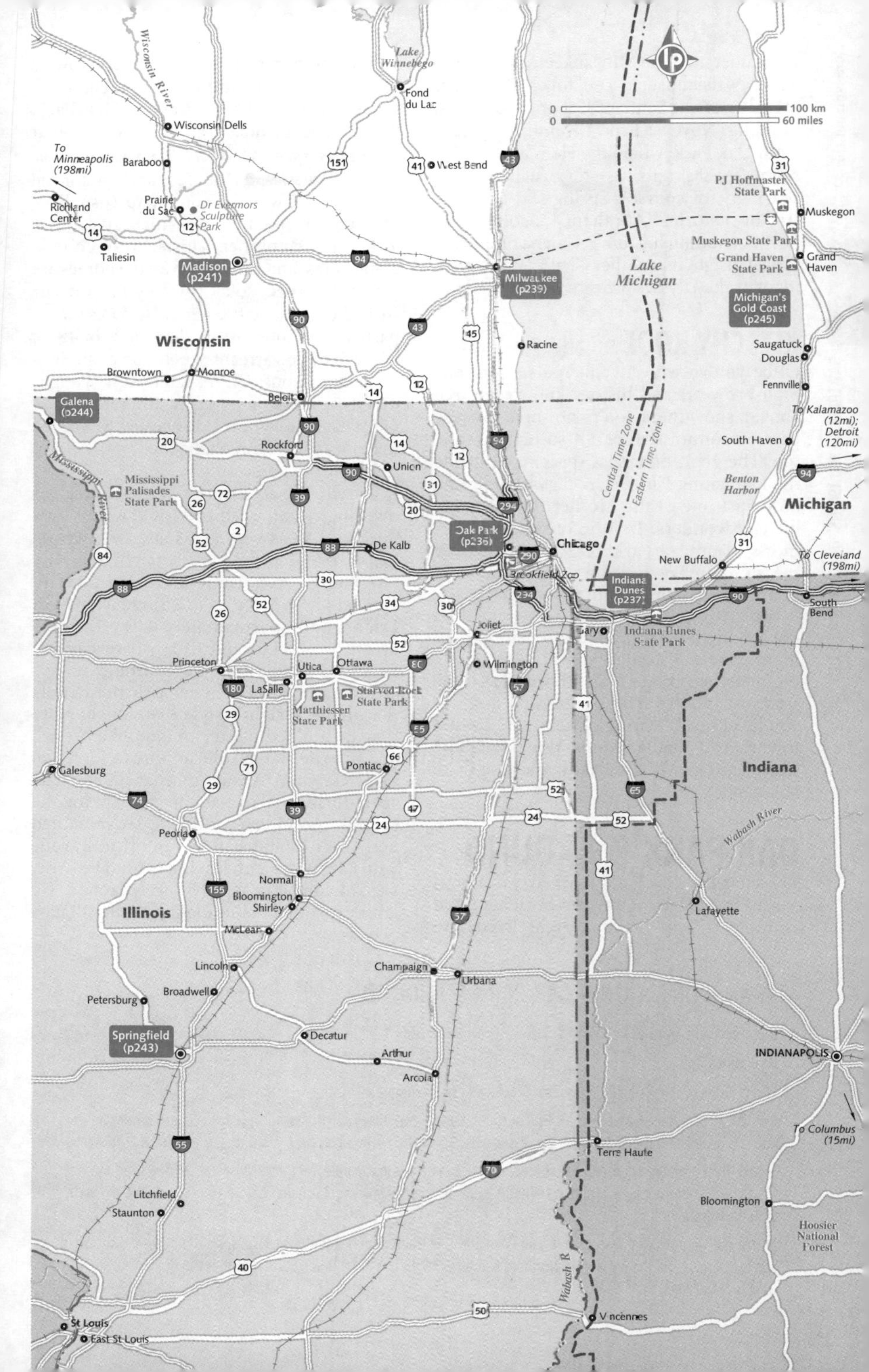

Lake Winnebago
Wisconsin River
Fond du Lac
0
100 km
0
60 miles
Wisconsin Dells
To Minneapolis (198mi)
Baraboo
West Bend
PJ Hoffmaster State Park
Muskegon
Richland Center
Prairie du Sac
Dr Evermors Sculpture Park
Muskegon State Park
Grand Haven State Park
Grand Haven
Taliesin
Madison (p241)
Milwaukee (p239)
Lake Michigan
Michigan's Gold Coast (p245)
Wisconsin
Racine
Saugatuck
Douglas
Fennville
Browntown
Monroe
Beloit
Galena (p244)
To Kalamazoo (12mi); Detroit (120mi)
Rockford
South Haven
Mississippi River
Union
Central Time Zone
Eastern Time Zone
Benton Harbor
Mississippi Palisades State Park
Michigan
Oak Park (p236)
De Kalb
Chicago
New Buffalo
To Cleveland (198mi)
Brookfield Zoo
Indiana Dunes (p237)
South Bend
Joliet
Gary
Indiana Dunes State Park
Princeton
Utica
Ottawa
Wilmington
LaSalle
Starved Rock State Park
Matthiessen State Park
Galesburg
Pontiac
Indiana
Wabash River
Peoria
Normal
Bloomington
Shirley
Lafayette
Illinois
McLean
Lincoln
Champaign
Urbana
Broadwell
Petersburg
Springfield (p243)
Decatur
Arthur
Arcola
INDIANAPOLIS
To Columbus (15mi)
Terre Haute
Litchfield
Staunton
Bloomington
Hoosier National Forest
Wabash R
St Louis
East St Louis
Vincennes

is his übersite. The Milwaukee Art Museum (p240) sports unusually cool folk and outsider art galleries in a Santiago Calatrava-designed building. Novelist Ernest Hemingway hails from Oak Park, where the Hemingway Museum (opposite) tells his story (using words sparingly, of course). Springfield houses a trio of historical Abraham Lincoln sights (p243), including his tomb. Galena offers historical insight on another Civil War-era president at the Ulysses S Grant home (p244).

KITSCHY KOOL

Once you've wowed your pals with your high-brow art and history knowledge (see above), show them you're no snob, because you're a connoisseur of not-so-high culture, too. The giant fiberglass spaceman outside the Launching Pad Drive-in (p243) on Route 66 is just one of the Mother Road's many kitschy wonders. In Wisconsin, Dr Evermor's Sculpture Park (p242) – crowned by the futuristic Forevertron – feels like the set of an old 'It Came From Outer Space' sci-fi flick. It doesn't get much wackier than the Racing Sausages (aka guys dressed in mondo meat costumes) at Miller Park (p240). Pig-bedecked Oink's Dutch Treat (p239) is the start of a kitschy array of roadside shops as you head north through Michigan's coastal towns. And finally, Annie Wiggins Ghost Tour (p244) provides a healthy dose of hoke in Galena.

OAK PARK & AROUND

The suburb of Oak Park spawned two famous sons: Ernest Hemingway was born here, and architect Frank Lloyd Wright lived and worked here from 1898 to 1908. The town's main sights revolve around both men.

During Wright's 10 years in Oak Park, he designed a whole heap of houses. Stop at the visitors center (☎ 888-625-7275; www.visitoakpark.com; 158 N Forest Ave; 10am-5pm) and ask for the architectural walking-tour map (usually a free, photocopied page), which gives their locations. Ten of them cluster within a mile along Forest and Chicago Aves; the homes are privately owned, so all gawking must occur from the sidewalk. Moore House (333 N Forest Ave) is particularly noteworthy. First built in 1895, it's Wright's bizarre interpretation of an English manor house. In his later years, Wright called the house 'repugnant' and said he had only taken the commission because he needed the money. He claimed that he walked out of his way to avoid passing it.

To actually get inside a Wright-designed dwelling, you'll need to visit the Frank Lloyd Wright Home & Studio (☎ 708-848-1976; www.wrightplus.org; 951 Chicago Ave; adult/child 4-10 $12/5) nearby on Chicago Ave. Tours are held at 11am, 1pm and 3pm Monday to Thursday; to 6pm Friday; and approximately every 20 minutes between 11am and 3:30pm Saturday and Sunday. The hour-long walk-through reveals a fascinating place, filled with the details that made Wright's style distinctive. Note how he molded plaster to look like bronze and how he stained cheap pine to look like rare hardwood. Always in financial trouble, spendthrift Wright was adept at making the ordinary seem extraordinary. He remained here until 1908, when he ran off to Europe with a female client, leaving behind his wife, six kids and his architecture practice. He later explained his infidelity, saying that as

TRANSPORTATION – OAK PARK & AROUND

Distance from Chicago To Oak Park 8 miles; to Brookfield Zoo 14 miles.

Direction West.

Travel time To Oak Park 20 minutes; to Brookfield Zoo 25 minutes.

Car To Oak Park, take I-290 west, exiting north on Harlem Ave; take Harlem Ave north to Lake St and turn right. For the zoo, go west on the Eisenhower Expressway (I-290) to the 1st Ave exit, then south to 31st and follow the signs.

El Take the Green Line to the Oak Park stop, which lands you about 1 mile from the visitors center. The trip (one way $2) takes 20 minutes; be aware that the train traverses some bleak neighborhoods before emerging into Oak Park's wide-lawn splendor.

Metra The Union Pacific West Line has an Oak Park stop; trains depart from Ogilvie Transportation Center. Brookfield Zoo is reachable via the Burlington Northern Santa Fe (BNSF) Line from Union Station; exit at the Hollywood stop (one way Oak Park/zoo $2.15/3.05).

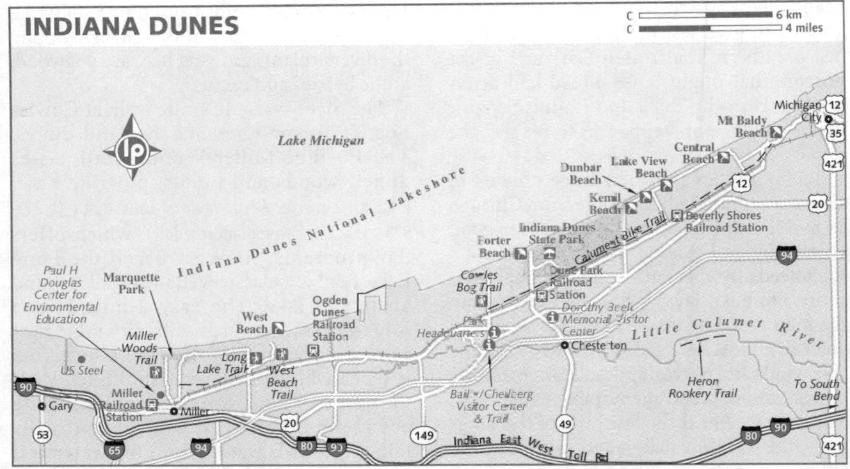

a 'thinking man,' he didn't have to follow the rules of the ordinary man. He set up shop next at Taliesin in Wisconsin, where he lived with his new lady until a deranged servant murdered her in 1914.

You can take a tour that combines the Home & Studio with a neighborhood walkabout. Self-guided audio tours are also available. Both the Home & Studio and the visitors center sell tickets for whatever combination you desire.

The **Unity Temple** (☎ 708-383-8873; www.unitytemple-utrf.org; 875 Lake St; adult/child 5 yrs & under/student $8/free/6; 🕑 10:30am-4:30pm Mon-Fri, 1-4pm Sat & Sun) is the only other Wright building that devotees can go inside; it requires a separate admission fee. If you're short on time or money, skip this one and head to the Home & Studio instead.

Despite Hemingway calling Oak Park a 'village of wide lawns and narrow minds,' the town still pays homage to him at the **Ernest Hemingway Museum** (☎ 708-848-2222; www.ehfop.org; 200 N Oak Park Ave; adult/child $7/5.50; 🕑 1-5pm Sun-Fri, 10am-5pm Sat). The exhibits begin with his middle-class Oak Park background and the innocent years before he went off to find adventure. The ensuing displays focus on his writings in Spain and during WWII. Admission includes entry to **Hemingway's birthplace** (☎ 708-848-2222; www.ehfop.org; 339 N Oak Park Ave; adult/child $7/5.50; 🕑 1-5pm Sun-Fri, 10am-5pm Sat), where you can see his first room. 'Papa' was born here in 1899 in the large, turreted home of his maternal grandparents.

To see the array of animals Hemingway likely shot and killed on his famed hunting expeditions, head southwest from Oak Park to the **Brookfield Zoo** (☎ 708-485-0263; www.brookfieldzoo.org; 8400 W 31st St, Brookfield; adult/child 3-11 yrs $10/6; 🕑 9:30am-6pm, shorter hrs Sep-May). With 2700 animals and 215 acres, the zoo can easily sustain a day's wanderings. More extensive than the free Lincoln Park Zoo in Chicago, Brookfield features dolphin shows, African- and Australian-themed exhibits, several primate areas, a kids' zoo and a ton more.

Because most visitors use the north gate and tend to stop at the nearby attractions first, you can avoid some of the crowds by starting in the southern part of the zoo and working back north.

These sights are only 20 to 25 minutes from downtown Chicago, but if you wish to overnight in the area, see p230 for lodging information.

INDIANA DUNES

Lake Michigan's prevailing winds created the 21 miles of sandy beaches and dunes that comprise **Indiana Dunes National Lakeshore** (☎ 800-959-9174; www.nps.gov/indu; admission free except West Beach, which charges per car $6). Behind the sands, large areas of woods and wetlands have become major wildlife habitats and the breeding grounds for an incredible variety of plant life. Everything from cacti to hardwood forests and pine trees sprouts here.

Preserving this rare ecosystem, which stretches from Gary east to Michigan City, has always been a struggle. The vast and stinky steel mills that pop up amid the bucolic beauty show which way the fight has often gone, and give visitors a whiff (literally – just breathe in that rotten Gary air) of the horrors that might have spread had activists like Dorothy Buell and Illinois Senator Paul Douglas not stepped in to protect the region.

Today the area attracts huge crowds in summer months, when people from Chicago to South Bend flock to the shores for good swimming and general frivolity. Swimming is allowed anywhere along the national lakeshore. On busy days, a short hike away from the folks clogging up developed beaches will yield an almost deserted strand. In winter the lake winds and pervasive desolation make the dunes a moody and memorable experience. You may well hear the low hum of the 'singing sands,' an unusual sound caused by the zillions of grains of sand hitting each other in the wind.

The best place to start your trip is the Dorothy Buell Memorial Visitor Center (☎ 219-926-7561; Hwy 49; 🕑 8:30am-5pm, to 6pm summer). It provides details on beaches plus free hiking, biking, birding and eco-tourism guides.

To receive these guides ahead of time, contact the Porter County Convention & Visitors Bureau (CVB; ☎ 800-283-8687; www.indianadunes.com). They'll send their maps, hiking guides and other information to you gratis.

From the visitor center, it's time to hit the sand. Most beaches are open from 7am to sunset daily. Of the developed ones, Central Beach is a good place to escape the masses, and it leads to a set of steep dune cliffs. Mt Baldy Beach boasts the highest dunes, with namesake Mt Baldy offering the best views all the way to Chicago from its 120ft peak. Don't look east or you'll see the environmental travesty of downtown Michigan City's coal-powered electric plant and huge cooling tower. This beach is by far the busiest of the lot. West Beach, which is nearest to Gary, draws fewer crowds than the others and features a number of nature hikes and trails. It's also the only beach with an on-duty lifeguard.

If you'd rather be hiking than sunbathing, the park service has done a fine job of developing trails through a range of terrain and environments. The Bailly/Chellberg Trail begins at the Bailly/Chellberg Visitor Center (☎ 219-926-7561; Mineral Springs Rd; 🕑 11am-4:30pm Sat & Sun) about two miles south of the beaches. The 2½-mile trail winds through the forest, passing restored log cabins from the 1820s and a farm built by Swedes in the 1870s. Among the diverse plants growing here are dogwood, arctic berries and cactus.

The nicely varied 5-mile walk at Cowles Bog Trail combines marshes and dunes. The 1½-mile Miller Woods Trail passes dunes, woods and ponds, plus the Paul H Douglas Center for Environmental Education (☎ 219-926-7561; call for program schedule), which offers day programs. At West Beach the Long Lake Trail is a classic wetlands walk around an inland lake. The easy 2-mile Heron Rookery Trail rewards with an amble past a breeding ground for the great blue heron; it's located inland, southeast of Buell Visitor Center. The best times for viewing are dawn and dusk, when you can catch the tall, regal birds wading into the water and spearing food with their pointy-sharp bills. Since the birds can be elusive, it's wise to stop into the Buell center first and have staff give you sighting tips.

Much of the national park area is good for cycling, although the traffic and the narrow shoulders on Hwy 12 can make that road dangerous. The Calumet Bike Trail runs west from near Michigan City almost to the Chellberg Farm in the middle of the national lakeshore. There is cross-country skiing inland, especially along the trails described above.

Indiana Dunes State Park (☎ 219-926-1952; www.dnr.in.gov/parklake; per car $4-10; 🕑 beaches 9am-sunset, park 7am-11pm, reduced hrs Sep-May) is a 2100-acre shoreside pocket within the national lakeshore; it's located at the end of Hwy 49, near Chesterton. It has more amenities, but also

TRANSPORTATION – INDIANA DUNES

Distance from Chicago 50 miles.

Direction Southeast.

Travel time 75 minutes.

Car Take I-90 through Gary to US 12; most sites are located off US 12. Note that I-90 is a toll road, so be prepared to pay $3 to $4 en route.

Metra The South Shore Line trains (☎ 800-356-2079; www.nictd.com) depart frequently from Millennium Station in the Loop and stop at Miller, Ogden Dunes, Dune Park and Beverly Shores (one way $5.50 to $7.50).

DETOUR: NEW BUFFALO

Just up US 12 from Indiana Dunes, across the Michigan border, the little town of New Buffalo beckons with its well-loved beach, dreamy ice cream and – believe it, people – surfing.

The novelty of surfing Lake Michigan can't be beat, and the laid-back dudes at Third Coast Surf Shop (☎ 269-932-4575; www.thirdcoastsurfshop.com; 22 S Smith St; 🕑 11am-6pm Mon-Fri, from 10am Sat & Sun, reduced hrs in winter) provide wetsuits and boards for surfing, boogie boarding and skimboarding (rentals per day $10 to $20). For novices, they offer 1½-hour lessons (surfing $45, skimboarding $35) right from the public beach from June through September. It's a great place to learn since the waves are nice and gentle in summer. The shop also rents bikes (per half day $15).

All that exercise earns visitors a dip or two at Oink's Dutch Treat (☎ 269-469-3535; 227 W Buffalo St), an ice cream shop plastered with pig memorabilia and scooping creamy flavors like Mackinac Island Fudge. For more substantial chow, get a wax-paper-wrapped cheeseburger, spicy curly fries and cold beer at Redamak's (☎ 269-469-4522; 616 E Buffalo St; burgers $3-5).

For lodging, check the Harbor County Lodging Association (☎ 800-352-7251; www.harborcountry.org/availability), or just motor another hour or so north to Saugatuck (p247).

more regulation and many more crowds. Away from its mobbed beaches, the park does offer secluded natural areas. In winter cross-country skiing is popular, while summertime brings out the hikers. Seven numbered trails zigzag over the sandscape: Trail 4 climbs up Mt Tom, the highest dune at 192ft; Trail 2 is good for spring flowers and ferns and is well-used by skiers; and Trail 8 surmounts three of the highest dunes, paying off with killer views of the region.

Unfortunately, the parks do not rent bicycles or skis, so you'll have to bring your own.

Other than a couple of beachfront snack bars you won't find much to eat in the parks, so stop at homey, Italian Lucrezia (☎ 219-926-5829; 428 S Calumet Rd; mains $12-21; 🕑 11am-10pm Sun-Thu, to 11pm Fri & Sat) in Chesterton or the sophisticated foodie-favorite Miller Bakery Café (☎ 219-938-2229; 555 Lake St; lunch mains $8-16, dinner mains $16-28; 🕑 lunch 11:30am-2pm Tue-Fri, dinner 5-9pm Tue-Thu, 5-10pm Fri & Sat, 4-8pm Sun) in Miller Beach.

Parking at the national lakeshore's beach lots is a nightmare on weekends unless you arrive before 10am; West Beach is your best bet, though it charges $6 per car. The state park has bigger lots. Or take the South Shore train from Chicago, which allows you to avoid the parking mess if you don't mind walking a mile or more from the various stations to the beaches.

It's certainly satisfying to visit the dunes as a day trip, but many folks prefer to linger and pitch a tent at the state park's campground (☎ 866-622-6746; www.camp.in.gov; campsites $17-28; 🕑 open year-round). Be sure to book ahead in summer.

MILWAUKEE

No one gives much consideration to Milwaukee, Wisconsin, standing as it does in Chicago's shadow, and that's a shame, because with its line-up of beer, motorcycles, world-class art and a ballpark with racing sausages, it makes a rollicking getaway.

Germans first settled the city in the 1840s. Many immigrants started small breweries soon thereafter, but the introduction of bulk-brewing technology in the 1890s turned beer into a major Milwaukee industry. Schlitz ('the beer that made Milwaukee famous'), Pabst and Miller were all based here at one time, but among the majors, only Miller remains today.

So why not make Miller Brewing Company (☎ 414-931-2337; www.millerbrewing.com; 4251 W State St; admission free; 🕑 10:30am-3:30pm Mon-Sat) your first stop, and join the legions of drinkers lined up for the free tours? Though the watery beer may not be your favorite, the factory impresses with its sheer scale: you'll visit the packaging plant where 2000 cans are filled each minute, and the warehouse where half a million cases chill while awaiting shipment. And then there's the generous tasting session at the tour's end, where you can down three full-size samples. Don't forget your ID.

For more swills, head to Sprecher Brewing Company (☎ 414-964-2739; www.sprecherbrewery.com; 701 W Glendale Ave; tours $3; 🕑 4pm Fri, noon-2pm Sat). The small microbrewery's tour includes a museum of memorabilia from long-gone Milwaukee suds-makers and a beer garden replete with oom-pah music. It's 5 miles north of downtown; reservations required.

TRANSPORTATION – MILWAUKEE

Distance from Chicago 92 miles.

Direction North.

Travel time 1½ hours.

Boat Milwaukee is the jumping-off point for the Lake Express ferry (☎ 866-914-1010; www.lake-express.com; mid-Apr-Oct), which sails to Muskegon, MI (one way adult/child $62/34.50, car/bicycle $72/10, 2½ hours), and provides easy access to Michigan's beach-lined Gold Coast (p245). The terminal is a few miles south of downtown; take I-794 East and follow the Port of Milwaukee signs.

Bus The drop-off for Megabus (☎ 877-462-6342; www.megabus.com/us) is at the downtown Amtrak station; frequent express buses run from Chicago to Milwaukee ($11, two hours). Badger Bus (☎ 414-276-7490; www.badgerbus.com; 635 N James Lovell St) goes to Madison ($17, 1½ hours); its terminal is near Amtrak.

Car Take I-90/94 west from downtown, and follow I-94 when it splits off. The interstate goes all the way into Milwaukee. It's a busy road, and travel times can be horrendous in peak hours. It's also a toll road part of the way, costing about $3.

Public transportation Providing efficient local bus services (fare $1.75), the Milwaukee County Transit System (☎ 414-344-6711; www.ridemcts.com) also has a free trolley that runs downtown in summer. Bus 31 goes to Miller Brewery from the corner of 6th and Washington Sts.

Train Perhaps the quickest way to Milwaukee given the snail-crawl pace of highway traffic is via Amtrak (☎ 800-872-7245; www.amtrak.com), which runs the Hiawatha train seven times per day to/from Chicago ($21, 1½ hours). The main station (☎ 414-271-0840; 433 W St Paul Ave) is downtown; there's also one at Milwaukee's airport (☎ 414-747-5300; www.mitchellairport.com).

In 1903 William Harley and Arthur Davidson, local Milwaukee schoolmates, built and sold their first Harley-Davidson motorcycle. A century later, the big bikes are a symbol of American manufacturing pride, and the Harley-Davidson Plant (☎ 414-343-7850; www.harley-davidson.com; 11700 W Capitol Dr; admission free; usually 9:30am-1pm Mon-Fri), in the suburb of Wauwatosa (20 minutes from downtown), is where the engines are built. The one-hour tours are kind of technical, but the ultimate payoff comes when you get to sit in the saddle of a vintage bike. No open-toed shoes are permitted.

More bikes (including Elvis'!) will be displayed downtown at the new Harley-Davidson Museum (www.h-dmuseum.com; cnr Canal & 6th Sts). It was under construction at press time, but is slated to open in 2008; check the website for updates.

Even those who aren't usual museum-goers will be struck by the lakeside Milwaukee Art Museum (☎ 414-224-3200; www.mam.org; 750 N Art Museum Dr; adult/child 13-18 yrs $8/4; 10am-5pm, to 8pm Thu), which features a stunning wing-like addition by Santiago Calatrava. It soars open and closed every day at noon, which is wild to see. There's a permanent display on Frank Lloyd Wright, and fabulous folk- and outsider-art galleries.

The Milwaukee Brewers play baseball at top-notch Miller Park (☎ 414-902-4000; www.milwaukeebrewers.com; 1 Brewers Way, near S 46th St; tickets $10-44), which has a retractable roof and real grass. It's famous for its 'Racing Sausages,' a group of people in giant sausage costumes who sprint down the field at the end of the 6th inning. Hot dogs and bratwursts come imbued with the Secret Stadium Sauce; no one knows for sure what it is, other than damn delicious.

Good places to scope for eats include N Old World 3rd St downtown; the fashionable East Side by the University of Wisconsin-Milwaukee; hip, Italian-based Brady Street by its intersection with N Farwell Ave; and the gentrified Third Ward, anchored along N Milwaukee St, south of I-94. The Friday night fish fry is a highly social tradition observed at restaurants throughout Wisconsin and all over Milwaukee. Frozen custard is another local specialty; it's like ice cream only smoother and richer. Kopp's (☎ 414-961-2006; 5373 N Port Washington Rd; 10:30am-11:30pm) is a popular purveyor, advertising flavors of the day (Midnight Chocolate Cake! Grand Marnier Blueberry Crisp!) from a flashing highway billboard. It's located in suburban Glendale, about 15 minutes north of downtown.

The city's festival schedule is endless. Summerfest (☎ 800-273-3378; www.summerfest.com; day pass $15) is the granddaddy, with 11 days of music and merriment in late June-early July. There's also PrideFest (www.pridefest.com; mid-Jun), Polish Fest (www.polishfest.org; late Jun), Irish Fest (www.irishfest.com; mid-Aug), German Fest (www.germanfest.com; late Jul) and a host of others. Call the visitors center for details.

INFORMATION

Milwaukee Visitors Center (☎ 800-554-1448; www.visitmilwaukee.org; 1st fl, 500 N Harbor Dr; 9am-5pm) Pick up maps and 'A Traveler's Guide to Wisconsin Cheese, Beer and Wine,' an exceptionally handy tool for eating and drinking your way through the rest of the state. Located in the Discovery World Bldg.

Wisconsin Milk Marketing Board (☎ 608-836-8820; www.wisdairy.com) Producer of the free guide mentioned above; contact the group if you want to receive it before your arrival – which we highly recommend.

EATING & DRINKING

Check the free, weekly Shepherd Express (www.shepherd-express.com) for additional restaurant and entertainment listings, or the online resource www.onmilwaukee.com.

Trocadero (☎ 414-272-0205; 1758 N Water St; mains $7-17; 11am-midnight Mon-Fri, from 9am Sat & Sun) A glorious wine list, cheese plates, crepes, baguettes with jam, mussels and *frites* – we're in Paris, *oui?* Nope, we're near Brady St at Trocadero, a romantic coffee house/restaurant/bar with a year-round patio (it's heated in winter).

Palm Tavern (☎ 414-744-0393; 2989 S Kinnickinnic Ave) Located in the south side neighborhood of Bay View, this warm, jazzy little bar has a mammoth selection of unusual beers and single-malt scotches.

Von Trier (☎ 414-272-1775; 2235 N Farwell Ave) Longstanding German favorite with plenty of brews on tap and a *biergarten*.

SLEEPING

Book ahead in summer to ensure you get a room.

Astor Hotel (☎ 800-558-0200; www.theastorhotel.com; 924 E Juneau Ave; r incl breakfast $99-129) The Astor, dating from 1918, has bright, spacious rooms, some with cool old furnishings, plus perks like free internet and a shuttle bus to nearby sights. It's located near the lake, east of downtown's core. Parking costs $4.

Best Western Inn Towne Hotel (☎ 414-224-8400; www.inntownehotel.com; 710 N Old World 3rd St; r from $89/99) It's operated by a chain, but this old hotel, in the heart of downtown, has good-quality rooms with a vintage ambience. Parking costs $10; wi-fi is free.

MADISON

Madison gets a lot of kudos – most walkable city, best road-biking city, most vegetarian friendly, gay friendly, environmentally friendly, and just plain all-round friendliest city in the USA. Ensconced on a narrow isthmus between Mendota and Monona lakes, it's a pretty combination of small, grassy state capital and liberal, bookish college town.

The heart of town is marked by x-shaped State Capitol (☎ 608-266-0382; admission free; 8am-6pm Mon-Fri, to 4pm Sat & Sun), the largest outside Washington, DC. Tours are available on the hour most days. On Saturday, Capitol Sq is overtaken by the Dane County Farmer's Market (www.dcfm.org; 6am-2pm Sat May-Nov), a good place to sample the Wisconsin specialties of cheese curds and beer-cooked bratwursts.

By all means, take advantage of the city's lakes and 200 miles of trails. For rentals, try Yellow Jersey (☎ 608-257-4737; www.yellowjersey.org; 419 State St; per day bikes $9.50; 10am-6pm Tue, Wed & Fri, to 8pm Mon & Thu, 9am-5pm Sat, noon-5pm Sun) for two-wheelers, and The Paddlin' Shop (☎ 608-284-0300; www.paddlin.com; 202 S Dickinson St; per day canoe or kayak $35-45; 10am-6pm Mon-Fri, to 5pm Sat & Sun) for water-faring craft. Both are near Capitol Sq (three blocks and 10 blocks, respectively).

State St runs from the capitol west to the University of Wisconsin. The lengthy avenue is lined with fair-trade coffee shops, parked bicycles and incense-wafting stores selling hackeysacks and flowing Indian skirts. An anomaly is the House of Wisconsin Cheese (☎ 608-255-5204; www.houseofwisconsincheese.com; 107 State St; 9am-8pm), which sells state-shaped cheddar blocks and foam rubber cheese-wedge hats among its pungent stock. State St also holds the impressive Museum of Contemporary Art (☎ 608-257-0158; www.mmoca.org; 227 State St; admission free; 11am-5pm Tue & Wed, to 8pm Thu & Fri, 10am-8pm Sat, noon-5pm Sun), with works by Frida Kahlo, Claes Oldenburg and others, plus a rooftop cinema that screens art films on summer Friday nights.

The University of Wisconsin campus has its own attractions, including the 1240-acre

TRANSPORTATION – MADISON

Distance from Chicago 150 miles.

Direction Northwest.

Travel time Three hours.

Bus Climb aboard Van Galder Bus (☎ 800-747-0994; www.vangalderbus.com), which runs between Chicago (either O'Hare or downtown) and Madison's Memorial Union (one way $26, 3 to 3½ hours) several times daily. Badger Bus (☎ 414-276-7490; www.badgerbus.com) goes to Milwaukee (one way $17, 1½ hours); it also originates at Memorial Union.

Car Take I-90/94 west out of Chicago; stay on I-90 when it splits off. Stay on the interstate going west to Rockford, then north. On the outskirts of Madison get onto US 18/12 west for about 6 miles, and then look for the Park St exit into downtown. Parts of I-90 require tolls.

Arboretum (☎ 608-263-7888; 1207 Seminole Hwy; admission free; 7am-10pm), dense with lilac, and the Memorial Union (☎ 608-265-3000; 800 Langdon St), with its festive lakeside terrace perfect for an outdoor drink. The Union also offers free live music, films and internet access.

Dr Evermor's Sculpture Park (admission free; 9am-5pm Mon & Thu-Sat, from noon Sun) sprawls 11 miles northwest of Madison on US 12. The doc welds old pipes, carburetors and other salvaged metal into a hallucinatory world of futuristic creatures and structures. The crowning glory is the giant, egg-domed Forevertron, cited by Guinness as the world's largest scrap-metal sculpture. The good doctor himself – aka Tom Every – is often around and happy to chat about his birds, dragons and other pieces of folk art. Look for sculptures along the highway marking the entrance.

Information

Madison Visitors Center (☎ 608-255-2537, 800-373-6376; www.visitmadison.com; 615 E Washington Ave; 8am-5pm Mon-Fri) Six blocks east of Capitol Sq, though you're likely to find all the info you need at the Memorial Union.

Eating

Café Soleil & L'Etoile (☎ 608-251-0500; 25 N Pinckney St; café mains $8-10, restaurant mains $29-35; closed Sun) All dishes use local, seasonal ingredients.

DETOUR: CHEESE & TALIESIN

Wisconsin is cheesy and proud of it, if you hadn't figured that out yet. The state pumps out 2.4 billion pounds of cheddar, gouda and other smelly goodness from its cow-speckled farmland. Local license plates read 'The Dairy State' with udder dignity. So embrace the cheese thing. And how better than via a road trip to the USA's largest concentration of cheesemakers, who happen to reside around Monroe, 60 miles south of Madison?

Follow your nose to Roth Käse (☎ 608-328-2122; www.rothkase.com; 657 Second St; 9am-6pm Mon-Fri, to 5pm Sat, 10am-5pm Sun), which creates unusual varieties like 'buttermilk blue.' Buy it at the onsite store, or watch 'em make it from the observation area (weekday mornings only). Several more producers also let you watch their process; get specifics from the 'Traveler's Guide to Wisconsin Cheese, Beer and Wine,' free from the Wisconsin Milk Marketing Board (☎ 608-836-8820; www.wisdairy.com), and available at shops and visitor centers throughout the state (or call and they'll send you one).

For serious R&R, spend the night at Inn Serendipity (☎ 608-329-7056; www.innserendipity.com; 7843 County P; r incl breakfast $100-115) on a five-acre working organic farm in Browntown, just west of Monroe. This two-room B&B is about as green as it gets. It's powered by solar and wind systems, the owners compost all food waste, and they've built their bathroom using recycled windshield glass for the tile.

Also in the vicinity, 40 miles west of Madison and 3 miles south of Spring Green, Taliesin was the home of native son Frank Lloyd Wright for most of his life, and is the site of his architectural school. It's now a major pilgrimage destination for fans and followers. The house was built in 1903, the Hillside Home School in 1932, and the visitors center (☎ 608-588-7900; www.taliesinpreservation.org; Hwy 23; tours $16-80; 9am-5:30pm May-Oct) in 1953. A wide range of guided tours cover various parts of the complex; reservations are required for the more lengthy ones. The one-hour Hillside Tour ($16, no reservation needed) is a good introduction. For additional Wright sights, see Oak Park (p236).

L'Etoile is the restaurant, open from 5:30 to 8pm. Soleil is the attached café, open 7am to 2:30pm, serving scrumptious sandwiches like trout salad on fresh-baked honey-oat bread and Wisconsin grilled cheeses on whole grain bread.

Himal Chuli (☎ 608-251-9225; 318 State St; mains $8-13; 11am-9pm Mon-Sat, noon-8pm Sun) Cheerful, cozy place serving homemade Nepali fare, including vegetarian dishes.

Sleeping

Arbor House (☎ 608-238-2981; www.arbor-house.com; 3402 Monroe St; r incl breakfast weekday $110-175, weekend $150-230) A wind-powered, energy-efficient-appliance-using, vegetarian-breakfast-serving B&B. It's located about 3 miles southwest of the capitol but accessible to public transportation. The owners will lend you mountain bikes, too.

University Inn (☎ 608-285-8040, 800-279-4881; www.universityinn.org; 441 N Frances St; r $89-129; P) The rooms are nothing special but the handy location by the State St action is; free internet access and wi-fi.

HI Madison Hostel (☎ 608-441-0144; www.madisonhostel.org; 141 S Butler St; dm $23, r $47) By the capitol; parking costs $5.

ROUTE 66 TO SPRINGFIELD

The classic highway from Chicago to Los Angeles once cut diagonally across Illinois to St Louis and beyond. Though now almost totally superseded by I-55, the old route – which is affectionately called Main St, USA – still exists in scattered sections, and its associated Americana survives in towns bypassed by the interstate. You'll encounter a serious trail of corn dogs, pies and other eats along the way, so get ready to loosen those belts.

The 'Mother Road' kicks off in downtown Chicago on Adams St just west of Michigan Ave. Our first stop: the Gemini Giant, a 28ft fiberglass spaceman proffering burgers and fries south of Joliet. Leave I-55 at Joliet Rd, following Hwy 53 southbound to Wilmington. This is where the Giant stands guard outside the Launching Pad Drive-In (☎ 815-476-6535; 810 E Baltimore St; items $2-5; 10am-9:30pm).

Motor down to Pontiac and on the outskirts look for the Log Cabin Inn (☎ 815-842-2903; 18700 Old Route 66; 5am-4pm Mon & Tue, to 8pm Wed-Fri, to 2pm Sat). When Route 66 was realigned, the restaurant was jacked up and rotated 180 degrees to face the new road. The Route 66 Hall of Fame (☎ 815-844-4566; 110 W Howard St; admission free; 11am-3pm Mon-Fri, 10am-4pm Sat) is also in town. Cruise by Bloomington and Normal and stop off in Shirley at Funk's Grove (☎ 309-874-3360; call for seasonal hrs), a 19th-century maple-syrup farm.

The small state capital of Springfield harbors a trio of Route 66 sights. All must stop to hail the corn-dog's birthplace at the Cozy Dog Drive In (☎ 217-525-1992; 2935 S 6th St; items $2-4; 8am-8pm Mon-Sat). It's a Route 66 legend, with all sorts of memorabilia and souvenirs, plus homemade doughnuts to chase down the main course. Shea's Gas Station Museum (☎ 217-522-0475; 2075 Peoria Rd; admission $2; 8am-4pm Tue-Fri, to noon Sat) lets visitors fill up with Route 66 pumps and signs. And there's nothing better on a warm summer evening than catching a flick under the stars at the Route 66 Drive In (☎ 217-698-0066; Recreation Dr; adult/child 4-12 yrs $5/3; nightly Jun-Aug, weekends mid-Apr-May & Sep).

Springfield also has a certifiable obsession with local hero Abraham Lincoln, who practiced law here from 1837 to 1861. The city's Abe-related sights offer an in-depth look at the man and his turbulent times, which only some cynics find overdone. Many of the attractions are walkable downtown and cost little to nothing. Get your bearings with maps from the central visitors center (☎ 800-545-7300; www.visitspringfieldillinois.com; 109 N 7th St; 8:30am-5pm Mon-Fri).

To visit the top-draw Lincoln Home, you must first pick up a ticket at the Lincoln Home Visitors Center (☎ 217-492-4150; www.nps.gov/liho; 426 S 7th St; admission free; 8:30am-5pm). The site is where Abe and Mary Lincoln lived from 1844 until they moved to the White House in 1861. You'll see considerably more than just the home: the whole block has been preserved, and several structures are open to visitors.

The Lincoln Presidential Library & Museum (☎ 217-558-8844; www.alplm.org; 212 N 6th St; adult/child 5-15 yrs $7.50/3.50; 9am-5pm) contains the most complete Lincoln collection in the world, everything from his Gettysburg Address and Emancipation Proclamation to his shaving mirror and briefcase. You'll have to wade through some Disney-esque exhibits to get to the good stuff.

TRANSPORTATION – SPRINGFIELD

Distance from Chicago To Wilmington 60 miles; to Springfield 200 miles.

Direction Southwest.

Travel time To Wilmington one hour; to Springfield 3½ hours.

Bus The Greyhound (☎ 800-231-2222; www.greyhound.com) runs frequent buses from Chicago to Springfield ($29-38, 4½ hours); the station (☎ 217-544-8466; 2351 S Dirkson Pkwy) is southeast of downtown.

Car Take I-55 south out of Chicago and follow it all the way to Springfield. Old Route 66 often parallels the interstate.

Train The Amtrak (☎ 800-872-7245; www.amtrak.com) runs five trains per day between Chicago and Springfield ($17 to $31, 3½ hours); the station (☎ 217-753-2013; cnr 3rd & Washington Sts) is downtown.

After his assassination, Lincoln's body was returned to Springfield, where it lies today. The impressive Lincoln's Tomb sits in Oak Ridge Cemetery (☎ 217-782-2717; admission free; 9am-5pm Mar-Oct, to 4pm Nov-Feb), north of downtown. The gleam on the nose of Lincoln's bust, created by visitors' touches, indicates the numbers of people who come to pay their respects.

Information

In addition to the resources below, get Lonely Planet's *Road Trip: Route 66* book, which will guide you all the way to LA, baby.

Route 66 Association of Illinois (www.il66assoc.org) Information on sights and events.

Historic Route 66 (www.historic66.com/illinois) Detailed driving directions from sight to sight.

Sleeping

The following options are in Springfield:

Inn at 835 (☎ 217-523-4466; www.innat835.com; 835 S 2nd St; r incl breakfast from $105-120) This 10-room B&B in an historic home offers the classiest digs in town.

Carpenter Street Hotel (☎ 217-789-9100, 888-779-9100; www.carpenterstreethotel.com; 525 N 6th St; r incl breakfast $72) It's a bland but well-priced option for downtown.

GALENA

Though just a speck on the map, Galena, Illinois, draws hordes of Chicagoans to its perfectly preserved, Civil War-era streets. The town spreads across wooded hillsides near the Mississippi River and manages to maintain its charm, despite a slew of tourist-oriented antique shops and restaurants.

Lead was mined in the upper Mississippi area as early as 1700, but industrial demands in the mid-19th century resulted in a boom. Galena (named for the lead sulfide ore) became a center for the industry and major river-port town, and businesses, hotels and mansions in Federal and Italianate styles shot up here. The boom ended abruptly after the Civil War, and Galena was all but deserted until restoration began in the 1960s.

The main visitors center (101 Bouthillier St) is on the eastern side of the Galena River, in the 1857 train depot. Get a walking guide, leave your car and explore on foot.

Elegant old Main St curves around the hillside and the historic heart of town. Among the sights is the Ulysses S Grant Home (☎ 815-777-3310; www.granthome.com; 500 Bouthillier St; adult/child $3/1; 9am-4:45pm Wed-Sun Apr-Oct, reduced hrs Nov-Mar), a gift from local Republicans to the victorious general at the end of the Civil War. Grant lived here until he became the 18th president of the United States. Tours are provided, sometimes conducted by a uniformed guy who pretends he 'is' Grant.

The elaborate Italianate Belvedere Mansion (☎ 815-777-0747; 1008 Park Ave; adult/child $10/3; 11am-4pm Mon-Fri, to 5pm Sat & Sun late May-Oct) is stuffed with antiques and holds a special claim to fame: it sports the green drapes from *Gone With the Wind* (remember the ones Scarlett O'Hara rips down and sews into a dress?).

On weekend evenings, set out on the hokey but fun Annie Wiggins Ghost Tour (☎ 815-777-0336; www.anniewiggins.com; 1004 Park Ave; 1hr tour $10; Fri & Sat evenings May-Oct). Yes, she wears a costume, but so does everyone in town, it seems.

Galena brims with B&Bs – you can't throw a quilt without it landing on a four-poster bed at one of the zillion properties in town. They add to the old-fashioned ambience, and it's easy to see why so many city dwellers pack up their cars on Friday, anxious to escape to the country and drift back into another, slower age (at least until Sunday).

En route to Galena, east of Rockford off I-90, is Union's Illinois Railway Museum (☎ 815-

TRANSPORTATION – GALENA

Distance from Chicago To Galena 165 miles; to Union 60 miles.

Direction Northwest.

Travel time To Galena three hours; to Union one hour 15 minutes.

Car Take I-90 west out of Chicago (tolls apply). Just before Rockford, follow US 51 and I-39 heading south for 3 miles, and then merge onto US 20 west, which runs all the way into Galena. To reach the rail museum, depart I-90 for US 20 at the Marengo exit; go northwest about 5 miles to Union Rd north and follow the signs.

923-4000; www.irm.org; US 20 to Union Rd; adult/child 3-11 yrs $6.50-10.50/$4.50-8.50; hrs vary Apr-Oct), one of the best of its kind in the US. The grounds boast more than 200 acres full of historic trains dating from the mid-1800s to the present. Models on display include steam, diesel and electric locomotives, plus passenger and freight cars, many of which are protected by large sheds. This is ground zero for the state's train nerds, and part of the fun is just watching the older patrons and museum volunteers giddily discussing the intricacies of each engine, coupler and car. Kids, too, go nuts here.

Information

Galena Visitors Center (☎ 815-777-4390, 877-464-2536; www.galena.org; 101 Bouthillier St; 9am-5pm Mon-Sat, from 10am Sun, extended hrs in summer)

Eating

Log Cabin (☎ 815-777-0393; 201 N Main St; mains $11-18; 4-10pm) Huge dinner portions served amid Americana ambience.

Clarks Again (☎ 815-777-4407; 200 N Main St; mains $3-7; 5am-1:30pm Sun-Fri, to 3pm Sat) Biscuit-and-gravy breakfasts or lunchtime sandwiches.

Sleeping

Most B&Bs cost at least $100 nightly, and they fill up on weekends. The visitors center does bookings; call or check the website.

DeSoto House Hotel (☎ 815-777-0090; www.desotohouse.com; 230 S Main St; r $128-200) Grant and Lincoln stayed in the well-furnished rooms, and you can, too. The hotel dates from 1855 and has wi-fi.

Grant Hills Motel (☎ 815-777-2116; www.granthills.com; US 20; r $65-75) A cozy motel 1.5 miles east of town, with fine views, a pool and a horseshoe pitch.

MICHIGAN'S GOLD COAST

Michigan's west coast – aka its Gold Coast – is the place to come to watch incredible sunsets while waves tickle your toes. The 300-mile shoreline features endless stretches of beach, coastal parks, orchards and small towns that boom during the summer tourist season.

Saugatuck – known for its strong arts community, numerous B&Bs and gay-friendly vibe – is one of the most popular resort areas. The best thing to do in Saugatuck is also the most affordable. Jump aboard the Saugatuck Chain Ferry (Water St; $1; 9am-9pm), and the operator will pull you across the Kalamazoo River. On the other side you can huff up the stairs to the grand views atop Mt Baldhead, a 200ft-high sand dune. Then race down the north side to beautiful Oval Beach. The Saugatuck Dune Rides (☎ 269-857-2253; www.saugatuckduneride.com; 6495 Blue Star Hwy; adult/child 3-10 $16/10; 10am-7:30pm Mon-Sat, noon-7:30 Sun Jul & Aug, to 5:30pm Apr-Jun & Oct) provide a half-hour of good, cheesy fun spent zipping through the sand.

TRANSPORTATION – MICHIGAN'S GOLD COAST

Distance from Chicago To Saugatuck 140 miles; to Grand Haven 170 miles; to Muskegon 185 miles.

Direction Northeast.

Travel time To Saugatuck 2½ hours; to Grand Haven 3 hours; to Muskegon 3 ¼hours.

Boat The Lake Express ferry (☎ 866-914-1010; www.lake-express.com; mid-Apr-Oct) sails from Muskegon to Milwaukee, Wisconsin (one way adult/child $62/34.50, car/bicycle $72/10, 2½ hours). Departure is from Muskegon's Great Lakes Marina (1920 Lakeshore Dr).

Car Take I-90 east toward Indiana for about 30 miles (be prepared to pay about $4 worth of tolls). After Gary, merge onto I-94 east, and stay on it for about 65 miles. After Benton Harbor merge onto I-196/US 31, and take it for about 40 miles, until you see exits for Saugatuck. The state parks are all off US 31 to the north.

DETOUR: MIDWESTERN METRO GETAWAYS

Minneapolis, Detroit and Cleveland aren't far from Chicago. They range from five to nine hours away by car, and little more than an hour by air if you cop a cheap flight (check Southwest or Northwest Airlines; the latter has hubs in Minneapolis and Detroit). Amtrak and Megabus also run to all three cities. Pick up a copy of Lonely Planet's *USA* for more in-depth explorations.

Detroit

Ah, the Motor City. Once the pride of the nation for its car savvy (GM, Ford and Chrysler all launched here), the city fell to pieces when the auto industry tanked. Today, once-grand buildings lie boarded up with trash blowing about their bases, and wide swaths of downtown are downright vacant. While this contributes to a sort of bombed-out Early East Berlin vibe, it's these same qualities that fuel a raw urban energy you won't find anywhere else.

The city sports a trio of top-tier attractions. Spend a day wandering through the Henry Ford Museum/Greenfield Village Complex (☎ 313-982-6001; www.thehenryford.org; 20900 Oakwood Blvd; adult/child 5-12 yrs $30/22; 🕑 9:30am-5pm, Ford open year-round, Greenfield Village closed in winter) in suburban Dearborn. The two museums contain a fascinating wealth of American culture such as the chair Lincoln was sitting in when he was assassinated, Edgar Allan Poe's writing desk, the bus on which Rosa Parks refused to give up her seat and, of course, vintage cars; parking is $5. The Motown Museum (☎ 313-875-2264; www.motownmuseum.com; 2648 W Grand Blvd; adult/child 4-11 $8/5; 🕑 10am-6pm Tue-Sat) is a string of unassuming houses that became known as 'Hitsville USA' after Berry Gordy began Motown Records – and the careers of Stevie Wonder, Marvin Gaye et al – with an $800 loan in 1959. Diego Rivera's mural *Detroit Industry* fills a room at the renowned and recently expanded Detroit Institute of Arts (☎ 313-833-7900; www.dia.org; 5200 Woodward Ave; adult/child 6-17 yrs $6/3; 🕑 10am-4pm Wed & Thu, 10am-9pm Fri, 10am-5pm Sat & Sun).

The 'coney' – a hot dog smothered with chili and onions – is a Detroit specialty. When the craving strikes (and it will), take care of business at Lafayette Coney Island (☎ 313-964-8198; 118 Lafayette Blvd; items $2.35-3.25; 🕑 7:30-4am Mon-Thu, to 5am Fri & Sat, 9:30-4am Sun). The minimalist menu consists of burgers, fries, pies, doughnuts and beer, in addition to the signature item. Cast-iron stomach required.

Detroit may be Motown, but in recent years it's been rap, techno and hard-edged rock that have pushed the city to the forefront of the music scene; homegrown stars include the White Stripes and Eminem. St Andrew's Hall (☎ 313-961-6358; www.standrewshall.com; 431 E Congress St) and Magic Stick (☎ 313-833-9700; www.majesticdetroit.com; 4120 Woodward Ave) are where the coolest bands plug in their amps.

The Inn on Ferry Street (☎ 313-871-6000; www.innonferrystreet.com; 84 E Ferry St; r incl breakfast from $124) harbors 40 guestrooms in a row of Victorian mansions right by the art museum. Free internet, wi-fi, hot breakfast and shuttle to downtown are included.

Cleveland

Does it or does it not rock? You'll have to visit to decide.

Certainly Cleveland's top attraction is the Rock & Roll Hall of Fame & Museum (☎ 216-781-7625, 888-764-7625; www.rockhall.com; 1 Key Plaza; adult/child 9-12 yrs $20/11; 🕑 10am-5:30pm, to 9pm Wed year-round, to 9pm Sat Jun-Aug). It's more than a collection of rock-star memorabilia, though it does have Janis Joplin's psychedelic Porsche and Ray Charles' sunglasses.

Several galleries line the Blue Star Hwy between Saugatuck and South Haven (yes, it's south, as the name implies, by about 20 miles), offering pottery, paintings, sculptures and glasswork. Blue Star Pottery (☎ 269-637-5787; 337 Blue Star Hwy; 🕑 11am-5pm Fri-Sun May-Nov, by appt rest of year) – known for its sturdy bowls and platters with leaf-print designs – stands out. The area also sports a slew of antique shops where you can buy old traffic lights, Victorian sleds or $100 china teacups. Start at the whopping, 50,000-sq-ft Blue Star Antique Pavilion (☎ 269-857-6041; 2948 Blue Star Hwy; 🕑 10am-6pm), which can absorb buyers and browsers alike for the better part of a day. If you're too lazy to drive far, mosey around downtown Saugatuck, near Water and Butler Sts, where more galleries and shops proliferate.

To commune with nature, head north to Grand Haven and Muskegon. Three state parks cluster between these two towns, all offering the opportunity to hike and camp on or near Lake Michigan beaches. Resort-style Grand Haven is all about silken sand,

Interactive multimedia exhibits trace the history and social context of rock music and the many performers who created it. Why is the museum in Cleveland? Because this is the hometown of Alan Freed, the disc jockey who popularized the term 'rock 'n' roll' in the early 1950s, and because the city lobbied hard and paid big. Be prepared for crowds.

Cultural attractions cluster around Case Western Reserve University (aka 'University Circle'), 5 miles east of downtown, including the excellent Cleveland Museum of Art (☎ 216-421-7340; www.clevelandart.org; 11150 East Blvd; admission free; ⌚ 10am-5pm Tue-Sun, to 9pm Wed & Fri). Busy Little Italy is along Mayfield Rd, near University Circle (look for the Rte 322 sign).

For stylish eating and drinking, head to the Ohio City and Tremont neighborhoods, which straddle I-90 south of downtown. West Side Market Café (☎ 216-579-6800; 1995 W 25th St; mains $5-8; ⌚ 7am-4pm Mon & Tue, to 9pm Wed-Sat, 10am-3pm Sun) is a smart stop if you're craving well-made breakfast and lunch fare, or cheap fish and chicken mains. The café is inside West Side Market itself, which overflows with fresh produce and prepared foods that are handy for picnicking or road-tripping. Great Lakes Brewing Company (☎ 216-771-4404; 2516 Market Ave; closed Sun) wins prizes for its brewed-on-the-premises beers. Added historical bonus: Eliot Ness got into a shootout with criminals here; ask the bartender to show you the bullet holes.

For sleeping try Brownstone Inn (☎ 216-426-1753; www.brownstoneinndowntown.com; 3649 Prospect Ave; r $75-135), a five-room B&B between downtown and University Circle.

Minneapolis

Minneapolis is the artiest town on the prairie, with all the trimmings of progressive prosperity – a cache of coffee shops, organic and ethnic eateries, swank art museums, and enough theaters to be nicknamed Mini-Apple (second only to the Big Apple, New York City). It's always happenin', even in winter.

Top attractions include the Walker Art Center (☎ 612-375-7622; www.walkerart.org; 725 Vineland Pl; adult/child 12-18 yrs $10/6, admission free Thu evening; ⌚ 11am-5pm Tue-Sun, to 9pm Thu & Fri), with big-name US painters and great US pop art, and the whimsical Sculpture Garden (admission free; ⌚ 6am-midnight) next door. Walk the 2-mile trail by St Anthony Falls (on the north edge of downtown at the foot of Portland Ave), the power source of the timber and flour mills that gave rise to this Mississippi River city. Within a mile or two of downtown, a ring of lakes circles the inner-city area. Cedar Lake, Lake of the Isles, Lake Calhoun and Lake Harriet are all surrounded by parks and paths.

Browse for food and drink in the punk-yuppie Uptown neighborhood. Bryant-Lake Bowl (☎ 612-825-3737; 810 W Lake St; sandwiches $6-9, mains $9-15; ⌚ 8-12:30am) has a divey interior but the food is high-class. Artisanal cheese plates, mock duck rolls, cornmeal-crusted walleye strips and organic oatmeal melt in the mouth, complemented by a wide-ranging beer selection (including several local brews). The onsite theater always has something intriguing and odd going on, too.

Acts such as Prince and protogrunge bands like Hüsker Dü and the Replacements cut their chops in Minneapolis. First Avenue & 7th St Entry (☎ 612-338-8388; www.first-ave.com; 701 1st Ave N) is the bedrock of the city's music scene, and it still pulls in top bands and big crowds. Triple Rock Social Club (☎ 612-333-7499; www.triplerocksocialclub.com; 629 Cedar Ave) is a popular punk-alternative club.

Cheery, 10-bedroom Wales House (☎ 612-331-3931; www.waleshouse.com; 1115 5th St SE; r with/without bathroom $55/65) caters to scholars at the nearby University of Minnesota, and is a fine place to lay your head; two-night minimum stay required.

boardwalks and lighthouses. Oh, and there's a giant musical fountain that squirts 90,000 gallons of water sky-high each evening in summer. Grand Haven State Park (☎ 616-847-1309; 1001 Harbor Ave; ⌚ 8am-11pm, closed Nov-Mar), off Franklin St from US 31, sprawls along the beach and is connected to downtown restaurants by a scenic walkway along the Grand River. Between Grand Haven and Muskegon, take US 31 to the Pontaluna Rd exit to get to PJ Hoffmaster State Park (☎ 231-798-3711; 6585 Lake Harbor Rd; ⌚ 8am-10pm), which features a 10-mile trail system with several sections that hug Lake Michigan. North of Muskegon is Muskegon State Park (☎ 231-744-3480; 3560 Memorial Dr; ⌚ 9am-10pm), off US 31 at the Hwy 120 exit, with 12 miles of trails through rugged, wooded dunes. The town of Muskegon itself is no great shakes, but it is the jumping-off point for the Lake Express ferry to Milwaukee (see p240).

For a more in-depth exploration of Michigan's Gold Coast, get Lonely Planet's *Road Trip: Lake Michigan*. Note all state parks (www.michigandnr.com/parksandtrails) require a vehicle permit (per day/year $8/29) to enter.

Information

Saugatuck Convention & Visitors Bureau (☎ 269-857-1701; www.saugatuck.com)

Eating

Marro's Italian Restaurant (☎ 269-857-4248; 147 Water St; pizzas $16-23; 🕓 5-10pm Tue-Sun) Gets props for its pizzas; located in downtown Saugatuck.

Crane's Pie Pantry (☎ 269-561-2297; 6054 124th Ave; 🕓 9am-8pm Mon-Sat, 11am-8pm Sun May-Oct, reduced hrs Nov-Apr) Off Hwy 89, a few miles south of Saugatuck, it's located smack-dab in the middle of a fruit orchard, which is where the peaches, apples, cherries and other luscious fillings come from.

Sleeping

B&Bs abound in Saugatuck. Most are tucked into century-old Victorian homes and range from $100 to $300 a night per couple in the summer high season.

Twin Gables Inn (☎ 269-857-4346, 800-231-2185; www.twingablesinn.com; 900 Lake St; r incl breakfast $126-220) This fifteen-room inn has pleasant views overlooking Lake Michigan.

Bayside Inn (☎ 269-857-4321; www.baysideinn.net; 618 Water St; r incl breakfast $100-190) A former boathouse with 10 rooms and an outdoor hot tub.

Pines Motorlodge (☎ 269-857-5211; www.thepinesmotorlodge.com; 56 Blue Star Hwy; r $95-165) A mom-and-pop motel with comfy rooms at Saugatuck's edge.

Michigan State Park campsite reservations (☎ 800-447-2757; www.midnrreservations.com; campsites $10-33, reservation fee $8).

TRANSPORTATION

Flights, tours and rail tickets can be booked online at www.lonelyplanet.com/travel_services.

AIR

O'Hare International Airport is the nation's second busiest airport, transporting about 80 million passengers a year. United Airlines has it's headquarters here, but scads more domestic and international airlines use the airport. Direct flights depart for London, Sydney, Tokyo… Midway Airport is mostly known as home to cut-rate carriers such as Southwest and ATA, but other domestic-only carriers operate here as well. Between the two airports you'll likely find a way here from there – wherever that is.

Foul weather can cause delays getting in and out of Chicago, especially from November through February. Call ahead and check your flight, but still head out to the airport. If the weather clears and the plane can leave earlier, it will. If you miss it, that's your responsibility. Non weather-related delays have plagued O'Hare in recent years. Runway expansion is in the works.

If you have an early flight, you might consider avoiding traffic and spending a night near the airport, see Airport Accommodations (p231) for more info.

Airlines

Airlines flying in and out of Chicago inlude:

Air Canada (☎ 888-247-2262; www.aircanada.ca)

Air France (☎ 800-237-2747; www.airfrance.com)

American Airlines (☎ 800-433-7300; www.aa.com)

ATA (American Trans Air; ☎ 800-883-5228; www.ata.com)

British Airways (☎ 800-247-9297; www.britishairways.com)

Continental Airlines (☎ 800-523-3273; www.continental.com)

Delta Airlines (☎ 800-221-1212; www.delta.com)

Frontier Airlines (☎ 800-432-1359; www.frontierairlines.com)

Japan Airlines (☎ 800-525-3663; www.jal.com)

KLM Royal Dutch Airlines (☎ 800-447-4747; www.klm.com)

Lufthansa (☎ 800-645-3880; www.lufthansa.com)

Northwest Airlines (☎ 800-225-2525; www.nwa.com)

Southwest Airlines (☎ 800-435-9792; www.southwest.com)

Spirit Airlines (☎ 800-772-7117; www.spiritair.com)

United Airlines (☎ 800-241-6522; www.united.com)

US Airways (☎ 800-428-4322; www.usairways.com)

CLIMATE CHANGE & TRAVEL

Climate change is a serious threat to the ecosystems that humans rely upon, and air travel is the fastest-growing contributor to the problem. Lonely Planet regards travel, overall, as a global benefit, but believes we all have a responsibility to limit our personal impact on global warming.

Flying & Climate Change

Pretty much every form of motor transport generates CO_2 (the main cause of human-induced climate change) but planes are far and away the worst offenders, not just because of the sheer distances they allow us to travel, but because they release greenhouse gases high into the atmosphere. The statistics are frightening: two people taking a return flight between Europe and the US will contribute as much to climate change as an average household's gas and electricity consumption over a whole year.

Carbon Offset Schemes

Climatecare.org and other websites use 'carbon calculators' that allow travellers to offset the greenhouse gases they are responsible for with contributions to energy-saving projects and other climate-friendly initiatives in the developing world – including projects in India, Honduras, Kazakhstan and Uganda.

Lonely Planet, together with Rough Guides and other concerned partners in the travel industry, supports the carbon offset scheme run by climatecare.org. Lonely Planet offsets all of its staff and author travel.

For more information check out our website: www.lonelyplanet.com.

Things Change...

The information in this chapter is particularly vulnerable to change. Check directly with the airline or a travel agent to make sure you understand how a fare (and ticket you may buy) works and be aware of the security requirements for international travel. Shop carefully. The details given in this chapter should be regarded as pointers and are not a substitute for your own careful, up-to-date research.

Virgin Atlantic (☎ 800-821-5438; www.virgin-atlantic.com)

In addition to the airline companies' own websites, which may have internet-only deals, a number of third-party sites can be helpful in finding flight discounts:

www.airfarewatchdog.com

www.expedia.com

www.hotwire.com

http://us.lastminute.com/

www.orbitz.com

www.priceline.com

www.smarterliving.com

www.travelocity.com

www.travelzoo.com

Airports

In conjunction with Mayor Daley's focus on making Chicago greener and cleaner, both airports have increased the number of recycling bins around the terminals. Posters and info center pamphlets educate visitors about ways to save energy while traveling.

O'HARE

The larger of the two airports, O'Hare International (ORD; ☎ 773-686-2200; www.ohare.com) is 17 miles northwest of the city. The four operational terminals (1, 2, 3 and 5) bustle day and night. Travel through the glass-and-steel Terminal 1 building, designed by architect Helmut Jahn, to Terminal 2 and you'll experience a psychedelic neon and colored glass moving-sidewalk.

ATMs and phones (including TTY phones) are available in every terminal. The airport has wireless internet access throughout ($6.95 per day). The bus-shuttle center is in the ground level of the central parking garage. Follow signs to get there from Terminals 1, 2 and 3. Terminal 5, the international terminal, has its own pickup area.

Airport services:

Airport information desks Terminals 1, 3 and 5.

Back Rub Hub (🕑 9am-9pm) Upper level, Terminal 3.

Children's Museum Exhibit Upper level, Terminal 2.

Currency exchange (☎ 773-462-9973) All terminals.

Police kiosk/lost-and-found Upper levels of all terminals.

Post Office (🕑 9am-5pm Mon-Fri) Upper level, Terminal 2.

Travelers & Immigrants Aid Office (☎ 773-894-2427; 🕑 8:30am-9pm Mon-Fri, from 10am Sat & Sun) Upper level of Terminal 2. Provides information, directions and special assistance.

UIC Medical Center (☎ 773-894-5100) Upper level, Terminal 2.

Visitor Information (🕑 9am-5pm) Lower level, all terminals. Brochures available 24/7.

MIDWAY

Fast-growing, but still a manageable-size, Midway Airport (MDW; ☎ 773-838-3003; www.flychicago.com) was redeveloped in the early 2000s and

AIRPORT SECURITY

Since the September 11, 2001 terrorist attacks, airport security in the US has adopted a zero-tolerance policy for even the slightest infractions of airport rules. As new threats arise, the Transportation Safety Administration (TSA; www.tsa.gov) changes the restrictions. Read signs at security entry points carefully, or check online. Prohibited items are confiscated and thrown away. Right now that includes pocket and other knives, and any liquid or gel that is larger than 3oz (shampoo, deodorant, drinks, etc). You're allowed to bring on cosmetic goo that is smaller than 3oz – but only if you put it in a quart size clear plastic bag that you take out of your carry-on and put in the tray when you go through security.

When suitcases are checked in at Midway or O'Hare, they must not be locked – unless you have a TSA-approved lock (marked with a red diamond insignia), sold in most luggage and department stores. The TSA has a master key to these.

Expect to have to take off your shoes and belt as you go through the metal detectors, and know that the people waving those wands over you are now federal employees; however inept they may seem, they can cause you no end of delays. Cracking jokes is not advised.

GETTING INTO TOWN

CTA train service is available from both airports, but it's a bit of a hike. So if you're lugging a load, shared shuttle van service is the way to go. Airport Express (☎ 888-284-3826; www.airportexpress.com) has a monopoly on services between the airports and downtown lodgings. Once in the center, you may have to ride around while others are dropped off before you. You may also have to wait until the van is full before you leave the airport. From O'Hare the fare is $27 per person ($19 a piece for two). Midway to the Loop costs $22 per person. For shuttle rides between Midway and O'Hare airports, use the Omega Shuttle (☎ 773-483-6634; per person $16).

Coach USA (☎ 800-248-8747; www.coachusa.com) buses serve southern Wisconsin, suburban Illinois and northwest Indiana from O'Hare and Midway airports.

O'Hare

The Chicago Transit Authority (CTA) offers 24-hour train service on the Blue Line to and from the Loop (about 45 minutes, $2). Unfortunately, the O'Hare station is buried under the world's largest parking garage. Finding it can be akin to navigating a maze – directional signs are variously marked as 'CTA,' 'Rapid Transit' and 'Trains to City.' Unless you are staying right in the Loop, you will likely have to transfer to complete your journey. A good alternative is to ride the El as close as you can get to your hotel and then take a taxi for the final few blocks.

Each terminal has one taxi stand outside the baggage-claim area; you may have to line up. The fare to Near North and the Loop runs about $35 to $45, including a 10% to 15% tip. Note that traffic affects the fare: meters keep running even when the car is at a standstill.

If you've rented a car, take I-190 east from the airport to I-90 east into the Loop.

Midway

You can take the CTA Orange Line from Midway to the Loop (about 30 minutes, $2). To reach the CTA station, follow the signs from the lower level baggage claim. You have to walk a ways through a not-very-climate-controlled parking garage to get there.

Follow the signs to 'ground transportation' to catch a taxi. Costs are based on the meter (there are no flat-rate rides), and will likely run about $25 to $30 plus tip into the Loop.

If you've rented a car at the airport, take S Cicero Ave north to I-55N east into town.

still has that shiny-new-airport smell. No matter which of the three concourses (A, B, C) you depart from, you enter and exit through the New Terminal, home to almost all of the airport's services and amenities. ATMs and pay phones (some TTY capable) are found throughout. Wireless internet access is available for $6.95 per day.

Airport police and Travelers Aid are in the New Terminal building. Additionally, there are two visitor information brochure kiosks; the first is in the lower level baggage-claim area, and the other is on the top floor, near the ATA counter.

BICYCLE

Riding along the 18.5-mile long Lakefront Bike Path is a great way to see the city. Though there are 120 miles of bike lanes around town, traffic can be less than respectful, making street peddling a bit more of a challenge. Request a free bike map from the City Department of Transportation (www.chicagobikes.org). Bikes rent for $8 an hour or $30-35 per day. You can arrange to pick up at one Bike Chicago (www.bikechicago.com) location and drop off at another; reserve online and you save money. Child seats and tandem bikes are available, as are guided tours.

Bikes are allowed on all CTA trains, save for during high-use commuter hours (7am to 9am and 4pm to 6pm Monday to Friday). Many CTA buses are equipped with a bike rack on the front that accommodates two bikes at a time.

Rental locations:

Bike Chicago Millennium Park (Map pp54–5; ☎ 888-245-3929; 239 E Randolph St; 6:30am-8pm Mon-Fri & 8am-8pm Sat & Sun Jun-Aug, 6:30am-7pm Mon-Fri & 9am-7pm Sat & Sun Apr-May & Sep-Oct; 6:30am-6:30pm Mon-Fri Nov-Mar; M Brown, Green, Orange or Purple Line to Randolph) The associated McDonald's Cycle Center has bike parking, lockers and showers for members ($20 per month).

Bike Chicago Navy Pier (Map pp54–5; ☎ 312-595-9600; 600 E Grand Ave; 8am-10pm Jun-Aug, 9am-7pm Apr-May & Sep-Oct; 66)

Bike Chicago North Ave Beach (Map pp76–7; ☎ 773-327-2706; 1603 N Lakeshore Dr; 8am-8pm Jun-Aug, 9am-7pm May & Sep; 151)

BOAT

Taking a Shoreline Sightseeing Water Taxi (☎ 312-222-9328; www.shorelinesightseeing.com; 10am-6pm) is an interesting alternative to walking or busing between major sights. The Lake Taxi transports you from the southwestern corner of Navy Pier to the front of the South Loop's Shedd Aquarium (one way adult/child $7/4). The River Taxi connects the Sears Tower with the mouth of the river at Gateway Park, just west of Navy Pier (one way adult/child $6/3). The Commuter Taxi picks up at the north side of the river, just east of the Michigan Ave bridge and floats along its merry way to the south side of Adams St, at the Sears Tower, and across from Union Station (one way $3).

The Chicago Water Taxi (☎ 312-337-1446; www.chicagowatertaxi.com; 6:30am-7pm) is another service, aimed primarily at commuters. It ferries you between the north shore of the river at Michigan Ave and the east river bank north of Madison St (near the Metra Ogilvie Transportation Center), stopping at La Salle/Clark en route. A one-way ride is $2, an all-day pass $4.

BUS

Long-distance bus carrier Greyhound (Map pp106–7; ☎ 312-408-5800, 800-231-2222; www.greyhound.com; 630 W Harrison St) sends dozens of buses in every direction every day, stopping along the way to pick up people traveling from small towns. Prices are least if you purchase with 21-day advance notice. Sample one-way fares and times include: Detroit ($27 to $35, six hours), Minneapolis ($36 to $61, 10 hours) and New York City ($54 to $91, 20 hours). The station's ticketing windows are open 24 hours. The Clinton El stop on the Blue Line is two blocks away.

Relatively new on the scene, low cost–oriented Megabus (☎ 877-462-6342; www.megabus.com/us) is giving Greyhound a run for its money to the Midwestern cities it serves. Booked ahead, a one way seat to Detroit or Cleveland (seven hours each) costs only $8, and service runs much more efficiently than the big dog (though less often). Megabuses depart from Union Station (Map pp54–5; 225 S Canal St).

Pace (www.pacebus.com) buses connect to outlying suburbs.

CAR & MOTORCYCLE

What's driving like in Chicago? Not pretty. Traffic is worst during morning rush hour, evening rush hour, the lunch hour, during a Bears game or a festival on weekends – oh, who are we kidding, cars can stack up at any hour on any day. Often you could crawl to your destination faster. As encompassing as Chicago public transportation system is, there's little reason to use a car, unless you're heading out of town.

Parking

Parking is another good reason to leave the car behind. Garages cost $20 and up a day, but will save you time and traffic tickets. Meter spots and on-street parking are plentiful in outlying areas, but the Loop, Near North, Lincoln Park and Lake View neighborhoods can require up to an hour of circling before you find a spot. Valet parking, even at $12, can be worth it in these congested neighborhoods. Some meter-free neighborhoods require resident parking passes, some don't. Read signs carefully. Most importantly: never park in a spot or a red curbed area marked 'Tow-Away.' Your car will be towed. Period. Tow-truck drivers in Chicago circle like vultures; fees start at $150, plus the cost of the cab ride to retrieve your car.

Rental

Just about every big name rental chain you can think of has outlets at both O'Hare and Midway airports, in addition to offices in town. If your taste runs to the more exotic and expensive, you might rent a Porsche Boxter or a Harley Davidson motorcycle from specialist firms.

You'll need a credit card to rent, and many agencies only do business with those 25 and older. Expect to pay $30 to $45 per day for a compact car, with rates going down somewhat if you rent for an entire week. Prices are also lower on weekends, sometimes dramatically so. Booking online has become commonplace (and firms may offer internet-only, no cancellation rates), but if it's last minute, calling might get you a better deal. At Hotwire (www.hotwire.com), an online booking agency, you can bid for lower rates. They guarantee the type of car, but they don't tell you the name of the rental agency (all well-known brands) until you've paid. You can't make any changes after you've committed, but we've seen rates from $13 to $23 per day accepted.

Most agencies' cars come with unlimited mileage; if they don't, ask about it – the per-mile costs can add up quickly. Also, be aware of redundant liability and medical insurance coverage. Many credit cards have built-in liability coverage on car rentals – check with yours before you agree to add supplemental insurance to your rental bill.

If you need a car only infrequently during a longer stay in Chicago, you might consider using **Zipcar** (☎ 866-494-7227; www.zipcar.com). You have to join ($50 annual fee) and pick up your ID card, but after that, all you have to do is call to reserve one of the cars parked in various locations around the city (business parking lots, residential areas). They'll give you the key access code and you return the car to the same parking spot at the agreed upon time (from $8 an hour). Cars are usually fuel-efficient models. Gas and insurance included.

Rental agencies:

Ace Rent a Car (☎ 800-323-3221; www.acerentacar.com) Off-airport independent, with lower than average rates. Call for airport shuttle (10 minutes to site)

Alamo (☎ 800-462-5266; www.alamo.com)

Avis (☎ 800-331-1212; www.avis.com)

Budget (☎ 800-527-0700; www.budget.com)

Chicago Exotic Car Rental (☎ 866-661-1054; www.chicagoexoticrentals.com) Ferraris, Hummers and Porsches go for anywhere from $250 to $2000 per day.

Dollar (☎ 800-800-4000; www.dollar.com)

Enterprise (☎ 800-867-4595; www.enterprise.com) Also has suburban locations; will pick you up from anywhere.

Hertz (☎ 800-654-3131; www.hertz.com)

Illinois Harley-Davidson (☎ 708-749-1500, 888-966-1500; www.eaglerider.com) Motorcycle rentals start at $125 per day.

National (☎ 800-227-7368; www.nationalcar.com)

Thrifty (☎ 800-527-7075; www.thrifty.com)

LOCAL TRANSPORTATION

The **Chicago Transit Authority** (CTA; ☎ 312-836-7000; www.transitchicago.com) runs all the El trains and local buses. The El train system is an efficient, air-conditioned way to get around Chicago, though only the Blue Line from O'Hare to the Loop and the Red Line from Howard to 95/Dan Ryan run trains 24 hours. You shouldn't have to wait more than 15 minutes for a train, but track construction meant to improve service may slow things down on some lines until 2009. Bus routes generally follow major thoroughfares north–south or east–west. Between the two systems, you can explore the furthest reaches of the city. Pick up useful, free system maps at all CTA stations, or plan your trip on their website.

For years, the CTA has been griping about insufficient funds, threatening to cut service and double rates if the state didn't bail them out. When a crisis point came, the Illinois legislature did just that, stalling fare hikes for a time. A rate increase of 10% each year for three years has been proposed, and Sunday service may be limited in the future.

For the time being, the fare for single adult riders on both CTA buses and the El is $2. The plastic card tickets have a magnetized strip that allows you to add as much fare as you'd like (up to $100). Fares (and transfers) are deducted automatically when you enter the El system or board the bus. The best bet for travelers is to buy a visitor pass: one day ($5), two days ($9), three days ($12), seven days ($20). These are available from vending machines found in both airport El stations and at visitor centers (p263), as well as at a few other stations and some hotels and hostels. The **Currency Exchange** (Map pp64–5; ☎ 312-944-4643; 62 E Chicago Ave; 24hr) also sells CTA passes (for cash only). If you buy them online at www3.yourcta.com, at least 10 days in advance they can be mailed to your residence.

The CTA *has* done a few things right in the past few years: so far they've put 20 diesel-electric buses into service (each has 90% reduced emissions over regular diesel), their headquarters are designed to exacting environmental standards, and they've been part of a bio-diesel bus test program.

During the summer months and Christmas holidays, the Chicago Department of Transportation runs a **Free Trolley** (www.cityofchicago.org/Transportation/trolleys/; 10am-6pm). Four routes connect the town's major sights: the blue trolley runs from Navy Pier to River North; the green trolley to/from the Loop and Museum Campus and Hyde Park; the red connects the Gold Coast with the Loop; and the yellow links Navy Pier with the Loop. Route maps are available online. The low-emission, trolleylike buses depart every 20 to 30 minutes. And yes, it's free. But be warned: on a hot summer day when you're packed in like sardines, you may wish you'd paid for public transport.

Taxi

Taxis are easy to find from the Loop through Lincoln Park. Simply stand on the curb and raise your arm to hail one. In other parts of the city, you can either call a cab or face what may be a long wait for one to happen along. Fares start at $2.25 when you get into the cab, $1.80 for each additional mile and about 40¢ per minute; the first additional passenger is $1, any extra passengers after that are 50¢ a piece. Drivers expect a 10% to 15% tip. All major companies accept credit cards. To report a taxi incident, take down the driver's name and cab number, and call the **Department of Customer Services Complaint Hotline** (☎ 311).

Reliable companies:

American-United Taxi (☎ 773-248-7600)

Flash Cab (☎ 773-561-1444; www.flashcab.com)

Yellow Cab (☎ 312-829-4222; www.yellowcabchicago.com)

TRAIN

Amtrak

Chicago's **Union Station** (Map pp54–5; 225 S Canal St) is the hub for **Amtrak** (☎ 800-872-7245; www.amtrak.com), and it has more connections than any other US city. Trains chug toward faraway cities like Los Angeles ($140, 43 hours), San Antonio ($113, 32 hours) and New York ($80, 18 hours). They also connect to closer Midwestern cities like Milwaukee ($21, 1½ hours) and Detroit ($27, 5½ hours). Booking several weeks in advance will usually save you money. Amtrak is faster than traveling by Greyhound, and much, much more comfortable.

Metra

A web of commuter trains running under the **Metra** (☎ 312-322-6777; www.metrarail.com) banner serves the 245 stations in the suburbs surrounding Chicago. Some of the Metra lines run frequent schedules seven days a week; others operate only during weekday rush hours. The four end-of-the-line Metra stations in Chicago are Ogilvie Transportation Center, Union Station, La Salle St Station and Millennium Station. Each station has schedules available for all the lines, as well as other information. Short trips start at $1.95; buy tickets from agents and machines at major stations.

DIRECTORY

BUSINESS HOURS

Normal business hours are:

Banks & most businesses 9am to 5pm Monday to Friday

Bars & pubs 11am to 2am, some bars until 4am or 5am

Restaurants 11am to 10pm

Shops 11am to 7pm Monday to Saturday, noon to 6pm Sunday

CHILDREN

From the dinosaurs at the Field Museum to the carousel on Navy Pier, to a bike ride along the lakefront and beach swim, Chicago will endlessly entertain children. Most museums have special areas to amuse and educate wee ones. See the boxed text on p67 for a list of Chicago's top kid-friendly attractions.

A good resource is **Chicago Parent** (www.chicagoparent.com), a free publication available at libraries, the Children's Museum and elsewhere. Also check out **Chicago Kids** (www.chicagokids.com), and **GoCityKids** (www.gocitykids.com), a helpful website that offers recommendations based on the weather that day, the level of intellectual rigor or athletic activity desired, and the child's age. The results can be sorted by neighborhood, making it a breeze to find something great for your kids to do after you've exhausted the delights of Navy Pier and all the museums.

For a comprehensive overview on traveling with kids, check out Lonely Planet's book *Travel With Children*.

Babysitting

Check with your hotel's concierge for a list of recommended sitters. **American Childcare Services** (☎ 312-644-7300; www.americanchildcare.com; per hr $18.50, plus $20 agency fee) provides professional babysitters who will come to your hotel (four-hour minimum service). It's recommended you book a couple days ahead of time.

CLIMATE

The nickname 'Windy City' actually has non-meteorological origins. It was coined by newspaper reporters in the late 1800s in reaction to the oft-blustery boastfulness of

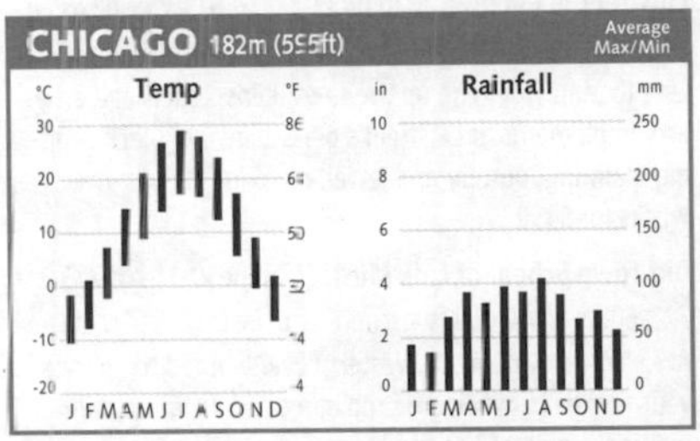

Chicago's politicians. Nevertheless, Chicago is windy, with everything from cool, God-sent lake breezes at the height of summer to skirt-raising gusts in the spring, to spine-chilling, nose-chiseling blasts of icy air in the winter. The city experiences all four seasons, with late spring and early fall being generally warm, clear and dry times. Winter and summer behave as expected, but early spring and late fall can freely mix pleasant days with rather wretched ones. Chicago has no true rainy season; its 34in of average annual precipitation are spread throughout the course of the year.

COURSES

You can learn a lot during your time in Chicago, from blues harmonica to improv to scarf crocheting.

If you'll be in town less than a week, try these options:

Chopping Block (Map pp50-1; ☎ 773-472-6700; www.thechoppingblock.net; 4747 N Lincoln Ave; Ⓜ Brown Line to Western) Offers both demonstration and hands-on cooking classes daily; wide-ranging topics include how to prepare locally sourced meals and how to amalgamate tailgate party chow for Bears games (two- to three-hour classes, $40-135). Classes are also held at the Merchandise Mart (Map pp64–5) outlet.

Second City (Map pp76–7; ☎ 312-664-3959; www.secondcity.com; 1616 N Wells St; Ⓜ Brown Line to Sedgwick) Laugh while learning to write and perform improv comedy at Second City's famed Training Center. Intensive Friday-to-Sunday workshops ($265) are offered frequently, along with traditional eight-week sessions. For the schedule, go to the website's 'Training Centers' link, then 'Chicago.'

Several local shops offer one-off classes; see Loopy Yarns (p135) for knitting, Beadniks (p130)

for jewelry making and Wolfbait & B-girls (p133) for fabric printing.

For those who will be in town for a longer duration (at least five weeks), try:

Lillstreet Art Center (Map pp50-1; ☎ 773-769-4226; www.lillstreet.com; 4401 N Ravenswood St; Ⓜ Brown Line to Montrose) Fire up the saws, kilns, easels and other arty implements at Lillstreet's glass-blowing, block-printing, painting, pottery and jewelry making classes; five weeks for $150.

Old Town School of Folk Music (Map pp50-1; ☎ 773-728-6000; www.oldtownschool.org/classes; 4544 N Lincoln Ave; Ⓜ Brown Line to Western) Ever wanted to impress your friends by wailing on the banjo, fiddle, blues harmonica or guitar? The Old Town School will teach you well; eight weeks for $150.

Speciman (☎ 773-489-4830; www.specimanproducts.com; 1240 N Homan Ave; 🚌 70) Sure you can learn to play the guitar (see Old Town, above), but why not go a step further and actually build your own stringed beauty? Six-week intensive luthier courses cost $3400.

CUSTOMS REGULATIONS

International travelers will be familiar with the red-and-green line system at O'Hare. Those with nothing to declare can opt for the green line, which is still subject to spot checks. Those with something to declare should definitely do so, because if you try to smuggle something in and are caught, your day will go downhill immediately. Penalties for drug smuggling are especially severe. Non-United States citizens over the age of 21 are allowed to import 1L of liquor and 200 cigarettes (or 100 non-Cuban cigars) duty free. Gifts may amount to no more than $100 in value. You may bring any amount of money less than $10,000 into or out of the US without declaration. Amounts greater than $10,000 must be declared.

Certain goods such as ivory and tortoiseshell anything are a no-no, as is drug paraphernalia. For more information, visit the website www.customs.gov.

DISCOUNT CARDS

Purchase the lump-sum CityPass (☎ 888-330-5008; www.citypass.com; adult/child 4-11 yrs $49.50/39) and save on admission fees for five of Chicago's most popular attractions: the Shedd Aquarium, Field Museum of Natural History, Adler Planetarium, Hancock Observatory and Museum of Science & Industry. You can buy the passes at the attractions themselves, or at Chicago's visitor centers (see Tourist Information, p263).

A CTA day pass (p253) provides savings on El and bus fares.

Students who present ID will often receive reduced museum admission. Discounts are also commonly offered for seniors, children and the disabled. In these cases, however, no special cards are issued (you get the savings on-site when you pay). American Auto Association (AAA) members frequently receive hotel and motel discounts, as well as other travel-related savings.

ELECTRICITY

Electric current in the US is 110-120V, 60Hz AC. Outlets accept North American standard plugs, which have two flat prongs and an occasional third round one. If your appliance is made for another system, you will need a converter or adapter. These are best bought in your home country. Otherwise, try a travel bookstore. Check www.kropla.com for further useful details on electricity and adaptors.

EMERGENCY

For all emergencies (police, ambulance, fire), call ☎ 911. For non-emergency police matters call ☎ 311.

GAY & LESBIAN TRAVELERS

Chicago has a flourishing gay and lesbian scene; for details, check the free weekly publications of Chicago Free Press (www.chicagofreepress.com) or Windy City Times (www.windycitymediagroup.com). The massive new Chicago Area Gay & Lesbian Chamber of Commerce (Map pp82–3; ☎ 773-303-0167; www.glchamber.org; 3656 N Halsted St; 🕑 9:30am-6pm Mon-Fri; Ⓜ Red Line to Addison) also provides useful visitor information. Chicago Greeter (see Organized Tours, p260) offers personalized sightseeing trips.

The biggest concentration of bars and clubs is on N Halsted St between Belmont Ave and Grace St, an area known as Boystown. Andersonville, aka Girls' Town, is another area with plenty of choices. For the gay and lesbian nightlife lowdown see p186.

HEALTH

No special vaccines are required or recommended for travel to the United States. All travelers should be up-to-date on routine immunizations. Because of the high level of hygiene, infectious diseases will not be a significant concern for most travelers.

Infectious diseases

WEST NILE VIRUS

These infections were unknown in the United States until a few years ago, but have now been reported in almost all 50 states. The virus is transmitted by culex mosquitoes, which are active in late summer and early fall and generally bite after dusk. Most infections are mild or asymptomatic, but the virus may infect the central nervous system, leading to fever, headache, confusion, lethargy, coma and sometimes death. There is no treatment for West Nile virus. For the latest update on the areas affected by West Nile, go to the website of the US Geological Survey (http://westnilemaps.usgs.gov/).

LYME DISEASE

This disease has been reported from many states, but most documented cases occur in the northeastern part of the country. A smaller number of cases occur in the northern Midwest. Lyme disease is transmitted by deer ticks, which are only 1mm to 2mm long. Most cases occur in the late spring and summer. The CDC has an informative, if slightly scary, web page on Lyme disease at www.cdc.gov/ncidod/dvbid/lyme/.

HIV/AIDS

As with most parts of the world, HIV infection occurs throughout the United States. You should never assume, on the basis of someone's background or appearance, that they're free of this or any other sexually transmitted disease. Be sure to use a condom for all sexual encounters.

Insurance

The United States offers possibly the finest health care in the world. The problem is that unless you have good insurance, it can be prohibitively expensive. It's essential you purchase travel health insurance if your regular policy doesn't cover you when you're abroad.

Bring any medications you may need in their original containers, clearly labeled. A signed, dated letter from your physician that describes all medical conditions and medications, including generic names, is also a good idea.

If your health insurance does not cover you for medical expenses abroad, consider supplemental insurance. Check the Lonely Planet website (www.lonelyplanet.com/bookings/insurance.do) for more information. Find out in advance if your insurance plan will make payments directly to providers or reimburse you later for overseas health expenditures.

Internet Resources

There is a wealth of travel health advice on the internet. The World Health Organization publishes a superb book, called *International Travel and Health*, which is revised annually and is available on line at no cost at www.who.int/ith/. Another website of general interest is MD Travel Health at www.mdtravelhealth.com, which provides complete travel health recommendations for every country, updated daily, also at no cost.

It's usually a good idea to consult your government's travel health website before departure, if one is available:

Australia (www.dfat.gov.au/travel/)

Canada (http://www.hc-sc.gc.ca/english/index.html)

United Kingdom (www.dh.gov.uk)

United States (www.cdc.gov/travel/)

HOLIDAYS

Chicago's governmental offices and services shut down on public holidays, as do some city shops. Locals celebrate many of the holidays with parades and other fanfare. To find out how you can join in the fun, see Festivals (p12). Major public holidays include the following:

New Year's Day January 1

Martin Luther King Jr Day Third Monday in January

President's Day Third Monday in February

Pulaski Day First Monday in March

Memorial Day Last Monday in May

Independence Day July 4

Labor Day First Monday in September

Columbus Day Second Monday in October

Veteran's Day November 11

Thanksgiving Day Fourth Thursday in November

Christmas Day December 25

INSURANCE

A travel insurance policy to cover theft, loss and medical problems is a good idea, especially when traveling in the US, where dismal medical coverage means routine trips to the doctor can cost the uninsured hundreds of dollars. Some policies specifically exclude 'dangerous' activities, which can include motorcycling.

You may prefer a policy that pays doctors or hospitals directly rather than requiring you to pay on the spot and claim later. If you have to claim later, ensure you keep all documentation.

Check that the policy covers ambulances or an emergency flight home.

INTERNET ACCESS

Public libraries remain the best bet for free wired internet access, with the Harold Washington Library (p60) the cream of the crop; get a 'day pass' at the counter.

For a while it looked like Chicago was going to get a municipal wi-fi network. Then the city figured out how much it was going to cost, and pulled the plug in mid 2007. Oh well – for free wi-fi there are always the public libraries. Bars and restaurants in Lincoln Park, Bucktown and Near North often have free wi-fi; try Map Room (p177) or Goose Island Brewery (p173). The Chicago Cultural Center (p58) also has it for free.

Hotels usually have wi-fi, though you'll often have to pay for in-room access (per day \$10 to \$15). Lobbies sometimes serve as free wi-fi zones. Public-use internet terminals are rare outside hostels and B&Bs. The one exception:

Screenz (Map pp76–7; ☎ 773-348-9300; 2717 N Clark St; per hr \$9; 🕑 8am-midnight Mon-Fri, from 9am Sat & Sun; Ⓜ Brown Line to Diversey) Do it all here: surf, download, burn CDs, print and scan.

LEGAL MATTERS

The basics of Chicago's legal system are identical to other US cities. If stopped and questioned by the police, you should cooperate, though you are not required to give them permission to search either your person or your car (though they can do both if they determine they have 'probable cause'). If arrested, you have the right to remain silent – which you should do – and the right to make one phone call from jail. If you don't have a lawyer or friend or family member to help you, call your consulate. The police will give you the number upon request.

It's generally against the law to have an open container of any alcoholic beverage in public, whether in a car, on the street, in a park or at the beach. But during festivals and other mass events, this rule is waived. The drinking age of 21 is pretty strictly enforced. If you're younger than 35 (or just look like it), carry an ID to fend off overzealous barkeeps and the like. The legal driving age is 16, the age of consent is 17 and the voting age is 18. There is zero tolerance at all times for any kind of drug use.

MAPS

Maps are widely sold at hotels, drug stores and newsstands. Try Lonely Planet's *Chicago* city map, a laminated map that folds into a compact size. Any bookstore, from Barbara's (p134) to Borders (p124) will carry it. You can pick up free maps of the Chicago transit system at any CTA station, or download one from www.transitchicago.com.

MEDICAL SERVICES

If you are ill or injured and suspect that the situation is in any way life threatening, call ☎ 911 immediately. This is a free call from any phone.

Clinics & Emergency Rooms

The following hospitals offer medical services through their emergency rooms. If your condition is not acute, call first, because many also operate clinics that can see you in a more timely and convenient manner. None of their services come cheap, so make sure you have insurance. If you are broke and don't have insurance, head to Stroger Cook County Hospital. If your problem is not life threatening, you will be seated in a waiting room where you will do just that, sit, for perhaps 12 hours while you're surrounded by people sicker than yourself.

Advocate Illinois Masonic Medical Center (Map pp82–3; ☎ 773-975-1600; 836 W Wellington Ave; Ⓜ Brown, Purple Line to Wellington)

Children's Memorial Hospital (Map pp76–7; ☎ 773-880-4000; 2300 N Lincoln Ave; Ⓜ Red, Brown, Purple Line to Fullerton)

Northwestern Memorial Hospital (Map pp64–5; ☎ 312-926-5188; 251 E Erie St; Ⓜ Red Line to Chicago)

Stroger Cook County Hospital (Map pp98–9; ☎ 312-864-6000; 1900 W Polk St; Ⓜ Blue Line to Medical Center)

University of Chicago Hospital (Map p114; ☎ 773-702-1000; 5841 S Maryland Ave; Ⓜ Metra to 55th-56th-57th)

Pharmacies

Walgreens pharmacies are convenient places to get your prescriptions filled. The following branches are open 24 hours:

Walgreens (Map pp64–5; ☎ 312-664-8686; 757 N Michigan Ave; Ⓜ Red Line to Chicago)

Walgreens (Map pp64–5; ☎ 312-587-1416; 641 N Clark St; Ⓜ Red Line to Grand)

MONEY

The US currency is the dollar ($), divided into 100 cents (¢). Coins come in denominations of 1¢ (penny), 5¢ (nickel), 10¢ (dime), 25¢ (quarter), 50¢ (half dollar – rare) and $1 (silver dollar – rare). Notes (bills) come in denominations of $1, $2 (rare), $5, $10, $20, $50 and $100.

See p17 for how your money will be spent in Chicago. For exchange rates, see Quick Reference on the inside front cover of this book.

ATMs

You can find ATMs everywhere in Chicago, with many convenience stores getting in on the action as well. All machines are connected to Cirrus and Plus, the world's two largest banking networks.

Unless you find an ATM belonging to your bank, you will be charged a fee of around $2 to withdraw money from one of the machines. The exchange rate you get by taking money out of the ATM is usually the very best available (though the fees may nullify that advantage).

Changing Cash & Traveler's Checks

You'll find that exchanging foreign cash and non-US dollar traveler's checks in Chicago is a hassle, although it can be done. One cautionary note: shortly after arriving in Chicago, you will begin noticing 'currency exchanges' on many street corners. These primarily serve people without bank accounts who want to cash checks, and will not exchange foreign currencies. Head instead to the following list of banks and exchange places.

Traveler's checks are usually just as good as cash in the US, provided they are in US dollars. Most places will accept them as long as you sign them in front of the cashier, waiter etc.

To exchange international monies or traveler's checks for dollars, you can visit the arrivals areas of O'Hare's Terminals 3 or 5, which have foreign-exchange services. Otherwise, you try one of the following places in the Loop:

American Express (Map pp54–5; ☎ 312-541-5440; 55 W Monroe St; ⏲ 8:30am-5:30pm Mon-Fri; Ⓜ Blue Line to Monroe)

Chase Building (Map pp54–5; ☎ 312-732-6009; 21 S Clark St; ⏲ 7:30am-5pm Mon-Fri; Ⓜ Blue Line to Washington)

Northern Trust Bank (Map pp54–5; ☎ 312-630-6000; 50 S LaSalle St; ⏲ 8am-5pm Mon-Fri; Ⓜ Brown, Orange, Purple Line to Washington)

Travelex (Map pp54–5; ☎ 312-807-4941; 19 S LaSalle St; ⏲ 9am-5pm Mon-Fri; Ⓜ Brown, Orange, Purple Line to Washington)

World's Money Exchange (Map pp54–5; ☎ 312-641-2151; Suite M-11, upper fl, 203 N LaSalle St; ⏲ 9am-5pm Mon-Fri; Ⓜ Blue, Green, Brown, Orange, Purple Line to Clark)

Credit Cards

Major credit cards are widely accepted by car-rental firms, hotels, restaurants, gas stations, shops, large grocery stores, movie theaters, ticket vendors, taxicabs and other places. In fact, you'll find certain transactions impossible to perform without a credit card: you can't reserve theater or other event tickets by phone without one, nor can you guarantee room reservations by phone, or rent a car. The most commonly accepted cards are Visa and MasterCard. American Express is widely accepted but not as universally as the first two. Discover and Diners Club cards are usually good for travel tickets, hotels and rental cars, but they're less commonly accepted in other situations.

If your credit card is lost or stolen, call the card issuer.

American Express (☎ 800-528-4800)

Diners Club (☎ 800-234-6377)

Discover (☎ 800-347-2683)

MasterCard (☎ 800-307-7309)

Visa (☎ 800-336-8472)

NEWSPAPERS & MAGAZINES

For further details on these publications, see p42.

Chicago Magazine (www.chicagomag.com) Monthly magazine with articles and culture coverage slanted toward upscale readers.

Chicago Reader (www.chicagoreader.com) Free weekly alternative newspaper with comprehensive arts and entertainment listings; widely available at bookstores, bars and coffee shops.

Chicago Sun-Times (www.suntimes.com) The Tribune's daily, tabloid-esque competitor.

Chicago Tribune (www.chicagotribune.com) The city's stalwart daily newspaper; its younger, trimmed-down version is *RedEye*.

Crain's Chicago Business (www.chicagobusiness.com) Weekly publication covering business news.

Time Out Chicago (www.timeoutchicago.com) Hip, service-oriented magazine with all-encompassing listings.

Venus Magazine (www.venuszine.com) Arts-oriented quarterly 'zine for women.

ORGANIZED TOURS

The general tours whip through the major sights in an hour or two. If you really want to get a feel for the city, the specialist excursions are a much better choice.

Boat tours run from roughly May through September; bus and walking tours operate year-round.

The Sports & Activities chapter has information on bicycle tours (p206) and kayak tours (p208).

General Tours

The **Chicago Trolley Co** (☎ 773-648-5000; www.chicagotrolley.com; tours $25) offers a guided two-hour, 13-mile tour that stops at all the major sights throughout downtown and the Near North. It's handy that you can hop on and off wherever you want, all day long. Call to find out which stop is closest to you.

Mercury Chicago Skyline Cruises (Map pp54–5; ☎ 312-332-1353; www.mercuryskylinecruiseline.com; tours $20; Ⓜ Red Line to Grand) and **Wendella Sightseeing Boats** (Map pp64–5; ☎ 312-337-1446; www.wendellaboats.com; tours $22; Ⓜ Red Line to Grand) both offer similar 90-minute tours of the river and lake. Be aware that passing through the locks to and from the lake can take up a fair part of the excursion. Mercury departs from the Michigan Ave Bridge's southeast corner; Wendella departs from the northwest corner. Though the companies advertise them as architecture tours, the information is perfunctory. Architecture lovers will get much better bang for their buck with Chicago Architecture Foundation boat tours (see below).

Mystic Blue Cruises (Map pp64–5; ☎ 877-299-7783; www.mysticbluecruises.com; tours from $25; 🚌 124) plies the lakefront, departing from Navy Pier. It caters to a younger crowd and offers lunch, dinner, cocktail and moonlight tours accompanied by DJs and music.

The four-masted schooner **Windy** (Map pp64–5; ☎ 312-595-5555; www.tallshipwindy.com; tours $27; 🚌 124) sets sail from Navy Pier. Passengers can play sailor by helping raise and lower the sails and by trying to steer the ship. With only the sound of the wind in your ears, these 90-minute tours are the most relaxing way to see the skyline from offshore.

Specialist Tours

The **Chicago Architecture Foundation** (CAF; Map pp54–5; ☎ 312-922-3432; www.architecture.org; 224 S Michigan Ave; tour prices vary; Ⓜ Brown, Green, Orange, Purple Line to Adams) runs the best tours in town, and there are heaps to choose from. Most popular are the 90-minute boat tours (weekday/weekend $26/28), departing from the Michigan Ave Bridge's southeast corner. The Historic Skyscrapers walking tour, departing daily at 10am (plus 3pm in summer) gives you the low-down on Chicago's most revered sky-high structures. The Modern Skyscrapers walking tour is another winner, departing at 1pm daily. Both take off from CAF's headquarters and cost $15. CAF also operates bus tours of Chicago, Prairie Ave, Hyde Park, Oak Park and other areas. Call or check the website for schedules.

Chicago Greeter (☎ 312-744-8000; www.chicagogreeter.com; tours free) pairs you with a local city dweller who takes you on a personal two- to four-hour tour customized by theme (architecture, history, gay and lesbian, and more) or neighborhood. Travel is by foot and/or public transportation; reserve seven business days in advance. **InstaGreeter** (🕒 10am-4pm Fri & Sat, 11am-4pm Sun; tours free) is the quicker version, offering one-hour tours on-the-spot from the **Cultural Center visitors center** (77 E Randolph St). Millennium Park also has a 'greeter' service; see p53 for details.

The Saturday morning **Chicago Neighborhood Tours** (☎ 312-742-1190; www.chgocitytours.com; tours $25) operated by the city's Department of Cultural Affairs are OK, but you pretty much just sit on a bus and stare out the window – though they do go into offbeat neighborhoods ignored by more mainstream companies. To join the four-hour jaunts, be at the Chicago Cultural Center Visitors Center (p263) at 9:30am for the 10am bus departure.

The Chicago Architecture Foundation sponsors the free **Loop Tour Train**, which is a great way to see Chicago's buildings and learn the elevated train's history. The 40-minute tours are held at 10am and 10:40am on Saturdays from May to September. Tickets are first-come, first-served starting at 9am at the Chicago Cultural Center Visitors Center (p263).

The comic, costumed **Untouchable Gangster Tours** (☎ 773-881-1195; www.gangstertour.com; tours $25) drives a van to some of Chicago's famous gangster sights. Confirm times and pick-up /departure points when booking.

The three-hour **Weird Chicago Tours** (Map pp64–5; ☎ 888-446-7859; www.weirdchicago.com; 600 N Clark St; tours $30; 8pm Thu-Sat; M Red Line to Grand) takes visitors to haunted sights, such as Resurrection Mary's hangout and the Sausage Factory murder location; there's also a pub tour.

Downloadable Tours

These walking tours are all available for free, so load'em up on your iPod and hit the road.

Chicago Loop Alliance (www.chicagoloopalliance.com) Offers three downloads taking in various downtown sights: Art Loop, Landmark Loop and Theater Loop.

Chicago Office of Tourism (www.downloadchicagotours.com) Check out the Buddy Guy-narrated blues tour.

Illinois Bureau of Tourism (www.onscreenillinois.com) Tour of famous movie sites such as *Blues Brothers, Ferris Bueller's Day Off* and *The Untouchables*.

PHOTOGRAPHY

Central Camera (p121) has it all: camera sales, supply sales, equipment repairs, traditional film processing and CD/DVD image transfers to free up digital camera memory card space. You can also buy digital camera memory cards at most Walgreens and Target stores, as well as transfer digital images to CDs at Walgreens.

POST

At press time, it cost 41¢ to mail a 1oz 1st-class letter within the US. Domestic postcards cost 26¢ to mail. It costs 69¢ to mail a 1oz letter to Canada or Mexico, 90¢ for other international destinations. Attach 69¢ of postage for postcards to Canada and Mexico, 90¢ for those going overseas.

Parcels mailed to foreign destinations from the US are subject to a variety of rates. First class can be very expensive. If you're not in a hurry, consider mailing your items 4th class, which goes by boat. Those rates can be very low, but delivery to Europe, for instance, takes six to eight weeks. If all you are sending is printed matter such as books, you qualify for an extra-cheap rate.

If you'd like to get mail while traveling but don't have an address, have it sent to you in Chicago via 'general delivery.' This is the same as poste restante. Letters should be addressed as follows: Your Name, c/o General Delivery (Station Name), Chicago IL (Zip Code), USA.

General-delivery mail is held for at least 10 days (sometimes as long as 30) before being returned to the sender. Bring photo ID when you come to pick up your mail. Full-service post offices that also accept general delivery include the following:

Main Post Office (Map pp54–5; ☎ 312-983-8182; 433 W Harrison St, Chicago, IL 60699; 24hr)

Fort Dearborn Station (Map pp64–5; ☎ 312-644-0485; 540 N Dearborn St, Chicago, IL 60610; 7:30am-5pm Mon-Fri, to 1pm Sat, 9am-2pm Sun)

Loop Station (Map pp54–5; ☎ 312-427-4225; 211 S Clark St, Chicago, IL 60604; 7am-6pm Mon-Fri)

Shipping Services

Shipping companies such as **UPS** (☎ domestic 800-742-5877, international 800-782-7892; www.ups.com) and **FedEx Kinko's** (☎ domestic 800-463-3339, international 800-247-4747; www.fedex.com) specialize in getting packages across the country and around the world in the blink of an eye. Call them to find the closest Chicago location to you.

RADIO

The Loop (97.9FM) Classic rock, where you'll find your Dido, Journey, Van Halen and U2.

WBEZ (91.5FM) National Public Radio affiliate airing news, political and cultural programs 24/7.

WGN (720AM) Local talk shows, plus broadcasts all of the Cubs games.

WHPK (88.5FM) University of Chicago's eclectic station of public affairs, rockabilly, calypso and beyond.

WSCR (670AM) Local sports 24/7; broadcasts all White Sox games.

WXRT (93.1FM) Modern, classic and local rock music.

www.vocalo.org Online station affiliated with WBEZ (see above) where listeners can interact with hosts and upload their own playlists and stories to the shows.

RELOCATING

If you're looking for a long-term rental while awaiting more permanent digs, see the ideas we've provided in the Sleeping chapter, (p214). A good web resource for finding fellow expats in Chicago is Meet Ups (www.meetup.com/cities/us/il/chicago/#Expatriates). For information on working in the Windy City, see p265.

SAFETY

Serious crime in Chicago has been dropping over the last few years, and the areas written about in this book are all reasonably safe during the day. At night, the lakefront, major parks and certain neighborhoods (especially south and west of the Loop) can become lonely and forbidding places. The Loop, Near North, Gold Coast, Old Town, Lincoln Park, Lake View and Bucktown, on the other hand, are tolerably safe (and bustling) night and day. For those who like to know before they go, you can visit www.chicagocrime.org, the pet project of a Chicago computer programmer. The site breaks down crime by type and neighborhood, and probably shouldn't be viewed by those who are on the fence about coming to the Windy City. (It's safe! We swear!)

TAXES

The basic sales tax is 9%. Some grocery items are taxed at only 2%, and newspapers and magazines, but not books, are tax-free. The hotel tax is 15.4%; the car-rental tax is 18%. And for meals in most parts of town, there's an extra 9.25% to 10.25% added to the bill (depending on location).

TELEPHONE

Area & Country Codes

The city has two area codes. The area code ☎ 312 serves the Loop and an area bounded roughly by North Ave to the north, Ashland Ave to the west and 16th St to the south. The rest of the city falls in area code ☎ 773. The northern suburbs use area code ☎ 847, suburbs to the west and south use ☎ 708, and the far west suburbs use ☎ 630.

The country code for the US is ☎ 1. The international access code is ☎ 011 for calls you dial directly.

Cell Phones

The only foreign phones that will work in the US (and Canada) are tri-band models operating on GSM 1900 and other frequencies. If you have a GSM tri-band phone, check with your service provider about using it in the US. Make sure to ask if roaming charges apply, as these can be hefty.

You can also rent a GSM 1900 compatible phone with a set amount of prepaid call time. T-Mobile (www.t-mobile.com) is one US company that provides this service, but it ain't cheap. Online retailers such as Telestial (www.telestial.com) and Planetfone (www.planetfone.com) sell phones. Most cost around $125, including voicemail, some prepaid minutes and a rechargeable SIM card. A good place in Chicago to poke around and possibly find a better deal is on Devon Ave (p130), where several shops sell cell phone equipment to a mostly Indian and European clientele.

Collect Calls

You can call collect (reverse the charges) from any phone; just dial ☎ 0 to begin the call. Rates, however, end up being *much* more expensive than walking to Walgreens or Jewel and purchasing a prepaid calling card. So if you have the cash to spring for a card, try to avoid making collect calls. Collect calls from the US to foreign countries are especially expensive, sometimes running $2 per minute. The operator should be able to tell you how much the rates will be before you place the call.

Dialing

All phone numbers within the USA and Canada consist of a three-digit area code followed by a seven-digit local number. If you are calling locally, just dial the seven-digit number. If you are calling from within the US to another area code, dial ☎ 1 + the three-digit area code + the seven-digit local number. In the city, if you don't use the area code when you should or you do use it when you shouldn't – both of which are common mistakes – you'll get an ear-shattering screech, followed by advice on what to dial.

To make an international call from Chicago (or anywhere in the USA), dial ☎011, then the country code, followed by the area code and phone number. To find out the country code of the place you're trying to call, look in the front of the local phone directory.

Toll-free phone numbers start with the area codes ☎800, ☎877 or ☎888. Numbers that begin with ☎900 will cost you a small fortune (up to several dollars per minute). You'll most often see such numbers advertised late at night on TV in ads asking, 'Lonely? Want to have some hot talk?'

Local directory assistance can be reached by calling ☎411. If you are looking for a number outside of your local area code but know what area code it falls under, dial ☎1 + the area code + 555-1212. These calls are no longer free, even from pay phones. For directory assistance for a toll-free phone number, dial ☎800-555-1212.

Pay Phones & Hotel Phones

Unfortunately, pay phones do not use the same high-tech card systems in the US that they do in Europe. This is fine for local calls, which cost 35¢ for about 10 minutes of talk time. But trying to make a long-distance call at a pay phone if you don't have a credit-card calling card or a prepaid calling card requires an outrageous amount of change. When using hotel phones, know that some places will charge up to $2 per local call. Ask in advance to avoid a shock later.

Prepaid Phone Cards

Prepaid phone cards usually offer some of the best per-minute rates for long-distance and international calling. They come in denominations of $5, $10, $20 and $50 and are widely sold in drugstores, supermarkets and convenience stores. Beware of cards with hidden charges such as 'activation fees' or per-call connection fees, and see if your card has a toll-free access number. A surcharge for calls made from public pay phones is common. AT&T sells a reliable phone card that's available at many retailers.

TIME

Chicago falls in the US Central Standard Time (CST) zone. 'Standard time' runs from the first Sunday in November to the second Sunday in March. 'Daylight saving time,' when clocks move ahead one hour, takes over for the rest of the year, from mid March to early November.

Chicago is one hour behind Eastern Standard Time (EST), which encompasses nearby Michigan and Indiana, apart from the northwestern corner of Indiana, which follows Chicago time. The border between the two zones is just east of the city.

The city is one hour ahead of Mountain Standard Time (MST), a zone that includes much of the Rocky Mountains, and two hours ahead of Pacific Standard Time (PST), the zone that includes California. Chicago is six hours behind Greenwich Mean Time (but remember daylight saving time).

TOILETS

There's not much in the way of public toilets. You can try the facilities at the visitors centers (see below), although they can be not-so-daisy-fresh. Another decent option are the Borders bookshops (p124) in the Loop and Gold Coast; you'll need to get the key from a staff member to enter.

TOURIST INFORMATION

The **Chicago Office of Tourism** (☎312-744-2400, 877-244-2246; www.cityofchicago.org/exploringchicago or www.choosechicago.com) provides a 24-hour hotline to answer questions about sights, events and lodging. It also operates two well-stocked visitors centers. It's tough to beat the one in the Chicago Cultural Center for sheer tonnage of multi-language maps and leaflets; friendly staff members and free wi-fi add to the beauty. The second location, in the Water Works Pumping Station, is close to the Near North and Gold Coast sights and shops. Both centers distribute the invaluable *Chicago Guidebook of Special Values* coupon book as well as sell CTA day passes (see p253); it's definitely worth your time to swing by and procure these items.

Chicago Cultural Center Visitors Center (Map pp54–5; 77 E Randolph St 🕑8am-7pm Mon-Thu, 8am-6pm Fri, 9am-6pm Sat, 10am-6pm Sun; Ⓜ Brown, Green, Orange Purple Line to Randolph) Many tours also depart from here.

Water Works Visitors Center (Map pp70–1; 163 E Pearson St; 🕑8am-7pm Mon-Thu, 8am-6pm Fri, 10am-6pm Sat, 10am-4pm Sun; Ⓜ Red Line to Chicago)

Internet Resources

As well as these listed below, the websites listed in the Newspapers & Magazines section (p260) are also good resources.

Craigslist Chicago (www.chicago.craigslist.org) Comprehensive listings for housing, jobs, items for sale etc.

Gaper's Block (www.gapersblock.com) The latest political and cultural happenings in the Windy City.

Green Maps (www.artic.edu/webspaces/greenmap/) Eateries, shops and other businesses that promote sustainable living choices in Chicago.

Hot Rooms (www.hotrooms.com) Chicago-centric hotel room consolidator.

LTH Forum (www.lthforum.com) Chit-chat about the restaurant scene from local foodies.

Metromix (www.metromix.com) *Chicago Tribune*-owned website with restaurant, bar and entertainment reviews.

TRAVELERS WITH DISABILITIES

Chicago can be a challenge for people with reduced mobility. The preponderance of older buildings means that doorways are narrow and stairs prevalent. All city buses are accessible, but many El stations are not. If you do find a station with an elevator, make sure that there's also one at your destination. To see a list of wheelchair-accessible El stations, check www.transitchicago.com/maps/accessible.html or call ☎ 888-968-7282 (press 5 for the Elevator Status Hotline).

For hotels, you're best off with the newer properties. But call the hotel itself – not the 800 number – and confirm that the room you want to reserve has the features you need. The phrase 'roll-in showers' is interpreted very loosely by some properties.

The **Mayor's Office for People with Disabilities** (☎ 312-744-7050, TTY 312-744-4964; www.cityofchicago.org/disabilities) is a good place to call to ask questions about the availability of services.

VISAS

A reciprocal visa-waiver program applies to citizens of certain countries, who may enter the US for stays of 90 days or fewer without having to obtain a visa. Currently these countries are Andorra, Australia, Austria, Belgium, Brunei, Denmark, Finland, France, Germany, Iceland, Ireland, Italy, Japan, Liechtenstein, Luxembourg, Monaco, the Netherlands, New Zealand, Norway, Portugal, San Marino, Singapore, Slovenia, Spain, Sweden, Switzerland and the UK.

In order to travel to the US visa-free, visitors from the above countries must have a machine-readable passport. If your passport cannot be scanned by a computer, you'll need to get a visa regardless. Consult with your airline or the closest US consulate or embassy for more information.

The main portal for US visa information is www.unitedstatesvisas.gov; this website is comprehensive, providing forms, contact information for US consulates abroad and even visa wait times calculated by country. The **US State Department** (www.travel.state.gov) also maintains comprehensive visa information.

As the US continues to fine-tune its national security guidelines, US entry requirements keep evolving as well. It is imperative that visitors double- and triple-check current regulations before coming to the country.

Visa Extensions

Tourists using visas are usually granted a six-month stay on first arrival. If you try to extend that time, the first assumption will be that you are working illegally, so come prepared with concrete evidence that you've been behaving like a model tourist: receipts to demonstrate you've been spending lots of your money from home in the US or ticket stubs that show you've been traveling extensively. Requests for visa extensions in Chicago are entertained at the office of **US Citizenship & Immigration Services** (Map pp54–5; ☎ 800-375-5283; www.uscis.gov; Suite 600, Kluczynski Bldg, Chicago Federal Center, 10 W Jackson Blvd; Ⓜ Red, Blue Line to Jackson). Meetings are all by appointment only, though, and to make an appointment, you have to visit the fine, robotic folks at http://infopass.uscis.gov. Be sure to get the paperwork moving well before your visa expires.

WOMEN TRAVELERS

Women will be safe alone in most parts of Chicago, though they should exercise a degree of caution and awareness of their surroundings.

The El is safe, even at night, though you might want to seek out more populated cars or the first car, to be closest to the driver.

In the commonly visited areas of Chicago, you should not encounter troubling attitudes from men. In bars some men will see a woman alone as a bid for companionship.

A polite 'no thank you' should suffice to send them away. Chicagoans are very friendly, so don't be afraid to protest loudly if someone is hassling you. It will probably send the offending party away and bring helpful Samaritans to your side.

WORK

It is very difficult for foreigners to get legal work in the United States. Securing your own work visa without a sponsor – meaning an employer – is next to impossible. If you do have a sponsor, the sponsor should normally be able to assist you, or do all the work themselves to secure your visa. Contact your embassy or consulate for more information.

If you're interested in doing some volunteer work while you're in town, check out the listings on the Chicago **Community Resource Network** (www.chicagovolunteer.net) or look through the opportunities listed in the community section of the **Craigslist message board** (www.chicago.craigslist.org).

BEHIND THE SCENES

THIS BOOK

This 5th edition of Chicago was coordinated and written by Karla Zimmerman, with contributions from Nate Cavalieri (Eating, Drinking, Entertainment, The Arts) and Lisa Dunford (Sleeping, Transportation, Walking Tours). Karla co-wrote the 4th edition with Chris Baty, who wrote the 3rd edition. Prior editions were written by Ryan Ver Berkmoes. This guidebook was commissioned in Lonely Planet's Oakland office, and produced by the following:

Commissioning Editor Jay Cooke

Coordinating Editor Elizabeth Anglin, Stephanie Ong

Coordinating Cartographer Sophie Richards, Julie Sheridan

Coordinating Layout Designer Aomi Hongo

Managing Editor Sasha Baskett, Geoff Howard

Managing Cartographer Alison Lyall

Managing Layout Designers Celia Wood

Assisting Cartographers Amanda Sierp, Jodie Whiteoak, Andrew Smith, Valentina Kremenchutskaya, Anita Banh & Fatima Basic

Cover Designer Marika Mercer

Project Manager Craig Kilburn

Thanks to Raph Richards, Laura Jane, Jacqueline McLeod, Lyahna Spencer & Wendy Wright

Cover photographs Travelers walking through airport corridor (blurred motion), Steve Dunwell/Getty Images (top); Millennium Park, Pritzker Pavilion, Giocoso Paolo/SIME 4Corners (bottom).

Internal photographs p4 (#3) Frances Dre, FlickR. All other photographs by Lonely Planet Images: p8 (#3) Charles Cook, p3 (#1), p5 (#2), p5 (#3), p6 (#4), p7 (#2), p7 (#4), p8 (#3), p8 (#2) Richard Cummins, p6 (#1) Rick Gerharter, p5 (#4), p4 (#1), p4 (#2), p8 (#1) Raymond Hillstrom, p2 (#1), p7 (#1) Richard I'Anson, p5 (#1), p6 (#2), p8 (#4) Ray Laskowitz, p7 (#3) John Sones

THANKS

KARLA ZIMMERMAN

Thanks to all my local amigos (you know who you are) for good-heartedly answering my relentless questions and sharing your favorite hot-spots. A tip of the hat to the kindly people at Chicago's Office of Tourism. Thanks to fellow *Chicago*ans Nate and Lisa for being such amazing troopers through the insanity. Jay, thanks pal, for idea-slinging and your Windy City boosterism. Thanks most of all to Eric Markowitz, the world's best partner-for-life, who fed and clothed me during the write-up.

NATE CAVALIERI

I owe a deep debt to my unfailing friends and hosts – Ben and Catrin, Jesse and Maria, Charlie – and everyone who showed me new corners of my favorite city, including an inspiring day splashing around in the fountain with Darrin and Emily. Thanks also for the friendly guidance of the folks at Lonely Planet including Jay Cooke, Karla Zimmerman and Lisa Dunford. Without the support of my

THE LONELY PLANET STORY

Fresh from an epic journey across Europe, Asia and Australia in 1972, Tony and Maureen Wheeler sat at their kitchen table stapling together notes. The first Lonely Planet guidebook, *Across Asia on the Cheap,* was born.

Travelers snapped up the guides. Inspired by their success, the Wheelers began publishing books to Southeast Asia, India and beyond. Demand was prodigious, and the Wheelers expanded the business rapidly to keep up. Over the years, Lonely Planet extended its coverage to every country and into the virtual world via lonelyplanet.com and the Thorn Tree message board.

As Lonely Planet became a globally loved brand, Tony and Maureen received several offers for the company. But it wasn't until 2007 that they found a partner whom they trusted to remain true to the company's principles of traveling widely, treading lightly and giving sustainably. In October of that year, BBC Worldwide acquired a 75% share in the company, pledging to uphold Lonely Planet's commitment to independent travel, trustworthy advice and editorial independence.

Today, Lonely Planet has offices in Melbourne, London and Oakland, with over 500 staff members and 300 authors. Tony and Maureen are still actively involved with Lonely Planet. They're travelling more often than ever, and they're devoting their spare time to charitable projects. And the company is still driven by the philosophy of *Across Asia on the Cheap:* 'All you've got to do is decide to go and the hardest part is over. So go!'

parents and partner, Florence, this project simply wouldn't have been possible.

LISA DUNFORD

Katie – you are the best sister ever. Thanks to you, Abby, Bryn and Brett Showalter for sheltering me. Samantha Thegze, a champagne toast to you for all your help. Uncle Bill (Thegze), I loved exploring books and building techniques together. Karla, it was great fun collaborating with you and Nate. Jay, thanks for all the ideas, and the opportunity. Thanks, too, to: Tracy and Tom Thegze, Alison Lyall, all the cartography and editing staff, and my love, Billy Dickman.

OUR READERS

Many thanks to the travelers who used the last edition and wrote to us with helpful hints, useful advice and interesting anecdotes:

Nicole Chaput, Paul Corradini, Linda Fraser, Sheryl Harawitz, Paul Lemons, Henrik Mitsch, Martha Molyneux, Sarah Oxenbridge, Lance Patford, Daniel Reigada, Claire Taylor, Weida Wang

SEND US YOUR FEEDBACK

We love to hear from travelers – your comments keep us on our toes and help make our books better. Our well-traveled team reads every word on what you loved or loathed about this book. Although we cannot reply individually to postal submissions, we always guarantee that your feedback goes straight to the appropriate authors, in time for the next edition. Each person who sends us information is thanked in the next edition – and the most useful submissions are rewarded with a free book.

To send us your updates – and find out about Lonely Planet events, newsletters and travel news – visit our award-winning website: www.lonelyplanet.com/contact.

Note: We may edit, reproduce and incorporate your comments in Lonely Planet products such as guidebooks, websites and digital products, so let us know if you don't want your comments reproduced or your name acknowledged. For a copy of our privacy policy visit www.lonelyplanet.com/privacy.

Notes

Notes

INDEX

See also separate indexes for:

000 map pages
000 photographs

000 map pages
000 photographs

ARTS

CLASSICAL MUSIC & OPERA

DANCE

FILM

READINGS & SPOKEN WORD

THEATER

EATING

AMERICAN

ASIAN

BAKERIES

BBQ

BREAKFAST

CHINESE

COFFEE SHOPS

COSTA RICAN

DELIS

DESSERT

ECLECTIC

FRENCH

FUSION

000 map pages
000 photographs

SPORTS & ACTIVITIES

BOWLING

DRIVE-INS

GOLF

GYMS

HEALTH DAY SPAS

BASEBALL

BASKETBALL

FOOTBALL

HOCKEY

SOCCER

WATERSPORTS

YOGA & PILATES

TOP PICKS

000 map pages
000 photographs

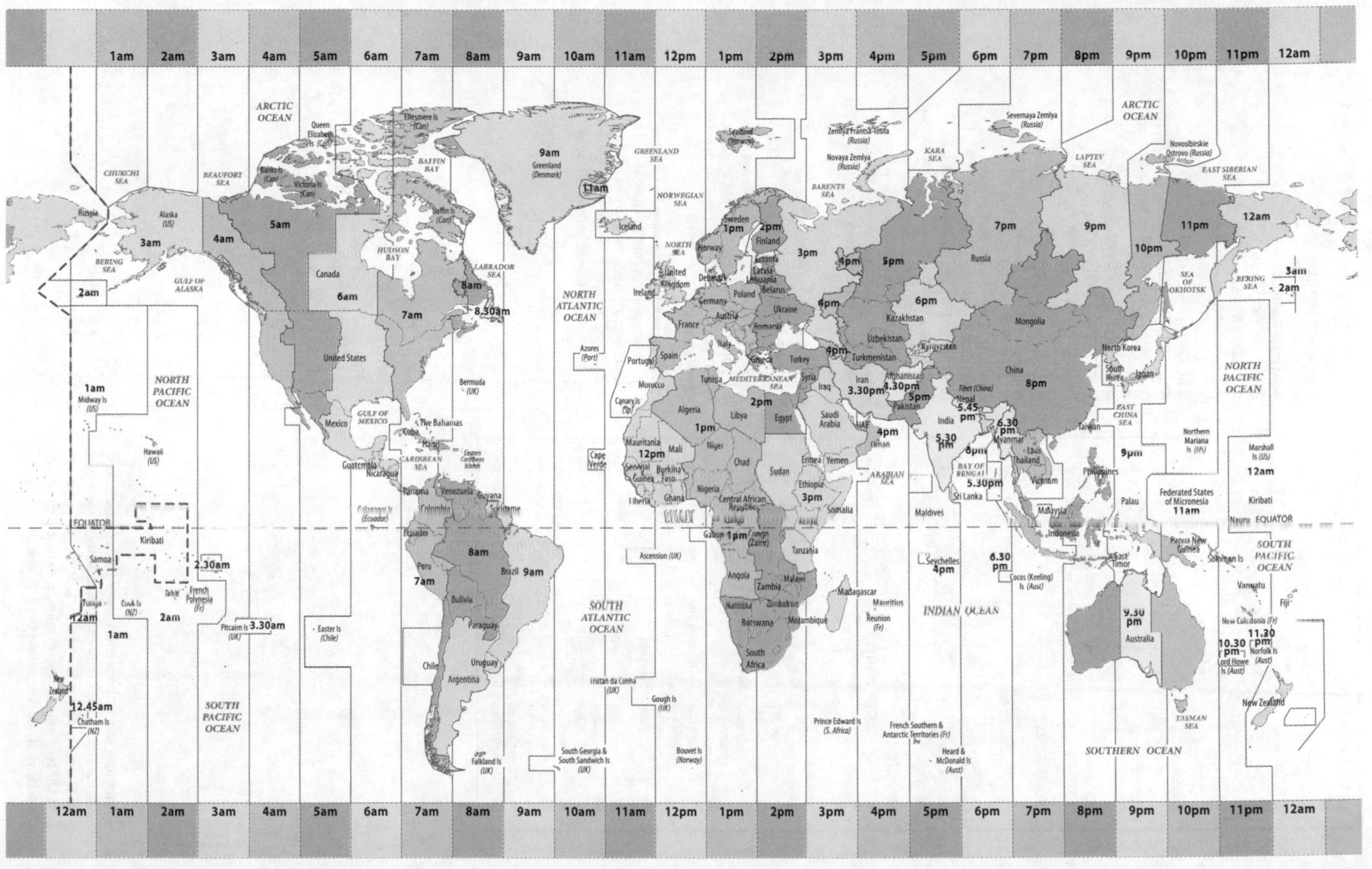

12am
1am
2am
3am
4am
5am
6am
7am
8am
9am
10am
11am
12pm
1pm
2pm
3pm
4pm
5pm
6pm
7pm
8pm
9pm
10pm
11pm
12am

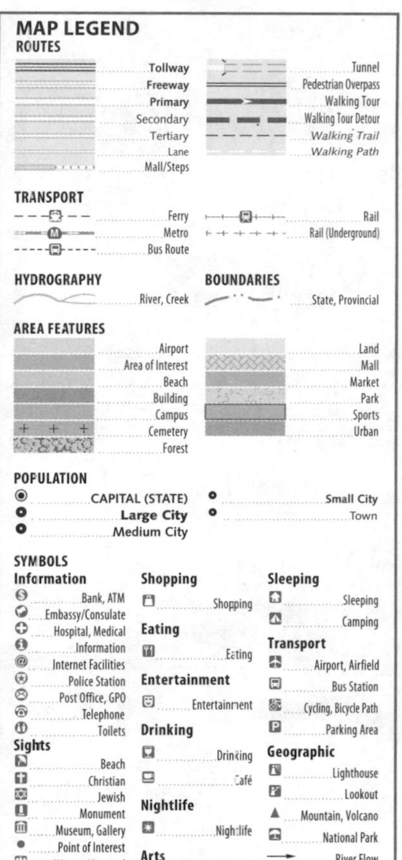

Published by Lonely Planet Publications Pty Ltd
ABN 36 005 607 983

Australia Head Office, Locked Bag 1, Footscray, Victoria 3011, ☎ 03 8379 8000, fax 03 8379 8111, talk2us@lonelyplanet.com.au

USA 150 Linden St, Oakland, CA 94607, ☎ 510 893 8555, toll free 800 275 8555, fax 510 893 8572, info@lonelyplanet.com

UK 2nd Floor, 186 City Road, London, ECV1 2NT, ☎ 020 7106 2100, fax 020 7106 2101, go@lonelyplanet.co.uk

Printed by Hang Tai Printing Company. Printed in China.